Unexpected Circumstances in European Contract Law

The recent financial crisis has caused many to question whether existing contracts may be adapted, terminated or renegotiated as a result of unexpected circumstances. The question is not a new one. In medieval times the notion of *clausula rebus sic stantibus* was developed to cope with such situations, and Germany introduced the theory of *Wegfall der Geschäftsgrundlage*. In England, the doctrine of frustration developed in the coronation cases provided one possible answer.

This comparative study explores the possibility of classifying jurisdictions as 'open' or 'closed' in this regard.

EWOUD HONDIUS is Professor of European Private Law at Utrecht University, the Netherlands.

HANS CHRISTOPH GRIGOLEIT holds a chair in civil law, commercial law, corporate law and private law theory at Ludwig-Maximilians-Universität Munich, Germany.

The Common Core of European Private Law

For the transnational lawyer the present European situation is equivalent to that of a traveller compelled to cross legal Europe using a number of different local maps. To assist lawyers in the journey beyond their own locality the Common Core of European Private Law Project was launched in 1993 at the University of Trento under the auspices of the late Professor Rudolf B. Schlesinger.

The aim of this collective scholarly enterprise is to unearth what is already common to the legal systems of European Union member states. Case studies widely circulated and discussed between lawyers of different traditions are employed to draw at least the main lines of a reliable map of the law of Europe.

Unexpected Circumstances in European Contract Law

Edited by

Ewoud Hondius
and
Hans Christoph Grigoleit

CAMBRIDGE
UNIVERSITY PRESS

CAMBRIDGE UNIVERSITY PRESS
Cambridge, New York, Melbourne, Madrid, Cape Town,
Singapore, São Paulo, Delhi, Tokyo, Mexico City

Cambridge University Press
The Edinburgh Building, Cambridge CB2 8RU, UK

Published in the United States of America by Cambridge University Press,
New York

www.cambridge.org
Information on this title: www.cambridge.org/9781107003408

First published 2011

Printed in the United Kingdom at the University Press, Cambridge

A catalogue record for this publication is available from the British Library

Library of Congress Cataloging in Publication data
Unexpected circumstances in European contract law / edited by Ewoud Hondius
and Hans Christoph Grigoleit.
p. cm. –
(The common core of European private law)
Includes bibliographical references and index.
ISBN 978-1-107-00340-8
1. Impossibility of performance – Europe. 2. Rebus sic stantibus
clause – Europe. 3. Vis major (Civil law) – Europe. I. Hondius, E. H., 1942–
II. Grigoleit, Hans Christoph. III. Title. IV. Series.
KJC1597.U64 2011
346.402–dc22

2010047276

ISBN 978-1-107-00340-8 Hardback

Contents

Contributors

Editors

EWOUD HONDIUS, Professor of European Private Law at the University of Utrecht, the Netherlands, and a member of the *Académie Internationale de Droit Comparé*.

AS HANS CHRISTOPH GRIGOLEIT is Professor of Civil Law, Commercial and Corporate Law and Private Law Theory at the University of Munich, Germany.

Authors of the reports

ODAVIA BUENO DIAZ, Lecturer, University of Amsterdam
MARTA CENINI, Assistant Professor of Private Law, University of Milan
ROBERT CLARK, Irish Law Commission, Dublin
JÚLIO GOMES, Professor of Law, Catholic Portuguese University, Porto
CARSTEN HERRESTHAL, Professor of Law, University of Regensburg
CLIONA KELLY, Lecturer in Law, National University of Ireland, Galway
BERT LEHRBERG, Professor of Law, University of Uppsala
BARBARA LUPPI, Assistant Professor of Economics, University of Modena and Reggio Emilia
BRIGITTA LURGER, Professor of Law, University of Graz
FRANCESCO MACARIO, Professor of Law, University of Foggia
LAURA MACGREGOR, Senior lecturer, University of Edinburgh
LUZ MARTÍNEZ VELENCOSO, Professor of Law, University of Valencia
VALENTINAS MIKELENAS, Professor of Law, University of Vilnius
KIM ØSTERGAARD, Senior researcher, Copenhagen School of Economics

FRANCESCO PARISI, Oppenheimer Wolff and Donnelly Professor of Law, University of Minnesota and Professor of Economics, University of Bologna
DENIS PHILIPPE, Professor of Law, Université Catholique de Louvain
ANTONIO PINTO MONTEIRO, Professor of Law, University of Coïmbra
ANDREAS THIER, Professor of Legal History, Ecclesiastical Law, Legal Theory and Private Law, University of Zurich
RAPHAEL THUNHART, Deputy Judge, Graz
LUBOŠ TICHÝ, Professor of Law, Charles' University of Prague
MATJAŽ TRATNIK, Professor of Law, University of Maribor
ANASTASSIOS VALTOUDIS, Professor of Law, Aristotle University of Thessaloniki
WILLEM WIGGERS, Senior Legal Consultant, Amsterdam

Contributors in the editing process

ELLA VAN DEN BRINK
TOBIAS MIETHANER
LOVRO TOMASIC

Books in the series

Unexpected Circumstances in European Contract Law
Edited by Ewoud Hondius and Hans Christoph Grigoleit
9781107003408

Personality Rights in European Tort Law
Edited by Gert Brüggemeier, Aurelia Colombi Ciacchi and Patrick O'Callaghan
9780521194914

Precontractual Liability in European Private Law
Edited by John Cartwright and Martijn Hesselink
9780521516013

Environmental Liability and Ecological Damage in European Law
Edited by Monika Hinteregger
9780521889971

The Enforcement of Competition Law in Europe
Edited by Thomas M.J. Möllers and Andreas Heinemann
9780521881104

Commercial Trusts in European Private Law
Edited by Michele Graziadei, Ugo Mattei and Lionel Smith
9780521849197

Mistake, Fraud and Duties to Inform in European Contract Law
Edited by Ruth Sefton-Green
9780521844239

Security Rights in Movable Property in European Private Law
Edited by Eva-Maria Kieninger
9780521839679

Pure Economic Loss in Europe
Edited by Mauro Bussani and Vernon Valentine Palmer
9780521824644

The Enforceability of Promises in European Contract Law
Edited by James Gordley
9780521790215

Good Faith in European Contract Law
Edited by Reinhard Zimmermann and Simon Whittaker
9780521771900

General editors' preface

This is the eleventh book in the series the *Common Core of European Private Law*. This project was launched in 1993 at the University of Trento under the auspices of the late Professor Rudolf B. Schlesinger. The methodology used in the Trento project is novel. By making use of case studies it goes beyond mere description to detailed enquiry into how most European Union legal systems resolve specific legal questions in practice, and leads to thorough comparison between those systems. It is our hope that these volumes will provide scholars with a valuable tool for research in comparative law and in their own legal systems. The collection of materials that the *Common Core* project is offering to the scholarly community is already quite extensive and will become even more so when more volumes are published. The availability of materials attempting a genuine analysis of how things are is, in our opinion, a prerequisite for a stimulating and critical discussion on how they should be. Perhaps in the future European private law will be authoritatively restated or even codified, as is envisaged in the Draft Common Frame of Reference. The analytical work carried on by the nearly 300 scholars involved in the *Common Core* project is a precious asset of knowledge and legitimisation for any such normative enterprise.

We must thank the editors and contributors to the results published so far. With a sense of deep gratitude we also wish to recall our late Honorary Editor, Professor Rudolf B. Schlesinger.

Preface

In 1993, the *Common Core of European Private Law* project was launched. Ever since, three groups convene every year to discuss themes to be taken up. In the group on contract law, the theme of unexpected circumstances was suggested on various occasions. As a matter of fact, one of the hypothetical cases dealt with in the very first theme that led to a published volume was about change of circumstances.[1] In 2001, the general editors of the series, Mauro Bussani and Ugo Mattei, asked Ewoud Hondius, later to be joined by Hans Christoph Grigoleit, to set up a group on this subject. National reporters were then selected, both from within the Trento/Torino participants and from outside the group.

At the group's first meeting in 2001 reporters for Belgium (Luc Vael), France (Anthony Chamboredon) - both later replaced by Denis Philippe (Belgium) - Germany (Carsten Herresthal), Italy (Francesco Macario), the Netherlands (Mirella Peletier, later replaced by Willem Wiggers), Portugal (Júlio Gomes and Antonio Pinto Monteiro) and Sweden (Bert Lehrberg) discussed a questionnaire to be sent out. During the meeting or at later stages, the charter members were joined by members for Austria (Brigitta Lurger), the Czech Republic (Luboš Tichý), Denmark (Kim Østergaard), England and Ireland (Robert Clark and Cliona Kelly), Greece (Anastassios Valtoudis), Lithuania (Valentinas Mikelenas), Scotland (Laura Macgregor), Slovenia (Matjaž Tratnik) and Spain (Odavia Bueno Diaz and Luz Martinez Velencozo). At various moments, it was also envisaged that national reports from Estonia, Finland, Hungary, Latvia, Luxemburg, Poland, Slovakia, Switzerland and Turkey would be included, but for various reasons these efforts failed to

[1] Reinhard Zimmermann and Simon Whittaker, *Good Faith in European Contract Law*, (Cambridge University Press, 2000), pp. 557–77.

materialise. From the very start, Francesco Parisi undertook to complete the project with a law and economics approach.

The group then set out to establish a questionnaire. Instead of using an autocratic method, whereby a general reporter comes up with a list of proposals, individual members of the group were invited to submit hypothetical cases, which were then subjected to approval by the group. The group first selected five 'hard core cases', which were later joined by ten other hypotheticals. In order not to burden reporters and readers with too many cases, some hypothetical cases were actually set up as combinations of two or more issues. Questions of remedies were not set out in separate hypotheticals, but rather dealt with as side issues in the core cases.

The core of the volume consists of these cases (Part III). They are preceded by an introductory part (Part I) and an overview (Part II) and concluded with an evaluation (Part IV). The introductory part (Part I) begins with a general comparative introduction in Chapter 1. In the history of Roman law and canonical law, the doctrine of *rebus sic stantibus* has played a role of importance.[2] This is reflected in Chapter 2 of Part I. Chapter 3 of Part I is devoted to a law and economics approach of unexpected circumstances.

In the editing process and in the comparative evaluation of the national reports we have received profound support from Ella van den Brink, at the time a student in the legal research master programme of the University of Utrecht, Tobias Miethaner, public attorney at the District Court of Munich, and Lovro Tomasic, PhD candidate at the University of Munich. In finalising the volume, the editors were furthermore assisted by Paul van Heijnsbroek, at the time a student in the legal research master programme of the University of Utrecht, by Rodrigo Momberg, PhD candidate at the University of Utrecht and by Wolfgang Sigler, candidate of law at the University of Regensburg.

The editors wish to thank the organisers of the annual common core conferences in Trento and Torino, Mauro Bussani and Ugo Mattei, for their intellectual support and Carla Boninsegna and Emanuela Amsler for their administrative assistance, as well as the publishers, in particular Finola O'Sullivan and Sinead Moloney, for their support. The linguistic support of Peter Morris and Kate Ollerenshaw is gratefully acknowledged.

The manuscript was completed in 2009, but an occasional reference to later publications has been added.

[2] See P. Abas, *Rebus sic stantibus*, (Deventer: Kluwer, 1989), p. 259 (in 1993 a German edition of this book was published by Heymann in Cologne).

Abbreviations

AAVV	Autores varios (various authors)
ABGB	Allgemeines Bürgerliches Gesetzbuch
AC	Appeal Cases
AcP	Archiv Civilistisches Praxis
Act.C	Actualidad Civil
ADC	Anuario de Derecho Civil
AJDA	L'actualité juridique: revue mensuelle: Droit administrative
AK	Civil Code [Greece]
All ER	All England Reports
AP	Areios Pagos (Supreme Court)[Greece]
BB	Betriebs Berater
BGB	Bürgerliches Gesetzbuch
BGBI	Bundes Gesetz Blatt
BGH	Bundesgerichtshof
BGHZ	Bundesgerichtshof Entscheidungen
BLR	Building Law Reports
BJ	Belgique Judiciare
BT-Ds	Bundestag Drucksachen
Bull.civ.	Bulletin des arrêts de la cour de cassation rendus en matiēre civile
Cass	Cassation; Cassazione
CC	Code civil, Codice civile, Código Civil
CE	Conseil d'Etat
Ch	Chancery
CLR	Commonwealth Law Reports
CO	Slovenian Code of Obligations
D	Recueil Dalloz

DB	Des Betrieb
DCFR	Draft Common Frame of Reference
DEE	Dilcaio Etairian kai Epichiriseon
DP	Dalloz Periodique
Eng Rep	English Reports
Erm	interpretation [Greece]
EvBl	Evidenzblatt der Rechtsmittelentscheidungen des Obersten Gerichtshofes [Austria]
FSR	Fleet Street Patent Law Reports
GP	Gazette du Palais
Hell D	Helliniki Dikaiosym
HR	Hoge Raad
ICC	International Chamber of Commerce
ILRM	Irish Law Reports Monthly
IR	Irish Reports
IRCL	Irish Reports Common Law
JBl	Juristische Blätter
JCB	Jurisprudence commercial de Belgique
JCP	Jurisclasseur périodique
Jlg	Revue de jurisprudence de Liège, Mons et Bruxelles
JLMB	Jurisprudence de Liège, Mons et Bruxelles
JT	Journal des Tribunaux
Jus	Juristische Schulung
JZ	Juristenzeitung
KB	King's Bench
KritE	Kritiki Epitheorisi
LM	Lindenmaier-Möhring, Nachschlagwerk des Bundesgerichtshofs.
MAC Clause	Material Adverse Change Clause
MDR	Monatsschrift für Deutsches Recht
NBR	New Brunswick Reports
NDik	Nomo Dikeon
NJ	Nederlandse Jurisprudentie
NJA	Nytt Juridiskt Arkir
NJW	Neue Juristische Wochenschrift
NoV	Nomiko Vima
NSWLR	New South Wales Law Reports
NZLR	New Zealand Law Reports
OGH	Oberlandesgericht

Pas	Pasicrisie
PECL	Principles of European Contract Law
Pir Nom	Piraiks Namologia
RCJB	Revue critique de jurisprudence belge
RDC	Revue de droit commercial belge
RDM	Revista de Derecho Mercantil
RGDC	Revue générale de droit civil belge
RGLJ	Revista General de Legislación y Jurisprudencia
RGZ	Reichsgericht Entscheidungen
RJ	Repertorio Jurisprudencia Aranzadi
RJC	Revista Juridica de Cataluna
RM	Rättsfall från Mourätterna
RRD	Revue régionale de droit
RTDCiv	Revue trimestrielle de droit civil
RW	Rechtskundig weekldad
SC	Sessions Cases
SLT	Scots Law Times
Sou	Statens Offentliga Utredningar
STS	Sentencia del Tribunal Supremo (Supreme Court Judgment)
SZ	Entscheidungen des österreichischen Obersten Gerichtshofes in Zivilsachen
TLR	Times Law Reports
TS	Tribunal Supremo
U	Ugeskrift for Retsvesen
WLR	Weekly Law Reports
WM	Wertpapier Mitteilungen
ZAS	Zeitschrift für Arbeits und Sozial recht
ZBI	Zentralblatt für die juristische Praxis
ZIP	Zeitschrift für Wirtschaftsrecht
ZMR	Zeitschrift für Miet und Rammrecht

PART I

Introduction and context

1 Introduction: An approach to the issues and doctrines relating to unexpected circumstances

EWOUD HONDIUS AND
HANS CHRISTOPH GRIGOLEIT

1. Setting the scene

A contract, once concluded, binds the parties and is intended to remain binding even if the circumstances change. For instance, if the financial position of one of the parties changes, his or her need for the object of the contract alters or the value of the object goes up or down, the validity of the contract itself will not be affected. However, some occurrences that go beyond the reasonable expectations of the parties may raise serious doubts as to the binding nature of contracts. For instance, what about the effect of events such as natural disasters, an oil crisis, an armed conflict or – to mention a quite recent significant event – a fundamental financial crisis? These or similar issues have been dealt with by courts in all European legal systems at some point and the historical perspective (cf. Chapter 2) reminds us that the issue of how to deal with unexpected circumstances has a long tradition in jurisprudence. In this Introduction we shall begin our comparative analysis with a survey of the central questions that dominate the issue of unexpected circumstances and prepare the ground for the more detailed analysis in the overview and case studies.

The eventualities of life are infinite and, therefore, the legal issues referring to unexpected circumstances present a kaleidoscopic picture. Still, it is possible to identify some categories of fact patterns that occur regularly and involve specific issues. Accordingly, in the questionnaire that was drafted as a starting point and that forms the backbone of our comparative analysis we have distinguished between four groups of unexpected circumstances that have proven to be of particular relevance in the context of private law:

- Group A: the equivalence of exchange is substantially affected;
- Group B: one party's use of contractual goods or services is substantially affected;

- Group C: failure of specific purposes (other than A and B);
- Group D: mutual mistake concerning the calculation underlying the contract.

In Group E some miscellaneous issues will be discussed.

2. *Pacta sunt servanda*

All jurisdictions dealt with in this volume – and most, if not all, other legal systems respecting individual liberties and the freedom of contract – are based on the principle that contractual obligations should be observed as the basis of contract law. In some jurisdictions with a statutory regime this principle has been codified, in others, like in common law jurisdictions, it is recognised on the basis of judicial tradition. The binding nature of contracts is traditionally referred to by the notion of *pacta sunt servanda* – the Latin of which perhaps misleadingly suggests that this was already a principle of Roman law, as we shall see in Chapter 2.

From a more general point of view, *pacta sunt servanda* is one aspect of the notion of individual autonomy. Under this idea individuals determine the rules governing their transactions by consent. It is a prerequisite of the freedom of contract that the rules that are consented to are binding on the relevant party as otherwise the agreement would be of little more than moral value and the functioning of contractual exchange would be endangered. Thus, freedom of contract corresponds with responsibility.

It would, of course, be irreconcilable with the principle of *pacta sunt servanda* if the validity of the contract was generally conditioned upon all the expectations of the parties and their realisation. This is particularly evident in light of the fact that the parties can generally examine the relevant information, assess the probability of uncertain events and specify the content of the contract according to their expectations and their willingness to take risks. On the other hand, in some cases the assessment of future developments and their comprehensive coverage by stipulations may be impossible or go beyond reasonable efforts.

Therefore, the issue of unexpected circumstances as it shall be explored in this volume refers to the limitations that are inherent in the contractual allocation of risks: it is not convincing to attribute the responsibility for the consequences of unexpected circumstances unilaterally to the burdened party based on the concept of *pacta sunt servanda* because a strict allocation of all exceptional events cannot be based on an autonomous act of contractual risk allocation. The limitations to contractual risk allocation are the reason why it is recognised in all European jurisdictions that the occurrence of unexpected circumstances may, under certain conditions, influence the validity of the rights and duties resulting from the contract. On the other hand, the principle of *pacta sunt servanda* and its fundamental function in a free society demand that the standard applied to loosening the binding terms of the contract must be restrictive.

3. General approach

In the different European jurisdictions, there are various legal concepts directed at achieving an equitable outcome where, due to unexpected circumstances, the strict stipulations of the contract or rules of law do not provide just results. Even though the objective of this study is to focus on the general phenomenon of unexpected circumstances rather than on specific doctrines, two important aspects will limit the scope of our analysis. First, the doctrines relevant in our context are directed at distributing risks arising from events that are not referred to specifically in the parties' agreement. It is not an issue of unexpected circumstances as defined for the purposes of this book if an eventuality materialises that has been specifically provided for in the contract even if the consequences may be burdensome to one party. Second, the concepts in question refer to events that are typically beyond the specific legal responsibility of either party. Cases of one-sided mistake or ('regular') breach of contract will be disregarded.

As far as the doctrinal solutions are concerned, two approaches that are used in the jurisdictions to deal with unexpected circumstances can be distinguished. On the one hand, cases of unexpected circumstances can be approached using conventional doctrines of contract law such as mistake, constructive interpretation, impossibility of performance and *laesio enormis* (cf. Section 4). On the other hand, in most legal systems there are doctrines that go beyond the conventional doctrines by identifying certain unexpected circumstances as an exception to the binding nature of the contract (cf. Section 5).

The latter doctrines are the most important source for our considerations and will prove to be essential in dealing with unexpected circumstances. Hence, they will play a major role in our comparative analysis. However, there is also a strong tendency to solve cases of unexpected circumstances using conventional contractual doctrines; these doctrines will play a significant role in the individual case reports.

4. 'Conventional' doctrines (relief based on the contract)

The doctrines in the first category refer to the contract itself as the basis for relief and will be referred to as conventional doctrines because they all apply generally and without specific regard to the unexpected and extraordinary nature of the event in question. Examples of such conventional doctrines are concepts such as (constructive) interpretation (especially implied terms), mistake, impossibility of performance and *laesio enormis*. In virtually all national reports, before addressing the unexpected event as such, the outcome of the case is assessed first based on conventional doctrines and many issues of unexpected circumstances are dealt with on the basis of such doctrines. These conventional doctrines do not openly address a conflict between the contractual agreement and the principles of equity but rather try to find a solution based on the (hypothetical) intentions of the parties that are adjusted to the unexpected event or on certain flaws in the mechanism of contracting such as mistake.

5. 'Exceptional' doctrines (relief based on extraordinary effects on the contract resulting from unexpected events)

The doctrines in the second category, on the other hand, provide relief for the burdened party on the basis of the extraordinary effects resulting from the unexpected circumstance in question. These doctrines are applied when relief cannot be derived from the parties' (hypothetical) intentions or from a flaw in the mechanism of contracting. It is the essence of these doctrines that they go beyond the contract itself, addressing the equity conflict between the (flawless but silent) contract and the extrinsic effects. Hence, the principle of equity is the basis of relief.

We call these doctrines exceptional because they openly derive an exception to the binding nature of the contract from the occurrence of an extrinsic effect. They can be put together under the heading *frustration of contract*. Frustration in this very broad sense means that the expectations of one or both parties have altered significantly after the conclusion of the contract and that this problem should be solved by a specific rule of law, separate from the contractual agreement. In a more technical sense, frustration of contract is a common law doctrine. In order to allow a first glance at the conceptual background, we shall outline this doctrine and some similar notions applied in various jurisdictions to solve problems of unexpected circumstances on a general level.

A. *Doctrine of Frustration*

The common law doctrine of frustration of contract is well explained in Lord Radcliffe's speech in *Davis Contractors Ltd* v. *Fareham UDC*[1] (see the England and Ireland, and Scotland sections of Chapter 4).

> Frustration occurs whenever the law recognises that without default of either party a contractual obligation has become incapable of being performed because the circumstances in which the performance is called for would render it a thing radically different from that which was undertaken in the contract. *Non haec in foedera veni.* It was not this that I promised to do.

Frustration is applied in cases which can generally be described as cases of impossibility but it is also extended to situations of frustration of purpose and illegality. While its scope potentially covers all unexpected circumstances, the courts are very reluctant to apply this doctrine. Only radical changes to the obligation will be taken into account under this doctrine.

The effect of frustration is to discharge the parties from future performance. In England, however, the effect is modified by the Law Reform (Frustrated Contracts) Act 1943, which allows for equitable compensation after the discharge of the contract.

B. Wegfall der Geschäftsgrundlage

In Germany, 'exceptional' relief is based on the notion of '*Wegfall der Geschäftsgrundlage*' that was introduced in legal literature, then recognised by the courts and finally codified in the German Civil Code with the reform of the German law of obligations (*Schuldrechtsreform*) that entered into force in 2002. In essence, the doctrine of *Wegfall der Geschäftsgrundlage* states that the binding character of the contract is suspended if the fundamental expectations of the parties are not fulfilled. These expectations may relate to matters already present at the time of contracting or to later events. Relief is only granted on the basis of *Wegfall der Geschäftsgrundlage* if the expectations are not accounted for in the contract or in more specific rules of law. If a case of *Wegfall der Geschäftsgrundlage* can be established, the court can either adjust the contractual obligation or allow a party to terminate the contract. The

[1] [1965] AC 696.

doctrine of *Wegfall der Geschäftsgrundlage* has been influential in many other jurisdictions, e.g. in Austria, Greece, Italy and Portugal.

C. Doctrine of assumptions

The doctrine of assumptions is applied in Denmark and Sweden and resembles the concept of *Geschäftsgrundlage*. Under this concept, a party may be relieved from its contractual obligations if the contract has unexpectedly become more burdensome. Similar to the German concept of *Geschäftsgrundlage*, the doctrine of assumptions can include mistakes at the time of conclusion as well as changes in circumstances after the conclusion of the contract. As far as the requirements of the doctrine are concerned, it bears a strong resemblance to the doctrine of *Geschäftsgrundlage*: in order to be operative, an assumption must be material and it must have been visible to the other party. If the doctrine applies, it generally allows a party to terminate the contract but the courts can also use it to adapt the contract. A concept that is very similar to the doctrine of assumptions and *Geschäftsgrundlage* is the doctrine of presupposition (*presupposizione*, *pressuposição*) which can be found in the legal systems of Italy and Portugal.

D. Clausula rebus sic stantibus

The doctrine of *clausula rebus sic stantibus*, as it is applied in Spain and Slovenia, focuses on circumstances that arise after the formation of the contract. It is applied in cases where performance has become extraordinarily burdensome (Spain) or where the balance of contractual obligations is fundamentally altered (Slovenia).

6. Legal consequences

Regardless of the respective doctrine, three different types of remedies can be distinguished in cases of a justified claim based on unexpected circumstances: the contract may be (i) terminated, (ii) adjusted or (iii) renegotiated.

A. Termination of the contract

A termination of the contract[2] provides for legal certainty in determining the consequences of the unexpected event as the rescission of the

[2] For simplification, we use the term 'termination' in the editors' comments to refer to all the different remedies that render the contract ineffective and may thereby lead to some kind of restitution (e.g., avoidance, rescission, cancellation etc.).

contract and the restitution of a (partial) exchange can be defined in an unambiguous way. In consequence, once a relevant claim has been accepted, there is little discretion left for the judge. The problem with termination is, however, that it only provides for an all-or-nothing solution, which might not always be appropriate taking into account the nature of the unexpected event and the resulting burdens. In particular, termination may completely shift the burden of the unexpected event to the party who would have benefited from it under the terms of the contract. Hence, jurisdictions that only offer termination as a remedy are more likely to apply very strict standards with regard to the requirements of entitlement to relief. The example of the doctrine of frustration in England, where the remedy of termination was complemented by compensation under the Law Reform (Frustrated Contracts) Act 1943, shows that such a lop-sided approach to the problem of unexpected circumstances is not very convincing.

B. Adjustment of the contract

The all-or-nothing approach of termination can be avoided if the terms of contracts are adjusted in accordance with the unexpected event and the principle of equity. An adjustment of the contract can be achieved by different methods. It can be qualified as an operation of law which the courts are called upon to carry out (e.g., the Netherlands, Spain, Sweden). An alternative mechanism is to entitle the burdened party to request adjustment which is then enforced by the courts (e.g., Germany, Italy). Another option is to combine termination of the contract with a claim of compensation for the party who would have benefited from the contract (e.g., England under the Law Reform (Frustrated Contracts) Act 1943). All the methods of adjustment have in common that they leave wide discretion to the courts in determining a fair allocation of risks related to the unexpected circumstances in accordance with the principle of equity. Therefore, the price of an equitable allocation of the risks is that courts strongly interfere with the parties' contractual dispositions. Consequently, the parties have little certainty with regard to the outcome of a lawsuit.

C. Renegotiation

The issue of court powers and of legal certainty may be solved if the adjustment of the contract is left to a process of renegotiation between the parties. It goes without saying that, in all jurisdictions, the contract can be saved if both parties decide to renegotiate and adjust their deal to unexpected circumstances. The problem with this solution is whether and how the law can enforce a duty to renegotiate. While most jurisdictions are reluctant to recognise a duty to renegotiate in good faith, the PECL formulates such a duty (Art. 6:111 (2) PECL). The difficulty of applying a duty to renegotiate in good faith is that there is no exact standard available to define the conduct that is required by the parties. In addition, a duty to renegotiate in good faith can never fully replace rules of law on termination or adjustment as renegotiations may fail even if they are conducted in good faith. Therefore, the duty to renegotiate must be complemented by a fall-back rule that involves the general problems of termination and adjustment, as can be seen in the PECL (Art. 6:111 (3) PECL). This technique was considered undesirably complicated and heavy-handed by the DCFR, which therefore does not impose an obligation to negotiate but makes it a requirement for a remedy under Art. III.-1:110 DCFR that the debtor should have attempted in good faith to achieve a reasonable and equitable adjustment by negotiation.[3]

7. 'Open' versus 'closed' legal systems

Our analysis, which is based on the general introductory sections of the national responses to our questionnaire as well as on general theoretical reflections on the problem of unexpected circumstances, has indicated that two aspects are essential in evaluating the general approach to problems of unexpected circumstances. The first relevant aspect is the question of whether a general exceptional doctrine addressing unexpected circumstances is available. The second relevant aspect is whether a mechanism for adjusting the contract is generally available as a remedy. As the solutions reached in the jurisdictions will vary based on whether a combination of these two conceptual aspects is available or not, we will distinguish between two groups of jurisdictions with regard to these two essential aspects: the 'open' and the 'closed' jurisdictions.

[3] Christian von Bar and Eric Clive (eds.), *Principles, Definitions and Model Rules of European Private Law/Draft Common Frame of Reference* (Munich: Sellier, 2009) vol. I, p. 113. See Gerrit De Geest, 'Specific Performance, Damages and Unforeseen Contingencies in the Draft Common Frame of Reference', in: Pierre Larouche and Filomena Chirico (eds.), *Economic Analysis of the DCFR/The Work of the Economic Impact Group within CoPECL* (Munich: Sellier, 2010) pp. 123–32.

We shall refer to those jurisdictions that have established a general 'exceptional' doctrine specifically addressing the issue of unexpected circumstances that can lead to an adjustment of the contract as 'open' legal systems. 'Closed' legal systems, conversely, are those jurisdictions that do not offer such a doctrine either because they do not have a general 'exceptional' remedy addressing unexpected circumstances or, even if they have such a doctrine (as most legal systems do), this doctrine cannot lead to an adjustment of the contract as a general rule.

This distinction leads to the following groups of jurisdictions:

(i) 'open' legal systems are those of Austria, Germany, Greece, Italy, Lithuania, the Netherlands, Portugal, Spain and Sweden. The DCFR and the other model codes specified below in more detail can also be qualified as an 'open' system.

(ii) 'closed' jurisdictions are those of Belgium, the Czech Republic, Denmark, England, France, Ireland, Scotland and Slovenia.

As the respective national doctrines are not very homogenous, such a distinction is inevitably somewhat rough. On a closer look, with the concept of frustration and the wide judicial discretion with regard to damages under the Law Reform (Frustrated Contracts) Act 1943, England arguably has many characteristics of an 'open' jurisdiction. However, due to the limited scope and the restrictive requirements of the doctrine of frustration, in terms of the doctrinal approach and the results achieved, England is more in line with the group of 'closed' jurisdictions and will therefore be found in this group.

It needs to be stressed that the distinction between 'open' and 'closed' jurisdictions is essentially a doctrinal distinction that is based on the nature of the legal concepts applied rather than on the results that are achieved in the cases in our questionnaire. It depends on the availability of an 'exceptional' concept providing for contractual adjustment as a general form of relief. Even though 'closed' legal systems tend to be more reluctant to grant relief in situations of unexpected circumstances, this is not necessarily always the case. There may be 'exceptional' concepts that allow for termination of the contract and, of course, cases of unexpected circumstances may be solved based on 'conventional' doctrines. In particular, an adjustment of the contract can often be achieved by constructive interpretation and therefore even in a 'closed' legal system the contract can be adapted. Likewise, in the 'open' jurisdictions, relief as such can be subject to strict requirements. Hence, the results reached in an 'open' jurisdiction can be more restrictive than in a 'closed' one. Finally, it should be noted that an application of 'conventional' concepts, which are widely discussed in both the 'open' and the 'closed' jurisdictions, may lead to a convergence between the two, all the more so as these 'conventional' concepts are applied in cases of unexpected circumstances by the 'open' jurisdictions as well.

As far as we are aware, the distinction between 'open' and 'closed' jurisdictions has not been used before with regard to the question whether or not a jurisdiction has established a general 'exceptional' doctrine specifically addressing the issue of unexpected circumstances that can lead to an adjustment of the contract. However, the distinction itself is widely in use for other areas of the law, such as property law. Here, the 'closed' system is sometimes referred to when denoting the impossibility of establishing new categories and types of limited property rights (*iura in re aliena*).[4] Likewise, the reverse possibility of any content entering into contracts even if such content does not qualifying into an existing category is occasionally referred to as the 'open' system of contract.[5]

8. Unexpected circumstances in supervening legislation and in model codes

As far as the explicit statutory recognition of unexpected circumstances is concerned, even within the 'open' jurisdictions there has been some reluctance to adopt 'exceptional' doctrines (Like *Wegfall der Geschäftsgrundlage*, the doctrine of assumptions and *clausula rebus sic stantibus*) into legislation. Only some jurisdictions have integrated the 'exceptional' concepts into codified law as a result of quite recent changes (e.g., Germany, Italy, the Netherlands and Portugal). This reluctance is remarkable because the respective concepts have been discussed and elaborated in jurisprudence for a long time (cf. Chapter 2 for more

[4] According to T. H. D. Struycken, *De numerus clausus in het goederenrecht*, PhD Nijmegen (Deventer: Kluwer, 2007) p. 812 '[t]he 1888 explanatory *Motive* to the draft text of the German BGB spoke of 812 "*die geschlossene Zahl*" of property rights. The words *numerus clausus* seem to have first been used by the German Franz Wieacker in 1938; they reappeared in several places at about the same time, in 1952 in Italy and in 1953 in the title of Bolgar's article which was published in the United States'. See also Bram Akkermans, *The Principle of* Numerus Clausus *in European Property Law*, PhD Maastricht (Antwerp: Intersentia, 2008) 657 pp.

[5] See P. S. Atiyah, *The Rise and Fall of Freedom of Contract* (Oxford: Clarendon Press, 1979) 791 pp.

details). The reason for this cautious approach is the high esteem for the sanctity of contracts.

In particular, general concepts addressing the issue of unexpected circumstances can be found in all relevant restatements and model codes of European contract law. The latest draft code, the DCFR, provides relief in cases of unexpected circumstances. Under Art. III. – 1:110 (2) DCFR the court may adjust or terminate the contract if performance 'becomes so onerous because of an exceptional change of circumstances that it would be manifestly unjust to hold the debtor to the obligation'. Similar rules have been proposed by:

- The Commission on European Contract Law (cf. Article 6.111 PECL);
- UNIDROIT (cf. Articles 6.2.1–6.2.3 of the Principles of International Commercial Contracts);
- the revision of the Principles of European Contract Law (PECL) by the Association Henri Capitant des Amis de la Culture Juridique Française and the Société de Législation Comparée (cf. Article 7:101); and
- the Avant-projet de Code européen des contrats (Gandolfi project) (cf. Article 157).

These model rules can be found in the Appendix.

In some legal systems judicial adjustment seems to have been admitted on a broader level by subjecting (even non-standard-term) agreements to general judicial control under a reasonableness test (cf. Sweden and Denmark). Once such a general form of relief is available to judges, many cases of unexpected circumstances tend to be assessed according to this general provision rather than according to the more case-specific concepts of the aforementioned doctrines. However, even under such a general statutory requirement of good faith, a more specific set of rules and principles dealing with unexpected circumstances should eventually be defined which will be in line with the exceptional doctrines discussed in Section 5.

9. Specific legislation and contract terms specifically addressing unexpected circumstances

Various jurisdictions have adopted specific rules, either in statutory regulation or in case-law, dealing with change of circumstances in certain contractual situations. For instance, in many jurisdictions, there is a special regulation with regard to labour contracts allowing the employee to terminate an employment contract when his interests have materially changed.

Alongside the legislation, in contractual practice certain clauses have been developed to address specifically the issue of unexpected circumstances. Even though such terms have become more and more common in the form of the so-called hardship clauses, they are not considered to be an element of the *lex mercatoria*. The parties' purpose behind the use of hardship clauses is to solve the issue of unexpected circumstances without intervention by the courts. However, inasmuch as vague standards are applied in hardship clauses, judicial intervention is unavoidable if amicable solutions cannot be achieved. A model hardship clause is provided by the International Chamber of Commerce (ICC). Another such common contract term with some affinity to the issue of unexpected circumstances is the so-called Material Adverse Change (MAC) clause used in contracts dealing with mergers and acquisitions. Yet, these clauses typically refer to the period between 'signing' and 'closing' and therefore they control issues that arise before the contract has become final.

10. Matters not dealt with

Changes of circumstances may become an issue not only in private law but also in administrative law. This field of law is not dealt with in this volume. It is worth mentioning, however, that, under French law, there is a famous contradiction between contract law and administrative law with regard to unexpected circumstances: while the French civil courts do not recognise the doctrine of *imprévision* as a mechanism to set aside a contract (*Canal de Craponne*), the administrative courts have applied it. Another example not dealt with in this volume is public international law. Article 61 of the Vienna Convention of the Law of Treaties of 1969 for instance deals with impossibility of performance and Article 62 deals with 'fundamental change of circumstances'.

2 Legal history

ANDREAS THIER

1. Unexpected change of circumstances: perspectives of legal history

From the historical perspective, basically three legal concepts are worth exploring with regard to the influence of an unexpected change of circumstances on legal transactions. The first one, the *clausula rebus sic stantibus* doctrine, has its roots in Roman philosophy and was developed as a normative rule during the Middle Ages. Second, the concept of (tacit) presupposition ('*Voraussetzungslehre*') emerged in the German legal discourse of the late nineteenth century. At the same time the third doctrine to be examined here, the idea of *frustration of contract*, was created by the English courts in order to cope not only with an unexpected change of circumstances in general, but also with cases of impossibility. In Section 2 below the Roman foundations of the *clausula* rule and the emergence of this doctrine during the period of the *ius commune*, which began in the thirteenth century will be discussed. Section 3 addresses the development of that doctrine in the Early Modern Period between the sixteenth and the eighteenth centuries. The final section will focus on the development during the nineteenth and the early twentieth centuries in which the doctrine of presupposition and the idea of frustration have come to the fore (section below).

2. The emergence of the *clausula* doctrine

In ancient Roman law the stability of contracts was one of the underlying principles of contract law.[1] Even though the parties could subject a contract to certain conditions, the Roman jurists did not recognise a

[1] For a (differentiating) survey see Reinhard Zimmermann, *The Law of Obligations. Roman Foundations of the Civilian Tradition* (Oxford/New York: Clarendon Press, 1990), pp. 578, 800.

specific doctrine relieving the parties of their obligations if unexpected circumstances occurred.[2] Hence Fritz Schulz, referring to the Roman law of sale, stated that there was an 'iron rule' of the binding power of (sales) contracts once they were concluded.[3] Against such a background it is not surprising that the first statements about the question of changing circumstances emerged in the philosophical discourse. Cicero (106 BC–43 BC) appears to be the first thinker to reflect on this situation.[4] He argued that it would be unethical to return a sword to its depositor if this depositor had become insane in the meantime.[5] That situation was, as Cicero stated, an example of numerous cases where the course of time would change something originally honourable into a dishonourable pattern.[6] As we shall see later the moralist essentials of this notion became influential especially in the Christian tradition and therefore also in the context of medieval canon law. It was, however, Seneca (4 BC–AD 65)[7] who created the formula of the *clausula rebus sic stantibus* by stating that 'all conditions must be the same as they were when I made the promise if you mean to hold me bound in honour to perform it'.[8]

Nevertheless, it was the sword example used by Cicero that was transmitted in the early tradition of Christian thought. Augustine of Hippo (AD 354–AD 430) inserted this case in a treaty on the psalms, stating that it would be 'evident' ('*manifestum*') that due to the changed mental

[2] Cf. Otto Fritze, 'Clausula rebus sic stantibus', (1900) 17 *Archiv für bürgerliches Recht*, 20–49, at 22 *et seq.*; Margarethe Beck-Mannagetta, 'Die clausula rebus sic stantibus und die Geschäftsgrundlage in der Dogmengeschichte', in: Bruno Paradisi (ed.), *La formazione storica del diritto moderno in Europa* (Florence: Leo S. Olschki, 1977), vol. III, pp. 1263–76, 1267 *et seq.*; for a survey see also Rudolf Meyer-Pritzl, '§§313–314: Störung der Geschäftsgrundlage. Kündigung von Dauerschuldverhältnissen aus wichtigem Grund', in: Mathias Schmoeckel, Joachim Rückert and Reinhard Zimmermann (eds.), *Historisch-Kritischer Kommentar zum BGB* (Tübingen: Mohr Siebeck, 2008), vol. II, n. 4.

[3] Fritz Schulz, *Classical Roman Law* (Oxford: Clarendon Press, 1951, repr. 1961), n. 917. In particular Schulz referred to the question whether the exchange of services could be reversed. Critical of this generalising statement, however, is Zimmermann, *Law of Obligations*, p. 800.

[4] For Cicero's position in the legal and philosophical discourse of his time see Jill Harries, *Cicero and the Jurists. From Citizens' Law to the Lawful State* (London: Duckworth, 2006), pp. 51–8 *et passim*, arguing that Cicero considered philosophy and rhetoric to be higher than jurisprudence.

[5] Cicero, De officiis 3, 95: *Si gladium quis apud te sana mente deposuerit, repetat insaniens, reddere peccatum sit, officium non reddere ...*

[6] Cicero, De officiis 3, 95: *Sic multa, quae honesta natura videntur esse, temporibus fiunt non honesta.*

[7] Brad Inwood, *Stoic Philosophy in Rome* (Oxford/New York: Clarendon Press, 2005).

[8] Seneca, De beneficiis, 4, 35, 3: *Omnia esse debent eadem, quae fuerunt quum promitterem, ut promittentis fidem teneas.*

condition of the depositor the sword would have to be kept at the depository.[9] This statement was transmitted in the textual context of medieval canon law.[10] This becomes clear in the *Decretum Gratiani* (composed around AD 1140), which marked the rise of a scientific medieval canonical jurisprudence.[11] The insertion of the Augustine text in Gratian's *Decretum*[12] appears to have been the starting point[13] for a debate between the medieval jurists concerning if and to what extent a change of circumstances would also result in a change of a contract. Johannes Teutonicus, the author of the *Glossa ordinaria* on Gratian's *Decretum*,[14] drew the conclusion from the Augustine text that every contract would be subject to the condition of constant circumstances.[15] Teutonicus applied this rule even to an oath sworn by a husband never to leave his wife and then noticing that his wife is betraying him. Pope Innocent III had already ruled that, for this case, the oath would be subject to the condition of the lawful behaviour of the wife.[16]

9 Augustine, Enarrationes in psalmos, 5, 7: *si cui gladius commendetur, et promittat se redditurum cum ille qui commendavit poposcerit; si forte gladium suum repetat furens, manifestum est tunc non esse reddendum, ne vel se occidat vel alios, donec ei sanitas restituatur.*

10 For the transmission of the Augustine text, mainly by Ivo of Chartres (AD 1040–AD 1117), see Linda Fowler-Magerl, *Clavis Canonum. Selected Canon Law Collections before 1140* (Hannover: Hahrsche Buchhandlung, 2005) (Monumenta Germaniae Historica, Hilfsmittel, 21), (for references in Ivo's Decretum, his Panormia and the so-called 'Tripartita', which was created at least in his environment).

11 See as a survey Thomas Duve, 'Corpus Iuris Canonici', in: Stanley N. Katz (ed.), *Oxford International Encyclopedia of Legal History*, (Oxford University Press, 2009), vol. II, pp. 218–225. See also Andreas Thier, 'Corpus Iuris Canonici', in: Albrecht Cordes, Heiner Lück and Dieter Werkmüller with philologic co-operation by Ruth Schmidt-Wiegand (eds.), *Handwörterbuch zur Deutschen Rechtsgeschichte*, (Berlin: 2nd edn, 2008), vol. I, pp. 894–901, 895–6.

12 *Decretum Gratiani*, Causa 22, Quaestio 2, c. 14.

13 The question of the medieval origins of the *clausula* doctrine has been controversially debated; see the survey in Beck-Mannagetta, 'Die clausula rebus sic stantibus', pp. 1268–70. It has also been argued that the major point of textual reference has been D. 12.4.8. See for this position Meyer-Pritzl, '§§313–314', n. 4, who, however, does not even mention the approach of Gratian's *Decretum*. See also Reinhard Zimmermann, '"Heard melodies are sweet, but those unheard are sweeter . . ." Conditio tacita, implied condition und die Fortbildung des europäischen Vertragsrechts', (1993) 193 *Archiv für die civilistische Praxis*, 121–73, 134.

14 For a short survey see Kenneth Pennington, Medieval Canonists, s. v. 'Johannes Teutonicus' http://faculty.cua.edu/pennington/1140i-p.htm.

15 Johannes Teutonicus, Gloss ad C. 22 q. 2 c. 14, ad v. 'furens', quoted from the Lyon edition of 1618, col. 1258: *Ergo semper subintelligitur haec conditio, si res in eodem statu manserit . . . Et est hic arg(umentum) quod propter novum casum datur auxilium . . .*

16 Decretal *Quemadmodum*, 2.24.25 . . . *quia in illo iuramento talis debet conditio subintelligi, si videlicet illa contra regulam desponsationis non venerit*; see for this decretal also Robert Feenstra, 'Impossibilitas and Clausula rebus sic stantibus. Some Aspects of Frustration

Commenting on this papal ruling, Teutonicus made it clear that 'many conditions have to be seen with oaths like these . . .' and referred to his formula *si res in eodem*.[17] Obviously, here the legal treatment of unexpected circumstances was grounded in the idea that the parties would establish rules for future developments which they did not foresee at the time of contracting.

A similar notion was discussed by the glossators of Roman law:[18] Accursius (AD 1182/5–AD 1260/3) created the formula *rebus sic se habentibus*, which was applied by Bartolus (AD 1313–AD 1357) to two cases and was widened by Baldus (AD 1327–AD 1400) to all cases of promises.[19] Similar to the canonistic tradition, Bartolus and in particular Baldus limited the binding power of a promise by postulating an implied tacit condition. Thus Baldus stated as a 'rule that every promise is to be understood with the circumstances being the same (*rebus sic se habentibus*)'.[20] Later on, the learned jurisprudence adopted these conceptions.[21] As Baldus' statement shows, the normative approach to unexpected circumstances now included interpretation (in terms of a kind of rebuttable presumption of the inclusion of an implied tacit condition). This becomes clear in particular in the writings of Philippus Decius (AD 1434–AD 1535).[22] He stated as a 'general rule that the words of a contract and of a statute are to be understood under the circumstances being and that they can therefore be contravened if a supervening event occurrs (*ex causa supervenienti*)'.[23] This

of Contract in Continental Legal History up to Grotius', in: Alan Watson (ed.), *Daube Noster, Essays in Legal History for David Daube* (Edinburgh/London: Scottish Academic Press/ Chatto and Windus, 1974), pp. 78–104, 82.

17 Johannes Teutonicus, 'Apparatus glossarum', in: Kenneth Pennington (ed.), *Compilationem tertiam*, Gloss ad 3 Comp. 2.15.11 ad v. subintelligenda condicio (Vatican City: Biblioteca Apostolica Vaticana, 1981 = Monumenta Iuris Canonici, ser. A, vol. 3), p. 285: . . . *quod plerumque condiciones intelliguntur in iuramentis ut hec* . . ..

18 Feenstra, 'Impossibilitas', pp. 82 *et seq.*

19 For a detailed analysis see Michael Rummel, *Die 'clausula rebus sic stantibus'. Eine dogmengeschichtliche Untersuchung unter Berücksichtigung der Zeit von der Rezeption im 14. Jahrhundert bis zum jüngeren Usus Modernus in der ersten Hälfte des 18. Jahrhunderts* (Baden-Baden: Nomos, 1991 = Fundamenta Juridica, 13), pp. 24–8.

20 Baldus de Ubaldis, 'Commentary ad D. 46.3.38, n. 2', in: Baldus de Ubaldis, *Commentaria Omnia* (Venice: 1599), vol. IV, fol. 36va: . . . *regulam, quod omnes promissio intelligitur rebus sic se habentibus.*

21 For a detailed analysis see Rummel, *Clausula*, pp. 38–66 with further reference.

22 For a short bio-bibliographical survey see Pennington Medieval Canonists, http:// faculty.cua.edu/pennington/1298l-z.htm.

23 Philippus Decius, Consilia sive responsa, consilium 335 n. 4, quoted from the edition Venedig 1570, fol. 364[ra]: *Et est regula communis quod verba contractus et statuti intelliguntur rebus sic stantibus ideo ex causa supervenienti contraveniri potest.*

kind of presupposition of an implied condition fits within the overall tendency of learned medieval jurisprudence in the area of contractual obligations: since the late twelfth century the principle of *pacta sunt servanda* had become the leading rule first for the canonists and later on for the legists.[24] According to this doctrine, the binding power of every contract was based on the power of the contractual promise. Hence, a unilateral withdrawal from a contract was based on the content of the promise itself and constructed as a tacit condition. The canon law doctrine regarding breaches of contract corresponded to this approach: every contractual promise was given under the tacit condition that the promisee complied with the duties created by his contractual promise. If the promisee failed to do so the promisor was no longer bound by his initial promise, because the condition of his promise had not been fulfilled.[25] Thus the legal remedy for a change of circumstances and also a breach of contract was derived from the idea of the contractual promise.[26] Sharply distinct from this doctrine was the medieval conception of error and mistake, which only referred to essential elements of the contract itself (comprising *error in negotio, in corpore, in persona*).[27]

3. The Early Modern period

The continuing rise of the *pacta sunt servanda* doctrine during the sixteenth and seventeenth centuries[28] resulted in a debate on the limits of binding contractual power. In the course of that debate

[24] For a survey see James Gordley, 'Good Faith in Contract Law in the Medieval ius commune', in: Reinhard Zimmermann and Simon Whittaker (eds.), *Good Faith in European Contract Law* (Cambridge University Press, 2000), pp. 93–117, 95–100; for a detailed discussion see Andreas Thier, '§ 311 Abs. 1 BGB', in: Schmoeckel, Rückert and Zimmermann (eds.), *Historisch-Kritischer Kommentar zum BGB*, vol. II, n. 11–14 with further references.

[25] In the canonist doctrine this condition was formulated with the words *si fides servetur*, cf. Georges Boyer, *Recherches Historiques sur la Résolution des Contrats (Origines de l'article 1184 C. Civ.)* (Paris: Hachette, 1924), pp. 221–42. For a survey see Andreas Thier, '§§346–359 BGB', in: Schmoeckel, Rückert and Zimmermann (eds.), *Historisch-Kritischer Kommentar zum BGB*, vol. II, n. 18.

[26] For a similar perspective see Zimmermann, *Law of Obligations*, pp. 580 *et seq.*

[27] Wolfgang Ernst, 'Irrtum. Ein Streifzug durch die Dogmengeschichte', in: Reinhard Zimmermann (ed.), *Störungen der Willensbildung bei Vertragschluss* (Tübingen: Mohr Siebeck, 2007), pp. 1–34, 11–17.

[28] For a survey see James Gordley, 'Some Perennial Problems', in: James Gordley (ed.), *The Enforceability of Promises in European Contract Law* (Cambridge University Press, 2001), pp. 1–21, 4–8, and Thier, '§311 Abs. 1 BGB', pp. 17–20.

the perspectives on the issues resulting from changes of circumstances shifted to the question whether and to what extent the contractual parties would include the altering conditions of their agreement in their contractual will. The starting point of this discussion was marked by Andreas Alciatus (AD 1492–AD 1550). He argued that the condition *rebus sic stantibus* was not always part of the will of the parties and that therefore also a change of their contractual will could not be assumed in every case of changing circumstances. Instead Alciatus distinguished between legal acts having been unilaterally set and acts based on a mutual agreement. In the case of a unilateral act a change of the party's will could be assumed if the party would presumably have disposed according to the new situation. In the case of mutual consent, however, the rule was not applicable in favour of only one party, as in this situation the will of both parties was crucial.[29] So, in Alciatus' concept the binding power of a contract and its basis in the originally concordant will of both parties prevailed – at least in tendency – over the interest of one single party to be relieved from its contractual obligations according to a change of circumstances.[30] But Alciatus made one important exception to his rule: if a new and not considered circumstance (*causa inconsiderata*) emerges, which *both* parties have presumably not preconceived, the rule of *rebus sic stantibus* will be applicable.[31] In this concept the idea of an implicit condition apparently lost ground. The emergence of an unexpected event was dealt with by an objective concept which had its basis not in the covenant itself but in the limits of the parties' foresight.

Initially, Alciatus' ideas found only little resonance in the jurisprudential debate.[32] Ulrich Zasius (AD 1461–AD 1535), for example, widened the concept of the *clausula rebus sic stantibus* stating 'as every agreement

[29] Andreas Alciatus, 'Tractatus de Praesumptionibus, praesumptio 16, n. 5 and 6', in: Andreas Alciatus, *Commentarii in aliquot Iuris civiles et Pontificii titulos* (Bale: 1557/1558, repr. Frankfurt/Main, 2004), vol. 4, col. 684: *Cum quaeritur an voluntas intelligitur, rebus sic stantibus aut sumus in actu dependente ex voluntate unius, et tunc si res incidat in casum, in quem verisimile sit disponenentem alias dispositurum, censetur mutata voluntas. . . . Aut loquimur in actu descendente ex voluntate duorum et non attenditur ista clausulae rebus sic stantibus, nec licet alteri mutare voluntatem.*

[30] For a more in-depth discussion of this complex doctrine see also Rummel, *Clausula*, pp. 80–5 with further reference.

[31] Alciatus, Tractatus, n. 6, col. 684: *Fallit . . .(scil. Regula), quando superveniet aliquis causa inconsiderata, de qua a partibus nihil verisimiliter esse agitatum.*

[32] Rummel, *Clausula*, pp. 85–95.

contains the tacit condition, i.e. *rebus sic stantibus*, a change of the things results in a change of the state of the agreement'.[33] Hugo Grotius (AD 1583–AD 1645), however, developed a more restrictive conception, which is, again, no coincidence: Grotius created a new doctrine of contract,[34] which he understood as a combination of a promise ('*promissio*') and the transfer thereof to the (potential) partner in the contract.[35] The *promissio* was also the starting point for Grotius' discussion of a limitation of contractual obligations by a *conditio tacita* and similar elements. Similar to Alciatius and some moral theologians[36] Grotius focused on the will of the promising party. He argued that the binding power of a promise was to be limited in two cases: if the underlying will of the obligation was defective or if a situation emerged that resulted in a contradiction to the will.[37] As part of the first restriction, the *defectus originarius voluntatis*, Grotius discussed the case of a 'failure of the reason (*ex cessatione rationis*), which alone and effectively moves the will'.[38] The difficulty here is the meaning of *ratio*. The term is sometimes interpreted as 'rationality' in general.[39] If this understanding is correct then Grotius would have introduced a new and very powerful device for

[33] Ulrich Zasius, 'Consilia, vol. 1, consilium 12, n. 81', in: Ulrich Zasius, *Opera omnia* (Lyon: 1550, repr. Aalen, 1966), vol. 6, col. 145: *tamen quia quaelibet conventione in se tacitam conditionem habet, scilicet rebus sic stantibus. . . unde rerum conditione mutata, iam et conventionis status mutatur.*

[34] For a detailed discussion see Malte Diesselhorst, *Die Lehre des Hugo Grotius vom Versprechen* (Cologne: Böhlau, 1959) (Forschungen zur neueren Privatrechtsgeschichte, vol. VI); Bruno Schmidlin, 'Die beiden Vertragsmodelle des europäischen Zivilrechts: das naturrechtliche Modell der Versprechensübertragung und das pandektistische Modell der vereinigten Willenserklärungen', in: Reinhard Zimmermann, Rolf Knütel and Jens Peter Meincke (eds.), *Rechtsgeschichte und Privatrechtsdogmatik* (Heidelberg: C.F. Müller, 1999), pp. 187, 190–193.

[35] Hugo Grotius, *De iure belli ac pacis libri tres in quibus ius naturae et gentium item iuris publici praecipua explicantur* (2nd edn, 1631, publ. by B. J. A. de Kanter-van Hettinga Tromp, 1939; Nd. 1993 newly edited based on the edition of 1646, by Robert Feenstra), pp. 335 *et seq.* (II, 11, §14): *Ut autem promissio jus transferat, acceptatio hic non minus quam in dominii translatione requiritur.* For this detail see also Thier, '§311', n. 17.

[36] Rummel, *Clausula*, pp. 96–101.

[37] Grotius, *De iure belli* p. 421 (II, 16, §22): *Restringens interpretatio (scil. promissionis) extra significationem verborum quae promissionem continent, aut ex defectu petitur originario voluntatis, aut ex casus emergentis repugnantia cum voluntate.*

[38] Grotius, *De iure belli*, p. 421 (II, 16, §22): . . . *ex cessatione rationis quae sola plene et efficaciter movit voluntatem.* The translation in the text stems from the translation in the anonymous English edition (1738), which was later edited by Jean Barbeyrac and, more recently edited by Richard Tuck, cf. Hugo Grotius, *The Rights of War and Peace* (Indianapolis: Liberty Fund, 2005), vol. II, p. 875.

[39] Rummel, *Clausula*, p. 103 with n. 390 and further reference.

the judicial control of contracts. *Ratio* (and its failure) would depend on the judgment of the court, thus being independent from the individual contract-related intentions of the parties. But another understanding of *ratio* is more likely: *ratio* might also be conceived as a reasonable motive. Evidence for this interpretation is given by Grotius' description of the relation between a promise and its *ratio.* A failure of reason is 'grounded on this, that what is contained in the promise, where such a particular reason is added or plainly implied, is not considered simply in itself, but as it falls under that reason.'[40] So, reason gave the promise its meaning and sense. But this did not mean that this specific sense had to comply with material rules of acting reasonably (e.g., to act ethically). Discussing this kind of *ratio* Grotius referred to the debate 'whether promises are to be understood with the tacit condition, if the things continue to be in the same posture'. But Grotius rejected this notion stating that the assumption of such a tacit condition 'has to be negated, unless it plainly appears that the present posture of things was included in that only reason we have talked of.'[41] At least with regard to a supervening change of circumstances Grotius did not adopt the former tradition in its original form:[42] Only if the expectation of an unchanged course of affairs is an element of the promisor's motive may the emergence of an unexpected event result in the rescission of the contract. Thus Grotius set clear limits to the *clausula* concept as only the frustration of the *specific* expectations of the promisor could trigger the rescission of the contract.[43]

There was, however, another Grotian clause for change of circumstances, the 'a new situation contradictory to the will' of the promisor (*repugnantia casus emergentis cum voluntate*).[44] It has been argued that this clause created new remedies for the modification or rescission of contracts in

40 Grotius, *De iure belli*, p. 421 (II, 16, §23): . . . *ex eo quod contentum in promissione, ubi ratio talis additur, aut de ea constat, non consideratur nude, sed quatenus sub ea ratione venit.* For the translation in the text see Grotius, *Rights*, p. 875.

41 Grotius, *De iure belli*, p. 422 (II, 16, §25): *Solet et hoc disputari, an promissa in se habeant tacitam conditionem, si res maneant quo funt loco: quod negandum est, nisi apertissime pateat, statum rerum praesentem in unica illa quam diximus ratione inclusum esse.* The translation in the text varies slightly from the translation in Grotius, *Rights*, p. 876.

42 There is apparently another perspective by Martin Josef Schermaier, *Die Bestimmung des wesentlichen Irrtums von den Glossatoren bis zum BGB* (Vienna/Cologne/Weimar: Böhlau Verlag, 2000 = Forschungen zur Neueren Privatrechtsgeschichte, vol. 29), p. 176, arguing that Grotius combined the *clausula* rule and elements of the traditional error doctrine '*in der Figur der conditio tacita*'.

43 For a similar view see Zimmermann, 'Heard melodies', 135.

44 Grotius, *De iure belli*, p. 422 (II, 16, §26). See also *ibid.* p. 421 (II, 16, §22).

Grotius' doctrine, because this clause would provide room to account for nearly every mistake as to future developments.[45] If this interpretation is correct, Grotius would, on the one hand, have limited the traditional *clausula rebus sic stantibus* rule while, on the other, have created a new and even further-ranging doctrine for a change of circumstances. But this understanding turns out to be arguable if we take a closer look at Grotius' text. A *repugnantia* against the will of the promising person could emerge in two situations: the fulfilment of a promise could violate a law as in the case of the sword, mentioned above. More important is the second case in which a contradiction to the original will emerges because the performance of the obligation appears to be too 'grievous and burdensome either regarding the condition of human nature absolutely considered or by a comparison of the person and the thing in question with the very end of the engagement'.[46] Grotius gave three examples for this situation: first, an object, lent out to someone, could be demanded before the end of the time-span fixed in the contract if the lender had an urgent need for it; second, the promise to provide military support could cease if the promising party was attacked itself; and third, the exemption from taxes must not to be understood as an exemption also from extraordinary subsidies in the situation of a 'pressing necessity of affairs'.[47] As these examples demonstrate, the doctrine of the *repugnantia casus emergentis cum voluntate* corresponded more with a – quite restrictive – concept of exoneration limited to singular circumstances. Grotius was the first jurist with a precise conception of these cases. But it did not apply to other cases of an unexpected change of circumstances. In general, it might be concluded that Grotius based the *clausula* rule on the will of the parties thus adopting essential elements of the former tradition. At the same time he also took a more objective approach (based apparently on an Aristotelian tradition of equity, which will not be discussed here[48]): by focusing on the *ratio* of a promise as a reference point for a change of

[45] Apparently in this direction see Schermaier, *Die Bestimmung des wesentlichen Irrtums*, pp. 176 *et seq.*; for a survey of other similar approaches see Rummel, *Clausula*, pp. 107 *et seq.*

[46] Grotius, *De iure belli*, p. 423 (II, 16, §27 n. 1): ... *nimis grave atque intolerabile: sive absolute spectata conditione humanae naturae, sive comparando personam et rem de qua agitur, cum ipso fine actus*; for the English version (slightly different from that in the text) see Grotius, *Rights*, pp. 877 *et seq.*

[47] Grotius, *De iure belli*, p. 423 (II, 16, §27 n. 1): ... *summa necessitas*; the expression in the text is derived from Grotius, *Rights*, p. 878.

[48] James Gordley, *The Philosophical Origins of Modern Contract Doctrine* (Oxford: Clarendon Press, 1991), pp. 89 *et seq.* and *passim.*

circumstances and its impact on the contract, Grotius developed (at least in principle) a more objective standard.

Grotius' doctrine became very influential in continental European jurisprudence in the seventeenth and eighteenth centuries.[49] Over time the doctrine was slightly modified. Heinrich von Cocceji (AD 1644–AD 1719),[50] for example, accepted the rule of the tacit condition, *si res maneant quo sunt in loco*, but tried to limit its application to the essentials of a contract (*substantia negotii*).[51] Other authors, however, argued in favour of a broad application of the *clausula rebus sic stantibus* rule. This is in particular true for Augustin Leyser (AD 1683–AD 1752), who combined natural law and the newly emerged doctrine of the *usus modernus pandectarum* in his writings. For the purposes of this report, Leyser is an interesting author because he argued – apparently for the first time – not only in favour of a rescission of the contract, but also in favour of a modification: a modification should take place if a promise contained not only one but multiple *rationes*. In this case it would be wiser, as Leyser put it, 'that the promise is not dissolved, but modified in order to adapt to the present time and condition'.[52] Leyser's contribution to the evolution of *clausula rebus sic stantibus* is important also with regard to another point: often referred to as a supporter of a nearly boundless application[53] of the *clausula* doctrine,[54] Leyser reflected on the dangerous consequences of exactly such a boundless practice of the *clausula* rule and warned against a *maximus abusus* thereof.[55] In order to

[49] For a short survey see Zimmermann, 'Heard melodies', 135.

[50] For an English account of Cocceji's biography and his influence on Prussian judicial reforms see Hermann Weill, 'Judicial Reform in Eighteenth Century Prussia: Samuel von Cocceji and the Unification of the Courts', (1960) 4 *The American Journal of Legal History*, 226–40; for a recent survey see Christoph Link, 'Menschenwürde und Gerechtigkeit als Staatszweck. Zum Werk Heinrich von Coccejis (1644–1719)', in: *Die Ordnung der Freiheit. Festschrift für Christian Starck zum siebzigsten Geburtstag* (Tübingen: Mohr Siebeck, 2007), 87–98.

[51] For a detailed discussion see Rummel, *Clausula*, pp. 110–16.

[52] Augustin Leyser, *Meditationes ad pandectas* (Leipzig: 1744), vol. 7, specimen 520, §5, p. 847: . . . *promissio non penitus remittenda, sed temperanda tamen, atque ad presente tempus et conditionem adcommodanda est.*

[53] Cf. his statement *omnis stipulatio intelligitur, rebus sic stantibus*; Leyser, *Meditationes*, Specimen 520, §1, p. 842.

[54] See e.g. Zimmermann, *Law of Obligations*, p. 580, and Meyer-Pritzl, '§§313–314', n. 5; for a former and influential similar argument, see Roderich von Stintzing and Ernst Landsberg, *Geschichte der Rechtswissenschaft, section 3, sub-volume 1: Das Zeitalter des Naturrechts (Ende 17. bis Anfang 19. Jahrhundert)* (Munich: 1898, repr. Aalen: 1978), pp. 210 *et seq.*

[55] Leyser, *Meditationes*, Specimen 520, §3, p. 843: *Neque est, quod cum aliquibus metuas, admissa hac doctrina, instabilem pactorum et promissorum omnium fidem fore Nihil enim est, quod metuas, si*

prevent this kind of abuse Leyser argued that a change of circumstances could result in a rescission of the contract only if three conditions were fulfilled: (i) the promise would not have been given if the new circumstance had been present at the time of the original contractual agreement; (ii) the party claiming a rescission of the contract must not have been responsible for the change of circumstances; and (iii) the change of circumstances could not have been foreseen and prevented by the parties.[56] Therefore, in this approach a more objective - and quite modern - approach was presented: the remedy for unexpected changes of circumstances was no longer sought in the idea of a tacit condition. Instead it was considered to be crucial whether and to what extent the risk of a future change of circumstances could be located in the sphere of a contracting party. If this risk was not attributable to either party a rescission (or modification) of the contract was only possible if the new circumstance was crucial for *both* parties.

Leyser's position appears to be typical of a general trend in Europe.[57] Even though the *clausula* rule was accepted in general, it was at the same time held that this doctrine was limited to essential changes of circumstances.[58] This also became clear in the great codifications of the late eighteenth century.[59] The Bavarian Codex Maximilianeus Bavaricus

modo magistratus officium suum facit, nec cuiuslibet circumstantiae mutationem pro justa contractus rescindi causa admittit . . .; Specimen 520, §4, p. 845: *Regulae, quam in praecedentibus commemoravi: quod omnis stipulatio rebus sic stantibus intelligatur, et mutate rerum facie, obligare desinat; maximus est abusus. Confugiunt ad eam, quotquot promissionis suae poenitet, et casum ac vicissitudinem qualemcumque, in rebus humanis indeclinabilem, inconstantiae suae causam obtendunt. Impudenter saepe. Et faciunt id tamen etiam in negotiis ac controversiis publicis . . .* For a similar approach to Leyser, see Klaus Luig, 'Richterkönigtum und Kadijurisprudenz im Zeitalter von Naturrecht und Usus modernus: Augustin Leyser (1683 - 1752)', in: *Das Profil des Juristen in der europäischen Tradition. Symposion aus Anlaß des 70. Geburtstages von Franz Wieacker* (Ebelsbach: Gremer, 1980), pp. 295–333, 325 *et seq.* and *passim.*

56 Leyser, *Meditationes*, Specimen 520, §3, p. 843: *. . . ut, si eadem rerum facies, quae nunc est ab initio adfuisset, alter nihil promisisset. Videndum praeterea, an mutatio haec sine omni eius, qui recedere a pacto cupit, culpa acciderit . . .*. Specimen 520, §4, p. 845 (Headline): *Mutatio rerum, quam paciscentes facile ab initio praevidere cavereque potuerunt, non tribuit justam recedendi ab obligatione causam.*

57 See as a survey: Helmut Coing, *Europäisches Privatrecht, Bd. I: Älteres gemeines Recht (1500–1800)* (Munich: C.H. Beck, 1985), p. 412, now corrected by the study by Rummel, *Clausula*, pp. 132–78.

58 Zimmermann, 'Heard melodies', 136, even argues that the *clausula* rule was going to vanish; another perspective - similar to the argument in the text - can be found in Meyer-Pritzel, '§§313–314', n. 5 with further references.

59 For a short survey regarding the legal treatment of unexpected circumstances in the late eighteenth century codifications see Beck-Mannagetta, 'Die clausula rebus sic stantibus', pp. 1274 *et seq.*

Civilis adopted Leyser's doctrine in part.[60] The General State Laws for the Prussian States (1794) ruled that if an unexpected change of circumstances made the attainment of the declared contractual purpose or the purpose of the nature of the contract impossible, every party could withdraw from the contract.[61] A similar rule was inserted in the Austrian General Civil Code, but it only referred to the law of preliminary contracts.[62]

Another approach, however, was adopted in English common law. Here, the idea of absolute liability in contract left no room for the impact of unexpected circumstances on the contract. The case of *Paradine* v. *Jayne*[63] established the tradition of absolute liability in contract and attributed the risk of unexpected circumstances to each party.[64] In *Paradine* v. *Jayne* a tenant had been expelled from his leased grounds by a foreign army and had claimed to be excused from rental payments. But the Court of the King's Bench rejected this argument. The judges held 'that as the lessee is to have the advantage of casual profits, so he must run the hazard of casual losses, and not lay the whole burthen of them upon his lessor.' The background of this argument was the idea of absolute binding contractual power, 'when the party by

60 See for a more in-depth discussion Jochen Emmert, *Auf der Suche nach den Grenzen vertraglicher Leistungspflichten* (Tübingen: Mohr Siebeck, 2001 = Beiträge zur Rechtsgeschichte des 20. Jahrhunderts, 32), pp. 152 *et seq.*

61 §378 I 5 ALR: *Wird jedoch durch eine solche unvorhergesehene Veränderung die Erreichung des ausdrücklich erklärten, oder aus der Natur des Geschäfts sich ergebenden Endzwecks beyder Theile unmöglich gemacht, so kann jeder derselben von dem noch nicht erfüllten Vertrage wieder abgehn.* §377 I 5 ALR laid down the rule that *in general* a change of circumstances would give no right to deny contractual duties: *Außer dem Fall einer wirklichen Unmöglichkeit, kann wegen veränderter Umstände, die Erfüllung eines Vertrags in der Regel nicht verweigert warden.* For a more in-depth discussion see Emmert, *Suche*, pp. 152–9.

62 *Die Verabredung, künftig erst einen Vertrag schließen zu wollen, ist nur dann verbindlich, wenn sowohl die Zeit der Abschließung, als die wesentlichen Stücke des Vertrages bestimmt, und die Umstände inzwischen nicht dergestalt verändert worden sind, daß dadurch der ausdrücklich bestimmte, oder aus den Umständen hervorleuchtende Zweck vereitelt, oder das Zutrauen des einen oder andern Theiles verloren wird.*

63 (1647) Aleyn 26 = [1558–1774] All ER 172; for a detailed discussion of *Paradine* v. *Jayne* and its antecedents, see David Ibbetson, 'Absolute Liability in Contract: the Antecedents of Paradine v. Jayne', in: *Consensus ad Idem. Essays in the Law of Contract in Honour of Guenter Treitel* (London: Sweet & Maxwell, 1996), pp. 3–37, *passim*, and Guenter Treitel, *Frustration and Force Majeure* (London: Sweet & Maxwell, 1994), 2–001–2–004.

64 For this common view of *Paradine* v. *Jayne* see, e.g., Grant Gilmore, *The Death of Contract* (Columbus: Ohio State University Press, 2nd edn, 1995), pp. 0.49–54 (also with a short survey on the parallel development in American contract law); Guenter Treitel, *The Law of Contract* (London: Sweet & Maxwell, 11th edn, 2003), p. 866, who calls this approach the 'doctrine of absolute contracts'.

his own contract creates a duty or charge upon himself, he is bound to make it good, if he may, notwithstanding any accident by inevitable necessity, because he might have provided against it by his contract.'[65] In this approach there was no room for the idea of tacit conditions or reasonable motives as possible reference points for a modification or a rescission of the contract in case of an unexpected change of circumstances. This judicial approach prevailed in England until the late nineteenth century even though minor exceptions to the *Paradine* rule had been granted by the courts.[66]

4. The nineteenth and early twentieth centuries

At the beginning of the nineteenth century the impact of the *clausula* doctrine was weak throughout Europe. As mentioned above, the German codifications and also the French Civil code exhibited varying degrees of reluctance to accept the idea of tacit conditions.[67] Instead the rules of error and impossibility covered cases of supervening events. This development was set forth in the contractual doctrine of the Historical School.[68] Here the binding power of the contractual will (or the protection of reliance on the contractual faith of the other party) left no room for the application of the *clausula* doctrine. This development was similar to the hostility of the pandestic doctrine towards the rescission of a contract in general.[69] It might be that the rapid economic change and the new dynamic of commerce fostered a change to these doctrinal standpoints, even though there is no clear evidence for this assumption in the available sources. However, during the late nineteenth century in Germany and in England new approaches to an unexpected change of circumstances emerged. While in Germany the crucial impulse was set by a legal author, Bernhard Windscheid (AD 1817–AD 1892), who presented the doctrine of presupposition ('*Voraussetzungslehre*'),[70] the development in the English common law was dominated by the courts, which began to apply the doctrine of frustration.

[65] *Paradine* v. *Jayne*, (1647) Aleyn 26.

[66] Treitel, *Frustration and Force Majeure*, 2-007-2-021.

[67] *Supra* at n. 59. See also Meyer-Pritzl, '§§313–314', n. 6.

[68] For a survey see Thier, '§311 BGB', nn. 19–21 with further references.

[69] For this phenomenon see Thier, '§§346–359 BGB', n. 24.

[70] Bernhard Windscheid, *Die Lehre des römischen Rechts von der Voraussetzung* (Dusseldorf: 1850); Bernhard Windscheid, 'Die Voraussetzung', (1892) 78 *Archiv für die civilistische Praxis*, 161–202. For a detailed discussion see Emmert, *Suche*, pp. 137–47.

The onset of the frustration doctrine was marked by the case of *Taylor* v. *Caldwell* in 1863:[71] the Surrey Gardens and Music Hall, rented by the plaintiff Taylor (and his partner Lewis) 'for the purpose of giving a series of four grand concerts and day and night fêtes at the Gardens', had been 'destroyed or so far damaged by accidental fire as to prevent' these 'entertainments'.[72] The plaintiffs demanded compensation for their losses (caused by their expenses in preparation and advertising).[73] Based on the *Paradine* rule this compensation would have had to be granted. Instead the court of the Queen's Bench rejected the claim: 'Although the civil law is not of itself authority in an English court', Blackburn, J stated, 'it affords great assistance in investigating the principles on which the law is grounded'.[74] In fact, Blackburn, J adopted this (as we have seen, former) tradition and stated that 'the contract is not to be construed as a positive contract, but as subject to an implied condition that the parties shall be excused in case, before breach, performance becomes impossible from the perishing of the thing without default of the contractor'.[75] As a consequence both parties were excused and their losses thus apportioned.[76] Later on, this rule[77] was applied not only to cases of impossibility,[78] but also to cases where the commercial *contractual purpose* was frustrated as in the famous coronation cases[79] like *Krell* v. *Henry*.[80] These cases – later recognised as typical cases of *frustration of purpose*[81] – arose as a consequence of the postponement of Edward VII's coronation and the eventual revision of its route.[82] Numerous contracts which had mostly been concluded in anticipation of the Royal Progress in order to provide facilities like seats or locations to watch the coronation became useless due to these events. Thus, as in *Krell* v. *Henry*, the question arose how to apportion the losses of this kind

[71] (1863) 3 *Best and Smith's Reports* 826. For a more in-depth discussion see Treitel, *Frustration and Force Majeure*, 2–024–2–028.

[72] (1863) 3 *Best and Smith's Reports* 826 (827). [73] *Ibid.* (827). [74] *Ibid.* (835).

[75] *Ibid.* (833 *et seq.*).

[76] For a more in-depth discussion see Treitel, *Frustration and Force Majeure*, 2–026–2–028, 2–039.

[77] For a survey of the impact of the *Taylor* doctrine on the development of the American jurisdiction, see the report in *Opera Co. of Boston, Inc.* v. *Wolf Trap Foundation for Performing Arts*, 817 F.2d 1094 (4th Cir. Va. 1987), 1097 with further references.

[78] Treitel, *Frustration and Force Majeure*, 3–001–5–058.

[79] For a survey see Treitel, *Law of Contracts*, pp. 867, 885–7, and for a more in-depth discussion Treitel, *Frustration and Force Majeure*, 7–005–7–013.

[80] (1903) 2 KB 740.

[81] See, e.g., Treitel, *Frustration and Force Majeure*, 7–001–7–004.

[82] See *Ibid.*, 7–005 for further details.

of supervening event. The Court of Appeal ruled that the cancellation of the procession discharged the contract because the procession was seen as 'going to the root of the contract, and essential to its performance'.[83] Even though the court extensively relied on Roman law, it might be remarked that the rationale of this decision was similar to Grotius' concept of a reasonable motive and its cessation due to a supervening event. For the purposes of this chapter it is, however, more important to note that the coronation cases apparently marked the height of a judicial development pointing towards the erosion of the sanctity of contract. In later decisions the English courts restricted the application of the *Krell* doctrine.[84] Thus 'in the interests of commercial certainty' the English courts gave the principle of the sanctity of a contract more and more importance.[85] Nevertheless, the evidence remains that by the late nineteenth century the idea of an implied condition[86] and thus an element of the former continental legal tradition had become part of the English law of contract.

In contrast, Windscheid's doctrine of presupposition did not suggest an implicit condition as the English courts had initially done. Instead Windscheid tried to restrict the *extent* of the contractual will by including 'presuppositions' in it. Windscheid distinguished conditions, motives and presuppositions in relation to the declaration of intent ('*Willenserklärung*'). They all had in common a restriction of contractual will. But while the condition meant 'only, if', the presupposition meant 'I want, but I would not want if not'.[87] Thus in the case of the presupposition the expectations of the parties became elements of the contract as far as they formed a part of the contractual will (and thus the declaration of intent). This approach marks a distinction between the *clausula* rule and the presupposition doctrine: while the *clausula* rule had been developed to protect the promisor against the *incertitude* of future developments, Windscheid focused on the *fulfilment* of the original intentions of the parties. If these expectations were frustrated, the party was given an *exceptio doli* and it could reclaim what it had given

[83] (1903) 2 KB 740 (748).

[84] Treitel, *Frustration and Force Majeure*, 7-014-7-033; Treitel, *Law of Contracts*, pp. 885-7, 898-908.

[85] Treitel, *Frustration and Force Majeure*, 2-037, with a short survey of the later developments.

[86] For a discussion of alternative constructions, which are, however, strongly connected to the idea of an implied condition see Treitel, *Law of Contracts*, pp. 920-3.

[87] Windscheid, 'Die Voraussetzung', 195.

to the other party in order to perform the contractual obligation. Windscheid's idea was, however, fiercely contested[88] and thus his attempt to insert a rule on presupposition into the German Civil Code failed. The principle of the sanctity of a contract was given more and essential importance.[89]

Nevertheless, German jurisprudence maintained its focus on cases of unexpected circumstances.[90] The most famous contribution to this discussion came from Paul Oertmann (AD 1865–AD 1938).[91] In his treatise on the '*Geschäftsgrundlage*' he took up elements of Windscheid's ideas:[92] The '*Geschäftsgrundlage*' was to be understood as the mutual consented presupposition of the contract. In this doctrine, a change of circumstances only had relevance for the contract if this circumstance was of importance for both parties. The German Reichsgericht adopted Oertmann's doctrine in 1921.[93] This development should perhaps be understood against the background of a new tendency of the courts, which had emerged since about the turn of the century arising in particular in the period since around 1920: the German courts[94] were ready to take social changes into account, particularly as the economic developments during and after World War I extensively changed the framework of many contracts. The most prominent example of this tendency is the so-called 'revaluation cases'.[95] From

[88] For a fierce criticicsm see Otto Lenel, 'Die Lehre von der Voraussetzung (im Hinblick auf den Entwurf eines bürgerlichen Gesetzbuchs)', (1889) 74 *Archiv für die civilistische Praxis*, 213–39, and Otto Lenel, 'Nochmals die Lehre von der Voraussetzung', (1892) 79 *Archiv für die civilistische Praxis*, 49–107. For a discussion of these debates see Emmert, *Suche*, pp. 143–7, and Ulrich Falk, *Ein Gelehrter wie Windscheid. Erkundungen auf den Feldern der Begriffsjurisprudenz* (Frankfurt am Main: Uittorio Klostenmann, 1989 = Ius Commune, Sonderhefte, Studien zur Europäischen Rechtsgeschichte, 38), pp. 210–14.

[89] Meyer-Pritzl, '§§313–314', nn. 10, 13.

[90] For a survey, see *ibid.*, nn. 14–17. For a parallel development in Italian jurisprudence (influenced by the German discourse), see Christian Reiter, *Vertrag und Geschäftsgrundlage im deutschen und italienischen Recht. Eine rechtsvergleichende Untersuchung zum Wandel des Vertragsbegriffs und seinen Auswirkungen auf die Regeln über den Wegfall der Geschäftsgrundlage in der neueren Rechtsgeschichte und im modernen Recht* (Tübingen: Mohr Siebeck, 2002 = Studien zum ausländischen und internationalen Privatrecht, 89), pp. 45–64.

[91] Rüdiger Brodhun, *Paul Ernst Wilhelm Oertmann (1865–1938): Leben, Werk, Rechtsverständnis sowie Gesetzeszwang und Richterfreiheit* (Baden-Baden: Nomos, 1999 = Fundamenta Juridica, vol. 34).

[92] Paul Oertmann, *Die Geschäftsgrundlage. Ein neuer Rechtsbegriff* (Leipzig: 1921).

[93] RGZ (3 February 1922) 103, 328, 332.

[94] For a parallel development in Italy see Reiter, *Vertrag und Geschäftsgrundlage*, pp. 64–75.

[95] See as a survey Frank Laudenklos, 'Aufwertungsrechtsprechung', in: *Handwörterbuch zur Deutschen Rechtsgeschichte I* (Berlin: 2nd edn, 2005), col. 345–7. For a more in-depth discussion

a theoretical point of view, one may refer this trend to the emergence of the so-called School of Free Right ('Freirechtsschule'),[96] whose followers endorsed the adoption of Oertmann's doctrine by the courts.[97] Eventually, in 2002, the German legislator incorporated the doctrine of '*Geschäftsgrundlage*' into the BGB (§313).

5. Conclusion

Initially, in the Roman context, dealing with unexpected circumstances was an ethical issue. Medieval canon and Roman law, however, took an approach based more on the parties' will thus creating the idea of a tacit condition. This approach mirrors the rise of the idea of the promise as the basis of the contract being introduced by medieval canon law.

In the Early Modern period the elementary function of the parties' will gained an even greater endorsement. It is indicative for this development that particularly the humanistic jurists (such as Andreas Alciatus) discussed the question of the *clausula rebus sic stantibus* in the context of the *interpretatio* of contractual will. This is shown, most clearly, in the Grotian rule that a change of circumstances can only have relevance - at least in principle - if it is related to the *ratio* of a party which was visible to the other party. The idea of a *repugnantia casus emergentis cum voluntate* is in certain ways also characteristic of this development: the expectations of the promising party - as far as they are included in its will - become the reference point for the further existence of the contract. It should be noted, however, that Grotius restricted the scope of this rule to some very specific cases.

By the eighteenth century, it had become clear to jurists that the *clausula* doctrine could be dangerous for the stability of contracts and promises. Nevertheless the authority of the tradition and - last but not least - the perception of a continuing dynamic change appeared to be too strong to abandon this doctrine in general. Augustin Leyser's statements and also the legislative provisions of the late eighteenth and the early nineteenth century revealed a tendency to limit the *clausula* doctrine particularly by the elements of fault and risk.

(including the developments in Austria, France and Switzerland) see Emmert, *Suche*, pp. 309–416.

[96] Luigi Lombardi Vallauri, *Geschichte des Freirechts* (Frankfurt am Main: Uittorio Kostermann, 1971 = Studien zur Philosophie und Literatur des neunzehnten Jahrhunderts, 10).

[97] For a positive judgement of the 'Geschäftsgrundlage' by the 'Freirechtsschule' see Meyer-Pritzl, '§§313–314', nn. 51–4.

The English common law went in another direction in this period. The idea of the absolute contract left no room for a rescission or modification of a contract due to unexpected circumstances: the contractors' absolute liability also extended to these kinds of complications and attributed their risk to the promisor.

The emergence of a new approach to contracts in the nineteenth century in continental Europe resulted initially in a decline of the *clausula* rule. Widespread hostility to the rescission of a contract resulted in a growing hostility to a consideration of the normative relevance of unexpected circumstances for the contractual promise. After 1850, however, Windscheid's idea of the tacit presupposition revived to a certain extent the Grotian tradition and increased the protection of the parties' contractual expectations. However, the principle of the sanctity of a contract was undermined by this kind of approach. Thus Windscheid's concept remained without immediate effect. In the long run, however, it triggered a discussion which apparently supported the emergence of a similar but more restrictive concept, the doctrine of the '*Geschäftsgrundlage*'. The intense social and, in particular, economic changes during the 1920s fostered the adoption of this doctrine by the German (and later also the Italian) courts.

While the *clausula* rule vanished in continental Europe, it found its way to the English courts. This can be demonstrated by cases like *Caldwell* v. *Taylor* and *Krell* v. *Henry* where the doctrine of frustration is based on the idea of an implied condition. However, the frustration concept was increasingly restricted in its further application by the common law courts. It appears as if the English courts – similar to some of their continental counterparts – were anxious to create a legal device for dealing with cases of unexpected circumstances but remained reluctant to use it.

3 Law and economics: the comparative law and economics of frustration in contracts

MARTA CENINI, BARBARA LUPPI,
FRANCESCO PARISI

1. Introduction

Frustration of purpose is a defence to the enforcement of a contractual obligation. Legal systems generally provide this defence when an unforeseen event undermines a party's purpose for entering into a contract. In many legal systems frustration of purpose is often treated and discussed jointly with the related doctrine of impossibility, which concerns situations where unforeseen events render impossible (practical impossibility) or far more burdensome (economic impossibility) the performance of the obligations specified in the contract. Although different in their substance, the economic analysis of the doctrines of frustration and impossibility share a common logic. In the following analysis we shall therefore treat these doctrines together.

When unexpected contingencies occur during the performance of a contract, there may be a divergence between what the parties have expressly agreed upon in the contract and what they have implicitly assumed was their contractual obligation in terms of assumption of risk. In other words, when there is a period of time between the conclusion of the contract and the performance of the parties, there may be a fundamental change of circumstances that makes the performance of the contract far more burdensome, or even physically impossible, for one party, or that completely frustrates the purpose of the contract for one party. The event that causes the change is, as said, unexpected or unforeseen and is not explicitly referred to in the parties' agreement. If it were in the parties' agreement, the general rules on breach of contract would apply. In all of these cases, the overarching question is whether the burdened party should be obligated to perform (or, if its performance has become impossible, pay damages) or whether it may be allowed to escape contractual liability by resorting to one of several 'contract defences'. Such defences might include the *rebus sic stantibus* ('things thus standing') clause under which a party's obligation under the contract is required to be fulfilled only when conditions are the same as they were when the contract was formed.

2. Review of the literature

Scholars understand that the right way to approach the problem requires that we pay attention to the risk problem and to the allocation of such a risk in accordance with the parties' intentions at the time they negotiated the agreement.[1]

Posner and Rosenfield[2] tried to show that when an event that is not chargeable to any of the two parties makes the performance of obligations by one party impossible or more burdensome, efficiency requires the allocation of such a risk to the party who can better bear it (the so called *superior risk bearer*). Several factors would determine who can bear the risk at the least cost: first, parties can often take precautions to decrease the probability that performance becomes impossible or to reduce the loss from the breach. In such a case, risk should be assigned to the party who can take precautions to reduce it at least cost. Second, even if no one can take precautions to reduce risk, someone can usually spread the risk by, for example, taking out an insurance policy. In such a case, the party who can spread the risk at least cost should be held liable.[3]

A person's ability to reduce and spread risk determines his or her cost of bearing it. Efficiency requires allocating the risk to the parties who can bear it at least cost. In this way, the cost of remote risks would be

[1] At first, courts (see *Taylor* v. *Caldwell*, 122 Eng. Rep. 309 (1863), which is generally recognised as the first case involving impossibility as a defence) framed the problem on the basis of the parties' will, investigating the intent of the parties at the time the contract was made. From this point of view, the occurrence or non-occurrence of the event is, although not expressed in the contract, an 'implicit condition' that was tacitly assumed by the parties. Recently, this point of view has been reproposed by N. Kim, 'Mistakes, Changed Circumstances and Intent' (22 January 2007), available at SSRN: http://ssrn.com/abstract=9587.

[2] R. A. Posner and A. M. Rosenfield, 'Impossibility and Related Doctrine in contract Law: An Economic Analysis', (1977) 6 *Journal of Legal Studies* 83. Related studies are also C.L. Bruce, 'An Economic Analysis of the Impossibility Doctrine', (1982) 11 *Journal of Legal Studies*, 311; R. Cooter and T. Ulen, *Law and Economics* (Reading, MA: Pearson Addison-Wesley, 5th edn, 2008), p. 276; P. Joskow, 'Commercial Impossibility, the Uranuim Market and the "Westinghouse" case', (1976) 6 *Journal of Legal Studies*, 119.

[3] Posner and Rosenfield, 'Impossibility and Related Doctrine in Contract Law', 90–2.

minimised while the contractual surplus would be maximised and would be divided between the parties.[4] Under this point of view, if the promisee is the superior risk bearer, the contract will be discharged; if it is the promisor who is the superior risk bearer, their performance failure will be considered as a normal breach of contract and will require expectation damages to be paid. When it is difficult to ascertain which of the two parties is the superior risk bearer (as happened, for example, in the famous coronation cases[5]), the authors suggest that as long as the performer is *generally* the superior risk bearer, assigning the risk to him in cases where there is doubt - that is, refusing discharge in those cases - can be expected to yield correct results more often than the contrary rule.[6]

Following a similar argument, other authors have pointed out that the parties may have a degree of risk aversion, which should be considered in the decision on who should bear the risk and on the amount of damages to be paid in case of breach of contract, an amount that may vary from full expectation damages to zero or even negative damages.[7] Sykes[8] suggested, for instance, that the remedy of discharge is efficient when the cost of performance has drastically increased and the promisor is risk adverse.

More recently, other studies have criticised these conclusions on a variety of grounds.[9] First, it has been pointed out that Posner's and

[4] Similarly, these authors also believe that when the contingency destroys the purpose of the contract, efficiency requires the allocation of the risk to the party who can bear it at least cost. Thus efficiency requires interpreting the doctrine of frustration of purpose as follows: if a contingency makes performance pointless, assign liability to the party who could bear the risk at least cost.

[5] The coronation cases were a group of appellate opinions in English cases, all arising out of contracts that had been made for accommodation for viewing the celebrations surrounding the coronation of King Edward VII, originally scheduled for 26 June 1902. The King fell ill, and the coronation was postponed until August. In general, the contracts were voided on the ground of frustration of purpose. Certain contracts which did not mention that the purpose was to view the coronation festivities were upheld, however. Here, it is clearly impossible to ascertain who is the superior risk bearer.

[6] Posner and Rosenfield, 'Impossibility and Related Doctrine in Contract Law', 111.

[7] M. J. White, 'Contract Breach and Contract Discharge due to Impossibility: A Unified Theory', (1988) 17 *Journal of Legal studies*, 353; and A. O. Sykes, 'The Doctrine of Commercial Impracticality in a Second-best World', (1990) 19 *Journal of Legal Studies*, 433 argued that the issue of impossibility and commercial impracticability is one aspect of the larger problem of the efficient remedies for breach of contract.

[8] Sykes, 'The Doctrine of Commercial Impracticability in a Second-best World', 433.

[9] See, among others, J. Gordley, 'Impossibility and changed and Unforeseen Circumstances', (2004) 52 *American Journal of Comparative Law*, 513–30.

Rosenfield's superior risk bearer criterion, especially in its final result (which, as we have said, generally allocates the risk to the performing party), re-proposes the *pacta sunt servanda* principle but in a more complex way: instead of simply saying that the performer is always liable, Posner and Rosenfield demanded that a fact-finder undertake an articulate inquiry about who is the superior risk bearer. This results, in most cases, in the same finding that would have been achieved under the *pacta sunt servanda* principle,[10] but there is still uncertainty. The uncertainty about who will be recognised as the superior risk bearer also leaves open the possibility that each party will rely on the other party to face the risk (or worse, that each party takes out insurance for the same risk).

Second, and more importantly, Trimarchi has shown that, when we are dealing with an upsetting of the economic equilibrium of the contract due to the occurrence of an extraordinary and unforeseeable event, the superior risk insurer criterion cannot work.[11] The principle of insurance (in its widest sense) lies basically in aggregating a number of homogeneous and uncorrelated risks with some statistical regularity that makes the overall losses in a given time-span predictable with a reasonable degree of accuracy.[12] The extraordinary and unforeseeable event is an absolute uncertainty rather than a calculable risk and more importantly it is not recurring. Besides this problem of statistical unpredictability, the fact that the risk has general consequences means that it hits several debtors, which is in contrast with the requirement that risks be of an independent nature before they can be insured against.

Trimarchi therefore, argues that the legal rule must be based on the situation resulting from the unanticipated occurrence, i.e. it is necessary to face the losses with an *ex post* perspective.[13] From this point of view, it appears preferable to give the burdened party the remedy of discharge. France, Belgium, the Czech Republic, Denmark, England, Ireland, Scotland and Slovenia have chosen this way, and Schwartz is

[10] M. Ambrosoli, *La sopravvenienza contrattuale* (Milan: Giuffrè, 2002), p. 60.

[11] P. Trimarchi, 'Commercial Impracticality in Contract Law: An Economic Analysis', (1991) 11 *International Review of Law and Economics*, 63.

[12] Moreover, Trimarchi suggests that the increase of performance costs very often corresponds to an analogous increase in the buyer's gain: in this case, the payment of expectation damages does not compensate the buyer for an actual loss but rather gives him an unexpected, extraordinary gain, which does not conform either to the principle of insurance or the *ex post* allocation of risks, Trimarchi 'Commercial Impracticality in Contract Law'.

[13] Trimarchi, 'Commercial Impracticality in Contract Law', 66.

favourable to this solution:[14] requiring performance of the condition of the contract or declaring the contract void seem the only practicable alternatives.

On the other hand, parties often have spent much money and time in the performance of the contract, and there may have been efficient allocation of resources resulting from the original contract. In order to preserve these benefits, there could be room left for re-negotiation of the contract in order to rebalance the economic interests upset by the contingency.[15]

As the non-burdened party is in a more advantageous position, it could try to exploit the situation and behave opportunistically. In such a case, the parties will only rebalance to an equal position if the burdened party has the ability to ask the judge to declare the contract void. For this reason, Italian law provides that the burdened party may ask the judge to void the contract and, only after this judicial claim and within the same trial, the other party may ask for the issue to be opened for renegotiation. This situation would also involve the intervention of the judge during the renegotiation.

Schwartz suggests that, in cases of frustration, it is preferable to induce the parties to enter into renegotiations rather than leave courts to adapt or rebalance the contract.[16] Courts, in fact, have imperfect information about market price, and most importantly about the subjective costs and benefits of the parties. Along similar lines, Gallo has proposed that, in order to facilitate this renegotiation, parties should insert into every contract a clause of revision of the agreement in case unexpected circumstances provoke a significant disequilibrium of the performance of the parties (the so-called hardship clause).[17] A default rule could impose such a clause, providing incentives to the parties for undertaking a bargain if they want to exclude the applicability of such a default rule. Unlike statutory provisions, a hardship clause would not call for the intervention of the judge, at least at the beginning.

[14] A. Schwartz, 'Relational Contracts in the Courts: An Analysis of Incomplete Agreements and Judicial Strategies', (1992) 21 *Journal of Legal studies*, 271; A. Schwartz, 'Law and Economics: l'approccio alla teariadel contratto', (1996) *Rivista critica del detetto privato*, 427, 446.

[15] Trimarchi, 'Commercial Impracticality in Contract Law'.

[16] Schwartz, 'Relational Contracts in the Courts'; Schwartz, 'Law and Economics'.

[17] P. Gallo, *Sopravvenienza coutrattuale e problem di gestione del Contratto* (Milan: Giuffrè, 1992).

Across Europe, most contracts provide that when the contingency occurs, parties have the duty to undergo bargaining in an attempt to rebalance the contract. Only after a failure of this private bargain may parties ask for judicial intervention. The risk of opportunistic behaviour of the advantaged party may be avoided by requiring that both of the parties act in good faith. In this regard, it is not consistent with Art. III.-1:110 DCFR, which requires only the debtor to behave in good faith. Along similar lines, the Association Henri Capitant developed a model solution according to which the parties must renegotiate the contract if it becomes deeply unbalanced during its execution due to a change of circumstances that could not reasonably be foreseen. Under this solution, the parties may terminate the contract by common agreement or ask for the intervention of the court only if the bargain fails 'in spite of the good faith of the contracting parties'.

3. The economics of frustration in contracts

When circumstances frustrate the purpose of a contract or render the performance of a contract impossible, the parties' contractual expectations are frustrated and a loss is incurred. In the face of such impossibility, legal rules determine which contracting party should bear the financial consequences of the impossibility. In the following, we consider the issue of optimal allocation of the cost of impossibility through the lens of economics. There are several issues that acquire relevance in the face of impossibility of performance. From an economic point of view these issues can be grouped in three main categories, namely: (i) risk allocation function, (ii) information harvesting function and (iii) incentive function.[18]

For each category, there are often two or more dimensions, each of which contributes to the determination of the optimal allocation of risk between the parties. These dimensions substantially affect the optimality of the allocation of risk in order to determine which party should bear the consequences of the frustration of the contract. Table 1 below shows that only for a small sub-set of situations does the same allocation of risk from impossibility yield the optimal balance between these

[18] These functions are similar to those that determine the optimal allocation of risk of failure through conventional and legal warranties, as discussed by F. Parisi, 'The Hanuanization of Legal Warranties in European Sales Law: An Economic Analysis', (2004) 52 *American Journal of Comparative Law*, 403–31.

competing normative goals. The restricted conditions under which each alternative allocation of risk yields optimal results in each dimension will be discussed in the remainder of this section.

In Table 1, we consider three alternative allocations of risk: one in which frustration provides a full defence for the promisor; another where the risk of impossibility is entirely borne by the promisor; and the third where the risk is spread between the parties. Further, the conditions under which the choice of allocation is immaterial are specified. The optimal allocation of the risk from impossibility will be determined by law-makers and by the contracting parties according to the relative weight attached to each of the three parameters of optimisation (i.e., optimal risk allocation, information disclosure and performance and reliance incentives). It is important to consider the choice of equilibrium level of allocation of risk that the parties would contractually agree upon under different conditions. As summarised in Table 1, from an economic point of view, the optimal frustration rule depends on (i) the risk propensities of the parties; (ii) the determinants of the probability of performance; and (iii) the private information available to the contracting parties.

From an economic incentive viewpoint, different frustration rules should be chosen in all such cases in order to create the optimal balance of these three factors.

In the following sections, we consider in greater detail the results outlined in Table 1, examining the equilibrium choice of contractual allocation of risk when the terms are negotiated by the parties in different environments. Such an optimal frustration rule coincides with the hypothetical bargained-for solution between parties and may provide some guidance for the understanding of the best legal allocation of risk between the parties. This discussion is concerned with both conventional allocations of risk, which are chosen and made into a contract by the parties in a transaction, and legal allocations of risk, which are created by operation of law in specified transactions.

A. Optimal allocation of the risk of frustration

First we consider the simplest case in which the probability of frustration is exogenous, in the sense that neither the promisor nor the promisee has any control over the likelihood of the occurrence of frustration or impossibility. Further assume that the information available to the contracting parties when the contract has been signed is symmetric. In this situation, the optimal frustration rule depends

Table 1: Determinants of an Optimal Frustration Rule

		Optimal Frustration Rule			
		Doesn't Matter	No Defence	Partial Defence	Full Defence
Economic Function	**Risk Allocation**	Both are risk neutral	Promisee is risk averse	Both are risk averse	Promisor is risk averse
	Harvesting Information	Symmetric information	Promisor has private information	Both have private information	Promisee has private information
	Incentives and Moral Hazard	Exogenous risk	Promisor's incentives	Bilateral incentives	Promisee's moral hazard

exclusively on the parties' attitude towards risk. In economic theory risk aversion defines the reluctance of a person to accept a fair bargain with uncertain payoffs and is captured analytically by the curvature of the utility function. A standard measure of risk aversion is the Arrow–Pratt absolute risk aversion index, defined as $ra = -\frac{U''}{U'}$. A person is risk neutral if the risk aversion index is zero, i.e., when $U'' = 0$, which corresponds to a linear utility function.

The possibility of a lost surplus from frustration of purpose or impossibility of performance represents an economic risk. When parties have the ability to diversify their risk by entering into a large number of contracts with independent risks, it is likely that they will face lower levels of risk aversion. In all these situations, the optimal allocation of the risk is exclusively determined by the relative risk aversion of the parties. The optimal allocation of the impossibility risk therefore depends on the circumstances of the contracting situation, and on the relative ability of parties to hedge their risk aversion through risk diversification or insurance. In this specific case, there are no information or incentive effects created by the frustration rule. Hence, we can distinguish two groups of cases.

The first group of cases includes situations of unilateral risk aversion. This may be the case where one of the two parties is a large contractor with a large portfolio of activities and risk or where one of the two parties can obtain effective insurance for the risk. Consider the case where one party, say the promisor or debtor, is risk neutral (hence $ra_D = 0$) and the other party, the promisee or creditor, is risk averse (hence $ra_C > 0$). Promisor and promisee have symmetric information and thus have similar expectations concerning the risk of frustration or impossibility. Since the probability of frustration is exogenous and cannot be influenced by either the promisor's level of care in the performance or the promisee's level of precaution, in this case the contracting parties would naturally bargain for a no defence scenario in case of frustration, and adopt similar safeguards to ensure alternative performance in case of impossibility. This means that in case of failure to perform, the debtor will have to pay full expectation damages. An opposite bargained-for solution is to be expected in the converse case of a risk-averse promisor and a risk-neutral promisee. Here, the promisee would be the best risk-bearer and thus – if all other conditions apply – the parties would naturally bargain for a contract with a full frustration or impossibility defence. The promisee serves as the promisor's insurer for these exogenous risks. Any other allocation of risk (e.g., no frustration defence or spreading the risk between the parties) would be Pareto inferior, since both parties could be made better off by shifting the entire risk on the risk-neutral party.

The second group of cases includes situations of bilateral risk aversion. Unlike the case in which both parties are risk-neutral, where alternative allocations of the risk will yield identical levels of aggregate utility (the parties are in fact indifferent to a zero-mean risk and will thus have no incentive to reallocate risk contractually), when both parties have some positive level of risk aversion ($ra_D > 0$ and $ra_C > 0$), the optimal frustration rule is likely to share the risk between the parties. Since risk aversion induces increasing marginal costs (in utility terms) with an increase in the value of the risk, parties would naturally bargain for a risk-sharing solution, with a resulting partial defence for frustration or impossibility.

B. Allocating risk to harvest information

Let's consider the different group of cases in which the risk is still exogenous but where the parties have different knowledge about the risk of frustration or impossibility and/or where they have different information about the financial consequences of non-performance. In this case, the person with better information has a higher accuracy in the estimate of the probability or the financial consequences of frustration. For the sake of expositional clarity, let's further assume that both parties are risk-neutral so that alternative allocations of risk are equally desirable from the risk-allocation point of view, discussed in Section A above. When operating under such an assumption, the only relevant criterion for choosing among different allocations of risk from impossibility is the effect that alternative rules may have on the parties' incentives and ability to reveal information. In the legal and economics literature, this function of conventional allocations of risk is known as signalling: the choice of frustration rule reveals truthful and credible information to the other party. This information-harvesting function materialises in different ways according to which of the two contracting parties has private information that is not known to the other. In the following, we consider the three possible combinations of asymmetric information and the role played by allocations of risk in each situation.

(a) Frustration rule as signal of promisor's confidence

Even though both contracting parties are aware that the probability of frustration is exogenous and is not influenced by their behaviour, they may have asymmetric information concerning the likelihood of frustration or impossibility. A promisor may have informational advantages due to economies of scale in the acquisition of information, or due to other natural advantages in forming an accurate estimate on the likelihood of frustration or impossibility of performance as specified in the contract. For the purpose of our analysis, imagine the simple case in which different producers are faced with a varying probability of frustration. In this case, the promisor has better information than the promisee concerning the realisation of conditions of impossibility.

The promisee expects the frustration rate to be equal to the market average, while the promisor has a more accurate expectation of the frustration rate for the specific contract. Analytically let us denote p_{MKT} with the average rate of frustration in the market. In the presence of asymmetric information on the promisor's side, the promisor has a more accurate knowledge of the probability of frustration in the specific contract. Let us denote p_i with the probability of frustration of the contract as estimated by promisor *i*. Promisors may face different exogenous frustration rates for a number of possible reasons. A promisor that expects to offer greater reliability compared to the average market expectation will have $p_i \leq p_{MKT}$; likewise, a promisor that estimates a greater risk of frustration compared to the market average will have $p_i > p_{MKT}$. Such asymmetric information creates a problem that is similar in nature to the lemons problem first considered by Akerlof.[19] In the presence of asymmetric information, the promisor's willingness to be liable (and to add the price of the allocation of risk to the sale price) is a credible signal of the information available to the promisor. Through the mechanism of contractual allocations of risk, individual promisors that face different exogenous probabilities of frustration will be able to offer observable and credible information to their promisees. Allocations of risk are a costly and thus credible signal which creates a separating equilibrium and can thus be seen as valuable tools for harvesting information.

From a practical standpoint, the signalling mechanism works because promisors know (or can more accurately estimate) the actual probability of defects of their products and can compute the expected cost of frustration risk. Promisors who face a higher risk of frustration, $p_i > p_{MKT}$, face higher costs for waiving a defence. Assuming enforceable allocation of

[19] G. A. Akerlof, 'The Market for Lemons: Qualitative Uncertainty and the Market Mechanism', (1970) 84 *Quality Journal of Economics*, 488–500.

risk contracts and assuming away situations of truncated liability (e.g., bankruptcy or dissolution of the manufacturer's company, etc.), each promisor is able to undertake the risk only if he or she can receive a price at least equal to the expected cost of future liability claims. This price mechanism will yield a separating equilibrium such that different types of promisors will be able to offer different types of coverage for the case of frustration or impossibility (hence they will choose different frustration rules or similar rules, but only at different prices). In turn, promisees will be able to infer the actual type of promisor from the observation of the allocation of risk that they offer, thus correcting the asymmetric information problem faced by the contracting parties. In this way, the choice of frustration rule serves a valuable information-harvesting function in the course of a transaction. As for the general case, this signalling allows for the transmission of credible information and it plays the general role of correcting information asymmetry between parties and facilitating trust.

(b) Frustration rule as signal of promisee's sensitivity to risk

While it is reasonable to assume that the promisor may have an informational advantage concerning the likelihood of frustration and events that may cause the impossibility of the contract, it may be natural to assume that the promisee may have private information concerning his or her ability to cope with non-performance and the potential harm that he or she would suffer in case of frustration of the contract.

From an economic point of view, interesting results can be obtained if the promisee possesses private information that is not available to the promisor. Following this line of thought, the choice of allocation of risk will not signal the promisor's private estimation of the risk, but rather the content of the private information of the promisee, namely the expected level of harm that he or she faces in case of contract frustration. Let's consider the case in which individual promisees face different levels of loss in the event of contract frustration. Let us denote L_H with the (high) level of loss experienced by a loss-sensitive promisee in case of frustration, and L_L with the (low) level of loss faced by a promisee with lower sensitivity to frustration. Let us assume that $L_H > L_L$. If promisors cannot differentiate a high-loss promisee from a low-loss promisee due to asymmetric information, a single allocation of risk will be offered to all promisees, based on the average expected loss. However, if frustration rules are derogable and alternative allocations of risk can be bargained for, the promisee's willingness to forgo liability coverage in exchange for a discount can signal the actual level of risk that he or she faces. Promisees facing a higher risk, i.e. characterised by a loss level equal to L_H, will bargain for a rule that shields them from the risk of frustration, while low-loss promisees, i.e. characterised by a loss level equal to L_L, will prefer to obtain a discount, forgoing full coverage. Also in this case, the contractual choice of a frustration rule may serve a socially valuable information-harvesting function.

(c) Frustration rules as matching devices

When both the promisor and the promisee have private information which is not known by the other contracting party, a bilateral asymmetric information problem arises. Consider a case where both information problems illustrated above are present, such that only the promisor knows the actual probability of frustration, and only the promisee knows the actual loss faced in case of frustration. Together, the combined presence of the two asymmetric information problems poses an interesting coordination problem. As generally shown by Spence[20] and as discussed by Wehrt[21] for the case of warranties, the solution of this problem is characterised by the Pareto optimal matching of different promisors and promisees. Promisors will choose different frustration rules, signalling their private information concerning the rate of frustration. Promisees will demand varying frustration rules, signalling their individual risk levels. In equilibrium, promisors with a higher expectation of frustration (i.e., $p_\iota > p_{MKT}$) will enter into contracts with promisees who face smaller individual losses (i.e., facing a loss equal to L_L in case of frustration), whereas more confident promisors (i.e., $p_\iota \leq p_{MKT}$) will enter into contracts with more sensitive promisees (i.e., characterised by a loss equal to L_H). If a continuous level of signalling is possible, the outcome will be Pareto-optimal, coinciding with the efficient matching of individual promisors and promisees that would occur in an ideal world of truthful disclosure and symmetric or observable information.

It is important to note that when the rules governing the effects of impossibility or frustration are not derogable by the parties, the signalling and matching functions discussed above cannot effectively be

[20] M. Spence, 'Consumer Misperceptions, Product Failure and Producer Liability', (1977) 44 *Review of Economic Studies*, 561–72.

[21] K. Wehrt, 'Warranties' in: Boudewijn Bouckaert and Gerit DeGeest (eds.), *Encyclopedia of Law and Economics*, (Aldershot: Elgar, 2000), pp. 179–95.

fulfilled, since all parties will be subject to such rules and no separating equilibria could be observed under such regimes.

C. Incentives and moral hazard

In real life, the probability and financial consequences of frustration can often be influenced by the behaviour of the parties. Promisors can hedge against contingencies that may affect their ability to perform in the face of unforeseen events through inventory and futures markets. Promisees can plan ahead to minimise the financial consequences of frustration. In this setting, we can distinguish three different scenarios: (i) situations of unilateral incentives where only the promisor influences the probability of frustration; (ii) situations of unilateral incentives where only the promisee influences the probability of frustration; and (iii) situations of bilateral incentives where both the promisor and the promisee influence the probability of such event. In all cases of endogenous risk, allocations of risk operate as incentives for the parties to invest in order to reduce the risk from impossibility. Allocation of risk may be seen as an instrument with which the parties control the efforts of the promisor and promisee to provide all the necessary conditions for the realisation of the contract. Similar to the previous cases, we will assume in the following analysis that the only consideration for the choice of a frustration rule is given by the effects of the rule on the incentives of the parties (i.e., we assume away the risk-allocation and information-harvesting functions of the rule).

The first and most natural case is the case in which only the promisor can effectively influence the probability of a frustration. In a unilateral promisor's incentive case, the only relevant variable is the effort of such party to reduce the likelihood of negative conditions that may cause the impossibility of the contract. Analytically, the promisor *i* can choose an effort level *e* that influences the probability of frustration $p_i(e)$. The higher the effort exerted by promisor *i*, the less likely the frustration of the contract will be. In analytical terms this is equivalent to assuming $p_i'(e) < 0$. In different contexts, the legal and economics literature terms this criterion of allocation of risk as the 'cheapest risk avoider' criterion. The intuition behind this concept is straightforward. Since the promisor is in the best position to minimise the risk from impossibility, it is desirable to shift on to such party the financial consequences associated with such event. Any mitigation or waiver of the promisor's liability for frustration or impossibility would undermine the optimal incentives to minimise this endogenous risk.

Situations of unilateral incentives where only the promisee influences the probability of frustration are probably less frequent but not impossible occurrences. This situation is modelled analytically as before, with the only difference that the effort level *e* is chosen by the promisee. With respect to the choice of frustration the considerations above apply in the converse. When only the promisee can affect the probability of a contract's impossibility or frustration, the rule should be chosen to create incentives on the promisee to minimise the likelihood or the economic harm that would follow from frustration. Predictably, the 'cheapest risk avoider' criterion in this case yields the converse optimal allocation of risk, rendering it desirable to shift on to such party the financial consequences associated with the event of contract frustration or impossibility. Any alternative rule would reduce or eliminate the promisee's incentives with an increase in the endogenous probability of impossibility or frustration.

It may occur that both the promisor and the promisee are in a position to influence the probability of contract impossibility or frustration. Situations of bilateral incentives are the result of a combination of the two unilateral problems considered above. Whenever the two incentive problems can be separated, the bilateral problem can be dealt with as a mere sum of two unilateral problems. This approach presupposes that it is possible to ascertain *ex post* whether a certain condition that materialises and causes the frustration of the contract is attributable to one or the other party. In this case, the optimal frustration rule would provide no defence and full promisee's coverage for all those risks which are under the control of the promisor and would instead provide a full defence for those risks which are affected by the behaviour of the promisee. In the market as we know it, however, a bilateral precaution problem cannot be easily reduced to the mere sum of the two elementary unilateral incentive problems. This is borne out in cases where both parties can influence the frustration or impossibility of the contract, with no opportunity to establish *ex post* the cause of such event. In all such cases where the causal contribution to the frustration cannot be ascertained *ex post*, the decoupling solution considered by Priest is not viable.[22] In these cases, no first best outcome can be created by a single frustration rule. A second best outcome can be pursued through partial

[22] G. L. Priest, 'A Theory of the consumer Product warranty', (1981) 90 *Yale Law Journal*, 1297–352, reprinted in Victor P. Goldberg (ed.), *Readings in the Economics of Contract Law* (Cambridge University Press, 1989), pp. 174–84.

allocations of risk and a partial defence which would leave the parties' incentives only partially aligned.

4. Legal solutions from an economic perspective

The member states of the European Union, as is well known, overcome the problems caused by the occurrence of an unexpected circumstance by providing several remedies varying from those linked to physical or practical impossibility,[23] to those linked to frustration of contract (*Zweckvereitelung, presupposizione*, doctrine of assumptions, and so on[24]), to those of economic impossibility (*Äquivalenzstörung,*[25] *eccessiva onerosità sopravvenuta, imprévision*, etc.).

In all of these remedies, it is always necessary that:

(1) there is an event, subsequent to contract formation,[26] that drastically changes the proportion of the performances of the two parties, making the performance of one party far more burdensome than it was at the time of contract formation or at worst impossible. This may happen, for example, when the costs of the performance becomes extraordinarily high, or inflation makes the cost of the labour and materials far higher;

(2) the contingency that causes the alteration is not chargeable to any of the parties and is extraordinary, exceptional, unforeseeable, unexpected, etc.. For some member states (especially Italy), it must be generally true that the event hits all the debtors and is able to affect the *market* price of the performance. Examples of extraordinary situations include high inflation, war, the opening or closing of a market, etc.;

(3) the contract is not aleatory and the occurrence materialises a risk that the parties have not referred to in the contract, or that one party has to

[23] Impossibility can be divided into three categories: practical impossibility, which is considered in Austria, Germany, Lithuania, Spain, Italy; legal impossibility, which is considered in Austria, Germany and Italy; and economic impossibility or commercial impracticability.

[24] Frustration of contract has been codified in several jurisdictions: Greece, Hungary, Lithuania, the Netherlands, Portugal. In some other jurisdictions, it is recognised at a judicial level (for example, in Italy).

[25] The doctrine of '*Zweckvereitelung*' and '*Äquivalenzstörung*' are part of the general concept of *objektive Geschäftsgrundlage* which was first elaborated by Larenz (K. Larenz, *Geschäftsgrundlage und Vertragserfüllung*, (Munich/Berlin: Beck, 1963); K. Larenz, *Lehrbuch des Schuldrechts*, (Munich/Berlin: Beck, 1962), vol. I, s. 230). This concept was at first acknowledged by courts and then by the legislator himself, who in 2002 codified it in the German Civil Code. In Austria also, it has been applied but not codified yet.

[26] In Sweden, the doctrine of assumptions includes both mistakes on conclusion and changes in circumstances after the conclusion of the contract.

> bear. This criterion takes into account the 'normal risk' of a contract, which can be determined by taking into account what kind of contract the parties have entered into (for instance, a sale between consumers; a sale between professionals; a contract between a contractor and a contracting firm in order to build a new house, an oil well, etc.; a contract between a supplier and a client, etc.) and in what kind of market. For example, in the market for some raw materials, a fluctuation in price equal to 200 per cent in a very brief period of time is a frequently recurring situation.[27]

It is clear that the set of situations considered by the member states of the European Union encompass only cases in which the risk of frustration or impossibility is exogenous and cannot be influenced, reduced or minimised by the behaviour of the parties. This means that the allocation of the risk on one or the other party cannot operate as an incentive for the party to invest in order to reduce such a risk. Furthermore, the scenarios considered generally involve parties with symmetric information, where neither party has private information about the probability or the financial consequences of the event.

This scenario is similar to what we consider in Section 3A. and the solution of the risk allocation problem seems to be found exclusively on the basis of parties' attitude towards risk. If a contingency occurs, the risk aversion of the promisee calls for full liability of the promisor; on the other hand, the risk aversion of the promisor requires that he or she may be allowed to escape contractual liability, as discussed in Table 1.

With regards to the set of situations considered by the doctrines of frustration and impossibility, it is not correct to assume that consumers are risk averse, while firms and professionals, who are contractors with a large portfolio of activities and risk, are risk neutral. As we have seen, these doctrines require for their applicability that the unforeseeable event causes a drastic change of the proportion of the performances of the two parties, making for instance the performance of one party far more burdensome than it was at the time of the contract. This means that if a firm or a professional is held liable and forced to perform or pay full expectation damages, this loss (which creates a windfall gain for the other party) would disrupt their economic and financial planning. This in turn would generate a net welfare loss. In other words, towards the

[27] Other requirements may be demanded: for instance, Spain requires that at least one party has not performed yet.

kind of risk that causes the so-called *distruption cost*,[28] neither firms nor professionals may be considered risk neutral.

In Section 3A, we have further noted that when both parties have some positive level of risk aversion, the optimal frustration rule is likely to share the risk between the parties. Yet, it is inefficient and often impractical to allocate the risk of unexpected contingency at the time the contract is made. Cooter and Ulen[29] and Pardolesi[30] have shown that the parties are rational in not discussing and allocating such remote and improbable risks and so it is efficient for the parties to ignore them, since the transaction costs involved would not be justified from an economic point of view given the low probability of these events. This idea is related to the necessary incompleteness of contracts: negotiating the allocation of risks imposes transaction costs with certainty while the occurrence of the risk is, in our case, remote and improbable. Parties will leave a gap in their contract if the cost of allocation of a risk is more than the cost of allocating a loss multiplied by the probability of a loss, which is the case with highly improbable post-contract contingencies. If the probability that the event occurs is low, it is less costly for parties to allocate the loss when it occurs than bear transaction costs with certainty in order to allocate the risk in the contract.[31]

For this reason, the remedy of discharge seems to be the only viable default allocation of the risk between the parties to prevent the net welfare loss. Both the parties will not be held to perform their obligation and they will forgo their right to counter-performance. Many of the European countries choose this solution, although by following different legal constructs or procedure.[32]

Renegotiation of the contract remains a viable *ex post* option to capture the benefits of the original contract whenever appropriate.[33] This

[28] Trimarchi, 'Commercial Impracticality in Contract Law', 52, 54.

[29] Cooter and Ulen, *Law and Economics*.

[30] R. Pardolesi, 'Regole di "default" e razionalità limitata: per un (diverso) approcio di analisi economica al diritto dei contratti', (1996) *Rivista Critica del diritto privato*, 451, 456.

[31] S. Shavell, 'Damages Measures for Breach of Contract', (1980) 11 *Bell Journal of Economics* 466.

[32] Belgium, the Czech Republic, Denmark, England, France, Ireland, Scotland and Slovenia are inclined to give the burdened party only the remedy of discharge.

[33] Austria, Germany, Greece, Hungary, Italy, Lithuania, the Netherlands, Portugal, Spain and Sweden leave room for the renegotiation or adjustment of the contract. In Italy, first the burdened party asks for the termination of the contract, and then the other party may offer an adjustment of the contract; under Austrian law, *Wegfall/Fehlen der Geschäftsgrundlage* entitles the disadvantaged party to either terminate the contract or to

would allow parties to face the transaction costs of renegotiation to reallocate the loss only when it materialises.

On the contrary, when the probability and financial consequences of frustration can be influenced by the behaviour of the parties or one or both of them have information that can affect the accurate estimation of the probability and financial consequences of the event, the economic functions of the frustration rules cannot be simultaneously fulfilled and often hinge upon the use of legal remedies as default rules that are freely derogable by the parties. When the rules governing the effects of impossibility or frustration are not derogable by the parties, several of the functions are compromised for the benefit of other functions (e.g., the trade-off we observed when discussing the risk allocation and incentive functions) or entirely lost (e.g., the loss of the signalling and matching functions observed when the applicable frustration remedies are made mandatory).

claim adjustment, in this case only if both parties would have concluded the contract with this different content had they anticipated the change of circumstances etc.

PART II

Overview

4 Overview: concepts dealing with unexpected circumstances

GERMANY AND RELATED JURISDICTIONS

Germany

A. *Introduction*

Under German law the most prominent, general and important concept dealing with the effects of unexpected circumstances on the contract is the doctrine of *Störung der Geschäftsgrundlage*.[1] This principle can roughly be described as an equitable relief that allows the courts to adapt or terminate a contract if the factual framework diverges fundamentally from the parties' expectations. The doctrine of *Störung der Geschäftsgrundlage* has been developed as a mechanism to define the limits of acceptable risk distribution by contractual stipulations. There are several other rules of a statutory or contractual nature dealing more specifically with the allocation of unexpected risks involved in a deal. It is widely accepted that the concept of *Störung der Geschäftsgrundlage* has a subsidiary character, i.e., it does not apply if the risk in question is provided for by either contractual or statutory provisions. The scope of the concept of *Störung der Geschäftsgrundlage* therefore depends on the application of those other legal rules.

B. *Legal doctrines bordering the concept of* Störung der Geschäftsgrundlage

(a) The rules of mistake (§§119 *et seq*. BGB)

Three characteristics of the German law of mistake have a decisive influence on the scope of application of the doctrine of *Störung der*

[1] In general the concept was referred to as *Wegfall der Geschäftsgrundlage* but nevertheless covered both the lack of the relevant circumstances at the time of formation and the interference with those circumstances after formation; the official heading of §313 BGB in which the concept has been codified therefore refers to *Störung der Geschäftsgrundlage* including both elements.

Geschäftsgrundlage. First, only certain kinds of errors are relevant, second, the consequence of a relevant mistake is only the avoidance of the contract, and, third, the party avoiding the contract may be liable for damages even if the mistake is mutual.

Theoretically, any unforeseen risk interfering with the contractual relationship may be considered a mistake if one adopts a broad definition including basic assumptions that may not have been specifically reflected at the time of dealing but are obviously crucial conditions to an economically reasonable transaction (e.g., maintenance of social stability, stable market development, value of currency etc.). Yet, under German law, the relevance of an error is defined restrictively in three provisions. Errors concerning the act of declaration (§119 I BGB) occur when a party misinterprets the objective meaning of its declaration or makes a slip. Such errors are rare and they do not impact on the issue of *Störung der Geschäftsgrundlage*. The same applies to errors caused by fraud (§123 BGB). The third type of error relates to the fundamental characteristics of the person (party) or the object of the transaction (§119 II BGB). This provision marks the borderline between wrongful expectations covered by the law of mistake on the one hand and expectations that potentially give rise to a claim of *Störung der Geschäftsgrundlage* on the other. Thus, it is noteworthy that, according to the prevailing opinion in legal literature, §119 II BGB covers only *characteristics present at the time of the declaration*, while future developments are generally not taken into consideration.[2] In addition, the prevailing opinion interprets the term 'characteristics of the person or the object' narrowly: the wrongful assumption must be *directly related to the person or the object* of the transaction; 'external' circumstances are relevant only in so far as they originate from qualities of the person or the contractual object. Wrongful assumptions lacking such a close relation are considered *irrelevant errors in motivation*, regardless of how fundamental they may ever have been to the formation of the contractual will.[3] Examples of irrelevant errors in motivation concern the inflation rate as well as other market developments or changes in the

[2] Cf. J. Ellenberger, '§119', in: O. Palandt *et al.* (eds.), *Bürgerliches Gesetzbuch* (Munich: Beck, 69th edn, 2010), n. 24; W. Hefermehl, '§119', in: H. T. Soergel *et al.* (eds.), *Bürgerliches Gesetzbuch* (Stuttgart: Kohlhammer, 13th edn, 1999), vol. 2, n. 64; for a different view see E. A. Kramer, '§119', in: F. J. Säcker *et al.*, *Münchener Kommentar zum Bürgerlichen Gesetzbuch* (Munich: Beck, 5th edn, 2006), vol. I/1, n. 118.

[3] Cf. Ellenberger, '§119', in: Palandt *et al.* (eds.), *Bürgerliches Gesetzbuch*, n. 24, 29; K. Larenz and M. Wolf, *Allgemeiner Teil des Bürgerlichen Rechts* (Munich: Beck, 9th edn, 2004), §36, nn. 2 *et seq.*

parties' purposes. Even an error concerning the value of the contractual object is considered irrelevant. The fact that value is irrelevant, however, is rather derived from the principles of a market economy than from the wording of §119 II BGB.[4]

As a consequence of a relevant error, the mistaken party may retroactively avoid its declaration and therefore the contract (§142 I BGB). As a general rule, the contract is avoided entirely unless the contract is severable and a partial upholding complies with the (hypothetical) will of the parties at the time of contracting (§139 BGB).[5] There is no rule providing for an adaptation of the contract by law as a more flexible alternative to general or partial rescission.

The party avoiding the contract is strictly liable for reliance damages incurred by the other party (§122 BGB), unless the other party was aware or negligently unaware of the error (§122 II BGB). Consequently, the party avoiding the contract unilaterally bears the losses resulting from the rescission.

(b) The concept of impossibility (§275 BGB)

Under German law, the creditor is generally entitled to specific performance. This right is excluded if specific performance is impossible. In this case, the debtor is liable for damages under certain circumstances. For the scope of the concept of *Störung der Geschäftsgrundlage*, it is important to understand that the rule of impossibility is interpreted restrictively and that the legal consequences of impossibility may inflexibly burden the creditor with the losses of non-performance.

As a general rule, the doctrine of impossibility applies where there is a natural or legal impediment to performance that the debtor cannot overcome by any means (§275 I BGB). The contract specifies the acts or results that constitute performance. Thus, circumstances which are not an insurmountable obstacle to an element of performance as stated in the contract do not give rise to an assertion of impossibility.

In some early judgments of the German Supreme Court (BGM), however, it was held that in a wider sense the doctrine should be extended to cases in which performance is *extraordinarily burdensome* to the debtor even though, theoretically, it could be exercised (so-called *economic impossibility*).[6]

[4] For a more specific reasoning see Kramer, '§119', in: Säcker *et al.*, *Münchener Kommentar zum Bürgerlichen Gesetzbuch*, vol. I/1, n. 132.

[5] Cf. J. Ellenberger, '§143', in: Palandt *et al.* (eds.), *Bürgerliches Gesetzbuch*, n. 2.

[6] Cf. RGZ 100, 134; RGZ 101, 74.

Yet, as soon as the principle of *Störung der Geschäftsgrundlage* had been established, this broad interpretation of impossibility was not upheld because the flexible remedies of *Störung der Geschäftsgrundlage* were considered to provide for more adequate solutions (see below).[7] The doctrine of impossibility applies, however, where the burden of performance on the debtor is not only extraordinarily high but also grossly *disproportionate* to the gains resulting to the creditor from upholding his right to performance (so-called *practical impossibility*).[8] This well-established rule was integrated into the BGB by the reform of the law of obligations enacted in 2002 (§275 II 1 BGB). It is emphasised in the legislative materials that the creditor's small interest is the decisive factor for applying the principle of impossibility, while the burden on the debtor by itself can only be a defence under the doctrine of *Störung der Geschäftsgrundlage*.[9] As an exception, a debtor of *personal services* is excused on the grounds of impossibility if he is unreasonably burdened by an impediment (§275 III BGB).

If performance is impossible for the debtor, he is relieved from specific performance (§275 BGB). However, the contract remains valid and the debtor is liable for damages, unless he can prove that he is not responsible for the impediment or – in cases of initial impossibility – for his ignorance as to the existence of the impediment (§§283, 280 I, 311a II BGB). In general, the debtor's responsibility is determined by the standard of negligence. A standard of strict liability is only adopted if it is explicitly or implicitly provided for in the contract (§276 I 1 BGB). If the debtor succeeds in rebutting the presumption of responsibility, he is completely relieved from his liability under the contract. As a consequence, the creditor is released from his contractual obligations as well (§326 BGB). This 'all-or-nothing' approach in cases in which an impediment is beyond the control of either party has contributed to the restrictive application of the doctrine of impossibility in favour of the more flexible concept of *Störung der Geschäftsgrundlage*.

(c) *Condictio ob rem* (§812 I 2 2nd alternative BGB)

Under §812 I 2 2nd alt. BGB, the benefits of a transfer can be reclaimed according to the provisions on unjust enrichment if 'the result intended

[7] Cf. C. Grüneberg,' §275', in: Palandt *et al.* (eds.), *Bürgerliches Gesetzbuch*, n. 21; K. Larenz, *Schuldrecht I* (Munich: Beck, 14th edn, 1987), §21 I e = pp. 318 *et seq.*

[8] Cf. Grüneberg, '§275', in: Palandt *et al.* (eds.), *Bürgerliches Gesetzbuch*, n. 22.

[9] Cf. BT-Ds. 14/6040, p. 130.

to be produced pursuant to the transaction does not materialise'. At first glance, this rule may seem to be of major importance with respect to the issue of frustration, but it has a very limited scope. It is common ground that §812 I 2 2nd alt. BGB is only applicable if the rules of contract law and the general rules on unjust enrichment do not apply. As a consequence, §812 I 2 2nd alt. BGB only refers to transactions under which the 'result intended to be produced' is not based upon a binding contractual promise. The reason for such an unusual transaction may be that the transferee does not want to be liable for the result to be produced or because a promise to do so would not be legally binding (e.g., promise of a testamentary disposition, §2302 BGB).[10] Even though the purpose in question is not an element of a binding promise of performance, a claim under §812 I 2 2nd alt. BGB is only valid if the parties have agreed to make the transaction dependent upon that particular purpose ('pursuant to the transaction').[11] Therefore, §812 I 2 2nd alt. BGB is not a general remedy with regard to cases in which unexpected circumstances interfere with the parties' plans.

It is disputed whether §812 I 2 2nd alt. BGB may be applied to 'regular' exchange contracts if the parties expect a certain result to be produced in addition to binding promises. In some older court decisions §812 I 2 2nd alt. BGB was applied to such cases and, consequently, the contract was rescinded as a whole.[12] However, the majority of modern scholarly opinion holds that specific expectations supplementing a binding contract should be governed by the rules of contractual interpretation (see below) and by the doctrine of *Störung der Geschäftsgrundlage*, whereas §812 I 2 2nd alt. BGB should not be applied.[13] The primary argument in this, again, is that the legal consequence of §812 I 2 2nd alt. BGB is an entire rescission of the transaction, while a more flexible adaptation is considered a more appropriate solution.

(d) Complementary interpretation of the contract ('*Ergänzende Vertragsauslegung*')

As already mentioned, the rules of *Störung der Geschäftsgrundlage* do not apply if a risk materialises which the contract attributes to one party.

[10] Cf. K. Larenz and C.-W. Canaris, *Lehrbuch des Schuldrechts*, (Munich: Beck, 13th edn, 1994), vol. II/2, §68 I 3a = S. 150 *et seq.*

[11] Cf. *Ibid.*, §68 I 3a = S. 151 *et seq.*

[12] Cf. BGH NJW 1973, 612; BGH MDR 1953, 33.

[13] Cf. Larenz and Canaris, *Schuldrecht II/2*, §68 I 3d = S. 153 *et seq.*; M. Lieb, '§812', in: P. Ulmer, *Münchener Kommentar zum Bürgerlichen Gesetzbuch* (Munich: Beck, 4th edn, 2004), nn. 165 *et seq.*

The precise content of the parties' declarations and of the contract, respectively, is to be determined according to the rules of interpretation. These rules primarily refer to the parties' *actual will* (§133 BGB), as it is recognisably, explicitly or implicitly, expressed in the declarations. If an actual and mutual will of the parties concerning a certain issue cannot be derived from the contract, the gap in the contract may be filled by reconstructing the *hypothetical will* of the parties[14] by complementary interpretation ('*ergänzende Vertragsauslegung*'). This is a method by which the solution to a certain question is extrapolated from the parties' will concerning other matters. Therefore, the contract itself is taken as the basis for adjudication. This concept allows the courts to sustain the contract while flexibly adapting it; in some decisions of the BGH a contract was adapted to unexpected circumstances.[15]

Unlike complementary interpretation, the doctrine of *Störung der Geschäftsgrundlage* is not based on the parties' will, but is considered to be a legal correction of the contract.[16] Therefore, under the concept of complementary interpretation, the circumstances giving rise to an adaptation or termination may be less grave than under the doctrine of *Störung der Geschäftsgrundlage*. Moreover, with respect to its subsidiary character, the doctrine of *Störung der Geschäftsgrundlage* applies only if there are no precise grounds for determining the parties' hypothetical will so that complementary interpretation is impossible. The distinction between both doctrines, however, often is very difficult to draw.[17] The hypothetical will of the parties is necessarily fictitious and can only be reconstructed by reference to what parties acting in good faith would have agreed upon in view of the particular circumstances (§§157, 242 BGB). By the same token, the principle of good faith is considered to be the source for the doctrine of *Störung der*

[14] Cf. BGHZ 9, 373 (277); BGHZ 77, 301 (304); D. Medicus, *Allgemeiner Teil des BGB* (Munich: Müller, 9th edn, 2006), nn. 338 *et seq.*; Larenz and Wolf, *Allgemeiner Teil*, §28, nn. 108 *et seq.*

[15] BGHZ 81, 135, 141; BGHZ 90, 69 (74); BGH WM 2000, 915 (916).

[16] Cf. K. Larenz, 'Ergänzende Vertragsauslegung und Rückgriff auf die Geschäftsgrundlage', (1983) *Karlsruher Forum*, 156 (160).

[17] E.g., in very similar cases, BGHZ 81, 135 (*ergänzende Vertragsauslegung*) and RGZ 163, 324, 333 *et seq.* (*Wegfall der Geschäftsgrundlage*). For a detailed discussion of the distinction see D. Medicus, 'Vertragsauslegung und Geschäftsgrundlage', in: H. H. Jakobs (eds.), *Festschrift für Werner Flume zum 70. Geburtstag: 12. September 1978* (Cologne: Schmidt, 1978), vol. I, pp. 629 *et seq.*

Geschäftsgrundlage as well, while it is commonly held that the hypothetical will of the parties is an important factor in determining the legal consequences of *Störung der Geschäftsgrundlage*.[18] Therefore, some scholars even deny any theoretical differences between both concepts.[19]

C. Development of the doctrine of Geschäftsgrundlage

At the time the German Civil Code (BGB) was created, there were essentially two different legal doctrines that permitted a party to set aside the contract after that performance had become extraordinarily onerous.

The first doctrine is known as *clausula rebus sic stantibus*.[20] According to this rule, which was recognised under the Gemeines Recht, contractual obligations are legally binding unless there is a fundamental change in the circumstances that the parties took into consideration at the time they entered into the contract. Thus, contractual promises are subject to the condition that the factual framework remains basically unchanged. Apart from a few specific provisions[21] (e.g., §321 BGB), the doctrine of *clausula rebus sic stantibus* was not established in the BGB since the legislators intended to emphasise the principle of *pacta sunt servanda*.[22]

The second doctrine is referred to as *laesio enormis*. This rule enables a party to set aside the contract if the contractual obligations are either initially extremely disproportionate or become so subsequent to the formation of the contract.[23] The doctrine of *laesio enormis* was explicitly rejected by the authors of the BGB, again, in favour of *pacta sunt servanda*.[24]

Thus, when the BGB came into force it lacked a general provision which set limits on the *pacta sunt servanda* rule in the case of the occurrence of unforeseen events or a particular hardship for one of the

[18] Cf. Larenz and Wolf, *Allgemeiner Teil*, §38, nn. 50 *et seq.*

[19] Cf. H. Nicklisch, 'Ergänzende Vertragsauslegung und Geschäftsgrundlagenlehre - ein einheitliches Rechtsinstitut zur Lückenfüllung ?', (1980) BB, 949 *et seq.*

[20] For further details of the rule *clausula rebus sic stantibus*, cf. G. Köbler, *Die clausula rebus sic stantibus als allgemeiner Rechtsgrundsatz* (Tübigen: J. C. B. Mohr, 1991); for the historical development of the *Geschäftsgrundlage*, cf. W. Fikentscher, *Die Geschäftsgrundlage als Frage des Vertragsrisikos* (Munich: Beck, 1971), pp. 1 *et seq.*

[21] Cf. §§321, 490, 593 *et seq.*, 519, 605 Nr. 1, 775 I Nr. 1, 779 BGB.

[22] Cf. RGZ 50, 255 (257); BGH NJW 1995, 1345 (1347); with regard to §313 BGB, cf. G. H. Roth, '§313', in: Säcker *et al.*, *Münchener Kommentar zum Bürgerlichen Gesetzbuch*, vol. 2, n. 16.

[23] T. Mayer-Maly, 'Renaissance der laesio enormis?', in: C.-W. Canaris and U. Diederichsen, *Festschrift für Karl Larenz zum 80. Geburtstag am 23 April 1983* (Munich: Beck, 1983), pp. 395 (396 *et seq.*).

[24] Cf. Motive II p. 322 = Mugdan II p. 178; RGZ 64, 181; R. Sack, '§138', in: J. V. Staudinger *et al.* (eds.), *Kommentar zum bürgerlichen Gesetzbuch und dem Einführungsgesetze* (Munich: Sellier and Berlin: DeGruyter, 2003), n. 230.

parties. Even though these aspects may fall within the scope of some other legal doctrines, such as impossibility (§275 BGB) or the rules of mistake (§§119 *et seq.* BGB), these doctrines operate within very narrow limits and only provide for an entire rescission of the transaction.

The strict idea of *pacta sunt servanda* laid down in the original form of the BGB turned out to be too harsh in the aftermath of World War I. At this juncture, due to the shortage of goods and galloping inflation, performance of contractual obligations was rendered extremely burdensome and the equivalence of exchange was distorted on a very large scale. The Reichsgericht (RG) first tried to alleviate certain instances of hardship by the so-called doctrine of *economic impossibility*. According to this doctrine the debtor of a non-monetary obligation was absolved from the contractual obligation if the nature of performance changed so radically as to render it something different from its nature at the time of formation.[25] Subsequently, the RG invoked the *clausula rebus sic stantibus* rule as well as the principle of good faith (§242 BGB) in cases in which the transaction was substantially affected and adjusted the contract, mainly by increasing the payment.[26] In some cases the adjustment was based upon the fact that performance would have ruined one of the parties financially; in some other cases the RG asserted that the payment fell completely short of being adequate.[27]

The further development was significantly influenced by Paul Oertmann's treatise in which he introduced the concept of *Geschäftsgrundlage*.[28] His concept was soon adopted by the courts and refined in numerous judgments.[29] The doctrine of *Geschäftsgrundlage* is a means to set aside the contractual stipulations if extraordinary and unexpected circumstances occur. There are three situations commonly defined as typical cases of *Geschäftsgrundlage*: first, cases in which the equivalence of the exchange is fundamentally distorted; second, cases in which one party's purpose as to the contractual subject matter is substantially affected; and, third, cases in which the parties share a

[25] Cf. RGZ 99, 259.
[26] Cf. RZG 99, 115; RGZ 100, 129 (131 *et seq.*); RGZ 103, 177 (178 *et seq.*).
[27] Cf. RGZ 100, 134 (135); RGZ 102, 272 (273); RGZ 103, 177 (179).
[28] P. Oertmann, *Die Geschäftsgrundlage* (Leipzig: Deichert, 1921).
[29] Cf. RGZ 103, 328 (332); BGHZ 25, 390 (392); BGHZ 40, 334 (335); BGH NJW 2001, 1204; for a different view, cf. W. Flume, *Allgemeiner Teil des Bürgerlichen Rechts, II. Das Rechtsgeschäft* (Berlin/Heidelberg/New York: Springer, 4th edn, 1992) §26 n. 3.

grave error.[30] With regard to the legal consequences, the doctrine of *Geschäftsgrundlage* primarily provides for the adjustment of the contract. Only if an adjustment is unfeasible is the entire contract set aside.

The reform of the law of obligations 2002[31] finally introduced the concept of *Störung der Geschäftsgrundlage* into the BGB (§313 BGB). However, the new statutory provision was not meant to modify the rules developed by the courts substantially. The legislators rather intended to codify the judge-made law without effecting substantial changes.[32] Thus, they tried to take over the conditions of a relevant *Störung der Geschäftsgrundlage* in §313 I and II BGB from the definitions developed by the courts and they structured the legal consequences accordingly in §313 I and III BGB, granting primarily adjustment of the contract and secondarily termination. The requirements of §313 BGB are explained in detail in the report on Case 1.

Austria

A. Introduction

In Austrian civil law, the doctrine of '*Wegfall der Geschäftsgrundlage*' (cessation of the basis of the contract) is considered to be the main legal device determining the legal consequences of an unexpected change of circumstances. It is not expressly mentioned in the Austrian Civil Code (Allgemeines Bürgerliches Gesetzbuch, ABGB), but is a creation of court decisions and literature. However, this doctrine is a subsidiary relief which is available only in cases where the respective risk is not allocated to one of the parties by special provisions of contract law.[33]

[30] Cf. BGHZ 122, 32 (34); BGHZ 131, 32 (39) (equivalence of exchange distorted); BGH NJW 1984, 1746 (purpose substantially affected); BGHZ 25, 392 (grave error); cf. G. H. Roth, '§313', in: Säcker *et al.*, *Münchener Kommentar zum Bürgerlichen Gesetzbuch*, vol. II, n. 147 *et seq.*, 213 *et seq.*, 223 *et seq.*; C. Grüneberg, '§313', in: Palandt *et al.* (eds.), *Bürgerliches Gesetzbuch*, nn. 38 *et seq.*, 25 *et seq.*, 35 *et seq.*

[31] Cf. BGBl. 2001 I pp. 3183 *et seq.*

[32] Cf. Regierungsbegründung BT-Ds. 14/6040, p. 175.

[33] Peter Rummel, '§ 901', in: Rummel (ed.), *Kommentar zum ABGB* (Vienna: Manz, 2000), vol. I, nn. 4, 6 with further references; F. Gschnitzer in: H. Klang (ed.), *Kommentar zum ABGB* (Vienna: Verlag der österreichischen Staatsdruckerei, 1968), vol. IV, p. 335; P. Rummel, 'Anmerkungen zum gemeinsamen Irrtum und zur Geschäftsgrundlage', (1981) *Juristische Blätter*, 1 (7, 10); H. Koziol and R. Welser, *Bürgerliches Recht* (Vienna: Manz, 2007), vol. I, p. 162; P. Apathy, '§ 901', in: M. Schwimann (ed.), *Kommentar zum ABGB* (Vienna: LexisNexis, 2006), vol. IV, n. 11; F. Bydlinski, 'Vertragsrechtliche Grundfragen des Industrieanlagenbaus', in: J. Aicher and K. Korinek (eds.), *Rechtsfragen des nationalen und internationalen Industrieanlagenbaus* (Vienna: Orac, 1991), p. 67 (115).

The Austrian Civil Code (ABGB) contains a variety of provisions which apply to particular types of contracts affected by an unexpected change of certain circumstances. Such specific provisions apply to labour contracts,[34] contracts for work and services,[35] lease contracts,[36] agency contracts,[37] mortgage/pledge agreements,[38] contracts of partnership,[39] donations[40] and others.[41] Similar provisions are also found in other statutes: for landlord and tenant contracts,[42] labour contracts,[43] insurance contracts[44] and construction contracts.[45] Besides these contract type related provisions, there exist certain general rules of contract law which may be applied by courts to change of circumstances situations as well: §871 ABGB (as to the subject matter of the contract), §901 ABGB (mistake in motive), §920 ABGB (impossibility), §918 ABGB (delay), §934 ABGB ('*laesio enormis*'), §1435 ABGB (*condictio causa data causa non secuta*) and the concepts of 'ordinary' or 'extraordinary' termination of long-term contracts.

In many areas the relationship between the above mentioned express statutory provisions and the doctrine of '*Wegfall der Geschäftsgrundlage*' is quite unclear. Officially the doctrine is applicable only subsidiarily. But nevertheless, as will be explained in the case studies below, in many cases Austrian courts apply statutory concepts and the doctrine of '*Wegfall der Geschäftsgrundlage*' side by side (cumulatively) to justify a certain result that they consider fair and reasonable in the particular circumstances. The following short introduction into the rules of Austrian civil law applying to change of circumstances situations will focus on the most important general concepts and rules needed to solve the case examples of the questionnaire, leaving aside the large number of other provisions regarding specific types of contracts.

B. *Impossibility and related doctrines*

In the course of World War I, the Austrian Oberster Gerichtshof (OGH) had to decide in many instances on the effects of hyperinflation and shortage of goods on contracts of sale which were entered into before

[34] §§1154b, 1155, 1161, 1162 ABGB. [35] §§1168, 1168a, 1171 ABGB.
[36] §§1096, 1104 *et seq.*, 1107 *et seq.*, 1112, 1116a, 1117, 1118, 1120 *et seq.* ABGB.
[37] §§1022, 1024 ABGB.
[38] §§458, 467 ABGB. [39] §§1189, 1205, 1206 *et seq.*, 1210 ABGB.
[40] §§947, 948 ABGB. [41] E.g., §§976, 1048 *et seq.* ABGB.
[42] §§7, 12a, 14, 29, 30 Mietrechtsgesetz. [43] §§8, 24–7 Angestelltengesetz.
[44] §§13, 23 *et seq.*, 41a, 51, 60 (2), 68, 69 Versicherungsvertragsgesetz.
[45] §5(3) Bauträgervertragsgesetz.

the outbreak of war. It was held that the seller is relieved from his duty to perform under the concept of 'impossibility' where the burden of performance had become grossly disproportionate to the counter-performance (the price) due to an unforeseeable change of the general economic circumstances and the seller would thus risk insolvency or financial ruin if he were forced to perform ('*Ruinrechtsprechung*').[46] In Austria, this historical approach, which was not upheld in modern private law, can be regarded as the predecessor of the doctrine of '*Wegfall der Geschäftsgrundlage*'.

Austrian doctrine generally distinguishes between 'initial impossibility' (existing already at the time of conclusion) and 'supervening impossibility' ('*anfängliche und nachträgliche Unmöglichkeit*').[47] According to contemporary doctrine 'impossibility' under §920 ABGB still includes not only factual or legal impossibility of performance, but also the so-called concept of '*economic* impossibility' ('*wirtschaftliche Unmöglichkeit*') in the sense of '*unaffordability*' ('*Unerschwinglichkeit*'). Thus, the debtor is entitled to avoid the contract, even if he is in fact able to perform, but performance is so extremely costly or otherwise burdensome for him that he cannot reasonably be expected to perform under these circumstances.[48] Under the concept of impossibility the debtor is relieved from his duty to perform. However, he has to pay back any counter-perform ance he has received under the contract.

C. *The concept of mistake*

If one adopts a broad definition of mistake, any unforeseen change of circumstances that are somehow connected to the contractual relationship can be regarded as a mistake about the assumptions of the parties concerning the contract. However, the Austrian concept of mistake is more restrictive. As a basic rule, only mistakes concerning the subject matter of the contract are legally relevant ('*Geschäftsirrtum*') and allow the mistaken party to avoid or modify the contract. This means that only mistakes with regard to his declaration of intent, the contractual partner or the object of the transaction are considered relevant. According to §871 ABGB, the mistaken party can invoke such a mistake if one of three alternative requirements is fulfilled: (i) the mistake must

[46] OGH, SZ 2/133; OGH, ZBl 1922/66; OGH, ZBl 1921/134 and 135; 28 June 1921, ZBl 1921/112; 1 July 1921, ZBl 1922/67; 20 December 1921, ZBl 1922/118; 27 February 1923, ZBl 1923/69.

[47] Koziol and Welser, *Bürgerliches Recht*, vol. I, pp. 170 *et seq.*

[48] R. Reischauer, '§920', in: Rummel, *Kommentar zum ABGB*, vol. I, n. 4 with further references.

have been caused by the other party, (ii) the mistake must have been evident to the other party due to the circumstances, or (iii) the mistake must have been discovered in due time (*'rechtzeitig aufgeklärt'*). Whether or not there is a right to avoid (or modify) the contract in cases of 'mutual mistakes' concerning the subject matter of the contract is controversial.[49]

Thus erroneous assumptions with respect to general future circumstances and developments do not qualify as mistakes regarding the subject matter of the contract (*'Geschäftsirrtum'*). §901 ABGB provides that – as a general rule – mistakes in the inducement/motives (*'Motivirrtum'*) of the mistaken party do not affect the validity of the contract. By way of an exception, such mistakes in the inducement/motives can be invoked in 'gratuitous' contracts (e.g., gifts), in all types of contracts where the parties incorporated the motive as a condition into the contract and in all types of contracts where the mistake was caused by fraud of the other party. Mistakes as to future developments are generally not taken into consideration. This means that in the majority of cases the Austrian concept of mistake is not a suitable instrument to deal with the impacts of unforeseen and exceptional events on contractual obligations.[50]

D. The doctrine of 'Wegfall der Geschäftsgrundlage'

Where circumstances, which are typical prerequisites pertaining to the purpose or nature of the contractual exchange, change, the principle of §901 ABGB was found to be grossly unfair, since this rule was formulated with regard to particular motives of only one of the parties turning out to be erroneous. Whereas in cases of an unexpected change of typical basic prerequisites of the contract an erroneous assumption of both parties that cannot be regarded as belonging exclusively to the sphere of only one of the parties can be found. Therefore, the undesirable gap left open by §901 ABGB was bridged by the introduction of the doctrine of '*Wegfall der Geschäftsgrundlage*' (frustration of contract, doctrine of *clausula rebus sic stantibus*, fundamental change of circumstances underlying the contract, cessation of the basis of the contract).

In its present form, this doctrine of '*Wegfall der Geschäftsgrundlage*' (cessation or lack of the basis of the contract) was developed by Pisko

[49] For further details see Case 13.

[50] R. Bollenberger, '§901', in: H. Koziol, P. Bydlinski and R. Bollenberger (eds.), *Kurzkommentar zum ABGB* (Vienna/New York: Springer, 2008), n. 6.

in 1934 by analogy with several provisions of the ABGB according to which a change of circumstances entitles a party to terminate the contract, and it was later adopted by the Austrian Oberster Gerichtshof (OGH).[51] Additionally, in the view of modern commentators, the '*Wegfall der Geschäftsgrundlage*' is based on the supplementary interpretation of the contract according to the hypothetical intention of the parties.[52] Contrary to the German Civil Code (§313 BGB), the doctrine of '*Wegfall der Geschäftsgrundlage*' has not yet been incorporated into the Austrian Civil Code. But it is nevertheless unanimously accepted by courts and scholars.

According to the definition presented by Oertmann,[53] which was adopted by Austrian court decisions,[54] the '*Geschäftsgrundlage*' is

> the idea of one of the parties, which became apparent at the conclusion of the contract, was recognised by the other party in its relevance, and not queried by the other party, or the common idea of all parties to the contract of the existence or the occurrence of circumstances which form the basis for the contractual intention of the parties.[55]

When these 'basic circumstances' or 'prerequisites for the contract' cease to exist, (i) a disruption of the equivalence of exchange or (ii) a

[51] §§936, 1052, 1170a and 947 *et seq.* ABGB; O. Pisko in: Klang (ed.), *Kommentar zum ABGB*, vol. II/2, p. 348; for further references see Rummel, '§901', in: Rummel (ed.), *Kommentar zum ABGB*, vol. I, nn. 4 *et seq.*

[52] Rummel, 'Anmerkungen zum gemeinsamen Irrtum und zur Geschäftsgrundlage' 7; Rummel, '§901', in: Rummel (ed.), *Kommentar zum ABGB*, vol. I, n. 6; Wolfgang Mazal, 'Zur Anpassung betrieblicher Alterspensionen', (1985) *Recht der Wirtschaft*, 52; Ferdinand Kerschner, 'Zum Wegfall der Geschäftsgrundlage bei unwiderruflichen Sozialleistungen', (1988) *Wirtschaftsrechtliche Blätter*, 211 *et seq.*

[53] Oertmann, *Die Geschäftsgrundlage*, p. 37; for further details see Koziol and Welser, *Bürgerliches Recht*, vol. I, p. 163, and Bollenberger, '§901', in: Koziol, P. Bydlinski and Bollenberger (eds.), *Kurzkommentar zum ABGB*, nn. 6 *et seq.*; Rummel, '§901', in: Rummel (ed.), *Kommentar zum ABGB*, vol I, n. 6; Attila Fenyves, *Der Einfluss geänderter Verhältnisse auf Langzeitverträge. Verhandlungen des Dreizehnten Österreichischen Juristentages* (Vienna: Manz, 1997), vol. II/1.

[54] OGH 2 December 1976, 7 Ob 802/76; OGH 20 April 1982, 5 Ob 796/81; OGH 8 July 1986, 5 Ob 537/86; OGH 24 February 1987, 2 Ob 534/86; OGH 13 May 1993, 8 Ob 1577/93; OGH 9 March 2000, 8 Ob 232/99x; G. Roth, 'Vom Wegfall der Geschäftsgrundlage zur richterlichen Vertragsanpassung', in: E. Bernat, E. Böhles and A. Weilinges (eds.) *Festschrift für Heinz Krejci zum 60. Geburtstag* (Vienna: Verap Öslehreich, 2001), 1251 (1253); Fenyves, *Geänderte Verhältnisse*, p. 12.

[55] 'Geschäftsgrundlage ist die beim Geschäftsabschluss zutage getretene und vom etwaigen Gegner in ihrer Bedeutsamkeit erkannte und nicht beanstandete Vorstellung eines Beteiligten oder die gemeinsame Vorstellung der mehreren Beteiligten vom Sein oder vom Eintritt gewisser Umstände, auf deren Grundlage der Geschäftswille sich aufbaut.'

disruption of the purpose of the contract can occur making it unreasonably burdensome for one of the parties to be obliged to perform the original contract without any changes.[56]

The prerequisites of the doctrine of '*Wegfall der Geschäftsgrundlage*' can be summarised as follows:

- Commentators and court decisions[57] start with the opinion of Pisko,[58] who names the following requirements: (i) prerequisites typical for the contract (objective basis of contract) cease to exist, (ii) this event was not foreseeable by the disadvantaged party, and (iii) it does not fall under the party's 'sphere' of responsibility (i.e., the party did not assume the risk for this event).
- Court decisions require a so-called 'double gap' ('*Doppellücke*'), i.e., a gap in the law (no default rules applicable to the present case exist) and a gap in the contract (complementary interpretation of the contract does not lead to a solution).[59]
- Legal writers and court decisions[60] have extended the doctrine of '*Wegfall der Geschäftsgrundlage*' beyond the concept of Pisko by also including the subjective common expectation of the parties (subjective basis of contract) which are not typical objective prerequisites of the contract.
- According to F. Bydlinski,[61] the change of circumstances must have a *strong* impact on the contractual situation (requirement of *gravity*), especially on the equivalence of the exchange or, in cases of disruption of purpose, on the burden of performance on one of the parties.[62]

Under Austrian law, '*Wegfall/Fehlen der Geschäftsgrundlage*' entitles the disadvantaged party to terminate/avoid the contract or to adjust the contract. If the '*Geschäftsgrundlage*' was missing from the beginning, the contract will be avoided with retrospective effect (*ex tunc*), if the

[56] Rummel, '§901', in: Rummel (ed.), *Kommentar zum ABGB*, vol. I, n. 4.

[57] Fenyves, *Geänderte Verhältnisse*, p. 40; Bollenberger in: Koziol, P. Bydlinski and Bollenberger (eds.), *Kurzkommentar zum ABGB*, nn. 7, 8; Rummel, '§901', in: Rummel (ed.), *Kommentar zum ABGB*, vol. I, n. 5 with further references.

[58] O. Pisko in: Klang (ed.), *Kommentar zum ABGB*, vol. II/2, pp. 348 *et seq.*

[59] Bollenberger '§901', in: Koziol, P. Bydlinski and Bollenberger (eds.), *Kurzkommentar zum ABGB*, n. 8; Fenyves, *Geänderte Verhältnisse*, pp. 79 *et seq.*, each with further references; Koziol and Welser, *Bürgerliches Recht*, vol. I, p. 166.

[60] Bollenberger '§901', in: Koziol, P. Bydlinski and Bollenberger (eds.), *Kurzkommentar zum ABGB*, n. 9; Fenyves, *Geänderte Verhältnisse*, pp. 57 *et seq.*, each with further references; Koziol and Welser, *Bürgerliches Recht*, vol. I, p. 165.

[61] F. Bydlinski, 'Zum Wegfall der Geschäftsgrundlage im österreichischen Recht', (1996) *Österreichisches Bankarchiv*, 499 (506 *et seq.*).

[62] Bollenberger '§901', in: Koziol, P. Bydlinski and Bollenberger (eds.), *Kurzkommentar zum ABGB*, nn. 10, 11 with further references.

'*Geschäftsgrundlage*' ceases to exist after the conclusion of the contract, the contract will be terminated with *ex nunc* effect. Long-term contracts that have already reached the performance stage normally can only be terminated with *ex nunc* effect.[63] The disadvantaged party is entitled to claim adjustment (modification) of the contract if both parties would have concluded the contract with this different content if they had anticipated the change of circumstances ('hypothesis test' by analogy with the law of mistake §872 ABGB).[64]

E. *Risk allocation by spheres*

With regard to contracts for work and services the ABGB gives the ordering party the principal responsibility for unexpected impediments to performance arising out of his sphere of responsibility (risk allocation by spheres). According to §1168 ABGB the ordering party is obliged to pay the contract price (minus the costs saved by the other party due to the non-execution of the work) where the execution of the work is prevented by 'circumstances belonging to his sphere'. Where such impediments make the performance more burdensome, the ordering party has to pay for additional costs. According to §§1168 *et seq.* ABGB, the ordering party is liable for a lack of personal participation, the defectiveness of materials provided and wrong directives given by him. Other events that have been found to fall within the ordering party's sphere of responsibility include the death of a sitter to be painted by an artist, non-delivery of the freight for carriage and the halt of construction work due to being denied building permission.[65] However, the limits of each party's responsibility seem quite unclear and are determined by the courts on a case by case basis.

F. *Termination of long term contracts*

Under long term contracts a change of circumstances may entitle a party to terminate the contract if there is a serious cause ('*wichtiger Grund*') that renders the performance unreasonably burdensome for this party and which could not be foreseen by the parties (extraordinary

[63] Rummel '§901', in: Rummel (ed.), *Kommentar zum ABGB*, vol. I, n. 6a.

[64] Koziol and Welser, *Bürgerliches Recht*, vol. I, p. 163; Rummel '§872', in: Rummel (ed.), *Kommentar zum ABGB*, vol. I, nn. 1, 7.

[65] For further examples see R. Rebhahn '§1168', in: Schwimann (ed.), *Kommentar zum ABGB*, vol. V, nn. 21 *et seq.*

right of termination).[66] The extraordinary right of termination is considered to be a general principle of Austrian contract law and is based on an analogy with several express provisions of the ABGB.[67] The different treatment of long-term contracts by Austrian contract law is justified by the long duration of the parties' obligations under the contract which makes it impossible for them to take into account all future developments.

G. *Complementary interpretation of contract*

Legal writers and some court decisions assert that the concept of '*Wegfall der Geschäftsgrundlage*' is subsidiary to a resolution based on the interpretation of the contract, including complementary interpretation ('*ergänzende Vertragsauslegung*').[68] In other words, if the question of how to deal with an unexpected circumstance can be answered by complementary interpretation of the contract, it will be solved solely on the basis of contract interpretation and no recourse to the concept of '*Wegfall der Geschäftsgrundlage*' is necessary.[69] Rummel[70] thinks that the dividing line between complementary interpretation and '*Wegfall der Geschäftsgrundlage*' is blurred, and that '*Wegfall der Geschäftsgrundlage*' is, in most cases, in fact the result of complementary interpretation.

The Netherlands

A. *Unforeseen circumstances*

The Dutch Civil Code (Burgerlijk Wetboek) contains specific provisions dealing with unexpected circumstances. The relevant provisions of the Dutch Civil Code are Art. 6:258, 6:259 and 6:260, which are systematically arranged in Book 6 of the Civil Code on obligations, under Title 5 on agreements in general, more specifically in the paragraph on the 'consequences of agreements'. According to its systematic location, the provision applies to all nominated contracts (e.g., sale, gift, lease, mandate, subcontract, agency, deposit, employment, contracting for (construction) work, partnership, suretyship, insurance, and transportation). Although

[66] Bollenberger '§859', in: Koziol, P. Bydlinski and Bollenberger (eds.), *Kurzkommentar zum ABGB*, n. 7.

[67] §§1162, 1117 *et seq.* and 1210 ABGB; Koziol and Welser, *Bürgerliches Recht*, vol. II, p. 9.

[68] Rummel '§901', in: Rummel (ed.), *Kommentar zum ABGB*, vol. I, nn. 6, 6a with further references.

[69] See the requirement of 'double gap' ('*Doppellücke*') mentioned above.

[70] Rummel '§901', in: Rummel (ed.), *Kommentar zum ABGB*, vol. I, n. 6.

statutory texts are not denominated, the legal concept embodied by the said articles is commonly referred to as 'unforeseen' or 'changed' circumstances.[71] The provisions on unforeseen circumstances are considered as *leges speciales* of the broader principle of 'reasonableness and fairness' (good faith). In fact, Art. 6:258 explicitly refers to reasonableness and fairness as a criterion for its application.

Art. 6:258 is the most important of the three provisions. At the request of a party to an agreement, a court may exercise the power to modify, partly or wholly, the consequences of an agreement, or terminate the agreement or any part thereof. Such a modification or termination can be based on unforeseen circumstances of such a nature that the other party may not expect the agreement to remain unmodified. The words 'may not expect' are measured against the general standard of 'reasonableness and fairness'. In short, the test is whether the circumstances were 'reasonably foreseeable and were somehow reflected in the agreement'. The court may give retrospective effect to its modifications or termination.[72] Furthermore, a court must not modify or terminate the agreement to the extent that the risk must still be borne by and for the account of the party that requests a modification or termination. The court should base such a refusal to modify or terminate on the nature of the agreement or on what would commonly be considered to be appropriate.

Art. 6:258 embodies two important criteria:

(i) The circumstances must have been 'unforeseen'. There is a discussion about what level of foreseeability is required. Obviously, in the ideal contracting world the parties would have all the time that is necessary to provide for all conceivable circumstances and they would know exactly what matters. But in reality, considerations of efficiency, the desired level of certainty measured against the likelihood of an event occurring (or not), the expertise of the parties and probably also some trust that both parties will overcome complications on an ad hoc basis, will inevitably give a hint as to the relevant criteria for the

[71] The Dutch law on changed circumstances is described in English in Arthur S. Hartkamp and Marianne M. M. Tillema, *Contract Law in the Netherlands* (Deventer: Kluwer, 1995), pp. 120–6; and in German in Piet Abas, *Rebus sic stantibus* (Cologne: Heymans, 1993), pp. 263–82. A comparison between Dutch law and the principles of European contract law can be found in Danny Busch in: Danny Busch, Ewoud Hondius, Hugo Van Kooten, Harriët Schelhaas and Wendy Schrama (eds.), *The Principles of European Contract Law and Dutch Law; A Commentary* (The Hague/London/Boston: Kluwer, 2002), pp. 285–9.

[72] It is within the court's discretionary power to give retrospective effect to its modification or termination: HR 11 July 2003, NJ 2004, 616.

foreseeability requirement. These are circumstances that may be taken into account when interpreting (the framework of) the agreement. Furthermore, unforeseeability often relates to circumstances that have changed, but it may equally well be that the parties had expected a change of certain circumstances which eventually did not take place.

Generally, circumstances will be considered 'unforeseen' if two conditions are met: (a) the relevant circumstances relate to the future as opposed to the moment of entering into the agreement; and (b) the circumstances have not become part of the contractual agreement (i.e., the parties have neither explicitly or implicitly provided for the particular circumstances nor allocated a particular risk in one way or another). Likewise the parties might actually have considered certain circumstances, but consciously left them aside as being hypothetical. In such a case, the criterion under (b) is nevertheless likely to be met. All in all, answering the question whether circumstances were foreseen requires a reasonable interpretation of the entire agreement.[73]

(ii) The circumstances must be such that the other party may not expect the agreement to remain unmodified (measured against the standard of reasonableness and fairness). Here, the aforementioned specification of the nature of the agreement and common opinion applies. This is, of course, a field where the court will exercise some level of discretion: it will investigate what parties of similar expertise, in similar circumstances, would have agreed upon. The principle of reasonableness and fairness, as reflected in Art. 3:12 Dutch Civil Code, requires the court to take into account generally accepted principles of law, any prevailing beliefs in the Netherlands, the interests of the persons concerned and even those of society as a whole.

Obviously, the two criteria are still highly abstract and therefore, given the impact of any modification to or termination of the contract, the court should act with reticence. The Dutch legislature has explained, and the Hoge Raad has confirmed,[74] that Art. 6:258 should be applied reluctantly (or with due care). This is in the first place because the modification (or termination) by the court constitutes a new situation for the parties: the court does not establish which terms are applicable between the parties, but creates a previously non-existent legal context. Moreover, despite the required reluctance (or care), the court's authority to modify or terminate an agreement is largely discretionary.[75]

[73] The standard for interpretation has been developed in case law: HR 13 March 1981, NJ 1981, 635 (*Haviltex*).

[74] HR 20 February 1998, NJ 1998, 493.

[75] HR 18 January 2002, NJ 2002, 106.

However, this does not mean that a court may disregard the parties' justified interests.[76] Furthermore, consistent with the systematic positioning in the Dutch Civil Code, there is a very subtle distinction: the court only modifies the consequences of an agreement and not the agreement itself (although this distinction is rather theoretical). Finally, the reluctance or care required when applying Art. 6:258 should not be exaggerated: if the statutory criteria are met, a modification or termination is justified.[77]

Dutch law does not as such acknowledge a principle of subsidiarity in respect of any remedy contained in Art. 6:258, but the court may be expected to determine a proportional solution in its judgment.[78] In practice, not only will the court be reluctant and careful in substituting its judgment 'instead of' the contractual framework, but it will also provide for appropriate safeguards for each party: Art. 6:260 (1) specifically provides that the court may impose conditions in relation to its modifications. Furthermore, Art. 6:260 (2) gives the court a discretionary power to allow any or all parties to terminate the modified agreement (e.g., if the modification would be inconvenient). In such a case, the court should limit such option in time (and the enforceability of the modification or partial termination would then be deferred until such a period has elapsed). Generally, a court should adhere as far as possible to what the parties would otherwise have agreed.

Art. 6:258 Dutch Civil Code is mandatory law: the parties cannot exclude its application. However, the parties may well attempt to address as many circumstances as they deem appropriate and efficient within the context of their agreement. In the legal practice of mergers and acquisitions, this has led to a tendency to be exhaustive: the buyer of a company will negotiate for as many warranties relating to the company's business as possible. Often, this triggers the buyer's lawyer to propose an elaborate set of the law firm's standard warranties. Even if the warranties are not accepted, one may question whether the mere

[76] This may be concluded from HR 5 January 2001, NJ 2001, 79; compare: L. Reurich, *Het wijzigen van overeenkomsten en de werking van de redelijkheid en billijkheid, Recht en praktijk 135* (Deventer: Kluwer, 2005), pp. 74–9.

[77] See for instance: HR 8 November 1996, NJ 1997, 217 (i.e., equal to a similarly worded principle under the former Art. 7A:1639w Dutch Civil Code for terminating an employment contract, Art. 6:258).

[78] As was emphasised by M. E. M. G. Peletier, *Rechterlijke vrijheid en partij-autonomie* (The Hague: PhD VU University Amsterdam, BJu Boom,1999), pp. 129–35 and see Jac. Hijma, C.C. van Dam, W. A. M. van Schendel and W. L. Valk, *Rechtshandeling en Overeenkomst, Studiereeks Burgerlijk Recht* (Deventer: Kluwer, 2007), n. 292.

proposal of such model warranties meets the criteria that certain circumstances have become part of or excluded from the contract. Ultimately, this is also a question of contract interpretation, governed by the case law-developed '*Haviltex* formulae'.[79]

Finally, Art. 6:258 embodies a general provision on unforeseen circumstances. Specific provisions can be found in family law (Art. 1:159 section 3 Dutch Civil Code), property law (Arts. 3:168 (3), 5:78 and 5:97), contract law relating to real property (Art. 6:259) and certain specific contracts, such as for contracting for (construction) work (Art. 7:753), employment law (Art. 7:685) or with regard to travel contracts (Art. 7:503–504).

B. *Mistake and hardship*

The concept of unforeseen circumstances is adjacent to other statutory provisions on mistake covered by Art. 6:228 and hardship addressed in Art. 6:78 Dutch Civil Code. Although the respective legal concepts are clearly delineated from the doctrine of unforeseen circumstances, there are also instances of overlap.

The doctrines of 'unforeseen circumstances' and 'mistake' are primarily distinguished by the moment at which the determinative circumstances came to exist: a mistake applies if the parties erred as to the actual facts or events at the moment they entered into the agreement (and the actual facts or events are such that the parties would not have entered into the agreement had they been known).[80] The default solutions for either doctrine are relatively similar: the effect of either doctrine is that the agreement, or a part thereof, is cancelled (i.e., it is deemed retroactively not to have existed at all). However, a cancellation is not effective if a party offers, in a timely fashion, appropriate compensation for the adverse effects of the mistake (Art. 6:230). As in cases of unforeseen circumstances, in cases of mistake, each party may request the court to modify the consequences of a cancellation.

It is more difficult to define the difference in scope between 'unforeseen circumstances' and the doctrine of 'hardship' (i.e., force majeure or an impossibility to perform in due time). The Dutch Civil Code distinguishes between temporary and permanent impossibility (Arts.

[79] The landmark case is HR 13 March 1981, NJ 1981, 635 (*Haviltex*).

[80] The statutory provision distinguishes between unilateral and mutual mistake in that it provides for specific criteria for the applicability of either variant (Art. 6:228 (1)(a) to (c)). The effects of mistake are, however, the same: the contract can be declared void ('*vernietigd*').

6:74 and 6:75). Depending on the nature of the hardship and on the expected time of performance, a termination may be dependent upon notice of default (Arts. 6:81 *et seq.*). It is irrelevant whether the force majeure event was foreseeable; the applicability of a hardship is determined in a negative sense by reference to the defaulting party's fault or to statutory law, legal acts or what would commonly be considered to be appropriate. Therefore, the defaulting party is liable if it should have foreseen the hardship. Because the impossibility does not need to be 'absolute', and may have a strong subjective aspect, it will often overlap with the doctrine of changed circumstances. If successfully invoked, a force majeure event will limit the defaulting party's liability, i.e., the defaulting party will only be liable to the extent that it has enjoyed a benefit it would not have enjoyed if the hardship had not occurred (i.e., the doctrine of unjustified enrichment will apply - Art. 6:212).

C. Reasonableness and fairness

Art. 6:258 Dutch Civil Code does not expressly impose a duty to renegotiate. However, many authors argue that the parties will normally have a duty to renegotiate, even if it is not provided for explicitly. Such a duty can be based on the aforementioned principle of reasonableness and fairness in Art. 6:248.[81] Also, in deciding whether a modification or termination is appropriate, a court may very well take into account the fact that a party has refused to renegotiate or even considered the appropriateness of a renegotiation.

As far as the difference between Art. 6:258 (on unforeseen circumstances) and Art. 6:248 is concerned, the principle of reasonableness and fairness may result in contractual provisions or even statutory law being set aside. The doctrine on unforeseen circumstances specifies the principle of reasonableness and fairness by giving less abstract criteria and by providing that the required modification or termination takes effect only after a court has so established since the court has the power to impose further conditions. Neither of the two legal concepts excludes the application of the other: For example, whilst an agreement could be modified on the basis of changed circumstances, this does not preclude

[81] See the literature referred to in Busch in: Busch, Hondius, Van Kooten, Schelhaas and Schrama (eds.), *The Principles of European Contract Law and Dutch Law. A Commentary*, p. 289.

a party from terminating the same agreement by invoking the principle of reasonableness and fairness.[82]

EASTERN EUROPEAN JURISDICTIONS

Slovenia

A. Introduction

The territory of today's Slovenia was a part of the Austro-Hungarian monarchy until 1919. Most of it belonged to the Austrian part when the Austrian Allgemeines Bürgerliches Gesetzbuch (ABGB) was enacted on 1 January 1812. A small territory in the north-east belonged to the Hungarian part and Hungarian law was applicable there. In 1919, Slovenia became a part of the Kingdom of Yugoslavia. The new state left the civil law uncodified and kept the existing legislation in force. Consequently, the ABGB remained in force until 1945. The new Communist regime abolished the old legislation in 1945, but due to the lack of new regulations, the old legal rules[83] remained applicable as long as they did not contravene the principles of the Yugoslav Constitution and the new Yugoslav legislation. This meant that for contracts between private persons, as well as for contracts between state enterprises, the rules of the ABGB remained applicable until the enactment of the Yugoslav Obligations Act in 1978.[84] The rules of the ABGB were sometimes modified in the case law in line with socialist ideas, especially in the fields of compensation for damages and unjust enrichment.

In the field of commercial contracts (between state enterprises) however, the so-called '*Splošne uzance za blagovni promet*' (General Commercial Usages) that were established by the Yugoslav State Arbitration in 1954 applied in most cases. The usages contained not merely commercial customary law, but also a number of general rules of the law of obligations.

Due to its federalist structure and to the division of legislative competences between the federal legislator and the legislators in the federal units, the idea of a civil code was abandoned in Yugoslavia and special codifications for separate parts of civil law were prepared instead.[85] The

[82] See also: HR 25 June 1999, NJ 1999, 602 (*VvE* v. *CSM*).
[83] They were not 'legislation', but applied as 'legal rules'.
[84] Zakon o obligacijskih razmerjih, Official Gazette 29/78.
[85] Meanwhile almost all law of obligations and a part of property law fell into the competence of the federal legislator, the law of successions and family law was within the competence of the legislators of the federal units.

law of obligations was regulated by the Obligations Act 1978, which was a federal statute based upon an extensive comparative research. Its strongest influence was still the Austrian ABGB, but it was also influenced by the German Bürgerliches Gesetzbuch (BGB), the Italian Codice Civile, the French Code Civil and some Eastern European codifications. After Yugoslavia had fallen apart in 1991, the Obligations Act remained in force until 1 January 2002 when the present Slovenian Code of Obligations (CO) was enacted.[86] It is important to note that it does not differ considerably from its predecessor. Its strong resemblance to the Obligations Act 1978 makes it possible to interpret most of its provisions based on the case law and literature of the Obligations Act 1978 (including case law and literature from other parts of the former Yugoslavia). This is particulary important for a small country like Slovenia with only few experts in the field of contract law. It will take some time before a sufficient amount of case law based on the CO 2002 will be available. The fact that Slovenian civil law has (mostly) been developed from the Austrian law makes it also possible to use Austrian literature as a source of interpretation and, to a limited extent, even Austrian case law. It is in fact quite usual that Slovenian authors, when writing about Slovenian civil law, refer to the doctrine and case law in Austria and in other countries with related legal systems, as well as to the doctrine in other parts of the former Yugoslavia.

B. *Change of circumstances*

The Slovenian legal system has adopted the principle, that if there is a significant change of circumstances (*clausula rebus sic stantibus*), it might not be just and reasonable to require that the parties perform their obligations in accordance with the contract. This concept mitigates the principle of *pacta sunt servanda* in cases where strict adherence to this principle might be too severe.[87] The Slovenian CO 2002 addresses the issue of change of circumstances in Arts. 112–15. The said provisions enable the court to dissolve a contract due to a change of circumstances on the demand of one of the parties. However, it is not possible to adjust

[86] Obligacijski zakonik, Official Gazette, 83/2001.

[87] M. Dolenc in: M. Juhart and N. Plavšak (eds.), *Obligacijski zakonik s komentarjem*, 4 vols. (Ljubljana: GV Založba, 2003), vol. I, p. 599; N. Plavšak, M. Juhart and R. Vrenčur, *Obligacijsko pravo, splošni del* (Ljubljana: GV Založba, 2009), pp. 421, 424.

the contract unless the other party proposes adjustment or, at least, gives its consent.[88]

An action on the grounds of a change of circumstances is granted under the following conditions: the change of circumstances must occur after the conclusion of a contract and render the performance of one of the parties more difficult, or frustrate the purpose of the contract.[89] The change of circumstances further has to be so significant that the contract obviously no longer complies with the expectations of both parties and it would be unjust, according to general opinion, to keep it in force as it was concluded.

The disadvantaged party is not allowed to ask for a termination of the contract if it could have been expected to take such circumstances into consideration when the contract was concluded, if it could have avoided them or if it could have averted their consequences. The same applies if the change of circumstances occurred after the performance by the disadvantaged party was due.

The Slovenian CO also provides for certain specific rules regarding the termination of long-term (and certain other) contractual relationships, which are related to the general rules on change of circumstances in Arts. 112–15 CO. Those rules are:

- Art. 333 (termination of long-term contracts concluded for an indefinite period of time)
- Art. 616 (termination of lease contracts concluded for an indefinite period of time)
- Art. 727 (termination of licensing contracts concluded for an indefinite period of time)
- Art. 830 (termination of agency contracts concluded for an indefinite period of time)
- Art. 648 (termination of work contracts)
- Art. 783 (termination of mandate)
- Art. 901(4) (termination of a contract on organised travel).

C. General right to terminate contractual relationships

The Slovenian CO provides for a general right to terminate creditor–debtor relationships (mainly contracts) that are not concluded for a definite period of time in Art. 333. According to this provision, each

[88] The other party cannot be forced to accept an adjustment. Slovenian Supreme Court, III Ips 17/93; Dolenc in: Juhart and Plavšak (eds.), *Obligacijski zakonik*, vol.1, p. 605.

[89] Kranjc in: Juhart and Plavšak (eds.), *Obligacijski zakonik*, vol. I, pp. 119–20; Plavšak, Juhart and Vrenčur, *Obligacijsko pravo, splošni del*, p. 423.

party may terminate a creditor–debtor relationship by notice when its duration is not stipulated. The notice may be given at any time, unless the time is inappropriate. The relationship is terminated when the notice period stipulated by the contract expires, or if no such period is stipulated in the contract after a customary or appropriate notice period expires. The parties may agree, however, that their relationship terminates upon the actual delivery of the termination notice unless provided otherwise by statute.

D. Mistake

Under the Slovenian CO a contract can be annulled on grounds of a mistake. Generally speaking, only mistakes about facts and/or circumstances that were essential for the conclusion of a contract are relevant. Erroneous assumptions must be related to facts and/or circumstances that exist at the time of the conclusion of the contract. A mistake related to future developments or future changes of circumstances is irrelevant. In such cases the rules regarding a change of circumstance might be applicable.

A contract concluded under the influence of mistake can be annulled if two cumulative requirements are met:[90]

- the mistake must be significant (essential); and
- the mistake must be justifiable.

According to Art. 46(1) CO, a mistake is significant if it relates to essential characteristics of the *object* of the contract or to the personal characteristics of the contractual partner (if such characteristics are essential for the conclusion of the contract). Furthermore, a mistake *may* be considered significant if it relates to circumstances that are decisive for the conclusion of the contract according to custom or according to the intention of the parties. It is generally accepted that such circumstances should be essential elements of the contract.[91]

The mistake must be *justifiable*, i.e., the mistaken party must act with sufficient care. Light carelessness (*culpa levis*) is sufficient to preclude the mistaken party from seeking annulment.[92] The standard of the care

[90] Dolenc in: Juhart and Plavšak (eds.), *Obligacijski zakonik*, vol. I, p. 346.

[91] A mistake related to the payment of the sales tax was not considered to be related to an essential element of the contract. Boris Strohsack, *Obligacijska razmerja* (Ljubljana: Uradni list RS, 2nd edn, 1992), vol. I, p. 123.

[92] M. Vedriš and P. Klarić, *Gradjansko pravo* (Zagreb: Narodne novine, 1998), p. 158; Dolenc in: Juhart and Plavšak (eds.), *Obligacijski zakonik*, vol. I, p. 349.

required depends on the position of the mistaken party in the contractual relation. If he is a *lay person*, the standard of an average, reasonable person is to be applied. If the mistaken party is a *professional*, the standard of professional care applies. This means that a mistake is only justifiable if it would not be discovered by the majority of professionals specialised in that field.[93]

When the above requirements are met, the contract is valid, but the mistaken party may seek annulment. The annulment has retroactive effect (*ex tunc*). However, the mistaken party may not seek annulment if the other party is willing to perform the contract as if there had been no mistake (Art. 46(4) CO). The action must be filed within one year after the reason for annulment has been discovered, but not later than three years after the conclusion of the contract (Art. 99 CO).

Article 46(3) CO provides for the right of compensation of damages for the other party if a contract is annulled on grounds of mistake and the other party acted in good faith. This right exists regardless of whether the mistaken party is responsible for the mistake or not.[94] This provision makes it clear that the mistaken party is liable even if it cannot be blamed for the mistake ('strict liability').

E. Equal value of performances (gross disparity)

In Slovenian law, the principle of equal value of performances ('*iustum pretium*', '*laesio enormis*', gross disparity) was enacted as one of the general principles of contract law (Art. 8 CO).[95] It applies to synallagmatic contracts. According to the second paragraph of this general provision, legislation will set out the cases in which the infringement of this principle has legal consequences. This principle is further recognised in Art. 118 CO. If there is a clear disproportionality between the value of obligations of both parties *at the time of conclusion* of a bilateral contract, the injured party may request the annulment of the contract, provided that it did not know or was not obliged to know about the disparity between the value of the mutual obligations at the time of the conclusion of the contract (Art. 118(1) CO). The other party can, however, 'save' the contract by offering a supplement to its obligation, so that proportionality is reached (Art. 118(4) CO).

[93] Plavšak, Juhart and Vrenčur, *Obligacijsko pravo, splošni del*, p. 208.

[94] However, if the mistake is caused by the mistaken party, the mistake will not be justifiable, which means that the annulment action will be denied.

[95] Juhart in: Juhart and Plavšak (eds.), *Obligacijski zakonik*, vol. I, p. 618.

The rules regarding *laesio enormis* are very similar to the rules regarding mistake. The legal consequences are the same. According to legal doctrine, *laesio enormis* refers to a special case of mistake, namely mistake in the *value of performances*.[96] The rules of Article 118 CO are specific rules that should be considered in order to determine whether or not a mistake regarding the value of the mutual obligations is relevant when a party bases its action for annulment on grounds of mistake.

Lithuania

A. Introduction

The Lithuanian private law system is a typical civil law system based on Roman law traditions. Like most of the private law systems of continental Europe, Lithuanian private law was and is codified.

The first known Lithuanian written source containing provisions on contract law is the Code of Laws of 1468, known as the Code of King Casimir or the Restatement of Laws of Casimir. However, the most famous sources of Lithuanian law, which among other provisions include the provisions on contract law, were the prominent Lithuanian statutes of 1529 (First Lithuanian Statute), 1566 (Second Lithuanian Statute) and 1588 (Third Lithuanian Statute). The Third Lithuanian Statute of 1588 was in force in the largest part of Lithuania for more than 250 years - until 1840 when it was replaced by Russian legislation. All three Lithuanian statutes contained many provisions on contract law: e.g., Arts. 1–31 of the Third Lithuanian Statute provided detailed provisions on contracts of sale, donation, lease, pledge, the rules on the formal requirements of contracts, proof of obligations, etc.

After the restoration of independence in 1918, for historic reasons, the reception of four different legal systems of civil law took place: the Russian civil legislation of 1840 was applied in the largest part of the territory of Lithuania; the Civil Code of France of 1804 was in force in the territory located on the left side of the river Nemunas; the German BGB was applied in the Klaipeda region; and the Restatement of the Civil Laws for Baltic provinces was in force in the Palanga and Zarasai regions.

During the Soviet period (1940–1990), the legal system in Lithuania was replaced by the Soviet legal system. From 1940 to 1964, the Civil

[96] *Ibid.*, p. 621; Strohsack, *Obligacijska razmerja*, p. 198; B.T. Blagojević and V. Krulj, *Komentar zakona o obligacionim odnosima* (Belgrade: Savremena Administracija, 1983), p. 412.

Code of the Russian Federation of 1922 was applied. In 1964 the Lithuanian Civil Code was adopted. However, due to the system of centralisation, this Civil Code was a copy of the Civil Code of the Russian Federation. The Civil Code of 1964, as amended in 1994, remained in force until 1 July 2001.[97] On 17 May 1994, Article 177 of this Code was supplemented with a new part on the modification or rescission of a contract in the event of a relevant change of circumstances. This amendment was explained by economic difficulties faced in the period of transition from the planned to the market economy.

On 18 July 2000 the Parliament of Lithuania adopted a new Civil Code of Lithuania (hereinafter CC) which entered into force on 1 July 2001.[98]

The rules of contract law are concentrated in Book 6 'Law of Obligations'. This Book consists of 1018 articles and is divided into four parts. Part One deals with general questions concerning the Law of Obligations (Arts. 6.1–6.151). Part Two establishes general provisions of the Law of Contracts (Arts. 6.154–6.228). This part was prepared on the basis of the UNIDROIT Principles of International Commercial Contracts. Part Three regulates civil liability (contractual and liability in tort – Arts. 6.245–6.304). Special chapters on the administration of the affairs of third parties and on the obligations regarding unfair enrichment are also included in this part. Part Four (Arts. 6.305–6.1018) covers specific types of contracts: sale, gifts, lease, financial leasing, use, carriage, loan, franchising, insurance, factoring, construction, services, etc.

As the new CC has been in force for only four years and the rules of the new CC are not applied retroactively, there are only a few leading cases of the Supreme Court in applying the new contractual rules.

B. The principle of pacta sunt servanda *and its exceptions*

The new CC clearly establishes the principle of *pacta sunt servanda*.[99] According to Art. 6.189 CC, a contract, which is concluded in accordance with the provisions of laws and is valid, has the force of law between its parties. The contract binds them not only as to what it expressly

[97] For a more detailed historic introduction to Lithuanian contract law see: Valentinas Mikelenas, 'Unification and Harmonisation of Law at the Turn of the Millennium: the Lithuanian Experience', (2000) 5 *Uniform Law Review*, 2, 253–61; Dalia Mikeleniene and Valentinas Mikelenas, 'Contracts. Lithuania', in: R. Blanpain (ed.), *International Encyclopaedia of Laws. Contracts*. (The Hague: Kluwer, 2004).

[98] Valstybės žinios (2000), *Official Gazette* No 74–2262.

[99] Valentinas Mikelenas. *Commentary on Book VI of the Civil Code*, (Vilnius: Justitia, 2003) (in Lithuanian).

provides, but also as to all the consequences deriving from its nature or determined by laws. A contract must be performed by the parties in a proper way and in good faith (Art. 6.200 CC). None of the parties may unilaterally refuse performance of its own obligation or modify the conditions of performance thereof except in the cases provided for by laws or by contract (Art. 6.59 CC). However, there are several exceptions to the principle of *pacta sunt servanda*.

(a) Changed circumstances

The performance of a contract can be hindered by circumstances which fundamentally alter the balance of the contractual obligations, i.e., either the cost of performance has essentially increased or the value thereof has essentially diminished. According to Art. 6.204 CC, the aggrieved party has the right to request modification of the contract in this case. Such request must be made immediately after the occurrence of the obstructions and the grounds on which the request is based. The request for modification of the contract does not in itself entitle the aggrieved party to suspend performance of the contract. If the parties fail to reach an agreement on the modification of the contractual obligations within a reasonable time, any of them may bring an action. The court may dissolve the contract and establish the date and terms of its dissolution or modify the conditions of the contract by restoring the balance of the contractual obligations of the parties. The Article reads as follows:

Article 6.204. Performance of contractual obligations upon a change of circumstances

1. If the performance of a contract becomes more onerous for one of the parties, this party shall be bound to perform the contract in accordance with the procedure established in the other Paragraphs of this Article.
2. The performance of a contract shall be considered obstructed under such circumstances which fundamentally alter the balance of the contractual obligations, i.e., either the cost of performance has essentially increased, or the value thereof has essentially diminished if:
   1) these circumstances occur or become known to the aggrieved party after the conclusion of the contract;
   2) these circumstances could not reasonably have been foreseen by the aggrieved party at the time of the conclusion of the contract;
   3) these circumstances are beyond the control of the aggrieved party;
   4) the risk of occurrence of these circumstances was not assumed by the aggrieved party.
3. If the performance of a contract becomes obstructed, the aggrieved party shall have the right to make a request to the other party for the

> modification of the contract. Such request shall have to be made immediately after the occurrence of the obstructions and the grounds on which the request is based indicated therein. The request for modification of the contract shall not in itself entitle the aggrieved party with the right to suspend performance of the contract. Where within a reasonable time, the parties fail to reach an agreement on the modification of the contractual obligations, any of them may bring an action in a court. The court may:
> 1) dissolve the contract and establish the date and terms of its dissolution;
> 2) modify the conditions of the contract with a view to restoring the balance of the contractual obligations of the parties.

(b) Mistake, fraud, duress and violation of good faith or public policy

The grounds for absolute or relative nullity of a contract are stated in Book 1 CC (Arts. 1.78–1.96 CC). There are several relevant grounds – mistake, fraud, duress, violation of good faith or public policy, incapacity, etc. According to Art. 1.90 CC, a contract influenced by an essential mistake may be declared void on the demand of the person whose consent is vitiated.

A mistake is an erroneous assumption of the essential facts of a transaction that existed at the moment when it was concluded. Such an error must relate to the nature, object or any other essential condition of the contract itself, the civil legal status of the other contracting party or any other circumstances. A fact is furthermore only essential if a person of normal diligence and attentiveness would not have made a transaction in a similar situation or would have made it on essentially different terms if he had known the real state. A fact is likewise essential in cases of a mutual mistake, if one party induced the error of the other without intention to deceive, or if one party was aware (or should have been aware) of the other party's mistake and the requirement to perform would contradict the principles of good faith, justice and reasonableness.

However, a mistake is not considered essential if it was caused by gross negligence of the mistaken party, or induced by circumstances, the risk of which was taken by the party or if, taking into account the concrete circumstances, the risk of mistake falls upon the particular party.[100]

[100] LAT (i.e., Supreme Court of Lithuania), Judgment of 18 February 2004, Case No 3K-3–107/2004.

The mistaken party also cannot claim annulment of a contract if its rights and interests may be adequately protected by invoking other remedies (Part 7, Art. 190), e.g., if it is possible to modify certain contract terms on another legal basis, such as on the basis of gross disparity of the parties (Art. 6.228 CC).[101]

In the case of annulment of a transaction concluded under the influence of an essential mistake, the provisions on restitution are applied (Art. 1.80(2) CC). The party upon whose action the transaction is declared void may, in addition to the annulment, also claim compensation for the expenses incurred or the damage to or loss of his property if this party proves that the mistake was caused by the fault of the other party.

Art. 1.91 CC provides for the opportunity to declare a contract null and void if a party, which entered into the contract by reason of necessity, assumed obligations under unfair conditions. For the application of this norm, several facts must be proved by the plaintiff – the disadvantaged contracting party: a state of necessity; a causal relation between the entry into the contract and the state of necessity; and a serious disproportion between the rights and the duties of the parties, i.e., the fact that the contract is advantageous for the defendant and extremely disadvantageous for the plaintiff.

Based on the same provision, a contract may be declared void by a court on the action of the aggrieved party if it was entered into due to fraud, duress, economic pressure or real threatening, or if it was concluded by a malicious agreement of the agent of one party with the other party.

(c) Impossibility of performance

In Lithuanian law, there are two kinds of impossibility of performance of an obligation: initial and supervening impossibility. If the performance was impossible from the beginning of the obligation, there can be no obligation and no contract. Art. 6.3 CC clearly establishes the principle of *impossibilium nulla obligatio est*.

In contrast, the consequences of a supervening impossibility depend on whether the impossibility was caused by one of the parties. If, in a bilateral contract, neither party is responsible for the impossibility, neither party may require performance as long as neither the law nor the contract provide otherwise (Art. 6.127 CC). In such case, each party

[101] LAT, Judgment of 24 September 2003, Case No 3K-3–863/2003.

has the right to claim restitution in kind without being entitled to claim the corresponding counter-performance. If, in a bilateral contract, the debtor of the particular obligation is responsible for the event leading to impossibility, the other party may revoke the contract and claim restitution in kind (to return everything that was performed), and ask for compensation for losses incurred by the non-performance of this obligation, as long as neither the law nor the contract provide otherwise. If, on the other hand, the creditor of the particular obligation is responsible for the event leading to impossibility, the other party has the right to demand counter-performance and compensation of damages (Art. 6.62 CC).

(d) Force majeure

Absolute or objective impossibility must be distinguished from force majeure. Impossibility is a ground for extinguishing the obligation. Force majeure is a ground for the release of the debtor from the obligation to compensate damages for non-performance. However, in many cases force majeure at the same time constitutes the impossibility of performance, e.g., if force majeure is of a permanent nature.

According to Art. 6.212 CC, a party is exempted from civil liability for non-performance of a contract if it proves that its non-performance was due to circumstances that were beyond its control and could not have been reasonably expected at the time the contract was concluded, and if these circumstances or consequences could not have been prevented. Force majeure does not include circumstances such as the absence of goods promised in the market, the lack of the necessary financial resources of the party, or the non-performance of the debtor's suppliers.

According to this definition, there are four necessary elements of force majeure: the existence of an event which renders the performance of a contract impossible; the imputability of this event to the debtor; the debtor's impossibility of escaping this event or its consequences; the unpredictability of this event by the parties at the moment of the formation of the contract.

If the impediment is temporary, the non-performing party is exempted from liability only for a reasonable period taking into account the effect of that impediment on the performance of the contract.

The party who failed to perform is obliged to inform the other party about the impediment and its influence on the possibility of performing the contract. If the other party does not receive a notice within a reasonable time after the non-performing party became or should have become aware of the impediment, the other party is entitled to claim damages resulting from the non-receipt of the notice.

(e) Gross disparity

According to Art. 6.228 CC, a party may avoid a contract or a separate term thereof if at the time of the conclusion of the contract, the contract or its term gives the other party an excessive unjustified advantage. In such cases regard must especially be had for the question if one party has taken an unfair advantage of the other party's dependent position or economic difficulties, urgent needs, economic weakness, lack of information or experience, or his inadvertence or inexperience in negotiations. Note must also be taken of the nature and purpose of the contract. Upon the request of the disadvantaged party, a court may revise the contract or a term and adapt them so that the contract or a separate term meet the requirements of fairness and reasonable standards of fair dealing practices. The court may modify the contract or a separate term upon the request of the party which has received the notice of the cancellation, provided that it informs the other party of its request promptly after having received such notice and before the other party has reasonably acted in reliance on the cancellation.[102]

(f) Principles of justice, reasonableness and good faith and the filling of gaps of a contract

According to Art. 1.5 CC, the court must act in accordance with the principles of justice, reasonableness and good faith if the law or an agreement between the parties provide for discretionary decisions by the court for certain issues. In any case, the court is guided by the principles of justice, reasonableness and good faith when interpreting and applying laws. The above mentioned article allows the court, when deciding contractual disputes, to modify contractual terms and to reach a reasonable and fair balance between the interests of both parties. Art. 6.195 CC provides that if the parties have failed to discuss certain conditions that are necessary for the performance of a contract, such gaps in the contract may be eliminated by a court in determining appropriate conditions by taking into account non-mandatory legal norms, the intentions of the parties, the purpose and essence of the contract and the criteria of good faith, reasonableness and justice.

[102] Valentinas Mikelenas, *Commentary on Book VI of the Civil Code*, p. 265 (in Lithuanian).

It is also possible to fill the gaps in contractual provisions on the basis of the doctrine of implied contract terms. According to Art. 6.196 CC, there are two kinds of contract conditions – express or implied. The implied conditions follow from the essence and purpose of the contract, the nature of the relationships established between the parties, the criteria of good faith, reasonableness and justice. Thus the court, when interpreting a contract, may establish an implied contractual term on the basis of the above-mentioned criteria.

Czech Republic

A. Introduction

Czech law distinguishes two situations which are exceptions to the basic principle of contract law '*pacta sunt servanda*': the impossibility of performance and frustration of the purpose of the contract. The first applies to the whole area of private law governed by the Civil and Commercial Codes; the second is incorporated only in the Commercial Code and relates solely to commercial law relations.[103]

The regulation of impossibility of performance is found in the mandatory provisions of the Civil Code (Section 575) which is supplemented by further provisions of the Civil Code (Sections 576 and 577).

For commercial relations this regulation is further supplemented by non-mandatory provisions of the Commercial Code (Sections 352–4). A provision for cases of international trade is given in Section 731(3) Commercial Code, which provides for absence of a permission in connection with the performance of the contract.

The current legal regulation (of the Civil and Commercial Codes) developed primarily on the basis of the previous International Trade Code. Originally, under the Austrian Civil Code (ABGB) (in effect until 31 December 1950) both doctrine and court practice in cases of changed circumstances applied §1447 ABGB (which deals with the disappearance of movable things). The so-called middle Civil Code (in effect 1951–63) took over the basic idea of §1447 of its predecessor and embodied it into its §334. A new regime was introduced by the

[103] The Commercial Code (Act No. 513/1991 Coll. as amended) regulates the status of entrepreneurs, business obligations and other relations connected with business activities. The Civil Code (Act No. 40/1964 Coll. as amended) is applicable when it proves impossible to resolve the issue according to the Commercial Code (Section 1 of the Commercial Code).

International Trade Code in Sections 245–50 (impossibility of performance) and Section 275 (frustration), which was in effect until 1992. Its concept was incorporated into Sections 575–7 of the Civil Code (the current law) and 352–4 (impossibility of performance) and Sections 356 and 357 Commercial Code (frustration).

Problems of unexpected circumstances have not been a subject of special attention of Czech legal theory. Even their appearance in court practice is rare.

B. Basic regulation in the Civil Code

The Civil Code provides for the impossibility of performance. It principally ensues from a conception which fundamentally – at least at first glance – undermines the general principle of contractual relations (*pacta sunt servanda*), since in its general clause it permits *rebus sic stantibus* (Section 575(1): 'If performance becomes impossible the debtor's obligation to perform shall extinguish'). While this clause fundamentally opens an option to revise the obligations of the parties and therefore change the contractual relations, the provision immediately following restricts this option. It relates to the same conditions under which an adaptation may be applied to the original obligation (duty) of the debtor, in other words it defines what can be understood as impossible performance. The provision of Section 575(2) Civil Code stipulates that 'performance is not impossible in cases including, without limitation, where such performance may be effected though under more difficult conditions, with greater costs or only after an agreed period of time'. This negative definition implies that application of the general clause is possible only under absolutely exceptional circumstances, even though these restrictions are defined in very vague, general terms, which can certainly be interpreted in different ways and thus may even be interpreted widely for considerations of impossibility of performance.

Finally the Civil Code imposes a notification obligation on the debtor (Section 577). The debtor is obliged, without undue delay after discovering a fact causing performance to be impossible, to notify such a fact to the creditor. If the debtor fails to do so or does so late, he becomes liable for the damage that is incurred by the creditor due to the fact that he was not informed in due time of the impossibility.

C. Supplementary regulation in the Commercial Code

As has already been said, the Commercial Code supplements the basic regulation of the Civil Code with non-mandatory provisions.

The Commercial Code provides that impossibility of performance is not established if the obligation can be performed with the help of some other person independent of the debtor (Section 352(1) Commercial Code). Furthermore, the Commercial Code provides for cases of additional unlawfulness of performance as a consequence of the promulgation of laws subsequent to the conclusion of the contract, which bar the debtor from performing his obligations under the contract or which require him to obtain official licences that the debtor, although he made best efforts to obtain them, was not granted (Section 352(2) Commercial Code).

The Commercial Code also sets forth a burden of proof in regard to the impossibility of performance that affects the debtor (Section 352(4) Commercial Code).

D. Specific problems of impossibility of performance and frustration

(a) Impossibility of performance

Czech doctrine concentrates primarily on qualification of the impossibility itself, its content and some of its consequences. It emphasises that impossibility of performance means the occurrence, after the creation of the contract, of a situation affecting the original contract and making it impossible to perform, thereby extinguishing some or all obligations under it. It therefore relates to subsequent impossibility. If performance has been impossible from the outset, i.e., the impossibility existed at the time of the creation of the contract, the contract would be deemed not made since it would be absolutely invalid.[104]

On the other hand, the so-called economic impossibility of performance is distinguished. In the case of such impossibility, the performance is objectively possible, but from the economic perspective it is so difficult that it definitely cannot be demanded from the debtor. If the obligation is performable, i.e., if impossibility is not factually or legally given, economic impossibility itself does not trigger the extinction of the obligation.

Extinction of an obligation is triggered only by the objective impossibility of the performance of the obligation. It is not sufficient that there is a subjective impossibility, i.e., the fact that the debtor himself cannot perform the obligation (e.g., fail to supply agricultural products

[104] M. Škárová in: Jehlička *et al.* (eds.), *Občanský zákoník, Komentář* (*Civil Code, Commentary*) (Prague: ASPI, 9th edn, 2004), p. 847; I. Pelikánová in: Pelikánová *et al.* (eds.), *Obchodní právo* (*Commercial Law*), (Prague: ASPI, 2nd edn, 1998), p. 218.

due to a crop failure). The obstruction to performance must be insurmountable.[105]

Impossibility of performance relates to and depends on the content of the obligation or subject of performance. Therefore the extinction of an obligation will clearly not come into consideration if its content is pecuniary performance or performance in specified types of items.[106]

The obligation extinguishes by operation of law itself. No action from the debtor is needed. In this connection one should also distinguish between impossibility of performance on the one hand and force majeure on the other. As to their factual basis they are very similar.

(b) Impossibility and force majeure

It is necessary to distinguish between impossibility of performance and force majeure: impossibility of performance causes an obligation to be extinguished, whereas force majeure releases the obligor from the obligation to compensate and does not relate to the existence of the obligations. Impossibility of performance presupposes a permanent inability to perform the obligation, whereas force majeure may arise in the case of both a permanent and a temporary obstacle hindering the performance of the obligation.

The legal literature distinguishes five positive and two negative elements of force majeure.[107] The positive elements of force majeure are that the circumstances:

- must occur after the creation of the obligation;
- must objectively prevent the performance of the obligation;
- must be of exceptional nature;
- must be unavoidable; and
- must precede the default.

The negative elements of force majeure are:

- the impossibility of performance must not be of subjective nature, i.e., on the side of the person who is obliged to perform; and
- the impediment must not be one that the obliged person by the nature of contract is obliged to overcome (e.g., the obligation to obtain necessary government licences).

[105] See Škárová in: Jehlička *et al.* (eds.), *Občansky zákoník, Komentář (Civil Code, Commentary)*, p. 847.

[106] See Section 575(2) Civil Code and Škárová in: Jehlička *et al.* (eds.), *Občansky zákoník, Komentář (Civil Code, Commentary)*, p. 848.

[107] L. Kopáč in: R. Bystrický *et al.* (eds.), *Právo mezinárodního obchodu (Law of the International Trade)* (Prague: 1967), pp. 311 *et seq.*

Impossibility of performance is triggered by a situation where the obligation cannot be performed on any ground whatsoever, whereas in cases of force majeure it is important to identify what caused the obstacle to performance to arise and whether that meets the specific criteria demanded by the law.

The claim for damages is, in the case of force majeure, governed by Section 353 of the Commercial Code ('A debtor whose obligation is discharged due to the impossibility of performance must provide compensation for any damage caused thereby to the creditor, unless the impossibility of performance is caused by circumstances including liability (Section 374). The provisions of Section 373 and subsequent sections apply *mutatis mutandis* to compensation for damage (i.e. damages).'). The extent of the indemnity is governed by Section 373 of the Commercial Code ('Whoever breaches a duty arising from a contractual relationship is obliged to provide compensation for the damage (i.e. damages) caused to the other party, unless he proves that such a breach was caused by circumstances excluding his liability.'). According to Section 352(4) Commercial Code it is the debtor who must prove the impossibility of performance. If the debtor is able to prove that the obstacle occurs independently of his will and prevents him from performing his obligation then he is exonerated from his liability for damages. Section 374 reads as follows:

(i) Circumstances excluding liability are an obstacle which arose independently of the obligated (liable) party's will and which prevent this party from performing its obligation, provided that it cannot be reasonably expected that the obligated party could avert or overcome such an obstacle or its consequences, and further that the occurrence of such an obstacle was unpredictable at the time when the obligated party undertook to perform such obligation.
(ii) An obstacle, which only arose during the time when the obligated party was in default with performance of its obligation, or which ensued from its financial situation, shall not exclude its liability.
(iii) The consequences excluding liability are limited only to the duration of the obstacle to which they relate.

(c) Frustration of the basic purpose of the contract

The Commercial Code also recognises the institution of frustration of the purpose of a contract (Section 356). For this to apply, three conditions must be met:

- the purpose must be basic and must be expressed in the contract,
- the frustration must have occurred as a consequence of a substantial change of circumstances,

- a change of the financial situation of the parties or a change in the market situation is not deemed to constitute a change of circumstances.

Frustration of the basic purpose of the contract does not extinguish the obligation. The obligation has not been terminated by operation of law, but the frustration represents the ground of withdrawal from the contract for the party who is affected by the frustration.[108]

The fundamental purpose of an agreement is the purpose without the performance of which the agreement would not have been concluded.[109] The consequences of a change of circumstances must be significant enough for the fundamental purpose to be frustrated in its entirety. It is not sufficient for the purpose of the agreement to be frustrated only in part.

The party entitled to withdraw from the agreement is that which was to perform the frustrated purpose under the agreement. From the nature of the matter it ensues that the notice to withdraw from the agreement must include a statement of the reason, i.e., the purpose which was frustrated.[110]

The claim for compensation by the party which did not withdraw from the agreement includes all the costs which it incurred in preparing for its obligations and which become purposeless upon the extinction of the agreement, as well as a claim for lost profit. The compensation claim is governed by Section 357 Commercial Code ('A party which has withdrawn from a contract under the provisions of Section 356 shall pay compensation to the other party for any damage caused to the latter by such withdrawal'). The extent of indemnity is governed by Section 379 Commercial Code ('Unless this Act provides otherwise, compensation shall be provided for the actual damage and for the lost profits'). The extinction of the agreement ensues as a consequence of the legal act of withdrawal from the agreement, and it is therefore not possible to assert circumstances excluding responsibility.[111]

The civil law approach is similar to the approach in the Commercial Code. The relevant sections are Sections 575–7 Civil Code.

[108] See in the same sense Pelikánová, in: Pelikánová *et al.* (eds.), *Obchodní právo* (*Commercial Law*), p. 218.

[109] See *ibid.*, p. 218.

[110] See L. Kopáč, *Obchodní kontrakty* (*Commercial Contracts*), (Prague: Spectrem, 1993), vol. II, p. 841.

[111] See M. Tomsa in: I. Štenglová, S. Plíva, and M. Tomsa (eds.), *Obchodní zákoník, Komentář* (*Commercial Code, Commentary*) (Prague: Linde, 11th edn, 2006), p. 1093.

(d) Mistake and change of circumstances

The Civil Code recognises only essential mistake in conducting juridical acts. According to Section 49a Civil Code a legal act is void if the promiser was acting in error, that error was crucial for the execution of his promise and the mistake was caused by the promisee or at least the promisee must have known about the error. If the error was caused by the addressee intentionally, then the legal act is invalid even if the error is not essential. It is necessary to point out that the legal act is not invalid *ex lege*, but is invalid only relatively.[112] It means that the legal act is valid till the acting person gives notice to the addressee invoking the relative invalidity.[113]

In Czech law, mistake as a legal category is traditionally linked with the formation of contract. Neither in the legal literature nor in the case law has a connection been made between a change of circumstances and a mistake in perception of it.

E. Characterisation of Czech law

In accordance with prior practice and theory, which were tied to the International Trade Code, even the current stance on impossibility of performance as a termination of the obligation is relatively rigid and restrictive.

This attitude is characterised by certain typical traits. Czech law does not pay any particular attention to long-term contractual relations. Although the provisions discussed above certainly relate to them, their existence undoubtedly deserves special attention, which is not given to them even by doctrine or judicial practice. Aside from impossibility of performance, Czech law also recognises a proposition for frustration of obligations (frustration of the purpose of a contract) (see above). This proposition, which is incorporated in the Commercial Code, must doubtless be understood in the context of the provisions on impossibility of performance, although neither theory nor practice do so.

F. Non-acceptance of the doctrine of Wegfall der Geschäftsgrundlage

Czech law does not recognise the doctrine of *Wegfall der Geschäftsgrundlage*. Even under the Austrian Civil Code (ABGB), this doctrine has not been applied in the former Czechoslovakia.[114]

112 See J. Švestka in: Jehlička *et al.* (eds.), (Civil Code) *Občanský zákoník Komentář (Commentary)*.

113 See Section 40a Civil Code.

114 See J. Sedláček, in: F. Rouček and J. Sedláček (eds.), *Komentář k československému obecnému zákoníku občanskému (Commentary on the Czechoslovak General Civil Code)* (Prague: vol. IV, 1936), pp. 244–50.

On the other hand, it is necessary to mention the theory of frustration. This is enshrined in the Commercial Code and must doubtless be understood in the context of the provision an impossibility of performance, although this is not the case in either theory or practice.[115]

G. *Consequences*

(a) Extinction, discharge, withdrawal

Impossibility of performance leads to the extinction of the obligation but it may not cause the total discharge of the debtor. The majority of authors regard the regulation (Section 575 Civil Code) as mandatory: the parties cannot stipulate otherwise.[116] This is a very absurd consequence.

If the impossibility of performance was caused by the debtor, even though the obligation extinguishes, the creditor still has the right to compensation in the form of damages for losses he incurs as a result of the non-performance of the obligation, unless the provisions of the Commercial Code apply, exonerating the debtor if the impossibility of performance was caused by circumstances excluding his responsibility, (Section 374 Commercial Code).[117]

Upon withdrawal from an agreement due to frustration of the purpose of the agreement, the obligations of both parties will be extinguished. If a party terminated the agreement prior to its extinction, any claim by the other party for damages will not be affected by the withdrawal, since the agreement was terminated by the notice of withdrawal rather than the frustrating event.

(b) Damages

The extinction of an obligation due to the impossibility of its performance has similar effects as a failure to perform; thus, creditors may incur losses. The debtor becomes obliged to compensate a creditor for these losses (Section 353 Commercial Code) but may release himself from this obligation if he proves that the impossibility of performance consists of an obstacle to performance which falls into the category of circumstances ruling out responsibility (force majeure).[118] This is replaced by

[115] See Pelikánová, in: Pelikánová *et al.* (eds.), *Obchodní Právo (Commercial Law)*, p. 218.

[116] See e.g., Škárová in: Jeblička *et al.* (eds.), *Občansky zākonik, Komentář (Civil Code Commentary)* p. 849 S. Dvořák, V. Knapp *et al.*, *Občanské právo hmotné* (*Civil law*) (Prague: Codex, 3rd edn, 2002), vol II., p. 160.

[117] See IV; B. above.

[118] See Tomsa, in: Stenglová, Plíva and Tomsa (eds.), *Obchodní zákoník Komentář (Commercial Code)*, p. 1091.

damage caused by extinction of an obligation which became incapable of being performed. The key factor is the causal connection between the extinction and the damage arising. It is not relevant for the calculation of damages what period of time the obligation was to be performed in, but losses are calculated from the time when the obligation permanently ceased to be performable. The regime under the Civil Code is different: the debtor is not liable for any loss if it, without any delay after having learned of circumstances causing perfomance to be impossible, notifies the creditor accordingly (Section 577 Civil Code).

A party that has withdrawn from the contract due to the frustration of the contractual purpose is obliged to pay compensation to the other party for the losses caused by such withdrawal (Section 357 Commercial Code).

(c) Claim for return of performance provided

If impossibility of performance causes a right to withdraw from the agreement, while the other party has already performed its obligation, such other party shall have a claim for the restitution of this performance. This claim is based on a special regulation of unjustified enrichment in the Civil Code.[119]

H. The principles of good faith and good morals and of fair conduct

Czech law is undoubtedly among those jurisdictions which deem a type-defined or pecuniary obligation as always performable with consideration to its subject. However, this clearly also relates to the issue of devaluation of money as a consequence of, for example, inflation or monetary reform. These cases must, however, be resolved on the basis of the principles of good faith mentioned previously.

Within the scope of given problems good faith is relevant as a principle of interpretation of juridical acts.[120] The definition of good faith in Czech law may be found in the decision of the Supreme Court (Nejvyšší soud) (Case Cz 42/87): 'Good faith is the conviction of the acquirer that he is acting lawfully when he acquires a certain thing'.[121]

A juridical act which conflicts with good morals is void.[122] In the context of a change of contractual circumstances it means that a

[119] See Sections 451 *et seq.* Civil Code.

[120] See Section 35(2) Civil Code: 'Juridical acts expressed in words shall be construed not only according to the verbal expressions, but particularly with regard to the will of the person who performed the act, provided that such will is not contrary to the wording'.

[121] However, this is the only court decision which has been published at the present time.

[122] See Judgment No. OP 8/2000, p. 21.

contract can be declared void from the date this conflict came into existence. In case law, good morals are defined as 'a group of social, cultural and legal rules which in long term perspective have a high degree of stability, reflect substantial historical tendencies, are shared by relevant parts of the society and have the nature of the basic rules'.[123] A conflict with good morals exists when a contract grossly offends public opinion.[124] This happens when in the case of a loan agreement the interest rate is evidently inadequate or if one party abuses an inexperienced party.[125] Unfortunately, no decision has been published yet which would assess the imbalance between the contracting parties as a consequence of the changed circumstances during the existing contractual relationship through the potential conflict with good morals. The length of the contractual relationship has not been taken into consideration in this context.[126]

Principles of fair business conduct (Section 265 Commercial Code)[127] have a similar controlling relevance as the principle of good morals in the Civil Code.[128] They should prevent grossly injust relationships. The consequences of the application of Section 266 are different compared with the application of the good morals principle.

I. No judicial interference and the new legislation

Under the highly restrictive conditions of assertion of the principle of *rebus sic stantibus* the basic consequence of assertion of this exception is the extinction of the obligation or, as the case may be, of the agreement. In this regard, the law breaks the principle of maintaining the agreement and favours the extinction thereof. Adaptation or adjustment of the agreement is not relevant. In this regard – in contrast to German and

[123] See the decision of the Supreme Court R26 C 2042. See the Judgment of the Supreme Court SJ62/1997.

[124] See Decision PR 7/1996.

[125] See Švestka, in: Jehlička *et al.* (eds.), *Občanský zákoník, Komentár (Civil Code Commentary)*, p. 234.

[126] See the same opinion shared by Pelikánová, in: Pelikánová *et al.* (eds.), *Obchodni právo (Commercial Law)*, p. 219; Škárová, in: Jehlička *et al.* (eds.), *Občansky zákonik, Komentář (Civil Code Commentary)*, pp. 847–9; Bytrický *et al.*, *Právo Mezinárodního obchodu (Law of the International Trade)*, p. 312; J. Dvořák, in: V. Knapp *et al.*, *Občanské právo hmotné (Civil law)*, (Prague: 3rd edn, 2002), vol. II., p. 161.

[127] Section 265 Commercial Code: Exercise of right which contradicts the principle of fair business conduct.

[128] Only one published decision could be found (PP 10/1997) which has only very general meaning saying that evidently inadequate interest may represent a conflict with the principle of fair business conduct.

Swiss practice – all judicial interference in the contractual relationship is ruled out.

The Draft Civil Code takes over the provisions on impossibility of performance from the current Commercial Code (see Sections 1730–2).[129]

SCANDINAVIAN JURISDICTIONS

Sweden

A. Basic characteristics of Swedish contract law

The authoritative sources of Swedish private law are legislative acts, preparatory works and case law. The *legislative acts* are, in principle, the major source of law. However, legislation is generally preceded by extensive *preparatory works*. Here, analyses are made of former and foreign law; general principles for the legislation are outlined; and detailed comments are submitted on how the new rules are to be understood and applied in varying situations. *Case law* is not formally binding for Swedish courts. However, the Supreme Court's rulings are still an essential and vital source for, and of, Swedish private law. In fact, the principles stipulated in these Supreme Court rulings – particularly in recent years – are usually strictly applied by lower courts. The most important supplementary source of law is academic commentaries (in fact, they are often important enough to be considered authoritative by the courts). Others are contracts, customs, etc.

Reasoning on the relevant values and the (legal) objectives of the law also form an important part of Swedish law. In this area, *the teleological judicial (and jurisprudential) method*, as expounded by the renowned professor of Swedish procedural law Per Olof Ekelöf, is very influential. According to this method, the (legal) objective of a rule of law is to be decisive for its application. Put simply, the general principle is that a statute should, in 'hard cases' ('*säreget fall*'), be applied in accordance with its objective.[130] This objective is established by observing the results of the statute when it is applied to 'clear cases' ('*klara fall*'). However, if the legal outcome of the proposed interpretation in a 'hard case' is incompatible with the legal system as a whole, the interpretation is incorrect. Such a teleological interpretation is objective in

[129] In the wording as of December 2007; see www.leblog.cz.

[130] For the following, see P. O. Ekelöf and H. Edelstam, *Rättegång. Första häftet* (Stockholm: Norstedts Juridik, 8th edn, 2002), pp. 79 *et seq.*; and B. Lehrberg, *Förutsättningsläran* (Uppsala: Iustus Förlag, 1989), pp. 64 *et seq.*

the sense that the purpose is established by observing the effect the rule has upon people's behaviour when applied in clear cases, and need not be identical with the aim the legislator had when issuing the rule. This method is used not only for interpretation of statutes but for all kinds of legal issues, regardless of what sources of law are involved. In preparatory works, academic commentaries and Supreme Court cases, different types of reasoning regarding the (legal) objectives of the rules of law and the consequences of different interpretations are often decisive for the conclusions.

The fact that Swedish legislation in the area of contract law is fragmented is often decisive for the legal methodology used with regards to contract law. There is no general civil code. The Contracts Act,[131] with its wide scope of application, deals only with a limited set of issues regarding the formation of contracts, agency[132] and invalidity of contracts. Legislation regarding the contracting parties' rights and duties, breach of contract, etc. is available only for a limited number of contract types: e.g., sale and purchase, rental and right to use of real estate, consumer services, credit sales and consumer credit. For other contracts, and for issues not dealt with in the legislation, the courts are often left to rely upon analogous applications of rules from legislation on other types of contracts, such as the Sales Act and on (analogies with) available cases and other available sources of law. With this aim, sophisticated methods for different kinds of analogies are used, particularly in case law and academic commentaries.

The hierarchy of rules and methods used to create rules for adjudication in individual cases in Swedish contract law can be described as follows:[133]

(1) mandatory legislation ('*tvingande lag*');
(2) interpretation ('*tolkning*') of the contract (based upon the parties' intentions, their contractual expressions and their impressions[134]);
(3) individual constructive interpretation ('*individuell utfyllning*') (based on the circumstances of the case);

[131] 'Lagen (1915:218) om avtal och andra rättshandlingar på förmögenhetsrättens område' (commonly referred to as 'avtalslagen').

[132] There is no proper English translation for the Swedish concept '*fullmakt*'.

[133] B. Lehrberg, *Avtalsrättens grundelement* (Uppsala: IBA Institutet för Bank- och Affärsjuridik, 2nd edn, 2006), pp. 297–8. Similar: A. Adlercreutz, *Avtalsrätt II* (Lund: Juristförlaget i Lund, 5th edn, 2001), p. 18.

[134] This includes the intention of a party as to the content of the contract, his impression of the other party's intention and what the parties actually expressed – for instance in a written contract or in an offer or acceptance.

(4) supplementary legislation and other supplementary rules applicable to the specific type of contract ('*dispositiv lag*');
(5) analogies from supplementary legislation for similar types of contracts ('*laganalogier*');
(6) general supplementary rules ('*allmänna utfyllande regler*') based on analogies with diverse sources of law (e.g., legislation, leading cases, preparatory works, academic commentaries, customs) in different areas of the law;
(7) general legal considerations ('*allmänna rättsliga överväganden*') for the construction of supplementary rules, most often on the basis of different forms of analogies;
(8) discretionary considerations ('*skönsmässiga överväganden*').

In particular, the general supplementary rules are often based on rather few cases from different areas of contract law, and are often abstract in their wording. In fact, the gap in the level of abstraction when compared to upcoming cases is so high that it is often argued that the general rules do not offer much guidance in individual cases except for pointing out the main direction of the analyses, e.g., whether to look for bad faith or negligent behaviour. Therefore, the analyses of hard cases are most often based on the details of the leading cases, which are thoroughly accounted for, rather than on a general principle directly applied.

Most cases of unexpected circumstances are dealt with under rules of breach of contract and other specific issues. Amongst the most important of these rules are the rules of avoidance on the basis of fraudulent or other foul behaviour at the formation of a contract in the Contracts Act[135] (Sections 30, 31 and 33) and the rules on breach of contract and force majeure and on obstacles ('*hinder*') to performance, e.g., in the Sales Act.[136] When these rules are not directly applicable, they are often applied analogously instead. Some of the analogies have such a wide range of application that they form general principles of contract law, most of which are summed up under the so-called doctrine of assumptions ('*förutsättningsläran*'). The general clause regarding unreasonable contract terms ('*oskäliga avtalsvillkor*') in Section 36 Contracts Act also has a wide scope of application. These are the two major methods on how to deal with unexpected circumstances in Swedish law. There is also a number of other principles with a rather wide range of application. For instance, contracts for intellectual property services can *in dubio*

135 Lag (1915:218) om avtal och andra rättshandlingar på förmögenhetsrättens område.
136 Köplagen (1990:931).

be unilaterally terminated at any time. Also, in some cases, a long-term contract can be cancelled due to extraordinary circumstances (*'viktig grund'*).

B. *Breach, force majeure and obstacles to performance*

When unexpected circumstances cause problems in contractual relations, this is generally because they interfere with one of the parties' performance. If that party is unable to duly fulfil their obligations under the contract, this will normally result in a breach of contract. In the event of a breach, the other party is generally entitled to diverse sanctions, such as to withhold performance, to terminate (i.e., cancel, rescind) the contract and to demand damages as compensation for the entire loss, including indirect or consequential losses, caused by the breach.

When it comes to impossibility (*'omöjlighet'*) and force majeure, some general principles originally based on the old Sales Act of 1905[137] are still considered effective, although less restrictive rules are normally an option. Thus, a party can never be obliged to perform the impossible. As a main rule, this principle applies whether performance is generally impossible or if it is only impossible for that particular party, although insolvency is excluded as ground for impossibility. Furthermore, relief is also granted in other cases of force majeure, i.e., performance can be considered impossible due to a circumstance which could not have been taken into account when the contract was concluded, such as the destruction of all goods of the kind the seller was to deliver, war, embargo on import or other comparable circumstances.

The principles laid down in the Sales Act of 1990 are somewhat less restrictive. Under Section 23, the buyer's right to require performance by the seller does not apply if there is an obstacle which the seller is unable to overcome, or if delivery demands sacrifices that are not reasonable in relation to the buyer's interest in receiving the goods. The main rule concerning damages under Section 27 is that the buyer is entitled to compensation for direct losses caused by the seller's breach of contract, where the seller is unable to prove that the delay is caused by an obstacle outside of his control which he could not reasonably have foreseen, and the consequences of which he could not reasonably have avoided or overcome. To what extent these principles can be applied analogously to other types of contracts is yet to be settled in Swedish

[137] See also Section 7 Bills of Exchange Act (lag (1936:81) om skuldebrev).

law. However, for many cases of changed circumstances less restrictive norms are available.

C. The doctrine of assumptions

The doctrine of assumptions (*'förutsättningsläran'*) in Swedish (and indeed, Scandinavian) law of contracts deals with the problem of unknown and unforeseen circumstances on the grounds that basic assumptions have failed. Although this doctrine is firmly established in traditional academic writing and in case law, it has been subject to criticism by some Swedish academic writers. The starting point of the doctrine of assumptions is that a party has entered into a contract unaware of certain facts that made the contract less profitable or more burdensome than expected or that events occurring after the conclusion of the contract – or the fact that an expected event has not occurred – have caused the same effect. The question is: is it possible for the disadvantaged party to avoid the contract because of these unknown circumstances or unforeseen occurrences?

The doctrine of assumptions can be applied irrespective of whether an assumption was erroneous when the contract was concluded (mistake[138]) or became erroneous only after the unexpected event occurred or the expected event did not (changed or unexpected circumstances). Traditionally, the distinction between these two cases is considered problematic, as well as generally being unimportant. The doctrine of assumptions is also applicable whether the party making the claim has acted upon an awareness of a known assumption, or the party simply did not know or foresee the facts or occurrences that would make the contract less profitable or more burdensome than assumed. Thus, the often misunderstood concept of 'assumption' can be characterised as a legal construction, making it easier to deal with various forms of mistakes and changed circumstances with the use of a single term.

Based on a thorough investigation of case law and legislation,[139] it is submitted that the doctrine of assumptions can be elaborated as a number of different rules. Four of these express basic requirements

[138] Mistake as to the content of the contract is dealt with in Section 32(1) Contracts Act. Under this section, the contract can be set aside if the addressee knew, or ought to have known, of the mistake.

[139] B. Lehrberg, *Förutsättningsläran. Allmänna betingelser för möjligheten att frånträda rättshandlingar på grund av okända eller oförutsedda omständigheter* (Uppsala: Iustus Förlag, 1989) and B. Lehrberg, *Avtalstolkning* (Uppsala: IBA Institutet för Bank- och Affärsjuridik, 5th edn, 2009), pp. 221 *et seq.* for later case law.

that, in principle, must always be fulfilled for the doctrine of assumptions to be applicable. They are:

(i) The assumption must be 'material'. The requirement of materiality is traditionally a subjective one. The disadvantaged party (claimant) must have acted upon the assumption, in the sense that the contract would not have been concluded, or would have been concluded only on (materially) different terms, had the true state of affairs been known to that party.

(ii) The assumption must be 'visible'. The defendant must have known, or ought to have known, both the existence of the assumption and the fact that it is material to the party making the assumption.

(iii) The claimant must have acted in 'good faith'. This is relevant in cases where the claimant has known that the 'assumption' was erroneous (where there really was no assumption at all), or that there was a considerable risk that it was. This involves so-called conscious risk-taking ('*medvetet risktagande*'), where the claimant has knowingly assumed the risk that the assumption could prove to be erroneous. For most – but not all – cases the rule also applies when the claimant did not know that the assumption was erroneous, but had such information available that they ought to have known it. In some exceptional cases, the defendant has a duty of investigation to find out if the assumption is valid or not. In these cases, the rule applies to the extent that this duty is not fulfilled.

(iv) The claimant must not have caused the non-realisation of their own assumption. If the claimant has caused the circumstances which have resulted in the claim for termination, the contract will remain, if the situation is not so exceptional that the behaviour appears entirely defensible and does not diverge from what the defendant is entitled to expect.

Traditionally, the doctrine of assumptions is based mostly on the writings of the Danish writer Henry Ussing.[140] In his view there is only one additional prerequisite: 'risk'. This states that it must be 'just and equitable' for the risk to be borne by the defendant. In practice, even if all four basic prerequisites (i-iv) are fulfilled, the assumption is unlikely to result in relief for the party making the claim.

For a descriptive overview of the diverse situations in which the application of the doctrine of assumptions could be considered, this typology of twelve different types of assumptions is introduced:

[140] Mainly H. Ussing, *Bristende Forudsætninger. Bidrag til Læren om Formueretslige Tilsagn* (Copenhagen: G. E. C. Gads Förlag, 1918) and H. Ussing, *Aftaler paa Formuerettens Omraade* (Copenhagen: G. E. C. Gads Förlag, 2nd, edn, 1945).

(i) the assumption that the defendant is bound by the contract;
(ii) the assumption that the defendant will fulfil their promise;
(iii) the assumption that performance of the contract will not fail to occur for some reason not connected to the defendant's fulfilment of their promise;
(iv) assumptions as to the quality or quantity of performance.
(v) other performance related assumptions;
(vi) assumptions regarding objectives of the contract other than performance;
(vii) the assumption that the claimant's own promise will not become unexpectedly burdensome per se;
(viii) the assumption that the claimant's fulfilment of his promise will be possible and not unexpectedly burdensome;
(ix) the assumption that the claimant's fulfilment will not be dangerous;
(x) the assumption that the performance of an obligation that requires the claimant to give something up will not turn out to require the giving up of something unexpectedly valuable to him;
(xi) the assumption that the claimant's resources will not diminish; and
(xii) assumptions relating to objectives other than economic values.

The most significant distinctions are between '*qualified performance assumptions*' (assumptions as to the performance; (i), (ii) and (iv)), '*ordinary performance assumptions*' ((iii) and (v)) and other assumptions ((vi)–(xii)). While qualified performance assumptions are often of legal relevance under the rules of breach of contract, and ordinary performance assumptions are occasionally judged as relevant in case law, other assumptions are only comparatively rarely of legal relevance.

As far as the prerequisite of 'risk' is concerned, it follows from case law that it must be 'just and equitable' *('lämpligt och rimligt')* that the 'risk' is placed on the defendant.[141] It is submitted that the following six grounds of termination/adjustment can be identified on the basis of case law, analogies from existing legislative provisions and legal doctrine:

(i) *Promise* and *warranty*. It is a firmly established rule that an assumption renders the contract void when it relates to matters which the defendant has promised to discharge, or to facts or events warranted to be in existence or to have occurred. Such promises and warranties are most common in relation to qualified performance assumptions, e.g., those which are connected to the performance of the defendant or related to circumstances of which the defendant has special knowledge not possessed by the claimant. They should, however, be subject to avoidance in other cases as well.

141 NJA 1981 p. 269.

(ii) *Clarifications*. Explicit transfers of information between the parties or other behaviour with the same effect render the contract void if they make an erroneous assumption 'well-founded', or if the defendant has been acting negligently, i.e., in a blameworthy way, towards the claimant while giving the information.

(iii) *Visible facts*. An assumption that is based upon facts visible to the defendant or that is shared by the claimant and defendant (common assumption, to be compared with common mistake) is subject to relief if the situation is analogous to the situation in which the defendant has given the claimant information. In relation to assumptions founded upon concrete facts, the defendant must thus have had such better knowledge about these facts that the claimant subjectively relied upon this better knowledge, and was objectively entitled to do so.

(iv) *Unexpected Profits*. An assumption is normally subject to relief in cases of unexpected profits under the following conditions:
 - the assumption is based upon facts visible to the defendant, or the assumption is common to the parties; and
 - the defendant, as a result of the fact that the assumption was erroneous, made a profit at the expense of the claimant; and
 - the purpose the claimant had in entering into the contract is not feasible, or the claimant has suffered a significant loss. It is further submitted that this third requirement need not normally be fulfilled if the assumption is a 'fulfilment assumption'. These are important rules when it comes to changed circumstances.

(v) *Fraud or bad faith at the formation of the contract*. The assumption is subject to relief when the defendant knew, or ought to have known, that the claimant acted upon an assumption that was not in accordance with the facts, and the defendant acted negligently by entering into the contract without informing the claimant of the facts.

(vi) *Negligent causation of the failure of the assumption*. The assumption is subject to relief when the defendant after the formation of the contract negligently caused the failure of the assumption. According to the main rule, the defendant is free to act as it wishes; the claimant has no special claim to require more of the defendant than respect for the claimant's interests to a reasonable degree given the circumstances. The defendant has a duty to pay regard to the assumption especially when it is 'well-founded' (often making it relevant under one or more of the rules mentioned above), but the rule concerning negligently causing failure of an assumption also applies in other cases where the defendant has acted in a blameworthy way towards the claimant, although this is not very common.

In general, the doctrine of assumptions is only applicable when the relevant mistake or unexpected circumstance is not already dealt with in the contract or in applicable supplementary contractual legislation (which does not include rules on invalidity of contracts).[142]

The mistaken party's remedy for the failure of a basic assumption is most commonly termination. A contract term could also be adjusted, but only to the effect of reducing an obligation (e.g., reducing the price) not of increasing an obligation (e.g., increasing the price) or creating a new obligation.[143] Damages are not a remedy under the doctrine of assumptions. The main rule is that damages follow in cases of breach of contract, but not in other cases of failure of basic assumptions.[144]

D. *Unreasonable contract terms*

Section 36 Contracts Act regarding unfair contract terms was introduced in 1976. Before that, a considerably more restrictive rule was applied, based upon an analogy with the former Section 8 Bills of Exchange Act,[145] and other similar rules. Section 36 not only deals with standard terms, but also with terms which have been individually negotiated. The section states that a contract term can be adjusted or disregarded in a particular case if it is unreasonable ('*oskälig*') with reference to the contents of the contract, the circumstances at the formation of the contract, circumstances arising later and other circumstances.

This rule can be used not only to adjust (or disregard) a specific unreasonable contract term with the effect of reducing an obligation – but also to modify the contract so that an obligation is increased or a new obligation implied. If the unreasonable term is of such importance to the contract that it cannot in its entirety be fairly upheld unchanged, other parts of the contract can be adjusted or it can be disregarded in its entirety. This makes Section 36 an important tool to adjust a contract to changed circumstances.

Applying the requirement of 'unreasonableness', the need to protect a consumer or another inferior party to a contract is especially to be taken into consideration. Some important modifications to the application of Section 36 are stated in a separate act on consumer contract terms.[146] If a contract term in a consumer contract has not been individually negotiated, Section 36 applies with modifications. For example an event that has occurred after the conclusion of the contract may not

[142] Lehrberg, *Förutsättningsläran*, pp. 168–72. [143] NJA 1989 p. 614.

[144] NJA 1928 p. 47, NJA 1936 p. 368 and NJA 1989 p. 614.

[145] Lag (1936:81) om skuldebrev.

[146] Lag (1994:1512) om avtalsvillkor i konsumentförhållanden (Sections 11–12).

be considered to the disadvantage of the consumer, with the effect that a contract clause that would otherwise have been considered unreasonable could not be adjusted or set aside.

It follows from the above that the application of the prerequisite that terms should not be 'unreasonable' is based upon the contractual situation as a whole. However, the application of Section 36 has to be directed at (at least) one specific contract clause. It is not possible to adjust the contract only because it is unreasonable in general if no specific unreasonable contract clause can be identified.[147]

The preparatory works to Section 36 and case law provide clear and straightforward solutions in a few cases only. In other cases, the application of the prerequisite that a clause should not, be 'unreasonable' is often a rather complicated task. However, some important guidelines are suggested in the preparatory works.

A contract clause can be deemed unreasonable solely on basis of the content of the contract. A contract clause can also be considered unreasonable per se, even if it is not accompanied by any aggravating circumstances. Some contractual clauses are even considered unreasonable regardless of the circumstances. Clauses that are in conflict with the law or public morals are usually mentioned, although not all such clauses are considered unreasonable. A clause which hands over the right to decide upon important issues to one of the parties is often considered unreasonable.[148] However, the judgment with respect to a specific contract clause often depends on the contents of the contract as a whole. A party who seems to have been treated unfairly in one clause is often compensated in another.

The circumstances at the formation of the contract also form part of the context in which a contract clause must be judged. It can be taken into consideration if a superior party has misused its position at the negotiations, for instance by behaving aggressively, taking the other party by surprise or using other unreasonable methods to make the inferior party enter into the contract. A disparity between the performances on both sides can also be a reason to intervene, although not in all cases, which is especially true in business relations.[149]

The legislator emphasises the importance of analysing whether the parties could have foreseen the changed circumstances at the time of

[147] NJA II 1976 n. 4 p. 249, and in case law: NJA 1989 p. 614.

[148] Prop. 1975/76:81 pp. 118 *et seq.*; and SOU 1974:83 pp. 148 *et seq.*

[149] Prop. 1975/76:81 pp. 125 *et seq.*; and SOU 1974:83 pp. 152 *et seq.*

formation of the contract. Therefore, there is more often reason to intervene in long-term contracts. However, the legislator stresses that not every circumstance that occurs subsequent to the time the agreement was entered into may call for the application of Section 36. In commercial relations, Section 36 has been rarely and cautiously applied.[150] Yet, the legislator also stresses that the rule must not be used to compensate for a party's superior power at the formation of the contract. To some degree Section 36 can be used to adjust contract terms to new legislation. This is especially true when it comes to contracts concluded for exceptionally long periods of time.[151]

Among other circumstances which could be used as measures to indicate if a contract clause might be unreasonable, rules of law, good commercial practice and other related contracts should be mentioned.

E. Specific rules for termination of long-term contracts

Some types of long-term contracts, e.g., rental contracts, collaboration agreements, insurance agreements and agreements on services, are normally subject to unilateral termination *('uppsägning')* under the contract terms without specific cause. Often, but not always, advance notice within a specific period of time is required.

Some types of long-term contracts are also subject to termination without notice under supplementary law, provided that the contract is valid until further notice ('*tills vidare*') and that other conditions have not been agreed regarding termination. This principle, based on analogies with Section 46 old Commission Act[152] and Chapter 2 Section 24(2) Partnership and Non-registered Partnership Act,[153] is considered applicable to contracts on rental and on intellectual property services in academic commentaries.[154]

Some other types of long-term contracts are also subject to relief, i.e., termination, without advance notice in the event of unexpected circumstances of an extraordinary magnitude, so-called '*viktig grund*'. This term is expressly used in Section 26 (i), (ii) of the Commercial Agents Act,[155]

[150] C. R. Von Post, *Studier kring 36 § avtalslagen med inriktning på rent kommersiella förhållanden* (Stockholm: Förlag Claes Roberg von Post and Jure, 1999), p. 298.

[151] Prop. 1975/76:81, pp. 126–8, and SOU 1974:83, pp. 156 *et seq.*

[152] Lag (1914:45) om kommission, recently substituted by kommissionslag (2009:865). See also Section 32 of the new Commission Act (kommissionslag (2009:865)).

[153] Lag (1980:1102) om handelsbolag och enkla bolag.

[154] See, e.g., J. Hellner R. Hager and A. H. Persson, *Speciell avtalsrätt II. Kontraktsrätt. Andra häftet. Allmänna ämnen* (Stockholm: Norstedts Juridik, 4th edn, 2006), p. 61.

[155] Lag (1991:351) om handelsagentur.

in Chapter 2 Section 25 of the Partnership and Non-registered Partnership Act[156] and in Section 35 (i)(ii) of the Commission Act.[157] In academic commentaries, it has been submitted that this principle of '*viktig grund*' might be applied analogously to some other types of long-term contracts; however, the scope of application as well as the content of this principle is unclear.[158] It is not clear for example, to what extent, or when, this principle goes beyond what follows from the doctrine of assumptions.[159]

Denmark

A. Introduction

The general principle under Danish law is that an agreement is binding upon the parties once it has been concluded (cf. Section 1 and DL 5-1-1 Contracts Act). Thus, a party to a contract bears the risk of unexpected circumstances arising after the formation of that contract and they necessarily make the contract more burdensome to fulfil. In general, it takes something extraordinary for the promisor in a contract to escape contractual obligations and liability after the formation of that contract. Another elementary principle in Danish law is the freedom of contract. In accordance with Danish law, the parties have the option of making a conditional promise, implying that if one or more conditions are not fulfilled the parties will not have entered into a valid contract or the fulfilment of that contract may be postponed.

In dealing with unexpected circumstances, the promisor in a contract can refer to Section 36 Contracts Act,[160] the doctrine of assumptions or Section 24 Sale of Goods Act, which deals with the question of force majeure.[161] It is generally accepted that the last mentioned is also

[156] Lag (1980:1102) om handelsbolag och enkla bolag.

[157] Kommissionslag (2009:865); The rule regarding '*viktig grund*' was also based on Section 51(2), and Section 52(2), of the old Commission Act, which referred to cases where it could not reasonably be required that the commission was upheld (*'icke rimligen kan påfordras att uppdraget skall bestå'*).

[158] See, e.g., Hellner, Hager and Persson, *Speciell avtalsrätt II.*, pp. 61–2, and K. Rodhe, *Om jämkning av kontrakt på grund av ändrade förhållanden. Förhandlingarna å det nittonde nordiska juristmötet i Stockholm den 23–25 augusti 1951* (Stockholm: Norstedts, 1952), Annex V, pp. 22–3.

[159] See, e.g., H. Nial, *Om handelsbolag och enkla bolag* (Stockholm: Norstedts Juridik, 3rd, edn, 1992), p. 262.

[160] Cf. Consolidated Act (Lovbekendtgørelse) n. 781 af 26 august 1996 om aftaler og andre retshandler på formuerettens område.

[161] Cf. Consolidated Act (Lovbkendtgørelse) n. 237 af 28 marts 2003 om køb.

applicable outside the scope of the Sale of Goods Act. Danish law does not provide for any general default rule relieving one party from its contractual obligations once they result in hardship. The promisor in a contract can only invoke hardship if the contract contains a rule specifically addressing the event of hardship. Otherwise, hardship as such is not a valid excuse or a basis for remedies. However, specific remedies may apply if a case of hardship also falls within the scope of application of Section 36 Contracts Act (unfair terms) or the doctrine of assumptions (see below sections II and III).

Sections 28–34 Contracts Act contain rules on avoidance due to fraud or other forms of reprehensible behaviour. Yet these rules deal with issues in conjunction with the formation of the contract, where it is crucial whether or not the promisee in the contract has acted in good faith. In general, these rules are not applicable to unexpected circumstances that may arise after the formation of the contract.

Besides the above-mentioned rules in Danish law, a Danish court might use different methods of interpretation in dealing with questions of unexpected circumstances. The principle of *in dubio contra stipulatorem* may especially be relevant in cases concerning unexpected circumstances. This issue is not dealt with directly in conjunction with the comments on the cases, but the Danish courts do tend to use different devices of interpretation in order to set a contract aside, to insert a provision in the contract or to adjust it.

B. *Unfair contract terms*

Section 36 Contracts Act is a rule which deals with unfair contractual stipulations. It states as follows:

> (1) A contract may be modified or set aside, in whole or in part, if it would be unreasonable or at variance with the principles of good faith to enforce it. The same applies to other juristic acts.
> (2) In making a decision under subsection (1) hereof, regard shall be had to the circumstances existing at the time when the contract was concluded, the terms of the contract and subsequent circumstances. (Unofficial translation)[162]

[162] The wording in Danish is: 'En aftale kan ændres eller tilsidesættes helt eller delvist, hvis det ville være urimeligt eller i strid med redelig handlemåde at gøre den gældende. Det samme gælder andre retshandler. Stk. 2. Ved afgørelsen efter stk. 1 tages hensyn til forholdene ved aftalens indgåelse, aftalens indhold og senere indtrufne omstændigheder.'

Section 36 Contracts Act was enacted in 1975 and came into force on 1 July of the same year.[163] In the preparatory work on Section 36 it was clearly stated that the section should cover economic crime (which was extensively debated at the time) and should protect consumers against unfair contract terms. Case law shows that Section 36 has been applied by the Danish courts, especially in conjunction with consumer cases. However, Section 36 has also been applied in numerous cases involving businesses. It is applied especially when the parties to the contract can be characterised as being stronger and weaker, respectively.

Section 36 was revised in 1994 and the revision came into force on 1 January 1995.[164] The wording of Section 36 was changed in the sense that the expression 'set aside' was replaced with the wording 'may be modified or set aside'. The revision was supposed to strengthen the obligation. This issue is more extensively debated in conjunction with Case 1. Directive 93/13/EC on unfair terms in consumer contracts was enacted in the Contracts Act as Sections 38a, 38c and 38d with the revision of Section 36 in 1994.

The most important notion in Section 36 Contracts Act is 'unreasonable' or 'at variance with good faith'. It is worth emphasising that the latter part of subsection 2 allows one to take subsequent circumstances (after the formation of the contract) into consideration if it transpires that upholding the contract would be considered unfair. The question of whether a contract violates Section 36 is not easily answered. In evaluating the contents of the contract the following factors are commonly - but not exclusively - referred to: the status of the parties, deviations from non-mandatory rules, the due care and diligence of a prudent businessman, and the application of standard conditions.

The application of Section 36 provides the courts with different options if a contract is considered to be unfair:

(i) certain terms in the contract may be set aside or made less strenuous;
(ii) the whole agreement may be set aside or made less strenuous;

[163] Cf. Lov nr. 250 af 12. juni 1975. The Danish considerations in conjunction with the preparatory work were influenced by the Swedish work of Jan Hellner in: 'Generalklausul I förmögenhetsrätten' (1974) SOU, 83. For more comprehensive general remarks on Section 36, see Lennart Lynge Andersen and Palle Bo Madsen, *Aftaler og mellemmænd*, (Copenhagen: Thomson, 5th edn, 2006), pp. 204 *et seq.*

[164] Cf. Lov nr. 1098 af 21. december 1994.

(iii) the application of the contract may be set aside in one particular situation, but will otherwise be maintained;[165] or

(iv) the contract may be amended.

Case law shows that since the enactment of Section 36 Contracts Act, the provision has been invoked quite frequently. One could argue that Section 36 is the most important source of law for setting a contract aside if unexpected circumstances render the transaction burdensome for the promisor after the formation of that contract.

C. *The doctrine of assumptions*

The application of the doctrine of assumptions[166] requires the fulfilment of three conditions.[167] A promisor is not bound by his promise if his assumption was determinable, perceptible and relevant. First, to establish an assumption, a determination must be made that the promisor would not have entered into the agreement had he known about the subsequent events at the time of concluding the contract. It is worth mentioning that an assumption is clearly different from a condition, which is an element of the contract. Second, an assumption is perceptible to the promisee if he realised or supposedly should have realised what was the assumption of the promisor. The courts have interpreted the doctrine of assumptions as including conscious as well as unconscious assumptions. Finally, the third condition concerning relevance is rather dealt with as a matter of risk assumption; specifically, it is determined whether the promisee should bear the risk of the assumption not materialising.

If the court applies the doctrine of assumptions, the contract is void and it might be possible to claim damages. Instead of setting aside the whole agreement, the courts may also adjust the obligation in order to lessen or increase it.[168] The doctrine of assumptions has been applied in several cases, even after the enactment of Section 36 Contracts Act.[169]

[165] Cf. Lunn and Trønning i *Juristen og Økonomen* (1975), p. 393.

[166] The doctrine of assumptions was inspired by Bernhard Windscheid from Germany, and was later taken up and developed by Henry Ussing in Denmark. See Ussing, *Bristende forudsætninger. Bidrag til Læren om Formueretlige Tilsagn*. The courts have subsequently directly or indirectly used the theory in their rulings. For further references, see Andersen and Madsen, *Aftaler og mellemmænd*, p. 193.

[167] For a more comprehensive discussion about the doctrine of assumptions, see the Swedish report. There is hardly any difference in the application of the doctrine of assumptions in Swedish and Danish law.

[168] Cf. Ussing, *Aftaler*, p. 481.

[169] See for instance U 1978.973V, U 1987.370V, U 1996.780H and U 1981.1070Ø. The last is interesting in the sense that the city court applies Section 36 Contracts Act, while the

A case from the High Court of Western Denmark from 1995[170] illustrates the notion behind the doctrine of assumptions quite clearly: a woman signed a contract to buy a vehicle in order to transport goods in connection with the purchase of a cafeteria. Unfortunately, she was not able to purchase the cafeteria as the authorities did not grant her the required Danish citizenship. Therefore, she cancelled the sales contract. According to the evidence adduced, the agent selling the vehicle was aware that the woman would be unable to buy it if she could not purchase the cafeteria. The assumption was, in other words, perceptible to the seller. However, the risk of not obtaining citizenship should have been borne by the buyer. Therefore, the fact that the assumption was determinable and perceptible did not give rise to the doctrine of assumption. The woman was therefore not entitled to cancel the sales contract.

Recent case law shows that the doctrine of assumptions is still influential in Danish law. In another case, a married couple had a child together, while the wife had an illegitimate child from a prior relationship.[171] The last will and testament of the couple contained a provision stating that if the husband died before his spouse, she was entitled to retain undivided possession of the estate until she died. Thereafter, the estate was meant to be divided equally between the two children. The husband died first and in connection with the administration of the estate it was discovered that the illegitimate child had violated the Danish Penal Code[172] by taking wrongful possession of the estate. This was possible since the wife was suffering from dementia. In a later court decision, the illegitimate child was ordered to repay DKK 160,000 to the wife. According to the Eastern High Court, this child was not entitled to

appeal court, the Danish High Court, applies the doctrine of assumptions. In connection with membership of a free church the person in question had entered into an obligation to pay 10 per cent of his income to the church. After three years, he left the church and claimed that he was no longer under the obligation to pay 10 per cent of his income to the church. Østre Landsret delivered a judgment in favour of the person applying the doctrine of assumptions.

170 U 1995.243V. See furthermore U 1995.277/2H where the doctrine of assumptions was used to change a contract comprising of discounts due to the decision of the Danish Competition Authorities.

171 U 2006.370Ø. In U 2001.1068H Højesteret rejected the application of the doctrine of assumptions in conjunction with a complex framework agreement on renting a conference hotel where the tenant was not able to comply with the budgeted turnover. In U 2005.716SH an investment agreement was not declared void due to fraud or the doctrine of assumptions.

172 Consolidated Act no. 1000, 5 October 2006 as amended by Section 1 of Act no. 527, 6 June 2007.

inherit anything, since it was the assumption of the deceased husband that such a wrongful act would never be committed by any of the children in accordance with the will.

Danish case law also shows that the parties to the conflict sometimes invoke both Section 36 Contracts Act and the doctrine of assumptions. This may apply if a subsequent event renders the stipulations in the contract unfair, on the one hand, and if the event is against the assumptions of the promisor, on the other. Such cases fall within the scope of Section 36 Contracts Act and of the doctrine of assumptions as well. In 2002, the Danish Supreme Court (Højesteret) delivered a judgment[173] in a case concerning the purchase of a car by a consumer. The contract contained a provision which obliged the consumer to pay 10 per cent of the purchase price as damages if he cancelled the contract without reason. The Højesteret stated that there was no reason whatsoever to apply the doctrine of assumptions since the parties had entered into an unconditional contract where the seller had no information about the buyer's assumptions. Instead, it applied Section 36 Contracts Act, admitting that the parties had entered into an agreement with the above provision, but it considered that the obligation to pay damages in favour of the seller was an unreasonable provision and so it was set aside. In another judgment rendered by the Højesteret in 2005[174] a different approach to the relationship between the two legal concepts might be noted. In this case, a number of agreements were set aside as being void in conjunction with a loan given to a bank, since, when the loan capital was requested, the bank had projected its financial situation to be much more optimistic than was actually the case. A majority of three judges of the Højesteret applied Section 36 Contracts Act since the agreements were considered unreasonable. A minority of two judges agreed with the result, but applied the doctrine of assumptions, since the risk of an incorrect assumption had to be borne by the bank.[175]

It might be argued in dealing with subsequent events that it is in accordance with Danish law to apply either Section 36 Contracts Act or the doctrine of assumptions depending on the case at hand, but as the case law actually shows, it is very difficult to make a very clear distinction. Today, Section 36 Contracts Act is the most important source of law in dealing with the question of unexpected circumstances after the

[173] U 2002.706H. [174] Cf. U 2005.1978H.

[175] See furthermore U 1993.923H where a majority of the judges applied the doctrine of assumptions instead of Section 36 Contracts Act.

formation of a contract has taken place. In the explanatory report[176] on Section 36 Contracts Act, it is clearly stated that Section 36 offers a more suitable solution with regard to unexpected circumstances than the doctrine of assumptions. In the explanatory report, it is even stated that the doctrine of assumptions is largely based on a legal fiction.[177] This implies, depending on the case, that it is possible to apply Section 36 Contracts Act and/or the doctrine of assumptions.[178] Section 36 is probably predominant as a source of law when it comes to cases between a stronger and a weaker party who contracted. The doctrine of assumptions is thus still part of Danish law if a case gives rise to questions concerning unexpected circumstances between businesses. There is, however, no doubt that Section 36 Contracts Act has gained 'territory' at the expense of the doctrine of assumptions. It should be borne in mind that the legal consequences of both concepts are basically the same.

D. *Force majeure*

While the application of Section 36 Contracts Act or the doctrine of assumptions might be fairly difficult to predict, it might be somewhat easier to demonstrate the possibilities of invoking force majeure. As mentioned above, Section 24 Sale of Goods Act contains a provision on force majeure in conjunction with a delay by the vendor.[179] Section 24 deals solely with the question of the vendor's liability with regard to unascertained goods[180] and is a non-mandatory rule. The vendor or the purchaser is liable (strict liability), unless the unexpected circumstances meet the three conditions of force majeure. First, the force majeure event was not predictable at the time the parties entered into the

[176] p. 25.

[177] For further reading and references, see Lennart Lynge Andersen and Palle Bo Madsen, *Aftaler og mellemmænd*, (Copenhagen: Thomson, 4th edn, 2001), p. 220.

[178] In U 1989.1039H the Danish Supreme Court delivered a judgment concerning a professional entrepreneur. The court preferred to rely on the doctrine of assumptions rather than applying Section 36 Contracts Act.

[179] In accordance with Section 43(3), Sale of Goods Act, the vendor is also entitled to invoke force majeure in conjunction with the delivery of defective goods. The purchaser can also invoke force majeure in accordance with Section 30 Sale of Goods Act.

[180] If the vendor in question delivers a specific good, Section 23 Sale of Goods Act is applied. The liability in accordance with Section 23 Sale of Goods Act is less restrictive compared to Section 24 Sale of Goods Act. For comprehensive general remarks on Section 24 Sale of Goods Act, see Jacob Nørager-Nielsen and Søren Theilgaard, *Købeloven med kommentarer* (Copenhagen: Gadd, 2nd edn, 1993), pp. 319 *et seq.*

agreement. It is by definition an unexpected event. Second, it is impossible to provide similar goods compared to the goods in question. In practice this implies that nobody is able to provide similar goods. In other words, it must be impossible to provide similar goods on the market. Third, the unexpected circumstances must be of an extraordinary and non-recurrent character such as war, natural disasters, riots, embargos and strikes. If the event takes place on a regular basis, it is not considered extraordinary.[181] If force majeure can be invoked, there is no obligation to pay damages.

The number of Danish cases applying the doctrine of force majeure is substantial. However, the case law is not perfectly precise and distinct. It is probably fair to state that the interpretation of the three conditions has become more open compared to the former strict interpretation of the provision.

In cases of delay, the buyer is entitled to terminate the contract if the delay is considered to be fundamental. With regard to agreements between businesses, any delay would be considered fundamental unless only a small fraction of the goods in question is concerned (cf. Section 21(3) Sale of Goods Act). The Sale of Goods Act contains no provision about the seller's obligation to perform in a case of force majeure. If the event prevents the vendor from performing the contract within a certain period of time, he still has an obligation to deliver. But if performance is not possible for more than six months, the contract would normally be regarded as having lapsed. If it is clear that the delivery of the goods in question is permanently impossible due to frustration, the obligation to deliver will also lapse. In order to minimise the loss due to force majeure, the seller is under an obligation to inform the buyer of the circumstances. Otherwise, he will be liable for such subsequent costs.

E. *Mistake and interpretation*

Section 32(1) Contracts Act contains a provision on mistake. As mentioned above, mistake is traditionally considered to be limited to the formation of the contract and it deals basically with the question whether the promisee has acted in good faith once he or she accepts the promise of the promisor.

[181] Compared to Art. 79 CISG, the liability within the scope of Section 24 Sale of Goods Act is stricter.

Danish law contains no general provisions on interpretation. Such rules have evolved through case law.[182] The main principle with respect to interpretation is the will of the parties. If it is possible to reach agreement on the meaning, such an interpretation will take place. In general, such a method of interpretation works as long as it is possible for the parties to find a mutual understanding. However, as soon as there is a dispute between the parties, this method is not very likely to succeed in practice. Thus, it is often more likely that an objective interpretation of the contract will prevail.[183] In connection with unexpected circumstances, the principle of *in dubio contra stipulatorem* is quite frequently applied by the courts.[184] This rule of interpretation is traditionally used to interpret the contract against the party who has drawn up the contract. However, this method of interpretation has also been used by the Højesteret in a case where the parties' lawyers, in connection with the splitting up of a public company, had drafted a contract containing a (jointly drawn) competition clause, which was later violated by one of the parties.[185] The principle of *in dubio contra stipulatorem* can be viewed as a source of law to relieve the party to a contract from an obligation if it becomes more burdensome to fulfil the contract after the formation of that contract. Like Section 36 Contracts Act, the doctrine of assumptions and the concept of force majeure, the use of *in dubio contra stipulatorem* is a way to 'escape' from, or at least to lessen the obligation of the promisor in a contract. This method of interpretation is very often applied in Danish case law either alone or in connection with the application of Section 36 Contracts Act. However, it cannot be said that the principle of *in dubio contra stipulatorem* is a general device to escape from a contract that has become burdensome as it requires that a contract is unclear, ambiguous or non-comprehensive.

[182] For a more comprehensive discussion on interpretation in Danish and Scandinavian law, see Ole Lando, Elisabeth Thuesen, Christina Tvarnø and Kim Østergaard, *Udenrigshandelens Kontrakter* (Copenhagen: Jurist-og öknomforbundet, 5th edn, 2006), pp. 112 *et seq*.

[183] See for instance U 2006.3316/1H. Furthermore, in this case the Danish Supreme Court also refused to apply the doctrine of assumptions.

[184] See for instance U 2001.655V and U 2003.618H. In the latter judgment delivered by the Højesteret an unclear clause was interpreted in such manner that the contracting party could choose which clause on limited liability should apply. See also U 1975.892Ø.

[185] Cf. U 2004.2899H.

ROMANIC–MEDITERRANEAN JURISDICTIONS

Italy

A. Introduction

There is no general principle in the Italian Civil Code that allows for a correction of the unjust effects of supervening and unforeseeable events on contracts (i.e., a modification of the original balance between the obligations). The necessary compromise between the traditional principle '*pacta sunt servanda*' (which embodies the idea of the 'sanctity' of contract) and the (more modern and apparently opposite) principle of '*clausula rebus sic stantibus*' has been found under Italian law according to the general rules on the 'excessive burden' set forth in the Civil Code (CC) in Arts. 1467–9. These rules were inserted by legislation in Book IV of the CC ('Obligations'), Title II ('Contracts in general'), Chapter XIV dedicated to the 'dissolution of the contract' ('*risoluzione del contratto*') due to non-performance, impossibility and, finally, excessive burden:

Art. 1467 CC 'Contract with obligations of both parties'

(1) In contracts for continuous or periodic performance or for deferred performance, if extraordinary and unforeseeable events make the performance of one of the parties excessively onerous, the party who owes such performance can demand dissolution of the contract, with the effects set forth in article 1458.
(2) Dissolution cannot be demanded if the supervening onerousness is part of the normal risk of the contract.
(3) A party, against whom dissolution is demanded, can avoid it by offering to modify equitably the conditions of the contract.

Art. 1468 CC 'Contracts with obligations of one party only'

In the case contemplated in the preceding article, if only one of the parties has assumed obligations, he can demand a reduction in his performance or a modification of the manner of performance, sufficient to restore it to an equitable basis.

Art. 1469 CC 'Aleatory contract'

The provisions of the preceding articles do not apply to contracts which are aleatory by their nature or by the intention of the parties.

The adoption of these rules in the Code is certainly due to the developments of the studies of some great German scholars of the nineteenth century. The most prominent of the scholars was Bernhard Windscheid, who investigated. '*Voraussetzung*', i.e., the implied intention of the parties that becomes a condition of the contract from a subjective perspective. It was furthermore influenced by the evolution of the '*rebus sic stantibus*' doctrine, which led to a more objective approach in considering the intention of the parties and also originated in the German legal discourse. This development was influenced by a famous work from the beginning of the twentieth century, in which Paul Oertmann introduced the concept of *Geschäftsgrundlage* (foundation of the transaction).

As far as the Italian legal tradition is concerned, one can say that the idea of the *Voraussetzung* (implied assumption of the existence of some circumstances), as well as the developments of this doctrine (such as the doctrine of the *Geschäftsgrundlage*) were imported in Italy by literally translating the original German word *Voraussetzung* into the Italian one '*presupposizione*'. The doctrine of the *presupposizione* soon became an attractive subject of study for those scholars who were particularly interested in analysing the general doctrine of the legal act, *negozio giuridico* (i.e., the *Rechtsgeschäft*) elaborated by the German doctrine of the nineteenth century. The doctrine was considered, in the very traditional view of the pandectistic school, as a declaration of the intention of the parties with the purpose of producing a legally binding consequence.

These developments analysing the weight which the law gives to the individual intention found a fundamental point of reference in the doctrine of the *presupposizione*. The impression of the devastating effects of both world wars on the economy led the Italian legislator to codify this doctrine by adding a new specific section in the CC dedicated to the *risoluzione per eccessiva onerosità*. Unknown to the previous Civil Code (dated 1865), such rules consider a change of circumstances as a reason for the legitimate dissolution or termination of the contract, provided that the strict requirements of the rules are met (cf. section III below).

It is clear that under Italian law the above relief can overlap with some more traditional remedies such as mistake (Arts. 1427 *et seq.* CC), the termination for supervening impossibility (Arts. 1463 *et seq.* CC) or the interpretation of the contract (Arts. 1362 *et seq.* CC). As far as mistake is concerned, the avoidance of the contract may be obtained only if the mistake extends to elements present *at the time* of the formation: the rules on mistake do not cover future developments that may prejudice a contractual party. Termination for supervening impossibility is only operable if the performance becomes impossible in a strict sense. The so-called concepts of 'economic impossibility' or the 'extraordinary difficulty' in rendering the performance are not legitimate reasons under the rules of Arts. 1463 *et seq.* CC. The need to mitigate such strict interpretation of the rules on supervening impossibility induced the legislator of the CC (dated 1942) to introduce the relief of termination for excessive burden (Arts. 1467 *et seq.* CC) described above.

Finally, the rules on the interpretation of contracts (Arts. 1362 *et seq.* CC) might be helpful to understand the scope of the risk that the parties have assumed. The hypothetical will of the parties can be reconstructed by considering the behaviour of a party acting in good faith under the specific circumstances.

The rationale of a solution leading to an 'all or nothing' result for the party whose performance has become excessively burdensome can probably be explained with reference to the prevailing role of the principle of the sanctity of the contract in the main civil law systems. This is particularly true in cases of bilateral contracts (the general rules on the dissolution or termination of contracts due to the breach or non-performance of the contractual obligations as well as to the supervening impossibility of the performance always concern bilateral contracts). In fact, if the contract is such that only one of the parties has assumed an obligation, a reduction of his performance or a modification of the manner of performance sufficient to restore it to an equitable basis may be demanded according to Art. 1468 CC. In this latter case, only the affected party may ask for the modification of the contract (which the court could impose on the counter-party).

B. *Specific Requirements*

(a) Contracts for continuous or periodic performance or for deferred performance

It should be noted that long-term contracts (e.g. supply or construction contracts) are subject to the above mentioned general rules, although the risk of extraordinary and unforeseeable events, which might have an impact on the contractual balance is much more important than in the instant (or discrete) transaction. For example, it is worth noting, however, that an important default rule of construction contracts (*appalto*, cf. Art. 1664 CC) considers the supervening hardship or difficulty in performance in order to set forth a remedy very different from that provided for by the general rules on excessive burden (see above, Arts. 1467–9 CC). If, as a result of unforeseeable circumstances, there have occurred such increases or reductions in the cost of the materials or of labour as to cause an increase or reduction of more than 10 per cent of the total price agreed upon, the independent contractor or the customer can request that the price be revised.

Italian case law has discussed (and admitted) a remedy in cases of real estate sales contracts if the parties have deferred the main performance (the delivery and/or the formal deed), even partially, without having decided about the risk of the supervening events. Often Italian courts have applied Art. 1467 CC to the preliminary sale of apartments to be built, in which the balance between the price agreed upon and the building costs had been materially affected (e.g., by inflation).[186]

Of course, the excessively onerous obligation must not have been performed yet.[187] Consequently, if the buyer has already received full payment, the remedy may not be invoked against the inflation that has accrued after the payment.[188] Further, relief is not granted if the requesting party is in breach of contract, e.g., if the supervening event could have been avoided if the performance had been at the time agreed upon.[189] Finally, according to Italian case law, the relevant change of circumstances must occur *after* the conclusion of the contract (see in the same sense Art. 6:111 (a) of the PECL). If the events are not 'supervening', but already exist at the date of the agreement and are merely unknown to the parties, other rules apply (e.g., those provided for mistake, according to the requirements set forth in the Italian CC).

(b) Excessive burden of performance - Art. 1467 CC

Even though Art. 1467 CC is a very general rule it defines better than the similar rule set forth in Art. 1664 CC (supervening hardship or difficulty in the performance of building contracts) under which conditions performance may be deemed 'excessively burdensome'.[190] Under Art. 1467 CC, there is no doubt that the imbalance must be remarkable with regard to the kind of agreement.[191]

Although Art. 1467 CC mentions the 'excessive burden of the performance', according to Italian case law the balance between the performances of the respective parties may be affected by an increase of the cost of the performance as well as by the loss of value of the agreed

[186] Cass., 15 December 1984, n. 6574; Cass. 4 November 1980, n. 5905, among many other similar judgments.

[187] Cass., 13 December 1980, n. 6470, 1981, I, 713.

[188] Cass., 13 May 1982, n. 3005.

[189] Cass., 13 December 1980, n. 6464; Cass. 15 December 1984, n. 6582.

[190] This provision only considers those increases or reductions in the cost of materials or labour, that exceed 10 per cent of the total price.

[191] Cass., 13 July 1984, n. 4114; 14 December 1982, n. 6867.

counter-performance.[192] The explicit provision of the PECL reflects the current application and interpretation of the rule at issue under Italian law. The remedy may be granted only if the performance is still excessively onerous at the time of the demand for the dissolution of the contract. After all, the burden could end or diminish before the party requests the discharge and the dissolution of the contract.[193] In such a case, the demand will be rejected.

Dealing with the concept of excessive burden, it should be said that Italian Law recognises the legal doctrine of *laesio enormis*. The relief given to the obliged party is the right to ask for a rescission of the disproportionate agreement (*rescissione*, Arts. 1447–52 CC), but *laesio enormis* is relevant only if the contractual obligations are initially disproportionate. It further provides that other requirements specifically indicated in Arts. 1447 and 1448 CC are met: the contract must have been concluded under the pressure of a personal danger or specific need of the prejudiced party. In other words, rescission is not granted if the contract became disproportionate subsequent to its formation; in this latter case the rules on *eccessiva onerosità* shall apply.

It is interesting to note that, although both the *ratio legis* and the wording of the rules about *laesio enormis* substantially differ from those provided for by the Civil Code in order to protect the obliged party against the supervening disproportion, Art. 1450 CC allows the defendant to avoid the rescission by an offer to modify the contract according to good faith. (Should the parties not agree about the offered modification, the Court has to terminate the contract.) Therefore, one can argue that the rules on the adaptation of contracts are familiar to Italian law and in the light of the system designed by the Civil Code (see Section D below).

(c) Supervening burden exceeding the normal risk of the contract and exclusion of aleatory contracts

Closely linked to the concept of 'excessive' burden is the provision contained in Art. 1467(2) CC, according to which dissolution cannot be demanded if the supervening onerousness is part of the 'normal' risk of the contract. This restriction is justified by the risk which each party assumes. Such a risk is implied as the law must limit any remedy aimed at modifying or setting aside a contract. As in other countries (e.g, in Germany, as far as the *Geschäftsgrundlage* is concerned, see section I

[192] Cass., 16 March 1981, n. 1465. [193] Cass., 27 January 1981, n. 608.

above), the doctrine of the normal risk, which characterises each kind of contract (and each specific agreement), is well established and developed in Italy.[194]

Pursuant to the above rule and the doctrine of the normal risk, a request for the dissolution of the contract has always been rejected by the courts if the alteration of the contractual balance did not exceed the foreseeable fluctuation of the market values, which includes a certain degree of inflation.[195] It is clear that any application of the said rule and/or the doctrine of the normal risk of the contract presupposes an extraordinary and unforeseeable character of the events. Accordingly, Art. 1469 CC sets forth that the preceding articles do not apply to contracts that are aleatory by their nature or by the intention of the parties.

(d) Extraordinary and unforeseeable events

With its reference to 'extraordinary and unforeseeable events', Italian law expresses the requirement that a change of circumstances must not have been taken into account at the time of the conclusion of the contract (see Art. 6:111 (b) PECL). The test of the 'extraordinary and unforeseeable' character of the event may be conducted only on a case by case basis: a regular inflation does not generally represent the disrupting event or the circumstance, but the rate of the inflation could be extraordinary and unforeseeable.[196] The limits fixed by the legislator determine a rather strict application of the said rule for the Italian courts: a strike of workers could be considered neither extraordinary nor unforeseeable, taking into account that the supplier bears the risk of the organisation of the enterprise (i.e., the strike could not exceed the usual contractual risk).

As a matter of fact, many supply contracts, particularly if they are long-term contracts, have hardship clauses that deal with usual contractual risks such as inflation or an increase/decrease of the cost of raw materials or a strike of the workers. The crucial question is whether the party – in exercise of due care – could reasonably be expected to have not only foreseen but also avoided the whole risk of supervening events

[194] Cf. R. Nicolò, 'Alea', in: *Enciclopedia del diritto* (Milan: Giuffrè, 1958), vol. I, p. 1026; later, M. Bessone, *Adempimento e rischio contrattuale* (Milan: Giuffrè, 1970), pp. 343 *et seq.*, who underlines the role of the general clause of good faith in this context; more recently, developing this latter perspective, V. Roppo, 'Il contratto', in: G. Ludica and P. Zatti *Trattato di diritto privato* (Milan: Giuffrè, 2001), p. 1037.

[195] Cass., 9 March 1985, n. 1913; Cass., 5 January 1983, n. 1.

[196] Cass., 8 June 1982, n. 3464; Cass., 16 November 1984, n. 5827; Cass., 5 February 1982, n. 670.

through the agreed hardship clause. Pursuant to Italian case law, even a complex indexation clause agreed upon in a long-term contract cannot exclude the application of the rules at issue (and therefore the dissolution of the contract) if the supervening events were so exceptional and unforeseeable that they frustrate even the agreed clause.[197] The only case for excluding the application of the remedy therefore remains that of an aleatory contract (see Section C above; see also the remarks on Case 15).

(e) Equitable modification of the conditions of the contract

Unlike Art. 6:111 PECL, the general rule set forth by Art. 1467(3) CC provides that only the party against whom the dissolution is demanded can decide whether or not to ask for the equitable modification of the contract in order to avoid its dissolution.[198] Art. 1664 CC (concerning the supervening events within the performance of a building contract), however, provides for a different rule, which seems to reflect more closely the rationale of the rule established by the PECL: the requesting party may exactly indicate the equitable modification, which will be subject to the evaluation of the court with regard to the situation existing at the time of the decision.[199] But pursuant to Italian case law, the party may also ask the court to determine an equitable modification, should the court not consider the suggested modification to be equitable.

As far as the extent of the adaptation is concerned, the equitable modification must take into account the normal risk of the contract and the court should therefore not exclude the consequence of the risk of a change of circumstances that the parties reasonably could have considered at the time of the conclusion of the contract,[200] according to Art. 6:111(3)(b) CC. This norm provides for a judicial adaptation distributing the losses and gains resulting from the change of circumstances between the parties in a just and equitable manner.

Although Art. 1467(3) CC does not expressly provide for an obligation to renegotiate with the aim of equitably adapting or modifying the affected contractual terms, it could be argued that, once the interest in avoiding the dissolution has been declared, both parties are entitled

197 Cass., 29 June 1981, n. 4249; Cass., 28 November 1958, n. 1373.
198 Cass., 29 October 1958, n. 3470; Cass. 30 April 1953, n. 1199.
199 Cass., 13 January 1984, n. 275.
200 F. Macario, *Adeguamento e rinegoziazione nei contratti a lungo termine* (Naples: Jovene, 1996), p. 267.

to propose to the counter-party to enter into a negotiation. In this case, if a party refuses to negotiate or if he breaks off negotiations contrary to good faith and the rules of fair dealing, the court can award damages for the loss suffered, in addition to the equitable modification of the contractual terms. This conclusion is supported by the general duty to perform in good faith (Arts. 1175 and 1375 CC). Of course, the above rule could be superseded if a duty to renegotiate with the aim of adapting the contract to the changes that have occurred is specifically agreed upon.

C. Conclusion

In the absence of specific rules in the Civil Code (as in §313 of the German BGB), a general principle stating the preference of Italian law for keeping the contract in force by means of modification could probably be recognised also in Italy and it could be said that such a principle must prevail over the rules that lead to the complete dissolution of the agreement. In this context, some rules on impossibility (e.g., partial impossibility, Art. 1464 CC) and mistake (e.g., maintenance of the rectified contract, Art. 1432 CC) seem to confirm this underlying principle of the Civil Code, as far as the general part of the rules of contract is concerned.

Furthermore, if we consider the rules set forth (within or outside the Civil Code, e.g., within statutes) for specific contracts, this attitude of Italian law appears even clearer and hardly disputable. A meaningful example of the above mentioned attitude of the Italian legislator is given by Art. 1664 CC, applicable to the cases of hardship in the performance of building contracts, which allows both parties to ask for a revision of the agreed price of the works if, due to unforeseeable circumstances, the costs of the raw materials or the workmanship increase or decrease by over 10 per cent of the agreed cost.

It is certainly true that Section III of Chapter XIV of the Civil Code regulates the legal consequence of hardship together with other kinds of 'dissolution/termination of the contract'. But if we go beyond the *prima facie* appearance, we can say that, although Italian law does not primarily provide for the adaptation of the contract, the legal means of pursuing the equitable adjustment of the contract instead of dissolving it plays a significant role in different situations, either through the various adaptation and/or renegotiations clauses or through the legislative rules aiming at the same purpose.

Recent comparative legal studies have underlined the European trend to harmonise the solutions given by the different countries to hardship towards the maintenance of the contract (so-called '*favor contractus*') through the adaptation of the relevant clauses, also in the light of the results of the economic analysis of law.[201]

Spain

A. Pacta sunt servanda *and the case law exception of* cláusula rebus sic stantibus

When Spanish courts deal with cases of unexpected changes of circumstances, the starting point of their considerations is respect for the principle of *pacta sunt servanda* (codified in Art. 1091 Spanish Civil Code (CC)). Due to the importance of this principle, Spanish civil law as a general rule refuses to grant relief on grounds of hardship. Contrary to the German development before the introduction of §313 BGB, the Spanish literature had not paid much attention to the remedy of the doctrine of the *clausula rebus sic stantibus* when there has been a change of circumstances.[202] Nevertheless, the Spanish courts have developed the doctrine of *clausula rebus sic stantibus* alongside the statutory instruments mentioned above. In the case of changed circumstances it allows a party who is unduly burdened to be discharged from a contract, or to request the adaptation of the contract to the new situation.

Both Spanish courts and legal literature (in line with the pronouncements of the judiciary) have referred to the application of the *rebus sic stantibus* clause as a remedy to correct the imbalance resulting from a change of circumstances in contracts. The clause implies an understanding that in every contract a tacit agreement exists, according to which the duty to perform the contract is only binding when the circumstances remain the same as they were at the moment when the contract was concluded (*contractus que habent tractum succesivum vel dependentiam de futuro rebus sic stantibus*).[203] However, the Tribunal Supremo (TS) has also dealt with cases where there has been an extraordinary alteration of circumstances by applying other doctrines such as excessive onerousness,[204] or the doctrine of the basis of the contract

[201] Cf. P. Gallo, *Sopravvenienze e problemi di gestione del contratto* (Milano: Giuffrè, 1992); more recently, F. P. Traisci, *Sopravvenienze contrattuali e rinegoziazione nei sistemi di civil e di common law* (Naples: Scientifiche Edizioni Italiane, 2003), p. 327.

[202] In Spain, there are not many doctrinal works especially devoted to the study of the *cláusula rebus sic stantibus*.

[203] See J Castán Tobeñas, *Derecho civil español, commúny foral* (Madrid: Reus, 2005), p. 621.

[204] STS of 23 April 1991, (RJ 1991, 3023).

being no longer present.[205] In its judgment of 6 October 1987,[206] the TS expressly stated that 'all of these doctrines serve as a way of re-establishing the reciprocity between the interests of the parties to the contract'. However, the doctrine of the *rebus* clause is the most important one.

Many lines of justification have been articulated to defend the use of the *rebus* clause despite the fact that it is opposed to the principle of the sanctity of contracts. Some authors argue that the clause exists in every contract because of the presumed will of the parties (a subjective explanation). Others have criticised this approach and have tried to provide an objective justification for the use of the clause. Professor Lasarte[207] reasserts that this remedy is just a concrete application of the general rule established by Art. 1258 CC ('integration rule').[208] This means that the ground of justification is not based on the will of the parties, but on the principle of good faith. Other authors, like Perez González, Alguer[209] and Arechederra,[210] explain that Art. 1258 CC allows an interpretation of the principle of the sanctity of contracts in a way that is compatible with the requirements of justice and equity. The TS has also tried to provide objective justifications when applying this remedy. In its judgment of 28 January 1970,[211] the Court affirmed that the clause is not contrary to the principle of the sanctity of contracts. However, in other judgments the Court has stated just the opposite.

All these attempts to justify the use of the clause do not seem to be enough for the TS to accept its general application. The principle of the sanctity of contracts prevails over the need to adjust the contract to the demands of equity. The attitude of the TS and, in general, of the Spanish contractual legal system towards the application of the *rebus sic stantibus* clause was made obvious when the TS characterised 'its application [as] a dangerous practice'.[212]

The conditions laid down by the courts for the application of the doctrine of the *rebus sic stantibus* clause are strict:

[205] STS of 15 March 1994, (RJ 1994, 1784). [206] RJ 1987, 6720.

[207] See C. Lasarte Álvarez, *Principios de derecho civil, t. 11, Derecho de obligaciones* (Madrid/Barcelona: Marcial Pons, 2009), p. 354.

[208] Article 1258 CC obliges the parties to comply not only with what they have expressly agreed upon but also with the requirements of good faith, general usage and the law.

[209] See Espert Sanz, p. 149.

[210] See L. I. Arechederra Aranzadi, *La equivalencia de las prestaciones en el derecho contractual* (Madrid: Moutecarvo, 1978), p. 15.

[211] RJ 1970, 324. [212] STS of 17 May 1957.

(i) The contract must be a long-term contract or a contract in which at least one of the parties has not yet performed.
(ii) The basis of the contract must have been altered. This is accepted if (a) the contract has become excessively burdensome for one of the parties, or (b) the purpose of the contract has been totally frustrated.
(iii) The change of circumstances must be extraordinary in nature and unforeseen, i.e., neither party could reasonably have taken the impediment into account at the time of concluding the contract.[213]
(iv) Furthermore, it is required that neither party has accepted the risk of the change of circumstances (as a contractual obligation).[214] The doctrine of the *cláusula rebus sic stantibus* is not applicable to aleatory contracts.
(v) The person invoking the change of circumstances must not be responsible for this change.[215]

The application of the *rebus* clause can have two different effects: (i) the adaptation of the contract restoring the equilibrium, or (ii) the termination of the contract. However, the courts prefer to adapt the contract. A termination is only granted when it is not possible to restore the balance between the performances.[216]

There are many decisions that recognise the possibility of an adaptation or termination of the contract on grounds of *cláusula rebus sic stantibus*, but only in an *obiter dictum*. However, the doctrine has only been significant in the eventual decision in a few judgments by the TS.[217] In most judgments in which an extraordinary alteration of the

[213] The TS has denied the application of the clause in the following decisions because the change was foreseeable: 16 October 1989 (RJ 6927); 18 September 1996 (RJ 1728); 14 December 1940 (RJ 1135); 26 March 1963 (RJ 2120); 31 November 1963 (RJ 4264) ; 10 December 1990 (RJ9927) ; 6 October 1987 (RJ 6720); 21 February 1990 (RJ 707); 26 October 1990 (RJ 8049); 23 April 1991 (RJ 3023); 4 February 1994 (RJ 910) and 29 May 1996 (RJ 3806).

[214] For instance, this was the reason for denying the application of the *cláusula rebus sic stantibus* in STS of 29 January 1996 (RJ 737) and STS of 23 June 1997 (RJ 5201).

[215] This was the reason for denying the application of the *cláusula rebus sic stantibus* in the following decisions of the TS: of 19 April 1985 (RJ 1804); of 17 May 1986 (RJ 2725); of 19 November 1994 (RJ 8539); of 10 February 1997 (RJ 665); and of 17 November 2000 (Act. C. 280).

[216] E. Rodríguez Rovira and J. Illescar, 'Apunte sobre la posbiel incidencia de las medidas de emergencia argentinas en las obligaciones sometidas a derecho español', (2002) 2 *Actualidad Jurídica Uría y Menéndez*, 113–18.

[217] STS of 11 June 1951 for an adaptation of the contract; STS of 23 November 1962 (RJ 5005) for an adaptation; STS of 28 January 1970 (RJ 324) for termination; STS of 9 July 1984 (RJ 3939) for an adaptation; STS of 23 March 1988 (RJ 2228) for termination; STS of 6 November 1992 (RJ 9226) for an adaptation; STS of 4 October 1996 (RJ 7032) for an adaptation. See also the decisions of the Audiencias Provinciales of: Valencia of 17 May 1991 (Act. C. 1991, 1055); Barcelona of 16 February 1993 (Act. C. 1993, 415); Navarre of 12 November 1998 (Elder. 1998, 31028).

circumstances has been accepted the TS has considered that the requirements for applying the clause had not been fulfilled.

B. Further exceptions to the principle of pacta sunt servanda

This reluctance to apply the clause is likely to have resulted in the Spanish legislator not codifying the remedy. There is no specific reference to the clause in the CC. In its judgment of 31 October 1963 (RJ 1963, 2120) the TS pointed out that the *rebus* clause had not been codified in the Spanish CC because it was contrary to the spirit of the code. The application of the remedy is *contra tenorem rationis* and this is why it has to be exceptional and restrictive.

However, it cannot be concluded that there is a complete lack of codified rules with regard to unexpected circumstances under Spanish civil law: a statutory exception to the principle of *pacta sunt servanda* is the doctrine of impossibility (Arts. 1182 *et seq.* CC). Furthermore, there are other statutory mechanisms that are to be taken into consideration concerning a change of circumstances, namely the exceptions of fortuitous event and force majeure as well as the doctrine of mistake. These might be means to excuse non-performance and they may thus limit the principle of *pacta sunt servanda.*

(a) Impossibility

With regard to an impossibility to perform, Art. 1182 indicates that an obligation to provide a certain good extinguishes if that good disappears or is destroyed without the debtor being responsible. Art. 1184 CC states that obligations to act extinguish when the performance is legally or factually impossible. Impossibility only exonerates the debtor when it was unforeseeable and due to a cause that could not be prevented.[218]

There are no clear boundaries between a case of impossibility to perform and a case of excessive onerousness and therefore one may apply the *rebus sic stantibus* doctrine under the guise of impossibility.[219] Excessive onerousness occurs where performance is still possible but the difficulties in performing are of such a magnitude that performance cannot reasonably be required from the debtor. Under Spanish law the impossibility to perform only excuses non-performance if it is absolute and objective, and not if it is merely onerous to perform. However, there

[218] L. Díez Picazo and A. Gullón Ballesteros, *Sistema de dereche civil* (Madrid: Tecnos, 2002), vol. II, p. 281.

[219] See Section B below.

have been court decisions in which an extraordinary difficulty in performing has been equated with an impossibility to perform. This was the case in SAP Lleida of 19 March 1998 (AC 1998, 576) where a contractor had difficulties in performing due to the characteristics of the soil he had to remove. The TS admitted the application of this approach in cases in which the performance of the contract would have created an unfair result.[220] In another decision the TS indicated that extraordinary difficulties in performing could not be invoked when the circumstances that caused it could have been foreseen. Furthermore, the TS indicated that an intervention by the authorities, which made it impossible to achieve the expected profits, was not an unforeseen circumstance since in the specific field (the construction of sea-going vessels) there was such an industrial risk inherent in a business area which is strongly regulated by the government. As far as the courts accept the exception of extraordinary difficulties, the TS equates such difficulties with the *rebus* clause with regard to the legal consequences: hence the contract is modified.

(b) Force Majeure

Furthermore, the exculpation (‘*incumplimiento no imputable*’) of a fortuitous event or force majeure has to be mentioned. On the basis of Art. 1105 CC, a party is not liable for non-performance if circumstances occur that were unforeseeable or that, although being foreseeable, could not have been prevented.

(c) Basis of the contract no longer present

The basis of the contract being no longer present is another doctrine to be considered. In Spanish law, the ‘*causa*’ is an essential element of the contract; when the *causa* is lacking, the contract is deemed not to exist (Art. 1261 CC). According to Art. 1274 CC, the *causa* for a party in onerous contracts is the performance or the promise of performance by the other party. The *causa* is generally understood in an objective sense as the aim that is typically pursued by the parties in each contract (for instance, in sales contracts, the delivery of goods in exchange for payment).[221] However, the Spanish judiciary and doctrine admit that the subjective aims of the parties can have juridical relevance if they were

[220] Cf. also STS of 17 May 1957 (RJ 1957, 2164) and 16 October 1989 (RJ 1989, 6927).

[221] Código Civil Comentado, 1997, p. 551; Díez Picazo and Gullón, *Sistema de derecho civil*, p. 47; J. L. Lacruz Berdejo *et al.*, t. II, *Derecho de obligaciones: contratos y cuasicontratos* (Madrid: Dykinson, 2009).

known to both parties and the parties have formulated the contract on the basis of these grounds.[222]

According to Díez Picazo, this doctrine is to be applied when an unforeseeable and extraordinary change of circumstances leads to the lapsing of the socio-economic basis of the contract. This would be the case if the balance between the corresponding performances is affected and if the common aim of the parties can no longer be attained (or the aim of one of the parties recognised by the other).[223] There are certain requirements which have to be met:

(i) the objective aim of the contract must disappear;
(ii) it must be evident to the other party that this aim was determinant for the party to contract; and
(iii) the party which invokes the application of this doctrine must not have had control over the circumstances which have led to the *causa* no longer being present.

(d) Mistake

Also, the doctrine of mistake (Art. 1266 CC) must be taken into account. According to Spanish case law, not every mistake renders a contract invalid on the ground of defective consent. In order to serve as a ground for annulling the contract, the following conditions must be met:

(i) the mistake must be fundamental, that is, it must concern a matter which was decisive for the mistaken party to enter into the contract;[224]
(ii) there must be a causal link between the mistake and the purpose of the contract ('*dolo causal*' or '*dolus grave*');[225]
(iii) the mistake must not be attributable to the party who has made it ('*excusable*'). A mistake is understood to be *excusable* when the party invoking the mistake could have avoided it by taking reasonable care.[226]

The consequences of a mistake depend on the *causa* of the contractual relationship. The relevance of a mistake is evaluated on the basis of the

[222] Cf. STS of 30 June 1948 (RJ 1948, 1115), STS of 11 July 1984 (RJ 1984, 3939), STS of 30 December 1985 (RJ 1985, 6620), STS of 19 January 1990 (RJ 1990, 19), STS of 20 April 1994 (RJ 1994, 3216), STS of 30 June 2000 (RJ 2000, 6747), STS of 10 April 2002 (Act. C. 2002, 492).

[223] Díez Picazo, *Fundamentos del Derecho*, p. 898.

[224] STS of 5 March 1960 (*RA* 950); STS of 15 October 1973 (*RA* 3797). Díez Picazo and Gullón, *Sistema de Derecho Civil*, Vol. II, p. 54; Albaladejo, *Derecho Civil I, Introducción y Parte general*, p. 632.

[225] STS of 14 June 1943 (RA 719).

[226] STS of 8 June 1968 (RA 3766); STS of 5 March 1962 (RA 1532). In the literature, see Díez Picazo and Gullón, *Sistema de Derecho Civil*, p. 54; Albaladejo, *Derecho Civil I*, p. 633.

specific nature of each contract and the behaviour of the contractual parties based on the principle of good faith (Art. 1258 CC). This evaluation is necessary because a mistake does not always lead to the same consequences. The question of whether it is adequate to exempt the party in error from its obligation to perform requires an analysis of the conflicting interests. In Spanish case law, there are many examples of decisions where the buyer purchased goods for a specific purpose, which then could not be used in the designated manner due to circumstances which already existed at the time of concluding the contract. In most of these cases, the courts declared the contract void on the ground of the defective consent of the buyer (STS of 27 October 1964 (RJ 1964, 4735) or 30 April 1997 (RJ 1997, 3863).

(e) Other specific provisions in the CC

There are several specific provisions in the CC that are applicable when a change of circumstances has taken place. As an example, some of the provisions that provide solutions to some situations in which a part of the contractual obligation becomes too onerous for one of the parties shall be mentioned:

- *Terms of payment*, Art. 1129 CC: the debtor loses his right to invoke a term for payment if (i) after the obligation has been contracted, he becomes insolvent, unless it has provided security for the debt; (ii) it fails to give the agreed security; or (iii) due to his own acts he has impaired such security or if the security perishes as a result of a fortuitous event, unless the security is immediately replaced.
- *Right to withhold delivery*, Art. 1467 CC: the seller is not obliged to deliver the sold objects when he is in imminent danger of not being paid due to the insolvency of the buyer.
- *Resolution of the sale*, Art. 1503 CC: if the seller has reasonable grounds to fear the loss of the sold immovable object and the price, he may immediately request the resolution of the sale.
- *Rent reduction*, Art. 1575 CC: the lessee has no right to a rent reduction due to the infertility of the hired land or the loss of fruits due to ordinary fortuitous events. However, the lessee has this right if he loses more than half of the fruits due to extraordinary and unforeseen fortuitous events, unless explicitly agreed otherwise. Extraordinary fortuitous events are: a fire, war, pests, unusual floods, a plague of locusts, an earthquake or any other unaccustomed events that the parties could not have rationally foreseen.
- *Rescission of the lease*, Art. 1558(3) CC: if in the case of repair work the part of the premises which the lessee and his family need as living space has become uninhabitable, the lessee may rescind the contract.

- *Resignation of the mandate*, Art 1736 CC: the agent may resign from the mandate contract by giving notice to the principal. If the principal suffers disadvantages as a result of the resignation, the agent must indemnify him, unless the agent resigned because he would have suffered a great detriment had he continued to perform the mandate.

(f) Specific Provisions in Navarre

Although it is not applicable at a national level, the Civil Code of Navarre, one of the several regional civil law systems that co-exist with the national civil law system in Spain, has codified a remedy that is applicable to a change of circumstances that affects the equilibrium of the contract and the equivalence of the mutual obligations. Article 493(3) of the said code states that the aggrieved party may claim an adjustment of the contract according to the demands of equity or may claim a termination.

Portugal

A Introduction

The problem of establishing the legal relevance of a supervening change of circumstances is an old preoccupation in Portuguese legislation; here, as in other areas, the national legal order has been shaped by many influences.

Historically, medieval literature, which had its origins in Roman law,[227] was the first influence: the doctrine of *clausula rebus sic stantibus* postulating the status quo with regard to certain circumstances had to be accepted as an implied term of every contract.[228] However, this theory raised vehement criticism. The concept was considered to be too vague[229] since such a resolutive condition could not convincingly be deduced from the intention of the parties, or conversely from law,[230] in which case the aforementioned clause becomes meaningless. Therefore, the effect of

[227] As proposed by Pfaff, for example. However, this theory is criticised by Luís Carvalho Fernandes, 'A Teoria da Imprevisão do Direito Civil Português', (1963) *Boletim do Ministério de Justiça*, 128, n. 19 at 28.

[228] António Menezes Cordeiro, *Da Alteração das Circunstâncias, a concretização do artigo 437 do Código civil à luz da jurisprudência posterior a 1974*, handout of 'Estudos em Memória do Prof. Doutor Paulo Cunha', (Lisbon: AAFDL, 1987), p. 12.

[229] Carvalho Fernandes, 'A Teoria', 29: 'very vague, in its field of application as well as in its foundation'.

[230] Menezes Cordeiro, *Da Alteração*, p. 12.

this doctrine in Portuguese law should not be overestimated. On this subject Menezes Cordeiro says that 'no clear influence of European legal reasoning can be identified in Portugal which would have enabled the admittance of *clausula rebus sic stantibus*'.[231] Carvalho Fernandes also considers that 'the theory of unexpected circumstances has not been generally accepted in any of the regulations' and only the initial grievance is addressed by them. This is despite the fact that occasionally solutions are found in line with *clausula rebus sic stantibus*: for example the solution found by the 'Ordenações Filiplinas' (which were in force before the first Portuguese 'Código Civil'): in Title XXIV a landlord was entitled to evict a tenant due to supervening home requirements.[232]

The first Portuguese Código Civil, which emerged in the nineteenth century (1867), does not contain the doctrine of *clausula rebus sic stantibus*. Quite in contrast, not only does it reinforce the binding nature of the contract and the necessity of immediate performance, but it also admits exceptions only in cases of accident and force majeure. Because of this, there were many who denied any relevance of supervening alterations apart from situations of accident and force majeure. Meanwhile, over time, there were other influences: in the area of public law ('*Direito Público*'),[233] and especially in the field of administrative contracts, the French doctrine of unexpected circumstances had a marked influence.[234]

But in the area of civil law, and ever since German civil law has become the dominant influence in Portugal, the doctrinal discussion has closely followed German developments. Thus, in the first instance, Windscheid's presupposition ('*pressuposição*') theory[235] and then the theory of the basis of the agreement ('*base negocial*') proposed by Oertmann and developed by a number of authors – such as Larenz, Lehmann and Kegel – the latter theory in many ways being a development of the former, had a remarkable, if not decisive, influence on our law. This point of view had a marked influence on the preparatory

[230] Menezes Cordeiro, *Da Alteração*, p. 12. [231] Menezes Cordeiro, *Da Alteração*, p. 21.

[232] Carvalho Fernandes, 'A Teoria', 174.

[233] See, in the area of administrative contracts, the diplomas mentioned by Carvalho Fernandes, 'A Teoria', 270 *et seq.*, in particular relating to the two world wars which took place last century.

[234] This fact can explain the thinking of authors like Marcelo Caetano. On the theories of Marcelo Caetano, see Carvalho Fernandes, 'A Teoria', 267 *et seq.*

[235] See, in Portuguese law, for all, António Menezes Cordeiro, *Da Boa Fé no direito civil* (Coimbra: Almedina, 1984), vol. II, pp. 967 *et seq.*

studies of the new Código Civil of 1966 (which is still in force and which was also inspired by the research of Antunes Varela).[236]

B. Article 437, n°1, Código Civil

Art. 437, n°1, Código Civil (CC) states that

> if the circumstances on which the parties based their decision to contract change unexpectedly,[237] the burdened party has a right to terminate the contract, or to alter it according to fair judgment, as long as the requirement of the obligations which it assumed seriously affects the principles of good faith and is not covered by the actual risks inherent in the contract.

The solution provided by Art. 437 CC thus represents a compromise solution between various historical lines of thought and has been criticised as lacking coherence. On the one hand, Art. 437, n°1 CC relies on an *unexpected* alteration in the 'circumstances, on which the parties based their decision to contract.'[238] Portuguese literature has maintained that the concept of unexpected circumstances is broader than that of unforseeability.[239] On the other hand, a right to terminate or modify the contract 'according to fair judgment' only exists 'as long as the requirement of the obligations seriously affects the principles of good faith and is not covered by the actual risks inherent in the contract'.[240]

There are those who believe that 'it has not been possible to achieve the inclusion of references to equal justice and good faith in one rule'[241] and that good faith should take precedence. But the reference to risks inherent in the contract is open to various interpretations. Some

[236] Antunes Varela, *Ineficácia do testamento e vontade conjectural do testador*, (Coimbra: Coimbra Editora, 1950), pp. 263 *et seq.* and pp. 323 *et seq.*

[237] The precise wording refers to an 'anomalous' ('abnormal') change that as such does not always have to be unforeseeable. As Pedro Pais de Vasconcelos has suggested, *Teoria Geral do Direito Civil* (Coimbra: Almedina, 3rd edn, 2005), p. 749, there may be circumstances that are anomalous and yet they might be foreseeable.

[238] Menezes Cordeiro, *Da Boa Fé*, p. 1106.

[239] Mário Júlio de Almeida Costa, *Direito das Obrigações* (Coimbra: Almedina 10th edn, 2006), p. 338.

[240] Portuguese jurisprudence has understood that the unexpected alteration of circumstances must cause an imbalance in fulfilment, making performance of the contract excessively onerous or difficult for one of the parties. Cf. for all, the Supreme Court ('Acordão do Supremo Tribunal de Justiça' of 18 January 1996, (1996) *Boletim do Ministério da Justiça*, n°453, 462, and 'Acordão do Supremo Tribunal de Justiça', (1997) *Boletim do Ministério da Justiça*, n°462, 412).

[241] Menezes Cordeiro, *Da Boa Fé*, p. 1108.

authors emphasise that an alteration of circumstances should not be included in the scope of the actual contract as a risk assumed by the parties.[242] Others, however, argue that the doctrine is only operative when other rules explicitly fail to provide other forms of support for losses suffered.[243] According to this view the provision of Art. 437 CC is only operative if the result is compatible with the nature of that particular contract and provided there are no specific rules for that type of contract.

According to the courts there are four requirements for Art. 437 CC to be applied:

(i) It is necessary that one of the elements of the so-called basis of the contract is affected by a supervening change.
(ii) That change must be anomalous or exceptional, i.e., a development which one would not conceive as a daily, normal change with regard to the features of that particular contract. This requirement, although autonomous, sometimes cannot easily be distinguished from the further requirements.
(iii) It must be contrary to the imperatives of good faith to uphold the contract without adaptation. The demand of one of the parties to respect the contract must be openly abusive. Some courts have invoked the principle of equality as well as the requirement of good faith in the enforcement of the contract.
(iv) The supervening change must not be covered by a risk inherent to the contract. This condition does not only relate to the type of the contract in question but it means that this relief must be subsidiary to the contractual clauses and other legal rules that establish consequences for the change of the contractual basis of that specific contract.

While certain aspects of Art. 437 CC are relatively uncontroversial – for instance that it cannot be applied by a court without a request of one of the parties[244] – others remain in a shroud of controversy and doubt.

[242] Almeida Costa, *Direito das Obrigações* pp. 340–1.

[243] See Menezes Cordeiro, *Da Boa Fé*, p. 1107. On this question see also Carlos Alberto da Mota Pinto and Paulo Mota Pinto, *Teoria Geral do Direito Civil* (Coimbra: Coimbra Editora, 4th edn, 2005), p. 613; Guilherme de Oliveira, 'Alteração das Circunstâncias, Risco e Abuso do Direito, a propósito de um Crédito de Tornas', (1989) *Colectânea de Jurisprudência*, 5, 19; Antunes Varela (with the collaboration of Henrique Mesquita), 'Resolução ou Modificação do Contrato por Alteração das Circunstâncias', (1982) *Colectânea de Jurisprudência*, 7 *et seq*. See also, António Pinto Monteiro and Júlio Gomes, 'Rebus sic stantibus – Hardship Clauses in Portuguese Law', (1998) 3 *European Review of Private Law*, 319, 328–9.

[244] 'Acórdão do Tribunal da Relação do Porto' of 15 July 2004, proc. 0433899, www.dgsi.pt. The court was prepared to accept that the abrupt decrease in the cost of cotton in the

This is true as far as the procedural mechanism to invoke the change of circumstances is concerned: some court decisions present it as a defence that may be invoked as a sort of exception ('*Einrede*'),[245] whereas others believe that the defendant has to invoke change of circumstances in a countersuit ('*reconventio*').[246] If the change of circumstances justifies the rescission ('*resolução*') of the contract, it seems that it is not subject to the general rules that apply to the rescission of contracts. Normally, rescission does not require a court action to be effective. Here, however, it seems that court action is required for the rescission to operate.[247] The retroactive effect of rescission also does not occur when the contract is rescinded as a result of a fundamental change of circumstances: either there is no retroactive effect whatsoever[248] or this effect is limited to the moment when the supervening event occurred or even, and perhaps better, the moment when the occurrence of the supervening event was invoked. Another controversial issue concerns the extent to which Art. 437 CC may or may not be applied to contracts that have already been performed. Some authors[249] and some court decisions[250] exclude the possibility of invoking Art. 437 CC when the contract has been fully performed, but the question is far from settled.

The most critical doctrinal view with regard to the present rule tends to underline the essential nature of the contractual distribution of risks, of the protection of reliance and of complementary interpretation

world market was a relevant change of circumstances, but the defendant simply ceased to perform and never invoked Art. 437 CC. As a result the court decided that it could not, by its own initiative, enquire whether there had been a cause for the termination or the modification of the contract.

245 'Acórdão do Supremo Tribunal de Justiça' of 19 March 1979, processo 067672 (1979) 285 *Boletim do Ministério de Justiça*, 234 and 'Acórdão do Supremo Tribunal de Justiça' of 18 May 1993, processo 083521, www.dgsi.pt.

246 'Acórdão do Tribunal da Relação do Porto' of 15 July 2004, processo 0433899, www.dgsi.pt.

247 'Acórdão do Supremo Tribunal de Justiça' of 10 December 1996, processo 94A470, (1997) 462 *Boletim do Ministério da Justiça*, 412: rescission based on change of circumstances requires a court action.

248 'Acórdão do STJ' of 16 May 2002, proc. 02B1145, www.dgsi.pt: no retroactivity.

249 Defending the proposition that Art. 437 CC may not be invoked if a contract has already been fully performed see L. Menezes Leitão, *Direito das Obrigações* (Coimbra: Almedina, 4th edn, 2006) vol. II, p. 136, n. 263 and Menezes Cordeiro, *Da Alteração das Circunstâncias*, p. 70; accepting that it is still possible to invoke Art. 437 CC exceptionally see Almeida Costa, *Direito das Obrigações*, p. 344 and C. Mota Pinto and P. Mota Pinto, *Teoria Geral do Direito Civil*, p 613,

250 'Acórdão do Supremo Tribunal de Justiça' of 20 May 1986, processo 073835, www.dgsi.pt: Art. 437 CC may not be invoked when the contract has been already fully performed.

('*ergänzende Vertragsauslegung*'). However, even from this point of view it is recognised that cases exist in which there may be 'radical alterations that were completely unexpected in a particular contractual situation'.[251] In such situations the only solution proposed is to share the loss equally. But the Portuguese courts mostly refer to Art. 437 CC and not to the complementary interpretation of contracts.

C. Further rules

The general rules on impossibility are of little help in these cases although they have priority over Art. 437 CC. But, in principle, even extreme difficulty or hardship to perform does not amount to impossibility since the Code does not subscribe in general to the doctrine of the limit of the debtor's sacrifice ('*Opfergrenze*').[252]

In addition to Art. 437 CC, one must also take into account Art. 252, n° 2. CC, since the latter also embodies the recognition of the doctrine of the basis of the transaction *('doutrina da base do negócio')* by Portuguese law. With regard to this distinction, it is important whether the error was prior or contemporaneous to the formation of the contract, or whether there is a change in the basis of the transaction after formation. In the first case the situation is one of error in the basis of the transaction ('*erro sobre a base do negócio*') (Art. 252, n° 2, CC); in the second case, the problem is one of presupposition ('*pressuposição*'), which the Código Civil covers in the rule for unexpected change of circumstances ('*alteração anormal das circunstâncias*'), on which the parties based their decision to enter into a contract (Art. 437 CC). In other words, the error refers to the present or the past, while the presupposition refers to the future.

Greece

A. Article 388 AK

The principle of the binding nature and the sanctity of contracts (*pacta sunt servanda*) is one of the most fundamental principles of the Greek

[251] Menezes Cordeiro, *Da Alteração*, p. 80.

[252] There are, nevertheless, a few rules that exceptionally take into account the serious difficulty to perform. For instance in a loan ('*mutuum*') of objects other than money (e.g., cereals, wine, olive oil) if it becomes extremely difficult for the debtor to give back things of the same kind he may choose instead to give back their value in money at the moment when restitution ought to take place (Art. 1149 CC).

Civil Code. Nevertheless, in certain cases the contractual commitment may prove to be overly harsh for one of the parties, particularly if the circumstances on which the contract is based have changed and, consequently, the balance of the contract is distorted to the detriment of one of the parties.[253] The Civil Code (Astikos Kodix (AK)) deals with this problem by an express provision in Art. 388 AK.[254] With this provision, the Greek legislator gives the parties a right to seek judicial dissolution or adjustment of a reciprocal contract.

Art. 388 AK reflects criteria resulting from classic theories and more modern doctrines, which have been developed internationally in the twentieth century (that is, basically, the German doctrine of the lapse of the transaction's underlying basis – '*Wegfall der Geschäftsgrundlage*'[255] – and the French theory of the unforeseen circumstances – '*théorie de l'imprévision*').[256] The basic idea, however, which is essential to the above article, is the concept of good faith ('*bona fides*'), established by the general and most basic provision of the Civil Code, that of Art. 288 AK. As a consequence, even in cases in which the strict requirements of Art. 388 AK are not met, it is still possible to resort to Art. 288 AK, if, in general terms, the performance and the maintenance of the contract violates the fundamental principle of good faith.[257] This, however, does not lessen the practical value of Art. 388 AK, given that this article demonstrates that the legislative intended for the judiciary to intervene in such cases.[258]

[253] See Michael Stathopoulos, *Contract Law in Hellas* (Athens: Kluwer Sakkoulas, 1995), n. 291.

[254] See Alexandros Litzeropoulos, *The Judicial Rulings as a Factor of Formation of Private Law* (Athens: Sakkoulas, 1932, repr. 2000), pp. 249–50; Ioannis Sakketas,'Art. 388' in: *ErmAK Interpretation of the Civil Code* (Athens: 1949), vol. II/A, n. 1; Asterios Georgiadis, *Law of Obligations – General Part* (Athens/Thessalonica: Sakkoula, 3rd edn, 2000), vol. II, pp. 129–30.

[255] This theory was first presented in a systematical way by Oertmann, *Die Geschäftsgrundlage*. For the partial acceptance of this doctrine by Art. 388 AK, see Sakketas, 'Art. 388', in: *ErmAK* n. 16; Ioannis Gasis, 'Waiver from the Article 388 AK', (1975) 23 NoV p. 705, 707; Nikolaos Papantoniou, *The Good Faith in Civil Law* (Athens: Sakkoulas, 1957, repr. 1997), p. 174; Ast. Georgiadis, *Law of Obligations*, p. 134.

[256] See also, Stathopoulos, *Contract Law*, n. 292.

[257] See M. Stathopoulos, *Law of Obligations – General Part* (Athens/Thessalonica: Sakkoula, 4th edn, 2004), §22 n. 3; Apostolos Georgiadis, *Law of Obligations – General Part* (1999), §33 n. 8; AP 1066/1996, HellD 38, p. 114; Thessalonica Appeal Court 1228/1997, HellD 38, p. 1959; Athens Appeal Court 9107/1995, HellD 38, p. 916; 11603/1995, HellD 38, p. 917.

[258] See Stathopoulos, *Law of Obligations*, §22 n. 3.

There are several special prerequisites for Art. 388 AK to be applicable:

(i) The contract must be reciprocal. The problem of an unforeseen change of circumstances in other obligations (e.g., in unilateral contracts) is regulated by the general provision of Art. 288 AK.[259]

(ii) The change must concern circumstances, on which the parties have based the conclusion of the contract, regarding the requirements of good faith and common usage. According to the prevailing opinion in legal literature,[260] these are the actual and legal facts whose importance emerges from the will of the parties (subjective criterion) and, simultaneously, from the main target and the function of the specific contract (objective criterion).[261] This is the so-called underlying basis of the contract but in a more objective interpretation.[262] The mere subjective importance of an unforeseen change is irrelevant according to Art. 143 AK.

(iii) The change must have been of a supervening nature, that is, it must have occurred after the formation of the contract. If the crucial circumstances are non-existent or the change of them has already taken place at the time of the formation and the parties are unaware of it, Art. 388 AK is not applicable. *De lege ferenda*, this restriction is hardly justified as the principle of *bona fides* necessitates (perhaps even more than in case of the subsequent change) the dissolution or adjustment of the contract.[263] However, in such cases the recourse to other provisions, which provide more or less equal protection, is possible, e.g. Art. 140 *et seq.* AK (mistake). Rather seldom, but not impossible, is the application of Art. 179 AK (exploitative contract).[264]

In particular, concerning the mistake of the parties, it should be pointed out that, if a mistake is *shared by both parties* and relates to facts,

[259] See Georgios Balis, *Law of Obligations – General Part* (Athens: Sakkoula, 3rd edn, 1969), p. 312; Sakketas, 'Art. 388', in: *ErmAK*, nn. 20–3; Panagiotes Zepos, *Law of Obligations – General Part* (Athens: Zacharopoulos, 2nd edn, 1955), p. 560; Stathopoulos, *Law of Obligations*, §22 n. 13; Ast. Georgiadis, *Law of Obligations*, vol. II, pp. 137–8; Ap. Georgiadis, *Law of Obligations*, §33 n. 9.

[260] For a different, purely objective approach see Case 2 below.

[261] In detail Sakketas, 'Art. 388', in: *ErmAK*, nn. 30–1; furthermore Balis, *Law of Obligations*, pp. 312–13; Stathopoulos, *Law of Obligations*, §22 n. 16; Ioannis Spyridakis, *Law of Obligations – General Part* (Athens: Sakkoula, 1994), pp. 314–15.

[262] See Stathopoulos, *Law of Obligations*, §22 nn. 14–16.

[263] See *ibid.* n. 20.

[264] See Zepos, *Law of Obligations*, p. 561; Georgios Michailidis-Nouaros, *Law of Obligations (university lessons)* (1957), pp. 215–16; N. Papantoniou, *General Principles of Civil Law* (3rd edn, 1983), pp. 401–3; Stathopoulos, *Law of Obligations*, § 22 nn. 20 *et seq.*; Ast. Georgiadis, *Law of Obligations*, vol. II, p. 139; Ap. Georgiadis, *Law of Obligations*, §33 n. 13; Spyridakis, *Law of Obligations*, p. 315.

which are crucial for the specific contract, the aggrieved party has the right to annul the contract pursuant to Art. 140 *et seq*. AK without any obligation whatsoever to compensate the other party.[265] This approach is supported by the judiciary and some legal writers.[266] According to another and more persuasive view,[267] though, Art. 288 AK is the relevant provision, which under stricter conditions, provides for an *ipso iure* adjustment or dissolution of the contract.

A *unilateral* error of a party, on the other hand, is dealt with directly by Arts. 140 *et seq*. AK. The party's error must either be due to a discrepancy between its will and its declaration (Arts. 140–1 AK: error as to the declaration) or to a false estimation of the qualities of a person or an object (Art. 142 AK: error as to the qualities). In the above cases, the mistaken party is provided with the right to judicial dissolution of the contract with retroactive effect. In contrast with Art. 388 or even 288 AK, there are no further requirements. The annulment of the contract, though, does not deprive the other party of any kind of protection. Usually, this party is entitled to claim damages suffered due to the frustration of its reliance in the validity of the contract (see Art. 145(1) AK). This is, in fact, a case of a negative interest. The quantum of damages is, however, limited to the party's positive interest (its interest in the performance of the contract, see Art. 145(1) AK).

(iv) The circumstances, which have brought about the change, should be exceptional as well as unforeseen. Unusual events of a natural, political, social or economic nature (or events related to such phenomena), even though they are not necessarily events of force majeure, are generally considered as exceptional.[268] The specific character of the circumstance is irrelevant (e.g., radical illness of a party). Circumstances are considered as unforeseen, if they have not and could not have been foreseen. According to a convincing view in legal literature, the unforseeability test is a subjective criterion.[269]

(v) The performance must have become so excessively onerous for the debtor in comparison with the counter-performance that it would be contrary to good faith for the other party to insist on the

[265] For further details see Case 13 below. [266] See in detail in Case 13 below.

[267] See in detail in Case 13 below.

[268] See Zepos, *Law of Obligations*, p. 562; Stathopoulos, *Law of Obligations*, §22 n. 24; Ast. Georgiadis, *Law of Obligations*, vol. II, p. 141; Ap. Georgiadis, *Law of Obligations*, §33 nn. 14–15. For a legitimation of the above criterion see in detail in Case 2 below.

[269] Cf. Ap. Georgiadis, *Law of Obligations*, §33 n. 17. The objective point of view, similarly with the objective approach of negligence, is supported by Martin Henssler, *Risiko als Vertragsgegenstand* (Tübingen: Mohr-Siebeck, 1994), p. 55, in the same legal context of German law.

performance.[270] The mere fact that the debtor suffers an unpredictable loss or that he faces difficulties in performance are not sufficient, although it is not required that he must be financially ruined by the transaction.[271] If the extreme burden of the fulfillment exceeds any tolerable limit and goes beyond the maximum economic sacrifice that can be demanded by the debtor (see also Art. 288 AK), it is a case of economic impossibility and Art. 380 AK applies.[272] Under these circumstances, both parties are released from their obligations *ipso iure* (rule of common release), while a judicial adjustment of the contract is excluded.[273]

B. *Conditions beyond those expressly required*

Beyond the conditions expressly required by Art. 388 AK, the prevailing opinion also demands:

(i) There must not be any contractual provision that allocates the risk of the situation in question between the parties (force majeure clauses etc.).[274] Still, the total allocation of risks to one of the contracting parties is null and void,[275] if this agreement does not serve – or is not justifiable by – the purpose of the contract (e.g., aleatory contracts).[276]

Of course, contractual agreements also comprise implied agreements which can arise from a complementary interpretation of the contract by virtue of Art. 200 AK. According to the case law, complementary interpretation requires a doubt or a lacuna in the contract.[277] The filling of this lacuna is not a case of an arbitrary choice or, on the other hand, of a pure objective decision. The juridical authority searches for the so-called 'hypothetical' or, in other words, 'normative will of the parties'. In particular, it speculates on what the parties would have agreed upon in good faith if they had foreseen the specific matter. Anything that characterises the specific contract should be taken into account (i.e., the explicit terms, the negotiations, the motivation and the interests of the parties, even the social context

[270] AP (plenary session) 9/1997, HellD 38, p. 767; AP 474/1997, HellD 38, p. 1826.
[271] See Balis, *Law of Obligations*, pp. 314 *et seq.*; Sakketas, 'Art. 388', in: *ErmAK*, n. 49; Spyridakis, *Law of Obligations*, p. 316.
[272] See Stathopoulos, *Law of Obligations*, §19 nn. 57 *et seq.*
[273] See *ibid.*, §22 n. 26; Ap. Georgiadis, *Law of Obligations*, §33 n. 19.
[274] See AP 494/1999, HellD 40, p. 1083.
[275] See Stathopoulos, *Contract Law*, n. 298.
[276] See Stathopoulos, *Law of Obligations*, §22 n. 40; Ap. Georgiadis, *Law of Obligations*, §33 n. 27.
[277] See AP 28/2007 (unpubl.); 1978/2006 (unpubl.); 1867/2006 (unpubl.); 1484/2006 (unpubl.).

under which the contract is being concluded).[278] If the above indications do not lead to a result or if there are no relevant indications, the lacuna is filled by the purely objective rules of the underlying basis of the contract.[279] It should be pointed out, though, that in the legal practice the theoretical difference between the purely objective rules of the underlying basis of the contract and the more subjective approach of complementary interpretation (e.g., according to the indications of the specific contract) is not always clear. After all, the basic idea of the two institutions is the one of *bona fides*.

(ii) The contract must not have been completely or at least partly been performed.[280] In exceptional cases, however, the application of Art. 388 AK may not be prohibited by the mere fact that the contract has already been fulfilled.[281]

A minority of legal writers[282] furthermore requires that the debtor must not have been at fault. This is based on Art. 344 §2 AK, according to which the debtor bears responsibility even for fortuitous events. Nevertheless, Art. 344 AK is not related to counter-performance and, moreover, to the destroyed balance of the performances. It only deals with the fact that the obligation does not become void if the debtor is at fault. Thus, the default of the debtor should not be considered a negative prerequisite for the doctrine of the unforeseen change of circumstances.[283]

If the above conditions are met, the debtor of the excessively onerous performance has a right to seek a judicial adjustment of the performance to the appropriate extent, or, if such an adjustment is impossible, the total or partial (only as to its still unfulfilled part) dissolution of the contract.[284] The judicial dissolution of the contract results in the

[278] See Marianos Karasis, *General Principles of the Civil Code*, (Athens Komotini: Sakkoulas, 1996), vol. I, n. C 383.

[279] See also Karasis, *General Principles*, vol. I, n. 394.

[280] See Sakketas, 'Art. 388', in: *ErmAK*, n. 55; George Oikonomopoulos, 'Unforeseen change of circumstances', (1972) 28 NDik, 321, 326 I; Ast. Georgiadis, *Law of Obligations*, vol. II, p. 142.

[281] See Stathopoulos, *Law of Obligations*, §22 n. 29.

[282] See Sakketas, 'Art. 388', in: *ErmAK*, n. 54; Zepos, *Law of Obligations*, p. 561 n. 2.

[283] See Balis, *Law of Obligations*, p. 313; Papantoniou, *The Good Faith*, pp. 179–80; Ast. Georgiadis, *Law of Obligations*, vol. II, p. 140; Stathopoulos, *Law of Obligations*, §22 n. 28; in detail I. Spyridakis, 'Unforeseen Change of Circumstances during the Default of the Debtor', (1978) 26 NoV, 1016 *et seq*.

[284] See Balis, *Law of Obligations*, p. 315; Michailidis-Nouaros, *Law of Obligations*, p. 218; Spyridakis, *Law of Obligations*, p. 317; in detail Panagiotes Theodoropoulos, 'The Judicial Power in Case of Unforeseen Change of Circumstances of the Contracts' (Article 388 AK) (1960) 1 HellD, 133 *et seq*., 344 *et seq*.

termination of the contractual obligations in the future and only in exceptional cases has retroactive effect.[285] As a consequence, an exchange of performances that has already taken place is reversed according to the provisions on unjust enrichment (Arts. 388 §2, 904 *et seq.*, 912 AK).[286]

FRANCE AND RELATED JURISDICTIONS

France

A. *The doctrine of* imprévision

(a) Definition

In the French discourse, the doctrine of *imprévision* is the most important concept dealing with the effects of unexpected circumstances on contractual obligations. This idea generally refers to cases in which unforeseen economic circumstances become apparent after a contract has been concluded and which make its performance extremely difficult or much more costly, but do not render it impossible.[287] The doctrine of *imprévision* can be based on the assumption that there is an economic imbalance between the contractual obligations at the time of performance. The doctrine is not applied to speculative contracts like stock exchange transactions, as this 'speculative' nature is part and

[285] See Stathopoulos, *Law of Obligations*, §22 n. 34.

[286] See Michailidis-Nouaros, *Law of Obligations*, p. 219; Stathopoulos, *Law of Obligations*, § 22 n. 35; Spyridakis, *Law of Obligations*, p. 318.

[287] J. Ghestin, *Les obligations, Effets* (Paris: LGDJ, 2001); P. Voirin, *De l'imprévision dans les rapports de droit privé*, Thesis (Nancy: 1922); E. Gaudin de la Grange, *La crise du contrat et le rôle du juge*, Thesis (Montpellier: 1935); P. Azard, 'L'instabilité monétaire et la notion d'équivalence dans les contrats', (1953) *I Jurisclasseur Périodique*, 1092; M. El Gammal, *L'adaptation du contrat aux circonstances économiques* (Paris: LGDJ, 1967); 'Le Rôle du juge en présence de problèmes problématiques', (1970) *Travaux Association R. Capitant*, t. XXII, and especially the report on the role of the judge in the face of economic problems in French law by B. Oppetit, 185n and the general report by R. Perrot, 260; P. Catala, 'Les effets de la dépréciation monétaire sur les rapports juridiques contractuels en droit civil français', (1971) *Travaux Ass. H. Capitant*, t. XXIII, 439, J. Ghestin and M. Billiau, *Le prix dans les contrats de longue duré* (Paris: LGDJ, 1990); J. L. Devolve, 'L'imprévision dans les contrats internationaux', (1988–90) *Travaux comité fr. DIP*, 147; L. Grynbaum, *Le contrat contingent*, Thesis (Paris: 1998); C. Jamin, 'Révision et intangibilité ou la double philosophie de l'article 1134 du code civil', (1998) 58 *Droit et Patrimoine*, 46 *et seq.*; H. Lecuyer, 'Le contrat, acte de prévision', (1999) *Mélanges Terré*, 643; R. David, 'L'imprévision dans les droits européens', (1974) *Mélanges Jauffret*, 211; D. Tallon, 'La révision du contrat pour imprévision au regard des enseignements récents du droit comparé', (1997) *Mélanges Sayag*, 403 *et seq.*, especially 406.

parcel of such contracts.[288] From a theoretical point of view the concept of *imprévision* is directed at resolving a conflict between commutative justice demanding a balanced exchange on the one side and, on the other, the principle of *pacta sunt servanda* which corresponds to the more general objective of legal certainty.

(b) Historical developments

In Roman law force majeure was a well accepted concept. Meanwhile, in the medieval period, the importance of commutative justice was stressed. Saint Thomas of Aquinus asserted that one who makes a promise and does not keep it because of changing conditions cannot be blamed for any unfaithfulness.[289] This view implied the notion of *clausula rebus sic stantibus*. According to this concept contracts providing for successive acts of performance over a future period of time must be understood as being subject to the condition that the circumstances will remain the same.[290] Post-glossators adopted this doctrine of *imprévision*, while Cujas and Pothier did not even mention it.[291] In the French Civil Code, the idea of *imprévision* was not recognised, which may be seen as the result of the influence of the historical school of Roman law, the natural law school and the liberal economy.[292] Art. 1134 Code Civil (Cciv) lays down the principle of the immutability or sanctity of contracts. The same idea underlies Art. 1793 Cciv. This confirms that the French position is inspired by the notion of the autonomy of will.[293] Historically, Art. 1134 Cciv is construed as a demarcation between the power of the courts and legislation forbidding judges from interfering with contracts and, therefore, reserving contractual justice for legislative regulation. In the Code Civil, however, very few provisions leave room for *imprévision* as contained in, in particular, Arts. 1769–73. In cases of the accidental destruction of the total or, at least, half of a

[288] Art. 7 al 2, 'Loi Faillot' 21 January 1918.

[289] Saint Thomas of Aquinus in his *Somme théologique*, IIa-IIae p. 110, arts. 3 to 5.

[290] The Latin adage is: '*contractus qui habent tractum successivum et dependentiam de futuro rebus sic stantibus intelleguntur*'.

[291] Voirin, *De l'imprévision*, pp. 46–7.

[292] Liberalism, as the predominant philosophical stream in the eighteenth century, gave rise to some ideas which were incompatible with a restrictive application of the *rebus sic stantibus* doctrine as provided by the canonists. *Pacta sunt servanda*, on the contrary, was perfectly coherent with the concept of *laissez faire*. Therefore the code enacted during this period did not adopt *rebus sic stantibus*.

[293] '*Le contrat est une emprise sur l'avenir*': G. Ripert, *La règle morale dans les obligations civiles*, n°84, p. 151.

harvest, a farmer may, under certain conditions, obtain a discount in the rental payments for agricultural land. However, the exceptions to the immutability principle were extended after the enactment of the Code Civil.

(c) Legislative exceptions

One will first notice an increasing number of legislative or judicial exceptions to the principle of the sanctity of contracts. Temporary legislation dealing specifically with hardship was enacted as a reaction to the world wars and economic crises. After the outbreak of World War I the legal literature looked for theoretical justifications to exculpate the debtor who could not perform his contractual obligations because it had become extremely burdensome. The concept of *rebus sic stantibus* attracted new interest and obtained legal acceptance in the 'Loi Faillot' (1918) relating to successive or postponed performance contracts concluded before 1914.[294] Furthermore, a growing number of statutes generally protecting the 'weaker parties' in contracts were enacted. Many of these statutes are directly related to the *imprévision* doctrine as is particularly the case with the Act of 30 July 1930 (Arts. 17 and 20) on insurance contracts. This is also the case with Art. 37 of the Act of 11 March 1957 on copyright (L.131–5 Code of Intellectual Property).[295] One may also refer to the Act of 3 July 1971 (Art. 833–1 Cciv[296]), the Act of 11 July 1975 on divorce reform (Art. 276 Cciv[297]), the Act of 4 July 1984 (Arts. 900–2 Cciv) and, finally, the Act of 25 January 1985, in its Art. 98(2).[298] All these examples demonstrate how far the principle of

[294] The Act of 21 January 1918, the 'Loi Faillot', allowed for the *résolution* (but not the *révision*) of contracts concluded before 1914 if one of the contractors had been the victim of a reasonable assumption when concluding the contract; see also the Act of March 1918 (regarding the modification of a lease for real property), as well as the Acts of 6 July 1925, 8 April 1933, 1 January 1924, 11 November 1932, 12 July 1933 and 22 April 1949, concerning contracts entered into before 2 September 1939 (relating to delivery, construction contracts, performance and successive or postponed contracts).

[295] Article 37 of the Act of 11 March 1957 provides that, having sold his exploitation rights, an author of intellectual work who has suffered a loss of more than seven twelfths due to a *lésion* or an insufficient prediction is entitled to claim a revision of the contract price.

[296] In succession or gratuity law contracts or unilateral contracts, Art. 855–1 Cciv. (based on the Act of 3 July 1971) provides for an adaptation of the contract under certain circumstances when the value of the contracted goods has increased or decreased by more than a quarter since the division.

[297] Amending maintenance payments for a spouse.

[298] In the case of a leasing contract including commitments by the lessee to acquire commercial establishments, when the lessee is not able to acquire the good due to a

the sanctity of contracts is subject to exceptions when major changes occur in society.

(d) Case law

Administrative law

The principle of sanctity also became subject to a large number of judicial exceptions. In France, in administrative law, the *imprévision* doctrine has been generally recognised since the famous decision in *Gaz de Bordeaux*[299] where the Conseil d'État, the highest Administrative Court, allowed a contract to be renegotiated when there were unexpected circumstances. In the absence of an agreement, administrative law grants an indemnity to a contracting party based on the principle of continuity of public services.[300] This applies in particular to transport, public works and distribution markets.[301] However, the contractual imbalance must have been caused by an event that is external and unforeseeable to the contracting parties and that event must result in an excessive burden for the contracting party. If the imbalance is permanent, the contract can be cancelled.[302]

The principle of inviolability established by the Cour de Cassation

Contrary to the administrative courts, the civil courts have consistently refused to recognise a revision on the basis of *imprévision*. However, a tendency can be observed that civil judges will also intervene even though the scope of their intervention is quite limited. In any case, this opposing view between civil and administrative courts shows how difficult the implementation of *imprévision* is in French law.

After coming close to recognising the *imprévision* doctrine at the beginning of the nineteenth century,[303] the Cour de Cassation, the

reason which is beyond his control. See L. Fin-Langer, *L'equilibre contractual* (Paris: LGDJ, 2002), pp. 367–75.

299 In the case '*Gaz de Bordeaux*', the Conseil d'État established the *imprévision* doctrine. An unpredictable increase in coal prices had disrupted the balance of a concession contract. The Administrative High Court granted damages to the concessionaire, CE 30 March 1916, DP 25 March 1916, S. 17 March 1916, *Les grands arrêts de la jurisprudence administrative*, 11th edn, n°50: Cf. : Annexes XXX.; J. Antoine, 'La mutabilité contractuelle née des faits nouveaux extérieurs aux parties', (2004) RFDA, 80.

300 CE. 5 November 1982, soc. Propétrol, AJDA, 1983, 259, conc. Labetouille.

301 The interpretation of a contract where a public body is involved is not governed by the rules of *droit civil* in France, but is a matter of *droit administratif*. So the reasoning of the Conseil d'État is different from that of the civil and commercial courts.

302 CE. 9 December 1932, Tramways de Cherbourg, DP 17 March 1933, *Les grands arrêts de la jurisprudence administrative*, 11th edn, n°50.

303 Req., 20 August 1838, S. 1838, 1, p. 973; DP 1838, 1, p. 380.

highest civil court, rejected the concept in 1856[304] and established the principle of the sanctity of contracts on 6 March 1876[305] in the famous case of '*Canal de Craponne*'.[306] The contracts in question, dating from 1560 and 1567, referred to the water supply for an irrigation canal in the plains of Arles at a fixed price. Much later, in the nineteenth century, confronted with inflation and an increase in labour costs, those in charge of canal maintenance requested that the price be increased. The Aix Court of Appeal confirmed the tribunal's judgment in which the price had been increased. However, this decision was overruled by the Cour de Cassation arguing that time and equity could not allow a judge to modify the agreement between the parties according to Art. 1134 Cciv.

Exceptions

The principle of the sanctity of contracts has been consistently adhered to by the highest civil courts. Yet, in a growing number of cases, judges have been allowed to revise contracts.

The civil courts generally take into consideration changed circumstances that render the performance of a contract more difficult and give the parties an incentive to renegotiate the terms of their contract.[307] The obligation to renegotiate is justified by the principle of good faith between the parties in the execution of a contract as laid down in Art. 1134 Cciv. The instability of the contract must be due to an exterior event after its conclusion and must not have been caused by either of the parties.

At this stage, great uncertainty still exists with regard to the conditions for the application of *imprévision*. It is particularly unclear whether or not these circumstances really have to be new and unforeseeable

[304] Cass. civ., 9 January 1856 (7 cases) DP 1856, 1, p. 33, report Nicias-Gaillard, which considered that an unpredictable increase in a contingent fee did not constitute force majeure since it would not make the performance of an insurance contract against the risks of military recruitment impossible. Despite changing circumstances, the contract should be declared valid: Cass. civ., 11 March 1856, DP 1856, 1, p. 100; 2 April 1856, DP 1856, 1, p. 101; 7 March 1859, 1, p. 118. See also Cass. civ., 24 March 1874 (2nd case), S. 1874, 1, p. 428.

[305] DP 1876, 1, p. 193, note A. Giboulot; S. 1876, 1, 161.

[306] Cass. civ., 6 March 1876, (*De Galliffet* v. *Commune de Pélissanne*) DP 76.1.195.S. Giboulot, 76.1.161, *Grands arrêts* n°94.

[307] Cf.: Cass. com., 3 November 1992, '*arrêt Huard*', Bull. civ. 1992 IV n° 338, p. 241, JCP; 24 November 1993, n° 46–7, p. 469. See also, Cass. com., 24 November 1998, Bull. civ. 1998 IV n° 277, p. 232, *JCPE*; 22 July 1999, n° 29, p. 1242, Obs. C. Jamin.

upon the conclusion of the contract and whether they have to be beyond the control of the parties.

A report (by Professor Catala and his team of distinguished legal scholars) recommending that the French Civil Code be reformed was submitted to the French Minister of Justice on 22 September 2005. It is currently still under discussion and the Ministry of Justice is preparing to revise the Civil Code based on this report.[308] The report does not expressly recognise the doctrine of *imprévision* because the drafters consider that the parties themselves have to foresee the difficulties in performing their obligations.[309] But the draft does introduce a rule that recognises the relevance of unexpected circumstances. Article 1135-1 of the draft Cciv allows the parties to insert a renegotiation clause in the case of unexpected circumstances that affect the equilibrium of the contract so that one of the parties loses its interest in performing the contract. Article 1135-2 Cciv provides that, in the absence of such a clause, the parties can request the president of the court of first instance to order a renegotiation. This draft article specifies that the negotiations must be conducted in good faith. If such negotiations are of no avail, the parties can terminate the contract. With reference to the UNIDROIT Principles, it has been suggested that such negotiations must be conducted on a constructive and timely basis.[310] It has been pointed out that the proposals for the adaptation of a contract must be in conformity with the original contractual framework. Damages can be claimed if one party does not negotiate in good faith.[311] There are many authors who argue in favour of the renegotiation of a contract by the judge if there are unexpected circumstances.[312]

The draft prepared by the Ministry of Justice goes further; in the case of failure of the renegotiation by the parties, the judge can not only terminate the contract (as recommended in the Catala report) but he is also entitled to revise it in agreement with the parties.

[308] See Art. 136 of the report presented by the Ministry of Justice in July 2008 to the Parliament.

[309] See commentary, p. 35, by A. Ghozi.

[310] S. Primont, *L'économie du contrat* (Aix-Marseille: Presses Universitaires, 2004), p. 272, n°414.

[311] *Ibid.*, p. 273.

[312] See for a revision of the contract by the judge: C. Jamin, 'Révision et intangibilité du contrat ou la double philosophie de l'article 1134 du code civil', (1998) *Droit et patrimoine*, 46, 55 *et seq.*; C. Thibierge-Guelfucci, 'Libres propos sur la transformation du droit des contrats', (1997) RTD. civ. 357, n° 11 s., 366; Ripert had previously written 'l'immutabilité du contrat apparaît comme un anachronisme', *La règle morale*, n° 84

B. *Other concepts*

Imprévision can be distinguished from other concepts which might also be relevant when it comes to a change of circumstances.

(a) Force majeure

In general, the courts are reluctant to equate an unforeseen event rendering the contract more onerous with an impossibility to perform. Accordingly, new circumstances which make the performance substantially more difficult do not constitute a case of force majeure.[313] However, some decisions have given this concept a wide interpretation so that it can be extended to cases of changed circumstances. To give an example, force majeure has been applied in cases of frustration of purpose. The famous case, well known in comparative law, of *Dispot Merlin* v. *Robillard* is the best example. A contract between the parties regulated an express service by road between Rouen and Paris. Two years later, with unexpected speed, a rail connection between these two cities was established. The judge allowed the contract to be terminated by applying the doctrine of force majeure.[314]

The way in which the doctrine of force majeure is applied depends on how the effects of an obligation are defined.[315] In one case, the lessor was released from his obligation to repair because the rented property could not be retained without excessive expenses. Although it did not make the performance of the contract impossible but merely more costly, it came close to a fortuitous loss. This was based on the definition

[313] See J. Carbonnier, *Les obligations* (Paris: PUF, 21st edn, 1998), vol. IV, n°144, p. 270; P. H. Antonmattéi, *Contribution à l'étude de la force majeure* (Paris: LGDJ, 1992), n°118, p. 82; Voirin, *De l'imprévision*, pp. 81–4, Cass. civ., 18 January 1950, 1950, I, p. 227.

[314] Comm. Rouen, 28 August 1843, upheld on appeal Rouen, 9 February 1844, D., 1845, p. 4.

[315] Applying the doctrine of force majeure, it is important to establish the content of an obligation. Tunc distinguishes between obligations of means and obligations to procure. If the contractual obligation qualifies as an obligation of means, the debtor is only liable if he is proved to be at fault, whereas with regard to obligations to procure, the debtor bears the burden of proof that he was not at fault. Nevertheless, Tunc considered that *imprévision*, on the one hand, and the determination of the content of an obligation, on the other, are distinct. While *imprévision* extends to the question whether the contract must be continued or terminated, this doctrine assesses the level of 'diligence' which is required in the performance of the obligation. Cf. A. Tunc, 'Force majeure et absence de faute en matière contractuelle', (1945) RTDCiv, 1945, 235; A. Tunc, 'La force majeure dans ses rapports avec le contenu de l'obligation contractuelle', (1946) JT, 1946, 313.

of the content of the lessor's obligation.[316] The obligation to repair was held not to extend to repairs caused by unforeseeable circumstances, which led to substantial expenses.

(b) *Cause*

A *cause* is the legal reason for an obligation, but it is also used as an expression for the motives or the counterpart of an obligation. In the absence of a *cause*, an obligation does not have to be performed. In the last few years, this concept has been applied more and more frequently.[317] The *cause* must be present at the formation of the contract so that future developments are consequently not taken into consideration. However, some situations are very close to the concepts of *imprévision* and frustration of purpose. If, for example, a patent does not lead to the results that the parties had sought in the contract, case law considers that the contract lacks any *cause*.[318] Similarly, a contract concluded between potential heirs and a genealogist was held to lack a *cause* when the heirs could have had knowledge of the succession without the intervention of a genealogist. A promise to sell agreed in 1908 but only invoked in 1965 was declared void due to a lack of *cause* because the price had become ridiculous.[319] In certain borderline cases, future circumstances can deprive a contract of its *cause*, which is seen as the purpose of the contract.[320]

(c) Mistake

A contract which has been concluded due to a mistake is void. A mistake is only considered relevant if (i) it determined the consent of the mistaken party, (ii) if it concerns essential qualities of the object of the contract, and (iii) if the mistaken party is not at fault. A unilateral mistake is not operable under the doctrine of mistake.[321] A mistake

[316] See, Y. Rouquet, 'De l'étendue de l'obligation d'entretien du bailleur', (2001) *Dalloz*, 3622.

[317] J. Ghestin, *La notion d'erreur en droit positif français actuel* (Paris: LGDJ, 1963), pp. 262 *et seq.* Cf. J.M. Guegen, 'Le renouveau de la cause en tant qu'instrument de justice contractuelle', (1999) D., 1999, 352; criticising this concept, see X. Lagarde, 'Sur l'utilité de la théorie de la cause', (2007) D., 740; the draft Catala maintains the concept of *cause* (see Arts. 1124–1126–1).

[318] Cass., 21 February 1837, S, 1837, I, p. 187; 22 August 1844, S, 1844, I, p. 831; Cass. req., 12 April 1861, S., I, p. 735. J. Ghestin, *L'erreur*, n. 220.

[319] Cass.civ., 20 February 1974, Bull.civ., III, n° 85, p. 65.

[320] See *Société pour l'extenstion et l'embellissement de la ville de Biarritz* v. *Guillaume*, quoted by E. de Gaudin de la Grande, 'La cause', *Jurisclasseur Périodique*, Art. 1131–3 C.civ.

[321] Cass. 24 April 2003, n° 01–17.458 (n° 503 FS-P+B), (2004) D, 450.

must be present at the formation of the contract; mistakes as to future circumstances cannot be taken into consideration. For example, the fact that an advertisement is not as successful as expected is not sufficient to apply the rules of mistake.[322]

A mistake concerning motives is only considered relevant if the motives and their realisation in the future become part of the contractual agreement. Some borderline cases concern the following situation: a piece of land was sold and the intention of the buyer was to build a house.[323] No guarantee was given by the seller that planning permission would be granted, but the property was sold at the normal price for building land. Furthermore, the seller knew of the buyer's plans. Planning permission was eventually refused, however. In the absence of a contractual guarantee the seller was not held liable. However, the doctrine of mistake was applied.[324] This case concerned circumstances which were present at the formation of the contract (no planning permission) although there were strongly related unexpected developments which subsequently occurred (the refusal of planning permission although both contracting parties had expected that it would be granted).

(d) *Sujétions imprévues* (unforeseen burden)

The doctrine of *sujétions imprévues* applies under similar conditions as *imprévision*, i.e., with regard to new circumstances that are unforeseeable and beyond the control of the parties leading to a substantial distortion of the contractual framework. But contrary to *imprévision*, it concerns ordinary circumstances which are a *natural* occurrence (for instance, the discovery of rocks in the ground) in a construction contract. Sporadically, the courts have extended this doctrine to cases where the circumstances did not have a natural essence. This has been the case with regard to the increased prices for raw materials.[325]

[322] See Cass., 16 May 1939, *Giurisprudenza comparata di diritto civile*, 1948, n°88 and obs. G. B. Funaioli. See J. Ghestin, *L'erreur*, p. 63.

[323] See also Rennes, 28 March 1999: The case also concerned a contract for the sale of land where planning permission was subsequently refused. The Court of Appeal decided that the lack of a possibility to build constituted a substantial quality of the land and applied the regime of hidden defects instead of the regime of mistake. An appeal was rejected, Cass.civ. 11 February 1981, Bull.civ., III, n°31.

[324] Riom, 17 May 1979, D., 1980, J, p. 12 with obs. G. A.

[325] See civ. Brussels, 11ch; 30 May 1969, *SABCA* v. *État belge*, unpublished, confirmed by Brussels, 4th ch., 10 December 1970, RG 1753, quoted by A. de Grand Ry, M A. Flamme and P. Mathei, n° 374, p. 607.

If the requirements of *sujétions imprévues* are met, French law recognises a change of circumstances and grants the contractor an indemnity.[326] Article 1793 Cciv provides that, in a construction contract, the price of the work cannot be modified when a lump-sum payment has been stipulated. This article has been subject to various exceptions in cases of a substantial disruption of the contractual argreement due to unforeseen circumstances.[327]

(e) Interpretation

According to Article 1156 Cciv, in the case of doubt, judges will interpret the will of the parties in order to determine the effects of a contract. Frequently, parties have not thought about various situations that give rise to a dispute and have not expressly covered this matter in the contract. Some authors have denounced the hypocrisy of determining a will that does not exist arguing that a more honest approach would be to construe a solution based on good faith or usage.[328] The *rebus sic stantibus* clause is related to interpretation. The parties only accept that they are bound by the contract on the basis of an implied term that the contract will not be binding if unforeseeable circumstances occur that render the performance of the contract extremely burdensome for one of the parties.[329]

Judges have, for instance, applied the mechanism of interpretation in the following case of unexpected circumstances: a labour contract signed before World War II contained a clause referring to the jurisdiction of Rouen. The war divided the country into two parts and the contracting parties were in the free zone of the country. The judge disregarded the competence clause and held that the court of Lyon had jurisdiction.[330]

(f) *Lésion*

The doctrine of *lésion* allows a party to rescind the contract when there is a profound imbalance between the values of the respective obligations

[326] F. Llorens, *Contract d'enterprise et marché de travaux publics* (Paris: LGDJ, 1981), p. 300; Cass. civ., 23 June 1873 and Cass. req, 20 April 1874, DP, 329; Cass. civ. 6 March 1967, JCP, IV, 58.

[327] L. Fin-Langer, *L'équilibre contractuel* (Paris: LGDJ, 2002), p. 384, n° 542; Cass., 8 March 1965, GP, 1997, 32 with obs. M. Peisse; Cass. civ., 12 March 1997, Bull, III, n°54; S. Primont, *L'économie*, p. 274.

[328] H. L. J. Mazeaud, M. de Juglart and F. Cliabas, *Leçons de droit civil* (Paris: Montchrestien, 1978), vol. II. n° 346; Llorens, *Contract d'enterprise*, p. 302; J. Maynau, *Les fictions de contrats dans le Code civil et depuis le Code civil*, Thesis (Montpellier: 1924), p. 146; F. Terre, *L'influence de la volonté individuelle et qualification* (Paris: LGDJ, 1957), p. 200.

[329] X. Bomsel, *La théorie de l'imprévision en droit civil français* (Paris: Jouve, 1922), p. 22.

[330] Cass. soc., 11 June 1942, DC, 1943, p. 135 with obs. J. Flour.

at the time of concluding the contract.[331] This doctrine is only recognised by the legislator under specific assumptions.[332] A change of circumstances after the conclusion of the contract, as a general rule, does not give rise to the notion of *lésion*.[333]

There are some cases, however, in which the courts have invoked *lésion* in a case of unexpected circumstances. For example, a judge resorted to *lésion* instead of *imprévision* to justify the rescission of a contract. The contract, concluded just before World War I, granted one of the parties an option to buy property some years later at a fixed price. The option could be cancelled within five years. Due to a significant depreciation in currency after World War I, the actual price represented only one third of the value of the original agreed price. In order to overcome this unjust result, the judge applied the doctrine of *lésion*.[334] This solution was confirmed by the legislator in the Act of 28 November 1949, according to which a *lésion*, in the case of a unilateral promise to sell, must be assessed at the time of performance.[335]

(g) Good faith and equity

The parties are bound by the content of a contract, but the contract must be performed in accordance with the norms derived from the law, usage and equity. The relationship between good faith (Article 1134(3) Cciv) and equity is not clearly defined. Good faith can entail an obligation to renegotiate a contract. However, the effects of good faith remain uncertain in French law.[336] However, it is admitted that, in principle, good faith cannot have a corrective effect.[337] In a recent decision, the Cour de Cassation refused to intervene concerning the content of contractual obligations.[338] The judge nevertheless sanctioned an unfair use of contractual rights. For example, it needs to be stressed as mentioned

[331] C. Chantepie, *La lésion*, (Paris: LGDJ, 2006), p. 1; Fin-Langer, '*L'équilibre contractuel*'; M. A. Perot-Morel, *De l'équilibre des prestations dans la conclusion du contrat* (Paris: Dalloz, 1961).

[332] For instance, in case of the sale of land, if the difference in value is higher than seven twelfths; Arts. 1674 *et seq.* Cciv.

[333] P. Voirin, *De l'imprévision*, pp. 70 *et seq.*; J. Ghestin, *Le contrat*, p. 451; B. Margo, *Lésion 'a posteriori' et imprévision dans les contrats*, Thesis (Paris: 1949), pp. 150–79.

[334] See Cass. req., 19 April 1926, S, 1926, I, p. 128. See Article 1674 Cciv.

[335] Art.1675 (2) Cciv.

[336] See B. Fauvarque-Cosson and S. Amrani Mekki, 'Droit des contrats', (2007) *Dalloz*, 2966.

[337] C. Albiges, *De l'équité en droit privé*, 200, n° 305 (Paris: LGDJ, 2000); concerning the distinction between Arts. 1134(3) and Art. 1135 Cciv, see P. Jacques, 'Regards sur l'article 1135 du Code civil', (2005) *Dalloz*, 295.

[338] Cass. com., 10 July 2007, n° 06–14.768, 2007, AJ 1955, obs. X. Delpech.

earlier that the obligation of renegotiation in case of change of circumstances is based on good faith.

Some authors propose that equity could have a corrective function so that the judge can adjust the contract in case of a change of circumstances.[339] Article 1135 Cciv permits a court to impose obligations on the parties on the basis of equity while Article 1134(3) Cciv concerns the behaviour of the parties in the performance of the contract.[340]

(h) Deferred payment

Debtors can incur difficulties in making payment due to unforeseeable circumstances. In such situations the judge is entitled to reschedule the payment according to Art. 1244–1 Cciv. This provision cannot be considered as a rule concerning unexpected circumstances because the content of the debtor's obligation remains unchanged.[341] However, in connection with the problems in performing obligations after World War I, some judges used this provision as a legal basis for correcting contractual obligations.[342]

(i) Unjust enrichment

The rules on unjust enrichment could have been considered as a legal basis for renegotiating a contract in case of an imbalance in the contractual obligations where one party would profit to the detriment of the other party who suffers a loss. The application of unjust enrichment is dependant upon four conditions, namely (i) an enrichment of one party, (ii) at the expense of the other party, (iii) a causal link between the enrichment and the expense, and (iv) subsidiarity, which means that this doctrine will not apply if the enrichment has a legal cause. This concept does not apply, in principle, to a change of circumstances because in such cases the unjust enrichment can be put down to a cause. The agreed terms of the contract provide a legal ground for the enrichment and the expense incurred.[343]

[339] Tallon, 'La révision du contrat'; F. Cherigny, *La révision judiciaire des conventions en droit privé français*, Thesis (Poitiers: 1994).

[340] Jacques, 'Regards sur l'artide 1135' 306, n° 163.

[341] D. Philippe, *Le Changement de circonstances et bouleversement de l'économie contractuelle* (Brussels: Bruylant, 1986), p. 143; Voirin, *De l'imprévision*, p. 208.

[342] M. Planiol and G. Ripert, *Traité pratique de droit civil française* (Paris: LGDJ, 1930), vol. VI, p. 549; P. Voirin, *De l'imprévision*, p. 208; Rouen, 19 May 1871 (the war between France and Germany), D., 1871, 2, 179.

[343] J. Ghestin, Ch. Jamin and M. Billiau, *Les effets du contrat* (Paris: LGDJ, 3rd edn, 2001), n° 312, p. 357.

Belgium

A. Imprévision

(a) Definition

In the Belgian legal discourse, the doctrine of *imprévision* is the focus of attention as a form of relief in cases in which one party is extraordinarily burdened by the contract due to unexpected circumstances. As in French law, this concept applies if new circumstances arise which are beyond the control of the parties and which were unforeseeable, render the contract substantially more burdensome or substantially alter the economic balance between the obligations of the parties.[344] The more general approach of frustration of purpose is not covered by this doctrine.

(b) Recognition in Belgian law

With regard to the historical development, the thoughts presented in the French section of this overview apply to Belgian law as well.

The Belgian Cour de Cassation does not recognise the doctrine of *imprévision.*[345] However, some lower courts have referred to this principle, but have rejected its application due to the fact that the conditions for its application have not been met.[346] In the literature, various authors argue that this principle should be recognised.[347]

[344] Cass., 30 October 1924, Pas., 1924, I, p. 565; H. De Page, *Traité élémentaire de droit civil belge* (Brussels: Bruylant, 3rd edn, 1964), p. 560. See for criticism of these definitions D. Philippe obs. comm. Brussels, 16 January 1979, JT, 1980, pp. 459 *et seq.*; L. Vael, 'Beschouwingen over het imprevisieleerstuk: omtrent de eventuele ontsluiting van de overeenkomst in geval van een gewijzigd contractueel verhoudingskader', in: Ludo Comelis *et al.* (eds.), *Liber Amicorum Tijdschrift voor Privaatrecht en Marcel Storme* (Ghent: Story Scientia, 2004), pp. 703 *et seq.*; P. Wéry, 'L'imprévision et ses succédanés', (1996) JLMB, 105; D. Philippe, *Le changement.*

[345] See Cass., 14 April 1994, Pas., 1994, I, p. 365; 30 June 2006, role n° C050/85F, www.jurudat.be. See also Cass., 7 February 1994, *Juridat*, JC94271_2, Pas., I, p.150; Cass., 4 September 2000, *Juridat*, JC00942_1, Pas., 2000, I, p.345; JL02CG1_2; Liège, 7e ch. 16 December 2002, JL02CG1_2; Cass., 20 April 2006, *Juridat*, JC064K1_6.

[346] S. Heremans, 'Le bouleversement de l'économie contractuelle à la suite d'un changement de circonstances : quelques éclairages nouveaux', (2000) RGDC, vol. II 573 with the analysis of various decisions, among others comm. Liège, 15 September 1995, RDC, 1998, p. 446; Wéry, 'L'imprévision et ses succédanés', 105.

[347] See A. Van Oevelen, 'Kroniek van het verbintenissenrecht' (1993–2004), RW, 1644; S. Heremans, 'Le bouleversement', 573; L. Vael, 'Beschouwingen', p. 703; C. Delforge, *La spécificité des contrats à long terme*, Thesis, (UCL, 2006), p. 247; E. De Bock, 'Stijgende metaalprijzen, is er tergemoetkoming' (2005) NJW, 477; D. Philippe, *Le changement*; J.-F. Romain, *Le principe de convention-loi (portée et limites): réflexions au sujet d'un nouveau paradigme contractuel – Les obligations contractuelles* (Brussels: Jeune barreau de Brussels, 2000), n° 38.1, p. 142.

Unlike in France, the Conseil d'État is not competent to deal with public contracts; therefore the restrictive approach of the Belgian Cour de Cassation concerning unforeseen circumstances would, in principle, also apply to public contracts.

We can underline a recent decision of the Supreme Court of 19 June 2009. In a long-term international contract, the price of raw materials rose sharply. The Court of Appeal proceeded to adapt the contract. This decision was confirmed by the Cour de Cassation. The court considered that on the basis of Art. 7 of the Vienna Convention, the international usages apply to the sale of goods. UNIDROIT principles are international usages. These principles recognise the adaptation of the contract in case of change of circumstances; consequently the contract could in this case be adapted on this basis. Furthermore, the Supreme Court considered that Art. 79 of the Vienna Convention, which exonerates the debtor in case of impediment, must have a broad interpretation and must also apply in cases of change of circumstances that render the performance of the contract substantially more burdensome.

(c) Specific legislation

After World War I, specific provisions with a temporary character were enacted, designed to alleviate the consequences of wartime hardship.[348] Furthermore, in specific sectors statutes were later enacted on a permanent basis in order to deal with unexpected circumstances concerning especially long-term contracts,[349] like lease contracts (Art. 7 of the Law of 16 February 1991 on residential leases, Art. 6 of the Law of 30 April 1951 on commercial leases,[350] Arts. 17 *et seq.* of the Law of 4 November 1969 on tenancies and leasehold property[351]), divorce by mutual consent (Art. 1288 of the Belgian Civil Code (Cciv)) or public works (Art. 16 of the general terms on public works). According to Art. 710 Cciv the judge can also order the expiry of a servitude when it has lost its purpose for the beneficiary.

[348] Act of 11 October 1919, *Moniteur belge*, 29 October 1919; see D. Philippe, *Le changement*, p. 156.

[349] S. Heremans, 'Le bouleversement', 473 *et seq.*; Philippe, *Le changement*, p. 156. De Bock, 'Stijgende Metaa Lprijzen', 477.

[350] See D. Philippe, *Le changement*, p. 162.

[351] Law of 15 June 1955 modified by the law of 2 July 1974.

B. Concepts dealing with unexpected circumstances

(a) Force majeure

Like the doctrine of *imprévision*, force majeure addresses circumstances arising after the formation of the contract and which were unforeseeable and beyond the control of the parties.[352] Force majeure is based on the notion that not only the equilibrium of the contract is distorted, but the actual performance of the contract is rendered impossible.[353] In contrast, *imprévision* only concerns an economic imbalance in the contract.[354]

The courts have often given a broad interpretation to the concept of impossibility and the position is that the debtor is not required to ruin himself by performing the contract.[355] Thus, for example, expensive renovations to living accommodation by a landlord due to new legislation have been considered as a case of force majeure. The judge considered that these expenses were disproportionate to the equilibrium of the contract.[356]

(b) *Caducité*

The doctrine of *caducité* applies if, after the formation of the contract, new circumstances arise that lead to a lacuna regarding an essential element of the contract (i.e., the subject-matter of the contract). *Caducité* does not necessarily require a distortion of the contractual equilibrium, as is the case with *imprévision*, or an impossibility to perform, like force majeure; furthermore, the new circumstances must not have been unforeseeable. *Caducité* allows the aggrieved party to terminate the contract *ex nunc*.[357] The lapsing of an index mechanism to determine

[352] A. Van Oevelen, *kroniek*, n° 40, 1659.

[353] See D. Philippe and S. Michaux, *La force majeure, Traité de droit des obligations* (Brussels: Kluwer, 2002).

[354] Brussels, (1st chambre) 25 January 2000, *Juridat*, JB41246_3.

[355] Comm. Brussels, 9 March 1981, JCB, 1982, p. 165.

[356] Civ. Brussels, 15 February 1973, JT, 1973, p. 258.

[357] Civ. Namur, 26 April 1990, RRD, 1990, p. 489; J. F. Romain, 'Clarifications concernant la théorie de la caducité des actes juridiques, en particulier des libéralités testamentaires, par disparition de leur cause-mobile determinant'; obs. under Cass., 21 January 2000, RCJB, 2004, p. 77; for a recent discussion on the application of this doctrine following the entering into force of regulation 1400/2002 in case of exclusive distribution agreements, comm. Brussels, 28 March 2006, JT, 2006, and observations P. Kileste and C. Staudt, p. 511; P.-A. Foriers, *La caducité des obligations contractuelles par disparition d'un élément essentiel à leur formation* (Brussels: Bruylant, 1998).

prices in a long-term supply contract has been considered to be an example of *caducité*.[358]

In a decision dated 16 November 1989, the Cour de Cassation admitted that the doctrine of *caducité* not only applies in cases where certain elements of the contract are absent, but also when the *cause*, i. e., the purpose of the contract, is frustrated, thereby converging with the notion of frustration of purpose. However, the decision mentioned above concerned a gratuitous contract and it is questionable whether this doctrine could also be applied with regard to non-gratuitous contracts. More recently, the Cour de Cassation has held in an important case that this doctrine is not relevant for non-gratuitous contracts.[359]

(c) *Sujétions imprévues*

The doctrine of *sujétions imprévues* applies in similar cases as *imprévision*. It also requires that newly arising circumstances, which were unforeseeable and beyond the control of the parties, disturb the framework of the contract. In contrast to *imprévision*, it concerns naturally occurring circumstances (e.g., the discovery of rocks in the ground) in a works contract. Under such conditions, Belgian law recognises a change of circumstances.[360] *Sujétions imprévues* has also been applied by the courts, although rarely, in cases where the circumstances were not ones which occurred naturally. This was the case with regard to price increases for raw materials, for example.[361]

(d) Good faith

Under Belgian law good faith requires collaboration and cooperation between the parties in the performance of the contract.

With regard to the performance of a contract, the concept of good faith is recognised by Art. 1134(3) Cciv, while the aspect of good faith

[358] See D. Philippe, 'Les clauses relatives au changement de circonstances dans les contrats à long terme' in: *La vie du contrat à prestations successives* (Brussels: Bruylant, 1991), p. 170.

[359] Rôle C980335F, N. Justel, F-20000121-7.

[360] Brussels, 8 March 2001, *Juridat*, JB01381_1, RG 95/AR. See for a recent application, Brussels, 4th ch, 3 April 2007, RG 1999/AR/2591.

[361] See civ. Brussels, 11ch. 30 May 1969, *SABCA* v. *Etat belge*, unpublished, confirmed by Brussels, 4th ch., 10 December 1970, RG, p. 1753, quoted by A. De Grand Ry, M.A. Flamme and P. Mathéi, *Droit administratif* (Brussels: Bruylant, 1989), n° p. 374, p. 607.

with regard to the completion of a contract is recognised by Art. 1135 Cciv.[362]

In the literature four different implications of good faith are distinguished, namely (i) completion, (ii) modification, (iii) derogation or (iv) adaptation of a contract. However, the Cour de Cassation has rejected the adaptive effect of good faith.[363] Sometimes the courts have decided that insisting on the performance of a contract that is not based on a just equilibrium is contrary to good faith.[364]

The completing effect of good faith can, in principle, be based on Art 1135 Cciv but only as far as this principle can accommodate a change of circumstances. For instance, when an unforeseen event occurs, the judge can complete the contract in order to provide a legal regime for this new circumstance.[365]

(e) Mistake

Mistake requires that a substantial element, which induced one of the parties to enter into the contract, was not present when the contract was concluded.[366] A mistake relating to future circumstances cannot be taken into consideration.[367]

A mistake as to motives is only accepted if such motives were integrated in the framework of the contract.[368] When, for example, a feasibility study carried out by the seller was a decisive element in the buyer entering into the contract, and the subsequent sales were not in line with the forecasts in the study, the Cour de Cassation held that the contract was void.[369]

The doctrine of *sujétions imprévues* has been based on mistake in civil law. Other cases can be cited: in the case of a transaction the judge can

[362] D. Philippe, 'De Rechter en de inhoud van de overeenkomst', in: *De overeenkomst vandaag en morgen* (Brussels: Kluwer, 1990), pp. 543 *et seq.*

[363] Cass., 7 February 1994, *Juridat*, JC94271_2, Pas., I p. 150; Cass., 4 September 2000, *Juridat*, JC00942_1, Pas., 2000, I, p. 345; JL02CG1_2; Liège, 7th ch., 16 December 2002, JL02CG1_2.

[364] Liège, 21 December 2001, JT, 2002, p. 564; see Liège 12 October 1999, JLMB, 99/1221.

[365] Philippe, *De inhoud.*

[366] See Cass., 24 September 2007; comm. Mons, 26 April 2004, *RGDC*, 2006, p. 241.

[367] See Ghent, 12 May 1923, Pas., 1924, II, p. 1; Brussels, 8 June 1972, Pas., 1972, II, p. 167.

[368] See Ghent, 5 April 1979, *Recueil general de l'enregistrement et du notariat* (1980), p. 436, n° 22551.

[369] Cass., 27 October 1995, Pas., 1995, I, p. 95, JT, 1996, 61 (this case is not so clear-cut because the feasilibity study had been carried out by the other party; the buyer could also have invoked misrepresentation); Cass., 3 March 1967, Pas., I, p. 811.

amend this transaction when there is a radical change of circumstances.[370]

(f) Cause

On the one hand, *cause* refers to the counterpart of an obligation. On the other hand, a *cause* is also defined as the motive for entering into the contract. The *cause* must be operable when a contract is concluded. Changes of circumstances occurring after the conclusion of the contract are disregarded.[371]

The concepts of *cause* and mistake can be clearly distinguished: a *cause* is the reason for entering into a contract whereas the concept of mistake refers to a false conception of important elements when contracting. There are, however, borderline situations between both concepts, in particular in cases of a mistake as to the *cause* of the contract.[372]

(g) Interpretation

The judge determines the will of the parties by interpretation on the basis of Art. 1156 Cciv.[373] If the concept of interpretation is given a wide scope, the judge can also determine what the parties implied in the contract when there has been a change of circumstances. There have indeed been decisions in which interpretation has been invoked as the legal basis for amending the contract in cases of changed circumstances.[374]

Furthermore, the presence of a tacit condition precedent can be implied by the judge on the basis of interpreting the contract. For instance, with the sale of land the parties may assume that planning permission will be granted. If planning permission is refused after the

[370] See Philippe, *Le Changement*, p. 183; Cass., 28 March 1974, Pas., I, p. 779.

[371] H. De Page, *Opinion*, p. 368, n. 18; P. Van Ommeslaghe, 'Observations sur la théorie de la cause dans la jurisprudence et la doctrine moderne', (1970) RCJB, 326; P. Van Ommeslaghe, 'Examen de jurisprudence', (1975) RCJB 462; Mons, 31 January 1979, JT, 1979, p. 643; D. Philippe, 'Economie contractuelle, cause, erreur et interprétation du contrat', (2002) *Mélanges J. Herbots*, 295.

[372] This leads to frequent discussions in the literature related to the justification and definition of the concept of cause. See Van Ommeslaghe, 'Théorie de la cause', 326.

[373] See for an analysis of the principles of interpretation in Belgian law, L. Cornil, concl. sub Cass., 4 April 1941, Pas., 1941, I, p. 120; Philippe, 'Economie contractuelle'.

[374] See Civ. Brussels, 24 May 1884, Pas., 1884, III, p. 247; see P. Orianne, *Le contrat de concession* (Novelles), p. 247; E. Causin, 'L'interprétation des contrats', in: Michel van de Kerchove (ed.), *L'interprétation en droit* (Brussels: Bruylant, 1978).

conclusion of the contract, the contract can be brought to an end *ex tunc* on the basis of the condition precedent doctrine.[375]

However, it is questionable whether the concept of interpretation can be given a very broad scope as parties often do not take a change of circumstances into consideration when drafting the contract. If the parties did not express their will at all on this issue, it is misleading to refer to the concept of interpretation. It would be better to speak of the completion of the contract and not of interpretation.[376]

(h) Abuse of rights

The doctrine of abuse of rights is applied when a person uses his legal position intentionally to cause harm to another person or to obtain an advantage which is disproportionate in comparison to the damage caused to another person.[377]

Based on the doctrine of abuse of rights, the courts might consider it abusive to insist on the performance of the contract if the debtor makes a substantial commercial loss and the creditor realises high profits.[378] Nevertheless, Belgian law does not recognise, in principle, unexpected circumstances on the basis of an abuse of rights.

(i) *Lésion*

The principle of *lésion* allows the contract to be rescinded when there is a profound imbalance between the value of the respective obligations at the time when the contract is concluded. As in France, this doctrine is only recognised in specific cases.[379] Furthermore, a change of circumstances after the conclusion of the contract generally cannot be taken into consideration.

However, there is also case law where the judge has applied the principle of *lésion* in the case of unexpected circumstances. For example, a judge relied on *lésion* instead of *imprévision* to justify the rescission of a contract. The contract, concluded just before World War I, granted one of the parties an option to buy property some years later at a fixed price. Due to a significant currency depreciation after World War I, the current monetary value represented only one third of the price agreed

[375] See Liège, 25 March 1970; J.Lg, 1970–1971, p. 115.
[376] See Philippe, *De inhoud*, pp. 543–59.
[377] P.-A. Foriers, 'Observations sur le thème de l'abus de droit en matière contractuelle', (1994) RCJB, 189–240.
[378] See L. Campion, *La théorie de l'abus des droits* (Brussels: Bruylant, 1925), n° 226–7.
[379] See H. De Page, *Traité elementaire*, n° 81.

upon at the time the option was granted. In order to overcome this unjust result, the judge applied *lésion*.[380]

(j) Unjust enrichment

This concept has been envisioned as a basis for a renegotiation of the contract when there is an imbalance in the contractual obligations; indeed, in this situation one party would be enriched to the detriment of the other.

Unjust enrichment can be applied under four conditions, namely (i) the enrichment of one party, (ii) the impoverishment of the other party, (iii) a causal link between both and (iv) subsidiarity. Subsidiarity means that the principle cannot apply if there is a valid legal reason for this enrichment. This concept does not apply, in principle, in cases of unexpected circumstances because the unjust enrichment has a legal cause, i.e., the contract, which can constitute a legal ground for the enrichment and impoverishment of the respective parties.

ENGLAND AND RELATED JURISDICTIONS

England and Ireland

A. Introduction

Both English and Irish contract law are rooted in the common law tradition. Until the foundation of the Irish state in 1922 the structural links between the Irish legal system and the English common law were extremely strong.[381] The administration of justice in Ireland revolved around the same court structure as that found in England and, with the abolition of the Irish Parliament in the 1800 Act of Union, the Westminster Parliament legislated for Ireland until 1922. As a result, some of the key statutes that were in force in Ireland, statutes that passed into Irish law in 1922 by way of transitional provisions in treaty law and under statute, were Westminster Parliament statutes. Indeed, the Sale of Goods Act 1893, as amended by subsequent Irish statutes,

[380] See Cass., 13 July 1923, Pas., 1923 with the conclusions of Terlinden, rejecting recourse against Brussels, 5 April 1922, Pas., 1922, II, p. 65, appeal by the judgment of civ. Brussels, 22 June 1921, Pas., 1923, II, p. 67; civ. Ghent, 23 May 1923, JT, 1921–1924, p. 490; civ. Liège, 10 July 1923, Pas., 1923, III, p. 145. This was an incorrect application of the doctrine of *lésion* because the imbalance was not present when the contract was concluded, but only when the contract was performed.

[381] See generally, R. Byrne and J. P. McCutcheon, *The Irish Legal System* (Dublin: Butterworths, 4th edn, 2001).

remains the basis of Irish sale of goods law. Cases decided by the English courts prior to 1922 are regarded as being of significant precedent value and the doctrine of *stare decisis* is followed by Irish courts. Post–1922 English cases are not binding on Irish courts but decisions of the English appellate courts, and the House of Lords in particular, have strong persuasive value. Cases from Australia, New Zealand and Canada have also been followed by Irish courts.

In the post–1922 period, Irish legislation in the area of contract has not been particularly noteworthy. In particular, Ireland has not legislated in the area of mistake or frustration. The answers to the questions are therefore based upon general common law or equitable principles. In England, too, this is an area mostly governed by common law principles, but there has been some legislative intervention, including in particular the Law Reform (Frustrated Contracts) Act 1943 which provides for the effects of frustration of contract. However, the 1943 Act is limited, in that only certain effects of the doctrine are dealt with – namely the adjustment of the financial position of the parties after they are discharged from their future contractual obligations – and it does not regulate the circumstances in which a contract is frustrated.

Due to the close connection and common tradition of Irish and English law, it appears to be appropriate to present a report on a common basis in the following. As far as differences between both jurisdictions exist, they are pointed out separately.

B. Doctrine of frustration

The idea that a change of circumstances may *of itself* lead to the adjustment or cessation of a contractual obligation is unknown to English and Irish law. A change of circumstances may have some effect within the context of an agreement if the events that have arisen make the bargain fundamentally different from that which was agreed. Concepts that give expression to this possibility are judge-made and include the doctrine of frustration, under which supervening events may have the effect of discharging the parties from future performance. This doctrine of frustration was initially based on implied contract theory, as laid down by Blackburn J. in the English case of *Taylor* v. *Caldwell*:

> When from the nature of the contract it appears that the parties must from the beginning have known that it could not be fulfilled unless when the time for the fulfilment of the contract arrived some particular specified thing continues to exist, so that when entering into the contract they must have contemplated

such continued existence as the foundation of what was to be done, then, in the absence of any express or implied warranty that the thing shall exist, the contract is to be considered a positive contract but *subject to the implied condition* that the parties shall be excused, in case, before breach, performance becomes impossible from the perishing of the thing without the default of the contractor.[382]

The implied term theory was endorsed in Ireland by O'Connor MR in *Cummings* v. *Stewart (No. 2)*.[383] However, the implied term theory is now generally rejected as being a legal fiction - the parties did not in fact contemplate the events which occurred, and furthermore it is virtually impossible to presume that, had they done so, they would have agreed on the effects of those events. Although alternative bases have been suggested,[384] the classic statement of the doctrine is that of Lord Radcliffe in *Davis Contractors Ltd* v. *Fareham UDC*:[385]

Frustration occurs whenever the law recognises that without default of either party a contractual obligation has become incapable of being performed because the circumstances in which the performance is called for would render it a thing radically different from that which was undertaken in the contract. *Non haec in foedera veni*. It was not this that I promised to do.[386]

This is essentially 'an objective test based upon the construction of the contract'.[387]

C. Mistake and implied terms

Frustration is perhaps the best known of the common law mechanisms for dealing with a change in circumstances, but the law relating to contractual mistake is also of importance, for example, when the parties are under varying degrees of misapprehension about the underlying factual or legal situation at the time of entering into the contract. While English and Irish courts do not recognise a general doctrine of good faith - indeed, there is a marked hostility to such a doctrine - judicial willingness to adjust contracts by implying terms into a contract, either on the basis of 'business efficacy' or on the presumed

382 (1863) 3 B & S 826, 833 (emphasis added). 383 [1913] 1 IR 95.

384 For example, Lord Sumner described the doctrine as 'a device by which the rules as to absolute contracts are reconciled with the special exceptions which justice demands': *Hirji Mulji* v. *Cheong Yue SS Co Ltd* [1926] AC 497, 510.

385 [1956] AC 696. 386 [1956] AC 696, 728–9.

387 Per Murphy J. in *Neville & Sons* v. *Guardian Builders Ltd* [1990] ILRM 601 (Ire.).

intention of the parties, can 'soften' the literal meaning of a contract, and, in practice, modify the agreement.

Scotland

A. *Historical development*

According to Lord Cooper, there are two main sources from which the modern Scottish principles of frustration have developed. The first is early cases on *rei interitus*, a term used to describe the situation where there has been '. . . destruction, total or partial, actual or constructive, of some specific thing essential to the performance [of the contract]'.[388] Numerous cases of *rei interitus* exist, particularly in the context of contracts of lease, but also of contracts of sale and hire. It was more usual to class relevant cases as part of the law of property rather than part of the law of contract. A very early discussion of *rei interitus* can be found in the works of one of the institutional writers, Craig.[389] He discusses the particular case of forfeiture of a feudal interest in land justified by the misconduct of the vassal. The case is explained by Craig by reference both to the *condictio causa data causa non secuta* (a remedy used to recover sums or goods given for a specific purpose where that purpose fails),[390] and by reference to *naturalis aequitas*.

The second source of the Scottish principles of frustration is the development of the *condictio causa data causa non secuta* in the works of the institutional writers Stair, Bankton, Erskine and Bell.[391] The *condictio* was subsequently applied in Scottish cases, particularly in the House of Lords case of *Cantiere San Rocco SA* v. *Clyde Shipbuilding & Engineering*

[388] See T. M. Cooper, 'Frustration of Contract in Scots Law', (1946) 28 *Journal of Comparative Legislation*, Pt III, 1, 2.

[389] Sir Thomas Craig, *The Jus Feudale*, original edition 1655 (Edinburgh: W Hodge, 1934).

[390] This action is considered further below. For analysis see G. D. MacCormack, 'The Condictio Causa Data Causa Non Secuta', in: R. Evans-Jones (ed.), *The Civil Law Tradition in Scotland* (Edinburgh: The Stair Society, 1995), p. 253.

[391] A. McDowall, Lord Bankton, *An Institute of the Laws of Scotland in Civil Rights: with Observations on the Agreement or Diversity between them and the Laws of England, (1751–1753)* (Edinburgh: The Stair Society, 1993–1995), vols. 41 and 43, I, pp. 8, 21; Stair, 1st Viscount, (James Dalrymple), *Institutions of the Law of Scotland*, D. M., Walker (ed.), (The University Presses of Glasgow and Edinburgh, 6th edn, 1981), vol. I, p. 7; J. Erskine, 'An Institute of the Law of Scotland', in: J. B. Nicholson (ed.), (Edinburgh: Butterworths/Law Society of Scotland, 8th edn, 1871; reprinted 1989) vol. III,1, p. 10; G. J. Bell, *Principles of the law of Scotland*, (W. Guthrie (ed.), 10th edn, 1899, reprinted with an introduction by W. M. Gordon) (Edinburgh: The Law Society of Scotland and Butterworths, 1989), paras 28 and 530.

Co[392] in 1923. The most influential institutional writer, Stair, discussed the *condictio* in the context of his discussion of the obligation of restitution, an obligation which is distinct from those arising under the law of contract.[393] He notes the use of the *condictio* to recover things given in contemplation of a marriage, where the marriage, which is the cause of the gift, fails to take place.[394]

In a landmark Scottish case,[395] Lord MacMillan approved the following definition of frustration drawn from a posthumous edition of Bell's *Principles of the Law of Scotland*:

> When by the nature of the contract its performance depends on the existence of a particular thing or state of things, the failure or destruction of that thing or state of things, without default on either side, liberates both parties.[396]

The modern formulation depends less on the existence of a particular thing and focuses more on the different nature of the contract in changed circumstances. It can be found in the speeches of Lords Reid and Radcliffe in the English House of Lords case *Davis Contractors Ltd* v. *Fareham UDC*:[397]

> Frustration occurs whenever the law recognises that without default of either party a contractual obligation has become incapable of being performed because the circumstances in which performance is called for would render it a thing radically different from that which was undertaken by the contract. *Non haec in foedera veni*. It was not this that I promised to do.[398]

While this leading definition of frustration is taken from an English House of Lords case the seeds of the new approach were sown in the earlier Scottish House of Lords case *James B Fraser & Co* v. *Denny, Mott & Dickson*.[399] Nevertheless, it remains important to bear in mind that the development of the Scottish principles of frustration has differed in significant respects from the English principles. Referring to Scots and English law, Lord Cooper commented:

[392] 1923 SC (HL) 105. [393] *Ibid.*

[394] See R. Evans-Jones, 'Unjust Enrichment, Contract and the Third Reception of Roman Law', (1993) 109 *Law Quarterly Review*, 663 where he argues that Stair's example was incorrectly applied in *Cantiere San Rocco SA* v. *Clyde Shipbuilding & Engineering Co* 1923 SC (HL) 105.

[395] *James B Fraser & Co* v. *Denny, Mott & Dickson* 1944 SC (HL) 35. [396] Bell, *Principles*, p. 29.

[397] [1956] AC 696. [398] [1956] AC 696, per Lord Radcliffe at 729.

[399] In the speeches of Lords Wright and Porter, 1944 SC (HL) 35.

Though two streams of thought have now in large measure coalesced, their sources lie far apart and each has flowed through its own juristic channel.[400]

Traces of the difference of development in Scotland and England are still visible, most obviously in the difference in rules of unjustified enrichment applied after a contract has been frustrated. In English law, the Law Reform (Frustrated Contracts) Act 1943 applies. In Scots law, the *condictio causa data causa non secuta* applies. This *condictio* has its roots in Roman equity, and provides the pursuer with a remedy to recover things given for a specific purpose where that purpose has failed.

B. Delimitation, borderline cases

It is difficult to identify the boundary line between cases of frustration and impossibility in Scots law. The terms are often used interchangeably. The term 'impossibility' is more commonly found in older texts where it is used as a heading to describe the treatment of legal and practical impossibility and also cases of change of circumstances.[401] By contrast, in a modern context, 'frustration' is the chapter-heading more commonly used. Again, in those more modern works such a chapter would usually encompass cases of impossibility in addition to change of circumstances. The leading modern text devotes only a short section to impossibility in Scots law.[402] New cases are much more likely to be analysed using the concept of frustration rather than impossibility.

It is necessary too to identify the dividing line between the principles of frustration and those of error. As a general rule, the principles of the law of error are most likely to be applicable where an error has prevented the parties from reaching consensus under the contract.[403] In cases of unexpected circumstances, the parties will usually have reached consensus, but the supervening circumstances render the obligations under the contract different from what was expected. The two concepts are almost aligned in one particular area, namely where the subject matter of the contract is destroyed. Where both parties erroneously believe the subject matter to be in existence at the date of formation, this is treated as a case of common error.[404] In theory at least,

400 See Cooper, 'Frustration of Contract' Pt III, 1.

401 See W. M. Gloag, *The Law of Contract* (Edinburgh: W. Green, 2nd edn, 1929), Chapter 19.

402 See W. W. McBryde, *The Law of Contract in Scotland* (Edinburgh: W Green, 3rd edn, 2007), paras 21–26 to 21–29.

403 *Ibid.*, para. 15–01. 404 *Ibid.*, para. 15–36.

such an error renders the contract void.[405] Where the subject matter is destroyed after formation, this is treated as a case of impossibility.[406]

In general in Scots law, there is no right to cancel a long-term contract. Parties may, of course, argue that a term should be implied into the contract providing them with a right to cancel such a contract. It seems that it is only possible to imply such a term in contracts of no fixed term. Where the contract has a fixed term, the courts would refuse to make such an implication because this would conflict with the express term providing the contract with a specific duration.[407]

C. Theoretical basis

There have been several different suggestions as to the theoretical basis of frustration. It seems that originally the legal basis of frustration in Scots law was the power of the court to find a 'just solution' in the circumstances.[408] Emphasis of this legal basis can be found in Lord Wright's approval in a Scottish House of Lords case[409] of Lord Sumner's statement that the doctrine of frustration is really '. . . a device by which the rules as to absolute contracts are reconciled with a special exception which justice demands'.[410] The practical application of that theory recognises that the parties must be released from a contract which, because of changed circumstances, would '. . . in substance be performance of a different contract from that to which the parties agreed'.[411] Although some modern authors continue to identify this as the correct legal basis,[412] this view is not borne out by the modern cases.

A second possible rationale is that the contract was conditional on the continued existence of the subject matter of the contract or the continuation of the existing state of things. It is this idea which lies at the heart of Bell's explanation quoted above.[413] This explanation is

[405] *Ibid.*, para. 15.-36 and see the discussion of the effect of such an error in Case 13.

[406] See *Leitch* v. *Edinburgh Ice and Cold Storage Co Ltd* [1900] 2 F. 904 involving destruction of goods, or *Cantors Properties (Scotland) Ltd* v. *Swears and Wells Ltd* 1978 SC 310 involving the destruction of leased subjects.

[407] McBryde, *Contract*, para. 9-10.

[408] See Cooper, 'Frustration of Contract', Pt III at 5.

[409] *James B Fraser* v. *Denny, Mott & Dickson* 1944 SC (HL) 35 per Lord Wright at 43.

[410] *Hirji Mulji* v. *Cheong Yue Steamship Co Ltd* [1926] AC 497 at 510.

[411] Lord Coulsfield *et al.*, *Gloag and Henderson The Law of Scotland* (Edinburgh: W Green & Son Limited, 12th edn, 2007), para. 11.02.

[412] See the concluding sentence of para. 880, A. D. M. Forte, 'Frustration', in: Sir Thomas Smith *et al.* (eds.), *The Laws of Scotland: Stair Memorial Encyclopaedia* (Edinburgh: Butterworths/Law Society of Scotland, 1987–96), vol XV.

[413] Bell, *Principles*, p. 29.

now discredited in England,[414] and, although it received some recognition in Scotland, it was discredited there early in the twentieth century.[415]

A third possible rationale is that contained in one of the leading modern textbooks, MacQueen and Thomson.[416] Their view could be seen as a development of Bell's view given that it relies on an implied resolutive condition that the contract will, when the time comes for performance, not be incapable of performance. In Scots law a resolutive condition is a condition which, if purified, brings the contract to an end.[417] The authors comment: 'If as a result of a subsequent event, performance of a contract becomes impossible, then the implied resolutive condition is purified and the contract is frustrated.'[418] In their view other implied resolutive conditions may exist providing that performance of the contract will not be illegal, nor radically different from what the parties anticipated at the moment of formation of contract. It is, however, difficult to find support for this view either in academic comment or modern case law.

It seems that the true theoretical basis is one which rests on the rules for construction or interpretation of a contract, the essence of which can be found in Lord Radcliffe's highly influential and oft-quoted speech from *Davis Contractors* quoted above.[419] The rules of interpretation are applied in order to construe the contract in the light of the circumstances in which it was made. This is then compared with the parties' obligations seen in the light of the new circumstances. Those circumstances will only be relevant if they are truly extraneous and do not involve fault on the part of either contracting party.[420]

[414] See E. Peel, *Treitel's Law of Contract* (London: Sweet & Maxwell, 12th edn, 2007), paras. 19–115 to 19–116.

[415] It was recognised in later editions of Bell, *Principles*, see 8th edn, edited by Guthrie, p. 29, but criticised by Gloag, see *Contract*, p. 343.

[416] H. L. MacQueen and J. M. Thomson, *Contract Law in Scotland* (Edinburgh: Totell Publishing, 2nd edn, 2007), para. 4.67.

[417] For the meaning of resolutive conditions see *ibid.*, paras 3.59–3.63.

[418] *Ibid.*, para. 4.70. A similar explanation can be found in some English texts – see Peel, *Treitel's Law of Contract*, paras. 19–118 to 19–119, under the heading 'Foundation of the Contract'.

[419] See also *National Carriers Ltd* v. *Panalpina (Northern) Limited* [1981] AC 675 per Lord Simon at 700.

[420] *Paal Wilson & Co A/S* v. *Partenreederei Hannah Blumenthal* [1983] 1 AC 854 per Lord Brandon at 909.

D. Contractual clauses

The contracting parties in a commercial situation may insert a force majeure clause in the contract. Such a clause will stipulate the consequences where performance becomes impossible for a wide variety of reasons such as war, acts of nature or strikes. The use of such clauses is common, particularly in maritime contracts and in the oil industry,[421] and indeed its usage is considered in the context of shipping in the answer to Case 5. Where such a clause applies, the contract will subsist notwithstanding the frustrating event. It may even provide a mechanism for renegotiation of the contract, an outcome which would not be possible at common law.

E. Administrative contracts

Administrative contracts are not treated as a special class in Scots law, and therefore no special rules apply to them. The general rules on frustration of contract would be applied.

F. Specific legislation

Frustration in Scots law is governed by common law principles rather than any specific statute. In particular it should be noted that the Act which may apply in English law to permit an equitable adjustment of the contracting parties' financial positions following frustration, the Law Reform (Frustrated Contracts) Act 1943, does not apply in Scotland.

G. Consequences

As already stated, a different regime applies in Scotland compared to England in the context of the consequences of frustration. Both systems analyse the effect on the contract in the same manner: the parties' future rights and obligations under the contract are discharged from the time at which the frustrating event occurs. However, rights accrued under the contract prior to the frustrating event can be enforced.

In English law, the terms of the Law Reform (Frustrated Contracts) Act 1943 can be applied following frustration to make equitable adjustments to the situation of the contracting parties. Scots law applies the *condictio causa data causa non secuta* following frustration, an issue which was confirmed by the institutional writers.[422] The *condictio* '... provides a remedy where someone has given money or property to another on

[421] McBryde, *Contract*, para. 21–15.
[422] Stair, *Institutions*, I, 7, 7; Bankton, *Institute*, 1, 8, 21; Erskine, *Institute*, III, 1, 10.

the clear understanding that the recipient will make counter-performance or that a particular event should occur. Should the counter-performance or event not take place, in principle the *condictio* lay to recover the value of what had been given'.[423] Following the Scottish House of Lords case of *Cantiere San Rocco SA* v. *Clyde Shipbuilding & Engineering Co*[424] in 1926, this view became 'embedded' as the modern rule applicable in cases of frustration of contract.

Despite its authoritative status, the usage of the *condictio* here has been strongly criticised. The most vocal critic has been Professor Evans-Jones, who argued that the House of Lords misapplied Roman law in *Cantiere*, and that the *condictio* has no place in situations of frustration of contract.[425] He pointed out that cases of frustration were previously resolved by applying only the principles of the law of contract, and more particularly the rules of allocation of risk in contract.

Others have criticised the remedy provided by the *condictio* for different reasons. In a famous article on the history of frustration in Scots law, Lord Cooper envisaged a much wider role for the Scottish courts in cases of frustration. He suggested that the court had the power to make equitable adjustments. This power existed, in his view, because the *condictio*, in common with other unjustified enrichment remedies, had a strong equitable basis. However, he conceded[426] that his suggestion was contrary to the rather narrower formulation of the remedy which can be found in the judgment of Lord President Inglis in the important case of *Watson & Co* v. *Shankland*.[427] Nevertheless, he argued that the point was left open in the later House of Lords case of *James B Fraser* v. *Denny, Mott and Dickson*.[428] Looking at the modern law, it seems highly unlikely that the Scottish courts have the ability to make equitable adjustments. Nor do the courts have the power, as is the case in some other systems, to amend the terms of the contract following frustration. The Scottish court's powers are limited to ordering reversal of the enrichment. This limited power has attracted criticism recently from MacQueen and Thomson, who express their dissatisfaction with the inability of the *condictio* to resolve cases where the losses of one party to the contract do not result in a benefit to the other party.[429] This limitation is amply illustrated by Case 2.

[423] MacCormack, 'Condictio Causa Data Causa Non Secuta', 253.
[424] 1923 SC (HL) 105. [425] Evans-Jones, 'Unjust Enrichment'.
[426] See Cooper, 'Frustration of Contract', Pt III, 1. [427] (1871) 10 M. 142.
[428] 1944 SC (HL) 35. [429] MacQueen and Thomson, *Contract Law* at para. 4.85.

PART III

The case studies

5 Questionnaire

A. EQUIVALENCE OF EXCHANGE IS DISTORTED

Case 1 *'Canal de Craponne'*

Long term agreement - devaluation of the price agreement

Early in the twentieth century, the farmers X and Y entered into a contract under which X promised to build and maintain an irrigation channel; Y was entitled to extract water at a fixed price. The contract was concluded for an unlimited period of time. Almost 100 years later, X's successors ask for an increase in the price arguing that due to inflation and a rise in the cost of maintenance as well as labour the agreed price has become completely inadequate.

Is the claim by X's successors justified? Are they, alternatively, entitled to terminate the contract?

Case 2 Extraordinary inflation

Hardship due to extraordinary inflation; hardship resulting from a foreign currency agreement

(a) *Extraordinary inflation*

X receives a loan from the Y-Bank. Under the agreement, the interest rate is fixed at 10 per cent for five years. In the twenty years immediately before the agreement, the rate of inflation had been relatively stable within a range of 1 to 6 per cent. In the third year after the conclusion of the agreement, the economic situation begins to destabilise and inflation rises quickly to 50 per cent.

Y-Bank asks for an adjustment or for a termination of the contract.

(b) *Variation: foreign currency agreement*

The loan agreement between X and the Y-Bank provides for repayment and interest in a foreign currency. In the ten years immediately before the agreement, the relevant exchange rate had been relatively stable within a range of 20 per cent. Subsequently, the national currency is devalued by 80 per cent compared to the foreign currency.

X asks for an adjustment or for a termination of the contract.

Case 3 Government intervention – tax increase

Post-contractual imposition of a tax

X and Y enter into a contract under which X promises to supply 120,000 litres of industrial spirit to Y. Subsequently, a statute is enacted by which an alcohol tax is imposed on the sale of industrial spirit. The statute provides that the seller has to pay the tax. The tax is so high that it even exceeds the price that X and Y have agreed upon.

Is X entitled to recover compensation for the additional costs, to adjust or to cancel the contract?

Case 4 Unexpected benefit

Long term lease – extraordinary increase of the rental value

Y leases business premises from X for a fixed period of fifteen years. Shortly after concluding the contract, the character of the area changes strongly and unexpectedly: a military airport located nearby is shut down and an enormous amount of public funds is invested in the area (infrastructure etc.). As a consequence, Y's business soars and his profits are 500 per cent of what he could reasonably have expected. By the same token, the rental value of comparable business premises in the same area rises to 500 per cent of the amount X and Y have agreed upon. X claims that the rental price should be adjusted accordingly or, alternatively, that the agreement should be terminated.

Is X's claim justified?

B. RECIPIENT'S USE OF CONTRACTUAL GOODS OR SERVICES IS SUBSTANTIALLY AFFECTED

Case 5 Destruction of cellar

Renovation of cellar becomes useless due to the destruction of the building by natural disaster

X agrees to refurbish Y's cellar into a wine cellar. The work is scheduled to start one month after the agreement. Before the work has started, Y's house is completely destroyed during a violent summer storm. However, the cellar of the house remains fully intact. Y immediately informs X and asks him not to perform. X insists on the agreement. He argues that Y's cellar is still intact, that he has reserved two weeks to carry out the work and that he has already purchased the necessary materials.

Is Y obliged to pay the contract price or, alternatively, to compensate X for his losses?

Case 6 Confiscation of petrol

Government intervention makes the use of a rented petrol station impossible

X leases a petrol station from Y. Due to the outbreak of war, the government confiscates all petrol in that area and it is impossible for X to obtain petrol from any source. As a result, X can make no use of the petrol station. He stops the payment on the lease.

Is X's refusal to pay the rent justified?

Case 7 Hotel reservation

Individual purpose of the visit frustrated; strike by airport personnel; general safety endangered; coronation case

X booked a room at Y's hotel, but:

(a) *The exhibition he wants to visit is cancelled at the very last moment.*
(b) *A terrorist movement declares that it is to launch a campaign against tourists in that town.*
(c) *An unforeseeable strike by airport personnel prevents X from travelling at the specified time to the city where the hotel is located.*
(d) *The coronation procession scheduled on the respective date is cancelled. The room has a view of the street where the procession was supposed to take place. Due to the extraordinary event, the agreed price is ten times higher than the regular price.*

Is X entitled to cancel the reservation?

Case 8 Shop rental

Renting a retail outlet; unexpected business environment at a shopping centre

X is the owner of a bookshop. He contracts with Y to rent business accommodation in X's shopping centre. The fixed period of the lease is five years. The shopping centre has just been built and a large part of the accommodation is still unoccupied. Both parties expect at the time of contracting that a variety of shops (the hotel and catering trade, retail sales) will be located there. One year later almost all the accommodation is rented, but three quarters of the shopping centre consists of restaurants and cafes. For that reason most potential customers visit the shopping centre after X closes the doors of his bookshop.

Is X entitled to an adjustment or to a termination of the contract?

Case 9 Beer supply agreement

Long-term supply of beer; beer sales are far below expectations

X, the owner of a bar, enters into an exclusive supply agreement with the brewery Y for a fixed period of fifteen years. Pursuant to the contract, X is obliged to accept and pay for a specific quantity of beer on a monthly basis, while he is allowed to use technical equipment and furnishings owned by Y. The consumption of beer, however, remains far below expectations. The bar is well attended but the 'Y beer' is unpopular amongst customers at X's bar. X requests an adjustment or the termination of the agreement.

Is X's claim justified?

Case 10 Export ban

Purchaser of technical equipment is affected by export ban

Firm X purchases technical equipment which is to be produced by firm Y. The parties know that firm X plans to resell the equipment to Iraq. At the time of contracting, exports to Iraq are illegal but the parties expect that the status quo will change before the time of delivery. The parties are aware that the equipment can only be sold to Iraq at a reasonable price. When firm Y has completed production and offers delivery, exports to Iraq are still illegal and no change is in sight. Firm X refuses acceptance and payment.

Is X's refusal to accept and pay justified?

C. FRUSTRATION OF SPECIFIED PURPOSES (OTHER THAN A OR B)

Case 11 Sale of real estate involving expectation of cultural use

Use of real estate by transferee does not comply with expectations of the transferor

X sells his family home to Y at a price far below its market value. Both parties assume that Y would dedicate the house to cultural purposes only. However, this assumption was not inserted in the contract as an explicit condition. Y changes his mind and gives it to one of his daughters instead.

Is X entitled to ask for the difference between the agreed price and the market value or, alternatively, to reclaim the house?

Case 12 Investment in spouse's house is frustrated by divorce

Equitable compensation if divorce laws lack a basis for compensation

Before X and Y marry, they enter into a prenuptial agreement, in which they agree on the separation of property. During the marriage X buys a house and X and Y use the house as their family home. The price of the house is €500,000. X is the sole proprietor of the house, but Y has contributed €100,000 to the purchase price. In addition, Y carries out extensive renovation work before they move in. The renovation would have cost €50,000 if professional services had been employed. After X and Y have lived together in the house for one year, they separate and then divorce. Divorce law does not provide a basis for compensation.

Is Y entitled to compensation for his contributions to the family home?

D. MUTUAL MISTAKE CONCERNING THE CALCULATION UNDERLYING THE CONTRACT

Case 13 Share deal – mutual mistake

False determination of the market value in a share deal

X holds shares of Z corporation. He agrees to sell the shares to Y at the current price as listed by the stock exchange on the day of contracting. In the written contract, the parties set a price of €10 per share. However, the actual price per share on the day of contracting is €12. The internet service, from which the parties derived the price, had displayed an incorrect number. When X discovers the correct price, he demands that the purchase price is to be increased to €12.

Can X ask for a price of €12 per share? Can he, alternatively, terminate the contract?

E. MISCELLANEOUS ISSUES

Case 14 Impediments of production beyond seller's control

Production of contractual goods is inhibited by a strike/ restriction of electricity supplies

X agrees to deliver some goods to Y at a certain date, but:

(a) *the workers of a subcontractor go on strike.*
(b) *due to problems with the state energy production and distribution system the government decides to cut the electricity supply at night thereby making it impossible to work at night.*

As a result, X cannot deliver the goods for an uncertain period of time. Is Y entitled to terminate the contract and to ask for damages?

Case 15 Disclaimer

Disclaimer concerning the rights arising from unexpected circumstances; other clauses related to unexpected circumstances

The construction company X agrees to build a double-floor building on Y's land for the price of €2,000,000. In the contract the parties stipulate a disclaimer which excludes 'all the rights of both parties arising from unexpected circumstances'. Two weeks after the construction work has begun a granite rock, which could not have been detected by the parties before the conclusion of the contract, is revealed on Y's land. As a result the costs of the construction increase by 300 per cent.

Can X ask for an adjustment of the contract or can he terminate the contract in spite of the disclaimer?

6 The case studies

A. EQUIVALENCE OF EXCHANGE IS DISTORTED

Case 1 *'Canal de Craponne'*

Long-term agreement – devaluation of the price agreement

Early in the twentieth century, the farmers X and Y entered into a contract under which X promised to build and maintain an irrigation channel; Y was entitled to extract water at a fixed price. The contract was concluded for an unlimited period of time. Almost 100 years later, X's successors ask for an increase in the price arguing that due to inflation and a rise in the cost of maintenance as well as labour the agreed price has become completely inadequate.

Is the claim by X's successors justified? Are they, alternatively, entitled to terminate the contract?

Germany and related jurisdictions

Germany

X's successors are entitled to claim adjustment under German law. Depending on the circumstances, X's successors may also have a right to terminate the contract.

I. In the given case, the parties did not include an express or implied provision for the impact of long-term inflation. The depreciation can also not be dealt with by interpreting the contract on the basis of the parties' hypothetical will. Thus, the contract itself cannot be drawn upon to eliminate the disproportionality between the contractual obligations caused by inflation.

II. Furthermore, X's successors are not absolved from the contractual obligation on the ground of *practical impossibility* (§275 II BGB). This rule would permit X's successors to refuse performance only if the burden of performance was completely disproportionate compared to Y's interest in the performance. The decisive criterion is whether the increased burden of performance incurred by X is somehow reflected by a corresponding gain for the creditor (Y). Applying this test to the case, the burden of performance is made up by the water costs as well as the maintenance and labour costs. It results in the availability of water for Y, a corresponding economic gain. Thus, the burden of performance is equivalent to the creditor's interest in the performance. The fact that the relation between the burden of performance and the payment is grossly disproportionate is irrelevant under §275 II BGB.[1]

III. 1. The core issue is the imbalance (disparity/discrepancy) between the burden of performance of X's successors and the payment. According to the prevailing case law[2] and the majority of legal writers[3] this imbalance falls within the scope of *Strung der Geschäftsgrundlage*. In this kind of case performance amounts to an unbearable hardship due to the imbalance between the obligations while there is no legal or physical impediment.[4] This reasoning is still valid after the reform of the Law of Obligations 2002.[5] Therefore the case is to be solved on the basis of §313 BGB.[6]

2. §313 I BGB does not define what constitutes the *Geschäftsgrundlage* of a contract. It is generally accepted that the rules of *Geschäftsgrundlage* are applicable to basic assumptions shared by both parties at the time of contracting. If the assumption is held by only one party, it must be recognisable to the other party and not contested by him. The assumption may refer to present or future circumstances as far as they are relevant for the contractual will while not provided for in the contract.[7]

[1] Cf. Regierungsbegründung BT-Ds. 14/6040, p. 130; C.-W. Canaris, 'Sondertagung Schuldrechtsmodernisierung', (2001) JZ 499, (502).

[2] Cf. BGH LM §242 (Bb) nn. 12, 50.

[3] Cf. C. Grüneberg, '§275', in: O. Palandt *et al.* (eds.), *Bürgerliches Gesetzbuch* (Munich: Beck, 69th edn, 2010), n. 21; H. Wiedemann, '§275', in: H. T. Soergel *et al.* (eds.), *Bürgerliches Gesetzbuch* (Stuttgart: Kohlhammer, 12th edn, 1990), n. 38; K. Larenz, *Schuldrecht I*, (Munich: Beck, 14th edn, 1987) §21 I e; for a different view, cf. Emmerich, '§275', in: F. J. Säcker, R. Rixecker *et al.*, *Münchener Kommentar zum Bürgerlichen Gesetzbuch* (Munich: Beck, 5th edn, 2007), vol. II, n. 28.

[4] Cf. Grüneberg, '§275', in: Palandt *et al.* (eds.), *Bürgerliches Gesetzbuch*, n. 21; Wiedemann, '§275', in: Soergel *et al.* (eds.), *Bürgerliches Gesetzbuch*, n. 38.

[5] Cf. Regierungsbegründung BT-Ds. 14/6040, p. 130.

[6] For a special rule concerned with the adjustment of leases, cf. §593 BGB.

[7] Cf. BGH NJW 2001, 1204, (1205).

3. With regard to mutual contracts, the equivalence of exchange is part of the *Geschäftsgrundlage* regardless of whether it can be inferred from the parties' conduct in a particular case. In a market economy, the equivalence of exchange is determined by the parties. However, the relationship of the objective value may be indicative of the parties' view. In the given case, inflation caused an unexpected distortion in the equivalence of exchange and thus affected the (objective) *Geschäftsgrundlage*.[8]

4. Furthermore, it is required that the *Geschäftsgrundlage* is *substantially* affected, i.e., a massive change in the relevant circumstances must have occurred (cf. §313 I BGB). Accordingly, as a general rule, *regular* inflation does not lead to the application of the doctrine. The impact of inflation on monetary obligations has to be assessed on the basis of two fundamental principles. First, the parties usually do foresee depreciation and therefore the creditor of a monetary obligation typically includes the depreciation of the currency value in his calculation of the interest rates.[9] Second, according to the so-called 'nominal value principle' the value of a monetary obligation must be determined on the basis of its nominal instead of its actual ('real') value.[10] Thus, the creditor of a monetary claim bears the risk of 'normal' depreciation. The reason is that the parties of a long-term contract are usually aware of the fact that the equivalence of exchange cannot be taken for granted over a long period of time.[11]

5. Yet, in exceptional cases, regular inflation may affect the *Geschäftsgrundlage* substantially. This is true if the equivalence of exchange is distorted by continuous inflation such as to exceed the risk taken by the creditor of a monetary claim and to render the agreement completely against his interest.[12] It was held by the courts that an increase in the general prices by 150 per cent over a period of thirty years is sufficient to constitute such a distortion. It is important to note that the price increase over the whole previous period of the contract

[8] Cf. Regierungsbegründung BT-Ds. 14/6040, p. 174; C. Grüneberg, '§313', in: Palandt *et al.* (eds.), *Bürgerliches Gesetzbuch*, nn. 26 *et seq.*; G. H. Roth, '§313', in: F. J. Säcker *et al.*, *Münchener Kommentar zum Bürgerlichen Gesetzbuch* (Munich: Beck, 5th edn, 2006), vol. II, nn. 147 *et seq.* For a different opinion, cf. W. Flume, *Allgemeiner Teil des Bürgerlichen Rechts, II. Das Rechtsgeschäft* (Berlin/Heidelberg/New York: Springer, 4th edn, 1992), §26 n. 5.

[9] Cf. for this argument BGH WM 1968, 1248; BGH WM 1973, 839; BGH WM 1976, 1034.

[10] Cf. Roth, '§313', in: Säcker *et al.*, *Münchener Kommentar zum Bürgerlichen Gesetzbuch*, vol. II, n. 149; for further details of the nominal value principle cf. BGHZ 61, 38; BGHZ 79, 194; C. Grüneberg, '§245', in: Palandt *et al.* (eds.), *Bürgerliches Gesetzbuch*, n. 15.

[11] Cf. BGHZ 86, 167 (169); BGHZ 77, 195 (196).

[12] Cf. BGHZ 77, 195 (198 *et seq.*); BGHZ 86, 167 (169); BGHZ 90, 227 (228).

must be considered.[13] With respect to contracts, which are supposed to cover the living expenses for one party, the courts have accepted even a lesser increase as sufficient.[14]

6. Furthermore, according to §313 BGB, one party must be *unreasonably burdened* by the contract if it is upheld as it was originally concluded. With regard to X's heirs, this condition is met. Neither the contract itself nor general legal rules allocate the risk of such a substantial distortion in the equivalence of exchange to them. It is true that with respect to mutual contracts the debtor generally bears the risk that performance becomes more expensive to him than he has expected. However, the cost increase X's successors are faced with cannot be regarded as a normal burden since it exceeds the decisive margin. The simple fact that the contract at hand is a long-term contract does not justify the suggestion that the debtor of the non-monetary performance must bear the risk of depreciation irrespective of the extent.

7. As the primary legal consequence of a relevant application of *Geschäftsgrundlage*, X's successors are entitled to ask for adjustment of the contract on the basis of §313 I, III BGB. The extent of the increase in the payment is to be determined dependent on the shift in the general economic conditions since the time of formation.[15] The courts determine this shift by calculating the mean rate between the price increase rate and the salary rise rate. Thus, the approach differs from the calculation adopted to determine whether performance is unreasonably onerous. As a result, the increased payment will generally exceed the 150 per cent margin which is relevant for the question as to whether performance is still reasonable.

8. X's successors are not entitled to terminate the contract.[16] Under the rules of *Geschäftsgrundlage*, termination is admitted only if the adjustment is impossible (§313 III BGB). As a general rule for long-term contracts, §314 BGB entitles either party to terminate the contract if he is unreasonably burdened by it. However, as long as an adjustment of the

[13] Cf. BGHZ 90, 227; BGHZ 111, 214 (216); BGHZ 119, 220 (222).

[14] Cf. BGH WM 1975, 1131; C. Grüneberg, '§313', in: Palandt *et al.* (eds.), *Bürgerliches Gesetzbuch*, n. 28.

[15] BGHZ 75, 279; BGHZ 77, 188; G. H. Roth, '§313', in: Säcker *et al.*, *Münchener Kommentar zum Bürgerlichen Gesetzbuch*, vol. II, n. 151; P. Bassenge, '§9a ErbbauRG', in: Palandt *et al.* (eds.), *Bürgerliches Gesetzbuch*, n. 7.

[16] Cf. for special provisions governing certain kinds of contracts, C. Grüneberg, '§314', in: Palandt *et al.* (eds.), *Bürgerliches Gesetzbuch*, n. 4; E. A. Kramer, 'Einleitung', in: Krüger, *Münchener Kommentar zum Bürgerlichen Gesetzbuch* (Munich: Beck, 5th edn, 2007), vol. II, n. 101; Regierungsbegründung BT-Ds. 14/6040, p. 177.

contract on the basis of §313 I BGB is possible, the latter is a *lex specialis* and §314 BGB may not be invoked.[17] Thus, the contract can be terminated only if the increase in the payment would amount to an unreasonable burden for Y. However, some scholars take the view that the party that incurs disadvantages from the adjustment is entitled to set aside the contract.[18]

Austria

Even if the fixed price has become inadequate, X's successors have no right to adjust the agreement, but they are entitled to terminate the contract due to its long-term nature, which may also enable them to renegotiate the contract with Y.

I. 1. In the present case the doctrine of '*Wegfall der Geschäftsgrundlage*' does not apply, since both parties were able to anticipate the depreciation of money. Regular inflation is no unexpected change of circumstances and therefore X's successors are not entitled to terminate the contract.[19] Furthermore, §988 ABGB provides that, for loan contracts, depreciation of money does not affect the nominal debt. This is considered a general principle of Austrian law. Therefore, pecuniary debts are independent of inflation (so-called 'nominal principle of money obligations').[20] As a basic rule, the creditor bears the risk of money depreciation.

2. Nevertheless, there are some exceptions. For example, a contractual obligation to pay support is dependent on inflation.[21] Furthermore, as a general rule, where the obligation to pay money shall enable the creditor to accomplish a certain purpose, the nominal obligation is adapted to inflation (obligation in value of money).[22] This exceptional adjustment to inflation is justified by the parties' intent, since the creditor would not be able to achieve the intended purpose otherwise.[23]

[17] Cf. Regierungsbegründung BT-Ds. 14/6040, p. 177; Grüneberg, '§314', in: Palandt *et al.* (eds.), *Bürgerliches Gesetzbuch*, n. 9.

[18] Cf. W. Flume, *Das Rechtsgeschäft*, §26 n. 4 b; for further details Roth, '§313', in: Krüger, *Münchener Kommentar zum Bürgerlichen Gesetzbuch*, vol. II, n. 105.

[19] OGH JBl 1979, 651 = EvBl 1979/220. [20] OGH SZ 3/61.

[21] Schubert, '§988', in: P. Rummel (ed.), *Kommentar zum ABGB* (Vienna: Manz, 2000), vol. I, n. 2.

[22] OGH JBl 1961, 86; OGH SZ 44/58.

[23] Franz Gschnitzer, Christian Faistenberger and Heinz Barta, *Schuldrecht Allgemeiner Teil* (Vienna: Springer, 1985), p. 60; Binder,'§988', in Schwimann (ed.), *Kommentar zum ABGB* (Vienna: LexisNexis), vol. IV, n. 21.

3. In the present case the obligation to pay money did not primarily intend to compensate X for his maintenance costs, but was fixed as a price for water drawn by Y. As a result X's successors have no right to increase the price of water unilaterally.

II. 1. However, the agreement is a 'long-term' contract ('*Dauerschuldverhältnis*'), which is a contract for the performance of a recurring (continuing) obligation for an indefinite period of time. According to the general principles of Austrian civil law such contracts can be terminated by each party after a reasonable period of notice without any particular cause (ordinary right of termination or '*ordentliche Kündigung*').[24]

2. Austrian courts and commentators hold that the parties must be aware of the fact that money devalues.[25] A creditor who fails to stipulate an index clause bears the risk of inflation. However, the right to terminate a long-term contract for an indefinite period of time by ordinary notice of termination can be explained by complementary interpretation of the contract ('*ergänzende Vertragsauslegung*') according to the hypothetical intention of the parties who failed to agree upon the modalities of termination. If a long-term contract is unlimited in time, it cannot be assumed that the parties wanted the contract to last forever. They generally cannot foresee events in the far future and how they will affect their willingness to stick to the contract. Their interests are therefore best protected by granting them an ordinary right of termination upon reasonable notice. Thus X's successors can point to their right to terminate the contract and invite Y to accept a higher price if he wants to avoid termination.

The Netherlands

Under Dutch law, X's successors have the option of either terminating or adjusting the agreement depending on the court's assessment.

First, a preliminary remark: the fact that X and Y died and had successors does not change the assessment of the case under Dutch law. Furthermore, the assessment below assumes that the successors of X and Y succeeded under general title. The reference to a 'transfer

[24] Helmut Koziol and Rudolf Welser, *Bürgerliches Recht*, (Vienna: Manz, 2007), vol. II, pp. 9, 109; F. Bydlinski, *Zulässigkeit und Schranken 'ewiger' und langdauernder Vertragsbindungen* (Vienna: LexisNexis, 1991), p. 11.

[25] OGH JBl 1979, 651 = EvBl 1979/220; F. Gschnitzer, in: H. Klang (ed.), *Kommentar zum ABGB* (Vienna: 1968), vol. IV/1, p. 339.

under general title' means that, by operation of law, a successor in title acquires rights and obligations in their entirety (i.e., effectively leaving the existing legal environment unchanged). In the current case it is assumed that the succession was by general title.[26]

I. 1. The Dutch statutory provisions on unforeseen circumstances specifically address cases involving real property. According to Art. 6:259, an agreement obliging a beneficiary or user of real estate to perform (or obliging a third party to be allowed to perform) in a certain manner may be amended or terminated by the court. This provision does not exclude Art. 6:258 Dutch Civil Code, which may be applied alternatively. Art. 6:259 does not apply to all patrimonial rights (i.e., property rights of '*houderschap*'), such as a lease and a ground lease. A court can amend or terminate a real estate-related contract: (i) if at least ten years have elapsed since the agreement was entered into and an unmodified continuation of the obligation would be contrary to the public interest, or (ii) if the beneficiary of the obligation has ceased to have a reasonable interest.

2. In the current case, however, Art. 6:259 does not apply: condition (ii) is certainly not met because obviously both X and Y will have a strong interest; furthermore, condition (i) is not very likely to be at stake due to its reference to the public interest. However, there is a provision that after ten years contractual obligations related to real estate can become subject to amendment. The 100 years in the current case considerably exceeds this ten-year period. Based on this assessment a court should not be overly reluctant to apply the general provision of Art. 6:258 on changed circumstances, even though the more specific provision of Art. 6:259 is not applicable.

[26] The distinction under Dutch law between succession under general title and under specific title is reflected in Art. 3:80 Dutch Civil Code. 'General titles' other than acquisition ('*erfopvolging*') are (matrimonial) joinder of estates ('*boedelmenging*'), merger ('*fusie*') or demerger ('*splitsing*') of legal entities. Specific titles, on the other hand, are the transfer of ownership ('*overdracht*'), the operation of statutes of limitations ('*verjaring*'), expropriation ('*onteigening*') and any other manner established by law (Art. 3:80 (3) Dutch Civil Code). If the successors of X and Y continued the respective contractual positions of their predecessors under specific title, then such positions would include the agreement in question only (i) if the obligations between X and Y were recorded in a notarial deed and registered in the public registers (Art. 6:252 Dutch Civil Code) or (ii) if the succession in the obligations relating to the real estate was provided for in the (consecutive) agreement(s) between Y and its subsequent successor(s) in title pertaining to the acquisition of the real estate (Art. 6:253).

II. 1. In this context it is important to point out how Dutch law generally deals with long-term agreements. First of all, Dutch law would consider the duration of the contract as undefined rather than unlimited. As opposed to contracts for a long duration, contracts with an undefined duration (both varieties are referred to as '*duurovereenkomst*') are particularly considered to be subject to amendment based on changed circumstances. More specifically, if the contract is not generally very detailed or otherwise does not provide comprehensively for an elaborate number of circumstances, most Dutch authors consider that at some (remote) point in time it is appropriate to either terminate or modify the provisions of such a contract. Moreover, two decisions of the Hoge Raad on changed circumstances point in this direction.

2. In the case of *Campina* v. *Jole*, Campina guaranteed that employees would not be made redundant but subsequently the company's business deteriorated and many employees had to be laid off. Jole challenged his dismissal on the ground that Campina had guaranteed his continued employment. The Hoge Raad established that the parties had not, in a rigid and unchangeable manner, carved their agreement into stone. Rather, they had opted for a more dynamic approach, whereby the duration of the various subsequent stages of their arrangement was left open for the time being.[27] This approach obviously affects an otherwise clear agreement in such a fundamental way that a court must be reluctant to embrace such an interpretation. A party arguing that the agreement was not intended to be for an indefinite period of time therefore bears the burden of proof that this was not the case. (In other words, the court should scrutinise the request of a party to amend a contract.) An amendment could also be effectively based on the general principle of reasonableness and fairness, or initiated on the basis of interpretation. This case law justifies the conclusion that also in the current case of X's irrigation channel, X and Y must be deemed never to have considered their arrangement to remain unmodified for a period even exceeding 100 years.

3. In the case *VvdE* v. *CSM*,[28] the Hoge Raad assessed the claim of a stock exchange to modify its stock exchange listing agreement with CSM. In *VvdE* v. *CSM*, the contentious agreement was rather lengthy and otherwise elaborate but no right to modify had been included. The Hoge

[27] An example of such a case: HR 19 November 1993, NJ 1994, 156 (*Campina* v. *Jole*), also addressed in HR 10 July 1989, NJ 1989, 786 (*FNV* v. *Campina*).
[28] NJ 1999, 602.

Raad established that it is irrelevant whether a party bases its claim on the general principle of reasonableness and fairness or on changed circumstances (i.e., Art. 6:258). A party may benefit from the criteria of Art. 6:258 by arguing that the litigated agreement requires amendment, but it may equally achieve the same result (or termination) on the basis of the more general principle of reasonableness and fairness (i.e., as reflected in Art. 6:248). Since the termination of the listing agreement was admissible, amendment pursuant to Art. 6:258 is likely to be also allowed.

4. Similarly, the agreement between X and Y was probably never intended to remain unchanged for over 100 years. Also, there was probably no other option for irrigation readily available. The requirements of Art. 6:258 Dutch Civil Code are likely to be met in the current case: (i) the 100 years without change was probably not intended and accordingly, the increase in the water price over such a period of time is an unforeseen element in the agreement. Furthermore, (ii) whereas the agreement relates to real estate but lasts for much longer than ten years (even beyond 100 years), Y's successors could not reasonably have expected the agreement of their predecessor to remain unmodified.

Eastern European jurisdictions

Slovenia

Under Slovenian law, X's successors do not have the right to ask the court to adjust the agreement (the price). They may, however, terminate the agreement by a simple notice, based upon Art. 333 CO. Alternatively, they can try to renegotiate the contract. The threat of termination on the side of X's successors might force Y's successors to accept a higher price.

I. X's successors cannot ask for an increase in the price on the basis of a complementary interpretation of the contract since such an instrument does not exist in Slovenian law. Contracts are interpreted according to their wording. Only in cases where the contractual provisions are disputed does Art. 82(2) provide that such provisions shall be interpreted in accordance with the parties' common intentions and with the principles of the law of obligations as set out in the CO.[29]

[29] N. Plavšak in: M. Juhart and N. Plavšak (eds.), *Obligacijski zakoniks Komentarjem* (Ljubljana: GV Založba, 2008), vol. I, pp. 494–5; Supreme Court of Slovenia, II IPS 145/94 and II IPS 741/95.

II. 1. In Slovenia, a claim to adapt a contract cannot be based on the concept of change of circumstances (Art. 112 CO). Instead, it would allow X's successors to terminate the contract if the change of circumstances occurred after the conclusion of the contract and rendered the performance more difficult for one of the parties, or if the purpose of the contract was frustrated.[30] The change of circumstances must be so significant that the contract obviously no longer complies with the expectations of both parties and that it would be unjust, according to general opinion, to keep the contract in force as it was concluded.

2. The disadvantaged party, however, is not allowed to invoke a change of circumstances if it should have taken such circumstances into consideration when the contract was concluded, if it could have avoided them or if it could have averted their consequences. The same applies if the change of circumstances occurred after the performance of the disadvantaged party was due.

3. In the present case, the change of circumstances consists in the devaluation of money. Article 371 CO expressly provides that pecuniary debts are independent of inflation (the principle of monetary nominalism). Exceptions are only possible upon agreement by both parties[31] so the *clausula* doctrine does not apply in cases of devaluation of money as a general rule. However, the principle of monetary nominalism was already codified in Art. 394 of the former Yugoslav Obligations Act 1978, according to which this principle only applies, '*unless statutorily provided otherwise*'. This left room for exceptions on grounds of a change of circumstances.[32] There is also case law relating to the said provision that allows for an action in cases of abnormal inflation. Yugoslav case law before 1978 also allowed for a dissolution of a contract in cases of considerable (abnormal, unexpected) changes of prices.[33] In addition, the Yugoslav currency was subject to a series of devaluations and even to hyperinflation (in the late 1980s). Therefore reasonable interpretation requires that the '*clausula*' is applicable to contracts that have been concluded well before the enactment of the present CO of 2002, at least in cases of extraordinary changes to the value of money. The principle

[30] Kranjc in: Juhart and Plavšak (eds.), *Obligacijski zakonik*, vol. I, pp. 119–20.

[31] And also in other areas of civil law, e.g., the obligation to pay maintenance.

[32] S. Cigoj, *Komentar obligacijskih razmerij*, 2 vols. (Ljubljana: ČZ Uradni list Republike Slovenije, 1984), vol. I, p. 441.

[33] A change of prices higher than 50 per cent and sometimes higher than 45 per cent (Supreme Yugoslav Commercial Court P 34/64, Zso 1964, 284; Supreme Slovenian Commercial Court 1127/74, 12 January 1975, Bilten VPS 1975, 4).

of monetary nominalism 'works' only where the currency is stable, but inflation can render this principle inequitable based on the requirements of good faith (Art. 5 CO).[34] The principle of equal value of performances (Art. 8, Art. 118 CO) only applies in cases of gross disparity existing at the time of the conclusion of a contract. In the present case there has been no extraordinary devaluation of money, but only normal inflation, which could have been anticipated by both parties at the time of conclusion of the contract.

III. In the case at hand, the contract has been concluded for an undefined period of time. Under Slovenian law, a long-term contract concluded for an undefined period of time may be terminated by notice of one of the parties (Art. 333 CO). X's successors must respect a reasonable period for notice.[35]

Lithuania

As the contract was concluded for an unlimited period of time, X's successors are entitled to terminate the contract on the basis of Art. 6.199 CC. According to this rule, a contract for an indefinite period of time may be terminated by either party, provided the party gives notice of his intention to the other party a reasonable time in advance, unless otherwise provided for by law or a contract. Alternatively, the contract may be adjusted.

I. According to Art. 6.190 CC, after the death or liquidation of one of the parties, the rights and duties arising from the contract pass to his heirs (successors) if it is permitted by the nature of the contract, law, or the contract itself. The contract at hand does not have a strictly personal (*intuitu personae)* character. Thus, it shall have the force of law for X's successors (Art. 6.189 CC). According to Art. 6.223(4) CC, a refusal of one party to perform a contract in whole or in part may be effected only in cases provided for by the law or the contract. As the contract does not include such a provision, X's successors are bound by it.

II. The contract concerned has created a monetary obligation between the parties. One of the peculiarities of the monetary obligation is the principle of nominalism established by Art. 6.873(6) CC. The essence of this principle is that an obligation to pay a sum of money

[34] T. Stanovnik, 'Denarni nominalizem, valorizacija in obresti', (1996) 5 *Podjetje in delo*, 617; S. Cigoj, *Teorija obligacij, Splošni del obligacijskega prava* (Ljubljana: ČZ Uradni list Republike Slovenije, 1998), p. 54.

[35] Juhart in: Juhart and Plavšak (eds.), *Obligacijski zakonik*, vol. I, pp. 441–3.

must be performed at its nominal value, unless a contract or law provides otherwise. The principle of nominalism means that ordinary ('regular') inflation has no effect on the rights and duties of the parties to the obligation. Thus, ordinary ('regular') inflation is not considered to be a changed circumstance according to Art. 6.204 CC, because (i) the parties could easily have foreseen ordinary ('regular') inflation, and (ii) they must bear the risk of ordinary ('regular') inflation.

III. When concluding a contract for an indefinite period, the parties usually provide for certain safeguards, e.g., the possibility of revising a contract upon the change of particular circumstances. In the case at hand, however, no provisions for the effect of normal inflation on the performance of the contract were established by the parties. Therefore, even applying a subjective method to the interpretation of a contract (pursuant to Art. 6.193(1) CC, it is necessary to seek the real intentions of the parties without being limited by the literal meaning of the words). It would be difficult to prove that the parties, when concluding the contract, intended to subject it to constant adaptation in accordance with normal inflation. A party could certainly invoke Art. 6.196 CC and attempt to prove that, taking into account the long-term character of a contract, an implied condition can be derived from the contract according to which the terms of the contract ought to be constantly modified with respect to normal inflation. Nevertheless, in the absence of the relevant court practice, it would be difficult to claim that the court would accept such an interpretation.

IV. 1. However, X's successors may ask for a modification of the contract and for an increase in the price on the basis of the principles of good faith, justice and reasonableness. According to Art. 6.223 CC, a contract may be modified by agreement of its parties. If one party refuses to modify the contract or does not respond to such a proposal within thirty days, an action for a judicial modification of a contract may be brought by the other party. The court may increase the price if the above mentioned situation violates the principles of good faith, justice and reasonableness. One can argue that the principles of good faith and justice require a modification of the price. This position can be based on the nature of the contract under discussion – the contract is concluded for an indefinite period and it has become onerous to one party. The principles of good faith and justice require that the originally established balance of the parties' interests is perpetuated throughout the duration of its validity. This position is also supported by a recent judgment of the Supreme Court. The Court indicated that any disputes related to the price agreement had to be based on the principles of good faith, justice and reasonableness, and that it was necessary to ensure that the price was reasonable and did not unjustly enrich one of the parties at the expense of the other.[36] Consequently, if due to normal inflation, the price becomes symbolic and no longer conforms to the market criteria, it becomes unreasonable and must be considered a violation of the balance of the parties' interests.

2. Indeed, modifying a contract in most cases improves the position of one party at the expense of the other. Thus, if the Court increases the price, Y may no longer be interested in the contract. As the contract is concluded for an indefinite period, Y may terminate the contract pursuant to Art. 6.199 CC.

Czech Republic

There are two ways in which the case may be resolved (in the case of a contract concluded for an indefinite period of time):

- **(i) X's successors may terminate the contract by notice pursuant to Section 582(2) Civil Code. The contract will be terminated upon the expiration of three months from the receipt of the notice by Y's successors, without any claims from either party arising from the termination.**
- **(ii) Depending on the facts (inflation rate), X's successors may be entitled to terminate the contract on the grounds that an extreme distortion of the equivalence of the exchange has occurred. Yet, X's successors have no right to adjust the contract.**

I. Termination of contracts that are concluded for an unlimited period of time is governed by the Civil Code Section 582. According to this provision, if a contract is concluded for an unlimited period of time and the subject of the contract consists in continuous or repeat performance or in an obligation to tolerate or to refrain from something, then such a contract may be terminated by a notice given at least three months of the end of the calendar quarter. There is no need to have a qualified reason for such termination.

II. This involves the issue of fairness, balance of performance, good faith and, not least, good morals. What is in conflict with good morals is that a party gains performance which he did not count on in good faith. Receipt of such performance can be deemed immoral, since it is not in

[36] LAT, Judgment of 9 January 2006, Case No 3K-7-3/2006.

conformity with the intentions of the parties to the contract and the subject of performance. The principle of good morals can be found in Section 39 Civil Code. According to the judgment of the Constitutional Court (Ústavní soud)[37] 'good morals' are an abstraction of ethical, generally observed and legitimate policies, whose observance is frequently guaranteed by law in the interest that every act be in accordance with the general moral principles of a democratic society. As a consequence of such a conflict with good morals, a contract may be declared void from the outset. In addition, Section 265 Commercial Code may apply, according to which conduct (or, more precisely, exercise of a right) that contravenes the principle of fair business shall not be protected by law.

Scandinavian jurisdictions

Sweden

In Sweden, X's successors may claim adjustment of the price or termination of the contract according to Section 36 Contracts Act. Termination may also be available under the doctrine of assumptions.

I. This is a typical case of changed circumstances, which also involves the specific problem of contractual liabilities unlimited in time. The failed assumption is an ordinary performance assumption of the category 'other assumptions regarding the performance' (see Chapter 4 for more detail). Assumptions of this type are comparatively often of legal relevance in case law. However, the main rule is – as for most types of assumptions – that they are not relevant. Under Swedish law there are traditionally two main methods of dealing with this kind of situation; the doctrine of assumptions and the rules on unfair contract terms. However, before 1976, these rules were very restrictive and, due to the traditional opinion, confirmed in the case NJA 1989 p. 614, the doctrine of assumptions could be applied only to avoid a contract, but not to claim for a price increase or for damages.[38] Therefore, traditional case law in this area is very restrictive.

II. 1. In Sweden, the specific issue of 'perpetual' contractual liabilities has been discussed in particular in connection with the Swedish

[37] Collection of Judgments and Rulings of the Constitutional Court, vol.11, C No.14.

[38] However, it is possible to be (partly, or entirely) released from a liability to perform under a promise, which would, in many cases, lead to a similar result.

Supreme Court case, NJA 1946 p. 679. In 1904, a railroad company promised an association of house owners a fixed price (equivalent to the typical price at that time) on railway tickets for the members of the association. In 1942, the company claimed compensation for higher prices, arguing that the assumptions on which the contract was based had failed due to an 'exorbitant' increase in costs. The court arrived at the conclusion that the company had not been able to prove any circumstance that could free it from its liabilities under the contract. The Supreme Court also referred to the judgment of a lower court, which had explicitly argued that the fact that the company had suffered a loss as a result of the application of the contract under changed economic circumstances did not give it a remedy, as it could not be assumed that the company had overlooked that possibility at the time the contract was entered into.

2. However, the renowned Justice Karlgren, in his dissenting opinion, argued that a promise unlimited in time could be terminated after a considerable time had passed and essential circumstances had changed in a way the parties had not foreseen, even if the same circumstances would not have given a remedy if the promise had not been of this peculiar nature. In this case, the value of money, taking into account the extended period of time and due to circumstances such as two world wars, had changed to an extent that could not reasonably have been foreseen. Therefore, termination was possible. However, it must also be considered that the company, by virtue of the promise, negotiated a higher price for the land, and that the promise was of great importance to the house owners. Therefore, the contract could be changed only gradually. The promise was to remain in force for five years and prices were to be raised thereafter with the difference between the promised and normal prices being eliminated in an additional ten years. It is submitted that this is much more in accordance with a modern view and that, today, the contract might even have been adjusted more radically under Section 36 Contracts Act.

III. 1. Under Section 36, a contract term can be adjusted or disregarded in a particular case (that is, the Court adjudicates on the matter as if the clause did not exist) if it is unreasonable ('*oskälig*') with reference to the contents of the contract, the circumstances at the conclusion of the contract, circumstances arising later and 'other circumstances'. According to the preparatory works, Section 36 can be used to modify long-term contracts, with 'perpetual contracts' specifically mentioned.[39] It can be used not only to adjust or disregard a specific unreasonable contract term to reduce an obligation; it is also possible to modify the contract to increase an obligation, or even to imply a new one.

2. The Swedish courts have applied Section 36 in a few cases where the circumstances were somewhat similar to the circumstances in this case.[40] In case NJA 1979 p. 731 the issue arose whether the price set out in a long-term contract could be modified due to inflation through an application of Section 36. In the early 1960s, some land areas were leased for forty-nine years, to be used for summer houses. The rent was SEK 50 for a year. The estate owner demanded compensation for SEK 400 and for an indexation clause to be added to the contract. The leaseholders made an admission to the amount of SEK 150, arguing that this would compensate for the long contract term, the increased costs and the changed value of money. The Supreme Court judged the case on the basis of the leaseholder's admission. The prices had already been low when the parties entered into the contract, but not unreasonable. The long contract term and prices in comparable lease contracts in the same district was not enough to adjust the price more than the leaseholders had admitted on the basis of increased costs and monetary inflation. The absence of an indexation clause was not considered to be unreasonable. However, the facts of NJA 1979 p. 731 have been considered by legal authors as such that could give rise to an application of Section 36.[41]

3. In case NJA 1994 p. 359 Section 36 was tested on a case of 'perpetual' promise. A contract entered into in 1954 stated that the owner of some land estates would not have to pay the municipality any fee for waste water sewerage. The contract was adjusted – but only on the basis of an admission – to the effect that the land owner would not have to pay any fee as long as he himself was living on the estate. The fact that the promise was 'perpetual' was not considered a ground for adjustment per se. Nor was the adoption of new administrative rules constituting a new fee system. However, the new fee system was to be taken into account, as the difference in relation to the fee did become greater over time. Still, the relevant contract clause was not considered to be

[39] Prop. 1975/76:81, p. 127; SOU 1974:83; pp. 156 *et seq.*, and K. Grönfors, *Avtalslagen* (Stockholm: CE Fritzes, 3rd edn, 1995), p. 235.

[40] See NJA 1979, 731; NJA 1983, 385; NJA 1994, 359, as well as RH 1980, 14.

[41] C.-R. Von Post, *Studier kring 36 § avtalslagen med inriktning på rent kommersiella förhållanden* (Stockholm: Förlag Claes Roberg von Post and Jure AB, 1999), p. 165.

unfair as of 1 January 1995, although the court indicated that the clause might become unfair at a later point in time.

4. On the basis of the long time that has passed, and the price trend – mainly caused by several great wars and revolutions which could not reasonably have been foreseen in the early 1900s – it must be presumed that the costs have increased considerably and that the price has become extremely low due to the changed value of money. Considering this and the fact that X's successors are obligated to maintain the irrigation channel, it is submitted that the claim for a higher price is justified under Section 36.

IV. An adjustment to a higher price under Section 36 must be related to the reasonable price. Therefore the interests of both parties need to be considered when the new price is decided, and the adjustment does not as such entitle Y to terminate the contract. On the other hand, it would be possible for the court to adjust the contract so that the new price is only binding if Y agrees to uphold the contract. However, such a special solution would probably only be used when special circumstances call for it.

V. If, on the other hand, X's successors wanted to seek a termination, they could argue that their obligation to maintain the irrigation channel is unfair. As these contract clauses correspond to each other, it is submitted that, if the price clause is unfair, this clause would also be considered unfair and that X's successors are therefore entitled to 'adjustment to zero', i.e., termination, instead.

VI. Another option is termination or adjustment of the liability to maintain the irrigation channel under the doctrine of assumptions. The ground most prevalent is that Y, as a result of the unexpected circumstance, made an unexpected profit at the expense of X's successors. Furthermore, it is required that X acted in 'good faith' and as the assumption is a performance assumption, good faith would suffice. It is submitted that, when possible, this rule should be applied in cases such as this, as it provides judges with more valuable guidance.

Denmark

In accordance with Section 36 Contracts Act X's successors are entitled to adjustment of the price agreement.

I. It is not possible to resolve the case by a complementary interpretation as the wording of the contract seems quite clear and leaves no doubt as to its interpretation. Thus, the application of *in dubio contra stipulatorem* is not likely to take place in this case.

II. 1. Danish law does not contain general statutory provisions that provide for the termination of contracts concluded for an unlimited period of time. However, case law allows for the termination of such contracts if six months' notice is given when the contract has been in force for a substantial period of time.[42] This would at least be the case when the contract has been concluded between professional partners. So far there is no reported case law with respect to contracts concluded for an unlimited period of time between a professional party and a consumer.

2. If the contract is concluded without any provision on termination, it may be terminated with one month's notice provided that the contract has been in force for a period of less than one year. In a contract that had been in force for less than eleven months, the Højesteret set the notification of termination at one month.[43]

III. The doctrine of assumptions is not applicable in this case because the conditions of the contract are clear and distinct.

IV. 1. Pursuant to Section 36 Contracts Act, the parties are bound by the content of the contract if its provisions are clear. However, it may be possible to adjust the contract if there is a distortion in the equivalence of exchange between the parties. With the revision of Section 36 Contracts Act in 1994, as mentioned in Chapter 4, it has become possible for the judge to increase an obligation. So far, case law is scarce concerning this issue.

2. However, in a case from 2004 the Western Danish High Court delivered a judgment regarding a lease contract concerning agricultural land.[44] In 1847 the original purchaser of the farm had the lease contract registered. The lease contract contained a provision according to which the current owner of the farm or any future owner had the obligation to lease a particular part of the farmland until the end of 2046. The lease contract contained no provisions with respect to termination or the determination of the rent, including the question of inflation. The annual rent for a rather substantial area of farm land was DKK 10. On 1 September 2001, the plaintiff bought the farm being fully aware of the content of the lease contract. He subsequently filed a lawsuit against the defendant claiming that the lease contract should be terminated

[42] Cf. U 2000.567H (eight years), U 2004.148H (forty years), U 1980.42H (eighteen years), U 1991.803SH (sixteen years), U 1976.947SH (twenty years). For a further discussion, see Ole Lando, Elisabeth Thuesen, Christina Tvarnø and Kim Østergaard, *Udenrigshandelens Kontrakter* (5th edn, 2006), pp. 277 *et seq.*

[43] Cf. 2000.1581H. [44] Cf. U 2004.2518V.

without notice, alternatively that the defendant should pay rent in accordance with the market value.

3. Pursuant to Section 36 Contracts Act, a contract may be modified or set aside in its entirety if it is considered unreasonable. When applying Section 36 it is possible to take into consideration the circumstances that prevailed when the contract was entered into, the contents of the contract and subsequent circumstances.[45] As the plaintiff was fully aware of the content of the lease contract, the Western High Court of Denmark decided that it was not possible to set aside the whole agreement in accordance with Section 36 Contracts Act. The plaintiff could not reasonably claim that the low rent for the farm land was an unexpected circumstance. However, the Western High Court did decide that the current rent was unfairly low and, in accordance with Section 36 Contracts Act, the rent was increased from DKK 10 to 8000, which was the amount that a sub-lessee paid to the defendant.

4. Assuming that the court adapts the price in favour of X's successors in the case at hand, Y's successors would be entitled to terminate the contract with six months' notice considering that the contract does not contain a provision on termination and has been in force for many years. Pursuant to Danish law, in general a contract that has been in force for more than five years can be terminated with a period of notice of six months.

5. Thus, in accordance with Danish law, it is possible to increase an obligation if it is considered unreasonable given the performance exchanged by the parties to the contract. The Western High Court stressed that since the plaintiff was fully aware of the content of the lease contract, it was not possible to terminate the contract in its entirety.

6. On the other hand, the Højesteret delivered a judgment in 2003 comprising a long-term oral agreement between the publisher of the Tintin comic book series and a translator, who was also the Vice President of the company for a certain period of time.[46] In the period between 1960 and 1975, the translator had translated twenty-three Tintin albums. He left his position in 1975 to work for another

[45] Section 36 Contracts Act was incorporated into the Act in 1975. At that point of time it was not possible to increase an obligation. This changed as of 1 January 1995 when Section 36 was revised by law no. 1098 of 21 December 1994. U 2004.2518 V is the first reported case where a Danish court has done so. Until this revision the agreement as provided in Case 1 would be regarded as being binding between the parties. See for instance U 1917.1 H.

[46] Cf. U 2003.23H.

publishing company. In conjunction with his departure, he signed a document with the publisher where he renounced any further and future rights concerning the translation of the twenty-three Tintin albums. By signing the document the translator received an additional amount of DKK 6,000. During the period from 1970–1974, the number of Tintin albums sold in Denmark exploded compared to the sales figures in the 1960s. The Højesteret stated in its decision that the agreement did not have any time limitations, and the translator, after he left his position, had not acted in a manner in which he could claim the additional payment of royalties since the agreement contained a provision by which he was paid a fixed salary in accordance with the number of pages translated. When the contract was entered into in 1960, it was not possible to predict the large turnover that would be generated by the Tintin albums, especially during the first part of the 1970s. However, since the translator did not take this profit potential into account in 1975 when he left the publisher, the Højesteret found that the publisher was entitled to print and sell additional numbers of the Tintin albums without any further payment to the translator.

7. Even though this case shows a distortion in the equivalence of exchange between the parties in a long-term contract, the Højesteret showed no inclination to apply Section 36 Contracts Act. The Højesteret applied a very objective interpretation of the contract between the parties and, since the contract was in no way ambiguous or unclear, it was possible to resolve the case based on the terms of the contract. The translator was paid according to the number of pages translated and he made no claims when he renounced his position. This Danish Supreme Court decision shows that if the parties have incorporated clear and unambiguous conditions in the agreement, they are bound by that agreement, even though future and unexpected profits solely benefit one of the parties to the contract.

Romanic-Mediterranean jurisdictions

Italy

In Italy, two remedies are available: renegotiation and termination. The obligation to renegotiate aims at avoiding the termination of the contract in compliance with good faith.[47] If both

[47] R. Sacco, 'Il contratto', in: R. Sacco (ed.), *Tratt. Sacco* (Turin: UTET, 2004), vol II, p. 686.

remedies (renegotiation and termination) can be validly enforced, X's successors have a free choice. Yet, once X seeks termination before a court, the modification of the contract terms can be offered by Y only and it cannot be disposed of by the judge by operation of law.[48]

I. This case deals with a long-term contract, in which the parties did not include an express provision for the impact of the inflation. Such a contractual term cannot be inferred by way of interpretation of the contract on the basis of the parties' hypothetical intention.[49]

II. Under Italian law, the creditor of a monetary claim bears the risk of the 'normal' depreciation (unless otherwise provided in the contractual terms, e.g., through index clauses). A further obstacle for X's successor is given by the so-called 'nominal value principle', pursuant to which the value of a monetary obligation is to be determined on the basis of its nominal instead of its real value.

III. 1. It should be considered, however, that pursuant to the previously mentioned Art. 1366 CC (interpretation of contractual clauses in good faith) X's successors could maintain that the long time of 100 years from the start of the contractual relationship itself implies the right to the adjustment/increase in the price, even if the parties would never have thought of it at the time of the formation of the consent. According to a similar line of reasoning one may apply (i) Art. 1374 CC (integration of the contractual effects), which provides for additional contractual terms beyond the parties' express declarations by means of mandatory rules, usage and equity,[50] or (ii) Art. 1375 CC (performance in good faith), which, in principle, leads to a duty to renegotiate the agreed price according to good faith. In fact, renegotiations avoid the need for the parties to perform the originally stipulated conditions that have subsequently become inequitable. They prevent the parties from the need to perform an illogical relationship, with no connections with its effective underlying conditions. X's successors therefore have the right to negotiate the adjustment of the contract terms.

2. Thus, if the contract itself gives X's successors no right to obtain an increase of the price due to inflation (which is a regular one, see below), we can say that the application of some general rules could induce the court to grant X's successors the requested increase of the price.

[48] F. Macario, *Adeguamentoe niregoziazione nei contratti a lungo termine* (Naples: Javene, 1996), 266.

[49] Cass., 16 March 1984, n. 1799.

[50] See overview (Chapter 4).

Although Art. 1467(3) CC does not expressly provide for an obligation to renegotiate with the aim of equitably adapting or modifying the affected contractual terms, it could be argued that, once an interest in avoiding the dissolution has been declared, each party is entitled to propose to the counter-party to enter into a negotiation. In this case, if a party refuses to negotiate or breaks off negotiations contrary to good faith and the rules of fair dealing, the court could award damages for the loss suffered, in addition to the equitable modification of the contractual terms. This conclusion could be grounded on the general duty to perform in good faith (Arts. 1175 and 1375 CC).[51]

IV. 1. In the case of a long-term contract with continuous or periodic performance, Art. 1373 CC provides that each party has a unilateral right to withdraw from the contract.

2. Alternatively, X's successors can pursue termination of the contract according to Art. 1467 CC. As the parties have agreed on a long-term contract, which is not yet completely performed, the case at issue would, in principle, fall within the scope of Art. 1467, since Italian case law has admitted that not only the increased cost of the performance (extremely onerous) but also the depreciation of the counter-performance allows a party to invoke the termination of the contract.[52] However, Italian case law[53] has stated that, as a general rule, a *regular* inflation does not represent a disrupting event or circumstance provided for by Art. 1467,[54] since the latter has to be 'extraordinary and unforeseeable'. Furthermore, Art. 1467(2) states that the termination may not be requested if the supervening hardship does not exceed the 'usual contractual risk' and we can assume that a contract concluded for an unlimited period of time implies a normal risk of depreciation.[55] Finally, one may find that inflation substantially affects the balance between the performances of the parties. Italian courts have admitted that inflation can be a reason for termination pursuant to Art. 1467 CC if the performance of the debtor has become extremely onerous or the counter-party's performance is extremely depreciated.[56] This must, however, be assessed on a case by case basis, considering the fundamental requirement that the rate of inflation be 'extraordinary and unforeseeable'. According to the prevailing

[51] Macario, *Adeguamento*, p. 349. [52] Cass., 05 February 1986, n. 670.
[53] Cass., 03 August 1990, n. 7833; Cass., 15 December 1984, n. 6574.
[54] F. Gambino, *Normalità dell'alea e fatti di conoscenza* (Milan: Giuffrè, 2001), p. 183.
[55] Cass., 09 March 1985, n. 1913. [56] Cass., 07 June 1991, n. 6452.

opinion, the claim of X's successors would be justified due to the length of the period of time.

Spain

It is unlikely that X's successors' claim for adjustment or termination of the contract would be justified because regular inflation is not an unforeseeable occurrence.

Most of the cases that have been dealt with by the TS concern situations of price inflation. The disadvantaged party claims that the contractual equilibrium has been disturbed and requests the termination of the contract or an adaptation of the price agreement to the new circumstances.

I. 1. The civil code does not include a general provision that grants the parties to a long-term contract without a time-limit a right to end the contract unilaterally. However, some specific provisions acknowledge such a right. Art 1583 CC concerning service contracts indicates that a contractual agreement for life is void. Contracts concluded for an indefinite period may be terminated (Art. 1732 CC regarding mandate contracts) after the expiration of a period determined by common usage (Art 1750 CC regarding a lending contract) or after a reasonable period of notice subject to good faith (Art. 1705 CC).

2. The Spanish courts have explicitly required that a reasonable period of notice must be observed with regard to the unilateral termination of distribution contracts. The TS has pointed out that the terminating party cannot exercise his right unilaterally.[57] For commercial agency contracts the right to unilaterally end a contract for an indefinite period is laid down in Art. 24(1) of the Act on Commercial Agency, which implements Art. 15(1) of the Directive on commercial agency. A statutory provision providing for a right to unilateral termination is also included in the Law on Rental Contracts of 1994, but only for a tenant of domestic property.

II. 1. A change in the real value of money is not generally deemed to be a sufficient ground for the application of the *rebus* clause by the TS. If the debt is a monetary one, the principle of nominal value is applied in Spanish law, so that the debt is calculated on the basis of its nominal instead of its real value. The debtor fulfils his payment obligation if he pays the agreed price irrespective of whether this sum reflects the

[57] STS of 24 February 1993 (RJ 1993 1298) and 25 January 1996 (RJ 1996, 319).

originally intended value of the obligation at the time of performance or if it has diminished due to inflation or currency devaluation.

2. Regarding these cases, the TS argues that the parties must contractually agree on terms which allow changes in the real value of money to be corrected, such as periodic revisions of the contract or stabilisation clauses.[58] Parties are expected to bear the risk of any variation in the real value of money. Therefore the Spanish courts do not generally grant relief or modify the contract if the excessive hardship is due to inflation because the increase in prices is not an unforeseeable circumstance.

3. There is a great number of judgments that deny the application of the doctrine of the *cláusula rebus sic stantibus* in this case, e.g., cases relating to the leasing of a mine[59] and to the leasing of an irrigation ditch to draw off water to supply fields.[60] In the latter judgment, the parties had contracted in 1925 and the fixed price for drawing off the water from the irrigation ditch was 250 pesetas (€1.50) per year. The lessor asked for the contract to be adapted claiming a price increase on the basis of the *rebus* clause. The court determined that the parties could have included a special clause to distribute the risk of inflation as a foreseeable circumstance in the contract.[61] According to the reasoning of the TS in this case, a contract is not to be modified 'only because time has passed and the continuous alteration of the circumstances has produced an alteration in the reciprocal values taken into account by the parties at the time the contract was concluded'.

4. However, in an exceptional case, a court modified a contract in a case concerning inflation.[62] In that case a husband had stated in his last will and testament that after his death his widow should periodically receive rent obtained from the exploitation of part of the inheritance. About forty years later, the courts decided that this amount should be increased because of inflation. This solution was based on Art. 1258 CC and the requirements of good faith: the basis of the contract had changed and this needed to be restored. On the basis of this case, it could be argued that even if normal inflation over a long period of time is the only change of circumstances (see the cases mentioned above), the (probably unforeseeable) effects of this inflation because of the

[58] STS of 15 March 1972 (RJ 1972, 1252).

[59] STS of 14 December 1940 (RJ 1940, 1135); STS of 31 November 1963 (RJ 1963, 4264).

[60] STS of 26 March 1963 (RJ 1963, 2120); STS of 10 December 1990 (RJ 1990, 9927).

[61] See for a similar Spanish case, STS of 26 March 1963 (RJ 1963, 2120).

[62] STS of 23 November 1962 (RJ 1962, 5005).

(abnormal) duration of the contract could require an adjustment of the contract based on good faith.

Portugal

X's successors can ask for an adjustment or a termination of the contract.

I. 1. If the *Canal de Craponne* case was a lease contract ('*locatio*'), the solution would be straightforward under Portuguese law since Art. 1025 CC expressly forbids an initial term of more than thirty years. Any period that is longer than the legal limit is reduced to thirty years by operation of law. According to legal literature, there is a general principle against perpetual contractual obligations as well as a right to terminate a contract without a fixed term unilaterally subject to the requirement of good faith, which includes giving reasonable notice to the other party. With regard to this principle it is true that the Code does permit perpetual leases, but it must be stressed that the debtor has the right (that cannot be waived) of transforming the periodic rent into a lump sum in order to terminate the contract unilaterally.

2. It must be recognised that the legal basis of this right of termination is somewhat uncertain since there are no general rules in the Civil Code on long-term contracts; in fact, they are a creation of literature. Again it is true that some rules exist that may be understood as an expression of such a principle – for instance a contract with an agent ('*mandatum*') may normally be terminated by the principal without the need for a ground or justification. However, those rules may be explained as resulting from the particular nature (for instance the fiduciary relationship) of that contract.

II. Assuming that the court denies a right to unilaterally terminate the contract, this case could be solved on the basis of Art. 437 CC. However, Portuguese courts have restricted its application to exceptional cases: even in cases where there is a change in the overall basis of the agreement (to use Kegel's expression), the positions taken have been very restrictive. The application of Art. 437 CC has in particular been rejected during the processes of de-settlement, nationalisation of companies and the closing of the 'Bolsa' (stock exchange) following the 1974 revolution.[63] More recently, its application was also rejected in a case in which

[63] Antonio Menezes Cordeiro, *Da Alteração das Circunstâncias, a cancretizacão do artigo 437: do Código civil à luz da jurisprudência posterior a 1974*, handout of 'Estudos em memória do Prof. Doutos Paulo Cunha (Lisbon: AAFDL, 1987), pp. 72–3 who sees a 'very restrictive tendency'.

the provider was the subject of a hostile take-over bid.[64] However considering the extremely long period of time that has lapsed, the courts probably would allow for the modification or rescission of the contract.

Greece

X's successors have the right to a judicial adjustment, which could result in an increase of the price.

I. Given that the contractual context provides no clear indication with regard to the adaptation of the contract, there is no room for complementary interpretation.

II. 1. Due to the major devaluation of the currency, X's successors have a right to an adjustment of the price according to Art. 288 AK, given that they are faced with a long-term, gradual, and as a result, also excessive devaluation. As the devaluation is of an excessive but not of an exceptional character, Art. 388 AK does not apply.[65] The perspective of a long-term contractual relationship makes the devaluation appear normal and foreseen. However, as mentioned before,[66] the crucial issue is not only whether the event was foreseeable but its implications for the allocation of the contractual risks and in this case the contract does not deal with the issues at stake.

2. The distortion is considered to be excessive only if the devaluation goes beyond the limit of 50 or 60 per cent[67] – which should be considered as a given in Case 1 – after the elapsed time of 100 years and the interference of two world wars. This kind of devaluation completely destroys the contractual apportionment of risks and makes the judicial re-allocation of the damages indispensable.[68]

3. The adjustment of the contract to the above conditions consists, according to Art. 288 AK, in a deviation from the fundamental principle of nominalism, which otherwise applies in the Greek currency system (see Art. 2 §3 compuls.L. 362/1945). In accordance with this principle,

64 'Acordão do Supremo Tribunal de Justiça' of 16 May 2002, Processo 02B1145, www.dgsi.pt. On this point in English, see A. Pinto Monteiro and Júlio Gomes, 'Rebus sic stantibus – Hardship Clauses in Portuguese Law', (1998) 3 *European Review of Private Law* 319 *et seq.*

65 See AP 382/1997, HellD 38, p. 1827; 678/1996, HellD 39, p. 593.

66 See above in the overview (Chapter 4).

67 See Iarnis Spyridakis, *Law of Obligations – General Part* (Athens: Sakkoula, 1994), p. 316; Stathopoulos, 'Art. 388', in: Ap. Georgiadis and M. Stathopoulos (eds.), *AK*, (Athens: 1978–1982) n. 29.

68 Loannis Sakketas, 'Art. 388' in: *ErmAK, Interpretation of the Civil Code* (Athens: 1949), n. 44.

the relevant value for the fulfillment of a monetary obligation is the nominal one, even if the currency has lost parts of its real value in the period between the conclusion of the contract and the fulfillment of the obligation.[69] Furthermore, the judicial intervention in the above case is an exception to the principle of subjective equivalence, which generally applies to contracts. From the perspective of the principle of subjective equivalence, the validity of a contract remains indisputable, even if the corresponding performances are not objectively equivalent. The institution of '*laesio enormis*' and the philosophical approach of a possibility to 'discover' the just price ('*justum praetium*') were not adopted by the Greek Civil Code.[70] Only under the strict conditions of Arts. 388 and 288 AK is the excessive objective disproportion between the corresponding performances to be taken into consideration. Otherwise, the strict application of the valorism principle would lead to an extreme injustice against the interests of the debtor who relies on the amount of his monetary obligation as specified in the contract.

III. Theoretically, the major disturbance of the contractual equilibrium could allow the parties to terminate the contract without notice. According to a broad principle, all long-term contractual relationships (as in Case 1) may be terminated by either party, if substantial reasons can be proved.[71] This principle derives from of a series of special provisions, which provide the parties of a long-term contract with a right to terminate it for substantial reason (e.g., Arts. 585, 588 and 594 AK for leases, Art. 672 AK for contracts of work and Art. 766 AK); and the excessive devaluation undoubtedly meets this requirement. The right of unilateral termination for a substantial reason rules out the consequence of adjusting the contract, which Art. 288 AK (and 388 AK) provides. Nevertheless, if the extraordinary termination deprives the counter-party from its right to ask for a juridical adjustment of the contract against bona fides, its exercise is forbidden as abusive (Art. 281

[69] See Gasis, 'Art. 291–292', in: n. 26; Stathopoulos, *Law of Obligations – General Part* (Athens/Thessalonica, 4th edn, 2004), §11 nn. 19, 37; Ap. Georgiadis, *General Principles of Civil Code* (Athens: Sakkoulas, 3rd edn, 2003), §8 n. 15; George Kallimopoulos, *The Law of Money* (Athens: Sakkoulas, 1993), p. 167.

[70] See Panagiotes Papanikolaou, *About the Limits of the Protective Intervention of the Judge in Contracts* (Athens, Sakkoulas, 1991), pp. 258 *et seq.*; G. Dellios, 'The Judicial Control of the Content of Consumers' Contracts and their Limits', in: *Consumers' Protection and System of Private Law* (Athens Thessalonica: Sakkoula, 2001), vol. II, pp. 351 *et seq.*

[71] See Kapodistrias, 'Introductory Notes 416–54', in: *ErmAK*, nn. 42 *et seq.*; Stathopoulos, *Law of Obligations*, §5 n. 85; Apostolos Georgiadis, *Law of Obligations – General Part*, §53 n. 10.

AK).[72] This seems to be the case in this situation. Therefore, the execution of the right of termination should be considered to be forbidden.

France and related jurisdictions

France

X's successors are entitled to terminate or to renegotiate the contract.

I. Following the principle of the sanctity of contracts, X's successors will, in principle, not be entitled to an adaptation of the terms of the contract. Even if performance leads to damages for the contractor because changed circumstances make the performance more costly than expected, respect for the creditor's legitimate expectations must prevail over any consideration of equity.[73] However, even though this principle has been approved by a part of the legal literature[74] and was restated by the Cour de Cassation,[75] the revision or termination of the contract might be possible (see II and III below).

II. A perpetual undertaking of services is contrary to Article 1780 Cciv.[76] According to this provision, a contract for services must be limited in time or to specified work. This prohibition in French law has been extended to other contracts and is currently considered to be a general principle of law.[77] Accordingly, X's successors would be allowed to terminate the contract.

[72] See Aristides Chiotellis, *The Legal Results' Determination in Case of the Disturbance of the Underlying Basis in Contractual Relationships*, Dissertation(1979/80) (Munich: Beck, 1981), pp. 162–3.

[73] Cf. D. M. Philippe, *Changement de circonstances et boulversement de l'économie contractuelle* (Brussels: Bruylant, 1986), *adde.*, on the conflict between contractual justice and legal security and A. Sériaux, 'Le futur contractuel', in: J. Austruy (ed.), *Le droit et le futur, Actes du 3e Colloque de l'Association française de philosophie du droit* (Paris: PUF, 1985), pp. 77 *et seq.*, *spec.* n°27 who considers that contractual justice only requires that voluntary unjust imbalances be rectified.

[74] G. Ripert, *La règle morale dans les obligations civiles*, n° 84. According to M. M. Malaurie *et al.*, *Les obligations* (Paris: Cujas, 2nd edn, 1990), n. 35, n° 619, *révision* is *a 'machine à faire exploser l'économie'*.

[75] In particular by its Commercial Chamber, on 3 January 1979, 18 December 1979 and 31 May 1988, revoking first instance judgments which were inclined to decide on equity. Cf.: Cass. com., 18 December 1979, Bull.civ. IV, n° 339; RTD civ. 1980, p. 780, obs. G. Cornu. See also Cass. civ., 15 November 1933, G P, 1934, I, p. 68 (refusal to apply the concept of *imprévision* to a contract concluded in 1845).

[76] J. Carbonnier, *Les obligations* (Paris: PUF, 21st edn, 1998), n° 6.3; O. Litty, *Inégalité des parties et durée du contrat* (Paris: LGDJ, 1999); Philippe, *Changement de circumstances*, p. 148.

[77] Litty, *Inégalité*, p. 321.

III. One could also invoke the concept of good faith. In this case, the heirs suffered significant losses by providing the service. The judge could, on this basis, grant an injunction to the parties so that they can renegotiate the contract.[78]

Belgium

X's successors are entitled to terminate the contract. Furthermore, their claim to adjust the price agreement to the changed circumstances is likely to be granted by the recognition of a duty to renegotiate.

I. Belgian law, like French law, does not recognise perpetual contracts. Therefore it can be assumed that judges would authorise a termination of this kind of contract by the debtor.

II. Second, beneficiaries can possibly renounce an inheritance. In this way, they can also avoid the consequences of a disadvantageous contract.

III. Third, one could invoke the principle that contracts have to be performed in good faith. If the strict performance of a contract is disproportionately onerous for one party or derisory for the other due to changed circumstances, the judge could consider that the principle of good faith is affected. In the case at hand, the beneficiaries suffered significant losses by providing the service in question; upholding the contract unaltered indeed seems to violate the principle of good faith. In order to meet the demands of good faith, a duty to renegotiate the contract might be derived from this principle. However, this solution is not as clear-cut or as certain as it is in France because in Belgium there is no case law like the case of *Huard*[79] and the following cases where parties have been obliged to renegotiate the contract when there are unexpected circumstances.

England and related jurisdictions

England and Ireland

The most likely solution to this question under English and Irish law is that X's successors have no right to renegotiate the consideration, nor will a court vary the price payable under the

[78] Cass., 16 June 2004; see on this problem, J. Azéma, *La durée des contrats successifs* (Paris: LGDJ 1969).

[79] Cass. Com 3 November 1992, *sté française des pétroles BP* v. *Huard*, JCP 1993, II, nr. 22614.

contract. However, Y's successors will not be able to hold the other contracting party to the contract forever, and the contract is likely to be held to be terminable upon giving reasonable notice, either by way of a process of construction of the agreement or by way of an implied term. Although it is not entirely clear, there would appear to be no reason why the exercise of a termination right by one contracting party against another would create a subsequent obligation to negotiate another contract.[80]

I. First, with regard to X's successors' claim to an increase in price, there is no statutory provision in England or Ireland which would allow X's successors to seek such an increase. Nor is a court at liberty to vary the terms of the contract to increase the price payable under the contract because of a change in circumstances. Thus, X's successors could not demand an increase in the price payable under the contract. X's successors could well seek to renegotiate the contract price but Y's successors in title would be in no way bound to enter into such negotiations. If Y's successors were to agree to make an additional payment in return for the continuing right to draw this water, recent English[81] and Irish[82] case law would recognise that such a promise would be binding upon Y's successors, but, absent such a voluntary agreement on the part of Y's successors, X's successors have no right to insist on a renegotiation of the contract price.

II. X could attempt to claim the reasonable value of the benefits conferred upon Y in the past, in the hope that this would be fixed at a value higher than the contract price. Such a *quantum meruit* claim is essentially a restitutionary claim, which might be sustained if, for example, the contract is void for uncertainty of terms,[83] or if no contract exists because of the absence of good consideration.[84] Similarly, if a contract is concluded on the basis of a common or mutual mistake,

[80] It would appear that in the *Staffordshire Water* case, the court expected the parties to renegotiate the price. However, the majority of the court was somewhat unclear on this issue, and it is likely that this conclusion was based on the particular facts of the case, including its statutory background.

[81] *Williams* v. *Roffey Bros. & Nicholls (Contractors) Ltd* [1990] 1 All ER 512 (Eng).

[82] *Trucks Machinery Sales Ltd* v. *Marubeni Komatsu Ltd*, Unreported, High Court, 23 February 1996. In Australia see *Musumeci* v. *Winadell Pty* (1994) 34 NSWLR 723 and in New Zealand see *Newmasters Ltd* v. *Ranier Investments* [1992] 2 NZLR 68 and *Antons Trawling Co* v. *Smith* [2003] 2 NZLR 23.

[83] *Folens & Co* v. *Minister for Education* [1984] ILRM 281.

[84] *Bradford* v. *Roulston* [1858] 8 IRCL 468.

which has the effect of rendering the contract void, subsequent performance of the contract before the mistake comes to light will entitle a court to uphold a *quantum meruit* claim.[85] However, these facts do not suggest a mistake of any kind.

Alternatively, X could claim that the contract was terminated at some point in the past, for example on the basis of frustration, and that the work he has done since then should be paid for on a restitutionary or *quantum meruit* basis, as opposed to at the contractual rate. However, it is not possible to base a frustration argument on the mere fact that many years have gone by and the contract is now more burdensome than it was at the time of its formation. Also, the fact that X and Y, and their successors, have to date performed the contract would probably prevent the success of any such argument.[86] However, even if this argument were to succeed, it would only represent a potential increase in the price payable for past services and could not provide a basis for a future increase in price.

III. 1. Third, with regard to X's successors' claim that they are entitled to terminate the contract, if the contract was a personal contract, then it would be at an end upon the death of X or Y. However, the facts indicate that the parties to the contract anticipate that the contract is *not* a personal contract. X and Y's successors have continued to observe the terms of the initial contract, so both parties would be estopped from asserting that the contractual obligations should be regarded as being personal to X and Y.

2. Neither English nor Irish statute law contains any general rule that allows a long-term contract to be terminated when the contract has been concluded for an unlimited period of time. It has already been mentioned that the doctrine of frustration of contract would not provide a remedy here. It is generally foreseeable that a long-term contract will be affected by factors such as inflation or changes in the market, and no supervening event has occurred on which to base a frustration argument.[87] Judicial intervention is possible only if the agreement *itself* contains a basis for permitting the court to conclude that the contract

[85] *Fanning* v. *Wicklow County Council*, Unreported, Irish High Court, 30 April 1984.

[86] See *Davis Contractors Ltd* v. *Fareham UDC* [1956] AC 696 (Eng). Such an argument was, however, successful in the Australian case of *Codelfa Construction Proprietary Ltd* v. *State Rail Authority of New South Wales* (1982) 149 CLR 337.

[87] Such a supervening event could potentially include a situation where inflation increases 'not at a trot or a canter, but at a gallop' *Wates Ltd* v. *Great London Council* [1983] 25 BLR 1, per Stephenson LJ at 35.

was not intended to run in perpetuity. The court may find that the parties never intended for the contract to bind the parties in perpetuity, but rather that it was intended that it could be terminated on the giving of reasonable notice. This could be done either on the basis of implied terms or simply on an interpretation of the contract.

3. The facts presented to us strongly resemble those that arose in the English case of *Staffordshire Area Health Authority* v. *South Staffordshire Waterworks Co.*[88] In that case a contract agreed in 1929 provided that the defendant water company would provide a hospital with water 'at all times hereafter'. The contract contained no provisions on termination. By the 1970s the agreement had become extremely burdensome on the defendant, owing to increases in water rates and the effects of inflation. The hospital authorities were paying 2.9p per gallon, whereas the ordinary rate payable was almost nineteen times that, at 55p per gallon. The defendant gave the hospital six months' notice to terminate the agreement, which the hospital refused to accept. The trial judge held the 1929 agreement was to run in perpetuity and the 1975 notice was invalid. The Court of Appeal reversed this decision. Taking a broad interpretation of the contract, the majority held the phrase 'at all times hereafter' was capable of meaning 'at all times hereafter during the subsistence of the agreement'.[89] Hence the contract was silent as to whether or not it was determinable by notice, and it was open to the court to find that it was so determinable. The majority was of the view that it was 'incredible'[90] that the defendants should have bound themselves to supply whatever the hospital required upon terms fixed once and for all, and concluded that the agreement was capable of termination on reasonable notice. Goff LJ cited with approval an important dictum from McNair J in *Martin-Baker Aircraft Co* v. *Canadian Flight Equipment Ltd*[91] where the learned judge said:

> I do not feel that a law merchant would normally look at such an agreement as this as being an agreement intended to constitute permanent relationships. For example, I have little doubt that the law merchant would regard a contract for sale of a hundred tons of coal monthly at a fixed price, no period being specified, as a contract determinable on reasonable notice.[92]

88 [1978] 1 WLR 1287 (Eng). 89 *Ibid.*, 1399.
90 *Ibid.*, 1402. 91 [1955] 2 All ER 722 (Eng.).
92 *Ibid.*, 733. This case was cited with approval by Peart J in *Dakota Packaging Ltd* v. *APH Manufacturing*, Unreported, Irish High Court, 10 October 2003, later overruled by the Irish Supreme Court but on another point.

This case can be contrasted with the New Zealand Court of Appeal's decision in *The Power Co Ltd* v. *Gore District Council*.[93] There, a 1927 deed set the price that the Power Company's predecessors in title could charge in supplying electricity to Gore District Council at one penny per unit. In this transaction Gore District Council were in fact also transferring assets to the Power Company and in the supervening period the Power Company enjoyed additional benefits from the relationship created through the deed. However, in 1995 the Power Company purported to give fifteen months' notice of termination of the agreement and Gore District Council refused to accept this notice of termination. The Power Company sought a declaration that the obligation was at an end, either because the deed was terminable on notice or through the doctrine of frustration. The Court of Appeal, however, pointed to an express term in the 1927 Deed which said that the deed was to be binding 'for all time hereafter'. This clause was held to be dispositive. It was not possible to 'read down' the clause, nor infer, as in *Staffordshire*, that the price was only to be payable during the currency of the agreement. Thus, the obligation was perpetual and it was not possible to terminate the contract on the giving of notice. On the issue of frustration the New Zealand Court of Appeal found that the high level of inflation throughout the 1970s and 1980s, and the fact that the supply of electricity to Gore District Council was now much more expensive, did not justify a finding of frustration, although the Court of Appeal did indicate that some sudden dramatic fall in the value of the currency might have such an effect.[94] Looking at the other benefits secured for the Power Company by the contract, it could not be said that the fixed cost of providing electricity rendered the contract fundamentally different. In an interesting piece of *obiter dicta*, the Court of Appeal suggested that private law concepts such as frustration were not readily applicable to contracts between public agencies where the state, through legislation for example, would be the most appropriate means of dealing with changing circumstances.[95]

[93] [1997] 1 NZLR 537.

[94] The Court here referred to the statement of Stephenson LJ in *Wates Ltd* v. *Greater London Council* that a contract could be frustrated if inflation increases 'not at a trot or a canter, but at a gallop'. [1983] 25 BLR 1, 35 (Eng).

[95] In a recent follow up decision on this dispute, the New Zealand High Court has held that subsequent regulatory legislation has not altered the binding nature of the 1927 deed: *Gore District Council* v. *The Power Co* [2003] 1 NZLR 697.

4. Whether or not an English or Irish court would take an approach similar to that in the *Staffordshire* case or the *Power Co Ltd* case would most likely depend on the facts of the case at hand, as the result in both essentially depended on the court's construction of the particular contract. However, in a case such as the one presented in the current hypothetical, where the contract is silent as to the duration of the contract, it is more likely that the court would follow the *Staffordshire* line of jurisprudence.

IV. While the majority in *Staffordshire* did not accept an implied term methodology, there are later cases in which changed circumstances do trigger the use of implied term reasoning. For example, in *Express Newspapers Plc* v. *Silverstone Circuits*[96] the English Court of Appeal held that where safety considerations at a motor racing circuit required the demolition of a bridge, a contract permitting a newspaper the exclusive right to advertise its product on the bridge did not afford the newspaper a right to prevent removal of the bridge. In the view of the Court of Appeal the licence to advertise on that bridge was subject to an implied term that the licence would terminate if at any time it became necessary to remove or destroy the bridge, for whatever reason.

V. Irish case law suggests that an implied term solution to this kind of problem is likely to be adopted. There is a significant body of jurisprudence drawn from cases in which continuing and recurring obligations arise under agreements that do not expressly deal with issues such as the duration of the contract or termination.[97] The leading case is *Irish Welding* v. *Philips Electrical (Ireland) Ltd.*,[98] in which a sole distributorship contract was silent on the issue of termination. Finlay P held that it was quite unrealistic to conclude that either party intended the agreement to be terminable at will and the learned judge ruled that this agreement was terminable upon giving reasonable notice; in this case a reasonable notice period was nine months. Nevertheless there are agreements that can be held to be perpetual[99] or to be by their nature irrevocable[100] or indeed terminable at will.[101] However, these will be the exception rather than the rule.

[96] *The Independent*, 16 June 1989 (Eng).
[97] For example, distributorship agreements and exclusive licences.
[98] Unreported, Irish High Court, 8 October 1976.
[99] *Watford Borough Council* v. *Watford RDC*, Reported in *The Times*, 18 December 1967 (Eng).
[100] *Harrods Ltd* v. *Harrods (Buenos Aires) Ltd* [1999] FSR 187 (Eng).
[101] Bare contractual licences for example.

Scotland

There appears to be no Scottish case on exactly the same facts as the *Canal de Craponne* case.[102] It is difficult to anticipate the decision which a Scottish court is likely to take on these facts. If a court chose to follow established Scottish law, X would not be released from the contract. This is because a Scottish court does not have the power to imply a term permitting termination on reasonable notice in contracts of unlimited duration. That said, however, a Scottish court might choose to follow the (English) authority of the *Staffordshire* case. If so, X would be released from the contract on the particular authority of that case, rather than through an application of the general concept of frustration of contract. The matter is an open question, and it is impossible to provide a definitive answer.

I. It is assumed that, for the purposes of this question, the contract expressly states that it has been entered into for an unlimited duration. Thus, the unlimited duration is an express term of the contract. This being the case, it is not possible to imply a term to the effect that the contract is terminable on notice by either party. The courts will not imply a term into a contract which would directly contradict an express term.[103] So also, a term could not be implied allowing the parties to vary the price where the actual price is stipulated by an express term.

II. 1. It is important to distinguish here between contracts entered into for an unlimited period and those entered into for an indefinite duration. As noted above, it is assumed that this question concerns a contract entered into for an unlimited duration. This being the case the court will not imply a term permitting termination on notice. Nor is there any statutory provision granting such a right. Contracts of long duration are relatively common in Scots law, particularly in the context of leases of heritable property. In such leases, the parties are expected to agree a rent for the entire duration, or include a mechanism in the lease for revisal of the rent in accordance with market rates during the whole

[102] With regard to the English case of *Staffordshire Area Health Authority* v. *South Staffordshire Waterworks Co*, which is likely to be treated as authoritative in Scotland, see the English and Irish report.

[103] *Cummings* v. *Charles Connell & Co (Shipbuilders) Ltd* 1968 SC 305, per Lord Clyde at 309 and Lord Guthrie at 311, both of whom cite W. M. Gloag, *The Law of Contract* (Edinburgh: W. Green, 2nd edn, 1929), p. 289; W. W. McBryde, *The Law of Contract in Scotland* (Edinburgh: W. Green, 3rd edn, 2007), para. 9–10.

duration of the lease. There are examples of cases where the court has, in effect, held that an agreement was to continue in perpetuity.[104]

2. By contrast, contracts entered into for an indefinite duration may be terminated on notice. McBryde identifies two opposing lines of authority,[105] one of which suggests that such termination requires reasonable notice[106] and the other that simple notice, whether reasonable or otherwise, is required.[107]

III. In Scots law, the fact that supervening events or a change in the law has made the contract more burdensome or less profitable is irrelevant.[108] Similarly, the fact that the contract has become more expensive to perform, or commercially less attractive for one party, is not relevant, and will not result in frustration of that contract.[109] Inflation alone cannot constitute frustration,[110] and a party cannot avoid his duty to perform a contract on the grounds of 'commercial impossibility'.[111]

Editors' comparative notes

The open jurisdictions

In most of the open jurisdictions, X is entitled to request an adjustment of the contract (Austria, Germany, Greece, Lithuania, the Netherlands, Portugal and Sweden). The adjustment allows the courts to save the basic bargain to the benefit of Y. In Italy, Y will be under an obligation to renegotiate the contract in good faith. As an alternative to adjustment, X may also terminate the contract. A potential exception is Germany, where – according to the doctrine of *Wegfall der Geschäftsgrundlage* – adjustment is generally regarded as the primary remedy.

The predominant criterion in the open jurisdictions is whether the inflation was foreseeable. 'Regular' inflation is not regarded as unforeseeable. This corresponds to the nominal value principle according to which the amount of a monetary debt is based on its nominal and not on its 'real' value. Excessive inflation, however, may be regarded as unforeseeable and therefore is a potential justification for adjustment. Nevertheless, the standards for determining the 'excessiveness' of

[104] *Bernards* v. *North British Railway Company* (1897) 5 SLT 116.
[105] McBryde, *Contract*, para. 9–16.
[106] *Fifeshire Road Trustees* v. *Cowdenbeath Coal Co* (1883) 11 R. 18.
[107] *Stewart & Co* v. *Rendall* (1899) 1 F. 1002. [108] *Holliday* v. *Scott* (1830) 8 S. 831.
[109] *Wilson* v. *Tennants* [1917] AC 495.
[110] *Wates Ltd* v. *Greater London Council* (1983) 25 BLR 1 (CA).
[111] *Hong-Kong and Whampoa Dock Co Ltd* v. *Netherton Shipping Co Ltd* 1909 SC 34.

inflation necessarily remain vague and somewhat arbitrary. The decisive point in the case at hand is that the inflation has accumulated over a long period of time. After 100 years, the price level will have changed drastically even if the yearly rates of inflation cannot be considered as excessive.

The rationale for the general willingness to grant relief seems to be the fact that the parties did not take the long-term effects of their contract into account even though they might have been foreseeable at the time of conclusion. As a consequence, one party has to bear the burden of an obligation that was originally not intended by the contracting parties.

The remedy of termination is generally available for long-term contracts. By granting a right to terminate the contract upon reasonable notice, most jurisdictions take into account that the parties are unable to foresee all future changes of circumstances. A right to terminate such contracts avoids placing unreasonable burdens on one party, which usually correspond with windfall profits for the other party. This rationale is clearly expressed in the Dutch response.

The closed jurisdictions

In the group of closed jurisdictions, the majority solution to this case is also a right to terminate the contract upon reasonable notice. As with the open jurisdictions, the main rationale for termination is the long-term nature of the contract. The answer is somewhat less certain in jurisdictions where the solution is based on implied terms of the contract, such as England, Ireland and Scotland, because the contract at hand does not lend itself to constructive interpretation. In these jurisdictions, the legal ground for granting a right to terminate the contract is not firmly established in the case law and quite disputed in legal literature.

With the exception of Denmark, where an increase of the rent is granted, adjustment is not an option in the closed jurisdictions. Belgium and France introduce an obligation to renegotiate the contract.

Conclusion

In the given case, all legal systems are likely to grant some form of relief as a result of the excessive change in the contractual equilibrium over such a long period of time. While termination is available as a remedy in most of the jurisdictions, a claim for adjustment of the contract is recognised only in some. Termination is the more 'radical' remedy because it simply sets the contractual agreement aside, whereas adjustment constitutes a more 'conservative' remedy as it can save a part of the contractual agreement. One should also consider that the availability of some form of adjustment is of particular significance in this case as X's channel and Y's piece of land are naturally bound together so that neither party can easily replace the other's consideration with a third party transaction.

Case 2 Extraordinary inflation

Hardship due to extraordinary inflation; hardship resulting from a foreign currency agreement

(a) *Extraordinary inflation*

X receives a loan from the Y-Bank. Under the agreement, the interest rate is fixed at 10 per cent for five years. In the twenty years immediately before the agreement, the rate of inflation had been relatively stable within a range of 1 to 6 per cent. In the third year after the conclusion of the agreement, the economic situation begins to destabilise and inflation rises quickly to 50 per cent.

Y-Bank asks for an adjustment or for a termination of the contract.

(b) *Variation: foreign currency agreement*

The loan agreement between X and the Y-Bank provides for repayment and interest in a foreign currency. In the ten years immediately before the agreement, the relevant exchange rate had been relatively stable within a range of 20 per cent. Subsequently, the national currency is devalued by 80 per cent compared to the foreign currency.

X asks for an adjustment or for a termination of the contract.

Germany and related jurisdictions

Germany

With regard to both cases, the aggrieved parties are entitled to an adjustment of the contract under German law.

(a) Extraordinary inflation

I. 1. In the given case, the contract does not contain an explicit clause providing for the impact of extraordinary inflation.[112] Furthermore, the

[112] Provisions that increase the interest rate in relation to currency inflation are limited by the Gesetz über das Verbot von Preisklauseln bei der Bestimmung von Geldschulden (Preisklauselgesetz) vom 7.9.2007, BGBl. I, p. 2248; cf. for further details C. Grüneberg, 'Anh zu §245', in: Palandt *et al.* (eds.), *Bürgerliches Gesetzbuch*; Roth, '§313', in: W. Krüger

inflation cannot be dealt with by interpretation of the contract on the basis of the parties' actual or hypothetical will. The concept of complementary interpretation is not applicable if there is no hint how to extrapolate a rule for the impact of extraordinary inflation from the contract. Thus, the contract itself can not be drawn upon.

2. A is not relieved from his contractual obligation on the ground of impossibility. The extraordinary inflation is not covered by the doctrine of *practical impossibility* (§275 II BGB). The relevant test is whether the burden of (specific) performance – the payment of the interest rates by X – is grossly disproportionate as compared to the bank's interest in the performance.[113] In this case, X's burden of performance is not increased because, due to inflation, the actual value of the repayment and of the interest in the third year is *less* than the value at the time of formation. Moreover, there is no imbalance between X's burden of performance and the bank's gain. A reduction of X's burden of performance, which is at stake in this case, is not covered by the concept of practical impossibility.

3. Y-Bank has no right to terminate the contract under the rule of §488 III BGB. This rule provides for the termination of a loan after three month's notice if the duration of the contract is not limited.[114] It has to be assumed that X and Y limited the duration of the contract. Moreover, Y-Bank may not terminate the contract due to extraordinary circumstances according to §490 I BGB. This right arises only if the financial circumstances of the debtor deteriorate or the given security decreases in value, both of which is not the case.

II. 1. As the requirements of those special provisions (§§488, 490 I BGB) are not met, the concept of *Geschäftsgrundlage* is applicable.[115] It is characteristic for this case that the nominally fixed interest rate has a substantially lower buying power at the time of performance than was expected by the parties at the time of formation. Thus, the debtor's contractual burden of performance is substantially mitigated.[116] This

et al., *Münchener Kommentar zum Bürgerlichen Gesetzbuch* (Munich: Beck, 5th edn, 2007), vol. II, nn. 163 *et seq.*; K. Larenz, *Schuldrecht I*, §12 V; K. Schmidt, 'Grundfragen der vertraglichen Wertsicherung', (1983) *ZIP*, 639.

113 For further details cf. Case 1 n. 2.

114 Cf. W. Weidenkaff, '§488', in: Palandt *et al.* (eds.), *Bürgerliches Gesetzbuch*, nn. 31 *et seq.*; R. Freitag, 'Die Beendigung des Darlehensvertrages nach dem Schuldrechtsmodernisierungsgesetz', (2001) WM, 2370.

115 Cf. §490 III BGB; W. Weidenkaff, '§490', in: Palandt *et al.* (eds.), *Bürgerliches Gesetzbuch*, n. 17; Freitag, 'Die Beendigung des Darlehensvertrages nach dem Schuldrechtsmodernisierungsgesetz'.

116 Cf. Larenz, *Schuldrecht I*, §10 II d, 12 VII.

case addresses the problem of the effect of an extraordinary inflation ('galloping inflation') on the contractual obligation, i.e., the discrepancy between the nominally fixed interest rate and its intended actual value.[117] According to prevailing case law [118] and the majority of legal writers,[119] the concept of *Geschäftsgrundlage* is applicable in such cases. This is also true after its codification in 2002 (see §313 BGB) as the legislative history of the reform act of 2002 explicitly refers to distortion of the equivalence of exchange by inflation.[120]

2. The concept of *Geschäftsgrundlage* requires a basic assumption that is shared by both parties at the time of formation or an assumption of one party, recognisable to and uncontested by the other party.[121] The concept of *Geschäftsgrundlage* is applicable if extraordinary inflation causes an unexpected distortion of the equivalence of exchange.[122]

3. In the given case, the requirement of a *substantial* effect is met. The parties to a long-term contract bear the risk of 'normal' depreciation.[123] In this case, the equivalence of exchange is distorted by an 'extraordinary' inflation. Due to the stability of conditions over a period of twenty years, the *extraordinary* inflation was not foreseeable and the parties supposedly did not include it in the calculation of the interest rates. Moreover, the nominal value principle comes to an end in an economic situation characterised by extraordinary inflation. In this situation the general economic interest of adhering to the nominal value principle is trumped by the individual interest of the creditor[124] as the currency has lost a substantial part of its function to provide measurement for the value of goods[125] and the nominal value principle would result in an essentially unjust solution for the creditor. Based on this reasoning, the courts allowed an adaptation of contracts in the times of extraordinary

[117] Cf. for the impact of a 'creeping inflation' on long term contracts, Case 1.

[118] Cf. RGZ 103, 328; 107, 78 (87); 145, 51; for a summary cf. Roth, '§313', in: Krüger, *Münchener Kommentar zum Bürgerlichen Gesetzbuch*, vol. II, nn. 147 *et seq.*

[119] Cf. Larenz, *Schuldrecht I*, §10 II d, 12 VII; Grüneberg, '§313', in: Palandt *et al.* (eds.), *Bürgerliches Gesetzbuch*, nn. 26 *et seq.*; Roth, '§313', in: Krüger, *Münchener Kommentar zum Bürgerlichen Gesetzbuch*, vol. II, nn. 147–9.

[120] Cf. Regierungsbegründung BT-Ds. 14/6040, p. 174.

[121] Cf. Case 1.

[122] Cf. Grüneberg, '§313', in: Palandt *et al.* (eds.), *Bürgerliches Gesetzbuch*, n. 27; Roth, '§313', in: Krüger, *Münchener Kommentar zum Bürgerlichen Gesetzbuch*, vol. II, nn. 148 *et seq.*; Larenz, *Schuldrecht I*, §10 II d, 12 VII; Regierungsbegründung BT-Ds. 14/6040, p. 174.

[123] For the limits of this risk allocation cf. Case 1.

[124] Cf. Roth, '§313', in: Krüger, *Münchener Kommentar zum Bürgerlichen Gesetzbuch*, vol. II, n. 149.

[125] For this argument cf. Larenz, *Schuldrecht I*, §12 VII.

inflation in Germany (1922/1923).[126] There was also an extensive discussion among legal writers about whether the increased inflation rates in the 1970s exceeded the decisive margin.[127] Even though courts allowed the adaptation of *some* specific kinds of long-term contracts,[128] they usually held that the inflation at that time did not rise to a level that makes an adaptation of the interest rate of (long-term) monetary obligations necessary by law.[129]

4. Y-Bank is *unreasonably burdened* by the contract because the risk of a substantial distortion due to extraordinary inflation is not allocated to the bank by contract nor by statute. Even though the creditor of a monetary obligation usually bears the risk of depreciation of the currency, this risk allocation covers only normal inflation.[130] Moreover, due to the long-term stable inflation, the parties could not foresee an extraordinary inflation.

5. The prime legal consequence of a finding of *Geschäftsgrundlage* is an adjustment of the contract on the basis of §313 I, III BGB. The usual adaptation is an increase of the debtor's payment with regard to the nominal sum of money and with regard to the interest rate. The courts increased the payment and held that the debtor does not have to pay the former value of his monetary obligation but a just amount that is allocated between the former and the actual value.[131] This amount is determined on the basis of the shift in the general economic conditions since the time of the formation. Hence, Y-Bank can ask for an adjustment of the contract by the court. Usually the parties will renegotiate the contract before a claim is filed. Nevertheless, according to the prevailing view in case law and in legal literature, there is no right to enforce a renegotiation of the contract under German law.

6. Y-Bank cannot terminate the contract based on the concept of *Geschäftsgrundlage* (§313 III BGB) since it can be adjusted to the circumstances. The general right to terminate a long-term contract without notice if the party is unreasonable burdened (§314 BGB) does

[126] Cf. note 420.

[127] Cf. Roth, '§313', in: Krüger, *Münchener Kommentar zum Bürgerlichen Gesetzbuch*, vol. II, n. 160.

[128] Cf. Case 1; for an overview cf. Roth, '§313', in: Krüger, *Münchener Kommentar zum Bürgerlichen Gesetzbuch*, vol. II, n. 159.

[129] Cf. BGH LM §242 (Ba) n. 94, 95.

[130] This risk allocation is justified by the fact that the usual depreciation of the currency value is known to the parties and can be included into the calculation; cf. Roth, '§313', in: Krüger, *Münchener Kommentar zum Bürgerlichen Gesetzbuch*, vol. II, n. 161.

[131] Cf. RGZ 100, 129; RGZ 107, 78 (86 *et seq.*) (other contracts than loans).

not apply because an adjustment of the contract according to §313 BGB is possible.

(a) Variation: foreign currency agreement

I. 1. The devaluation of the national currency altered the exchange rate between the two currencies substantially and led to an increased burden for the debtor. This is also true with regard to §244 BGB. According to this provision the debtor may perform a foreign currency obligation in Euros unless the parties explicitly stipulated for a payment in the foreign currency. But even if §244 BGB is applicable the foreign currency still provides for the *value* of the debt.[132] Cases like the one at hand are – according to the courts[133] and the majority opinion of legal writers[134] – covered by §313 BGB.

2. The equivalence of exchange is part of the *Geschäftsgrundlage*, which is affected by the devaluation of the national currency. The *Geschäftsgrundlage* was affected substantially: the parties may foresee a change in the exchange rate and the contractual agreement implicitly allocates this risk to the affected party. Thus, X as the debtor of a foreign currency obligation bears the risk of 'normal' changes in the exchange rate that increase his burden of obligation. However, this risk allocation does not apply if the change in the exchange rate exceeds the normal range by a long way.[135] With regard to foreign currency agreements, the courts accept a substantial affection of the *Geschäftsgrundlage* – compared with cases of an extraordinary inflation – under a test quite easy to pass. In the 1930s the courts held that the devaluation of the national currency by 30 per cent qualified for a substantial affection of the *Geschäftsgrundlage*.[136] In a single decision even a devaluation of only 13 per cent was held enough.[137] Legal writers, however, consider this

[132] For the general legal background of foreign currency agreements cf. Grüneberg, '§245', in: Palandt *et al.* (eds.), *Bürgerliches Gesetzbuch*, nn. 17 *et seq.*; S. Grundmann, '§245', in: Krüger, *Münchener Kommentar zum Bürgerlichen Gesetzbuch*, vol. II, nn. 88 *et seq.*; G. Maier-Reimer, 'Fremdwährungsverbindlichkeiten', (1985) NJW 2049.

[133] Cf. RGZ 141, 216; RGZ 147, 289; RGZ 155, 137; RGZ 163, 334; BGH WM 1965, 843.

[134] Cf. Roth, '§313', in: Krüger, *Münchener Kommentar zum Bürgerlichen Gesetzbuch*, vol. II, nn. 148 *et seq.*; Grüneberg, '§313', in: Palandt *et al.* (eds.), *Bürgerliches Gesetzbuch*, n. 27.

[135] Cf. Grüneberg, '§313', in: Palandt *et al.* (eds.), *Bürgerliches Gesetzbuch*, n. 34.

[136] Cf. RGZ 141, 212 (216); RGZ 163, 324 (333); RGZ 155, 137.

[137] Cf. RGZ 147, 286 (289).

not significant enough to justify an amendment of the agreement.[138] In the given case, the depreciation is four times higher than the stable range over the last twenty years; neither the contract nor the law therefore allocates the risk at hand.

3. Furthermore, Y is *unreasonably burdened* if the contract is upheld in spite of the devaluation.[139] Even though some speculative elements *may* be inherent in a foreign currency obligation, this does not provide sufficient grounds for an allocation of the risk to X. Thus, X can ask for an adjustment of the contract on the basis of §313 I, III BGB.[140]

Austria

The Y-Bank is not entitled to termination or adjustment of the loan contract. With regard to the variation: X bears the risk of devaluation of the national currency and is obliged to fulfill his contractual obligations. The contract will not be adjusted.

(a) Extraordinary inflation

I. 1.§988 ABGB provides that depreciation of money does not increase the numerical obligation of repayment. Nevertheless, according to general principles of Austrian law 'long-term contracts' ('*Dauerschuldverhältnisse*') can be terminated if there is a serious cause ('*wichtiger Grund*') that renders performance unreasonably burdensome for one party (extraordinary right of termination of long-term contract or '*außerordentliche Kündigung*').[141]

2. In view of the inflation in consequence of World War II, the Austrian OGH held that extraordinary changes of monetary value making the performance of an obligation unacceptable to one party constitute a sufficient cause which entitles the burdened party to terminate a long-term contract.[142] Alternatively, a party to a long-term contract is entitled to invoke '*Wegfall der Geschäftsgrundlage*' if an extraordinary depreciation of money occurs that could not have been foreseen by

[138] Cf. Grüneberg, '§313', in: Palandt *et al.* (eds.), *Bürgerliches Gesetzbuch*, n. 27; cf. also BGH WM 1965, 843: devaluation of 4.76 per cent does not qualify for a substantial affection of the *Geschäftsgrundlage*.

[139] For the decisive criteria see above.

[140] Before the concept of *Geschäftsgrundlage* was codified, the courts held that the party burdened by the devaluation could claim a partial compensation. Nevertheless, this was only applied to contracts for the mutual exchange of goods and money but not to loans Cf. RGZ 145, 51. This distinction is neither codified in §313 nor it is upheld by the courts and legal writers.

[141] Koziol and Welser, *Bürgerliches Recht*, vol. II, p. 9. [142] OGH, JBl 1961, 188.

the parties at the time of contract conclusion.[143] As far as other contracts (mere exchange of goods or services and money) are concerned, the depreciation of money must cause a serious imbalance between the performances which is ruinous for the aggrieved party.[144] If this is not the case, the contract cannot be terminated on the basis of '*Wegfall der Geschäftsgrundlage*'.

3. A loan contract is, in principle, a long-term contract: the debtor 'rents' a sum of money from the creditor; the debtor's obligations are twofold: he has to pay a monthly or annual 'rent' (interest payment) and he has to pay back the sum received. The obligation to return the rented object (the repayment of the capital) is not typical for a long-term contract. Handing over and returning the object (i.e., the sum of money) merely provides the basis for performance of the long-term 'lease', where a sum of money is provided in exchange for interest payment. The main performances in a long-term loan contract are, therefore, the provision of credit and the interest payment. If the imbalance of the agreed performances in a loan contract is at stake, the value of these two main performances must be assessed and compared. The depreciation of the capital sum itself is a different issue to be analysed separately. It may cause a serious imbalance of exchange as well, but the exchange under scrutiny here is of a different nature. It does not include a time element; the parties merely intend to restore the object of the 'rent' at the end of the rental period.

4. In this case, inflation does not render the main exchange (use of money against interest) inadequate. While the money provided to the debtor loses its value, the individual interest rates paid in exchange depreciate as well. What is actually distorted in this case, is the give-and-return relationship concerning the capital sum of the loan. This is not a long-term exchange with recurring obligations (as the main exchange relationship) and cannot simply be left intact for the past three years and terminated for the future. Termination or adjustment of the whole contract on the basis of '*Wegfall der Geschäftsgrundlage*' is only possible if the performance of the contract is ruinous for the aggrieved party. Assuming that it is not, Y-Bank is not entitled to terminate or adjust the contract.

5. According to the prevailing Austrian opinion, the legal consequence of a '*Wegfall der Geschäftsgrundlage*' can be either termination or

[143] Günter Ertl, *Inflation, Privatrecht und Wertsicherung* (Vienna: Manz, 1980), p. 235.
[144] Rummel, '§920', in: Rummel (ed.), *Kommentar zum ABGB*, vol. I, n. 4.

adjustment of the contract.[145] Some authors even give priority to the adjustment of the contract.[146] If the consequences of an unchanged continuation of performances of the loan were really disastrous or ruinous for Y-Bank, the adequate remedy would certainly be an adjustment and not a termination of the contract (because the latter would force the debtor to repay the whole outstanding capital at once). Adjustment could mean that part of the inflation rate of 50 per cent is taken into account when recalculating the capital that has to be repaid at the end of the loan period. Even though there is no formal 'right to renegotiate' under Austrian contract law, the parties are, of course, not prevented from seeking agreement on a change of the contract.

(b) Variation: foreign currency agreement

I. 1. The doctrines of '*Wegfall der Geschäftsgrundlage*' or extraordinary termination do not apply where the change of circumstances (the serious cause) is part of a risk assumed by one of the parties.[147] Foreign currency agreements are speculative in character. By entering into a foreign currency agreement the parties willingly accept the advantages and risks of fluctuating exchange rates.[148] Therefore increasing exchange rates are within the sphere of risk of the debtor and do not entitle him to terminate the contract under Austrian law. Such contractual allocations of risks will be considered invalid only if they violate the principle of good faith and public morality ('*gute Sitten*') of §879 ABGB (see Cases 9 and 15 below). This does not seem to be the case here.

2. Where the requirements of '*Wegfall der Geschäftsgrundlage*' are not met, termination and adjustment are excluded. The aggrieved party (X) is not entitled to demand adjustment of the contract.

II. 1. Whether or not unpredictable and extraordinary events entitle a party to adjust or terminate the contract is a question of contractual risk allocation.[149] If the risk of inflation was not assumed by one of the parties of a long-term contract of limited duration, an unexpected

[145] Rummel, '§901', in: Rummel (ed.), *Kommentar zum ABGB*, vol. I, n. 6a with further references; Koziol and Welser, *Bürgerliches Recht*, vol. I, p. 166.

[146] Rummel, '§901', in: Rummel (ed.), *Kommentar zum ABGB*, vol. I, n. 6a with further references.

[147] Apathy, '§901', in: Schwimann (ed.), *Kommentar zum ABGB*, vol. IV, n. 8.

[148] Ertl, *Inflation, Privatrecht und Wertsicherung*, p. 235.

[149] See F. Bydlinski, *Zulässigkeit und Schranken*, p. 15; Fenyves, *Der Einfluss geänderter Verhältnisse auf Langzeitverträge, Gutachten für den 13. ÖJT*, p. 98; Bernd Schilcher, 'Geschäftsgrundlage und Anpassungsklauseln im Zivilrecht', (1999) VR, 32, 34.

extraordinary increase in inflation may give the disadvantaged party the right of extraordinary termination of the contract. In cases of strong inflation, exchange contracts that are not long-term contracts can be adjusted or terminated on the basis of '*Wegfall der Geschäftsgrundlage*' only if the disadvantaged party otherwise suffers ruinous consequences. If, however, one party assumed a particular risk of change under the contract and this speculation turns out to be unfavourable, that party nevertheless has to absorb this risk.

The Netherlands

Under Dutch law, the fluctuating interest rate is within Y-Bank's sphere of responsibility. X can refuse to renegotiate and a court should reject Y-Bank's request to terminate the loan. With regard to the variation, it is likely that X will also be bound to the contract.

(a) Extraordinary inflation

I. 1. Under Dutch law, if the matter is within X-Bank's sphere of business, a court should reject any modification or termination requested by Y-Bank. Even if a change of circumstances occurs within Y-Bank's sphere of responsibility, it would not be considered appropriate to attribute the risk of such circumstances to X. According to Art. 6:258 Dutch Civil Code (on unforeseen circumstances) a court should adopt a reluctant approach.

2. However, the case can also be described as follows: Y-Bank lends an amount against fixed interest to X and itself obtains a loan to finance this transaction. If such financing could have been obtained under a (lower) fixed interest rate, this means that Y-Bank has speculated on better market conditions than the loan conditions vis-à-vis X. Such a means of financing the loan is entirely within the sphere of Y-Bank's responsibility and there is no reason to attribute such a risk to X.[150]

[150] The case might be different if (exceptionally) it was X who required Y-Bank to ascertain the payment of the principal amount of its loan in a particular, agreed manner. This is realistic in loan propositions for 'project finance' or larger transactions such as public tenders or major acquisitions. Indeed, such examples might display an involvement of the party seeking financing from a lender. But even then, it is still highly questionable whether this would justify shifting any part of the financing risk to X. Case 2 does not contain any elements pointing to the fact that X had interfered in this financing arrangement of the bank, or even that X was aware of the risks assumed by Y Bank.

3. According to Dutch law on unexpected circumstances the termination or amendment of an agreement can be based on the nature of that agreement. In this respect, the type of loan may be relevant for determining how any risks should be allocated. Mortgage loans, for example, tend to be provided out of a portfolio fund on the basis of standard conditions that imply a certain risk profile.[151] The nature of such a loan agreement does not reasonably justify that X bears the risk of circumstances that have not been incorporated in the loan. The doctrine of unforeseen circumstances may apply in individual cases, but not in cases that affect a large group of persons. If a government has not deemed regulatory interference appropriate, there is no reason for a court to interfere in individual cases. The broader context of changed circumstances, affecting large groups in society, would instead imply that X can reasonably expect that the contract will remain unchanged.[152]

(b) Variation: foreign currency agreement

I. Under Dutch law, an amendment of the contract (or a duty to renegotiate) is not likely to be granted. Termination, however, would be appropriate, as well as a damages claim by Y-Bank for early repayment.

II. As in almost every country in the world, the Dutch legislature has adopted the nominal value theory.[153] According to this principle, monetary debts are to be performed in the currency and amount agreed. Accordingly, the creditor (Y-Bank) bears the risk of a devaluation and the debtor (X) bears the negative effects of a revaluation unless statutory law, usage or a legal act, including a contract, provide for another scheme of risk allocation (Art. 6:111 Dutch Civil Code). Since the case

[151] In such cases investors subscribe to participate in the fund and in this game of 'supply and demand' an interest rate or interest calculation formula is determined. The bank that governs such a fund is responsible for lending the fund's money in accordance with the standard conditions. In such a context, it is not Y-Bank that suffers the consequences but the investors. If they would be entitled to be compensated, directly or indirectly, this would be on the basis of a special provision in the conditions for subscribing to the fund or a misleading prospectus. Either ground is entirely within the sphere of the bank's responsibility. Now X wanted to borrow money; and the bank offered a fixed interest rate for five years. At best, the fund's standard conditions allow for a limited number of options, such as a fixed term of five or ten years and some administrative cost-related negotiable terms. For the rest, the loan conditions are determined by the standard conditions of the funds, which are non-negotiable for X.

[152] *Asser Hartkamp & Sieburgh*, 6-III 2010, nr. 450. no. 338.

[153] W. A. K. Rank, *Geld, geldschuld en betaling, Serie recht en praktijk no. 94* (Deventer: Kluwer, 1996), pp. 115 *et seq.*

is clear as to the currency, the issue is a typical case of unforeseen circumstances. In view of the strong adherence to the nominal value theory it is doubtful that a court would amend the contract.[154]

III. 1. The main question is whether the agreement can be modified or terminated on the basis of the extraordinary currency devaluation. The statutory basis for such modification or termination would be Art. 6:258 Dutch Civil Code. The application of this rule depends on (i) whether the currency risks were (reasonably) foreseeable, and (ii) whether the currency fluctuations were of such a nature that Y-Bank could not reasonably expect the loan agreement to remain unchanged. Forseeability may be dependent on the factual question of which party wanted to provide for repayment and interest payment in the foreign currency (and probably why): the answer would point to the person who requested the uncommon situation. If X requested such repayment, it does not seem likely that a renegotiation or amendment of the loan is justified since it was this party which required the 'unusual' currency. Therefore it would be appropriate also to attribute the risk of currency fluctuation to X.

2. It is questionable whether the negative consequences of currency fluctuations should be shifted to the risk and account of Y-Bank. Y-Bank did not expect to be burdened with the risk of fluctuation and it did not have to anticipate this. However, the relatively large impact of the exchange rate may well be a sufficient ground for granting early termination. In such a case, Y-Bank is likely to be entitled to damages. However, the amount of such damages is not likely to be very high. Most loan agreements provide for early repayment clauses (or limited repayment rights) with rules on penalties. Obviously, such penalties indicate the bottom end of the bank's interest in not having the loan agreement terminated. Such clauses could therefore serve as reference points in determining Y-Bank's maximum damages (if any) in the event of a renegotiation or amendment of the loan.

Eastern European jurisdictions

Slovenia

Y-Bank is not entitled to terminate the loan agreement. With regard to the variation, X has to bear the risk of devaluation of the national currency.

[154] HR 2 January 1931, NJ 1931, 274 (Mark is Mark) m.n. E. M. Meijers.

I. Since Yugoslavia, as well as Slovenia, has known very high inflation until recently, it is quite difficult to give a definite answer to the questions regarding this case. Until the introduction of the Euro in Slovenia, it has been usual to apply variable interest rates, which were also related to the inflation-index or foreign exchange clauses (DEM, USD, CHF, €) or a combination of them in all loan contracts. Cases like the one described above have not occurred in practice.

(a) Extraordinary inflation

I. As the loan contract has been concluded for a *definite* period of time, Art. 333 is not applicable. There is also no extraordinary right to terminate the contract. X may, however, be allowed to repay the whole debt before maturity.[155] Slovenian law does not allow for an untimely termination of contracts that have been concluded for a definite period of time in general. This is only allowed in case of a change of circumstances.

II. 1. Art. 371 CO introduces the nominal principle for pecuniary debts. There is also case law that expressly refuses to apply the *clausula* rule with regard to banking contracts.[156] The same line is followed by the Slovenian Supreme Court[157] which held that it was not possible to demand dissolution of a contract when the performance of pecuniary debts has become more difficult. A pecuniary obligation is a 'generic' and not a 'specific' obligation. According to the Supreme Court, the performance of a generic obligation can only become impossible for reasons which are outside of the debtor's sphere of risk. It is therefore, in the court's view, not possible to demand dissolution of a contract on grounds of a change of circumstances in cases of generic obligations (such as the obligation to pay a sum of money). This decision (and the reasoning) has, however, been criticised and could be overruled by a new decision of the Supreme Court. As has been discussed above in Case 1, strict application of the principle of pecuniary nominalism might contravene the principle of good faith in Art. 5 CO. However, as of yet there is no case law that could give any guidance in this respect. The principle of equal value of performances (Art. 8 *j*° Art. 118 CO) would not apply in this case, because this principle applies only to gross disparity existing at the time of the conclusion of a contract.

[155] Many Slovenian banks allow for the repayment of the whole debt, sometimes even without extra cost.

[156] Yugoslav Supreme Commercial Court Sl 2111/71.

[157] Slovenian Supreme Court III IPS 17/93.

2. It is not possible to enforce renegotiation or an adjustment of a contract in cases of a change of circumstances. A party may always suggest it, but it always depends on the will of the other party.[158]

(b) Variation: foreign currency agreement

I. The *clausula* rule of Art. 112 CO does not apply to contracts where one of the parties expressly (or implicitly) assumes a certain risk, such as in this case, the risk of devaluation of X's national currency. Since inflation has always been a problem in Yugoslavia and until recently also in Slovenia, it has been common practice in Slovenia until the introduction of the Euro, and before 1991 in Yugoslavia, that credit contracts included a foreign currency clause (DEM, USD, CHF, €).

Lithuania

Under Lithuanian law, the contract may be terminated but Y-bank will be under an obligation to pay compensation that amounts to the other party's performance interest, as a general rule. Relief could be granted under the doctrine of changed circumstances; however, there is no relevant court practice in Lithuania. Relief is less likely to be granted in the case of a foreign currency agreement.

(a) Extraordinary inflation

I. Art. 6.217(4) CC permits a party to apply to the court for the dissolution of a contract. This is an independent mechanism to dissolve a contract in the event of a non-essential breach by the other party. It also applies if the other party is not in breach, e.g., if the requesting party has no interest in the contract any more. However, in such cases the requesting party must compensate damages incurred by the other party due to the dissolution of the contract. There are no exceptions for loan agreements or contracts concluded for an indefinite time. Thus, loan agreements may in general also be terminated. The only exception is established for consumer contracts, where the creditor's right to terminate a contract is limited (Art. 6.889 CC).

II. 1. In this case, Art. 6.204 CC on changed circumstances could formally be applied because the extraordinary inflation fundamentally alters the balance of contractual obligations. However, Y-Bank must

[158] Slovenian Supreme Court II IPS 496/93 and III IPS 124/98.

prove that the extraordinary inflation occurred after the conclusion of the contract. In this case, there is no difficulty for the bank to prove this circumstance. Y-Bank must also prove that it could not reasonably have foreseen the extraordinary inflation at the time of the conclusion of the contract. This condition is quite difficult for the bank to prove as a bank is considered to be a professional, and the court practice applies different behavioural standards to consumers and professionals.[159] Therefore, the court may refuse to accept the demands of the bank on the assumption that the bank, as a professional, could have predicted such an extraordinary inflation. Furthermore, Y-Bank must prove that it did not assume the risk of extraordinary inflation under the contract. This condition may also be difficult for the bank to prove for two reasons. First, courts acknowledge that business involves risks, and the activity of a bank is subject to even greater risks, therefore banks are expected to assume the risks of a sudden increase of inflation as well.[160] Second, in consumer contracts, the banks in Lithuania usually include a clause that permits them to change the rate of interest unilaterally. Therefore, the circumstance that a fixed rate of interest is established in the contract without any provisions for its change may be viewed by the court as evidence that the bank has assumed the risk of a sudden increase of inflation. However, there is no court practice or a doctrine of law in Lithuania to prove this conclusion.

2. If the loan agreement is a consumer contract pursuant to Art. 6.889 CC, the bank is not entitled to demand termination of the contract and the court, guided by the arguments presented above and taking the protection of the consumer's interests as its priority, would most probably refuse to satisfy the demand of the bank for a modification of the contract. However, there still is no relevant court practice in Lithuania.

III. Pursuant to Art. 6.204(3) CC, the aggrieved party is entitled to request negotiations for a modification of the contract if the prerequisites of a change of circumstances are met. The court, however, has no right to compel the other party to negotiate. Therefore, if this other party refuses to enter into negotiation, the only way left for the aggrieved party is to bring an action for the dissolution or modification of the contract.

[159] LAT, Judgment of 13 June 2001, Case No 3K-3-645/2001.
[160] LAT, Judgment of 28 October 2004, Case No 3K-3-535/2004.

(a) Variation: foreign currency agreement

I. This situation is similar to the one discussed above. The only difference is that the parties have chosen a foreign currency instead of their national currency. The choice of a foreign currency entails greater risks, which means that the parties have to assume greater risks as well. Currency value fluctuation against the currency of various other countries is a customary and widespread phenomenon. There is also one more important aspect – the parties failed to include a clause on the change of currency exchange rates, leading one to hold that the parties have assumed the risks. In Lithuania, problems of this kind were often brought to court as initially the national currency – litas – was pegged to the US dollar and a great number of loans were issued in US dollars; later the litas was pegged to the Euro. The fluctuation of the dollar resulted in a number of disputes related to the application of interest rates. The courts predominantly used the nominalism principle without taking into account the currency fluctuations. They stated that the parties, failing to specifically determine this issue in their agreement, had to assume the whole risks so that Art. 6.204 CC could not be invoked.[161] Therefore the court probably would reject X's arguments to apply Art. 6.204 CC due to the assumption that X has taken the risk. Instead, it would apply the nominalism principle established in Art. 6.873 CC as the basic rule.

Czech Republic

Y-Bank may be entitled to terminate the contract by notice, provided that the contract is not time-limited. If a bank terminates the loan agreement, it is not necessary to give any grounds on which the notice is based. Besides this right, it is unlikely that Czech courts will grant relief in cases of excessive inflation or (as presented in the variation) devaluation of the currency.

I. The situation is similar to Case 1. Czech law, including case law, has no standardised criteria relating to the level of inflation and degree of devaluation of currency that must be reached before relief is applicable. This relates both to domestic and foreign currencies.

II. Provided that the loan agreement in question has been concluded for an indefinite period of time, Section 582(2) Civil Code applies. According to this provision, the agreement can be terminated by notice.

[161] LAT, Judgment of 15 September 2003, Case No 3K-3–813/2003.

III. 1. There exists no rule which would enable renegotiation of the contractual terms to be sought. As a very extraordinary solution, it would be conceivable to consider a conflict with the principles of fair business relations or, as the case may be, with good morals. According to Section 265, Commercial Code exercise of a right contrary to the principles of fair business relations does not enjoy legal protection.[162] This means that claims conflicting with the principles of fair business relations cannot be enforced. In parallel to this situation, Section 39 Civil Code provides that contracts or other juridical acts contrary to good morals are invalid.

2. Both good morals and the principles of fair business relations are objective categories independent of any subjective awareness of the parties. Based on the scarce case law to date, for example, a decision of two of three shareholders, without the consent of the third, which led to the sale of real property in the ownership of the company for a price significantly lower than could have been obtained at the given time and place is contrary to good morals. Similarly, a cooperative's statutes stipulating a waiting period of ten years for paying out a settlement share to members leaving the cooperative are regarded as contrary to good morals.[163]

3. These conclusions are based on the assumption (and it is no doubt a correct assumption) that parties establishing a long-term legal relationship should take into account any circumstances that could influence their position during the term of the contract. Therefore, they assume a reasonable portion of the risk. This is built on the fact that the parties – as diligent administrators paying due care to their property – will reflect these circumstances in the contract. Moreover, banks and other professionals entering into long-term relationships (e.g., insurance companies) typically have special tools for coping with the risk situations (risk management). Another question is whether the law should regulate these relationships, in certain (e.g., consumer) cases even by means of mandatory rules. It can be assumed that the law should especially

[162] An obviously disproportionate amout of interest may represent such a contradiction with the principles of fair business conduct (M. Tomsa in: I. Štenglová, S. Plíva and M. Tamsa (eds.), *Obchodní zákoní Komentář (Commercial Code, Commentary)* (Prague: Linde, 11th edn, 2006), p. 989). However, there is still no relevant case law. It is obvious that the contradiction can exist from the time when a contract has been formed, but it can also arise during the existence of the contract (during the relationship based thereon).

[163] See the judgment of the Supreme Court No. R 51/2001.

cover situations into which consumers can fall (the draft Civil Code unfortunately does not take into account regulation of this kind). For example, in long-term contracts for services (power supply purchases etc.), where consumers do not have the option to choose another supplier, the need to foresee a need for renegotiation, exchange rate clauses or termination of the contract proves extremely necessary.[164]

4. Within the framework of our topic, the application of provisions on good morals or principles of fair business relations is in practice very limited, because these institutions are intended above all for cases of a different type. Otherwise, it would be conceivable, under completely extraordinary circumstances (e.g., in the case of an exceptional change in the exchange rate by orders of magnitude), that the principle of good morals or fair business relations would function so that the bank could request that the credit be paid back in instalments, the value of which would correspond to the purpose of the loan contract as it was agreed before the change of circumstances. Thus, the principles would function as an argument against the debtor's defence that he is required to pay substantially more than stipulated in the contract.

Scandinavian jurisdictions

Sweden

Under Swedish law, in the initial case the contract would be upheld, while an adjustment may be granted in the variation.

I. There is no right, under Swedish law, to demand renegotiation unless specifically provided for in the contract. Nor is there a general right to terminate a loan contract, or long-term contracts in general. The principle regarding termination in the event of unexpected circumstances of an extraordinary magnitude, so-called '*viktig grund*', is most likely not applicable. The impact of the old Banking Business Act in these cases will be disregarded.[165] Therefore, the issue in both cases is

[164] In the case of consumers, the solution is *inter alia* based on the protection against unfair contract terms (see section 56 Civil Code).

[165] Under the Banking Business Act (Bankrörelselagen (1987:617)) certain restrictions were imposed on the banks' credit agreements, with the result that such agreements were normally entered into for a period not exceeding one year. Thereafter the loans were automatically prolonged if not terminated. However, longer credits were allowed to a certain maximum amount, varying for each bank. Furthermore, no time limitation is imposed under the Banking and Financing Business Act (lagen (2004:297)

whether termination or adjustment is possible under the doctrine of assumptions, or Section 36 Contracts Act.

II. 1. It is important to note that the two situations are of entirely different types, although there are some superficial similarities between the cases (and also between the types). In case 2(a), the value of the performance Y-Bank is entitled to has decreased. This is a case of failure of an ordinary performance assumption of the same type as in Case 1 above. In this case, the assumption has to do with Y-Bank's use of the performance received. Assumptions of this type are comparatively often considered to be of legal relevance in case law. However, according to the general rule, they are not relevant.

2. In case 2(b), from a formal point of view, which accepts the national currency as standard, the worth of the amount X has to pay has increased. This is a case of failure of a basic assumption as to X's own promise, which has become unexpectedly burdensome per se. From an alternative - perhaps more realistic - point of view, the worth of X's assets has rapidly declined due to devaluation. This is a case of failure of the basic assumption that the claimant's resources will not diminish. From both perspectives, the assumption is not a performance assumption, and it is true that assumptions of this kind are normally not of legal relevance, although exceptional cases do exist.

(a) Extraordinary inflation

I. 1. As the rate is fixed, Y-Bank has assumed the risk of a higher inflation rate under the agreement. This would normally exclude the application of the doctrine of assumptions. However, in this case the inflation is most likely beyond what the parties can be considered to have contracted for when agreeing on the fixed rent. Under the doctrine of assumptions termination may be possible, but not an adjustment to increase the rate of interest payable.

2. Case 2(a) concerns an assumption as to Y-Bank's use of the performance received. As there are no other specific grounds to deem the assumption to be legally relevant, the main argument under the doctrine of assumptions is that X has made a profit at the expense of Y-Bank. There are quite a few older Swedish cases supporting this principle,[166] some of which have already been presented in the analysis of Case 1

om bank- och finansieringsrörelse). This answer therefore disregards the impact of the old rules on these cases.

166 See especially, NJA 1946 p. 679, NJA 1956 p. 136, NJA 1983 p. 385, and NJA 1994 p. 359, as well as RH 1980, 14.

above. Two cases will be dealt with more extensively here, as they resemble the present case.[167]

3. In the case NJA 1930 p. 507 I, a licence fee for 1923–1925, contracted in 1895 to be paid in German Marks, was adjusted. Since 1914 the value of the Mark had been declining until it was practically worthless in the autumn of 1923. In 1924 the Reichsmark was established as the new monetary unit of Germany. One Reichsmark held the value of one billion old Marks. The Supreme Court noted that the German Supreme Court had adjusted claims in old Marks since 1923, arguing that payment at the nominal value would be contrary to good faith. In 1925, rules of adjustments of claims in old Marks had been established in Germany. Under these rules, licence fees were to be adjusted in accordance with the general principles of civil law. Referring to this, the Supreme Court concluded that the licence fee was not to be decided by the contract clause but by general principles of civil law. Considering all relevant circumstances, and especially that the value of the licence rights had not been affected by the decline of the Mark, the full value as before the decline was to be paid. However, the fees for 1923 were adjusted to half their value, to compensate for the decline in value they would have been subject to in the hand of the receiver had they been paid in 1923.

4. The outcome was in the opposite direction in the case NJA 1930 p. 507 II, where an insurance amount was not adjusted, although it was to be paid in German Marks in 1927. The insurance premium had been paid in full in 1917 and the insurance company had invested the money in claims in Marks. The Supreme Court was referring to 'principles of Swedish Law'.

5. It should be mentioned that the insurer in the latter case did not make any profit at the expense of the insured, as the insurance premium had also become worthless. In the first case, the value of the licence rights had not been affected by the decline of the Mark, so the licence-holder would have made a profit should he not have had to pay for them. On the basis of the case law, the most important prerequisite in cases like Case 2(a) is that the other party has made a profit at the expense of the disadvantaged party. In Case 2(a), there is no such profit.

[167] The cases NJA 1983 p. 385, NJA 1994 p. 359 and RH 1980, 14 are similar and support the same conclusions. See B. Lehrberg, *Förutsättningsläran* (Uppsala: Iustus Förlag, 1989), pp. 419–29.

Therefore the contract will not be terminated under the doctrine of assumptions.

II. Under Section 36 Contracts Act, the agreed interest may be modified or set aside if it is unreasonable with reference to the contents of the contract, the circumstances at the formation of the contract, circumstances arising later and other circumstances. The fundamental alteration of the equilibrium of the contract that would normally result from increased inflation, which Y-Bank could not have foreseen, would probably in many cases be sufficient per se to render a contract clause unreasonable. However, a bank is legally bound to guard its assets against risks and consequently to keep a portfolio of financial assets and obligations, which is, as a whole, much less vulnerable to inflation than that of a normal private person or company. Therefore, the impact of the increased inflation on a bank would probably be much less severe. A fixed interest rate is also the established way to eliminate the risk of a highly volatile interest rate. This kind of risk elimination is not only acceptable, but highly desirable, and should not be made impossible by frequent use of Section 36. The Court would conclude that some restraint is indeed justified, considering the major impact on the country's economy of an inflation of this magnitude. Many people would suffer great losses as a result of such inflation, and contract law cannot generally solve their problems. An attempt in that direction might only risk causing more harm. The outcome is far from obvious, but the best guess is that the contract would stand.

(b) Variation: foreign currency agreement

I. 1. This is an assumption as to X's own promise, which has become unexpectedly burdensome per se (or maybe, from a more informal point of view, an assumption as to the value of X's own resources). Under the loan agreement X has to pay five times as much in national currency as would have been the case if the rate of exchange had remained unchanged. As the assumption does not refer to the performance X expected under the contract, it should typically be somewhat more difficult to have the contract adjusted than in Case 2(a). This is, however, not true in these specific cases. While Y-Bank in Case 2(a) was asking for an extension of X's contractual liability (and termination would give a similar result for X), X is in this latter case merely asking for a reduction of his own liability.

2. The main prerequisites under the doctrine of assumptions are for this case that Y-Bank has, as a result of the fact that the assumption

failed, made a profit at the expense of X and that X has suffered a significant loss. Formally these prerequisites are fulfilled, and it is likely that the contract would be adjusted or terminated under the doctrine of assumptions. In relation to Section 36 Contracts Act, I believe the court would argue in a similar way, should X choose to rely on that rule instead.

3. This said, it could be of some importance if X is a consumer or another inferior party, an ordinary tradesman or a financial institution. If X is a financial institution, a Swedish court would probably consider some of the arguments concerning the risks of trade in financial markets that were applied above in relation to Case 2(a). If X is, on the other hand, a consumer etc., Section 36 is to be applied much less restrictively than if X is a tradesman. Such a differentiation under Section 36 would also influence the application of the doctrine of assumptions.

Denmark

Under Danish law, Y-Bank has to bear the risk of inflation as it is a 'professional' party with regard to financial transactions. In the variation, X is more likely to be granted relief as he is not acting as a 'professional' with regard to financial transactions.

I. As mentioned in the general remarks, Danish law does not contain any general rule creating an obligation to renegotiate a contract due to hardship. Neither is there any default rule in Danish law that applies in cases of hardship. In such circumstances as these, a Danish court might apply the doctrine of assumptions or Section 36 Contracts Act.

(a) Extraordinary inflation

I. 1. In practice these problems would arise very rarely with regard to small loans as banks in Denmark normally reserve the right to rescind the contract. If banks are dealing with loans of substantial amounts, they will not have the possibility to rescind the contract. However, the agreements provide that the interest rate fluctuates in accordance with the going rate in order to cover the bank's costs and a certain risk margin. In doing so, banks are able to protect themselves from the risk of high inflation. If the parties have entered into agreements such as the one in question, the case would normally be decided in accordance with a traditional interpretation of the contract.

2. If the loan contract has been concluded for a fixed period of time, there is normally no possibility to terminate the loan contract due to

extraordinary circumstances.[168] X's interest is traditionally protected as X is entitled to pay the full sum of the loan to the bank at any time.

3. Case law in this particular area of the law is indeed rare. However, the Højesteret decided in a case in 2003 that the doctrine of assumptions was not applicable.[169] A Danish company produced vegetable oil and bought raw materials in different places, including Malaysia. In June 1998, the Danish company entered into two agreements with the Danish branch of a French bank in order to protect itself against changes in the exchange rate between the USD and MYR. In accordance with the agreement, the bank should have provided a certain amount of MYR in March 1999. The exchange rate was 1 USD against 4.4 MYR. However, due to a financial crisis the Malaysian government intervened and set the exchange rate at 1 USD against 3.8 MYR on 1 September 1998. At a meeting of the Singapore Foreign Exchange Market Committee on the next day, the participating banks agreed that any outstanding agreements should be exchanged at the rate of 1 USD against 4.0 MYR. These guidelines were signed on 3 September by the ACI, a worldwide organisation representing banks. Because of a press release from the Malaysian National Bank asking companies to carry out any exchange rate agreements before 9 September, the Danish company asked the bank to fulfil the agreements that the parties had entered into in June 1998. In the meantime, the Malaysian National Bank withdrew this request. Thus, the Danish company withdrew its own request from the bank. However, the bank had already fulfilled the agreement in accordance with the agreements made by the ACI the day before.

4. Subsequently, the Danish company claimed damages primarily on the basis that the exchange rate was not in accordance with the original agreement (approx. USD 169,000). Alternatively the Danish company claimed damages in accordance with the official exchange rate on the date when the bank 'fulfilled' the obligation (approx. USD 151,000). The Højesteret held that the bank was entitled to fulfil the agreement in accordance with the request made by the Danish company, even though it had subsequently withdrawn its request. The reason for this was that at the time of the withdrawal, the bank had already fulfilled the original

[168] Cf. Andreas Tamasauskas, *Erhvervslivets låneoptagelse* (Copenhagen: Gjellerup, 1st edn, 2006), pp. 204 *et seq.*

[169] Cf. U 2003.112H.

request. The remaining issue was whether the bank was entitled to fulfil the request in accordance with the exchange rate, which was recommended by the ACI, or in accordance with the original contract. First of all, at the actual point in time it was possible to provide MYR. Second, the Højesteret stated that the Danish company was not bound by the recommendations issued by the ACI. Conclusively, the Court found that the agreement between the Danish company and the bank had similarities to insurance contracts, and since the Danish company had no information about the financial market in Asia prior to contracting and during the formation of the original contracts, the bank had to bear the risk of certain obstacles in providing MYR. Thus, it was not possible to invoke the doctrine of assumptions on behalf of the bank and the Danish company was granted damages equal to USD 151,000.

5. It may be noted that the case could not be resolved on the basis of force majeure, since it was possible to provide MYR. The Højesteret also rejected the application of the doctrine of assumptions since the condition of relevance had not been fulfilled.[170] The Danish company should not bear the risk of developments on the financial market in Asia, as it did not have the relevant information. The bank had to bear the risk because it did not take the necessary precautions to avoid this asymmetry of information. The Højesteret delivered the right judgment, since the bank as the 'professional' party was in a better position to take this matter into consideration before the stipulation in the loan agreement took effect. Neither party invoked Section 36 Contracts Act. It is not applicable to the case, since it is very difficult to argue that the bank should be protected as it is a professional on the financial markets.

(b) Variation: foreign currency agreement

I. With respect to the variation the burdened party is not the bank but the customer. Thus, the chances of X being granted relief are better on the basis of the aforementioned arguments, as X is not a 'professional' in financial transactions while the bank is in a better position to appraise the risks resulting from a foreign currency agreement.

[170] With regard to this condition see the overview (Chapter 4).

Romanic-Mediterranean jurisdictions

Italy

Y-Bank may be allowed to terminate the contract or to ask for an adjustment in the original case. This solution is less likely to be applied in the case of a foreign currency agreement.

(a) Extraordinary inflation

I. Under Italian law there is no statutory provision that provides for an extraordinary termination of a long-term contract: in the case of long-term contracts with continuous or periodic performances, Art. 1373 CC provides that each party has a unilateral right to withdraw from the contract. As regards loan contracts including short-term loans, the possibility of terminating a loan agreement financing the purchase of a house prematurely by individuals (without penalties) has been affirmed.[171]

II. 1. With reference to the case at issue, it must be said that the Supreme Court used to exclude the application of the remedy set forth by Art. 1467 CC to loan agreements since they do not constitute a performance and a counter-performance, but they may be classified as unilateral contracts, since the only relevant obligation is that of the borrower to repay the loan. But more recent studies have admitted the remedy.[172] Assuming that the remedy is applicable, it must be remembered that *regular* inflation, as a general rule, does not represent a disrupting event or circumstance provided for by Art. 1467 CC since it should be 'extraordinary and unforeseeable'. Furthermore, Art. 1467(2) CC states that the termination may not be asked if the supervening distortion of the contractual balance between performance and counter-performance does not exceed the 'usual contractual risk'. Therefore, it is clear that both parties bear the normal risk of depreciation of the money as well as of the inflation within a certain limit.

2. Italian courts have therefore decided that inflation may be a reason for termination pursuant to Art. 1467 CC (i.e., because the performance of the debtor has become extremely onerous or the counter-party's performance is extremely depreciated) only on a case-by-case basis,

[171] See Law 2 April 2007, No. 40.

[172] C.G. Terranova, *L'eccessiva onerosità nei contratti*, *Commentario Schlesinger* (Milan: Giuffrè, 1995), pp. 72 *et seq.*

considering the fundamental requirement given by the 'extraordinary and unforeseeable' character of the rate of the inflation.

3. Should this be the case, Y-Bank could in principle ask for a dissolution of the contract and the borrower could ask for its renegotiation and/or adjustment (see below) with the aim of an equitable distribution of the consequences of the extraordinary inflation. However, it may not be excluded that the conclusion of a loan agreement with a fixed interest rate would be interpreted as an implied assumption of the risk of inflation by an Italian court, even an extraordinary one, and consequently Y-Bank would not be entitled to ask for the dissolution of the contract by virtue of Art. 1467 CC. The prevailing opinion in case law and literature regards inflation as an extraordinary and unforeseeable event. Hence, it is deemed that the contract can be terminated pursuant to Art. 1467 CC.[173]

III. 1. As already said,[174] a general duty to renegotiate and/or to adjust the contract is not provided for under Italian law: however, the renegotiation and/or adaptation of the contract may be reached through the general rule set forth by Art. 1467(3) CC. Unlike Art. 6:111 PECL, the said rule provides that only the party from whom the dissolution is demanded can decide whether or not to ask for the equitable modification of the contract in order to avoid its dissolution.[175]

2. The requesting party may indicate exactly the equitable modification, which will be subject to the evaluation of the court with regard to the situation existing at the time of the decision.[176] But pursuant to Italian case law, the party may also ask the court to determine the equitable modification, should the court not consider the suggested modification to be equitable. As far as the contents of the adaptation are concerned, equitable modification must take into account the normal risk of the contract and the court should therefore not exclude the consequence of the risk of a change of circumstances that the parties could reasonably have considered at the time of the conclusion of the contract.[177]

[173] Cass., 23 June 1995, n. 7145, *Foro it.*, comments by F. Macario, *Inflazione, fluttuazioni del mercato ed eccessiva onerosità.*

[174] See above overview (Chapter 4).

[175] Cass., 29 October 1958, n. 3470; Cass., 30 April 1953, n. 1199.

[176] Cass., 13 January 1984, n. 275.

[177] Cf. Macario, *Adeguamento*, p. 272, similarly to the reasonable solution given by Art. 6:111(3)(b), which provides the judicial adaptation in order to distribute the losses and gains resulting from the change of circumstances between the parties in a just and equitable manner.

3. Although Art. 1467(3) CC does not expressly provide an obligation to renegotiate with the aim of equitably adapting or modifying the affected contractual terms, it could be argued that, once the interest in avoiding the dissolution has been declared, both parties are entitled to propose to the counter-party to enter into a negotiation. In this case, if a party refuses to negotiate or if he breaks off the negotiations contrary to good faith and the rules of fair dealing,[178] the court could award damages for the loss suffered, in addition to the equitable modification of the contractual terms.[179] This conclusion can be based on the general duty to perform in good faith (Arts. 1175 and 1375 CC). Of course, the above rule could be superseded if a duty to renegotiate with the aim of adapting the contract to the occurred changes is specifically agreed upon.

(b) Variation: foreign currency agreement

I. 1. The above arguments (Case 2(a)) also apply to this variation. It should be added that the agreement for the repayment and the interest in a foreign currency may fall under the provision of Art. 1469 CC, which excludes the application of Art. 1467 CC on aleatory contracts.

2. Italian courts recently have decided many cases where an unforeseen and unforeseeable extraordinary fluctuation of the ECU value, due to political decisions taken by the Italian Government, determined a strong distortion of the agreed equivalence of exchange within loan agreements concluded with reference to the value of the ECU. Upon the demand of the borrowers, the said unforeseeable and extraordinary fluctuation of the ECU with regard to the Italian currency has not been considered a valid reason to have the loan agreements renegotiated or adjusted by the court (nor dissolved according to Art. 1467 CC), since the free choice of the borrowers (and of the banks of course) to link the reimbursement to the value of the ECU determined the assumption of the risk of fluctuation, even the unusual and extraordinary one which actually happened: the parties have concluded – this was the decision of various courts[180] – an aleatory contract, pursuant to the above-mentioned Art. 1469 CC.

[178] Sacco, *Il contratto*, vol. II, p. 686.

[179] Macario, *Adeguamento*, p. 266; S. D'Andrea, *L'offerta di equa modificazione* (Milan: Giuffrè, 2006), p. 179.

[180] Trib. Turin 15 October 1996, Trib. Naples 1 March 1997, Trib. Rome 20 January 1997, Trib. Pescara 20 January 1997.

Spain

The legal evaluation of the case at hand is somewhat uncertain under Spanish law. The nominal value principle applies, as a general rule. However, some case law suggests that relief could be granted in cases of inflation or currency devaluation in long-term contracts.

I. The civil code does not contain special provisions to regulate the termination of loan contracts (Arts. 1753–7 regarding loans of money or other fungibles). It is therefore subject to the general contract law rules regarding the termination of contracts.[181]

II. 1. Spanish courts do not generally grant relief or modify a contract when a party is burdened with excessive hardship if this is due to inflation.[182] The reason for this is that a price increase is not deemed by the judiciary to be an unforeseeable circumstance. However, in one case the TS modified a monetary obligation even though the inflation was foreseeable.[183] This was justified because of the long duration of the contract and the unforeseeable effects of inflation that occurred over such a long period of time. On this basis, one can argue that in cases in which inflation is extraordinary and could not have been foreseen, the courts may apply the *rebus* doctrine because in this situation the requirements are met. This is indeed the opinion of Diez Picazo.[184] According to this author, if a currency devaluation could not have been foreseen and the other requirements are met, the doctrine of the *rebus* clause applies.[185]

[181] For concepts according to which a contract concluded for a definite period may be brought to an end in exceptional situations see the overview (Chapter 5).

[182] See the list of decisions in Case 1.

[183] STS of 23 November 1962 (RJ 1962, 5005). See Case 1.

[184] Díez Picazo, *Fundamentos del Derecho Carl Patinavel* (Madrid: Curtas, 1996), p. 271.

[185] In an article regarding the impact of the emergency measures taken by the Argentinian authorities in response to the economic, social and political crisis of 2001 on contracts subject to Spanish law, the authors discuss whether the *rebus* doctrine could apply. The measures included the devaluation of the Argentinian currency and a modification of the regime of preferred creditors, mainly in favour of the debtors. The authors indicate that a strict application of the requirements of the *rebus* clause would not allow its application because the emergency measures do not always imply an imbalance between the corresponding performances. However, they maintain that the *rebus* clause could apply if its scope was broadened to include cases in which the common aim of the parties in concluding the contract or the *causa* of the contract disappears: E. Rodríguez Rovira and J. Illescas, 'Apuente sobre la posbiel incidencia de las medidas de emergencia argentinas en las obligaciones sometidas a derecho español', (2002) 2 *Actualidad Juńdia Uría y Menéndez* 117.

2. As indicated above, the courts have held that the application of the *rebus* doctrine should in the first place lead to a modification of the contract.[186] The price has accordingly been modified in decisions in which the *rebus* doctrine was applied because the obligation of the debtor had become excessively onerous.[187] But the Supreme Court has granted a termination of the contract when it was impossible to restore the balance between performances, for example because the debtor had become insolvent.[188] This approach is not shared by Díez Picazo, who argues that in mutual contracts the excessive onerousness of the performances should lead to the termination of the contract.[189]

Portugal

Under Portuguese law, no relief will be available in the original case or in the variation.

(a) Extraordinary inflation

I. The law does not impose a duty to renegotiate a contract on the parties, even in cases of long-term contracts. But if the foundations of the contract suffer a fundamental change it is possible, according to Art. 437 CC, to ask the court to adjust or, alternatively, rescind the contract. Art. 437 CC requires a change in one of the circumstances that were the basis of the contract. This change must not be normal and must result in an unfair outcome if the contract was kept unaltered. Finally, the change must be beyond the risks that were assumed by the party according to the contract.

However, nowadays inflation cannot usually be regarded as an exceptional circumstance.[190] Therefore it is doubtful whether this rise in prices and even this sudden increase in the rate of inflation is enough to qualify for relief under Art. 437 CC, especially since Y is a bank and therefore a professional, which is expected to take care of its own interests by introducing an appropriate contractual clause. Portuguese courts have not been receptive to a revision of contracts due to inflation. Nevertheless, it can be argued that it would be wrong to discard inflation as a potential ground for the termination or the modification of the

[186] STS of 23 April 1991, *Id Cendoj*: 28079110011991100268.

[187] STS of 23 November 1962 (RJ 1962, 5005) and 6 November 1992 (RJ 1992, 9226), and of the AP Navarre of 12 November 1998 (Elder. 1998, 31028).

[188] STS of 23 March 1988 (RJ 1988, 2228).

[189] Díez Picazo, *Fundamentos del Derecho*, p. 899.

[190] See, for instance, Acórdão do STJ of 19 March 1991, processo 080035, www.dgsi.pt.

contract.[191] However, it is extremely difficult to predict the courts' answer in such a case, as there are no clear guidelines as to the amount or rate of inflation that might be considered exceptional. This applies especially if the risk of high inflation was considered to be inherent to the deal and the parties had, for instance, considered an indexation clause but finally agreed upon a fixed interest rate. The courts would also deny the relevance of inflation if at the time of entering into the agreement there were already visible signs of economic and/or political instability that made an abrupt increase in inflation not an unexpected event.[192]

(b) Variation: foreign currency agreement

II. The variation to this case (the foreign currency agreement) will be solved similarly (i.e., no remedy will be available). In this case, however, there is a further reason to be sceptical about Art. 437 CC: contracts in a foreign currency seem to have a speculative element, or at least to be associated with an inherent risk (*alea*). According to its wording, Art. 437 CC is not operative when the supervening events are within the risks inherent in the contract.[193]

Greece

Y-Bank has the right to a judicial adjustment of the contract pursuant to Art. 388 AK, but it has no right to enforce a renegotiation of the contract. As regards the variation, X can demand the judicial adjustment of the contract pursuant to Art. 388 AK, but has no right to enforce a renegotiation of the contract.

[191] See António Pinto Monteiro, 'Inflação e Direito Civil', in *Estudos em Homenagem ao Prof. Doutor Ferrer-Correia, Boletim da Faculdade de Direito da Universidade de Coimbra* (Coimbra: Almedina, 1989), special issue, vol. II, pp. 871 *et seq.*, 888. As the writer suggests, in spite of the so-called nominalism principle in the field of monetary obligations, it may happen that the erosion in the value of money is so drastic that commutative justice itself and the respect for the economic balance found by the parties require an adjustment of the contract (p. 883).

[192] Acórdão do Tribunal da Relação de Lisboa of 04 December 1990, processo 0033851, www.dgsi.pt. In the case of a contract entered into in 1976, in the aftermath of the revolution and the subsequent political and economic instability, the increase of inflation was foreseeable.

[193] For instance in a contract in which one assumes the contractual duty to pay a rent for the duration of the other party's life, Art. 437 cannot be invoked: see Acórdão do STJ of 07 February 1980, processo 068367 (1980) 294 *Boletim do Ministério da Justiça*, p. 308.

(a) Extraordinary inflation

I. Usually, there is no actual intention of the parties, either explicit or implicit, to base a loan contract on a general requirement of economic stability. At the time of the formation, the economic stability may influence the parties' considerations only by chance.[194] And the fact that economic stability is, among other things, a logical prerequisite, does not prove that the parties rely on this (unless we accept a fictitious will).[195] Furthermore, the inevitable contractual lacuna cannot be closed by complementary interpretation according to Art. 200 AK, as there are no objective or subjective indications in the contractual framework. This lacuna, however, might reveal that the underlying basis of a contract is in fact composed of purely objective criteria, and especially of the contractual allocation of risks.[196] Thus, the underlying basis of a contract might be considered as consisting of every legal or real fact, the absence of which destroys this risk allocation scheme. This scheme is determined by the explicit or implicit, agreements between the parties, the statutory rules and the, more or less, speculative or personal features of the contract.

II. As mentioned above, if contrary to good faith the extraordinary termination prevents the other party from his right to ask for a juridical adjustment of the contract, the exercise of the termination will be deemed abusive and therefore precluded (Art. 281 AK). Only if the borrower is incapable of fulfilling the adjusted obligation, can the

[194] As well as the political, environmental etc. stability.

[195] With regard to the limited boundaries of human knowledge and prediction, see E. Kaufmann, *The Essence of International Law and the Clausula rebus sic stantibus* (Tubigen: Miohr 1911, repr. 1964), p. 84; against the so-called '*pseudo-psychologisches*' criterion – which is founded predominantly by Paul Oertmann – see also G. Kegel, H. Rupp and K. Zweigertk, *The Influence of War on Contracts in the Jurisdiction of Germany* (Berlin: de Gruyter, 1941), pp. 108–9; K. Larenz, *Schuldrecht I*, pp. 10, 323–4; Fikentscher, *Die Geschäftsgnindlape als Frage des Uertragsrisikos* (Munich: Beck, 1971), pp. 6, 7, 15–16. Contra K. Simantiras, *General Principles of Civil Law* (Athens-Komotini: Sakkoulas, 4th edn, 1988), p. 551 n. 737.

[196] For the unique trustworthy criterion Ernst Rabel, *The Law of Sales of Merchandises* (Berlin: de Gruyter, 1936, repr. 1957), vol. I, p. 357 (ind. 1). See also N. Papanikolaou, 'The Measure of Onerousity of the Performance and the Extent of the Adjusting Intervention of the Judge in the Contract according to Art. 388 AK ', (1985) 33 NoV, 940, 942 I, 944–5; A. Valtoudis, *Sale of Enterprise. Precontractual, Contractual and Out of Unjust Enrichment Liability* (Athens/Thessalonica: Sakkoula, 2005), pp. 300 *et seq*. and also, even though indirectly, AP 678/1996, HellD 39, p. 593, 593 II; 1066/1996, HellD 38, p. 114, 115 I.

contract be terminated.[197] Therefore, the termination of the contract is excluded in the case at hand.

III. 1. The unforeseen rise of the inflation to 50 per cent excessively disturbs the functional equilibrium of the corresponding performances.[198] The unexpected economic crisis is an undeniable case of an 'unexpected change of circumstances'. Thus, Y-Bank has the right to seek an adjustment of the contract and, especially, an increase of the interest, by virtue of Art. 388 AK. The adaptation of the contract is always considered prior to its dissolution. The judge is obliged to select the path of least intervention in the existing contract. This does not emerge from the text of Art. 388 or even 288 AK. Nevertheless, it is based on the so-called '*favor contractus*' principle and on the general principle of proportionality.[199]

2. In any case, Y-Bank has no right to enforce the renegotiation of the contract, in contrast to the approach of some legal writers.[200] The prevailing version of this approach – which is found especially in German literature[201] – supports the ancillary and bilateral obligation of the parties to renegotiate the terms of the contract, disregarding the result. If a party refuses to cooperate, the other party is entitled either to refuse performance of his obligation (exception *non adimpleti contractus*, see Art. 374 AK), or to recover damages (due to the default of the other party[202] or to the so-called 'improper performance' or 'positive breach of contract'[203]), or, even, to rescind, making the adjustment of the contract impossible. There are some disadvantages, though, which make this approach implausible: specifically, it seems to violate the rule of the *ipso iure* adjustment of a burdensome contract, in cases where Art. 288 AK applies.[204] Furthermore, in practical terms, it also punishes the party who refuses to renegotiate by depriving them of the benefits of an adjusted contract. Finally, the party who took advantage of the unexpected change of circumstances might elude a judicial intervention by half-hearted negotiations.

197 See generally Stathopoulos 'Art. 388', in: Georgiadis and Stathopoulos (eds.), *AK*, n. 22.

198 See ad hoc Spyridakis, *Law of Obligations*, p. 316.

199 See Stathopoulos, *Law of Obligations*, §22 n. 33.

200 See Leonides Georgakopoulos, 'Liabilities and risk of sale of 100% of shares of a limited company', (1995) DEE 30, 31 II.

201 See above all Norbert Horn, 'Renegotiation obligation', (1981) 181 AcP, 255, 256 *et seq.* In details, Andreas Nelle, *Renegotiation Obligations* (Munich: Beck, 1993), *passim* and especially pp. 173 *et seq.*, 260 *et seq.*, 303 *et seq.*, 331 *et seq.*

202 See Georgakopoulos, 'Liabilities and risk of sale', 31 II.

203 See Horn, 'Renegotiation obligation', 286 *et seq.*

204 See above overview (Chapter 4).

(b) Variation: foreign currency agreement

I. The above solution may also apply to the foreign currency agreement. The aleatory feature of the specific contract has no influence on this judgment given the seriousness of the economic crisis.

France and related jurisdictions

France

In both cases there is no right to terminate the contract or to request adjustment under French law.

(a) Extraordinary inflation

I. In French civil law, the civil courts do not recognise the theory of unexpected circumstances and avoid any modifications regarding loan contracts. According to the reasoning in the '*Canal de Craponne*' case,[205] any judicial revision of contracts is prohibited. It is therefore impossible for a party to unilaterally request an adjustment of a loan contract to re-establish the financial balance which was destroyed by monetary instability. This applies even if a country is experiencing galloping inflation or if the national currency has been devalued in comparison with a foreign currency. This rule aims to persuade parties to be cautious and to foresee any possible changing circumstances in the contract. In our case, the parties should have inserted indexation clauses.

II. The revision of a contract in the case of extraordinary inflation has been rejected under French law.[206] The fact that circumstances are unpredictable is not sufficient to allow the revision of the contract. This solution is based not only on the rejection of the doctrine of *imprévision*, but also on the principle of monetary nominalism as expressed in Art. 1895 Cciv. According to this principle, the nominal value and not the real value (taking into account depreciation) is considered by the law of obligations.[207] This solution is supported by further arguments: interventions in the monetary system fall under

[205] Cf.: Cass., 6 March 1876, cf. : case n° 1.

[206] See *Travaux de l'Association Capitant*, 1953 and 1971.

[207] H. J. L. Mazeaud, n° 869; see on monetary depreciation in general, among others, H. Cabrillac, *De quelles incidences des variations monétaires sur la règle de droit privé* (Aix-en-Provence, 1937); J. Carbonnier, *Le principe du nominalisme monétaire et ses limites en droit français*, Travaux et conferences (Brussels: Larcier, 1960), VIII, pp. 113–26; see on monetary depreciation in contractual relations, *Travaux de l'Association Capitant*, 1953 et 1971; J. Ph. Levy, *Jurisclasseur civil*, Art 1895 C. civ., 1977; see on indexation, J. P. Doucet,

the competence of the State's economic policy. Furthermore, monetary depreciation is a general phenomenon and cannot be solved by the courts on a case-by-case basis.

(b) Variation: foreign currency agreement

I. This solution will also apply if the loan is expressed in foreign currency,[208] apart from the additional considerations which are linked to the national economic policy.

Belgium

Y-Bank is not entitled to request a renegotiation or adjustment of the contract.

(a) Extraordinary inflation

I. In Belgian law, a contract cannot be adjusted in cases of extraordinary inflation.[209] The unpredictability of the circumstances is not sufficient to allow a revision of the contract.

L'indexation (Paris: LGDJ, 1965), vol. 61; E. S. de la Marniere, 'Observations sur l'indexation comme mesure de valeur', (1977) RTD civ, 1977, 54.

[208] CE, 8 November 1935, S., 1936, 3, p. 48 and p. 313 with note by J. Delpech (depreciation of the pound in the thirties); depreciation of the rouble after 1971, Cass. Civ., 25 February 1929, *Clunet*, p. 1306; G. Van Hecke, *Problèmes juridiques des emprunts internationaux* (Leiden: E. J. Brill, 2nd edn, 1964).

[209] See the following authors: S. David-Constant, 'Erosion monétaire et droit privé', (1977) *Annales de Droit*, 443–57; H. De Page, 'Avis', (1924) BJ, 374; H. De Page, *Traité elementaire de droit civil belge* (Brussels: Bruylant, 3rd edn, 1964), vol. II, n° 569, p. 578; J. Dubaere, 'Het principe van het monetaire nominalisme', (1978–9) *Iura Falconis*, pp. 57–76; R. Piret, *Les variations monétaires et leurs répercussions en droit privé belge* (Brussels and Lawain, 1935); R. Piret ,'La réadaptation monétaire du 21 septembre 1949 et les conflits de droit privé', (1949) J T 491; R. Piret, 'L'influence des variations monétaires en matière de contrats de prêts et de rente viagère', (1953) *Travaux de l'Association Capitant*, 131 *et seq.*, 134 and 135; Y. Schoentjes-Merchiers, *De waardebeveiligingsclausule in het recht van de landen der europese economische gemeenschap* (Brussels, 1968); Y. Schoentjes-Merchiers, 'Les effets des variations monétaires sur les rapports juridiques contractuels en droit civil et en droit commercial belge', (1971) *Travaux de l'Association H. Capitant*, 355 *et seq.*, 375–7; Y. Schoentjes-Merchiers, 'Geld, tijd, waarde en recht, De Rechtsbescherming tegen de waardeschommelingen van het geld', in: *Recht in beweging*, t. II, pp. 831–47, 842–3; R. Vandeputte, *De overeenkomst*, pp. 186 *et seq.*; G. Van Hecke, 'L'influence des variations monétaires en matière de contrats de prêts et de rente viagère et en matière de contrats administratif', (1953) *Travaux de l'Association H. Capitant*, (Brussels: Larcier, 1977) 219 *et seq.*; R. Zondervan, 'L'inflation: le droit et les faits', (1977) *Mélanges J. Baugniet*, pp. 917–68.

In the case law, the following decisions refused to take depreciation into consideration: civ. Brussels, 7 February 1924, BJ, 1924, p. 384; Brussels, 3 May 1927 and 13 January 1928, comm. Brussels, 8 December 1925, JCB, 1928, pp. 28–43; Brussels, 20 February 1932, Pas., 1932, II, p. 226. The following decision, on the contrary, gave

II. This solution is based not only on the rejection of the doctrine of *imprévision* but also on the principle of a monetary nominal value as expressed in Art. 1895 Cciv. This principle means that in the law of obligations the nominal value and not the real value (consideration being given to the depreciation) is taken into account.

(b) Variation: foreign currency agreement

III. This solution will also apply in cases of depreciation of foreign currency, i.e., if the loan is expressed in foreign currency.[210]

England and related jurisdictions

England and Ireland

Under English and Irish law, the contract is not frustrated. Y-Bank has no remedy and must perform the contract. The variation concerning the foreign currency agreement will make little difference to the result and it is unlikely that X would be able to obtain a renegotiation or adjustment of the contract.

The contract would be upheld in both cases.

These hypothetical questions present a variation from the situation referred to in the Case.

(a) Extraordinary inflation

In the present case the parties have negotiated a loan agreement in which X has received a loan from the Y-Bank, with the interest rate fixed at 10 per cent for five years. The unexpected circumstance that has arisen is a sharp rise in inflation, so much so that by the third year the inflation rate has quickly risen to 50 per cent.

I. There would appear to be no statutory basis in either England or Ireland on which Y-Bank could seek to terminate or vary the loan agreement. Nor would the courts adapt contracts to take account of inflation, as the theory of nominalism is a fundamental part of contract law.[211] Instead, it is assumed that the parties themselves have provided for inflation. Nor, generally speaking, would a rise in inflation cause a contract to be frustrated or terminated. However, there may be support

effect to monetary depreciation civ. Brussels, 3 January 1938, Pas., 1938, III, p. 138. (3); H. De Page, avis sous civ. Brussels, 7 February 1924, BJ, 1924, pp. 361 *et seq*. See (1953 and 1971) *Travaux de l'association Capitant*.

[210] G. Van Hecke, *Problèmes juridiques des emprunts internationaux* (Leiden, E. J. Brill, 1964).

[211] See F. A. Mann, *The Legal Aspect of Money* (Oxford: Clarendon Press, 5th edn, 1992), pp. 86 *et seq*.

for the view that a sharp and sudden rise in inflation may have the effect of frustrating a contract. In *The Power Co Ltd* v. *Gore District Council*[212] the New Zealand Court of Appeal agreed with Stephenson LJ in *Wates Ltd* v. *GLC*[213] that a contract could be frustrated if inflation increases 'not at a trot or a canter, but at a gallop'.[214]

II. The issue is thus whether it would be appropriate to permit the Y-Bank to invoke the doctrine of frustration in this case. There are reasons why this may not be the proper thing to do here. Formation of the loan contract puts the lender in the position of controlling the terms of the contract. It would have been quite possible for the Y-Bank to insist upon contracting with A on the foot of a clause which would require X to submit to interest variations in certain circumstances. In this case Y-Bank were prepared to contract on the basis of a fixed interest rate. The situation is analogous to that in *Davis Contractors Ltd* v. *Fareham UDC*.[215] Here a contractor submitted a fixed price tender, which was accepted. Later events made the contract a loss making one and he sought to have the contract declared frustrated. The House of Lords held that because the contractor could have tendered a price variation clause he could not now turn around and avoid the contract merely because performance had become more expensive or burdensome. This is a general principle that does not readily admit any exceptions thereto. Thus, it is highly unlikely that this contract would be frustrated or that the court would vary or adjust the contract to take account of the high rate of inflation. In the unlikely event that the contract was frustrated, the effect would be to discharge all unperformed contractual obligations. Renegotiation or adjustment is not within the scope of English or Irish law.

(b) Variation: foreign currency agreement

I. This question varies from the first situation in that it relates to a devaluation of the foreign currency, and it is X, the debtor, and not Y-Bank, the creditor, who is seeking a renegotiation and adjustment of the contract. However, these variations would make little difference to the result and it is unlikely that X would be able to obtain a renegotiation or adjustment of the contract.

II. There is no general statutory relief available to X unless X is a consumer, in which case there may be a limited form of relief. In Ireland, the Consumer Credit Act 1995 gives consumers the right to

[212] [1997] 1 NZLR 537. [213] [1983] 25 BLR 1 (Eng).
[214] [1983] 25 BLR 1, 35 (Eng). [215] [1956] AC 696 (Eng).

terminate a consumer credit agreement such as a loan in certain instances, essentially by paying off the debt early and giving notice in writing of their intention to terminate, and in such a situation the consumer is entitled to a reduction in the cost of credit.[216] A similar facility exists in English law.[217] It might be that X would utilise this specific release mechanism in appropriate circumstances, although it would not necessarily be much use to X in the current situation if the national currency has already devalued.

It is unlikely that the courts would adjust the contract or terminate it under the doctrine of frustration. The case of *Anderson* v. *Equitable Life Assurance Society*[218] illustrates the strict approach of the common law courts to the devaluation of currency. The plaintiff's husband had in 1887 taken out a life insurance policy, whereby in return for payment of an annual premium of 2,300 German Marks for twenty years, the insurance company promised to pay 60,000 Marks on the death of the insured. The insured died in 1922, by which stage hyperinflation meant that German Marks had become worthless. The English Court of Appeal refused to revalorise the amount promised, and the plaintiff widow recovered nothing.[219] Similarly, in the question presented, the variation in foreign currency values would most likely not trigger any frustration of that contract. Even if the contract was frustrated, this would not give rise to an adjustment or renegotiation of the contract, but rather the contracting parties would simply be discharged as to any future obligations and would have to look to the law of restitution for any subsequent relief.

Scotland

As under English and Irish law the contract is not frustrated. Y-Bank has no remedy and must perform the contract under Scottish Law. Foreign currency agreements are treated accordingly so that X will be bound to the conditions of the contract in the variation as well.

[216] Section 52.

[217] Sections 94–7 Consumer Credit Act 1974. See also the Consumer Credit (Rebate on Early Settlement) Regulations 1983 (SI 1983/1562 as amended by SI 1989/596).

[218] [1926] 42 TLR 302.

[219] The English courts would, however, allow revalorisation where German law was said to be the proper law of the contract: *Kornatzki* v. *Oppenheimer* [1937] 4 All ER 133.

(a) Extraordinary inflation

I. Inflation which is classed as 'normal' does not provide grounds for frustration in Scots and English law.[220] Although it seems to be recognised in principle that, by contrast, frustration which is 'extreme' can provide grounds for frustration, no writer, whether Scots or English, seems able to cite an example of 'extreme' as opposed to 'normal' inflation. Having analysed the English case law, Treitel concludes that it is an open question whether inflation which amounts to a 'radical difference' from anything the parties contemplated might amount to frustration.[221] He is at pains to emphasise the extreme nature of the inflation which would be required.[222] There is no reason to suppose that the attitude of the courts would be any different in the foreign currency agreement variation.

(b) Variation: foreign currency agreement

I. Similarly, in the variation concerning a foreign currency agreement, the contract is not frustrated. X has no remedy and must perform the contract.

Editors' comparative notes

The open jurisdictions

Under the majority of the open legal systems, Y may claim adjustment or termination of the contract in situation (a). The reason for this is that an excessive and unforeseen inflation has altered the balance or equilibrium of the contract and thus made the contract extremely burdensome for Y. The exceptions to this solution are Austria, the Netherlands, Portugal and, perhaps, Spain. In the Netherlands, this case is regarded as a matter for the legislature to solve and not for the judiciary, whereas in Austria the change is not regarded as sufficiently serious to justify intervention. The Spanish reporter states that there is some case law suggesting that a contract can be terminated or adjusted but it is uncertain whether the conditions for intervention are met in this case.

220 *British Movietonenews Ltd* v. *London and District Cinemas* [1952] AC 166; *Wates Ltd* v. *Greater London Council* (1983) 25 BLR 1 (CA).

221 Treitel, *Frustration and Force Majeure* (London: Sweet & Maxwell, 2004), para. 6–045, see also Denning LJ in *Staffordshire Area Health Authority* v. *South Staffordshire Water Works Co* [1978] 1 WLR 1387 at 1397–8, where he cites Mann, *The Legal Aspect of Money*, p. 100.

222 See Treitel, *Frustration and Force Majeure*, para. 6–046.

In situation (b) most jurisdictions offer a similar approach. While, again, the majority of the open jurisdictions grants relief, the opposite position is remarkably represented by Austria, where foreign currency agreements are likely to be regarded as speculative trading, which is regarded to fall within the debtor's sphere of responsibility. Hence, he is not entitled to adjustment or termination of the contract unless he suffers ruinous losses. Some other reports support the Austrian position arguing that courts might be more reluctant to intervene in foreign currency agreements (cf. Italy, Lithuania, Portugal).

The closed jurisdictions

The closed jurisdictions deny adjustment and termination in both fact patterns of Case 2 (with the potential exception of the Czech Republic). The reasons given for this restrictive result differ. Belgium and France reject the doctrine of *imprévision* and invoke the principle of monetary nominalism to this end. The common law systems of England and Ireland and the mixed jurisdiction of Scotland report that the contract is not frustrated. However, the reporters admit that the case law is not quite settled and that there is a chance that courts might intervene in cases of more excessive inflation. In Slovenia, some case law suggests that banking contracts will be excluded from the *clausula* rule in the civil code.

Conclusion

In this case, we can observe a general reluctance to grant relief in the 'closed' as well as in the 'open' jurisdictions. The latter (with the exception of Austria, the Netherlands and Spain) offer the claimant a right to terminate the contract because of an excessive and unforeseen inflation or because devaluation goes beyond the contractually intended risk allocation and alters the contractual equilibrium. In the closed jurisdictions the claimants are mostly left without a remedy. The contract is considered not to be frustrated by the inflation by the clear majority of these jurisdictions.

As far as the distinction between extreme inflation (situation (a)) and currency devaluation (situation (b)) is concerned, the solutions are generally very similar. Only a few jurisdictions apply stricter standards to foreign currency agreements due to their speculative nature (Austria, Italy, Lithuania, Portugal).

Case 3 Government intervention – tax increase

Post-contractual imposition of a tax

X and Y enter into a contract under which X promises to supply 120,000 litres of industrial spirit to Y. Subsequently, a statute is enacted by which an alcohol tax is imposed on the sale of industrial spirit. The statute provides that the seller has to pay the tax. The tax is so high that it even exceeds the price that X and Y have agreed upon.

Is X entitled to recover compensation for the additional costs, to adjust or to cancel the contract?

Germany and related jurisdictions

Germany

X is primarily entitled to an adjustment of the contract prices according to the rules of *Geschäftsgrundlage* (§313 I, III BGB). In cases of government intervention, the courts often divide the loss that results from the intervention equally.[223] Thus, if it is possible to share the burden reasonably by an adaptation of the contract, X is not entitled to terminate the contract.

I. Parties often allocate the burden of an amendment to the tax laws by a specific clause in the agreement; this is especially true for contracts that are very complex or that deal with issues that are typically subject to tax law amendments.[224] In the case at hand, the contract itself does not provide for an *explicit* clause about the imposition of any tax. Furthermore, *complementary interpretation* of the contract does not offer a solution because there is no element in the actual or hypothetical will of the parties that allows a court to determine how they would have dealt with this post-contractual government intervention at the time of formation.

II. 1. The core issue of the case, the distortion of equivalence of the contractual obligations due to a governmental intervention, i.e., the post-contractual imposition of a tax, is covered by the concept of *Geschäftsgrundlage* (§313 BGB). According to the courts[225] and the majority

[223] Cf. Roth, '§313', in: Krüger,*Münchener Kommentar zum Bürgerlichen Gesetzbuch*, vol. II, nn. 177 *et seq*. for further references.

[224] For examples cf. Grüneberg, '§313', in: Palandt *et al*. (eds.), *Bürgerliches Gesetzbuch*, n. 34.

[225] Cf. BGH LM §242 BGB (Bb) n. 33; BGH WM 1984, 432 (export of beer to Iran); BGH NJW 1980, 1912 (1914); for further references cf. Grüneberg, '§313', in: Palandt *et al*. (eds.), *Bürgerliches Gesetzbuch*, n. 34.

opinion of the legal writers,[226] the general rules governing a distortion of equivalence[227] also apply if it is caused by a government intervention. There are several categories of cases of governmental intervention. First, the expropriation of land from its owner has to be mentioned.[228] The specific issue of these cases results from the direct intervention in ownership by the government. In other lines of cases the impact of the governmental act is only indirect. Second, the change of a long-term line of precedents of the BGH can justify intervention.[229] Third, the majority of cases deals with a change of statutes and its impact on the contractual obligations.[230]

2. In general, the concept of *Geschäftsgrundlage* requires a basic assumption that is shared by both parties at the time of formation or the assumption of one party recognisable to and uncontested by the other. If the legal framework after formation does not develop in compliance with the parties' expectations, there is an interference with the *Geschäftsgrundlage* (§313 I BGB). The post-contractual imposition of a tax on X results in an unexpected distortion of the equivalence of exchange and thus affects the *Geschäftsgrundlage*.[231]

3. Furthermore, the impact of the change on the *Geschäftsgrundlage* has to be substantial, i.e., there has to be a massive change in the relevant circumstances (see §313 I BGB). Regarding the amendment of tax laws, no precise standard has been developed by the courts or by legal writers. Nevertheless, in the other lines of cases dealing with specific kinds of governmental intervention there are some decisions that render a distortion of the equivalence of 15 per cent sufficient.[232] It has to be

[226] Cf. *ibid.*, n. 34; Roth, '§313', in: Krüger, *Münchener Kommentar zum Bürgerlichen Gesetzbuch*, vol. II, nn. 171 *et seq.*

[227] Cf. for those rules Case 1.

[228] Cf. for further details Roth, '§313', in: Krüger, *Münchener Kommentar zum Bürgerlichen Gesetzbuch*, vol. II, nn. 175 *et seq.*; another direct intervention is the governmental change of the currency value of monetary obligations, cf. for those cases *ibid.*, vol. II, n. 186 *et seq.*

[229] Cf. BGHZ 58, 362; BGHZ 70, 298; BGH *NJW* 1983, 1548 (1551); cf. Grüneberg, '§313', in: Palandt *et al.* (eds.), *Bürgerliches Gesetzbuch*, n. 34.

[230] Some legal writers consider the impact of the reunification of Germany as another line of cases, cf. Roth, '§313', in: Krüger, *Münchener Kommentar zum Bürgerlichen Gesetzbuch*, vol. II, nn. 182 et seq.

[231] Cf. Case 1. Cf. for the application of *Geschäftsgrundlage* by the imposition of taxes Roth, '§313', in: Krüger, *Münchener Kommentar zum Bürgerlichen Gesetzbuch*, vol. II, n. 180; Grüneberg, '§313', in: Palandt *et al.* (eds.), *Bürgerliches Gesetzbuch*, n. 34; Larenz, *Schuldrecht I*, §21 II.

[232] Cf. BGH LM §242 BGB (Bb) n. 40.

doubted whether the courts would apply this test today.[233] Nevertheless, in the case at hand, there is a substantial impact on the *Geschäftsgrundlage* even if one applies a strict test because the tax imposed on seller X exceeds the price agreed upon for the spirit and results in a substantial loss for X.

4. Additionally, one party must be unreasonably burdened by the contract if it is upheld as originally concluded. In this case there is neither a contractual nor a statutory provision that allocates this risk of a substantial distortion in the equivalence of exchange to the seller. Nevertheless, tax law is very often subject to amendments and especially the imposition of taxes as well as the rescission of tax benefits always has a substantial effect on the equivalence of the contractual obligations.[234] Moreover, tax burdens and tax benefits are usually part of the calculation of one or both parties and an error in the calculation usually is allocated to the affected party.[235] Thus, the courts as well as legal writers[236] apply the concept of *Geschäftsgrundlage* with caution to those cases. While some writers generally allocate the risk of tax law amendments to the affected party,[237] the majority acknowledges cases of shared burden but they apply a strict test: an unreasonable burden requires that the parties somehow included the results imposed by tax law into the contract[238] or that the agreement was founded on the *actual* expectation that the legal framework of the tax law will not be altered.[239] It is doubtful whether the case at hand would pass this test as X and Y did not *actually* base the agreement on the expectation that the tax law will not be amended. A more liberal test draws on two issues: the exceptionality of the amendment and the extent to which the equivalence of exchange is distorted.[240] Applying this test, the

[233] For critics, see also Roth, '§313', in: W. Krüger, *Münchener Kommentar zum Bürgerlichen Gesetzbuch*, vol. II, nn. 172, 181.

[234] Thus, some writers conclude that the parties often include an implicit clause into the contract that allocates the risk to the burdened party, e.g., Roth, '§313', in: Krüger, *Münchener Kommentar zum Bürgerlichen Gesetzbuch*, vol. II, n. 180.

[235] Cf. *ibid.*, vol. II, nn. 180, 194 *et seq.*

[236] Cf. Grüneberg, '§313', in: Palandt *et al.* (eds.), *Bürgerliches Gesetzbuch*, n. 34; for a more liberal approach cf. Roth, '§313', in: W. Krüger, *Münchener Kommentar zum Bürgerlichen Gesetzbuch*, vol. II, n. 180.

[237] Cf. *ibid.*, vol. II, n. 180.

[238] Cf. BGH NJW 1951, 517; OLG Hamburg MDR 1955, 226; for critics cf. Roth, '§313', in: Krüger, *Münchener Kommentar zum Bürgerlichen Gesetzbuch*, vol. II, n. 180.

[239] Cf. BGH NJW 1961, 1081; Grüneberg, '§313', in: Palandt *et al.* (eds.), *Bürgerliches Gesetzbuch*, n. 34; for critics cf. Roth, '§313', in: W. Krüger, *Münchener Kommentar zum Bürgerlichen Gesetzbuch*, n. 180.

[240] Cf. *ibid.* vol. II, n. 180.

presumably unforeseeable imposition of a very high tax as well as the fact that it exceeds not only X's profit but also the contractual price is relevant.

Austria

Under Austrian law, X is entitled to terminate the contract, but there is no right to recover compensation for the additional costs.

I. 1. In several decisions the Austrian OGH held that an amendment of a statute does not affect the '*Geschäftsgrundlage*' of an agreement. For example, the change of landlord and tenant law does not entitle the landlord to terminate an existing tenancy contract.[241] Nevertheless, this rule does not apply where certain legal provisions are an essential basis of the contract.[242]

2. In the present case both parties assumed that there would be no tax liability, which was the basis of their price agreement. Such a case falls within the scope of '*Wegfall der Geschäftsgrundlage*' as a newly imposed alcohol tax is an unexpected change of circumstances that causes a considerable imbalance of performances.[243]

3. By analogy with the law of mistake, '*Wegfall der Geschäftsgrundlage*' entitles a party to adjust the contract if only a minor aspect of the contract is affected and the adjustment is in accordance with the hypothetical intentions of both the parties (§872 ABGB).[244] In the present case, no adjustment of the price agreement is possible, because one cannot assume that Y would have bought the spirit at a considerably higher price. Therefore X cannot claim compensation for the additional costs from Y. Where no adjustment is suitable, the burdened party (X) is only entitled to terminate the contract.

II. The government's intervention does not fall within one of the parties' area of assumed risk and was not predictable. From X's point of view the performance of the contract including the obligation to pay taxes would cause an unreasonable burden for him, since he would sustain serious financial loss.[245] According to the rules of

[241] OGH, EvBl 1970/203 = Miet 22.508.

[242] OGH, EvBl 1971/2 = JBl 1970, 420; OGH, EvBl 1972/142; OGH, ZAS 1978, 22.

[243] Koziol and Welser, *Bürgerliches Recht*, vol. I, p. 162 and Apathy, '§901', in: Schwimann (ed.), *Kommentar zum ABGB*, vol. IV, n. 8.

[244] Koziol and Welser, *Bürgerliches Recht*, vol. I, p. 165; Rummel, '§872', in: Rummel (ed.), *Kommentar zum ABGB*, vol. I, nn. 1, 7.

[245] See OGH 17 March 1970, SZ 43/63 = JBl 1970, 420 = EvBl 1971/2.

'*Wegfall der Geschäftsgrundlage*' this situation justifies the termination of the contract.

The Netherlands

Under Dutch law, X is not very likely to receive compensation for the additional tax payments; likewise, he will most likely not be allowed to terminate the contract.

I. 1. Under Dutch law, X is not very likely to receive compensation for the additional tax payments or to be given a right to terminate the contract under the doctrine of changed circumstances (Art. 6:258). Several criteria of Art. 6:258 are met: the imposition of a tax on industrial alcohol was a future circumstance; the enacted statute was clearly unforeseeable because, most likely, X would never have contracted on the basis of this (unusual) provision if X had known of the statutory change. Also, the Hoge Raad confirmed that such an amendment of the law may constitute a change of circumstances within the meaning of Art. 6:258.[246] This judgment concerned new provisions in rent law and similar solutions were achieved by the lower courts in the area of tax law. Also, if there is an indication that the parties considered their agreement not to be 'carved in stone' but rather an outline of principles governing their (supply) relationship, an amendment to take account of the enacted taxes is probable. Such a claim should be based on the case *FNV* v. *Campina*,[247] in which an arrangement between the employees' union and Campina to keep a certain plant open was amended by the court after the imposition of an EU superlevy. The court considered the superlevy to be fundamental, unforeseeable (i.e., it could not have been taken into account when the agreement was reached) and part of an arrangement that the unions saw as a collective labour agreement. Internal notes by the unions provided evidence that they had always considered the arrangement to be of a general nature and had been advocating the flexibility it embodied. Hence the court, confirmed by the Hoge Raad, allowed an amendment so that the distribution centre could be shut down.

2. However, a court might come to a different conclusion in cases where each of the contracting parties (but in any event X) is a major company with professional tax and legal departments. If Y had known about any pending legislation, the contract would have been voidable by X on the ground of fraud or abuse of circumstances (Art. 3:44 Dutch

[246] HR 14 June 1996, NJ 1996, 729. [247] HR 10 July 1989, NJ 1989, 786 (*FNV* v. *Campina*).

Civil Code) or on the ground of mistake due to Y's failure to inform X. Such a duty to inform may well exist under these circumstances (Art. 6:228). According to Art. 6:258(2) Dutch Civil Code if Y did not know about any pending legislation, the question would be whether 'the nature of the agreement' or 'what would commonly be considered to be appropriate' determines that X should bear the risk. In the case of a mere sales agreement it is not very likely that a court will readily interfere with the intentions of the government, especially if both parties are professionals.

3. The most likely result of the case would be for a court to refuse any modification or termination of the transaction.

II. 1. The case is relatively exceptional as regards its factual setting: in practice, almost inevitably and without much negotiation, contracts provide that taxes are to be borne by the buyer rather than the seller. This may be different for a party that was eager to sell (at a certain price or sales volume) and which was willing to accept *all* risks, even as regards such undisputed matters as taxes.[248]

2. If X and Y agree that X should deliver 'DDP' (i.e., pursuant to Incoterm 'Delivered Duty Paid'),[249] the seller will bear all risks in connection

[248] Competition amongst raw material suppliers is often severe. In order to be competitive, suppliers must focus on their 'operational excellence' (i.e., in markets with low profit margins the challenge is to achieve customer-customised deliveries, to act quickly and reduce costs, with a focus on process improvement, supply-chain optimisation and achieving efficiencies in other time-consuming operations). This means that such suppliers concentrate on 'what matters' and assume the risk of less important factors or as factors with less impact for the benefit of a higher profit margin or lower product cost. At the same time, in the industry of bulk raw materials (like industrial spirit) it is common to provide for plain risk allocations, even in an unusual matter. This may be explained by the fact that one party may have better 'access' to a cheap solution than the other, leading to an allocation of risks that matches such access options. This does not mean, however, that normal contract provisions should be replaced by extraordinary stipulations such as in the case of X and Y. In this case, it may be assumed that X has not had the supply contract reviewed by a lawyer. This failure may well be responsible from a cost optimisation point of view, but anyhow embodies the risk that X enters into an unreasonable contract. Such a decision is of course for the risk and account of X.

[249] International Chamber of Commerce (ICC), *Incoterms 2000*, ICC publication N° 560 (Paris: 1999). In short, the term says that '"Delivered duty paid" means that the seller delivers the goods to the buyer, cleared for import, and not unloaded from any arriving means of transport at the named place of destination. The seller has to bear all the costs and risks involved in bringing the goods thereto including, where applicable, any "duty" (which term includes the responsibility for and the risks of the carrying out of customs formalities and the payment formalities, customs duties, taxes and other charges) for import in the country of destination.'

with the delivery at the port of destination.[250] The essential difference between DDP and the first alternative Incoterm, 'DDU' ('Delivered Duty Unpaid'), is precisely in the allocation of duties, customs, taxes and other charges. In practice, those in the sourcing business are very well aware of the scope and nature of each Incoterm. Under Dutch law, it must therefore be assumed that the parties have actually considered the impact of taxes. Although the case does not provide any details, it may well be that X could source its industrial spirit from another supplier or country and thereby avoid the burdensome taxes. Moreover, providing for such a 'second source' would typically be X's business responsibility. All these considerations suggest that X assumed the risk and that it bears the consequences of the enacted statute.

3. Accordingly, the contract cannot be amended or cancelled under Art. 6:258.[251]

Eastern European jurisdictions

Slovenia

Under Slovenian law X is entitled to terminate the contract but he cannot recover the additional costs.

I. In this case both parties have concluded the contract based on the presumption that there would be no changes in taxation. The enactment of a new tax does not fall within one of the parties' areas of assumed risks, it was not predictable and none of the parties could have taken it into account when they were negotiating the contract (price). The performance of the contract including the obligation to pay

250 The parties may or may not have specifically excluded VAT, as the DDP term explicitly allows. The choice for delivery DDP may well be made because both parties believed that X, rather than Y, is familiar with various administrative procedures and uncertainties in the country from where the industrial spirit is sourced and that X has the best access to all kinds of solutions in order to deliver in good time.

251 To some extent, the above considerations may be turned around: a decision to choose DDP and not DDU would be made for X's expertise in importing the industrial alcohol more expeditiously (and therefore more cheaply), so as not to burden X with highly exceptional tax impositions. The taxation of the seller seems to be highly exceptional: normally, taxes are charged to the supplier but payable by the seller. Also, if there was only one country from which to source the alcohol, and therefore all suppliers had to suffer from the tax (and if their and X's customers would all be picking up the additional tax bill, which is not very likely), there may be a reason to modify the consequences of the contract between X and Y.

taxes causes an unreasonable burden for X. Therefore, the imposition of the tax is an extraneous change of circumstances that gives ground for an action based on Article 112 CO ('*clausula* rule'). Yugoslav case law accepted even a change in existing taxation as a relevant change of circumstances; it is, however, unclear how high the rise of taxes must be to justify relief.[252]

II. Under Slovenian law it is not possible for a party to demand adjustment of the contract on the basis of change of circumstances. Adjustment of the contract by the court is nevertheless possible if the other party proposes it, or at least, if it gives its consent.[253] It is, however, highly unlikely that Y would buy the spirit at a considerably higher price, because his cost profit scheme was based upon a much lower price.

Lithuania

Under Lithuanian Law, this case would not be recognised as force majeure or as an essential change of circumstances. Therefore X cannot request an adaptation or a termination of the contract.

I 1. X may theoretically ask for a modification of the contract or its termination on the basis of Art. 6.204 CC because the tax fundamentally alters the balance of the contractual obligations: (i) the enactment occurred after the conclusion of the contract; however, X must further prove that (ii) this intervention could not have reasonably been foreseen at the time of the conclusion of the contract; and that (iii) the risk of occurrence of such government intervention was not assumed by him.

2. The plaintiff would find it rather difficult to prove circumstances (ii) and (iii) because there is no uniform attitude in the Lithuanian court practice in evaluating the activity of the government or the parliament. First, there have been instances when the court regarded amendments of laws or tax changes as force majeure.[254] Second, in contrast, there have also been cases where the court did not accept the introduction of new taxes as either force majeure or an essential change of circumstances and refused to apply Art. 6.204 CC. For instance, the court did

[252] A rise of taxes by 0.5 per cent has been declared as insufficient (Supreme Yugoslav Commercial Court Sl 1820/62, 22 August 1962. Cigoj, *Komentar obligacijskih razmerij*, p. 441.

[253] Dolenc in: Juhart and Plavšak (eds.), *Obligacijski zakonik*, vol. I, pp. 605–6; Slovenian Supreme Court II Ips 910/93.

[254] LAT, Judgment of 12 April 2006, Case No 3K-3-273/2006.

not consider an introduction of 5 and 18 per cent VAT on goods an essential change of circumstances and refused to modify the terms of a contract pursuant to Art. 6.204 CC.[255] In addition, as the Lithuanian legal situation, including tax laws, is amended very frequently, the court may hold that X was able to foresee such a change.

II. If X proves these circumstances, he may request the modification of the contract or alternatively terminate the contract on the basis of Art. 6.204 CC. If the court decides to modify the contract, the effects of the new tax would be divided between both parties, i.e., the court would not increase the price by the full tax, but most probably to only about 50 per cent of the sum of the tax. It is the purpose of Art. 6.204 CC to restore the balance of the contractual obligations not just to protect the interests of one party.

Czech Republic

The conditions for termination of the contract are met, provided that the main purpose of the contract (which has been frustrated) was expressly (specifically) stipulated in the contract. But, under Section 357 Commercial Code, the debtor will have to compensate his contractual partner for the damage caused by the termination.

I. The Commercial Code theory of frustration may play a role here.[256] In view of the amount of taxation, which the parties could not have foreseen, it is possible to consider the option of withdrawing from the contract on the grounds of frustration of the purpose thereof. The Commercial Code's rule on frustration of the purpose of the contract can be applied if three conditions are met. First, the main purpose of the contract must be frustrated; second, the main purpose must be specifically stipulated in the contract; and third, a pure change of the financial situation of one of the parties is not deemed to be a change of circumstances. The main purpose of the contract is to sell industrial spirit for the agreed price and to realise a profit from the sale. Although a major increase in alcohol tax is in itself not a reason to terminate the contract, in the light of the cited Commercial Code provision the basic purpose of the contract is frustrated and the frustration is not caused by a change in

[255] LAT, Judgment of 8 February 2006, Case No 3K-3–107/2006.

[256] See Section 356f Commercial Code; however, no detailed analysis exists in the literature.

the financial position of one of the parties or a change in the economic or market conditions, so the contract may be withdrawn from.

II. In view of the conflict with the principles of fair business conduct, claims can become unenforceable.[257] Fair business conduct is discussed above and the same principles apply in this case.[258] However, any claim for compensation by way of damages is out of the question here since the prerequisites would not be met.

Scandinavian jurisdictions

Sweden

Under Swedish Law the contract can be adjusted or perhaps terminated under Section 36 Contracts Act.

I. In this case, it is assumed that the seller X would not have to pay the tax if the contract was terminated, which is not necessarily in accordance with Swedish law.[259] Generally, Swedish law is somewhat restrictive when it comes to allowing a party to a contract to avoid taxation by claiming that the contract is void.[260]

II. The doctrine of assumptions cannot be applied to increase the seller's compensation, but only for avoidance, i.e., termination or limitation of a liability. This requires a specific ground, such as that the buyer made a profit at the expense of the seller. In this case no such profit has occurred. Nor is there any other specific ground for the application of the doctrine of assumptions. There is a slight possibility that the doctrine of assumptions possibly could still be applied on the basis that the parties would have contracted otherwise, had they known about the tax, but that appears an unlikely outcome.

III. 1. Under Section 36 Contracts Act, the price clause may be modified or set aside if it is deemed unreasonable with reference to the contents of

257 Provided that enacting the alcohol tax was upredictable.

258 We suppose that the delivery of 120,000 litres is a single (unrepeated) performance and therefore the contract is not long-term agreement.

259 Cf. NJA 1982 p. 493 I-II, where the Supreme Court maintained that the responsibility to pay tax on gifts was unconditional of the fact that the gifts were void under rules or principles of civil law as the tax had turned out to be much higher than the parties had assumed.

260 Compare NJA 1986 p. 205, stating that a judgment on cancellation of a purchase of real estate contract could not be based upon the defendant's admission, when the claim was obviously not legally founded, and NJA 1993 p. 319, where a purchase of real estate which had resulted in disastrous tax effects was considered void under general principles of civil law (probably the doctrine of assumptions).

the contract, the circumstances at the formation of the contract, circumstances arising later and other circumstances. As the tax is so high that it even exceeds the agreed price, and the seller will thus actually have to pay for delivering the industrial spirits, the distortion of the equilibrium of the contract is of such a magnitude that it would in most cases render the price unreasonable per se. However, this is not a normal situation. The effects of the new tax statute can be assumed to have been considered when it was enacted, and its effects on the purchase do not appear extraordinary. This calls for some restraint. Still, the economic consequences are not reasonable, and it is submitted that they render the price unreasonable. It would therefore be possible to adjust the contract to compensate for the tax, or to terminate the contract.

2. The aim of an adjustment under Section 36 is to arrive at a reasonable price. Consequently, the price should be adjusted so that the additional tax is shared between the parties – although the seller would still have to pay a greater part of the tax, as the burden is originally placed on him. However, if the unreasonable price is of such importance to the contract that the rest of it could not fairly be upheld unchanged, the contract can be adjusted in other parts, or terminated (i.e., adjusted to zero). Here, the court may consider whether the buyer would still want to buy, and whether the seller would still want to sell, the same quantities of industrial spirit if the contract was terminated. If so, an adjustment might be preferred to termination.

Denmark

No relief is available under Danish law.

I. As a main principle, X is obliged to deliver the industrial spirit in accordance with the agreement, even though an alcohol tax has been imposed by Danish law after the contract was entered into.

II. X might invoke economic force majeure in accordance with Section 24 Sale of Goods Act. Case law, however, clearly shows that even though prices may have risen by four or five times, X has the obligation to deliver in accordance with the contract.[261] The literature does not support any other solution, since in accordance with Danish law industrial spirit is regarded as a generic good, for which X is strictly liable.[262] In other words, as a starting point, X bears the risk if the price

[261] See for instance U 1922.858 H, 1942.214 SH, and 1965.631 H.

[262] For a comprehensive discussion on this issue, see Jacob Nørager-Nielsen and Søren Theilgaard, *Købeloven med kommentarer* (Copenhagen: Gadd, 2nd edn, 1993), pp. 350 *et seq.*

has risen due to government intervention. In the contract X could have reserved the right to increase the price of the goods in the case of any government intervention, which X did not do, even though he could have incorporated such a provision. Government intervention is traditionally considered as possible third party intervention in Danish contract law, which the parties can take into consideration in the provisions of the contract. That would especially be the case if the contract required the approval of any public body in order to become valid between the parties. Any literature on this issue is very scarce in Denmark. The literature focuses more on the interaction between the public and private sector.[263]

III. X might alternatively invoke the application of Section 36 Contracts Act. However, no case law has been reported with respect to this issue. In the contract X could have very easily reserved the right to increase the price due to the enactment of any tax legislation. If X invokes the application of Section 36 Contracts Act, he could argue that the fulfilment of the contract would be unreasonable. This might be considered a valid argument, but there is no good reason why Y should be more likely to bear the economic risk than X. After all, it might be presumed that X as the vendor is familiar with the market for industrial spirit and should consider the possibility of any government intervention. He must thus bear the risk of changed circumstances if the parties have not incorporated any such provision in the contract between them. Y is not necessarily familiar with the market for industrial spirit. It is quite likely that, in a future case, a party would refer to the application of Section 36 Danish Contracts Act, but such an application should be rejected in accordance with Danish law.

Romanic-Mediterranean jurisdictions

Italy

X is entitled to terminate the contract and he may, alternatively, receive compensation for his additional costs.

I. If the tax is actually so high that it even exceeds the price X and Y have agreed upon, X is certainly entitled, under Italian law, to terminate the contract according to Art. 1467 CC.[264] It is not a modification of the

[263] See, however, Karsten Naundrup Olesen, *Samfundsloddet* (Copenhagen: Thomson, 1st edn, 2003).

[264] See above, Case 1, and overview (Chapter 4).

fiscal law as such but the actual impact of the law on the contractual balance that allows the seller to invoke the termination. As far as the requirements of Art. 1467 CC are concerned, in the case at issue the specific supervening burden is not part of the normal risk of the contract and therefore it cannot be said that the seller has (implicitly) assumed the risk of the post-contractual imposition of an alcohol tax on the sale of industrial spirit.[265] A variation falling within the normal risk of the contract would not amount to a valid cause for termination. Indeed, the parties bear the burden to foresee the existence of a reasonable margin of risk related to any contractual covenant (meaning that any obligation may become more or less burdensome).[266]

II. A right to compensation for the additional costs suffered by the seller is not provided by Italian law, which does not explicitly recognise the adaptation or adjustment of the contract in the case of hardship (or similar cases). The seller is entitled to terminate the contract, as already said. However, since the party from whom the dissolution is demanded can avoid it by offering an equitable modification of the conditions of the contract (Art. 1467 13 CC),[267] a compensation for the additional costs may result indirectly from the equitable modification offered by Y (and accepted by X or, alternatively, decided by the court upon the demand of Y). Paragraph 3 does not establish a clear rule of rebalancing, but rather enables the judge to determine an equitable modification. This could induce the court to divide the supervening burden equally between the parties.

Spain

X is likely to be granted compensation for the increase in tax or to be allowed to terminate the contract.

I. There are no specific rules regarding the allocation of risk if the change of circumstances results from government intervention. In Spanish commercial practice, parties typically agree on how the risk is to be allocated in a case of force majeure which renders the performance impossible. But parties usually do not agree on how to allocate the risk in cases which do not amount to force majeure. If there is no contractually specified risk allocation in cases of changed

[265] Cf. Cass., 4 March 1998, n. 2386, where the Supreme Court has decided that a supervening EU tax levied on the import of olive oil from Greece does not exceed the normal contractual risk.

[266] F. Gambino, *Normalità*, p. 151.

[267] See above, Case 1, and overview (Chapter 4).

circumstances, the risk is borne by the party whose performance becomes more onerous.

II. 1. According to a decision by the TS, it has to be determined whether the risk has to be borne by the debtor when it comes to a changed situation due to government intervention.[268] In this case, the court did not apply the doctrine of the extraordinary difficulty in performing in order to exonerate the debtor from his liability. The risk was attributed to him as the type of activity he carried out (the construction of seagoing vessels) is known to be strongly influenced by governmental measures.

2. However, there is another decision by the TS that resembles this case.[269] The parties had concluded a lease contract to operate an amusement arcade. After the conclusion of the contract, a new tax on the operation of this particular business was imposed. Therefore the lessee wanted to terminate the contract. The court rejected such a claim arguing that this modification was not unforeseeable and the equilibrium of the contract was not excessively affected. Following this line of reasoning, the court might have decided to the contrary in the case at hand. After all, the tax was so high that it even exceeded the price that X and Y had agreed upon. Assuming that the imposition of the tax was not foreseeable, the court could have decided to terminate or modify the contract in order to restore the equilibrium.

3. As indicated above, the *rebus* doctrine leads in the first place to the modification of the contract. Only when it is impossible to restore the balance will the courts grant a termination.

Portugal

X is entitled to recover compensation for the additional costs or to terminate the contract.

I. The imposition of a tax qualifies as a change of the basis of the contract, according to Art. 437 CC. It is possibly even an unforeseeable event[270] and one that substantially shifts the balance between performance and counter-performance. It is largely recognised by legal literature[271] that new statutes or changes in the legal system itself, may represent a change of the foundation of the contract.

[268] Decision of 16 October 1989 (id. Cendoj. 28079110011989100911).

[269] Decision of 18 September 1996 18-9-1996 (RJ 1996, 1728).

[270] Although all that is required as previously stated is an anomalous change or turn of events, and not necessarily an unforeseeable one.

[271] See, for instance, Pires de Lima and Antunes Varela, *Código Civil Anotado* (Almedina: Coimbra Editora, 4th edn, 1987), vol. I, with the collaboration of M. Henrique

II. The priority of adjustment over termination is not clearly expressed in Art. 437 CC. Recently Oliveira Ascensão has suggested that the adjustment of the contract is only possible if no party to the contract expresses an opposition to the modification of the agreement. Otherwise, the judge could not impose the adjustment and rescission would be the only remedy available. However, the law normally favours the upholding of contracts and the legal provisions suggest that the court has the right to carry out a modification of the contract.[272] However, the case law is not yet settled. First, cases in which Art. 437 CC has been invoked successfully are extremely rare and, second, the decisions do not mention an express opposition of a contractual partner to any modification envisaged by the court. Nevertheless, in a case like this we believe the court would be particularly sensitive to reasons presented by the parties to terminate the contract, especially taking into account that the Civil Code protects the buyer against unforeseen increases in the price.

Greece

Under Greek law, the contract will be adjusted and the tax burden will most likely be distributed evenly between the parties. X has no right to claim compensation.

I. As a consequence of the sudden imposition of the alcohol taxes, X's obligation to perform becomes extremely onerous. The unforeseen change in the tax legislation, which makes the performance excessively onerous for the debtor, is one of the most characteristic cases within the scope of Art. 388 AK.[273] In this case, the judge has to try to adjust the contract.[274] The aim of this adjustment is not to adapt the sum of the taxes to the price of the contract fully (the claim based on Art. 388 AK is

Mesquita, p. 415, and Luís Menezes Leitão, *Direito das Obrigações* (Almedina: Coimbra Editora, 4th edn, 2006), vol. II, p. 135, who states that completely unforeseeable changes in the law may represent a change in the foundation of the contract. As an example of a change in the law that was deemed a reason to invoke Art. 437, see Acórdão do Supremo Tribunal de Justiça of 6 April 1978 (1978) 276 *Boletim do Ministério da Justiça*, 253 (whereby the statute that suspended the right to demand the demolition of certain buildings was considered to be a relevant change of circumstances).

[272] José de Oliveira Ascensão, 'Onerosidade Excessiva por Alteração das Circunstâncias', (2005) 65 *Revista da Ordem dos Advogados*, 625 *et seq*. Pais de Vasconcelos, *Teoria Geral de Direito Civil* (Coimbra: Almedina, 10th edn, 2006), p. 751, defends the priority of modification of the contract over its termination and invokes the black letter of the law and the *favor negotii*.

[273] See Stathopoulos, *Law of Obligations*, §22 n. 18.

[274] See also above under Case 2.

not a compensation claim) but to restore the balance of the corresponding performances according to good faith by raising the amount of the counter-performance. Therefore, the possibility of an equal distribution of the tax between the parties is not out of the question. It depends on the buyers' financial situation. If the latter is able to carry the extra burden, an adjustment of the price is the adequate solution. If not, the court is obliged to declare the dissolution of the contract.

II. Undeniably, X has no right to compensation given that, as already mentioned, the adjustment of a contract does not aim at the compensation of the damaged party, but at the restoration of the disturbed equilibrium of the performances.[275]

France and related jurisdictions

France

A French court might be inclined to divide the burden of the new tax between both parties based on the principle of good faith.

I. A new tax will not be considered as force majeure as the fact that the performance of the contract becomes substantially more onerous is not sufficient to apply the force majeure doctrine.[276] This event will not allow a revision of the contract. The seller must bear the consequences of this new tax as expressly prescribed by the statute.

II. However, since the recent decisions of the French Cour de Cassation, it is not unlikely that the judge will interfere by imposing an obligation on the buyer to renegotiate. This obligation is based on good faith. The court considered that a party is obliged to renegotiate a contract in cases of an unforeseeable change of circumstances that distorts the contractual equilibrium.[277] As a consequence, a part of the new tax will be attributed to the buyer. The exact burden of the new tax will be decided on an equitable basis, depending on the circumstances of the case.[278] However, the current case law is too scarce to determine a specific reasoning which will be followed by the courts.

[275] See Stathopoulos, 'Art. 388', in: Georgiadis and Stathopoulos (eds.), *AK*, n. 22.

[276] See above [section 2.1] and references.

[277] Cass. com., 3 November 1992, Cass. com., 24 November 1998,: Cass., 1st Ch. Civ. 16 March 2004.

[278] In administrative law, the burden of unexpected circumstances is mostly borne by the public authority; generally only 5 per cent of the new burden has to be borne by the party contracting with the public authority; see Cons. Etat, 30 November 1928, *Société le*

Belgium

X might be able to recover compensation for the additional costs based on the principle of good faith in Belgian law. However, this result is unlikely.

I. The enactment of the statute does not give rise to a revision of the contract. There is no reason to deviate from the clear provisions of the contract. The consequences of this new tax must be borne by the seller.

II. This new tax will not be considered as force majeure. The fact that the performance of the contract becomes substantially more onerous is not sufficient to apply the principle of force majeure.

III. However, it is not excluded, although it is improbable, that the judge will allow a revision of the price on the basis of the interpretation of the contract, good faith or the concept of abuse of rights.[279]

England and related jurisdictions

England and Ireland

X is neither entitled to terminate the contract nor can he obtain compensation for his additional costs.

I. 1. X may attempt to claim that the contract is frustrated and that he is thus discharged from his contractual obligations because the contract is now much more expensive to perform than was originally thought. However, it is unlikely that such a claim will succeed.

2. There are a number of judicial statements to the effect that contractual parties will not be discharged merely because the contract is more onerous to perform than was originally contemplated. In *Zuphen and Others* v. *Kelly Technical Services Ltd*,[280] Murphy J in the Irish High Court reiterated the statement of Lord Radcliffe in *Davis Contractors Ltd* v. *Fareham Urban District Council*:

> It is not hardship or inconvenience or a material loss itself which calls the principles of frustration into play. There must have been such a change in the significance of the obligation that the thing undertaken would, if performed, be a different thing from that contracted for.

Centre électrique, Rec. 1928, p. 1228; 1 July 1949, *Ministère de la Guerre*, Rec. 1949, p. 318; Philippe, *Changement de circonstances*, p. 97.

[279] See *ibid.*, pp. 176, 180, 185, 191; see also the French report (taking into consideration, however, that the Belgian case law does not contain decisions such as the French case of *Huard and others* (Cass. com., 3 November 1992, *Sté francaise des pétrdes BP* v. *Huard*, JCP 1993 II no. 22614) where a duty to renegotiate the contract was acknowledged).

[280] [2000] ELR 277, 291.

In *Neville and Sons Ltd* v. *Guardian Builders Ltd*[281] the Irish Supreme Court held that the mere fact that a contract was more onerous to perform than was originally contemplated did not mean it was frustrated. Blayney J approved the following statement of Lord Simon in *National Carriers Ltd* v. *Panalpina (Northern) Ltd*:[282]

Frustration of a contract takes places when there supervenes an event (without default of either party and for which the contract makes no sufficient provision) which so significantly changes the nature *(not merely the expense or onerousness)* of the outstanding contractual rights and/or obligations from what the parties could reasonably have contemplated at the time of its execution that it would be unjust to hold them to the literal sense of its stipulations in the new circumstances; in such case the law declares both parties to be discharged from further performance.

3. In England, there have been a series of decisions supporting this proposition. In *Tsakiroglou* v. *Noblee and Thorl*[283] the cost to the seller of performing a contract of sale was dramatically increased by the closure of the Suez Canal, and yet the contract was not frustrated. In *Brauer and Co Ltd* v. *James Clark (Brush Materials) Ltd*[284] the expenses of a seller of goods were increased by the unforeseen cost of obtaining an export licence and again the contract was not discharged. Lord Denning stated:

[A]ny person who sells goods forward must be ready himself to bear any increase in the market price. It would be a strange thing if a seller could insist on the contract if the price fell, and could escape his own obligations if it rose. It would do away with the whole point of forward contracts altogether.[285]

4. In *Blockow Vaughan and Co* v. *Compania Minera de Sierra Minera*[286] the defendant, who had contracted to sell iron ore to the plaintiff, was not discharged when his costs were greatly increased by an unforeseen increase in the cost of freight. Swinfen Eady LJ in the Court of Appeal stated:

A mere rise in the price of a commodity to be supplied, or in the rate of freight, [is] not alone a sufficient excuse for non delivery. A person [is] not entitled to be excused from the performance of a contract merely because it had become more costly to perform it.

[281] [1995] 1 ILRM 1, 7. [282] [1981] AC 675, 700 (emphasis added).
[283] [1961] 2 All ER 179 (Eng). [284] [1952] 2 All ER 497 (Eng).
[285] [1952] 2 All ER 497, 501 (Eng). [286] (1916) 33 TLR 111 (Eng).

5. Similarly, an increase in the cost of supplying goods caused by an unforeseen reduction in supply and/or rise in the price of goods will not discharge a seller. In one case,[287] the defendants had agreed to sell wheat to the plaintiffs. The subsequent actions of the Argentinian government meant the sellers could only perform the contract by buying wheat at a much higher price than that for which they had contracted to resell it. However, they were still not discharged from their contractual obligations. In *S Instone & Co Ltd* v. *Speeding Marshall & Co Ltd*[288] an agreement to sell coal was not discharged when, because of war, the price of coal was increased by 88 per cent. In *Greenway Brothers Ltd* v. *SF Jones and Co*[289] the defendant, who had contracted to sell spelter, was not excused even though, owing to the outbreak of war, the defendant could only get the spelter at an 'abnormal price'. In *Tennants (Lancashire) Ltd* v. *C S Wilson and Co Ltd*[290] the defendants had entered an agreement to supply magnesium chloride to the plaintiffs. The outbreak of war in 1914 caused a shortage in supply and hence a rise in prices. A clause in the contract provided that deliveries could be suspended pending any contingencies 'beyond the control of the sellers or buyers ... causing a short supply of labour, fuel, raw material, or manufactured produce, or otherwise preventing or hindering the manufacture or delivery of the article'. It was held that the shortage in the supply of magnesium chloride justified the suspension of performance, but that *on its own*, a rise in price 'even if very great'[291] would not constitute a hindrance to delivery within the meaning of the condition. It is also clear that such a rise in price would not frustrate the contract. Earl Loreburn stated:

> I cannot regard shortage of cash or inability to buy at a remunerative price as a contingency beyond the sellers' control. The argument that a man can be excused from performance of his contract when it becomes 'commercially' impossible ... seems to me a dangerous contention which ought not to be admitted unless the parties have plainly contracted to that effect.[292]

6. Cases from other common law jurisdictions also indicate that X will not be able to consider himself discharged from the contract purely

[287] *Exportelisa SA* v. *Guiseppe and Figli Soc Coll* [1978] 1 Lloyd's Rep 433 (Eng).
[288] (1915) 32 TLR 202 (Eng). [289] (1915) 32 TLR 184 (Eng).
[290] [1917] AC 495. Applied in *Peter Dixon & Sons Ltd* v. *Henderson Craig & Co Ltd* [1919] 2 KB 778 (both Eng).
[291] [1917] AC 495, 509 per Lord Finlay LC. [292] [1917] AC 495, 510.

because of increased costs and expenses.[293] The New Zealand decision of *Waiwera Cooperative Dairy Co* v. *Wright Stepheson and Co*[294] is directly on point. Here, a contract for the sale of cheese was not terminated even when the seller's expenses were greatly increased by an extra tax placed on butter fat, one of the constituents of cheese.

7. However, it should be noted that it has been suggested that an increase in costs may be so onerous as to discharge a party from his contractual obligations. It was thus suggested by the English Court of Appeal in *Brauer and Co Ltd* v. *James Clark (Brush Materials) Ltd*[295] that if the cost to the seller of obtaining an export licence was 'a hundred times as much as the contract price' then it would be possible that the seller would be discharged. There is also some fairly weak English authority for the proposition that an alteration of the law putting a burden on one of two contracting parties, in the course of carrying out his contract, entitles that party to repudiate the contract if the alteration is made by Parliament ad hoc: *Levenshulme UDC* v. *Manchester Corporation*.[296] However, it is unlikely that this would be applied in the context of a general tax being properly applied to all sellers of industrial alcohol.

II. 1. Any attempt by X to claim compensation for his additional costs will involve a judicial variation of the terms of the contract. However, English and Irish courts do not have the power to vary contracts in this way. If a document does not reflect the agreement that was actually struck, then the courts may rectify the written document,[297] but the courts do not have a general power to 'rectify' the terms of the agreement itself.[298] Similarly, in *British Movietonews Ltd* v. *London and District Cinemas Ltd*[299] the House of Lords made clear that a court has no discretion to qualify the contract for the purpose of doing what seems to it to be just and reasonable. Thus, X may be able to renegotiate the contract with Y so as to cover his increased costs, but Y will not be obliged to enter into such negotiations or form a new contract. If no new agreement is reached, X will simply have to perform or pay damages for breach of contract.

[293] See for example: *Delta Food Processors Ltd* v. *East Pacific Enterprises Ltd* [1980] BCLR 13; *Graham* v. *Wagman* [1976] 73 DLR (3d) 667; *Samuel* v. *Black Lake Asbestos* [1920] 58 DLR 27; *Tingley* v. *McKeen* [1954] 4 DLR 392 (All Canadian).

[294] [1917] NZLR 178. [295] [1952] 2 All ER 497 (Eng). [296] (1908) 72 JP 470 (Eng).

[297] See: *Nolan* v. *Graves and Hamilton* [1946] IR 377.

[298] See: *Irish Life Assurance Co Ltd* v. *Dublin Land Securities Ltd* [1989] IR 253.

[299] [1956] AC 166 (Eng).

2. *E. Hulton and Co Ltd* v. *Chadwick and Taylor*[300] provides a good example of an agreement being renegotiated in light of an unforeseen change of circumstances. The defendants agreed in 1913 to supply the plaintiffs with paper. When war broke out in 1914, it cost the defendants more to supply the paper. The defendants refused to supply paper except at increased prices, which as a result of a compromise the plaintiffs agreed to pay. It was held that this new agreement was binding as it was supported by fresh consideration.[301] However, it was clear that the defendant would have been in breach of contract if the new agreement had not been reached. The fact that the seller's costs had increased would have been irrelevant.

Scotland

X is neither entitled to claim compensation for additional costs nor is he allowed he terminate the contract.

I. 1. In Scots law, the fact that supervening events or a change in the law have made the contract more burdensome or less profitable is generally irrelevant.[302] Thus, in one case, a change in legislation which increased the specification of a bridge to be constructed over a railway, thus making performance of the construction contract more expensive for the construction company, did not frustrate the contract.[303] In the context of his discussion of legislation which rendered a contract '... more burdensome, or the advantages stipulated far less lucrative'[304] Gloag notes that:

> The validity of a contract is, however, not affected by a change in the law which does not make performance impossible, but does alter the value of the rights conferred, or the burden of the obligation imposed.[305]

2. Another leading Scottish author, T. B. Smith, confirmed this view: 'A rise in prices ... will not avoid a contract, though the position of one party may be seriously affected.'[306] Gloag added a qualification,

[300] [1918] 34 TLR 230 (Eng).
[301] See now *Williams* v. *Roffey Bros & Nicholls (Contractors) Ltd* [1990] 1 All ER 512 (Eng) and *Trucks Machinery Sales Ltd.* v. *Marubeni Komatsu Ltd.*, Unreported, Irish High Court, 23 February 1996.
[302] *Holliday* v. *Scott* (1830) 8 S. 831.
[303] *Summerlee & Mossend Iron & Steel Co* v. *Caledonian Rly Co* 1909 SC 536.
[304] Gloag, *Contract*, p. 340. [305] *Ibid.*, p. 342.
[306] T. B. Smith, *A Short Commentary on the Law of Scotland* (Edinburgh: W. Green, 1962), p. 848.

suggesting that if a legislative change completely transformed the nature of the obligation imposed then the contract may be frustrated.[307]

3. The above approach is visible in many Scottish cases.[308] One particular case, in which the court refused to find that the contract had been frustrated, is on very similar facts to those at issue here.[309] In the Scottish case, however, the increase in the spirit tax levied was not of as high a degree as in this example.

II. 1. The effect of the legislation may, however, be much more severe, so that one or both of the parties may find performance impossible as opposed to merely more expensive. In that event, the contract is frustrated and the parties are released from their future obligations under the contract, although accrued rights will remain enforceable.[310] It is suggested that the courts would treat this case as falling within the former class, i.e., that the contract is merely more burdensome or expensive to perform, and therefore that the contract would not be frustrated. X would not be entitled to claim compensation for additional costs nor to cancel the contract. Instead, X would be bound to perform the contract.

2. In practice, a statute which would potentially have a significantly detrimental effect on contracts in mid-performance would almost certainly contain transitional provisions to temper this effect.[311]

Editors' comparative notes

The open jurisdictions

In the majority of the open jurisdictions, X may terminate or adjust the contract because the tax was unforeseeable and its effects are excessive as compared to the contract price. In most of the open jurisdictions, the tax is not regarded as falling within any party's sphere of responsibility. Potential exceptions are the Netherlands and Lithuania, where a remedy could be available, in principle, but is held to be very unlikely in this case.

[307] Gloag, *Contract*, p. 342, fn. 3.

[308] *Bowhill Coal Co* v. *Tobias* (1902) 5 F 262, *Sumerlee & Mossend Iron & Steel Co* v. *Caledonian Rly Co* 1909 SC 536. See also the Privy Council case of *Hangkam Kwingtong Woo* v. *Liu Lan Fong* [1951] AC 536.

[309] *Maclelland* v. *Adam & Mathie* 1795 14 M. 247.

[310] *Lindsay* v. *Bett* 25 R. 1155; *Caledonian Insurance Co* v. *Matheson's Trs* (1901) 3 F. 865, per the Lord President, the Rt. Hon. J. B. Balfour at 871 and per Lord Kinnear at 872; *James B Fraser & Co Ltd* v. *Denny, Mott and Dickson Ltd* 1944 SC (HL) 35; *George Packman & Sons* v. *Dunbar's Trs* 1977 SLT 140; Gloag, *Contract*, p. 340; Smith, *Short Commentary*, p. 848.

[311] For an example of this approach see *Bowhill Coal Co* v. *Tobias* (1902) 5 F. 262.

Most jurisdictions try to save the contractual agreement if it is possible to find a distribution of the additional burden that leads to an economically viable situation for both parties (cf. Germany, Greece, Portugal). In fact, in Germany and Greece, this is regarded to be the preferable solution and termination is possible only if the adjustment turns out to be too burdensome for X. On the other hand, Austria offers no possibility of adjustment, but only termination. This is justified by the fact that a major aspect of the contract is affected and that it cannot be assumed that Y would have agreed to a much higher price.

The closed jurisdictions

Contrary to the open jurisdictions, no clear tendency can be found in the group of closed jurisdictions. In the common law jurisdictions and in Scotland, for example, the contract is not considered to be frustrated but merely burdensome for one party, which leaves X with no remedies at all. The effect of statutory changes on contracts is regarded to be a problem that is to be addressed by the legislator rather than by the courts (cf. the Scottish report). In Belgium and Denmark, X is also left without a remedy. Under French law, on the other hand, the parties are under an obligation to adjust the contract by renegotiation, which is derived from the principle of good faith. Under Slovenian law (and potentially also under the law of the Czech Republic), X may terminate the contract.

Conclusion

In the case of government intervention, we can observe a tendency to grant relief. In the open jurisdictions, X may generally adjust or terminate the contract because its balance has been altered by the unforeseen and excessive tax. Even in the group of closed jurisdictions, the case for relief is quite strong (Czech Republic, France and Slovenia). It is particularly remarkable that in the given case the French approach to recognise an obligation to renegotiate, based on the principle of good faith, comes quite close to the tendency observed amongst the open jurisdictions.

Case 4 Unexpected benefit

Long-term lease – extraordinary increase of the rental value

Y leases business premises from X for a fixed period of fifteen years. Shortly after concluding the contract, the character of the area changes strongly and unexpectedly: a military airport located nearby is shut down and an enormous amount of public funds is invested in the area (infrastructure etc.). As a consequence, Y's business soars and his profits are 500 per cent of what he could reasonably have expected. By the same token, the rental value of comparable business premises in the same area rises to 500 per cent of the amount X and Y have agreed upon. X claims that the rental price should be adjusted accordingly or, alternatively, that the agreement should be terminated.

Is X's claim justified?

Germany and related jurisdictions

Germany

X may ask for an adjustment of the stipulated price according to §313 I BGB unless an increase of the rent is an undue burden for Y. In the latter case X may terminate the contract (cf. §313 III BGB).

I. In the given case, the contract does not contain an explicit clause with regard to a change of the character of the area. Neither are there any contractual clauses that could justify a complementary interpretation of the agreement (§§133, 157 BGB). Furthermore, if business premises are the subject matter of the lease, there are no statutory provisions that allow the lessor to adapt the lease if the average lease for comparable business premises rises.[312]

II. In general, a substantial change of the circumstances may result in a right to terminate a lease for serious cause without notice (cf. §543 BGB). However, §543 BGB only provides for a right to terminate the contract but not for an amendment of the contractual obligation of Y, i.e., an increase of the rent. Additionally, there is no right to terminate the contract under this rule if the risk of the change of circumstances is allocated to one party by contract or by law.[313] The test for the risk allocation is the same as the one under the concept of

[312] Cf. M. Schulz, in: W. R. Bub and M. Treier, *Handbuch der Geschäfts- und Wohnraummiete* (Munich: Beck, 1999) III.A n. 257; regarding the lease of living accommodation the lessor may adapt the lease according to §§558–60 BGB. These rules cover an increase of the average level of the lease for comparable accommodation (§§558–558e BGB), a modernisation of the accommodation by the lessor (§§559–559b BGB) and an increase in the general costs of the lessor (§560 BGB).

[313] Cf. BGH NJW 1996, 714; W. Weidenkaff, '§543', in: Palandt *et al.* (eds.), *Bürgerliches Gesetzbuch*, n. 32.

'*Geschäftsgrundlage*' (§313 BGB). Thus, if §313 BGB results in a right to terminate the lease, the termination can also be based on §543 BGB. But §313 III BGB also provides for the preeminence of an adaptation of the contract over its termination while the same test applies. According to the majority opinion of legal writers, §543 BGB therefore is superseded by §313 BGB if an adaptation of the contract is reasonable.

III. 1. With respect to mutual contracts, the equivalence of exchange is part of the *Geschäftsgrundlage* regardless whether this can be inferred from the parties' conduct in the particular case.[314] In the given case, it is likely that the parties founded the assumed equivalence of exchange on the mutual expectation that the character of the area would not change for the duration of the contract. Nevertheless, it is sufficient that both parties assumed that the area would not change without further reflection.[315]

2. There is a substantial affection of the *Geschäftsgrundlage* because the altered character of the area qualifies as a massive change in the relevant circumstances (cf. §313 I BGB). This is true for both the equivalence of exchange and the special circumstances of the contract. The average rent equals five times the amount the parties contracted for. If the parties had foreseen this alteration at the time of formation, X would not have agreed to the contract. The distortion of equivalence of exchange by an unexpected *improvement* of the contractual subject matter is covered by the concept of *Geschäftsgrundlage* in general.[316]

3. Furthermore, X must be unreasonably burdened by the contract. In general, the risk of an unexpected loss or benefit is allocated to the affected party.[317] Thus, as a general rule, under §313 BGB a rise in value does not trigger a right to adapt the price.[318] Nevertheless, if the equivalence of exchange is fundamentally distorted, this general allocation of the risk does not apply.[319]

4. With regard to contracts for sale, in the situation at hand the question arises whether the concept of *Geschäftsgrundlage* also applies

[314] Cf. Case 1; Grüneberg, '§313', in: Palandt *et al.* (eds.), *Bürgerliches Gesetzbuch*, n. 25.

[315] Cf. BGH NJW 1996, 990 (992). [316] Cf. BGH NJW 1996, 990 (991).

[317] Cf. BGH WM 1969, 137 (*Förderzins für Rohöl*); Roth, '§313', in: Krüger (ed.), *Münchener Kommentar zum Bürgerlichen Gesetzbuch*, vol. II, n. 204; Grüneberg, '§313', in: Palandt *et al.* (eds.), *Bürgerliches Gesetzbuch*, n. 33.

[318] Cf. BGH WM 1968, 1248; BGH WM 1973, 839 (substantial rise of land value between closing and performance).

[319] Cf. BGH DB 1963, 448 (increase of stock value); BGH BB 1970, 1192 (increase of share value).

if the equivalence of exchange is distorted *after* the conclusion of the contract. In general, this concept may apply in exceptional cases after the conclusion of the contract.[320] Nevertheless, according to the courts and the majority of legal writers, in a contract for sale the risk of how the value of the subject matter of the contract develops in the future is - in principle - allocated by law to the buyer.[321] This risk allocation concurs also with the parties' reasonable expectation.

5. In the given case, X and Y entered into a long-term contract. Even though parties to a long-term contract cannot reasonably expect that there will be no change in the equivalence of exchange, this reasoning allocates only the risk of minor changes to the equivalence of exchange. Thus, in long-term contracts, a grave change of the equivalence results in an unreasonable burden for one party.[322] To apply this rule to a contract for lease, the courts and legal writers in general require that the contract was concluded for a long period of time,[323] i.e., at least ten years. Otherwise the resulting burden for one party does not qualify as unreasonable unless the price has changed extraordinarily since the contract will end in the near future and the party may have a general contractual right to terminate the contract. With regard to contracts that exceed this duration, legal writers[324] apply the rules that govern cases of leases in perpetuity ('*Erbpacht*'). However, a lower standard for a relevant change of equivalence is applied since, in lease contracts, the parties normally expect only a minor change of equivalence. As a result, in the given case, the stipulated rent amounts to only one fifth of the fair rental value and thus the distortion of the equivalence of exchange qualifies as an unreasonable burden for X because the parties contracted for a period of fifteen years and the distortion of the equivalence occurred shortly after conclusion.

[320] BGHZ 74, 370 (373); BGH LM §242 BGB (Bb) n. 83; H. Köhler, 'Störung der Geschäftsgrundlage', in: C.-W. Canaris *et al.* (eds.), *50 Jahre Bundesgerichtshof – Festgabe aus der Wissenschaft* (Munich: Beck, 2000), vol. I, pp. 295 (318 *et seq.*); more restrictive K. Larenz, *Geschäftsgrundlage und Vertragserfüllung* (Munich: Beck, 3rd edn, 1963), pp. 138 *et seq.*

[321] Cf. with regard to an increased value BGH NJW 1991, 1345; s.a. BGHZ 113, 310 (314); Roth, '§313', in: Krüger (eds.), *Münchener Kommentar zum Bürgerlichen Gesetzbuch*, vol. II, n. 203; for an exception cf. BGHZ 74, 370 *et seq.* (*Kauf von Bauerwartungsland*).

[322] Cf. BGH LM §242 BGB (Bb) n. 39.

[323] Cf. BGHZ 90, 227; BGHZ 86, 167; BGH NJW 1981, 1668; Schulz, in: Bub and Treier, *Handbuch der Geschäfts- und Wohnraummiete*, III.A n. 258.

[324] Cf. *ibid.*

Austria

Under Austrian law, X is neither entitled to an adjustment of the rent nor will he be allowed to terminate the contract.

I. Where a lease contract is made for a definite period of time, no party is entitled to terminate the contract earlier, unless there is a good cause making the performance of the contract unreasonably burdensome for this party (extraordinary right of termination).[325] The Austrian OGH held that a change of commercial circumstances and marketing opportunities is no good cause to terminate a long-term lease of business premises prematurely, since the parties were able to foresee such developments and accepted this risk.[326] For the same reason the doctrine of '*Wegfall der Geschäftsgrundlage*' is not applicable.[327]

II. Where parties agree on a lease of business premises for a definite period of time without a stipulation that entitles the parties to terminate the contract earlier, it is presumed that each party willingly accepts the risk of changing marketing opportunities.[328]

The Netherlands

Dutch case law imposes a high burden for an adjustment of the contract, which is unlikely to be met in the present case.

I. Under Dutch law, X is bound by the terms of the lease. He receives precisely what was agreed upon in the lease agreement. Since X agreed to the fifteen-year lease, one has to assume that he is compensated for the costs relating to the lease. In this case there is no evidence that X's cost base is adversely affected. Rather, the case indicates that the value of the (leased) premises has increased considerably.

II. Generally, Dutch law protects a lessee against a landlord who fails to comply with his duty to maintain the rented premises properly. Whilst in cases of a lease of housing accommodation the lessee is well protected against a landlord's opportunistic behaviour (Arts. 7:249 and 7:251–7 Dutch Civil Code), for offices and other commercial premises such strong protection is less evident. The rent can be adjusted if the rent for commercial premises does not correspond to the rent for similar premises in the area (Arts. 7:303–5 Dutch Civil Code), but such a claim for an adjustment is only allowed after a certain period of time

325 See §1116 ABGB and Koziol and Welser, *Bürgerliches Recht*, vol. II, p. 9.
326 OGH, JBl 1982, 142.
327 Apathy '§901', in: Schwimann (ed.), *Kommentar zum ABGB*, vol. IV, n. 8.
328 OGH, JBl 1982, 142.

(Art. 7:303 section 1(a)): five years after the date of the lease agreement (or a preceding judicial rent adjustment).

III. 1. However, Art. 6:258 Dutch Civil Code or the overriding principle of reasonableness and fairness in Art. 6:248 are still applicable. At least theoretically, there may be exceptional circumstances leading to exceptionally unreasonable situations.[329] But these provisions are unlikely to be of use to X: although the Hoge Raad has dealt with cases of contract amendment, in these cases specific legal rules were applicable (i.e., an adjustment was either admissible after the lapse of the lease term, or after the above five-year term) or the rulings were based on a distinction between parts of the rent base. If the adjustment was related to a service part of the rent it was deemed appropriate. If it was related to business premises only, an adjustment was dependent upon the requirements of Art. 7:303.[330]

2. In cases relating to statutory provisions, the Hoge Raad has determined that an objective standard (i.e., a comparison with leases in the area) would apply rather than the provisions of the lease agreement. Where an adjustment is requested for service-related elements, the court is free to adhere closely to the lease agreement. Under Art. 6:258, X's case does not lead to an unacceptable situation. Even though the circumstances have changed rather beneficially for Y, the benefit is of such a nature that Y may reasonably expect the lease to remain unchanged. Furthermore, the nature of the lease contract, which extends for a limited albeit long period of time, does not justify an untimely rent adjustment.

Eastern European jurisdictions

Slovenia

X is not entitled to request an adjustment of the price nor to terminate the contract.

I. Since the lease contract was concluded for a *definite* period of time, Art. 333 (providing for the right of termination of long-term contracts concluded for an *indefinite* period of time) is not applicable. The same is

[329] See: M. F. A. Evers, *Huurrecht bedrijfsruimten* (Deventer: Kluwer, 2003), p. 134 and P. Abas, *C. Asser's Handleiding tot de beoefening van het Nederlands Burgerlijk Recht, Bijzondere overeenkomsten, Huur* (2004), n. 302.

[330] HR 6 November 1992, NJ 1993, 578 and HR 20 April 2001, NJ 2001, 361 (*De Kring Wezenbeek*), respectively.

true for Art. 616, containing a similar rule regarding lease contracts. As the lease contract was concluded for a definite period of time, it is not possible for the parties to terminate the contract before that period has elapsed, except on ground of a change of circumstances.

II. In the present case, the new circumstances do not render the performance of one of the parties more burdensome, neither do they frustrate the purpose of the contract. The consequence of the change of circumstances is only that the transaction has become less profitable from the lessor's point of view. A change of business opportunities in the area was unpredictable for both parties. Since they did not include any clauses in their contract that deal with such changes, it can be assumed that they both accepted that risk. This means that the basic requirements for an action based on a change of circumstances under Art. 112 CO are not met. Furthermore, a rise of prices is not an unexpected circumstance. Case law also confirms that a rise of lease prices for immovables is a circumstance that should always be taken into consideration, especially by parties who perform commercial activities.[331]

Lithuania

No relief is granted under Lithuanian law.

I. 1. The lease contract is not only governed by the rules of the General Part of the Contract Law, but by special rules in Arts. 6.477–6.536 CC as well. Article 6.487(5) CC establishes that, unless otherwise provided for by the lease contract or the laws, the rent may be changed by the parties within the periods they agreed upon, but not more often than twice a year. Thus, a modification of the rent could be possible only if such a possibility is provided for by the contract.

2. There is only a limited possibility to terminate a lease contract because the law generally protects the weaker party – the lessee. According to Art. 6.497 CC, the lessor has the right to bring an action for the dissolution of a lease contract before the end of the term if: (i) the lessee uses the leased object in violation of the contract or not according to its designation; (ii) the lessee intentionally or negligently worsens the state of the leased object; (iii) the lessee fails to pay the rent; (iv) the lessee fails to repair the leased premises in those cases where the laws or the contract oblige him to do so; or (v) for other grounds provided for by the lease contract. Thus, the CC does not provide for the right of the

[331] Slovenian Supreme Court II Ips 358/95, January 23rd 1997; Dolenc in: Juhart and Plavšak (eds.), *Obligacijski zakonik*, vol. I, p. 608.

lessor to terminate a lease contract concluded for an indefinite period as a consequence of changes in the market of lease prices. Nevertheless, both the CC and the principle of freedom of contract allow the parties to stipulate in their contract such a basis for its dissolution.

II. Consequently, if the parties have failed to incorporate a mechanism to review the rent in their lease contract, the chances for X to invoke Art. 6.204 CC are quite limited for two reasons. First, both the defendant and the court may reject the request for modification or termination of the contract on the grounds that X, as a businessman, could reasonably be expected to predict the possibility of a change in the rent level within a period of fifteen years. Second, the demand of X may be also rejected on the grounds that X, in failing to include a contractual clause on the periodical revision of the rent, has assumed the risks. However, as in Case 1, X could request a revision of the rent referring to the general principle of good faith (Arts. 1.5, 6.158, 6.200 CC) with regard to the fact that the rent is considerably lower than the market price. However, in the absence of any relevant court practice, a court is unlikely to find X's arguments acceptable.

Czech Republic

No relief is granted under Czech law.

I. 1. In principle there is no right to extraordinary termination of a long-term contract in this case. It is relevant that, although the parties concluded a long-term contract, it was for a definite period of time (fifteen years), because Czech law distinguishes between contracts for an indefinite term and contracts for a definite period of time. Only the former can be terminated by notice.

2. The Act on lease of non-residential premises, which applies here, follows these principles.[332] A lease contract ends upon the lapse of the time stipulated in the lease contract (Section 9(1) of the Act). In other words, Czech law in principle excludes termination of lease contracts concluded for a limited period of time prior to expiry of their term.

II. An option for how to deal with the case is to avoid the contract as a consequence of a conflict with good morals (Section 39 Civil Code). The amount of rent has been set forth in certain terms with respect to the current rent-level in the respective locality and probably also taking into account the profit which Y could realise using the premises. From the time from which both the rent value and Y's profit became

[332] See the Section 582 Civil Code cited in Case 1.

disproportionate to comparable premises in the locality, the contract could in principle be regarded as void. Unfortunately, there is no case law covering this type of situation.

III. In the case where parties enter into a contract for a definite term (excluding the right of unilateral termination), one can presume that they take over the risk of any change of the relevant market conditions.

Scandinavian jurisdictions

Sweden

X's claim for an adjustment of the contract price or for a termination of the contract is not justified under Swedish law.

I. A lease of business premises would qualify as rent of real estate ('*hyra av fast egendom*') under Chapter 12 Section 1(1) Code of Land Laws.[333] For contracts on rental of real estate there is extensive regulation in Chapter 12 of the Code of Land Laws. The landlord is entitled to cancel the contract in some cases of the tenant's breach. These rules are exhaustive and rather restrictive.

II. The question of risk allocation in cases of unexpected benefit has not been dealt with explicitly in Swedish legislation, case law or literature. The rules, cases and analyses all seem to be at least implicitly based on the assumption that relief is sought by a party who has suffered losses or inconveniences as a result of a breach of contract or other unexpected circumstances. Nor does Swedish law provide for relief just because a party to a contract has made a business mistake like this. The assumption that a party's own performance is not more valuable than assumed is most often irrelevant, especially when it comes to assumptions concerning the future development of the value.

III. The doctrine of assumptions might be applied to adjust a contract on the basis of an unexpected profit that the defendant has made at the expense of the claimant. But this also requires that the claimant has suffered a loss,[334] which, in this case, he has not.[335]

IV. It must also be noted that the prerequisite that the clause should not be unreasonable in Section 36 Contracts Act is, at least to date, understood as 'unreasonably burdensome' and that it does not apply

[333] Jordabalken.
[334] B. Lehrberg, *Förutsättningsläran* (Uppsala: Iustus Förlag, 1989), pp. 373 *et seq.*
[335] Cases on this scheme are mentioned in the comments to Case 1 and 2 above. See, e.g., NJA 1930 p. 507 I and II; NJA 1979 p. 731; NJA 1983 p. 385 and RH 1980:14.

in situations where the only reason for its application would be that it might seem unfair that one party makes a profit while the other party does not. This limitation does not follow from the law or the preparatory works, nor has it been expressly laid down in case law. Therefore, it is possible that this view might change in the future. However, as such a change is yet to take place, one has to assume that the contract would stand under Section 36.

Denmark

Under Danish law, this is not a case of force majeure. X is left without a remedy.

I. Unless Y has committed fraud (cf. Section 30 Contracts Act) when entering into the contract, X is 'only' entitled to receive the rent in accordance with the lease contract. Danish law does not contain a rule that allows one to collect the profits made by others in the market. X and Y could have provided a provision in the contract, according to which Y has the obligation to pay rent in a certain manner in accordance with the turnover or the profit which Y generated by leasing the business premises. This would be in accordance with the freedom of contract between two professional parties. X was simply not able to calculate the bright future in this area when the parties entered into the contract. As a main principle, X must bear this risk when the contract does not provide otherwise.

II. Since the contract was concluded for a fixed period of fifteen years, X is not entitled to terminate the contract due to extraordinary circumstances or the like. Only if Y fails to pay the rent in accordance with the contract would this constitute a fundamental breach of contract that entitles X to terminate the contract without any further notice.

III. However, the Section 13 Danish Commercial Tenancy Act[336] contains a provision on the obligation to pay the market rent. If the parties have agreed that Section 13 Commercial Tenancy Act is not applicable to the lease contract, Y has the obligation to pay the rent for the fixed period of fifteen years pursuant to the contract. If, on the contrary, the parties have agreed that Section 13 Commercial Tenancy Act is applicable to the contract, the tenant has the obligation to pay the market rent for the business premises, provided that the rent in question is substantially lower or higher than the market rent. In the case at hand, the tenant unexpectedly has a very successful business, which entitles

[336] Cf. Lov no. 934 20 December 1999 om leje af erhvervslokaler mv.

Y to demand a rent which is comparable to the market rent. Pursuant to Section 13(2) such an increase in the market rent will first take effect four years after the conclusion of the contract and four years after Y has invoked the increased market rent.[337]

IV. In the case at hand, it is not possible to invoke economic force majeure, even though the performance of the contract imposes a substantial economic burden upon X considering the opportunity to rent the premises to an alternative tenant. All the case law concerning economic force majeure has dealt very directly with cases where the party in question had to pay an additional substantial amount of money, which is not the case here.

V. X might invoke the application of Section 36 Contracts Act in order to increase the rent. However, no case law, at least not at this present time, supports this point of view. It is very unlikely that Section 36 Contracts Act could be applicable in a case like this. Normally, X would at least have more information about the premises and the surroundings than Y. X has the option of investigating whether the relevant public bodies have made any plans for such an area. Such plans are in accordance with district plans published in accordance with Danish law. If X stipulates or negotiates the contract he can reserve the right to adjust the rent in accordance with similar facilities in the area, simply by including this as a condition in the contract. The inclusion of such a provision in the contract would normally exclude the application of Section 36 Contracts Act.

Romanic-Mediterranean jurisdictions

Italy

X can choose between the renegotiation of the rent and the termination of the contract.

I. The rules on mistake may not be applied to the case at issue in principle since the strong change in the nature of the leased area occurred after the formation of the contract.

II. As already said above, Art. 1467 CC provides a special right of termination in cases of an excessive burden, but the general provision related to long term contracts is Art. 1373 CC, which provides that each

[337] For a more comprehensive discussion, see Karin Laursen, *Erhvervslejeret* (Copenhagen: Thomson, 2003), and Kim Frost, *Systematisk oversigt i lejeret* (Copenhagen: Thomson, 1st edn, 2005).

party has a unilateral right to withdraw from the contract. In matters of lease contracts, Art. 4 l. 392/1978 also has to be taken into account. This provision allows each party to withdraw from the contract, the only requirement being a six-month notice. This does not result in an indemnification for Y, unless otherwise provided for by the parties.

III. The change of the character of the area where the leased business premises are settled furthermore entitles X to ask for the termination of the lease on the basis of Art. 1467 CC, since the supervening change is material and unexpected. It must be considered that the parties of a long-term contract, as in the case at issue, implicitly assume the risk of some changes in the contract; however, if they result in an unusual burden for one party, the latter is entitled to terminate the contract.[338] The main problem is to balance the consideration of the two parties: unexpected benefits certainly fall under Art. 1467 CC,[339] since the point of view to be taken into account with regard to a termination claim is that of the counter-party, which suffers a disadvantage due to supervening extraordinary events.

IV. 1. An alternative remedy for the adjustment of the lease is not provided for under Italian law, but this result could be obtained through the equitable modification of the contract offered by Y in the course of a renegotiation of the contract.[340] In the case at issue X does not actually complain about the 'excessive burden of the performance' due by him/her, but the loss of profit deriving from the supervening event. Although Art. 1467 CC mentions the 'excessive burden of the performance', according to Italian case law, the court may evaluate the alteration of the balance between the obligations, which may be due to the increase of the cost of the performance as well as to the loss of value of the agreed counter-performance.[341]

2. Often Italian courts have decided cases where the character of the land was altered after the conclusion of the sale agreement by virtue of supervening urban and planning rules and the legal reasoning turned around '*presupposizione*'[342] and mutual mistake.[343] The concept of *presupposizione* has a larger field of application than the rules of Art. 1467 CC, so that the courts use the concept of *presupposizione* in cases where

[338] M. Granieri, *Il tempo e il contratto* (Milan: Giuffrè, 2007).
[339] Cass., 13 July 1984, n. 4114; Sacco, *Il contratto*, II, p. 686.
[340] See above, Cases 1 and 3, and overview (Chapter 4).
[341] Cass., 16 March 1981, n. 1465.
[342] See above Cases 1 and 3, and overview (Chapter 4).
[343] Cass., 21 July 1980, n. 4775; Cass., 9 February 1985, n. 1064.

1467 CC cannot be applied. The two remedies are alternative, as the renegotiation obligations aim at avoiding the termination of the contract, in compliance with the good faith principle.[344] If both remedies (renegotiation and termination) can be validly enforced, X has a free choice, and the path taken would depend on X's underlying interest (i.e., whether X would prefer to keep the contractual relationship in place or, rather, to terminate it). Yet, once X seeks termination before a court, the modification of the contract terms can be offered by Y only and not disposed of by the judge.[345]

Spain

The court will probably decide to adjust the contract and increase the rent in order to restore the balance of the exchange.

I. 1. According to the Ley de Arrendamientos Urbanos of 24 November 1994 (LAU), contracts for the lease of business premises are governed by the *lex contractus*.[346] The LAU explicitly indicates that the regulation of the lease of commercial premises is to be left to the contractual autonomy of the parties. The different regimes are justified by the different economic situations to which they related.

2. The LAU grants the tenant a right to unilaterally terminate the contract (Article 11). According to this article, if the lease has been agreed for a period of more than five years, the tenant can terminate the relationship after five years have passed and if he notifies the landlord at least two months in advance.

II. 1. In the case under consideration, where the main circumstances of the contract vary so extraordinarily, the *rebus* doctrine can be considered due to the change in the character of the area and the consequential increase in the rental value.

2. However, the Spanish judiciary are very strict in applying the *rebus* doctrine, and it is not certain whether the courts would consider this change of circumstances as a ground to modify the agreement. There is a clear example of how cautious the Spanish legal system is regarding

[344] Sacco, *Il contratto*, II, p. 686. [345] Macario, *Adeguamento*, p. 266.

[346] The LAU is the Act on urban lease contracts, Act 29/1994 of 24 November 1994. All leases relating to housing in Spain are regulated by this Act. The Act covers issues relating to the lease of domestic and commercial property as well as long and short-term holiday lease contracts. It modifies the previous act of 1964 which introduced a protective regime for the tenant with regard to the leasing of domestic property. For example, the lease of a house must be for a minimum period of five years to ensure a certain degree of stability for families who rent a house and to provide an incentive for renting property.

the modification of rent in lease contracts. Indeed, the LAU states that it is impossible to automatically adapt the rent in lease contracts concluded before the LAU entered into effect (1994). Even though there is a glaring economic imbalance between the performance of the landlord and that of the tenant, the legislator only allows such rent to be progressively increased in accordance with the consumer price index. The legislator, followed by the judiciary, gives preference to the interests of tenants who have been renting a particular property for a long time to the detriment of the owners who do not receive an adequate counter-performance.[347]

3. This approach is underlined by an example from the case law,[348] where a tenant sought the application of the *rebus* doctrine in order to decrease the rent. The tenant, a company which leased properties in order to sub-lease them to tourists, argued that there had been a decline in tourism in the area. The court concluded that this was inherent in the commercial risk taken by the tenant. It was a change of circumstances that can be foreseen by the parties and therefore there was no ground to apply the modifying effects of the *rebus* doctrine.

4. Following the line of reasoning in this judgment, there might be a different result in the case under consideration. There is not only an extraordinary change of circumstances as the rental value has risen by 500 per cent and the rental benefits have increased by 500 per cent. In the situation at hand, the parties could not have expected this extraordinary variation in the circumstances due to the closure of the airport and the enormous investment in the infrastructure. They could not therefore have foreseen this situation in the contract. The further requirements of the *rebus* doctrine are also met: the party suffering from the change of circumstances has not caused this change, and there is no better means to resolve the situation than to apply the *rebus* doctrine.

Portugal

X's claim is justified under Portuguese law.

I. It is debatable whether this case falls within the scope of Art. 437 CC. It has been suggested that this rule is mainly concerned with cases where supervening circumstances make it much more difficult or

[347] See for example the decision of the Tribunal Constitucional of 17 March 1994 (RTC 1994, 89).

[348] SAP Tarragona of 10 January 1992 (AC 1992, 360).

onerous for one of the parties to perform.[349] Others, however, consider that the possibility of asking for a modification of the contract under Art. 437 CC is not restricted to cases where one or both of the contractual partners suffer losses as a result of supervening events. It may also occur whenever the economic balance of the contract is seriously compromised by unforeseeable circumstances.[350] The changes were unexpected in our case. In spite of the fact that both parties were traders and professionals, it seems that such a fundamental change in the area might be taken as sufficient to justify the intervention of the court. As far as we can determine there is no judicial precedent (i.e., no case where there is no increased hardship for the performance).

Greece

X can either request an adjustment of the contract or terminate the contract if Y is not willing to pay an increased rent.

I. By virtue of Art. 288 AK, a party has the right to an extraordinary termination without notice, based on a substantial reason, which proves the function and maintenance of the contract to be against the requirements of good faith.[351] The unforeseen und excessively onerous imbalance between the contractual obligations, which affects the above lease, constitutes a substantial reason giving rise to a right to terminate the contract by X. Nevertheless, the right of termination should not be exercised contrary to the requirements of good faith (see Art. 281 AK, which forbids the abusive exercise of a right). If Y is able and willing to pay an increased rent, the contract may also be adjusted.

II. Instead of termination, X has the right to an adjustment of the contract, which presupposes not only a substantial reason, but is furthermore subject to the strict conditions of Art. 388 AK. The

[349] Máro Júlio de Almeida Costa, *Direito das Obrigações* (Coimbra Almedina: 10th edn, 2006), p. 339. The writer acknowledges, however, that Art. 437 may apply to cases where there is no threat of economic ruin, but a serious threat to the person of the debtor or an excessive sacrifice.

[350] Giulherme de Oliveira, 'Alteração das Circunstâncias, Risco e Alruso do Directo, a propósato de un Crēdito de Tomas', (1989) *Colectânea de Jurispredência*, 65, 625 *et seq.*, 637.

[351] For the application of Art. 288 AK in a business lease see AP (plenary session) 9/1997, HellD 38, p. 767; AP 63/2000, NoV 48, 1573; 494/1999, HellD 40, p. 1083; 474/1997, HellD 38, p. 1826; 1066/1996, HellD 38, p. 114. See also George Archaniotakis, *The Business Lease* (Athens/Thessalonika: Sakkoula, 2003), vol. II, pp. 14–15, 113 *et seq.*; Ap. Georgiadis, *Law of Obligations*, vol. I, §29 nn. 19 *et seq.* Against the application of Art. 288 AK, due to the special statutory rule of Art. 5 §4 of the Decree 34/1995 for business leases, AP 1062/1996, HellD 38, p. 115.

requirement for the application of Art 388 AK is an unforeseen and excessively onerous imbalance between the corresponding obligations.[352] This prerequisite is met in this case, even though the aggrieved party does not, as regularly, suffer positive damages due to the performance of the contract but loses a great deal of profits, which would not have been lost if the subsequent change of the circumstances had been predicted.

France and related jurisdictions

France

Under French law, the contract will be adjusted to the changed circumstances according to the provisions in the Commercial Code. If these special provisions do not apply, the court might require the parties to renegotiate the contract subject to the principle of good faith.

I. 1. If the law on commercial leases applies, the contract can be adjusted as described hereunder (Art. 23–8 of the Decree of 30 September 1993, inserted in articles L-145–33 to L-145–39 of the Commercial Code).[353] In our case, it is likely that these provisions will apply. According to these rules, an adaptation of the lease price can take place every three years when there is a variation of more than 10 per cent between the lease price and the rental value as measured by the market value in the area where the property is located. In this case, developments on the real estate market at this place due to changed circumstances are taken into consideration.

2. If the court orders the parties to renegotiate in good faith, the consequences of a failure to renegotiate are somewhat vague. One can refer to a case of 30 April 1976 where the Court of Appeal considered that one of the parties had not negotiated in good faith and ordered the parties to continue their negotiation in the presence of an observer. A more recent decision, pronounced by the appeal court of Nancy on 26 September 2007, confirmed this first decision. If the parties do negotiate in good faith and cannot find a solution to their dispute, the contract might be maintained. However, the case law is not clear on

[352] See also above in the overview (Chapter 4).

[353] The law on commercial leases aims to protect the customer. It only applies if the lease refers to the customer's place of business. Cf. L. Ruet, *Les baux commerciaux* (Paris: Defrénois, 2006), p. 35, n48.

this point and the Catala draft[354] provides that in the case of a failure in the negotiations, the parties can terminate the contract.[355]

II. If the above-mentioned provisions do not apply, the law does not provide for a revision mechanism; the principle of *pacta sunt servanda* would be observed. However, the quoted new case law on the obligation to renegotiate might lead to a different result.

Belgium

X can request an adjustment of the price under Belgian law.

I. 1. The solution depends on whether the law on commercial leases, which provides a special regulation in Art. 6 of the Law of 30 April 1951, is applicable. The law on commercial leases only applies to retail leases if the location of the premises is relevant for access by consumers.

2. If the law on commercial leases applies, Art. 6 will allow a revision of the rent under certain conditions every three years if unforeseeable circumstances occur after the conclusion of the contract[356] or if a difference of 15 per cent between the initial rent and the actual value of the lease occurs. Here, the unpredictable change in the character of the area brings about a massive increase in the rental value of the business premises. Article 6 can therefore be applied and the price amended. As this provision is mandatory, the parties cannot derogate from it.

II. If the law on commercial leases is generally not applicable (e.g., if there is no contact with the clientele in the leased premises), a revision of the price will normally be rejected.

England and related jurisdictions

England and Ireland

It is highly unlikely that X will be entitled to adjust the lease or to terminate the agreement.

I. 1. The agreement between X and Y is a commercial venture, which happens to have turned out better for Y than the parties could have expected. However, this on its own is unlikely to persuade the courts that the agreement should be adjusted or terminated.

[354] Ruet, *Les baux commerciaux*, p. 131, n° 199.

[355] See B. Fauvarque-Cosson, 'La réforme du droit français des contrats: perspective comparative', (2006) *Revue de droit des contrats*, I, p. 162.

[356] See among others Justice de Paix, Liège, 6 June 2002, *JLMB.*, 2002, p. 1823; C. E. de Fresart, 'La révision triennale du loyer', in: A. Benat *et al.* (eds.), *Le bail commercial* (Brussels: la Charte, 2008), p. 156.

2. The courts have shown a reluctance to help parties who simply make a bad bargain, even where the fact that they entered into a bad bargain is only subsequently realised. In the Irish case of *Fitzsimons* v. *O'Hanlon*[357] the plaintiffs accepted a sum of money in settlement of a claim to an inheritance. It was subsequently discovered that the deceased had actually left behind more money than was originally thought, with the result that the defendants made an unexpected windfall profit. The plaintiffs' attempt to rectify their agreement to increase their share in the inheritance failed. The Irish High Court viewed the issues in terms of the doctrine of mistake but it was clear it would not interfere with a contract in order to simply increase the benefit to the plaintiffs. Budd J stressed that 'it is in the interest of commercial convenience that, in general, apparent contracts should be enforced'.

3. The fact that a lessee can take advantage of any profits resulting from the lease has never been seriously questioned. As a general principle, the lessee takes the risk that a lease will not be profitable (and so it is unlikely that the lease will be frustrated if it is less than profitable) and the lessor takes the risk that the lessee may unexpectedly benefit or profit from the lease (and so it is unlikely that the lease will be frustrated if it is more profitable than expected). In *Paradine* v. *Jane*[358] it was stated: '[A]s the lessee is to *have the advantage of casual profits*, so he must run the hazard of casual losses, and not lay the whole [burden] of them upon his lessor.'[359]

4. X may be able to adjust the rent owed by Y if the lease contains a rent review clause. A lessor in a similar situation to X protected himself with a rent review clause in the New Zealand case of *Maori Trustee* v. *Prentice*.[360] The lessee had entered into a long lease, with the rent to be reviewed after sixteen years. Within that time, certain unpredicted events occurred, such as the development of certain forestry interests nearby, which substantially increased the valuation of the premises. Rent was thus increased from NZD1,000 a year to NZD15,690 a year. The lessee's farming operation could not run with this extra expense, and the lessee vacated the property. The lessee argued that the rental increase was so great as to frustrate the lease. Williams J in the High Court accepted that the doctrine of frustration may apply to leases.[361]

357 [1999] 2 ILRM 551.

358 [1647] Reported Aleyn, 26; Steyn 47; 82 ER 897; [1558 – 1774] All ER Rep 172; A.K.R Kiralfy, *A Source Book of English law* (London: Sweet and Maxwell, 1957), p. 22.

359 Aleyn, pp. 27–28 (emphasis added).

360 [1992] 3 NZLR 344. 361 [1992] 3 NZLR 344, 353.

However, he noted that in order for the doctrine to apply, 'there needs to be some wholly extraordinary and unforeseen event which in effect destroys the whole basis of the contract.'[362] Here, the lessee had embarked on a commercial venture, and had taken on the lease knowing that it contained a rent review clause, thus accepting the risk of a high increase in rental. Hence he could not claim that the lease had been frustrated by the increase in rent, and the lessor was entitled to rely on the rent review clause after the sixteen years had lapsed. Thus, if X and Y had included a rent review clause in their agreement, this would reflect the new value of the lease. However, it is also clear from the judgment in *Maori Trustee* v. *Prentice* that even if there had been no rent review clause then the lessor could not have terminated the lease simply because the lease was worth a lot more than he was receiving for it. In fact, it appears that for much of the initial sixteen years of the lease (i.e., the period before the rent review clause took effect) the rent paid by the lessee was 'unduly low' but there was no question of the lessor being able to terminate the lease because of this.

5. In short, in the context of a commercial venture such as this the lessor will be said to have taken the risk of the value of the land increasing, in the same way as the lessee is said to take the risk of the value of land falling.

6. One final possibility open to X is to argue that there is an implied term in the lease providing that the lease could be terminated on the giving of reasonable notice. This would be subject to the earlier remarks on reasonable notice (see Case 1).

Scotland

X would have no right to either terminate the lease or to adjust the rent. The tenant would be entitled to performance of the lease for the remainder of the agreed period on the basis of the terms set in the contract.

I. 1. Generally there is no rule in Scots law which requires contracts to be either terminated or adjusted because performance becomes more beneficial than anticipated from the standpoint of one party. There have been attempts in the past to use the law of unjustified enrichment to this end, most particularly in the case of *Edinburgh District Tramways C Ltd* v. *Courtenay*.[363] Tramways had let advertising space on tramcars to Courtenay, an advertising contractor. It was agreed that Courtenay

[362] [1992] 3 NZLR 344, 354. [363] 1909 SC 99.

would bear the cost of the running boards for the adverts in addition to providing the adverts themselves.[364] Subsequently, new tramcars were designed by Tramways which had built-in running boards. The new boards were introduced primarily for safety reasons, but it was also possible to use the outside of the boards for the adverts. Because the contractor no longer needed to provide the boards, performance of the contract became much less expensive for them – in other words they had made a 'windfall' profit. Tramways sought to recover the cost of the boards from the contractor. The claim, brought in recompense (an unjustified enrichment action) was unsuccessful. A recompense action would only have been relevant had Tramways suffered a loss, which they had not. Similarly, in the example given above, X has suffered no loss, and so cannot use the law of unjustified enrichment to recover a gain made by Y.

2. Reference should be made to the case of *Wilkie* v. *Bethune*,[365] in which an employer had agreed to pay his servant in potatoes. A dramatic rise in the price of potatoes occurred, which was caused by a failure of crops in 1846. Had the servant been paid in potatoes, he would have received a performance which would be worth much more in real terms than the parties had originally anticipated. Such performance would have placed an onerous burden on the employer. The court held that the servant was entitled to a sum that would purchase an equivalent amount of food other than potatoes. The court reached this result by applying a very particular interpretation to the contract. The case is not an example of a general power to amend contractual terms where performance becomes more onerous than the parties had originally contemplated.

3. In practice, leases of commercial property almost invariably contain rent review clauses providing that the rent will be reviewed at agreed intervals, usually of five years. Had the lease in the example contained such rent review provisions, the rental under the lease could have been adjusted to reflect market rates.

Editors' comparative notes

The open jurisdictions

In the case involving an unexpected benefit the findings amongst the open jurisdictions are quite divided. Under some open systems, X is

[364] It should be explained that the sides of the upper deck of buses were open at this stage. The running boards would be inserted so that the adverts could be affixed to the bus.

[365] (1848) 11 D. 132.

entitled to claim either adjustment or termination of the contract (Germany, Greece, Italy, Portugal and Spain). In these jurisdictions, the same standards appear to apply to excessive benefits as to excessive burdens. The focus is not placed on the burden that the change of circumstances creates for one party but on the unforeseeable nature of the change. Accordingly, the doctrines applied are not regarded as an equitable form of relief for unreasonable burdens but rather as a means to address issues that the parties have mutually failed to foresee in their original agreement. The German report draws a parallel to cases of lease contracts for an unlimited period of time where adjustment is generally possible.

The other group of open jurisdictions, consisting of Austria, Lithuania, the Netherlands and Sweden, offers no remedy at all. This result is justified by the fact that X made a business mistake, the risk of which falls within his sphere: a change of market values is regarded to fall within the allocation of risks in the agreement and therefore no relief is granted. It is stressed that the contract was concluded for a fixed time period and that the parties have failed to include a price adjustment clause in the contract.

The closed jurisdictions

The closed jurisdictions generally deny relief in the case of unexpected benefits. This solution is based on the lease's commercial context. In line with the reasoning of some of the open jurisdictions the Scottish and the Slovenian reporters notice that the parties did not include a rent review clause, which would be common in commercial practice. However, a remedy is not ruled out as a matter of principle. The English and Irish report, for example, points out that relief could theoretically be granted on the grounds of frustration if the value of the leased premises and the price were out of proportion; however, the reporter also suggests that such judicial intervention would be highly unlikely under the facts of this case. The reporter for Belgium and France indicates that specific legislation on commercial leases may possibly be a basis for adjustment of the contract. Also, under French law, a court may require the parties to renegotiate the contract.

Conclusion

In the case of unexpected benefits, there is even more reservation towards setting aside the contract than in cases of unexpected burdens. A clear tendency for relief can only be identified in some of the open jurisdictions (Germany, Greece, Italy, Portugal and Spain) while the other open legal systems (Austria, Lithuania, the Netherlands and Sweden) and all the closed jurisdictions provide no firm basis for judicial intervention. It appears that one-sided windfall profits do not elicit the same equity considerations as excessive losses.

B. RECIPIENT'S USE OF CONTRACTUAL GOODS OR SERVICES IS SUBSTANTIALLY AFFECTED

Case 5 Destruction of cellar

Renovation of cellar becomes useless due to the destruction of the building by natural disaster

X agrees to refurbish Y's cellar into a wine cellar. The work is scheduled to start one month after the agreement. Before the work has started, Y's house is completely destroyed during a violent summer storm. However, the cellar of the house remains fully intact. Y immediately informs X and asks him not to perform. X insists on the agreement. He argues that Y's cellar is still intact, that he has reserved two weeks to carry out the work and that he has already purchased the necessary materials.

Is Y obliged to pay the contract price or, alternatively, to compensate X for his losses?

Germany and related jurisdictions

Germany

Under German law, an equitable solution is likely according to which Y has to cover X's expenses and half of the profits that X would have gained from the contract.

I. 1. In this contract, the parties have not explicitly provided for the destruction of the house. In particular, the existence of the building is not a condition to the contract as would be required under §158 BGB. Without further provisions, X and Y have taken for granted that the building will remain undamaged.

2. Furthermore, the contract is not subject to complementary interpretation according to §§133, 157 BGB as far as the destruction of the house is concerned. The concept of complementary interpretation allows the courts to fill gaps in the contract by reference to the will of the parties. There must be substantial hints in the contractual

provisions to determine a hypothetical will of the parties.[366] In the given case, the agreement between X and Y does not contain sufficient hints.

3. The rules on impossibility (§§275, 326 BGB) are not applicable because the cellar is still intact and therefore performance is not impossible.

II. 1. However, Y can terminate the contract on the basis of the (non-compulsary) statutory provisions concerning contracts for work and labour. X is contractually obliged to refurbish the cellar into a wine-cellar, i.e., to accomplish a particular result. Therefore, the contract between X and Y is a contract for work and labour (§§631 *et seq*. BGB). According to §649 I BGB, Y is entitled to terminate the contract before the accomplishment of the result at any time without notice and without giving reasons.[367]

2. If terminated, X's economic interest in the contract is protected under §649 II BGB: as a general rule, he is entitled to claim the contract price.[368] Only if there are specific gains caused by the early termination of the contract, i.e., if he saves expenses or benefits from using his capacities for other projects, are these gains deducted from the claim. The same applies if X does not use his capacities otherwise, even though he was able to do so. In this case, X has already purchased the necessary materials; the value of these materials does not have to be deducted from X's claim, unless he can use them otherwise. The facts do not suggest another opportunity for X to use his capacities during the relevant two weeks. Therefore, even if Y terminates the contract according to §649 I BGB, he is obliged to pay the agreed sum according to §649 II BGB.

III. 1. An alternative to terminating the contract is provided by the concept of *Störung der Geschäftsgrundlage* (§313 BGB). Under this regime the contract is principally upheld and adapted to the unexpected circumstances. An adaptation of the contract might be advantageous

[366] Cf. J. Ellenberger, '§157', in: Palandt *et al.* (eds.), *Bürgerliches Gesetzbuch*, n. 3; BGHZ 127, 138 (142); cf. for the limits between complementary interpretation and §313 BGB, Köhler, 'Störung der Geschäftsgrundlage', pp. 295 (304 *et seq.*); D. Medicus, 'Vertragsauslegung and Geschäftsgrundlage', in: M.M. Jacobs *et al.* (eds.), *Festschrift für Wenes Flume zum 70. Geburtstag: 12 September 1978* (Cologne: Schmidt, 1978), pp. 629 *et seq.*

[367] Cf. BGH *NJW* 1997, 259; H. Sprau, '§649', in: Palandt *et al.* (eds.), *Bürgerliches Gesetzbuch*, n. 1.

[368] Cf. BGHZ 140, 263.

for Y because he may be relieved partly from his contractual obligation under this doctrine.

2. The issue in this case is referred to as *Vereitelung des Verwendungszwecks* (frustration of purpose) by the judiciary and legal authors.[369] This term expresses the fact that the contractual obligation can be performed in theory, but it has become practically useless with regard to the purpose of the creditor. As a general rule, it is legally irrelevant whether or not either party can make use of the contractual subject matter in the way he has expected. In other words: each party bears the risk that his purposes can be realised, unless the purpose in question is stipulated in the contract.[370] Only in exceptional cases have the courts considered frustration of purpose as *Störung der Geschäftsgrundlage* according to §313 BGB.[371]

3. According to the prevailing opinion, the concept of *Geschäftsgrundlage* can be applied to assumptions related to existing or future circumstances as long as the contractual will of the parties is based on such circumstances, even if the parties have not specifically provided for these assumptions. The parties either have to share these assumptions or at least one party must be aware that the other considers them to be the basis of the contract.

4. Furthermore, the courts have required a specific justification for the – at least partial – shift in the risk concerning frustration of purpose. In the view of the courts, it qualifies as justification if the debtor has contributed to the frustration of purpose on the side of the creditor.[372] Additionally, another qualification results if one party's purpose of use is so closely related to the other party's interest that the latter party's claim of his contractual rights qualifies for a *venire contra factum proprium*. This was held in a case in which one party's remuneration had been increased because of the other party's use of the contractual subject matter.[373] Another example

[369] Cf. Roth, '§313', in: Krüger (eds.), *Münchener Kommentar zum Bürgerlichen Gesetzbuch*, vol. II, nn. 213 *et seq.*; V. Emmerich, '§275', in: Krüger (ed.), *Münchener Kommentar zum Bürgerlichen Gesetzbuch*, vol. II, nn. 151 et seq.; Grüneberg, '§313', in: Palandt *et al.* (eds.), *Bürgerliches Gesetzbuch*, nn. 35 *et seq.*; Köhler, 'Störung der Geschäftsgrundlage', pp. 295 (303 *et seq.*).

[370] Cf. Roth, '§313', in: Krüger (ed.), *Münchener Kommentar zum Bürgerlichen Gesetzbuch*, vol. II, n. 215; BGHZ 71, 293; BGHZ 74, 370.

[371] Cf. BGH LM §242 BGB (Bb) n. 12 (*Bohrhämmer*); BGH NJW 1984, 1746 (*Iran*); BGH JZ 1966, 409 (*Fertighaus*); BGH LM §242 BGB (Bb) n. 54 (*Gaststätteninventar*); BGH NJW 1998, 1701 (*Militärboote*).

[372] Cf. BGH LM §242 BGB (Bb) n. 36 (*Bohrhämmer*).

[373] Cf. BGH WM 1967, 561 (*Automatenkauf*); K. Larenz, *Schuldrecht I*, §21 II; Grüneberg, '§313', in: Palandt *et al.* (eds.), *Bürgerliches Gesetzbuch*, n. 37; cf. Case 7.

where a shift in the risk of frustration has been justified concerns cases of the so-called *Große Geschäftsgrundlage*. This expression refers to substantial changes in political, economic and social conditions, such as war, conditions similar to war, natural disasters, government intervention and similar cases of force majeure.[374] These conditions alter the contractual framework fundamentally and they are not consistent with the regular scope of the contractual and statutory risk allocation scheme. Furthermore, the resulting burden on one of the parties is purely accidental.

5. In the given case, the destruction of the house during the storm has completely frustrated Y's purpose of the contract. The storm can be qualified as a case of *Große Geschäftsgrundlage* because it involves an unusual act of nature and burdens Y accidentally.[375] Therefore the rules of *Störung der Geschäftsgrundlage* are applicable in this case.

6. Hence, Y can ask for an adaptation of the contract according to §313 BGB. The adaptation is supposed to provide for a fair division of the risk between the two parties. The specific method of adaptation depends upon the circumstances of the case. The courts have divided the damage between the parties,[376] adapted the contract price on the basis of an alternative use of the contractual subject matter[377] or set aside the contract in return for compensation.[378] Only in exceptional cases was the disadvantaged party allowed to avoid the contract without any indemnity. This is only legitimate if the other party is not severely burdened by the avoidance of the contract or if unusual circumstances justify that the other party bears the risk exclusively.[379]

Austria

Under Austrian law, Y is obliged to pay the contract price, which is reduced by the amount of the expenses saved by X due to fact that he does not execute his work. Y can request that X does not execute the work.

I. 1. The agreement in our case is a contract for work and services, to which special provisions of the ABGB apply. According to §1168 ABGB a

[374] Cf. *ibid.*, n. 5; Roth, '§313', in: Krüger (ed.), *Münchener Kommentar zum Bürgerlichen Gesetzbuch*, vol. II, nn. 49 *et seq.*

[375] This would be different if the condition of the house had contributed to the collapse. However, the facts given do not support this assumption.

[376] Cf. BGH LM §242 BGB (Bb) n. 12 (*Bohrhämmer*). [377] Cf. BGH WM 1967, 561.

[378] Cf. BGH NJW 1998, 1701 (*Militärboote*). [379] Cf. BGH LM §242 BGB n. 36, 54.

contractor keeps his claim for payment as long as he is ready to fulfill his obligation but is prevented from performance by circumstances arising in the customer's sphere of responsibility. However, according to §1168 ABGB, the customer is entitled to deduct from the contract price all expenses saved by the contractor due to the non-performance of his work obligations. These legal consequences are triggered by the mere fact that the work is not executed due to circumstances in the sphere of the customer. It therefore does not make any difference whether the execution of the work is rendered factually impossible by these circumstances or whether the customer chooses to prevent the execution in the light of his new situation. More than that, it is generally held that the customer is entitled to refuse acceptance of the work even without cause.[380] Therefore Y is entitled to countermand the work.

2. According to §1168a ABGB it falls within the customer's sphere of responsibility to ensure that materials provided to execute the work are appropriate. In particular, the customer is responsible for the premises where the work shall be done.[381] Under Austrian law there is no doubt that the destruction of the house by the storm falls within Y's sphere of responsibility. As a result, Y is obliged to pay the contract price, but is entitled to deduct any expenses saved by X.[382]

II. Under Austrian law '*Wegfall der Geschäftsgrundlage*' is a subsidiary doctrine which only applies where more specific provisions do not exist.[383] Where §1168 ABGB is applicable (service contract and 'circumstances in the sphere of the ordering party') it will determine the distribution of risks and exclude '*Wegfall der Geschäftsgrundlage*'. §1168 ABGB does not apply in cases where the provider is not ready to perform or where the circumstances preventing the execution of the work cannot be considered to fall within the sphere of the ordering party.

III. From an Austrian point of view the right to countermand services is justified by the fact that a debtor is generally obliged to perform but has no right to perform.[384] §§1168 and 1168a ABGB are default rules that provide a specific risk allocation between the parties of a work or services

380 OGH, GlUNF 6648; OGH, SZ 2/87; 1.2.1972, SZ 45/11 = EvBl 1972/200 = JBl 1973, 309; 24.5.1972, EvBl 1972/331.

381 OGH, wbl 1987, 219; OGH, SZ 71/142.

382 For further details M. Bydlinski, '§1168', in: H. Koziol, P. Bydlinski and R. Bollenberger (eds.), *Kurzkommentar zum ABGB* (Vienna/New York: Springer, 2008), n. 4.

383 Rummel, '§901', in: Rummel (ed.), *Kommentar zum ABGB*, vol. I, nn. 4, 6 with further references.

384 Heinz Krejci, '§1168', in: Rummel (ed.), *Kommentar zum ABGB*, vol. I, n. 11.

contract.[385] Each party is responsible for his voluntary contributions to the execution of the work and all events that prevent such contributions – even without or against his will – nevertheless belong to the sphere of the respective party. Since X was ready to perform his obligation in compliance with the contract, he shall not lose his claim for payment. All expenses and costs saved by X are deducted from his claim for payment in order to prevent the contractor from receiving a windfall benefit.

The Netherlands

Given the relatively strong protection of consumers under Dutch law, Y will probably be released from his obligation to pay the full contract price, but not from the obligation to compensate X for the actual expenses and work done in connection with already finalised work.

I. Under Dutch law, Y is only obliged to compensate X for his costs (the recently adopted Art. 7:757 Dutch Civil Code[386]). According to traditional opinions in the Dutch legal literature there is an insufficient basis for the argument that X should substantially share Y's loss, whereas, at the same time, Y is (at least partly) excused under the statutory provisions on creditor default according to Art. 6:58.

II. 1. If performance under a construction contract becomes impossible because the goods that are the subject of the contracted work perish or become lost without the contractor (i.e., X) being responsible for that fact or event, the contractor is entitled to a proportional part of the contracted sum pro rata according to the work already completed according to Art. 7:757 Dutch Civil Code. To assess Y's payment obligation it is appropriate to distinguish between X's contractual expenses in obtaining custom-made materials, expenses that cannot be reallocated (e.g., to another project), expenses that are compensated by alternative work or third party orders and X's contractual profit. This is also reflected in Art. 7:764 Dutch Civil Code, which deals with the principal's right to terminate and the obligation to compensate for expenditure incurred.

2. Unrecoverable costs for customised products (e.g., if X had manufactured specially designed wall tiles or created metal structures customised for Y's cellar) are borne by the principal, Y. The same will apply

[385] See M. Bydlinski, '§1168', in: Koziol, P. Bydlinski, and Bollenberger (eds.), *Kurzkommentar zum ABGB*, n. 1.

[386] The enactment of the provisions for contracts for (construction) work in Title 7.12 Dutch Civil Code came into force on 1 September 2003, but only applied to existing contracts as of 1 September 2006.

to any building plans that X may have made in connection with the construction work (although this is normally done by independent architects and construction firms).

III. However, general legal concepts can reduce the amount that Y ultimately has to pay to X. Such legal concepts include the generic duty that 'a party should make reasonable efforts to reduce its counter-part's damages as much as reasonably possible' and X's (potential) claim for damages will be reduced to damages that X actually suffered in terms of expenses, i.e., if X had an alternative project to which he could assign his employees and materials, the costs of the materials and labour that is re-used would not be considered as 'damages'. The courts will look for such alternatives, especially in economic circumstances where it is difficult to find employees or when the materials used for the cellar are reusable materials for which there is a market. These are elements of contractual loyalty that the parties may reasonably expect from each other under exceptional circumstances. Accordingly Y's obligation to pay (a part of) the contract price is likely to be reduced. X's reduction of Y's payment obligation could also, at least partly, be based on the legal concept of unjustified enrichment (Art. 6:212 Dutch Civil Code).

IV. Pursuant to Art. 7:764 Dutch Civil Code, Y is entitled to terminate the construction agreement at any time. Whereas Art. 7:757 addresses both parties' rights in the case of force majeure, Art. 7:764 deals with the principal's right to terminate and its consequences. This latter article would become relevant if Y entered into an agreement with a third party contractor for the reconstruction of the entire house. In such cases, Y is still obliged by the construction contract with X and X might therefore claim that, in connection with such house reconstruction work, X can be expected to reconstruct the cellar. Article 7:764(2) provides that, in the case of termination, Y has to pay the full contract price reduced by any savings that X can achieve. If the contract price contains costs or expenses to be incurred by X, Y's payment obligation shall consist of the actual costs which X incurred, whether for materials or labour, and the profit agreed for the entire construction work. As regards this latter compensation element, a court will be reluctant to grant this by analogy with Art. 7:757.

V. Under the doctrine of unforeseen circumstances (Art. 6:258(2) section 2 Dutch Civil Code), Y's claim will fail because the unforeseen circumstances which occurred fall entirely within Y's sphere of responsibility.[387]

[387] However, one may successfully argue that, according to common opinion, a contract amendment under Art. 6:258 requires the same result as Art. 7:757.

Eastern European jurisdictions

Slovenia

Under Slovenian law, Y can terminate the contract, but he must pay compensation to X, which amounts to the contract price. He is, however, entitled to deduct the costs that X saved because he did not have to perform the work.

I. The concept of impossibility (Arts. 116, 117 CO) does not apply to this case, because the mutual performances (i.e., the refurbishing of the cellar and the payment of the contract price) have not become impossible for the parties. Y's cellar can still be refurbished by X as it remains fully intact.

II. 1. From Y's point of view, the purpose of the contract has been frustrated. Frustration of purpose is a concept covered by the '*clausula* rule', regulated in Arts. 112–15 CO. However, these general rules only apply in the absence of a specific rule. In this case specific provisions of the CO regarding contracts for work apply. Article 648 CO provides for an unconditional right of the customer to terminate a contract before the work is finished. This right could be regarded as an application of the '*clausula* principle' where the customer, in a contract for work, recognises that the pursued purpose has become frustrated. On the other hand, Art. 648 CO is much wider than Arts. 112–15 CO, since it provides for an unlimited right to terminate the contract even for no (objectively) valid reason.

2. According to Art. 648 CO, the customer (Y), exercising his right to terminate the contract, must, however, pay the contractor (X) the agreed price, from which he is allowed to deduct costs X would have incurred, had the contract been performed. Y can also deduct any benefits X has from using the released capacities due to the non-performance of the terminated contract. These deductions aim to prevent the contractor from being unjustly enriched.

Lithuania

Y has a right to terminate the contract. As the contract is terminated due to force majeure, Y is not obliged to compensate X for the damages he incurred.

I. As the cellar remains fully intact and can still be refurbished by X, the case does not fall within the scope of the doctrine of impossibility.

II. 1. An agreement concerning the refurbishment of a cellar falls under Arts. 6.644–6.671 CC on building (construction) contracts.

According to Art. 6.658(4) CC, the customer has the right to terminate the contract in serious circumstances. As a consequence, if the customer is responsible for termination the customer has to pay the contractor for the completed work and to compensate the contractor for any losses. In calculating the damages, regard needs to be had to what the contractor has saved due to the termination of the contract. Thus, the sums saved by the contractor will have to be subtracted from the damages. This legal regulation is explained by the fact that the customer is usually regarded as the weaker party of the contract of independent work.

2. According to Art. 6.658 CC, force majeure unquestionably is an important reason which enables the customer to terminate the contract. Under Art. 6.212 CC, circumstances qualify as force majeure if they objectively render the performance of one party impossible. In this case it is evident that the wine cellar itself without the building is of no use to the customer. Therefore, from the position of the customer, the contract has lost its purpose. In certain cases, the loss of purpose may be qualified as force majeure.[388] Second, these circumstances must have been beyond the control of a party to the contract. This applies to ecological events like the summer storm at hand. A further prerequisite is that these circumstances could not have reasonably been predicted by the party at the time when the contract was concluded. The destruction of buildings due to natural forces is an extraordinary event. It could not have been foreseen by Y when he entered into the contract with X. Finally, the party must not have been able to avoid these circumstances. There are no indications that Y could have avoided the destruction of the house. Thus, Y is able to terminate the contract. As the work has not been started, X has no right to demand the contract price.

3. The contractor's claim for damages depends on whether the customer is responsible for the termination of the contract (Art. 6.248 CC). As the summer storm qualifies as force majeure, Y is not liable (Arts. 6.212, 6.248 CC). Therefore, X is not entitled to damages either.

III. Art. 6.204 CC is a general norm, while Art. 6.658 CC contains a specific regulation of force majeure with regard to construction contracts. In case of a collision between general and special norms, priority is given to the special norm. Therefore, Art. 6.204 CC is not applicable at hand.

[388] Valentinas Mikelenas, *Commentary on Book VI of the Civil Code* (Vilnius: Justitia, 2003), p. 265 (in Lithuanian).

Czech Republic

Y is obliged to pay the contract price, which shall be reduced by the amount saved due to non-performance and the amount he has or could have earned in an alternative transaction.

I. The provisions dealing with the impossibility of performance cannot be applied in the present case, since the performance is still possible.[389] In other words, Y is obliged to pay the contract price.

II. The relevant contract is a contract for work. Under Section 641(1) Civil Code the contractor shall receive the agreed price, even if the work was not performed, provided that the contractor was willing to perform the work and was prevented from the performance by circumstances on the side of the customer. Thus, the ordering party is obliged to pay the contracted sum, although he has not received anything under the contract himself. The purpose of this regulation is to provide the contractor with compensation for the performance that he failed to complete without fault.[390] X's willingness to perform requires that X was not only ready to do the work, including ready to procur the necessary material, but also able to complete the work within the agreed time.[391] However, the compensation shall be lowered by what the contractor (X) saved by non-performance of the work, and also by what he was able to earn in another way; i.e., by the income achieved for the period during which the contractor would otherwise have been performing the work for Y, and also by the possible income that he intentionally omitted to earn in the time in which he would have otherwise been carrying out the work for Y.[392]

III. The provision of the Commercial Code on frustration of the purpose of a contract (Section 356) will not apply, if the purpose of the contract is not expressed in it.

Scandinavian jurisdictions

Sweden

Y is not obliged to pay the contract price, as he is entitled to terminate the contract, but Y must compensate X for the work

[389] See M. Škárová in: Jehlička *et al.* (eds.), *Občanský Zākoník, Kamentář (Civil Code, Commentary)* (Prague: ASPI, 9th edn, 2004), p. 847.

[390] See *ibid.*, p. 957. [391] See *ibid.*, p. 958.

[392] See L. Kopáč, in: R. Bystrický *et al.* (eds.), *Právo Mezinārodního obchodu (Law of International Trade)* (Prague: 1967), p. 214.

he has already done or that has to be done notwithstanding termination.

I. X performs work on a building within the course of his business for a private citizen, Y. Therefore the Swedish Consumer Services Act applies (Section 1).[393] This Act is mandatory in favour of the consumer (Section 3). The consumer is, pursuant to Section 42, entitled to terminate *('avbeställa')* the contract. However, the craftsman is entitled to compensation for the work he has already done or still has to do, notwithstanding termination. This compensation should amount to the price that would have been demanded if the contract had only included the work that has actually been done (first paragraph). The craftsman is normally also entitled to compensation for his costs for the remaining part of the service, and for other losses caused by the fact that he has been unable to accept other assignments. Compensation may arise or in other ways specific to the contract. This right to compensation does not apply in cases where the consumer's purpose is not realisable because the object of the service has been damaged or lost for reasons other than the consumer's negligence, as is the case here (second paragraph). The craftsman is not under this latter rule entitled to more than the loss caused by the termination (third paragraph).

Denmark

The main principle in Danish contract law is that, once the parties have entered into a binding agreement, it must be fulfilled. In line with this principle, there is a possibility of obtaining specific performance or even an injunction to perform. However, in the case at hand X will not be entitled to claim the contract price, since the performance of the contract makes no sense. X is entitled to damages.

I. The doctrine of assumptions is very likely to be applied in this case. As mentioned in the overview (Chapter 4), the doctrine of assumptions requires that three conditions are fulfilled. The promisor is not bound by his promise if his assumption was determinable, perceptible and relevant. If Y does not intend to rebuild the house, the promise made by him is determinable in the sense that Y would never have made the promise or, in other words, would never have concluded the contract with X if he had known about the subsequent circumstances causing the demolition of his house. In addition, X's expectations were also easily perceptible for

[393] Konsumenttjänstlagen (1985:716).

X. The critical, third question is whether X should bear the risk of these unexpected circumstances. Danish case law does not contain a case which is similar to the one at hand. If the doctrine of assumptions is applied, the court would most likely set aside the entire agreement and compensate X for damages pursuant to the principle of reliance interest.

II. 1. The rules of force majeure might be relevant to the given case, but are less likely to be applied than the doctrine of assumptions. They are provided for in Section 27(3) AB 92 (General conditions for building and construction activities) and Section 24 Sale of Goods Act respectively. The agreement between X and Y would normally be considered to be a contract for work and materials, which is outside the scope of the Sale of Goods Act. In most cases, the parties would have chosen to apply AB 92. Otherwise the Sale of Goods Act would be applied by analogy. The main difference between the concept of force majeure in the Sale of Goods Act and AB 92 is that AB 92 additionally includes provisions on vandalism. Therefore, the application of AB 92 does not make a difference to the solution of the present case.

2. In accordance with Section 27(3) AB 92 (by analogy Section 24 Sale of Goods Act), the contractor cannot claim damages if the unexpected circumstances can be characterised as force majeure. As mentioned in the general remarks, three conditions must be fulfilled in order to invoke force majeure. The event must not have been predictable at the time when the parties entered into the agreement. Second, it must have been impossible to provide a similar good compared to the good in question. Finally, the unexpected circumstances must be of an extraordinary and non-recurrent character. Case law concerning Section 27(3) AB 92 and Section 24 Sale of Goods Act shows a very strict interpretation of the three conditions which must be fulfilled in order to constitute/establish force majeure. Therefore, X's claim for damages is not excluded due to force majeure.

Romanic–Mediterranean jurisdictions

Italy

Y may terminate the contract but he must indemnify X with regard to the expenses actually incurred, the works actually performed and the loss of profit.

I. On the basis that the parties have neither explicitly provided for the destruction of the house, nor implicitly assumed the existence of Y's house, Y is obliged to respect the contract with X. In other words, the agreement between X and Y does not contain elements to determine, by way of interpretation of the parties' intention (Arts. 1362 *et seq.* CC), the consequences of the destruction of the house. The doctrine of implied assumption (*presupposizione*) requires that the parties have either shared these assumptions or at least one party was aware that the other considered them a foundation of the contract.

II. Y is not entitled to avoid the contract according to the rules of mistake (Arts. 1427 *et seq.* CC), since the parties have never discussed the case of the house being destroyed and/or the connection between the house and the works in the cellar. Furthermore, the fact that the cellar is still intact after the disappearance of the house prevents Y from taking legal action in order to be discharged according to the rules of impossibility (Arts. 1463 *et seq.* CC). The performance is in fact not impossible for X or Y.

III. Under the circumstances, Y is entitled to terminate the contract pursuant to the rules concerning building contracts (*appalto*, Arts. 1655 *et seq.* CC). Of course, X is contractually obliged to refurbish the cellar into a wine-cellar, i.e., to accomplish a particular result and Y is obliged to pay the contract price. However, according to Art. 1671 CC, Y may terminate the contract before the service has been performed at any time without a term of notice and without giving reasons for the decision to withdraw. In this case, X's economic interest in the contract is fully respected by the law: Y has to indemnify X with regard to the expenses actually incurred, the works actually performed and the loss of profit. In the calculation of the damages suffered by X, specific gains caused by the early termination of the contract should be deducted according to the general rule of '*compensatio lucri cum damno*' i.e., if he saves expenses or benefits from using his released capacities for other projects.

IV. 1. Finally, since the case at issue presents the typical characters of frustration of purpose as far as Y is concerned, due to supervening unexpected events, it should be examined whether or not the remedy of termination under Art. 1467 CC is applicable because the performance has become extremely onerous. Art. 1467 CC can be invoked alternatively to Art. 1671 CC.

2. As a matter of fact, the contractual obligations can be performed, but the performance of X has become practically useless with regard to the purposes of Y. This implies that the payment of the contractual price could be deemed, from the point of view of Y, extremely onerous.

However, Art. 1467 CC grants a right to termination of the contract only if the disproportion is objective, and if it did not result from the modification of the criteria with which the party, having regard to its personal conditions, assesses the contract obligation. It is irrelevant whether or not either party can actually use such performance in the way he has expected, unless this issue is covered by the agreement. Since this does not seem to be the case (see above), the frustration of purpose of Y would not result in a legitimate reason for discharge from the contractual obligation (payment of the agreed price).

Spain

Under Spanish law, the client (Y) is entitled to terminate the contract provided that he pays the contractor for his expenses concerning the construction work, for the work already done and for 15 per cent of the benefit the contractor would have obtained if he had completed the construction work.

I. This is not a case of impossibility according to Spanish law. Article 1105 CC is not relevant as the cellar is still is in good order and X is therefore able to perform.

II. As X is obliged to refurbish Y's cellar, the special provisions for building contracts apply.[394] In this case, the court would apply Art. 1594 CC allowing the client to terminate the contract without justification at any time, provided he indemnifies the building contractor for the works he has done, the expenses he has incurred concerning the construction and the benefit that the contractor would obtain from the execution of the works.[395] This benefit has been generally fixed by courts at 15 per cent of the benefit that the contractor would have obtained had the construction work been completed. Furthermore, under Spanish law there is a duty for the party to mitigate damage (Art. 1107 CC) which has also been acknowledged in the case law of the TS.[396]

III. The doctrine of *cláusula rebus sic stantibus* is not applicable in this case because the rules of the CC are considered to provide for an implicit distribution of the risk in building contracts.[397]

394 Building contracts are regulated in Arts. 1588–1600 CC and in the Statute on Building Work of 15 November 1999, Ley General de la Edificación.

395 Article 1594 CC: *El dueño puede desistir, por su sola voluntad, de la construcción de la obra aunque se haya empezado, indemnizando al contratista de todos sus gastos, trabajo y utilidad que pudiera obtener de ella.*

396 28 January 2000 (Art. 454); 14 May 2003 (Art. 4749) and 23 May 2005 (Art. 6364).

397 For instance, in German law, the equivalent would be §649 BGB.

Portugal

Under Portuguese law, the owner (in our case, Y) may terminate the contract but he will be required to compensate the other party (X) for work carried out and expenses incurred.

I. As the cellar has not been destroyed, X is still able to perform. Therefore, the rules of impossibility are not applicable or, at least, are not directly applicable (as stated later on, some have suggested that those rules may be applied by analogy to fill in a legal gap).

II. The case suggests that the said contract would represent, in Portuguese law, a building contract ('*empreitada*'). As this is a building contract, Y can order the work to be discontinued ('*desistir da obra*') under the terms of Art. 1229 CC if the building, but not the basement, is accidentally destroyed. This article allows the owner to 'discontinue the work at any time, even if work has begun, provided that he compensates the contractor for his expenses and labour and for the profit he would have received from the work'. The compensation includes the resulting loss ('*dano emergente*') – the contractor's expenses and labour to date – as well as the loss of profit ('*lucro cessante*'), which seems to refer to the loss of profit for the entire work.[398] In this case Y would have to pay the agreed price having deducted the actual cost of the building work still to be done.

III. 1. It is important to ascertain, however, whether the loss of interest in receiving the contractual goods or services ('*prestação*') on the part of the recipient allows him to terminate the contract according to general principles regardless of Art. 1229 CC. Here, Y was 'forced' to discontinue due to external circumstances that frustrated his intended purpose. The situation described – it is still possible to modify the basement, but the rest of the building has been completely destroyed – is similar to a situation of loss of the purpose of rendering the service ('*Zweckfortfall*').[399] Portuguese literature has been sensitive to the

[398] Pires de Lima and Antunes Varela, *Código Civil Anotado*, p. 908.

[399] Such a situation was expressly considered by Professor Vaz Serra in a draft project in a rule called *desaparecimento do interesse do credor* (loss of recipient's interest) with the following wording: 'n°1 – The obligation ceases when the recipient's interest justifying it disappears. This can be said to be the case when the purpose of the obligation can no longer be achieved or when it is attained by means unconnected with the obligation and the recipient has no right to compensation; n°2 – The recipient's interest and the purpose of the obligation, in the situation envisaged in the previous paragraph, should be able to be deduced from the content of the transaction'. This rule, however, was not admitted in the final draft of the Código Civil. See Adriano Vaz Serra, 'Impossibilidade

problem and is debating the question of what should be understood by *impossibilidade de cumprimento* (impossibility of performance) and what is the most appropriate understanding of *prestação* (rendering of contractual services) (in a similar way to the discussions in Germany about the distinction between '*Leistungshandlung*' and '*Leistungserfolg*' and the problems of '*Zweckvereitelung*' and '*Zweckerreichung*').[400]

2. Antunes Varela[401] concludes that 'in many cases there are extraneous elements or exterior circumstances that are integral to or a condition of the actions of the party in such a way that if these are not present, a true impossibility of rendering the service can occur'. Baptista Machado, and following in his path, Ribeiro de Faria,[402] underline the difference that exists between certain obligations that are *neutral* in terms of purpose (which is typically the case in sale and purchase obligations) and others, in which, due to the actual type of contract or to the agreement between the parties, *the provider* ('*devedor*') *accepts the possibility of a connection between the rendering of his service and a determined purpose or aim of the recipient* ('*credor*') by which 'the rendering of this service becomes *impossible* from the moment that the intended purpose is not able to be achieved'. In the words of Baptista Machado, the fulfillment of contractual goods or services obligations is *finalised* when 'the provider accepts that the rendering of the contractual goods or services is tied to an individual and specific aim (or when the rendering of these, because of their very nature, can only have a specific and determined purpose)'.[403] Thus, in this situation there would be a common acceptance of the risk of the transactional plan if the purpose was frustrated by circumstances not attributable to either party. In line with

Superveniente por Causa não Imputável ao Devedor e Desaparecimento do Interesse do Credor', (1955) n° 46, *Boletim do Ministério da Justiça*, 5 at 140.

400 See, for example, F. Wieacker, 'Leistungshandlung und Leistungserfolg im bürgerlichen Schuldrecht', in: *Festschrift für Nipperdey* (Munich, Berlin: Beck,1965), vol. 1, pp. 783 *et seq.*; V. Beuthien, *Zweckerreichung und Zweckstörung im Schuldverhältnis* (Tübingen: Mohr Sieback, 1969); M. Köhler, *Unmöglickeit und Geschäftsgrundlage bei Zweckstörungen im Schuldverhältnis* (Munich: Beck, 1971); for all, Larenz, *Schuldrecht* I pp. 320 *et seq.*

401 Antunes Varela, *Das Obrigações em Geral* (Coimbra: Coimbra Editora, 7th edn, 1997), vol. 2, pp. 75–6.

402 Jorge Ribeiro de Faria, *Direito das Obrigações* (Coimbra: Coimbra Editora, 1990), vol. II, pp. 360 *et seq.*

403 João Baptista Machado, 'Risco contratual e mora do credor (risco da perda do valor-utilidade ou do rendimento da prestação e de desperdício da capacidade de prestar vinculada)', in: *Estudos em Homenagem do Prof. Doutor A. Ferrer-Correia* (1989), vol. 2, special issue of the *Boletim da Faculdade de Direito da Universidade de Coimbra*, 71 at 81, n. 16.

this, Baptista Machado considers that in these cases 'the provider renounces the profit from the transaction', and is entitled only *to be compensated for the work and expenses that he has already carried out* (cf. Art. 1227 CC).[404]

3. To sum up, for Baptista Machado, a distinction has to be made between the impossibility of rendering the contractual goods and services and the impossibility of their fulfilment: there are situations in which it is still possible to carry out the contractual goods or services, but where this cannot count as fulfilment, thus constituting an impossibility of fulfilment ('*impossibilidade de cumprimento*'). Other authors, such as Antunes Varela rely on Art. 468, n°1, CC, on benevolent intervention in another's affairs ('*negotiorum gestio*'), to justify the right of the provider to compensation.[405] In any case, Art. 437 CC is probably not needed to solve a case like this, since it is of a subsidiary nature. Most of the authors fill in the legal gap by applying either the rules on impossibility or the rules on *negotiorum gestio*. It must also be stressed that Art. 437 CC is more concerned with the adaptation of the contract or its adjustment than with the splitting of the losses.

IV. To summarise, in Portuguese law, in spite of the difficulties of a legal basis (rules on impossibility applicable by analogy or rules on *negotiorum gestio* by analogy, too[406]), X will be compensated for losses suffered according to the dominant view in legal literature.[407] This is a case of frustration of purpose ('*frustração do fim da prestação*') which is not expressly provided for in law. The lacuna can be filled by analogy, either by means of Art. 468, n°1, CC on management of another's affairs, or

[404] For a comparison see Maria de Lurdes Pereira, *Conceito de Prestação e Destino da Contraprestação* (Coimbra: Coimbra Editora, 2001), pp. 90 *et seq*., Calvão da Silva, *Cumprimento e sanção pecuniária compulsória* (Coimbra: Coimbra Editora, 1987), pp. 82 *et seq*., Menezes Leitão, *Direito das Obrigações, II* (Coimbra: Coimbra Editora, 2002), pp. 116 et seq., and António Pinto Monteiro, *Cláusula penal e indemnização* (Coimbra: Coimbra Editor, 1990), p. 112, n. 245.

[405] Antunes Varela, *Das Obrigações em Geral*, p. 85.

[406] The analogy is that the manager of another's affairs (*gestor*) is also entitled to the reimbursement of expenses that were necessary and to payment of his labour (if he was a professional) if the undertaking of the management was useful at the start ('*utiliter coepta*') even if without fault of the *gestor* the management fails and there is no final benefit for the principal ('*dominus*').

[407] Although isolated here in the context of Portuguese law, Vaz Serra, very unexpectedly, appears to opt for the possibility of the resolution of the contract through alteration in circumstances (Art. 437 CC): if the execution of the contract in the altered circumstances becomes absolutely senseless (as occurs in the cases of 'frustration of the purpose') the contract is resoluble (Annotation of the 'Acórdão' of 6 April 1978 (1978–1979) 111 *Revista de Legislação e de Jurisprudência*, p. 345 at p. 348).

preferably by means of Art. 1227 CC, on the impossibility of carrying out the work in the building contract.

Greece

Y will have to pay the contract price but will be allowed to deduct any expenses saved or profits realised by X due to the cancellation of the work.

I. In a reciprocal contract, every party undertakes an obligation to perform (direct legal cause) in order to acquire the counter-performance (indirect legal cause). The indirect legal cause results from the contract itself.[408] For that reason, its abnormal development is dealt with by the provisions on impossibility, default or defects.[409] Nevertheless, the transfer of goods itself does not constitute the final purpose. It is only a way for the parties to satisfy their needs and financial goals (so-called 'secondary' or 'substantial causes'). For example, In the case at hand, Y might aim to take advantage of the refurbished cellar for reasons of pleasure. Under the reservation of a special provision, the error in this motivation, in this so-called 'secondary cause', does not influence the validity of the contract according to Art. 143 AK.[410] The commitment of a contract (*pacta sunt servanda*) demands the protection of the party, even if the 'secondary causes' of the other party are frustrated.[411] The only exception to this allocation of risks is a collapse of the underlying basis of the contract due to unexpected circumstances.

II. 1. In the present case, Y's specific purpose of using the refurbished cellar did not become, one way or another, part of the agreement. Thus, the frustration of Y's purpose of use of the cellar does not result in any kind of non-fulfilment – e.g., non-fault impossibility of Y to perform – and so the 'risk of use' has to be borne by B.[412]

2. On the other hand, it is possible to unilaterally terminate a contract for work at any time before the completion of the work according to

[408] See Fikentscher, *Die Geschäftsgrundlage*, p. 26.

[409] See Ulrich Huber, 'Contractual goal, contractual content and underlying basis of the contract', (1972) JuS p. 58 II.

[410] Whether the unlawfulness of the cause may influence the validity of the contract, is a different one. See A. Litzeropoulos, *Elements of Law of Obligations (university lectures)* (Athens: 1960), vol II, p. 320.

[411] See Nikolaos Papantoniou, *The Good Faith in Civil Law* (Athens: Sakkoulas, 1957, repr. 1997), p. 175; 'Stathopoulos, Essential error for the annulment of the contract', (1995)1 KritE, p. 110. See also indicatively Valtoudis, *Sale of Enterprise*, pp. 296–7.

[412] See generally Karassis, *Law of Contract*, p. 101/2.

Art. 700 AK. In fact, Y's refusal to accept X's performance might be interpreted, according to good faith (Art. 173, 200 AK), as an implicit exercise of this right of termination. Y, however, will be obliged to pay the agreed price, apart from expenses which the contractor has saved due to the cancellation of the work (e.g., wages of employees) or alternative profits he intentionally does not realise (Art. 700 §2 AK).[413] By no means, whatsoever - not even alternatively to the price - should Y be obliged to pay any pecuniary compensation, that is the 'positive interest' or (non-) performance damages in the form either of positive damages ('*damnum emergens*') or of lost profits ('*lucrum cessans*').[414]

III. It is disputable whether the frustration of Y's purpose of use of the performance affects the underlying basis of the contract, in other words, whether, as already mentioned, it distorts the contractual allocation of risks due to unexpected circumstances. One could argue, for example, that if Y has no other place to live, the frustration of purpose should be considered as a serious disturbance of the contractual justice according to Art. 388 AK. As a result, the court could declare the termination of the contract and, possibly, impose an obligation on Y to compensate X for his frustrated expenses. It is, however, far from certain that these requirements are met in this case.

France and related jurisdictions

France

Under French law, Y will most likely be required to pay the contract price.

I. The contract must be performed. The destruction of the house does not qualify as force majeure as the work can still be performed. In particular, frustration of purpose as a ground for the termination of a contract is not recognised under French law. The later use of the works falls within the risks to be borne by the principal.

II. Mistake requires a false representation of substantial elements of the contract.[415] In this case, when entering into the contract, Y thought

[413] See Kardaras, 'Art. 700', in: Georgiadis and Stathopoulos (eds.), *AK*, n. 5, 8–9; Ioannes Deligiannis and Panagiotes Kornilakis, *Law of Obligations. Special Part* (Thessalonica: Sakkoula, 1992), vol. II, p. 306/7, p. 316.

[414] See Deligiannis and Kornilakis, *Law of Obligations*, vol. II, p. 313.

[415] Cass., 22 February 1978, *JCP*., 1978, II, 18925 decided that a discrepancy between the contract and what would appear, thereafter, to be the reality, can lead to the principle of mistake being applied.

that the cellar would be useful as part of the house. This expectation has been frustrated as the house was destroyed. However, the mistake was not present when the contract was concluded; at that moment, the house had not been destroyed.

III. The concept of *cause* refers to the motives for entering into a contract. However, such motives must also be present at the time of concluding the contract. Thus, the destruction of the house after the conclusion of the contract is not relevant for the application of the *cause*.

IV. The judge could also consider that the contractor had not acted in good faith or abused his legal position by claiming performance which appears to be useless for the principal. Abuse of right applies when there is a substantial breach of proportionality between the advantage of the performance for the one party and the burden for the other. Different facts can be taken into consideration, e.g., whether Y was quickly able to rebuild the house, whether it was easy for X to find other work or whether X incurred expenses by beginning the work. An abuse of rights is, of course, the exception and it is far from certain that the judge will apply this concept.

Belgium

Y will most likely be obliged to pay the contract price or to compensate X for his losses under Belgian law.

I. The destruction cannot be considered as force majeure because the work can still be performed. Frustration of purpose is not recognised as a ground for the termination of a contract as is the case in French law. The later use of the works falls within the ambit of risks to be borne by the principal.

II. Mistake implies a false conception of substantial elements of the contract.[416] In this case, when entering into the contract, Y thought that the cellar could be used in his house. This is no longer possible as the house has been destroyed. However, the mistake was not present during the conclusion of the contract and cannot apply in this case.

III. The concept of *cause* refers to the motives for entering into the contract. It was Y's intention to use the cellar when living in the house. However, circumstances occurring after the conclusion of the contract are not relevant under the doctrine of *cause*. Thus, the destruction of the house after the conclusion of the contract is not relevant for the application of *cause*.

[416] See also Cass., 22 February 1978, *JCP*., 1978, II, 18925.

IV. The judge could also consider that the contractor had not acted in good faith or abused his legal position by claiming the performance of a work, which appears to be useless as far as the principal is concerned. Abuse of rights means a substantial breach of proportionality between the advantage of the performance for one party and the disadvantage for the other. The solution will depend on factual elements; different facts can be taken into consideration, e.g., the possibility for Y to rebuild the house rapidly, the possibility for X to find other work easily or whether X has to incur expenses by beginning the work. However, an abuse of rights is an exception to the rule and it is rather improbable that the judge will apply this concept.

England and related jurisdictions

England and Ireland

The solution of the case is similar in English and Irish law although the underlying legal reasoning diverges slightly. The contract is frustrated by virtue of the destruction of the dwelling. The construction contract was dependent for its existence upon the continued presence of Y's house. On the facts as given, Y is not liable for breach of contract and does not have to pay X the contract price or compensate X for wasted expenditure on materials. If a sum was paid or payable to X in advance of the storm, Y should be able to recover the sum paid, or refuse to pay it if it was payable. In this situation X might be able to retain or claim a sum to cover the cost of the materials purchased, provided such expenditure was incurred in reliance on the advance payment and the materials were in fact wasted and of no other use to X.

I. X has agreed to refurbish Y's cellar into a wine cellar. This is a construction contract or a contract for services. The formation and performance of a contract of this kind are governed exclusively by reference to common law principles. Statute law in both England and Ireland requires the supplier of a service to meet certain implied statutory terms as to the service providers' ability to perform the service, but on these facts these statutory provisions are not relevant.[417] Section 6 Sale of Goods Act 1893 renders contracts for the sale of

[417] In Ireland, see the Sale of Goods and Supply of Services Act 1980, Section 39. In England, see the Supply of Goods and Services Act 1982, Sections 12–16.

goods void when, without the knowledge of the seller, the goods have perished before the formation of the contract, and section 7 avoids contracts for the sale of specific goods which perish after the formation of the contract but before the risk has passed to the buyer.[418] However, these provisions only apply to the sale of goods and would have no application to this question.

II. The general doctrine of frustration of contract is raised by the facts of this case. As discussed in the overview (Chapter 4), over the years there have been various theories as to the basis of this doctrine, from the 'implied term theory' to Lord Radcliffe's theory in *Davis Contractors*,[419] based on the objective construction of the contract. Despite its reliance on the implied term theory, the doctrine is well illustrated by the case of *Taylor* v. *Caldwell*.[420] There the defendants were to let the plaintiffs have the use of the Surrey Gardens and Music Hall 'for the purpose of giving four grand concerts' on 17 June, 15 July, 5 August and 19 August 1861. The defendants also agreed to maintain side shows in the Gardens on those dates. On 11 June the Music Hall was destroyed by fire, through no fault of the defendants,[421] and it thus became impossible to give the concerts. The plaintiffs brought an action for breach of contract, and sought damages in respect of the expenses which they had incurred in advertising and preparing for the concerts. Their claim was dismissed on the ground that there was an implied term in the contract that performance would be excused if the Music Hall was destroyed. It should be noted that performance was completely excused in this case, including performance of that part of the contract which was still technically capable of performance, i.e., the provision of side shows in the Gardens. Thus, if the plaintiffs had brought an action for the defendant's failure to provide the side shows in the Gardens, the action would most likely have failed on the basis that the contract as a whole was frustrated, and not merely that part relating to the Music Hall. It is also clear in this case that the destruction of the Hall excused both parties: 'both parties are excused, the plaintiffs from taking the

[418] In England, Sections 6 and 7 of the Sale of Goods Act 1893 are now to be found in Sections 6 and 7 of the Sale of Goods Act 1979.

[419] [1956] AC 696.

[420] (1863) 3 B&S 826 (Eng). See the discussion in Treitel, *Frustration and Force Majeure* at pp. 37–57.

[421] It seems that the fire was caused by the carelessness of a plumber in leaving an unattended flame in the roof of the Hall. See Treitel, *Frustration and Force Majeure* (1994) at p. 37.

Gardens and paying the money, the defendants from performing their promise to give the use of the Hall and Gardens and other things'.[422] Thus, it would have technically made little difference if the defendants had brought the action for breach of contract, for example, because of the plaintiff's failure to pay the agreed price for the Hall, or even a proportionate part of the price for the Gardens which were still available for use. Such an action would most likely also have failed on the basis of the implied term theory.

III. The issue in this problem is whether the heavy summer storm, which has destroyed Y's house but, miraculously perhaps, has left the cellar undamaged, is 'a frustrating event'. Implied contract theory cases such as *Taylor* v. *Caldwell* would regard this event as discharging the contract as between X and Y. The storm would be regarded as destroying an essential element in the contract, namely the building that the wine cellar was intended to be a constituent part of. Under the construction of the contract theory, a court would regard the intention of the parties as envisaging that the cellar conversion would allow Y to enjoy his/her domestic life all the more. If Y has no home then 'the obligation undertaken [by X] would, if performed, be a different thing from that contracted for'.[423] Nor would a heavy summer storm, of such magnitude and consequences, be an event that the parties could have expected. This case could alternatively be viewed as a case of 'frustration of purpose', and thus similar to the 'coronation cases', discussed below in relation to Case 7. Such an analysis would most likely lead to a similar result.[424]

IV. 1. In conclusion, even under the narrowest possible theoretical perspective, the service contract between X and Y is frustrated by the storm and its consequences. The discharge of contract takes place automatically, by operation of law and, while in practice one party may serve notice that the contract is discharged, service of notice is not required or conceptually relevant.

2. The consequences of frustration must now be considered. The doctrine of frustration means that both parties are discharged from performing the contract, and neither can bring an action for breach of contract against the other. Thus, as in *Taylor* v. *Caldwell*, X cannot sue Y for the contract price, or for damages to cover the cost of the

[422] (1863) 3 B&S 826, 840 per Blackburn J.

[423] Lord Radcliffe in *Davis Contractors* v. *Fareham UDC* [1956] AC 696 at 729 (Eng).

[424] See *La Cumbre Golf Club* v. *Santa Barbara Hotel Co* 271 P. 2d 476 (1928, US).

materials purchased or the loss of the two weeks he had reserved to complete the work.

3. The common law doctrine of frustration is prospective in its effects; rights that have already fallen due at the time of discharge of the contract cannot be avoided in the name of frustration.[425] So, if Y, prior to the frustrating event, was liable to have paid X any part of the contract price, that portion, or instalment, would still be payable, at least according to the accrued rights theory and the line of case law that is marked by *Chandler* v. *Webster*,[426] an English 'coronation case'. However, in a later English case, *Fibrosa*,[427] the House of Lords reversed the rule in *Chandler* v. *Webster*. It was held that a court could order the return of money that was paid in advance of discharge if the payor has received none of the benefit expected by him, i.e., if there was a complete failure of performance. The corollary of this was that, if such money was payable in advance of discharge, it would no longer be payable if the payor would receive none of the benefit expected by him.

4. In England, the Law Reform (Frustrated Contracts) Act 1943 was enacted shortly after the *Fibrosa* decision. Section 1(2) of the 1943 Act provides that sums paid under the contract in advance of the frustrating event may be recovered by the payor, and sums payable in advance of the frustrating event shall cease to be so payable. If the payee has incurred expenses the court may allow him to retain part or all of the advance sum to cover these expenses. Section 1(2) differed from the common law position under *Fibrosa* in that under the Act the payor's right to recover sums paid in advance is not dependent on there being a failure of consideration (i.e., complete non performance by the payee) and it is possible for the payee to retain a sum to cover his expenses. Thus, under the Act, if X was paid in advance of the frustrating event, X would have to return the sum paid to Y, or if a sum was payable to X it would cease to be so payable, but X could apply to the court to allow him to retain part or all of the advance sum to cover his expenses, namely the cost of purchasing the materials. However, as this essentially means that Y shoulders X's loss, the courts will not always grant this, particularly if Y has also incurred expenses or loss,[428] or if X can recoup his loss elsewhere, for example by using the materials on another project.

[425] See *Herman* v. *SS Vicia* [1942] IR 304. [426] [1904]1 KB 493 (Eng).
[427] *Fibrosa Spolka Akcyjna* v. *Fairbairn Lawson Combe Barbour Ltd* [1942] 2 All ER 122.
[428] See *Gamerco* v. *ICM/Fair Warning* [1995] 1 WLR 1226.

5. In Ireland, the law is unclear on this issue. There is no equivalent of the Law Reform (Frustrated Contracts) Act 1943 and no Irish court has ruled on this point. However, it is likely that the courts would favour *Fibrosa* to *Chandler* v. *Webster*, as the latter is now viewed as little more than an anomaly in the development of the law of unjust enrichment and the Irish courts will allow recovery of money paid where there has been a total failure of performance.[429] There is clearly a total failure of consideration in this case as Y has received none of the bargained for performance. Thus, Y could recover any money paid to X in advance of the storm, and would not have to pay it if it were payable. The fact that X bought materials would not be relevant here, as the important question would be whether X had provided any of the bargained for performance. This can be seen in *Fibrosa* where it was held that there was a total failure of consideration (performance) even though the sellers of the machinery had incurred expenses in constructing the machinery.[430] X might be able to retain a sum to cover his expenses on the basis of the defence of change of position.[431] However, X would not be able to rely on such expenditure to the extent that it was not in fact wasted, or if it was not made in reliance on the payment of the advance sum.

Scotland

X has no remedy against Y (neither based on contract nor on unjustified enrichment).

I. 1. Case 5 is an example of 'frustration of purpose', in other words where '. . . supervening events have so greatly reduced the value to him [i.e., the recipient of goods or services] of the other party's performance that he should no longer be bound to accept it and to pay the agreed price.'[432] The contract would be frustrated, thus releasing both parties from future performance from the moment of the frustrating event, i.e., the destruction of the house. The parties would be automatically released from their future obligations and neither would need to provide notice to the other.

2. Two important Scottish cases are potentially in point here. The cases mark a step in the development from a limited notion of frustration, applying to cases of *rei interitus* (destruction of leased subjects),

[429] See *United Dominions Trust (Ireland) Ltd* v. *Shannon Caravans Ltd* [1976] IR 225.
[430] Although on the facts of the case the machinery could be sold on to a third party.
[431] See *Westdeutsche Landesbank* v. *Islington BC* [1994] 4 All ER 890, 914 per Hobhouse J.
[432] Peel, *Treitel's Law of Contract*, para. 19-041.

towards what was treated as 'constructive' *rei interitus*. The idea developed in these two cases is that where the supervening event so markedly affects the performance of the contract, this is the equivalent of destruction of the subject. The first case is *Tay Salmon Fisheries Co Ltd* v. *Speedie*[433] in which a fishing company was the tenant of salmon fishings under a lease for nineteen fishing seasons. The area within which the fishings would take place was converted by law into a zone for aerial gunnery and bombing practice. The right to fishings granted by the lease was thereby rendered incapable of use by the tenant. It was held that, because the landlord was unable to provide the tenant with possession of the leased subject, the tenant was entitled to abandon the lease. Lord Sands commented:

> I think that the tenants are not entitled to resile from the lease, unless they are in a position to show that the exercise of their right under the lease has been so curtailed, not merely theoretically but practically, as to be substantially destroyed, or so completely altered, not merely in legal quality but in practical operation, as to change the character of the subject.[434]

Tay Salmon is not a case of actual *rei interitus* given that the salmon fishings continued to exist. It was simply impossible for the tenant to exercise this right. So similarly, in Case 5 the change in circumstances has resulted in Y being entirely unable to enjoy the services of X. Performance in accordance with the contract would be utterly changed in nature and would provide Y with something different from what was anticipated when the contract was entered into.

3. The second relevant Scottish case is *Mackeson* v. *Boyd*[435] in which a tenant had taken a lease of a furnished house for nineteen years from 1926. Following the outbreak of war, the house was requisitioned by military authorities and the tenant was excluded from the premises. The tenant raised an action of declarator that the lease had ceased to bind him. The court found in favour of the tenant, indicating that there had been '... constructive total destruction' of the subject let.[436] As in the previous case, the subject was not destroyed. Nevertheless, the tenant was unable to obtain the benefit of the landlord's performance.

4. On the authority of the two cases discussed above, it is suggested that the contract in Case 5 is frustrated, on grounds of frustration of

[433] 1929 SC 593. [434] *Ibid.* [435] 1942 SC 56.
[436] *Ibid.*, per the Lord President (Normand) at 61.

purpose. X's performance is practically worthless for Y. Both parties will be released from performance of the contract.

5. Given that frustration frees the parties from future performance, Y is not required to pay the contract price. The contract is not rendered void nor voidable by the frustrating event. Rights which have accrued under the contract prior to the frustrating event can be enforced. X's purchase of materials seems to be preparatory work only. The contract will probably not contain an obligation on Y to pay for the materials which would be enforceable by X. Thus, the fact that one can enforce accrued rights notwithstanding frustration is of little use to X. X cannot recover the cost of materials from Y.

II. The *condictio causa data causa non secuta* is potentially available as a remedy where sums expended for a particular purpose can be repaid where that purpose fails. As already explained, this remedy is limited in scope, applying only to require the enriched party to return the enrichment. This action is, however, of no assistance to X. Y has not been enriched. The facts suggest that the materials have not been delivered to Y. There is no mechanism in Scots law which would require Y to pay a sum representing X's wasted expenditure. X therefore has no remedy in Scots law. The deficiency of Scots law in this respect has been commented on as follows:

> ... principles of unjustified enrichment cannot accommodate losses arising from one party's expenditure in expectation of performance of a contract, if this expenditure has not resulted in a benefit to the other party. In these circumstances it is thought that a legislative regime is required to provide an equitable readjustment of any losses which the parties have sustained because their contract has been frustrated.[437]

Editors' comparative notes

The open jurisdictions

Y may terminate the contract in all the open jurisdictions. This is generally based on provisions on contracts for work and services in the civil codes concerned. The essential question, however, is whether and to what extent Y has to compensate X as a result of his termination.

[437] MacQueen and Thomson, *Contract Law*, para. 4.85.

In most of the open jurisdictions, the amount of compensation is calculated by taking the contract price as the basis from which the expenses that X saves by not having to perform are deducted. This is the solution in Austria, Germany, Greece, Italy, the Netherlands, Portugal and Spain. On the basis of this calculation, X will be awarded the profits that he was entitled to realise under the contract.

However, some of the reporters indicate that even though Y is in principle entitled to claim the expected profits the amount may be reduced because the reason for the termination of the contractual exchange is a natural disaster and thus a cause beyond X's foresight and control (Germany, the Netherlands, Portugal and Spain). In Lithuania, Y appears to be even fully discharged from any compensation because of the supervening event. Under German law, the equitable reduction of the compensation is based on the doctrine of *Störung der Geschäftsgrundlage* and is likely to lead to a compensation that covers X's full expenses, but only half of his profits. By contrast, the Austrian and the Greek reporters comment that the doctrine of *Geschäftsgrundlage* cannot be used to reduce X's claim for his contractual profits as the rules on contracts for works entitle the contractor to full compensation of his expected profits. In Greece, this is considered to be a more specific allocation of risk which has priority over the equitable rules of *Geschäftsgrundlage*.

The closed jurisdictions

In all the closed jurisdictions, with perhaps the exception of Belgium and France, Y may terminate the contract and thereby prevent the contract from being performed. Again, the decisive question is whether and to what extent Y has to compensate X.

Y can terminate the contract regardless of frustration but must compensate X for the profits X could have expected under the contract in Belgium, Czech Republic, Denmark and Slovenia; a similar approach can be observed in the French and the Belgian report.

In England, Ireland and Scotland, on the other hand, the contract can be avoided based on the doctrine of frustration of purpose. England and Ireland will allow for an equitable distribution of the losses. Under Scottish law, the doctrine of *condictio causa data causa non secuta* is resorted to as the potential basis of compensation after termination of the contract. Yet, a valid claim under this doctrine would only be available if Y was enriched by the cancelled exchange. As Y is not enriched in our case, this doctrine will not allow Y to claim compensation.

Conclusions

In all jurisdictions (with perhaps the exception of Belgium and France), Y may cancel the contract for works so that the contract will not be performed in kind. The rationale is that the destruction of the house has rendered the works useless. Therefore the decisive question is only whether and to what extent Y must compensate X.

There is a strong tendency in both the open and the closed jurisdictions that Y is entitled to compensation on the basis of his contractual profits (contract price less expenses). Yet, there is a significant division with regard to the extent of compensation: in some of the open and closed jurisdictions, X will be awarded the full profits to be expected under the contract and no equitable reduction is granted to Y (Belgium, Czech Republic, Denmark and Slovenia; cf. also France). This 'full profit approach' can be contrasted with the position that X's claim for his contractual profits has to be adjusted by some form of equitable reduction (England, Germany, Ireland, the Netherlands, Spain, Sweden). Only very few reports indicate that due to termination of the contract, there is no basis for compensation at all (Lithuania, Scotland).

It is remarkable that, in this case, by adjusting the amount of compensation payable after the contract has been discharged by frustration, the closed jurisdictions of England and Ireland present a result that is comparable to an adjustment of the contract granted by many of the open jurisdictions.

Case 6 Confiscation of petrol

Government intervention makes the use of a rented petrol station impossible

X leases a petrol station from Y. Due to the outbreak of war, the government confiscates all petrol in that area and it is impossible for X to obtain petrol from any source. As a result, X can make no use of the petrol station. He stops the payment on the lease.

Is X's refusal to pay the rent justified?

Germany and related jurisdictions

Germany

X can primarily ask for an adjustment of the contract according to §313 I BGB. In the given case, it might be appropriate to

suspend the contract for the duration of the confiscation. In addition, the losses of either party should be calculated; if Y's losses exceed X's loss, Y should be entitled to claim compensation for half of this difference.[438]

I. 1. The rules on mistake (§119 BGB) do not apply because the agreement is consistent with X's actual will at the time of contracting (see §119 I BGB) and the impossibility of obtaining petrol from any source obviously does not qualify under §119 II BGB as a 'quality' of the petrol station, the subject-matter of the contract.[439]

2. The rules on impossibility (§§275, 326 BGB) are not applicable either. X still has possession of the petrol station, i.e., the specific performance of Y's contractual obligation is possible.

II. 1. If the parties contracted the lease for a fixed period of time, it has to be considered whether X can terminate early only on grounds that justify a termination without notice (§542 II BGB). In the given case, the requirements of §542 II BGB are not met. There is no substantial defect as to the quality of the petrol station that amounts to an 'important reason' by statutory qualification (§543 II no. 1 BGB) nor is there an 'important reason' according to the general rule (§543 I 2 BGB).[440] The latter provision requires that the important reason emanates from the sphere of the *other* party,[441] which is *not* true with regard to the impossibility to obtain petrol. Additionally, the consequences of a mere termination of the contract are inequitable in the given case. If the contract is terminated, the losses resulting from war and confiscation are attributed solely to Y. Furthermore, termination cancels the contract for the rest of its regular duration while the confiscation may only be of a temporary nature. Therefore, a more flexible relief is preferable.

2. If the parties did not limit the period of the lease in the contract, X has the right to terminate the contract according to §580a II BGB because the petrol station qualifies as business premises. Therefore, X can terminate the contract with a six month notice at the end of March, July, September

[438] However, the decision RGZ 94, 267 holds that the lessee is relieved completely from his obligation to pay the rent for the time during which the gas station cannot be used.

[439] For further details about the requirements of §119 II BGB see Cases 5 and 8.

[440] The general right to terminate long-term contracts for valid reasons and without notice (§314 BGB) is subsidiary to the special provisions about the termination of a lease without notice in §543 II BGB; cf. C. Grüneberg, '§314', in: Palandt *et al.* (eds.), *Bürgerliches Gesetzbuch* n. 6.

[441] Cf. W. Weidenkaff, '§543', in: Palandt *et al.* (eds.), *Bürgerliches Gesetzbuch* n. 5; for further details cf. Case 8.

or December.[442] The right to terminate the contract without notice according to §543 BGB is also applicable to leases without a limited duration; nevertheless its conditions are not met in the given case.

III. 1. Since the issue in the case at hand is a frustration of purpose ('*Vereitelung des Verwendungszwecks*') the concept of *Störung der Geschäftsgrundlage* (§313 BGB) may provide an equitable solution.[443] In general, this concept is not superseded by the right to terminate the lease without notice according to §543 BGB.[444] An 'important reason' emanating from the sphere of the *burdened* party or from the *neutral* sphere may render it unreasonable for one party to be bound by the contract considering all circumstances and balancing the interest of both parties. The burdened party may therefore terminate the contract on the basis of §313 III BGB unless the adaptation of the contract is reasonable.

2. First, there has to be a basic assumption shared by both parties at the time of contracting or at least an assumption of X recognisable to Y and uncontested by him. It might be argued that the possibility of obtaining petrol qualifies as a basic assumption. However, the actual assumption shared by both parties was the absence of war as, in general, Y is not concerned with X's sources of supply. Both parties share the fundamental assumption that the economy will not be disrupted by war. The outbreak of a war falls within the scope of the so-called '*Große Geschäftsgrundlage*'. This expression refers to grave changes in the political, economic, and social conditions.[445] These conditions alter the contractual framework fundamentally and they are beyond the regular scope of the contractual and statutory risk allocation. Furthermore, the resulting burden for one party is purely accidental. The '*Große Geschäftsgrundlage*' is a subdivision of the so-called '*objektive Geschäftsgrundlage*',[446] which includes all circumstances and conditions

[442] Cf. W. Weidenkaff, '§580a', in: Palandt *et al.* (eds.), *Bürgerliches Gesetzbuch*, nn. 13 *et seq.* If the contract is a usufructuary lease according to §581 BGB the contract can only be terminated with a six month notice period at the end of every anniversary of the commencement of the contract.

[443] For general remarks about the frustration of purpose cf. Case 5.

[444] Cf. W. Weidenkaff, '§543', in: Palandt *et al.* (eds.), *Bürgerliches Gesetzbuch*, n. 8.

[445] Like war, conditions similar to war, natural disasters and government intervention; cf. Grüneberg, '§313', in: Palandt *et al.* (eds.), *Bürgerliches Gesetzbuch*, n. 5; Roth, '§313', in: Krüger (ed.), *Münchener Kommentar zum Bürgerlichen Gesetzbuch*, vol. II, nn. 49 *et seq.*, 189 *et seq.*

[446] Cf. Grüneberg, '§313', in: Palandt *et al.* (eds.), *Bürgerliches Gesetzbuch*, n. 4; Larenz, *Schuldrecht I*, §21 II = p. 324; for critics cf. Roth, '§313', in: Krüger (ed.), *Münchener Kommentar zum Bürgerlichen Gesetzbuch*, vol. II, nn. 49 *et seq.*

that form (from an objective point of view) the necessary foundations of the contract. The absence of those conditions normally renders the contractual agreement useless. According to the majority opinion in legal writing the parties do not have to ground the agreement explicitly on those fundamental conditions either in the wording of the agreement or by reference to it during the negotiations.[447] Thus, this term covers all conditions that form the basis of the contractual agreement as a matter of fact.

3. Second, there is no doubt that the circumstances in question were of a substantial effect on the *Geschäftsgrundlage*, i.e., there has been a massive change of the relevant circumstances. If the parties had foreseen the outbreak of the war and the confiscation of all petrol in the area at the time of formation, X would not have entered into the contract.

4. Third, if the contract is upheld as originally agreed upon, X is *unreasonably burdened*. As a general rule, the lessee bears the risk that he can achieve his purpose of use.[448] This general risk allocation is also valid for commercial leases.[449] Only in exceptional cases did the courts consider the availability of raw material needed for the production of goods as '*Geschäftsgrundlage*' in the case of a lease of a factory.[450]

5. Nevertheless, in the given case, X's purpose of use is frustrated by the outbreak of the war and the confiscation of all petrol. This alteration of circumstances results in an excessive and inappropriate burden for X. This substantial change in the social condition is neither allocated by the contract nor the statutory law of obligations. Thus, the frustration of purpose by a grave affection of the so-called '*Große Geschäftsgrundlage*' substantially deviates from the 'normal' cases of frustration of purpose. It fundamentally alters the basis of the contractual framework. Additionally, the resulting burden for X is purely accidental. Therefore, the conditions of a relevant *Grundlagenstörung* are met.[451]

6. However, it has to be mentioned that the rules of '*Störung der Geschäftsgrundlage*' are *not* applicable if the grave alteration of the social or economic circumstances does not result in a distortion of the

[447] Cf. BGHZ 131, 209 (215); Larenz, *Schuldrecht I*, §21 II = p. 324; Grüneberg, '§313', in: Palandt *et al.* (eds.), *Bürgerliches Gesetzbuch*, n. 4.

[448] BGH NJW 1981, 2405 (2406); BGH NJW 1970, 1313; Roth, '§313', in: Krüger (ed.), *Münchener Kommentar zum Bürgerlichen Gesetzbuch*, vol. II, n. 203; Grüneberg, '§313', in: Palandt *et al.* (eds.), *Bürgerliches Gesetzbuch*, n. 36.

[449] Cf. Case 8.

[450] Cf. BGH NJW 1958, 785; see also BGH NJW 1953, 1751 (*Bootshaus*).

[451] Cf. Grüneberg, '§313', in: Palandt *et al.* (eds.), *Bürgerliches Gesetzbuch*, nn. 5, 36 *et seq.*

equivalence of exchange,[452] a frustration of purpose or a hardship for one party, i.e., an undue burden with regard to specific performance. This concept cannot serve as a device for the judiciary to relieve the (financial) burden resulting from social or economic catastrophes in general.[453]

Austria

Under Austrian law, a special rule for lease contracts provides that the lessee (X) does not have to pay rent when the premises cannot be used due to extraordinary circumstances like war, fire and the like. The rules on mistake do not provide any relief here, because a mistake, misconception or lack of knowledge of future events does not qualify as a relevant mistake under §871 ABGB (no '*Geschäftsirrtum*').[454] The rules on impossibility do not apply either.

I. §1104 ABGB provides that where a leased property cannot be used as a result of extraordinary events, such as conflagration, war, epidemics, large area flooding, thunderstorms or general crop failure, no rent has to be paid. The application of §1104 ABGB requires adverse circumstances that affect a plurality of persons and prevent the lessee from using the leased property as intended.[455] The Austrian OGH already held that confiscations due to military measures fall within the scope of §1104 ABGB.[456] Therefore X's refusal to pay the rent is justified under Austrian Law.

II. Under Austrian law '*Wegfall der Geschäftsgrundlage*' is a subsidiary doctrine that only applies where more specific provisions do not exist.[457] Therefore, §1104 ABGB on lease contracts has priority in this case. The Austrian legislator assigned the risk that the leased property is not usable to the lessor regardless of fault. This includes events by force majeure.[458] This strict rule is obviously justified by social and economic reasons in view

[452] Cf. Cases 1–4.

[453] Cf. Grüneberg, '§313', in: Palandt *et al.* (eds.), *Bürgerliches Gesetzbuch*, n. 5.

[454] Rummel, '§871', in: Rummel (ed.), *Kommentar zum ABGB*, vol. I, n 9; Koziol and Welser, *Bürgerliches Recht*, vol. I, pp. 162 *et seq.*

[455] Würth, '§1104', in: Rummel (ed.), *Kommentar zum ABGB*, vol. I, n. 4; Iro, '§1104', in: Koziol, P. Bydlinski, and Bollenberger (eds.), *Kurzkommentar zum ABGB*, n. 2.

[456] OGH, EvBl 1957, 237 = Miet 4988.

[457] Rummel, '§901', in: Rummel (ed.), *Kommentar zum ABGB*, vol. I, nn. 4, 6 with further references.

[458] *Bericht der Kommission für Justizgegenstände über die Gesetzesvorlage betreffend die Änderung und Ergänzung einiger Bestimmungen des ABGB*, 78 Blg Sten Prot HH 21. Sess (1912) p. 199.

of agricultural properties. In many cases a lessee who innocently loses his profits from the leased premises will be unable to pay the rent. He might be driven into financial ruin if he had to pay the rent. The legislator has chosen to provide protection for him in such cases assuming that the risk may be more easily absorbed by the lessor than by the lessee whose business will most likely be ruined under such circumstances.

The Netherlands

X is not allowed to refuse payment. A war affects life in many ways and large groups of the society will suffer the consequences. If the government confiscates all petrol in a certain area, X has a claim against the government but not against Y who incidentally happens to lease land or petrol stations. It would be contrary to reasonableness and fairness to correct the consequences of the war for the incidental benefit of X only.

I. The ultimate remedy for X might be an early termination of the lease. If Y refuses such a termination, Dutch law provides for early termination only in connection with persistent or material default by the lessee. Furthermore, specific termination rights exist for lease contracts with a duration of more than two years. In all cases, the termination of a commercial lease contract is relatively difficult if it is not linked to the duration of the lease. In case of a longer duration, the *clausula rebus sic stantibus* doctrine (codified in Art. 6:258 Dutch Civil Code) might apply.

II. 1. Art. 6:258 applies if the relevant circumstances (i.e., the cutting off of petrol supplies due to war) are unforeseen and not reasonably foreseeable; also, such circumstances must be highly prohibitive for X's business. However, X is free to undertake alternative activities in the petrol station. Furthermore, the case does not contain elements that would require a shift of the risks involved in X's business to Y's business: the availability of petrol is a risk associated with the business of running a petrol station whereas the risk of a refusal to grant a permit to build petrol stations or of all petrol station lessees being declared bankrupt is typical for Y's business. The case then turns to the question whether the lease contract implied a certain risk allocation that the consequences of its materialisation should be for the account of either or both parties.

2. This question has been discussed comprehensively in the literature where scholars refer freely to foreign treatises such as Larenz's *Geschäftsgrundlage und Vertragserfüllung*, or the well-known English coronation cases.

III. The law on agricultural leaseholds might point to a solution for the present case. There, the recently introduced rule in Art. 7:330 specifically provides that an adjustment of the lease cannot be based on circumstances for which the lessee can insure itself, for which it is able to have recourse against a third party or which are otherwise within the sphere of the lessee's responsibility. In the current case, the lessee should be entitled to claim damages from the government (for the confiscation of any fuel). Similarly, inspiration may be found in transportation law. Article 8:396 Dutch Civil Code provides that each party may terminate the contract if circumstances such as war occur on the side of the carrier.[459] These sources of inspiration tend to disfavour X, who should have recourse against the government. Furthermore, the principle of reasonableness and fairness would require that circumstances that affect society as a whole be compensated generally rather than being corrected on a case-by-case basis. Furthermore, it is contrary to the standard of reasonableness and fairness to assign particular risks of X's business to Y, in other words the availability of petrol is a risk which falls within X's sphere of responsibility.

IV. X might argue that he is affected by force majeure (i.e., a temporary or lasting impossibility) making it impossible to perform (on time). Articles 6:74 and 75 Dutch Civil Code, however, attribute the consequences of such impossibility entirely to X. The war or the unavailability of petrol may excuse payment on the agreed day, but will certainly not entitle X to cancel instalments or reduce the lease sum. If there is a clear relation between the lease sum and the possibility of exploiting the petrol station as such, there may be a ground to shift part of the risk to Y. But there are no indications that could justify such a 'complementary interpretation' of the contract.[460]

[459] Cf. H. C. F. Schoordijk, *Het algemeen gedeelte van het verbintenissenrecht naar het Nieuw Burgerlijk Wetboek* (Deventer: Kluwer, 1979), pp. 528 *et seq.*; P. Abas, *Rebus sic stantibus* (Deventer: Kluwer, 1989), pp. 215 *et seq.*

[460] The solution might be different if Y had a contract with the government obliging him to distribute petrol in a certain manner, both in terms of exploiting petrol stations and in terms of distributing petrol amongst its franchisees in the petrol reseller chain. In that case, Y is the principal of the franchise chain as well as the supplier of petrol (and the purchasing of petrol will likely be an exclusive obligation or tied with other franchise-related obligations and benefits). In such a case, Y has a greater responsibility than the mere renting of petrol stations (or land). It remains doubtful, however, whether X's refusal to pay rent is justified by the impossibility of reselling petrol or rather by the connected breach by X of not supplying petrol (even if such supply is not subject to an exclusive purchase obligation – which would anyhow be contrary to competition law prohibitions).

Eastern European jurisdictions

Slovenia

X is entitled to demand termination of the contract on grounds of a change of circumstances (Arts. 112–15 CO). If the contract is concluded for an indefinite period of time, X has the right to terminate the contract by notice (Art. 616 CO).

I. The rules regarding impossibility (Art. 116 CO) are not applicable in the present case, because the performances of the parties have not become impossible. It is still possible for Y to let the petrol station to X. It is only the commercial use intended by both parties that has become impossible.

II. The rules regarding mistake (Art. 46 CO) are also inapplicable, because there were no irregularities as to the formation of the will of the parties at the time of conclusion of the contract. Furthermore, the fact that it is impossible to obtain petrol cannot be considered as a characteristic of a petrol station. It is rather a circumstance that occurred after the conclusion of the contract and mistakes regarding future developments do not allow for an action on grounds of mistake.

III. The rules with respect to warranty for defects of the object of the lease (Art. 597 CO) are inapplicable, because the impossibility of obtaining petrol cannot be considered a defect of the petrol station. The same is true regarding the rules on force majeure (Art. 617 CO).

IV. 1. Under Slovenian law, X is entitled to terminate the contract according to the rules of unexpected circumstances. In the present case both parties have concluded the contract, based on the presumption, that X would be able to exploit the petrol station in the usual way (i.e., selling fuel). Due to government intervention this has become impossible. From X's point of view, the purpose he pursued has been frustrated. The change of circumstances is so significant that the contract obviously no longer complies with the expectations of both parties and it would be unjust, according to general opinion, to keep it in force as it was concluded (as required by Art. 112(1) CO). A confiscation of petrol due to an outbreak of war is generally speaking not a circumstance that should normally be taken into consideration. It might be different, if there were a war or an acute threat of war in the country where the parties are operating.[461]

[461] There is, however, no (known) case law dealing with contracts concluded during or just before the war in former Yugoslavia, dealing with this issue.

2. If the court dissolves the contract, it will award Y (upon his request) compensation of a just part of damages suffered by the dissolution of the contract. 'Just' means that general rules regarding compensation by way of damages (including the lost profit) are not applicable. The amount of just compensation is left to the discretion of the court but it may not amount to full compensation (Art. 112(5) CO).[462]

Lithuania

The contract can be terminated or adjusted under Lithuanian law.

I. In this case, the doctrine of mistake is not applicable, as mistake requires that the relevant facts existed at the time when the contract was concluded (Art. 1.90 CC). Neither the war nor the relevant actions of the government existed at the time when the contract was concluded.

II. The doctrine of impossibility is also not applicable in this case, as it is acknowledged that a monetary obligation can always be performed.[463] It is specifically emphasised in Art. 6.212 CC that the lack of financial resources does not constitute a situation of force majeure. Similarly, X had no right to suspend performance of his monetary obligation either, as according to Art. 6.58 CC, it is only possible to suspend the performance of an obligation in the case of a failure of the other party to perform its obligations.

III. The general norms of the CC on the termination of a lease contract, which would also be applicable to this case, establish the right of a lessee to dissolve a lease if the leased object becomes unfit for use by virtue of a circumstance the lessee is not liable for (Art. 6.498 (2) CC). The concept 'unfit for use' ought to be interpreted in its narrow sense, i.e., unfit to be used for the purpose for which it has been leased. The lease contract was concluded for the purpose of selling petrol, but the war and the actions of the government made it impossible to acquire petrol. Thus the petrol station is no longer fit to be used for its purpose. The shortage of petrol cannot be attributed to X, so the war and the actions of the government should be regarded as force majeure. This conclusion is also supported by a judgment of the Supreme Court of Lithuania: the plaintiff leased a piece of land for the construction of a petrol station. However, after the contract was concluded, the local municipality changed the purpose of the land and the construction of a petrol station

[462] Dolenc in: Juhart and Plavšak (eds.), *Obligacijski zakonik*, vol. I, p. 607.
[463] Mikelenas, *The Law of Obligations. Part I*, p. 183.

on that particular plot was forbidden. The lessee demanded the dissolution of the lease contract on the basis of Art. 6.498(2) CC and the relevant court practice arguing that the change of circumstances would make it impossible for him to use the land for the contractually stipulated purpose. The court supported his view and acknowledged his right to dissolve the contract.[464] As the contract is being dissolved due to circumstances which constitute force majeure, Y is not entitled to demand compensation for the income he did not receive or any other losses.

IV. As Art. 6.498(2) CC is a special norm in respect of Art. 6.204 CC, the dissolution of the contract will not be governed by Art. 6.204 CC. If Y is interested in preserving the contract he could refer to Art. 6.487(1) CC. This norm allows the lessee to demand a reduction of the rent if due to circumstances he is not responsible for, the conditions of the use of the object have essentially worsened. In this case, Y is not able to use the petrol station for its purpose due to force majeure. Consequently, he is entitled to demand not only a reduction of the payment, but also to be exempted from the payment of the whole rent for the period he is not able to sell petrol. Thus, both the dissolution of the lease and its modification are regulated by special norms of the CC. Therefore, Art. 6.204 CC as the general norm is not applicable in this case.

Czech Republic

X may withdraw from the lease contract either on the grounds of frustration of the purpose of contract (provided the purpose is expressed therein) or because the petrol station (the subject matter of the lease) became unfit for the agreed use. Since the outbreak of war and subsequent confiscation can be considered force majeure, Y's liability for damage is likely to be excluded.

I. As explained in the overview (Chapter 4), the concept of 'mistake' presupposes that the other contracting party caused the mistake of the first party or at least knew of the mistake (Section 49a Civil Code).

II. If the basic purpose expressed in the contract was frustrated by fundamental change of circumstances, then the affected party can withdraw from the contract (Section 356 Commercial Code).

III. Under Section 679(1) Civil Code, a lease contract may also be terminated by the lessee if the property becomes unfit for the agreed or usual use and/or becomes unusable.

464 LAT, Judgment of 20 October 2003, Case No 3K-3–896/2003.

IV. The outbreak of war is a typical circumstance having the character of force majeure. In this situation, the lessee may withdraw from the lease agreement without further consequences. It is the lessor who bears the risk of such an event. According to Section 374(1) Commercial Code,[465] liability for damage is excluded.

Scandinavian jurisdictions

Sweden

Under Swedish law, X is entitled to termination with nine month's notice under the general rules on rent of real estate. There may also be sufficient other grounds for termination without such a long notice period.

I. In this case the 'lease of a petrol station' is to be considered a rent of real estate ('*hyra av fast egendom*') under Chapter 12 Section 1(1) Code of Land Laws. The rental period is unspecified. Such a contract is, under Chapter 12 Section 3(1) indefinitely binding ('*obestämd tid*'), and requires notice for termination. The time of notice would, under Section 4(1)(ii), normally be nine months.[466]

II. The confiscation of petrol relates to an ordinary performance assumption, which has to do with X's use of the performance received from Y. None of the rules on extraordinary termination in Chapter 12 of the Code of Land Laws are applicable. Nor is the landlord's responsibility for the quality of the rented object relevant in this case.

III. War is generally not force majeure to a monetary obligation, as the war does not make it more difficult to effect the payment. In the event of war, danger of war or other exceptional conditions as set out in the Moratorium Act,[467] the government is entitled to designate a moratorium as to payment obligations. However, this only postpones the duty to fulfil the obligation.

IV. Under the doctrine of assumptions, a contract may be terminated if an erroneous assumption related to the performance received (a 'performance assumption') is based upon facts that are visible to the

465 Tomsa in: Štenglová, Pliva and Tausa (eds.), *Obchcdní zākauík Komeutář*, p. 1093.

466 The notice must be in writing, under Section 8(1) if the rental has lasted for more than three months (however, an oral notice from X would have been sufficient if confirmed by Y in writing). Simply stopping the payments does not qualify as notice.

467 Lag (1940:300) angående förordnande om anstånd med betalning av gäld m.m. (moratorielag).

other party, or the assumption is common to the parties and the other party – as a result of the fact that the assumption was erroneous – made a profit at the expense of the deprived party. At least in older case law, the requirement for profit has been considered to have been met when, in a long-term contract where compensation is paid continually, the value of the performance has decreased.[468] Under this rule, termination would be possible in this case.

V. The war and the confiscation of petrol are changed circumstances, which could be considered under Section 36 Contracts Act, which is applicable not only when a contract term is unfair as such but also when its application in a specific case is unfair due to changed circumstances. It is difficult to say how a Swedish court would approach an extraordinary case like this. It might be of importance whether the war and its consequences as to petrol were foreseeable for the parties at the time of the formation of the contract. On the other hand, it is possible that the war would be considered a ground for adjustment per se. It is also possible that the contract would be considered unreasonable only after the expiration of some time, when the amount X has to pay has become high enough.

VI. The principle that a long-term contract can normally be cancelled following the occurrence of extraordinary circumstances (‘*viktig grund*’) would probably be applied considering the impact of the war on X’s use of the petrol station. However, the scope of application as well as the content of this principle is unclear.

Denmark

Under Danish law, the contract can be set aside by a court based on Section 36 Contracts Act or on the doctrine of assumptions.

I. In dealing with subsequent circumstances, it is not possible to invoke mistake in accordance with Section 32(1) Contracts Act. Upon the formation of the contract, neither X nor Y had any information concerning future government intervention.

II. The rules of impossibility can be invoked in this case if it is not possible for any petrol station in Denmark to provide fuel due to government intervention. However, X must be able to prove that nobody in Denmark is able to provide petrol (objective impossibility). Such governmental intervention would normally be considered force majeure

[468] See especially NJA 1918 p. 467, and Lehrberg, *Förutsättningsläran*, pp. 421–2. See also NJA 1911 p. 593. Compare NJA 1893 p. 433 and NJA 1916 p. 357.

provided the parties were not aware of such governmental intervention when the contract was entered into. Danish case law confirms that governmental confiscation amounts to force majeure in a time of war.[469] The condition of frustration is also fulfilled in the given case, which is a crucial factor that is rarely present in Danish case law. X is entitled to stop the payments to Y, but X must give notice to Y and explain why he considers himself entitled to do so. As discussed in the general remarks, the lapsing of a contract in conjunction with force majeure normally requires a period of six months. If X immediately stops the payments upon governmental confiscation, one could argue that he is violating the contract if he is not certain that the governmental confiscation will last for more than six months. X would then be liable towards Y.

III. As in Case 5, one could argue that the doctrine of assumptions should be applied to this case, again with the crucial question of whether Y should bear the risk of the governmental confiscation of the petrol.

IV. When Section 36 was incorporated in the Contracts Act, the provision gave rise to a substantial amount of case law with respect to agreements between oil companies, on the one hand, and petrol dealers on the other, since petrol dealers are considered to be in an inferior position compared to oil companies.[470] In 1985, the Danish Parliament (Folketinget) passed specific legislation to protect petrol dealers.[471] The legislation provides for specific rules; for instance on termination, competition clauses, minimum turnover and opening hours. Even though this specific legislation has diminished the relevance of Section 36 Contracts Act, the Act on Petrol Dealers does not deal with the issue in question.

V. If the petrol dealer only sells petrol and fuel-related products, which is very rarely the case in Denmark, the petrol dealer could, as the weaker party to the contract, invoke Section 36 Contracts Act or the doctrine of assumptions. The court could easily apply either rule, especially if it turns out that the war is a prolonged one. Thus, the contract would be set aside in its entirety.

[469] Cf. U 1923.343H, U 1945.738H, and U 1946.1241H.

[470] Cf. U 1987.243 H, U 1987.250 H, U 1987.526 H, U 1987.531 H, U 1988.1036 H, and U 1988.1042 H.

[471] Cf. Lov 1985-06-06 nr. 234 om benzinforhandlerkontrakter, which has been revised twice by L 1989-07-07 no. 376 and L 2000-05-31 no. 433.

Romanic-Mediterranean jurisdictions

Italy

X's refusal to pay the rent might be justified under Italian law.

I. The rules about mistake do not apply to the case at hand because, as already said,[472] mistake is relevant only if it concerns elements present at the time of the declaration, and does not cover future developments.

X's refusal to pay the rent is not justified as such. The confiscation of all petrol, due to the outbreak of the war, which determines the impossibility for X to obtain petrol from any source in that area, does not imply that the performance due by X is impossible. In fact, the payment of a sum of money may not be considered impossible in principle and therefore X may not refuse to pay and take legal action in order to be discharged according to the rules of impossibility (Arts. 1463 *et seq.* CC).

II. Although X is not entitled to terminate the contract, X has a unilateral right to withdraw from the contract as it is a lease contract (Arts. 1373(2) CC *et seq.*, Art. 4 l. 392/1978). The only requirement is six-month's notice, without any indemnification to Y, unless otherwise agreed in the contract.

III. 1. The case at issue presents the typical characteristics of frustration of purpose due to supervening unexpected events as far as the performance of X is concerned. This allows the application of the Italian doctrine of the implied condition, i.e., *presupposizione*.

2. It should therefore be examined whether or not the remedy of termination is applicable because the performance has become extremely onerous (Art. 1467 CC). As a matter of fact, the contractual obligations of both parties can be performed, but Y's performance has become substantially useless with regard to the purposes of X. This implies that the payment of the agreed rent could be deemed, assuming X's point of view, 'extremely onerous' (i.e., the payment is unreasonable, since the petrol station may not be actually used according to the contractual purpose). However, Art. 1467 CC allows for termination only if the burden is excessive and definitively produces an objective disproportion between the performances and thus Italian courts would grant this remedy only if the exceptional situation that renders the lease of the petrol station unreasonable (the war and the following confiscation of the petrol) lasts a certain period of time and the sum

[472] See Overview (Chapter 4).

that X has to pay becomes really disproportionate with regard to the interest of both parties.[473]

3. Italian courts have examined the possibility of raising a mere objection (in the case at issue, by X) against the request of an excessively onerous performance. The Supreme Court has decided in both ways[474] that it is allowed (or respectively not allowed) for the debtor to raise the objection of the excessive burden of the performance, independently of the request for the dissolution of the contract pursuant to Art. 1467 CC.[475] The current major opinion is, however, that the objection for excessive burden raised by the debtor against the request of performance must be formulated as a request for the dissolution of the contract.[476]

Spain

X's refusal to pay the rent is likely to be justified.

I. There is no specific statutory provision allowing one to terminate such a lease contract. A unilateral cancellation is only possible for the tenant of domestic property or if the contract was concluded for an indefinite period (see Case 5).

II. If Article 1105 CC on force majeure could be applied, X would be relieved from liability and his non-performance would be excused. However, this mechanism only applies if we consider that, unable to operate the petrol station, X has no means to pay the rent. In Spanish commercial practice, parties typically stipulate the consequences of force majeure. Therefore, it is unlikely that X can successfully invoke Article 1105 CC.

III. This is not a situation of mistake because the circumstances – the governmental confiscation of petrol due to war – were not present at the time the contract was concluded.

IV. In fact, this is a case in which the *causa* for X to contract disappears since he can no longer operate the petrol station for which he is paying rent. X no longer has a contractual interest in this agreement. The main requirements for the application of the disappearance of the basis of the

[473] Coll. arb., 12.08.1993, *Nuova giur. civ. comm.*, with observations by Cavanna, *Mutato contesto normativo e risoluzione per eccessiva onerosità*; Cass., 25 February 1993, n. 2338.

[474] Cass., 08 June 1984, n. 3450; and the opposite Cass., 13 December 1980, n. 6470.

[475] See above, Case 1, and overview (Chapter 4). For further information: Macario, 'Le sopravvenienze', in: Roppo (ed.), *Trattato del cautratto* (Milan: Giuffrè, 2006), ud. V, pp. 2, 653.

[476] Cass., 22 October 1998, n. 5724; Cass., 6 April 1987, n. 3321.

contract will apply: (i) the objective aim of the contract has lapsed as he can no longer operate the petrol station; (ii) it is evident to the other party that the intention to operate the petrol station was the decisive reason for X to contract; (iii) the party invoking the doctrine, X, has had no control over the events that have led to the disappearance of the *causa* (in fact, they were caused by a governmental measure); and, finally, (iv) the circumstances which led to the disappearance of the *causa* were unforeseeable.

Portugal

X can terminate the contract and refuse payment under Portuguese law.

I. It is economically impossible to operate a petrol station if, as a result of a war, the government confiscates all petrol. The problem is not one of legal impossibility – the government did not forbid the sale of petrol to the general public – but one of practical and economic impossibility (petrol becomes scarce and difficult to obtain in the market). However, in Portugal such a problem is not addressed by reference to the rules of impossibility of performance (it is still possible to perform and hardship, even rather serious, does not amount to impossibility) under Art. 437 CC.

II. 1. A war is an anomalous change of events. Due to the scarcity of petrol available to the civil population, to leave such a contract unchanged would amount to a result that is at odds with the requirement of good faith and to the economic balance that existed between performance and counter-performance. The case bears resemblance to a case decided by the Tribunal da Relação de Coimbra in 2006.[477] The owner of a petrol station and parking area adjacent to a major national road let the premises for a restaurant at a high monthly rent. The contract was entered into for a fixed period of five years but it could be renewed. At the time of conclusion there was a rumour in the media that a new highway might be built nearby. However, its precise location was still uncertain. Later on, the highway was built almost parallel to the road, diverting the vast majority of the clients of the petrol station – evidence was given of a loss of 90 per cent of the customers – and consequently also of the restaurant. The tenant informed the owner that he was not interested in renewing the contract but was also late with regard to the payment of the instalments concerning the last three

[477] 'Acórdão da Relação de Coimbra' of 31 January 2006, www.dgsi.pt.

months of the contract after the new highway had already diverted most customers. As the owner did not voluntarily agree on a price reduction, the case had to be solved by the court. The court decided in favour of the plaintiff, arguing that a reduction in the price was imperative in order to avoid an unjust result. The court decided that the reduction of the price should be proportional to the decrease of traffic.

2. The case illustrates the four requirements of Art. 437 CC: First, there was a supervening change in one of the circumstances that concerned the basis of the contract. It is not necessary to show conclusively that the intensity of the traffic was decisive for the will to contract; such an event is part of the objective basis of the contract. The purpose and the object of the contract was the fact that a restaurant formed part of a gas station and parking area adjacent to a main road. It is not necessary for such an event to result from the express will of the parties. Second, an anomalous change occurred when the highway was constructed parallel to the previous road. If the construction of the highway had already been foreseeable when the contract was agreed upon by the parties, the anomalous change would not necessarily have been unpredictable. Third, to keep the contract in force or even to keep it unchanged would have amounted to a result that would have been contrary to good faith. Furthermore, due to the extensive reduction of custumers, the landlord's performance is no longer an adequate counter-performance to the price. The fourth requirement is that the risk must not be inherent in the contract.

3. In practice, Art. 437 CC is conceived as subsidiary to other rules, namely contractual rules of adaptation of the contract, but also to other legal rules, such as the ones on the performance of the contracts. However, even if there are contractual rules, the courts will still apply Art. 437 CC and modify or terminate the contract if they believe that the adaptation rules, for instance, are themselves 'distorted' by a supervening change of the basis of the contract and that the application of such a clause would still lead to a result clearly contrary to good faith. The same applies to other legal rules: in this case, for instance, Art. 1040(2) CC concerning lease contracts establishes that if the usability of the object is affected, the lessee is entitled to a reduction of the rent if the reduction of the use extended to more than one sixth of the duration of the contract. In this case that did not occur since the contract lasted for five years and the reduction caused by the construction of highway lasted only for the final three months. However, the court still decided that Art. 437 CC could be invoked. The parallels of

this judgment and the case at hand suggest that Art. 437 CC can also be applied in the latter.

Greece

X may either terminate the contract based on a substantial reason pursuant to the principle of good faith (Art. 288 AK)[478] or request a judicial adjustment of the contract, resulting in a suspension of the contractual obligations. Under these conditions X can refuse to pay the rent.

I. The rules of mistake, especially as to the qualities of the contractual object (see Art. 142 AK) are not applicable. The availability of petrol cannot be considered a quality of the station. The same applies for the rules of impossibility, given that the debtor is in the position to provide the station to X.

II. Y is not in breach of any of his contractual obligations (see Art. 574 AK). X's refusal to pay the rent cannot be justified. In the given circumstances, Art. 596 §1 AK cannot be applied. According to this provision, the lessee is obliged to pay the rent, even if he is not using the leased object due to personal impediments. This general provision of the Civil Code also applies in the case of business leases given that the existing special legislation for the business lease (L Decree 34/1995) has no provision relevant to the issue whatsoever.[479]

III. On the contrary, general impediments or cases of force majeure that prevent a party from the use of the leased object for the agreed purpose, dismiss the lessee from the obligation to pay the rent.[480] The frustration of X's purpose to use the leased object was unpredictable and, furthermore, makes the use of the petrol station senseless. In other words, there is a substantial reason, which makes the maintenance of the contract an onerous burden for X giving him the right to terminate or suspend the validity of the contract.

[478] For the application of Art. 288 AK in business lease see Case 4.

[479] See Art 44 L.Degree 34/1995 and AP 182/2002, DEE 2002, 662; AP 491/1998, HellDni 1998, 1589; AP 1481/1996, HellDni 1997, 596; Panagiotes Filios, *Business Lease* (Athens-Komotini: Sakkoulas, 9th edn, 1996), §51 A-B pp. 184 *et seq.*; George Archaniotakis, *The Business Lease* (Athens/Thessalonica: Sakkoula, 2002), vol. I pp. 16–17 and vol. II (2003), p. 2, 99, 134; Ap. Georgiadis, *Law of Obligations – Special Part*, §29 n. 50.

[480] See Ap. Georgiadis, *Law of Obligations – Special Part*, vol. I, §24 n. 37; Konstantinos Kafkas, *Law of Obligations* (Athens: Sakkoula, 1975), vol. I, p. 326/7; M.G. Rapsomanikis, in: Georgiadis and Stathopoulos, *AK*, Art. 595–6 n. 5.

France and related jurisdictions

France

According to French law, X's refusal to pay the rent is justified.

I. Article 1722 Cciv allows a party to rescind a contract in the case of a partial or total impossibility of using the premises. In our case, the petrol station still exists, but it can no longer be used. Case law has extended the scope of Art. 1722 Cciv to cases where it is definitely and absolutely impossible to use the good according to its purpose.[481] The application of this provision will depend on how long the government measures are expected to last. If the duration is short, the lessee can invoke force majeure which results in the suspension of the contract when the obstacle is temporary. The judge will then have to determine whether the confiscation of the petrol is within the sphere of risks to be borne by the lessee.[482]

Belgium

X's refusal to pay the rent is justified under Belgian law.

I. Article 1722 Cciv allows a contract to be rescinded in the case of a partial or total impossibility of using the premises. Case law has extended the scope of Art. 1722 Cciv to cases where it is definitely and absolutely impossible to use goods according to their destination. A legal impossibility based on new government regulations falls within the scope of application of this provision.[483] The judge has to determine whether or not the confiscation of the fuel falls within the sphere of risks to be borne by the lessee. The consequences of Art. 1722 Cciv depend on the duration of the measures taken by the government. If they are temporary, the contract will be suspended; if the exploitation

[481] See Cass., 2 July 2003, *D.*, 2004, p. 1411;

[482] It is difficult to be more precise on this point because the concept of the allocation of risks is not frequently applied by the case law or discussed by legal authors in France.

[483] Cass., 9 January 1919, Pas., I, 1919, p. 82, BJ, 1919, p. 231; Cass., 5 July 1923, Pas., 1923, I, p. 410; comp. Cass., 27 June 1946, Pas., I, p. 270, RCJB, 1947, pp. 268 *et seq.*, conclusions of M. R. Hayoit de Termicourt, and observations of A. de Bersaques, Brussels, 21 April 1916 and 29 December 1915, Pas., 1915–1916, II, p. 254; civ. Bruges, 26 February 1917, Pas., 1918, III, p. 295 (the mere diminution of the clientele due to war does not lead to the application of Art. 1722 Cciv); civ. Liège, 21 January 1921, Pas., 1922, III, p. 61; See Cass., 5 December 1996, JLMB, 1997, p. 64. See P.-A. Foriers, *La caducité*, Thesis (Brussels: PUB, 1998); P.-A. Foriers, 'La caducité revisitée, A propos de l'arrêt du 21 janvier 2000', 2000 *JT*, 676.

of the petrol station is impossible and this is irreversible, the contract will be brought to an end.

II. The doctrine of *caducité* could also apply when there is a legal impossibility to perform the contract.[484] The lessee could be released on this basis. However, *caducité* is not applicable in cases of temporary obstacles.[485]

England and related jurisdictions

England and Ireland

The chances of X being discharged from the lease are increased if (i) there is an express term in the contract which states that the petrol station can only be used for the sale of petrol, or if such a term can be implied into the contract,[486] and (ii) X's inability to sell petrol lasts for a significant duration in the context of the lease as a whole. However even then X will have to counter the argument that he took the commercial risk that the lease would turn out to be unprofitable.

I. There is no legislation in either England or Ireland[487] which deals directly with this situation, and so we must turn to the common law doctrine of frustration as applied to leases.

II. 1. In 1943 in *Groome* v. *Fodhla Printing Co*[488] Black J in the Irish Supreme Court adopted the traditional common law approach of doubting whether the doctrine of frustration could be applied to leases.[489] This is based upon the theoretical argument that a lease grants an estate, or an interest, in land, and that the estate or interest survives physical destruction of the land or property. However, this was before

[484] Cass., 28 November 1980, Pas., 1981, I, 369, *RCJB*, 1987 and the note by P.-A. Foriers.

[485] It is difficult to be more precise on this point because the concept of the allocation of risks is not frequently applied by the case law or discussed by legal authors in Belgium.

[486] Such a term could be implied if there is no other sensible use for a petrol station, or if the station could not be readily converted to some other business use without breaching the lease or planning laws for example.

[487] In Ireland, Section 40 Landlord and Tenant Amendment (Ireland) Act 1860, generally known as 'Deasy's Act', gives a tenant the right to surrender the tenancy if the subject matter of the lease is destroyed or if it is incapable of beneficial occupation 'by accidental fire or other inevitable accident.'

[488] [1943] IR 380, 414.

[489] See also English cases such as *Matthey* v. *Curling* [1922] 2 AC 180; *London & Estates* v. *Schlesinger* [1916] 1 KB 20; *Youngmin* v. *Heath* [1974] 1 WLR 135.

the decision in *National Carriers Ltd* v. *Panalpina (Northern) Ltd*[490] in which the House of Lords accepted the possibility that a lease could be frustrated. Although there is no direct Irish authority on this issue, in *Neville & Sons Ltd* v. *Guardian Builders Ltd*[491] Blayney J in the Supreme Court approved significant dicta from *National Carriers Ltd* v. *Panalpina (Northern) Ltd*[492] and it is thus highly unlikely that there is an absolute ban on the application of the doctrine of frustration to lease. However, there does not yet appear to have been either an English or Irish case where a lease has been terminated by the common law doctrine of frustration.

2. It is probable that in a case where 'some vast convulsion of nature swallowed up the property altogether . . .'[493] or where it is lost due to coastal erosion,[494] or where there is total destruction of an upper floor flat by fire or earthquake[495] that a court would find the lease had been frustrated. There is some indication from other jurisdictions that a lease may be frustrated in circumstances less serious than this.[496] However, here the land and premises remain fully intact, and X can merely claim frustration of purpose. The chances of successfully claiming frustration of the purpose of a lease are small. X may be able to claim that the lease is frustrated if it can be proved that it is the common purpose of both parties that is frustrated. It will however be difficult to prove this unless an express term of the lease restricts the use of the premises to a particular purpose. For example, in *Cricklewood Property and Investment Trust Ltd* v. *Leighton Investment Trust Ltd*[502] Viscount Simon LC in the House of Lords suggested that if a lease is expressed to be for the purpose of building, or the like, and legislation is passed prohibiting building on the land, then the lease might be frustrated.[497]

3. A series of United States cases provide the classic example of a lease being frustrated because the purpose of the lease, as expressly stated in the lease, can no longer be carried out. These cases involved the lease of a liquour saloon, where the lease expressly restricted the use of the

490 [1981] AC 675 (Eng). 491 [1995] 1 ILRM 1, 7–8. 492 [1981] AC 675 (Eng).

493 *Cricklewood Property and Investment Trust Ltd* v. *Leighton Investment Trust Ltd* [1945] AC 221 per Viscount Simon LC at p. 229, (Eng).

494 See *National Carriers* per Lord Hailsham of Marylebone at p. 691, per Lord Simon of Glaisdale at p. 701.

495 See *National Carriers* per Lord Hailsham of Marylebone at p. 690.

496 E.g. *Turner* v. *Clark* 1983 NBR (2d) LEXIS 949; 49 NBR (2d) 340; 129 APR. 340. Here the New Brunswick Court of Appeal held that a residential lease was frustrated when an accidental fire severely damaged a leased apartment, rendering it unfit for occupancy.

497 [1945] AC 221, 229.

premises to the business of selling liquour. When prohibition[498] rendered this use illegal, lessees of saloons claimed that they were no longer under an obligation to pay rent, and that their leases had terminated, because of subsequent illegality and/or frustration of purpose. Whether such a claim would succeed generally depended on the construction of the lease, in particular on whether the lessee was completely restricted in his use of the premises or whether there was an alternative use for the premises. For example, in *Industrial Development and Land Co* v. *Goldschmidt*[499] the lease of a premises provided that the lessee was to 'use and occupy the said premises for the purpose of conducting thereon a general winery and/or wholesale and/or retail liquor business'. The tenant further covenanted that he 'would not suffer or permit the said premises to be used for any other purpose.' When prohibition rendered the sale of alcohol illegal and impossible the lease was discharged and the lessee was relieved from the payment of rent. In *Doherty* v. *Monroe Eckstein Brewing Co*[500] the lease provided that 'the only business to be carried on in the said premises is the saloon business' and again prohibition was held to discharge the lease. The fact that the lessee could still carry on subsidiary activities was held to be irrelevant. The principle purpose of the lease had been frustrated and this was enough. However, even these cases had their limits: if only one of several uses became impossible[501] or if the lease merely became unprofitable for the lessee[502] the lease was not frustrated.

4. Other jurisdictions have not been so understanding of the lessee's predicament. In *Vancouver Breweries* v. *Dana*[503] the Supreme Court of Canada refused to find that the loss of a liquour licence for a leased premises put an end to the lease or relieved the lessee from liability for rent. In *Corby* v. *McCarthy*[504] the New Zealand Court of Appeal held that a tenant was not discharged from his liability to pay the balance of a premium under a lease of a licensed hotel premises when the licence was lost. This was despite the fact that the lease contained covenants to

[498] E.g., the prohibition of the sale of intoxicating liquor under the 18th Amendment to the Constitution.

[499] 206 p. 134 (1922).

[500] 198 App div 708, 191 NY Supp 59 (1st Dept, 1921).

[501] *Grace* v. *Croninger* 55 P 2d 940 (1936); *Conklin* v. *Silver* 187 Iowa 819, 174 NW 573, 7 ALR 832 (1919).

[502] *Lloyd* v. *Murphy* 153 P (2d) 47, 25 Cal (2d) 48 (1944); reproduced in: Kessler and Gilmore, *Contracts, Cases and Materials* (Boston: Little Bran & Co, 2nd edn, 1970), p. 774; *Frazier* v. *Collins* 300 Ky 18, 187 SW 2d 816 (1945); *Essex Lincoln Garage* v. *City of Boston* 342 Mass 719, 175 NE 2d 466 (1961); *Mitchell* v. *Ceazan Tires* 153 P 2d 53 (1944).

[503] [1915] 26 DLR 665; 52 SCR 134.

[504] [1904] 23 NZLR 725.

carry on the premises as a licensed premises, and not to use them or allow them to be used for any other purpose. In the English case of *Grimsdick* v. *Sweetman*,[505] the obligation to pay rent for the lease of a beerhouse continued even when the licence to sell alcohol was subsequently revoked by an Act of Parliament. This was despite the fact that the tenant had expressly covenanted to 'continue the said premises as a beerhouse.' However, it should be noted that the lessee had been paid compensation for the loss of the licence, and the premises could still be used to some extent as a bakery and living quarters. Furthermore, it does not appear that the tenant was held liable for breach of his covenant.

5. Finally, whether or not the lease is frustrated may depend on the duration of the lease. In a situation where the lease is long term, the likelihood of frustration is greatly reduced.[506] Any interruption in the lessee's enjoyment of the land is more likely to be temporary and not sufficiently serious to warrant discharge. More generally, a long-term lease will be considered similar to a purchase of land, and it will generally be implied that the lessee took the risk of changes in circumstances affecting the lease. This is illustrated by the House of Lords decision in *National Carriers* v. *Panalpina*.[507] Here, a warehouse was demised to the defendants for a period of ten years from January 1974. The only access to the warehouse was by a street which was closed in May 1979, for a likely period of twenty months. In an action by the plaintiffs for recovery of unpaid rent, the defendants claimed that the lease had been frustrated by the closure of the street, which had rendered the warehouse useless for their purposes. It was held that although the doctrine of frustration was in principle applicable to leases, in the present case, given the likely duration of the interruption in contrast to the length of the lease itself, the lease was not frustrated.

Scotland

Under Scottish law, the contract is frustrated. Accordingly X can refuse the payment.

I. 1. In general, a shortage of supplies does not frustrate a contract.[508] Petrol would usually be classed as 'generic goods', replaceable from other sources. Substitute performance would be possible, and the contract of lease would not be frustrated. However, this example is not a

[505] [1909] 2 KB 740. [506] See Treitel, *Frustration and Force Majeure*, p. 400.
[507] [1981] AC 675. [508] *Blacklock & McArthur* v. *Kirk* 1919 SC 57.

case of mere shortage, but rather a complete inability to buy and sell petrol. Substitute performance is impossible. This is likely to be treated as a case of impossibility in Scots law.

2. It is likely that the court would decide that the lease in Case 6 is impossible to perform and thus frustrated only where *all* potential purposes for which the subjects could be let are impossible. The important question therefore is a practical one, namely whether the tenant has the ability to carry out a different trade from a petrol station. If it were decided that no other trade could be carried out from petrol station premises then the test would be fulfilled and the contract in Case 6 would be affected by impossibility of performance. The parties would be released from their obligations under the contract.

II. Case 6 is perhaps analogous to cases of *rei interitus*, or frustration of a contract due to destruction of the subject matter of the contract, discussed above.[509] Bell explained:

> . . . when by the nature of the contract its performance depends on the existence of a particular thing or state of things, the failure or destruction of that thing or state of things, without default on either side, liberates both parties.[510]

At one time, the scope for frustration in such circumstances was extremely limited.[511] This view prevailed until relatively recently, as is illustrated by the following quote from Paton and Cameron, writing in 1967:

> It is settled that the doctrine of *rei interitus* does not apply where it is merely the purpose for which the subjects have been let that has become impossible, and thus that a tenant is not entitled to an abatement of rent, or to rescission of the lease, where, for example, the licence of a hotel, the subject of the lease has been revoked, or the imposition by legislation of a close season has proved injurious to a salmon fishery.[512]

This restrictive view is illustrated in cases such as *Hart's Trs* v. *Arrol*,[513] in which a tenant carrying on a business of wine and spirit merchant failed to achieve a renewal of his licence. This occurred three and a half years

509 See also *Holliday* v. *Scott* (1830) 8 S. 831.

510 Bell, *Principles*, s.29.

511 *John Milligan & Co Ltd* v. *Ayr Harbour Trustees* 1915 SC 937, per Lord Justice-Clerk Macdonald at 948 and Lord Salvesan at 952. See also *Union Totalisator Co Ltd* v. *Scott* 1951 SLT (Notes) 5, per Lord Sorn.

512 G. Paton and G. Cameron, *The Law of Landlord and Tenant in Scotland* (Edinburgh: W. Green & Son, 1967), citing *Donald* v. *Leitch* (1886) 13 R. 790; *Hart's Trustees* v. *Arrol* (1903) 6 F 36; and *Holliday* v. *Scott* (1830) 8 S. 831.

513 (1903) 6 F. 36.

into a ten-year lease. Lord McLaren effectively ruled out *rei interitus*. However, their Lordships may have been influenced by the fact that the landlord in question had already waived the limitation on use of the premises as a wine and spirit merchants only.[514] It would therefore have been open to the tenant to carry out a different trade from the premises.

2. More recently, there are examples of leases being frustrated on the grounds of impossibility of performance,[515] one of which is a leading House of Lords case, *Denny Mott & Dickson* v. *James B Fraser & Co*.[516] JBF and DMD had entered into an agreement which comprised three elements:

- (i) JBF would let their timber-yard to DMD;
- (ii) JBF would purchase all of its timber supplies from DMD;
- (iii) on the occurrence of certain agreed events, the agreement would terminate and DMD would have the option to purchase the timber-yard.

Upon the outbreak of war in 1939, an order prohibiting the supply of timber was passed. Thus, element (ii) became impossible to perform. Their Lordships focused on whether the agreement was composite or severable, concluding that it was composite. The lease was indistinguishable from the trading agreement and so the entire lease fell when one part was frustrated.[517] Case 6 is analogous – the impossibility affects both the lease and the tenant's ability to trade.

3. Looking at the modern case law as a whole, the key issue appears to be whether the limitation imposed by the frustrating event in effect totally destroys the utility of the lease, or whether the tenant remains, at least in part, able to perform his business.[518] In Case 6 the tenant is completely unable to perform his business, and, arguing by analogy with *Denny Mott & Dickson* v. *James B Fraser & Co*,[519] the Scottish courts are likely to find that the lease in Case 6 is frustrated.

[514] McBryde certainly indicates that this is a relevant consideration, see *Contract*, at para. 21–33.

[515] See, for example, *Tay Salmon Fisheries Co* v. *Speedie* 1929 S.C. 593.

[516] 1944 SC (HL) 35.

[517] *Ibid*., per Lord Wright at 45. Only Lord Jamieson, who delivered his dissenting judgment in the Inner House, directly addresses this point, noting that the principle underlying the authorities is that '. . . the supervening event must be such as to destroy the commercial adventure or purpose for which the contract was entered into, or to bring about such a change in the conditions under which the parties negotiated as to destroy the basis or foundation on which the contract was concluded.' 1943 SC 293 at 335.

[518] *Holliday* v. *Scott* (1830) 8 S. 831.

[519] 1944 SC (HL) 35.

III. 1. In the above analysis of Case 6, it is assumed that the outbreak of war will result in an interruption of the tenant's ability to trade for a lengthy period. The legal analysis would differ in the perhaps unlikely event that war would be likely to be of short duration. In the English case of *National Carriers* v. *Panalpina (Northern) Limited*[520] the tenant was evicted from the subjects of let for a period of eighteen months where the entire duration of the lease was ten years. This was insufficient to frustrate the lease, Lord Hailsham suggesting that arguments of this type rarely succeed.[521] Lord Wright analysed the extent of interruption necessary for frustration to apply as follows:

> ... the real principle which applies in cases of commercial responsibility is that business men must not be left in indefinite suspense. If there is a reasonable probability from the nature of the interruption that it will be of an indefinite duration, they ought to be free to turn their assets, their plant and equipment and their business operations into activities which are open to them, and to be free from commitments which are struck with sterility for an uncertain future period.[522]

2. There appears to be no mechanism in terms of which the obligations under the lease can be merely suspended temporarily for the duration of the war. Rather, the options for the court are to decide either that the lease stands in its current form (if the duration of the interruption is likely to be short) or is frustrated entirely (if the duration is likely to be long).

3. Provided that the duration of the war is likely to be long, the courts would find the lease in Case 6 to be frustrated. X and Y would be released from the obligations under the lease in the future, i.e., after the occurrence of the outbreak of war. Any rights which had accrued under the lease prior to the outbreak of war would remain enforceable. Thus, X can stop payment of rent as from the date of the outbreak of war but would be liable for rent which had accrued prior to that date.

Editors' comparative notes

The open jurisdictions

X may terminate the contract with Y in all of the open jurisdictions and thus his refusal to pay is justified.

[520] [1981] AC 675. [521] *Ibid.*, at 692.

[522] *Ibid.*, per Lord Wright at 47. See also Peel, *Treitel's Law of Contract*, paras. 19–017 and 19–018.

Most jurisdictions offer a general right to terminate lease agreements subject to notice. However, such a right has no immediate effect (cf., e.g., Italy). In Austria termination is not subject to notice because there is a specific provision in the Civil Code which states that no rent has to be paid if the leased property cannot be used as a result of an extraordinary event. Similarly, in Lithuania there are specific provisions in the law of leases addressing the unexpected change of circumstances in question that allow for adjustment and termination.

Apart from specific provisions on leases, a right to terminate due to an unexpected change of circumstances is generally accepted in the open jurisdictions based on their 'exceptional' doctrines: the government intervention was not foreseen and was beyond X's control and risk.

As an alternative to termination, adjustment is available in Germany, Greece and Lithuania. It is based on the same rationale as termination. The adjustment will probably consist in the suspension of the contract for the duration of the confiscation. Once again, under German law adjustment has priority over termination, as a general rule; termination is only admissible if the adjustment is unreasonable.

The closed jurisdictions

In almost all of the closed jurisdictions, X is entitled to termination as well. This solution is primarily based on the force majeure character of the government intervention due to which the contract is frustrated as it no longer complies with the parties' expectations. In France and Belgium the notion of impossibility is applied to the case at hand leading to a discharge of the contractual obligations. The English and Irish reporter, however, indicates some uncertainty as the doctrine of frustration has not been applied to lease contracts by the courts yet. Based on rulings in other common law jurisdictions (United States, New Zealand) relief is more likely to be granted if the confiscation persists for a high proportion of the entire length of the lease.

Conclusion

In the case of a government intervention which renders using the rented object impossible, we can observe a uniform tendency in favour of relief in all jurisdictions. X is entitled to terminate the contract and can justly refuse payment. In some reports, however (Netherlands, England, and Ireland, Scotland), it is emphasised that strict standards apply. In some of the open jurisdictions, there are specific rules on lease contracts addressing the change of circumstances (Austria, Lithuania).

Adjustment of the contract is available only in some of the open jurisdictions and is likely to lead to a suspension of the contract for as long as the confiscation lasts.

Case 7 Hotel reservation

Individual purpose of the visit frustrated; strike at the airport; general safety endangered; coronation case

X booked a room at Y's hotel, but:

(a) *The exhibition he wants to visit is cancelled at the very last moment.*
(b) *A terrorist movement declares that it is to launch a campaign against tourists in that town.*
(c) *An unforeseeable strike by airport personnel prevents X from travelling at the specified time to the city where the hotel is located.*
(d) *The coronation procession scheduled on the respective date is cancelled. The room has a view of the street where the procession was supposed to take place. Due to the extraordinary event, the agreed price is ten times higher than the regular price.*

Is X entitled to cancel the reservation?

Germany and related jurisdictions

Germany

X is not entitled to cancel the reservation in Cases 7(a) - 7(c). He may terminate the contract in the case of the procession (7(d)) but will be under an obligation to reimburse Y for any expenses incurred.

(a) Cancellation of the exhibition

I. 1. The parties did not explicitly provide for the cancellation of the exhibition in the contract. There is no indication of a condition in the contract that the exhibition takes place (§158 BGB) or for a contractual right of rescission in case the exhibition is cancelled (§346 BGB).[523] In the case at hand, X and Y have taken it for granted that the exhibition will take place without further deliberation.

[523] For further details regarding the contractual right of rescission cf. R. Gaier, '§346', in: Krüger (ed.), *Münchener Kommentar zum Bürgerlichen Gesetzbuch*, vol. II, nn. 4–9.

2. The gap in the contract resulting from the unforeseen cancellation of the exhibition cannot be filled by applying the concept of *complementary interpretation* (§§133, 157 BGB).[524] This concept requires concrete grounds in the contractual provisions for determining a hypothetical will of the parties if the purpose is frustrated.

3. Moreover, X cannot avoid the contract on the basis of mistake (§119 BGB), because there was no relevant mistake according to §119 II BGB.[525] It is doubtful whether X had any specific assumption concerning a cancellation of the exhibition. Additionally, §119 II BGB requires that the mistake refers to a 'quality' of the subject matter of the contract.[526] The question whether or not the exhibition actually takes place cannot be considered a 'quality' of the room in Y's hotel; it is merely an external fact that is irrelevant under §119 II BGB.[527] Thus, even a specific misconception of X with regard to the exhibition is an irrelevant error as to the motives.

II. The first issue of the case is whether the rules of impossibility (§§275, 323, 326 BGB) are applicable. To deny the obligation of specific performance in accordance with §275 I BGB, the precise subject-matter of Ys specific performance must be determined by interpreting the agreement. According to a minority opinion[528] the lessor's specific performance is not confined to assigning possession to X, but also includes the obligation to provide the room in a manner that X can use it for his individual purpose. According to the majority opinion, contractual obligation has to be construed narrowly, at least unless the price for the room is increased because of the exhibition.[529] This opinion refers to §537 I BGB. According to this rule, the lessee has to pay the rent even if his purpose of use is frustrated for personal reasons. Thus, the risk of frustration of an individual purpose of use is allocated to the lessee and it is not part of the contractual obligation of the lessor.

III. 1. Finally, the concept of *Störung der Geschäftsgrundlage* (§313 BGB) does not provide for a right of X to cancel the reservation. Even though this concept may result in a termination of the contract if the

[524] Cf. Case 5 for further details of the concept of complementary interpretation.

[525] Cf. for details on §119 I BGB Case 6. [526] Cf. for details on §119 II BGB Case 6.

[527] Cf. J. Ellenberger, '§119', in: Palandt *et al.* (eds.), *Bürgerliches Gesetzbuch*, n. 27; for further details cf. Case 8.

[528] Cf. V. Beuthien, *Zweckerreichung und Zweckstörung im Schuldverhältnis* (Tübigen: Mohr Siebeck, 1969), p. 166 *et seq.*, 195.

[529] Cf. Larenz, *Schuldrecht I*, §21 II; W. Weidenkaff, '§535', in: Palandt *et al.* (eds.), *Bürgerliches Gesetzbuch*, n. 17.

adaptation of the contract is not reasonable, there is no relevant impact on the '*Geschäftsgrundlage*' in the given case.

2. The issue at hand is the frustration of purpose ('*Vereitelung des Verwendungszwecks*'),[530] i.e., Y can perform in theory, while performance has become practically useless with regard to X's purposes.

3. First, it is doubtful whether the taking place of the exhibition qualifies as a *Geschäftsgrundlage* of the contract between X and Y. The exhibition must be a basic assumption shared by both parties at the time of contracting or at least an assumption of X recognisable for Y and uncontested by him. There is no information that Y knew about X's intention to visit the exhibition during his stay at the hotel. Even if Y was aware of X's intention the exhibition preferably should not be considered as *Geschäftsgrundlage* because in general Y does not have to be concerned with his guests' reasons for the stay in his hotel. X's intention should therefore be considered only as an element in the motivation of one party that is irrelevant under the concept of *Störung der Geschäftsgrundlage*.

4. Second, even if the exhibition is considered as a *Geschäftsgrundlage* of the contract that is substantially affected by the cancellation, X is not unreasonably burdened by the cancellation. As a general rule, each party bears the risk that his purposes can be achieved unless the purpose in question is stipulated in the contract.[531] Moreover, the frustration of the purpose of the lessee is provided for in §537 BGB. According to this rule, the burden of a frustration of purpose is on the lessee if the reason refers to his personal circumstances. The case at hand is a standard example of this rule.[532] The same applies if the use of rented premises is frustrated or the premises are inappropriate for the intended use of the lessee.[533]

(b) Terrorist movement

I. In this case, there is no contractual provision about the threat of a terrorist movement. Therefore X has no right to rescind the contract. Nor can the absence of any menace be qualified as a condition of the contract. Additionally, under the rules of mistake, as set out above,

[530] Cf. for further details Case 5. [531] Cf. Case 5.

[532] Cf. OLG Braunschweig NJW 1976, 570; NJW 1976, 970; Grüneberg, '§313', in: Palandt *et al.* (eds.), *Bürgerliches Gesetzbuch*, n. 36; but see also BGH NJW 1977, 386.

[533] Cf. OLG Brandenburg ZMR 1999, 97; OLG Celle MDR 1999, 799.

X cannot avoid the contract on the basis of §119 I, II BGB because there is no relevant mistake with regard to the agreement.

II. Additionally, specific performance is possible, i.e., Y can transfer possession to X. Thus, the rules of impossibility do not apply. Y is also not liable under a warranty according to §§536, 536a BGB since there is no defect in the hotel room. The terrorist threat is not directly related to the 'quality' of the room, i.e., its physical or actual condition.[534]

III. 1. The main issue at stake is whether X can terminate the contract applying the concept of *Störung der Geschäftsgrundlage* (§313 BGB) because his intended use of the room is frustrated by the terrorist threat (frustration of purpose; *Störung des Verwendungszwecks*). It is doubtful whether the majority opinion would apply the so-called '*Große Geschäftsgrundlage*'[535] in the case of a mere announcement of terrorist attacks. Usually, only war and warlike social conditions fall within the scope of this doctrine. Nevertheless, the absence of terrorist assaults may be considered as a circumstance, that is (from an objective point of view) a necessary foundation of the contract and thus an element of the so-called '*objektive Geschäftsgrundlage*'.[536]

2. Even if the threat can be qualified as having a substantial impact on the (objective) *Geschäftsgrundlage*, under the given facts, X is not exposed to an unreasonable burden under the contract. As a general rule, the lessee bears the risk of frustration of his purpose of use.[537] If the so-called '*Große Geschäftsgrundlage*' is affected, the burden is exceptionally shifted. Nevertheless, this does not apply in the given case. Otherwise a mere terrorist threat would result in a right for X to terminate the contract, shift the burden on Y and deprive him of any profit under the contract. Moreover, the risk related to a mere terrorist threat on tourists is a day-to-day risk that everyone is exposed to. This may be different if there is not just a (general) threat but if a terrorist campaign is actually running against tourists in that place. In these cases there is a grave alteration of the circumstances. In such a case, X may terminate the contract; in return he has to indemnify Y for his expenses and a half of his lost profits.

[534] Even if the contract between X and Y qualified for an all-inclusive tour (§651a *et seq.* BGB; cf. also RL 90/314/EWG) only a concrete interference with the specific performance would result in a liability for warranty of Y; cf. H. Sprau, '§651j', in: Palandt *et al.* (eds.), *Bürgerliches Gesetzbuch*, n. 3.

[535] I.e., substantial changes of political, economic or social conditions; cf. Case 6.

[536] Cf. Case 6. [537] Cf. Case 6.

IV. This evaluation is backed by the special provision of §651j BGB that applies to package holidays. According to this rule, the parties may terminate such holidays if they are affected or only endangered by circumstances amounting to force majeure. If the contract is terminated under this rule, the tour operator has no claim for payment but is indemnified for his expenses. He has to provide for transportation bringing the traveller back home. Additional costs of the transportation as well as other additional expenses are shared between both parties (§651j II BGB). Nevertheless, according to the majority opinion, this rule does not apply in case of a single terrorist attack.[538] This result is different if there are several terrorist attacks on tourists in that town or region.[539]

(c) Strike at the airport

I. The strike only affects X's ability to reach and make use of the contractual subject matter. Thus, there are no grounds for relevant mistake under §119 BGB and the concept of impossibility does not apply as the transportation risk and the general risk not to be able to use the object of the lease must be borne by the lessee under §537 BGB. The rule of §537 BGB also indicates that there is no sufficient argument to apply the notion of *Störung der Geschäftsgrundlage* (§313 BGB). For there is only relief under §313 BGB if the incident goes beyond the 'regular' distribution of risk and §537 BGB allocates the transportation risk to the lessee. There would only be a reason to apply §313 BGB if the incident did not only affect X's journey to the hotel, but nobody could reach the hotel, e.g., if the region of the hotel was cut off by an earthquake, landslide or war.[540] As in our case there is no indication of such an event, X is not entitled to cancellation.

(d) Coronation procession

I. 1. With regard to the characteristics of this particular case, a minority opinion argues that the rules on impossibility (§§275, 326 BGB) are applicable.[541] According to this opinion, Y's contractual obligation

[538] Cf. Sprau, '§651j', in: Palandt *et al.* (eds.), *Bürgerliches Gesetzbuch*, n. 3; for a different opinion cf. O. Tempel, 'Zur Kündigung von Reiseverträgen wegen terroristischer Anschläge', (1998) NJW, 1827 *et seq.*

[539] Cf. AG Düsseldorf, MDR 2000, 201; AG Worms, NJW-RR 2001, 348.

[540] Cf. W. Weidenkaff, '§537', in: Palandt *et al.* (eds.), *Bürgerliches Gesetzbuch*, nn. 4 *et seq.*

[541] Cf. W. Flume, *Das Rechtsgeschäft*, §26 n. 3; Beuthien, *Zweckerreichung und Zweckstörung im Schuldverhältnis*, pp. 166 *et seq.*, 195.

encompasses not only the transfer of possession of the room but the transfer of possession in a way that the contractual subject-matter (the room) is suitable for the intended purpose of use (view of the procession). The latter is impossible due to the cancellation of the coronation procession.

2. The majority opinion[542] limits the contractual obligation to the transfer of possession. Otherwise Y's obligation would factually include that X can achieve his purpose of use even though Y did not promise that the procession would take place. Moreover, the cancellation of the coronation procession would burden Y unilaterally. Finally, by rendering the contractual obligation impossible the minority opinion denies X the right to use the room for a different purpose (e.g., vacation).

II. X cannot refuse to pay the agreed price according to §821 BGB because there is no contractual agreement between the parties that payment is dependent on the coronation procession ('*Zweckvereinbarung*' or agreement on a certain purpose). According to this rule, the debtor can deny specific performance if he is entitled to repayment because the creditor will be unjustifably enriched by specific performance. In the given case, however, X cannot claim restitution according to the principles of *condictio ob rem* (§812 I 2 Alt. 2 BGB):[543] there is no *explicit* or *implicit* agreement between the parties that Y's right to claim the lease depends on the possibility of seeing the procession. The possibility of seeing the procession was known to both parties, as it was the reason for the increased price. Nevertheless, the taking place of the procession did not become part of their '*Zweckvereinbarung*' (agreement on a certain purpose).

III. 1. According to the unanimous opinion, X does not have to pay the price agreed upon.[544] The majority opinion derives this solution from the concept of *Störung der Geschäftsgrundlage*. According to this view, the taking place of the coronation is part of the *Geschäftsgrundlage* (§313 BGB) of this contract.[545] In the given case, the contractual agreement of the parties is based on this mutual assumption as is evident from the price agreed upon.

542 Cf. Larenz, *Geschäftsgrundlage*, p. 173; Larenz, *Schuldrecht I*, §21 II *et seq*.

543 Cf. for further details Case 11.

544 Cf. Roth, '§313', in: Krüger (ed.), *Münchener Kommentar zum Bürgerlichen Gesetzbuch*, vol. II, n. 213.

545 Larenz, *Schuldrecht I*, §21 II et seq.; Köhler, *Unmöglichkeit und Geschäftsgrundlage*, pp. 176 *et seq*.

2. If the contract were upheld as originally concluded, it would amount to an unreasonable burden for X. Indeed, cases where the purpose of use of one party is closely related to the other party's interest are exceptional cases, in which the frustration of purpose amounts to a *Störung der Geschäftsgrundlage*. Accordingly, the risk is shifted on both parties so that the latter party's claim of his contractual rights amounts to *venire contra factum proprium* (§242 BGB).[546] With regard to leases this is true if nobody would have leased the object but for the specific event. Thus, in the case of a lease of a private balcony the risk shifts on both parties if the event is cancelled.[547] Also, if the intended use affects the price, the risk shifts from the lessee to the lessor[548] since he (partly) bears the risk of frustration of purpose. In those cases the lessee either increases the price due to the event or participates in the revenue from the intended use.[549] In the given case the agreed price is ten times higher than the normal price. Thus, it is reasonable to shift the risk of frustration of purpose. However, the primary legal result is an adaptation of the contract (§313 I BGB). Thus, the contract price may be reduced to the normal price if X has another purpose of use for the hotel room (e.g., vacation). If X has no use for the room he may terminate the contract (§313 III BGB), in which case an indemnification of Y's expenses is equitable.

Austria

X has no right to terminate the agreement in Case 7 (a) and (c). He may terminate the contract in Case 7(b) and (d).

(a) Cancellation of the exhibition

I. X was not mistaken as to the contents of the contract, but as to his own motives that led him to conclude the contract. §901 ABGB provides that – as a general rule – mistakes in the inducement/motives of the mistaken party do not affect the validity of the contract. This includes mistakes as to future developments. Furthermore, X is not entitled to invoke '*Wegfall der Geschäftsgrundlage*'. This doctrine is only applied if the existence of particular circumstances was an important basis or background of the contract from the perspective of both parties (plus

[546] Cf. Larenz, *Schuldrecht I*, §21 II. [547] Cf. *ibid.*

[548] Cf. BGH LM §242 BGB(Bb) n. 83 (*Krönungszug*).

[549] Cf. Grüneberg, '§313', in: Palandt *et al.* (eds.), *Bürgerliches Gesetzbuch*, n. 37: lessee of a music hall participates in the revenue from the event.

unforeseeability, plus no risk assumption).[550] X's plan to visit the exhibition is not a common basis of the contract for both parties, but rather a unilateral motive only of X. Mistakes as to unilateral motives are dealt with by §901 ABGB ('*Motivirrtum*'), according to which no relief is granted to the mistaken.

II. The same result is also achieved if we follow one Austrian decision[551] and apply §1168 ABGB to the hotel reservation contract.[552] As a special provision of risk allocation, §1168 ABGB leaves no room for the doctrine of '*Wegfall der Geschäftsgrundlage*' (see Case 5 above). Y is ready to perform and the circumstances that prevent performance of the contract are within the ordering party's (i.e., X's) sphere of responsibility. If X decides to cancel the journey, §1168 ABGB will entitle Y to claim the contract price, reduced, however, by the amount of expenses saved or profits made by Y instead, for instance by letting the room to another guest.

III. As the hotel reservation is a mixed contract (lease and services) and therefore also has a lease element §1107 ABGB, one of the lease contract provisions of the ABGB, might also be applicable. §1107 ABGB provides that where a lessee is prevented from using the leased property due to obstacles or accidents, he is nevertheless obliged to pay the rent. This argument underlines the result achieved according to §1168 ABGB. In a hotel reservation contract its service contract nature is preponderant over its lease character and therefore the more detailed provision in §1168 ABGB should be applied.

(b) Terrorist movement

I. It is generally held by Austrian courts and commentators that personal security is an essential requirement in an accommodation contract.[553] The Austrian OGH held that terrorist activities amount to force

[550] Rummel, '§901', in: Rummel (ed.), *Kommentar zum ABGB*, vol. I, n. 6a; If the '*Geschäftsgrundlage*' was not there from the beginning the contract will be *avoided* with retrospective effect (*ex tunc*), if the '*Geschäftsgrundlage*' disappears after the conclusion of the contract the contract will be *terminated* with *ex nunc* effect. Long-term contracts (already in the stage of performance) can normally only be terminated with *ex nunc* effect.

[551] LGZ Wien, Miet 45.156.

[552] A hotel reservation is not a typical lease, nor a typical work and service contract, but rather a mixed lease services contract with a stronger service element. Therefore §1168 ABGB as part of the work and service contract provisions (§§1151 *et seq.* ABGB) applies.

[553] See Gundula Peer, 'Der Wegfall der Geschäftsgrundlage im Reisevertragsrecht', (1994) *Zeitschrift für Rechtsvergleichung, Internationales Privatrecht und Europarecht*, 177, 179.

majeure and affect the '*Geschäftsgrundlage*' of such contracts if a journey to the contractual destination is unacceptable from the traveller's point of view.[554] Therefore, X is entitled to cancel the reservation if the threat is serious and exceeds the standard risk of terrorism for tourists in that country.[555] Accordingly it was held that a journey is unacceptable where the state department gave a warning.[556]

II. §1168 ABGB is not applicable to this case because terrorist attacks cannot be considered to be in the sphere of the ordering party. According to §1168 ABGB it falls within the ordering party's sphere of responsibility to ensure that performance by the provider is possible (see Case (a) above) and that necessary materials are provided. However, terrorist attacks or other dangerous circumstances at the destination of a travel contract are not in the ordering party's sphere of responsibilities. These latter circumstances fall within a 'neutral sphere' and call for the application of the doctrine of '*Wegfall der Geschäftsgrundlage*'.

(c) Strike at the airport

I. The strike of airport personnel is certainly an unpredictable change of circumstances. Nevertheless, the doctrine of '*Wegfall der Geschäftsgrundlage*' does not apply, since the risk of being prevented from travelling to the city where the hotel is located falls within X's sphere of responsbility. The journey to the hotel is part of the 'circumstances in the sphere of the ordering party' in the sense of §1168 ABGB. According to this provision X is obliged to pay the contract price, but is entitled to deduct from it any expenses saved or profits made by Y due to the fact that X does not use the room (as in Case (a)).

(d) Coronation procession

I. Although the coronation case was originally decided in England, it is the textbook example of '*Wegfall der Geschäftsgrundlage*' also in Austria.[557] According to the Austrian view, the termination of the contract is justified after the coronation has been cancelled, the procession being a general prerequisite or underlying presumption of the contract

[554] OGH, ZVR 1999/110; OGH, ZVR 2003/19.

[555] Michael Wukoschitz, 'Bombenterror auf Tourismusziele – "Allgemeines Lebensrisiko" des Reisenden oder Wegfall der Geschäftsgrundlage', (1996) *Recht der Wirtschaft*, 399, 402; Ingrid Bläumauer, 'ETA-Bomben & MKS – Storno des Reisevertrages', (2001) *Recht der Wirtschaft*, 322.

[556] See Pilz, 'SARS: Rücktritt vom Pauschalreisevertrag', (2003) *Ecolex*, 327.

[557] Koziol and Welser, *Bürgerliches Recht*, vol. I, p. 162.

for both parties. The cancellation was not foreseeable and does not fall within the lessee customer's area of assumed risk. The cancellation is not an event in the sphere of the ordering party in the sense of §1168 ABGB (see Case (b) above), therefore this provision is not applicable. X is entitled to cancel the reservation without having to pay the price. The doctrine of impossibility is not invoked here, because the taking place of the procession was not a performance contracted for by X. Under the contract, Y was not obliged to provide the hotel room *with* the coronation procession outside. Thus, it cannot be stated that one of the contractual performances has become impossible.

General

I. The issue then becomes one of whether the contract would be terminated or adjusted: adjustment of the contract would lead to a reduction of the 'coronation rent' down to the regular price of the hotel room. By analogy with the law of mistake, the contract will be terminated or adjusted depending on what the parties would have agreed on, if they had anticipated the unforeseeable event (see also Case 11). In this case, the parties would certainly not have concluded the contract. Therefore, X is entitled to demand termination of the contract.

II. 1. From an Austrian point of view, whether or not X is entitled to cancel the reservation is a question of risk allocation.[558] In the absence of any particular contract provisions this risk allocation is determined by §1168 ABGB. Circumstances which pertain only to the customer's motive to conclude the contract or his willingness, readiness or personal ability to make performance possible are 'circumstances in the sphere of the ordering party' in the sense of §1168 ABGB. Accordingly, the risk is assigned to the ordering party, X. Since Y did not even know that X booked the room because of a special exhibition (Case (a)) or that he was going to arrive by plane (Case (c)), these circumstances are not bilaterally accepted prerequisites of the contract and do not affect the validity of the agreement. As a result, the frustration of X's expectations is at his own risk.

2. On the other hand, the safety of tourists in the town where the hotel is located (Case (b)) and the taking place of the coronation procession (Case (d)) are not 'circumstances' in the sense of §1168 ABGB, which

[558] For the following argumentation G. Roth, 'Stornierung von Hotelreservierungen', (1991) *Juristische Blätter*, 1, 5, and Monika Gimpel-Hinteregger, 'Schulschikurse und Schneemangel', (1991) *Juristische Blätter*, 7, 12.

is therefore not applicable here. The named events belong to a 'neutral sphere'. The doctrine of '*Wegfall der Geschäftsgrundlage*' applies to them. The circumstances of Cases (b) and (d) are presumably bilaterally accepted (implied) prerequisites of X's booking the room. Neither party is responsible for the terrorist activities or the cancellation of the procession. Since both parties are presumed to have accepted these circumstances to be a basic prerequisite of the contract, the frustration of these expectations entitles X to cancel the reservation. The risk of these unforeseeable events that cannot be allocated to any party's sphere of responsibility has to be borne by Y.

The Netherlands

In Case 7, Dutch law will lead to the following results:

(a) X has no right to terminate the agreement;
(b) X is entitled to cancel the reservation;
(c) The fact that X cannot travel to the hotel is not a sufficient ground to cancel the reservation; and
(d) X is entitled to terminate the contract.

(a) Cancellation of the exhibition

I. The hotel reservation establishes an agreement which might qualify as a 'mixed' contract containing elements of a service and a lease contract. To the extent that it concerns a 'lease', Title 4 of Book 7 of the Dutch Civil Code applies. Since Title 7.4 does not address the 'unforeseen circumstances' of the case, the issue must be addressed under the generic Art. 6:258 Dutch Civil Code on unforeseen circumstances.

II. 1. In order to assess whether a party is entitled to terminate an agreement, a change of circumstances giving rise to such a termination should not be considered to be for the risk and account of one of the parties (Art. 6:258(2) Dutch Civil Code). In other words, such circumstances should somehow be a 'part of' the agreement. The fact that an exhibition is cancelled is not at all a typical part of a hotel reservation. Therefore, the cancelled exhibition is a matter which falls entirely within X's sphere of responsibility and is not covered by the agreement between X and Y. Accordingly, X is not entitled to cancel the reservation. Obviously, if Y is able to let the room to someone else, X's obligation to pay rent is reduced by the number of days the cancelled room is let to that third party because X is only obliged to pay damages as a consequence of the cancellation and not as such to pay the rent in the case of termination.

2. This may be different if the visit to the exhibition is packaged together with a reservation at Y's hotel. For instance, if Y's hotel has made arrangements with the organiser of the exhibition, i.e., by offering a discount to visitors who have bought tickets for the exhibition as well. In such a case it is evident that booking the hotel room is related to the exhibition.[559] In such a case, both the exhibition and the room reservation are intertwined in such a manner that if one is incidentally cancelled, the visitor should have the right to cancel the room as well. Although this would be a matter of interpreting 'connected legal relationships'[560] and not necessarily of 'changed circumstances', the application of one doctrine does not contradict the outcome of the other. Assuming that the cancellation of the exhibition was not foreseen, Y cannot reasonably expect that the hotel reservation is upheld. Since such an event does not fall within either party's sphere of responsibility, X should be entitled to terminate on the ground of changed circumstances.

(b) Terrorist movement

I. Strictly speaking, Case (b) does not concern a frustration of X's goal as envisaged by the hotel reservation (visiting the hotel for unspecified reasons), but a situation affecting X's willingness to visit the city. Dutch law on unforeseen circumstances would most probably respect that the declaration by the terrorist movement was unforeseeable and probably even that Y cannot reasonably expect X, in view of the prevailing principle of reasonableness and fairness (embodied in Art. 6:248 Dutch Civil Code), to remain bound by the reservation. However, the application of the doctrine of unexpected circumstances requires that the circumstances do not fall within X's sphere of responsibility (cf. Art. 6:258(2) Dutch Civil Code).

II. If the hotel in our case typically deals with tourists, X might argue that Y somehow assumed the risks involved in the tourist trade. That would be the case if the hotel reservation was not booked through a travel agency but by X personally. This would bring the case to the second condition of Art. 6:258(2), being that according to the nature of the contract the risk is attributed to X. This latter argument could be

559 It may even be that Y's hotel is fully booked by visitors to the exhibition.

560 The Dutch law on linked legal relationships (or groups of contracts) has been developed entirely in the case law: HR 23 January 1998, NJ 1999, 97 (*Jans* v. *Fiat Credit Nederland*).

turned around by reference to specific 'travel contracts' (Title 7.7A Dutch Civil Code),[561] although the case does not (seem to) qualify as a travel contract. If it did, X would have a right to terminate the contract under Art. 7:503. According to this statutory provision, X would be entitled to invoke the termination right at all times and with immediate effect and, furthermore, be entitled to a repayment or waiver of the contractual travel sum (or, to the extent X had already enjoyed part of the trip, a pro rata part of the travel sum). Assuming that the declaration by the terrorist movement is of an extraordinary nature (i.e., this might be different if X intended to visit a hotel in certain parts of Afghanistan or Iraq), it seems appropriate either to allow X to cancel the hotel reservation at no cost or to provide that X and Y share the disadvantage resulting from that event, for instance by modifying the agreed price.[562] The termination or amendment of the hotel reservation costs should then be based on Art. 6:258 due to the application of the principle of reasonableness and fairness (or the assessment under this article whether part of the risk should be allocated to X) under Art. 6:258; Art. 7:503 Dutch Civil Code on travel contracts may by analogy direct the solution in X's favour.

(c) Strike at the airport

I. It is not likely that X can prevent Y from charging X's credit card for the hotel reservation. Only if Y was involved in the travel arrangement through the airport would this have been different. The case is largely individually related to X, since other persons could equally arrive from other airports, at other times or by other means of travel. The requirement that the unforeseen circumstance must not be 'in the sphere' of the claimant (Art. 6:258) is not met. The determination of within whose

[561] A travel contract as defined in Art. 7:500 Dutch Civil Code entails a contract with a travel agency for a combination of at least two elements of (i) traveling; (ii) an overnight stay or stay for a period exceeding 24 hours; or (iii) tourist services (which services are a substantial part of the contracted trip).

[562] In the Netherlands most travel organisations use standard terms containing a clause on the annulment of the contract in case of war, a catastrophe etc. Often the risk is spread among the parties. Arbitral cases have dealt with the applicability of such clauses. See: Geschillencommissie Reizen (binding advice), 9 January 1987, *Tijdschrift voor Arbitrage* 1988, n. 10 (the Soviet Union after Chernobyl); Geschillencommissie Reizen (binding advice), 6 March 1990 *Tijdschrift voor Consumentenrecht* 1990, p. 238 (China after the Tianamen Square demonstrations), and Geschillencommissie Reizen (binding advice), 16 December 1991, TvC 1992, pp. 97, 102 and 105 (the former Yugoslavia during the civil war).

sphere the unforeseen circumstances should fall has been addressed in all the relevant literary works.[563]

(d) Coronation procession

I. 1. The case gives rise to several questions: should X pay any sum at all or, in other words, does X have a right to terminate the contract? If any sum were to be paid by X, would that be the normal price or the higher, contracted price? Would it make a difference if X actually comes to the hotel but for other purposes? These questions are relevant even in the case of termination, since Art. 6:260 Dutch Civil Code provides that any amendment or termination of an agreement by a court based on changed circumstances may be made subject to certain conditions, including the payment of compensation (i.e., in the current case the compensation of Y).

2. If X booked the hotel for purposes other than viewing the coronation procession (from X's room), there is no reason to adjust the price downwards if the coronation happens not to take place for any reason. In such a case, Art. 6:258 on changed circumstances would not apply since X has assumed the higher price for the need to have a room anyhow, even against an extraordinarily high price. The nature of the agreement, the letting of a hotel room against a high price, is within the sphere of X's responsibility rather than that of both parties.

3. If X has come to enjoy the coronation procession, it seems inappropriate to charge the difference between the regular room price and the coronation day price (i.e., ten times the regular price): both parties must be deemed to have anticipated the coronation as this is reflected in the agreed price. (Whether this is indeed the case is a matter of interpretation according to the general provisions in Arts. 3:33 and 35 Dutch Civil Code.) It may even be argued that, like the exhibition, the non-occurrence of the coronation is incidental to the hotel owner and should therefore be considered to be a circumstance that largely falls within Y's sphere of responsibility. If that view was indeed adopted by a Dutch court, X should not be required to pay more than the regular price. This point of view is not likely to be adopted within the framework of Art. 6:258 Dutch Civil Code, on which a solution of the case is based.

[563] See for instance: Schoordijk, *Het algemeen gedeelte*, pp. 524–529; or *Asser Hartkamp*, Seburgh 6-III* 2010, nn. 241 (on mistake), 443–4.

II. Finally, the question is whether X may terminate and avoid paying any amount at all. The answer to this question follows the same pattern as discussed for Case 7(b). It seems appropriate that Y charges a certain cancellation fee, covering at least administrative expenses and probably some compensation for available (extra) personnel. It may equally be possible that a Dutch court would reject such claims for compensation and allow a cancellation in all respects.[564]

Eastern European jurisdictions

Slovenia

X is not entitled to cancel the reservation and has to pay the full price in Case 7(a) and 7(c). In contrast, X is entitled to terminate the contract in Case 7(d).

(a) Cancellation of the exhibition

I. Article 40(1) CO expressly provides that the motives that form the basis of a synallagmatic contract do not affect its validity.[565] It is therefore not possible to demand annulment of the contract on grounds of mistake of motive. Moreover, the taking place of a specific event is generally not regarded as a typical prerequisite of an accommodation contract. X could have negotiated a specific contractual provision if he wanted this motive to be part of the contract. Consequently, in this case X alone bears the risk that the event is cancelled.

II. The '*clausula* rule' (Art. 112 CO) does not apply, because the change of circumstances did not affect the expectations of *both* parties since Y did not know about X's plan to visit the exhibition.

III. Article 648 CO regarding the termination of contracts for work could be applied to this contract by analogy.[566] According to this provision, X has the right to terminate the contract, but has to pay the contract price. He will, however, be able to deduct the expenses saved or profits made by Y, for instance by letting the room to another guest.

[564] The case, derived from English case law, is referred to as an example of unforeseen circumstances in the Dutch legislative notes to Art. 6:258 Dutch Civil Code.

[565] Synallagmatic (bilateral) contracts are contracts from which mutual obligations for both parties arise, such as sale, lease etc.

[566] This issue has not (yet) been decided by the case law nor discussed in the literature.

(b) Terrorist movement

I. 1. X could demand dissolution of the contract on grounds of a change of circumstances (Art. 112 CO). In the present case, the terrorist movement announced the attacks after the conclusion of the contract. This circumstance frustrates the purpose of the contract, because in a contract concerning a journey it is assumed that a tourist can move freely without putting his life and health in danger. Terrorist attacks are circumstances that do not fall within the sphere of either party. It may be arguable whether terrorist attacks nowadays are unexpected. But as they can occur anywhere and during any journey, the possibility of terrorist attacks did not have to be taken into consideration at the time of conclusion of the contract. Therefore X may demand dissolution of the contract on grounds of change of circumstances (Art. 112 CO).

2. If the court dissolved the contract, it would award Y (upon his request) the compensation of a just part of damages suffered by the dissolution of the contract (cf. Case 6 above). The court's discretion is wide enough to take into account the savings Y has made due to X's cancellation.

II. 1. If Y had been involved in arranging the travel, it might, however, be possible to apply the specific rules of the CO regarding contracts for organised travel by analogy.[567] In accordance with Art. 901(1) CO, the traveller is allowed to terminate the contract at any moment and, as a consequence, the organiser of the travel is entitled to reimbursement of certain costs, subject to paras. 2–5. In accordance with Art. 901(4) CO, the organiser is only reimbursed for administrative costs of organising the journey if the traveller terminated the contract due to circumstances that could not be avoided or averted and that would have prevented him from concluding the contract, if he had known them at the time of the conclusion of the contract. A terrorist attack, announced after the conclusion of the contract, could certainly qualify as such circumstance. In this case, X only has to pay the expenses Y has had when he made the reservation.

2. If it is applicable, the more specific rule in Art. 901 will override the general rule of Art. 112 CO. For X, an action on grounds of Art. 901 CO will be more advantageous in general, because X only has to pay the administrative cost of reservation. Under Art. 112 CO X would have to pay a part of the damage Y has suffered due to X's cancellation.

[567] There is, however, no case law (yet) to support this view.

(c) Strike at the airport

I. The strike of airport personnel is an unexpected change of circumstances, but it does not give ground for termination of contract, based upon Art. 112 CO. The risk of delays or even impossibility to travel is in the sphere of the customer, as is the risk of choice of the means of transportation.[568] Problems regarding transportation are considered as normal risks.[569]

(d) Coronation procession

I. The rules of impossibility do not apply, because the performance remains possible for both parties. Only the performance by the lessor has lost every sense for the lessee, since he will not be able to watch the coronation procession.

II. 1. Normally such a mistake in motive is not a sufficient ground for nullification of a contract, but in this case the expectation of the coronation procession was obviously a purpose (cause, '*causa*') of the contract for both parties.[570]

2. The fact that the rent is ten times higher than the usual price indicates that the lessor accepted that the taking place of the procession was a substantial part of the contract. X can therefore demand termination of the contract, on grounds of the '*clausula* rule' (Art. 112 CO).[571] An adaption of the contract (e.g., reduction of the price to the normal level) is possible, but only upon the agreement of both parties. It is, however, very unlikely that the lessee would still be interested in renting the room.

Lithuania

(a) X is entitled to cancel the reservation according to Art. 6.721 CC. He must compensate Y for any reasonable expenses Y incurred, as well as the income the hotel was deprived of if the room could not be leased otherwise for the concerned period (Art. 6.249 CC).
(b) X is exempted from civil liability.
(c) X is entitled to cancel the reservation if he proves that there was no other transport available to reach the hotel in due time.
(d) X will be discharged from his obligation under the contract.

[568] Cigoj, *Komentar obligacijskih razmerij*, p. 456. In this case there are alternative ways of transportation possible.

[569] Cigoj, *Teorija obligacij*, pp. 337–8.

[570] *Ibid.*, p. 601.

[571] One of the coronation cases, namely *Krell* v. *Henry* [1903] 2 KB 740 (CA), has been cited as a standard example of a case where termination on grounds of the '*clausula* rule' is allowed. Dolenc in: Juhart and Plavšak (eds.), *Obligacijski zakonik*, vol. I, pp. 601–2.

General

I. Booking a room in a hotel constitutes a mixed contract which has the features of two kinds of contracts – a lease contract and a contract for services. According to Art. 6.721(1) CC (which is applicable in the present case), the client, i.e., X, has the right to unilaterally terminate the contract even though the provision of the services by the provider is already in progress. In this case, X is bound to pay a part of the agreed price that corresponds to the rendered services and to compensate Y for other reasonable expenses incurred for the purpose of the performance before he received notice of the termination.

II. It should also be noted that hotels in Lithuania generally include standard contract terms that determine the consequences arising from the non-arrival of a client (usually, the client is obliged to pay a certain part of the price for his failure to arrive as a penalty). Therefore, the conclusions presented below are only applicable when the consequences of cancellation are not determined in the contract.

(a) Cancellation of the exhibition

I. Visiting the exhibition was the sole motive of X for entering into the contract. This motive was not known to Y. According to the Lithuanian doctrine, the motive or contractual goal is relevant only if it is known to both parties of the contract.[572] Therefore, even the notion of implied conditions (Art. 6.196(2) CC) cannot be applied in this situation. Furthermore, the performance of the contract by X is still possible without any complications. Thus, the rules of impossibility do not apply in this case.

II. Nevertheless, X is entitled to cancel the reservation according to Art. 6.721 CC as outlined above. As he has terminated the contract before having made use of the hotel room, he does not have to pay the rent pro rata. Instead, he must compensate Y for any reasonable expenses Y incurred, as well as the income the hotel was deprived of if the room could not be let otherwise for the period concerned (Art. 6.249 CC).

III. As the termination of a contract is regulated by a special norm (Art. 6.721 CC), Art. 6.204 cannot be applied in this situation either. Neither can X demand modification of the contract in accordance with Art. 6.204 CC, as he could have predicted the postponement of the

[572] Alfonsas Vileita *et al.*, *Commentary on Book I of the Civil Code* (Vilnius: Justitia), p. 198 (in Lithuanian).

exhibition and, by his failure to inform the hotel about the purpose of his trip, he assumed the possible risks.

(b) Terrorist movement

I. X is able to pay for the reserved room and to stay in the hotel. Thus, there is no impossibility of performance in this case.

II. However, X might be entitled to cancel the reservation and not be liable for damages if he proves that the threat of a terrorist attack is an event of force majeure. Serious threats to life, including serious threats of terrorist attacks qualify as events of force majeure (Art. 6.212).[573] The situation conforms to the conditions of force majeure defined in Art. 6.212 CC, as: (i) the information about a possible terrorist attack against tourists was received after the reservation; (ii) those circumstances were beyond X's control and could not have reasonably been predicted by him; (iii) X was not in the position to prevent a terrorist attack; (iv) the performance of the contract, i.e., his arrival in the hotel would have entailed a serious threat to X's life and health, especially having in mind the spread of terrorism and its real danger in the modern world. As life and health are of highest value, the principle of reasonableness requires that a person may not be forced to perform a contract at a risk to his health and life.

III. As has been mentioned, force majeure exempts from civil liability (Art. 6.253(2) CC). Consequently, no fault can be attributed to X for the fact that the obligations are not performed. Thus he is to be exempted from civil liability, as this requires a fault of one party (Art. 6.248 CC).

(c) Strike at the airport

I. The doctrines of impossibility of performance and mistake cannot be applied in this case.

II. Instead, X is entitled to cancel the reservation. The strike at the airport qualifies as an event of force majeure if X proves that there was no other transport available to reach the hotel in due time. In such case, X is not liable in respect of Y's hotel. This conclusion is based on the fact that, according to Art. 6.212 CC, strike in this situation is attributed to the circumstances of force majeure, as: (i) X could not have predicted it; (ii) it was beyond his control; (iii) X was not in the position to prevent it; (iv) the risk in this case is transferred to the hotel, as X (on the assumption that he is a customer) is considered to be the weaker

[573] Mikelenas, *Commentary on Book VI of the Civil Code*, p. 235.

party. The difference between Case 7(c) and Case 7(a) is that in Case 7(a) X is still able to visit a city in which he booked the hotel. Article 6.721 CC is not applicable in this case, because although it allows a customer to terminate a contract without any reasons it also establishes the duty of the customer to pay part of the price and compensate the hotel proprietor for his losses.

(d) Coronation procession

I. In this case, the contract under discussion could be qualified as a contract which created a conditional obligation (Arts. 6.30–6.32 CC). Until the condition – coronation procession – is not fulfilled, Y cannot require performance. In this case, the obligations of the parties extinguish without causing any liability for the non-performance of the condition. This conclusion is made on the assumption that Y was aware of X's intention to watch the coronation procession. Even if the hotel had not been aware of this circumstance, X could refer to Art. 6.196 CC. The reservation time (at the time of the coronation procession) and the price of the room (ten times higher than usual) constitutes obvious evidence that the contract contained an implied condition: X was prepared to perform the contract only if the coronation procession occurred at the set time. If the court does not support this position, X might invoke other legal instruments.

II. The doctrine of impossibility is not applicable in this case as X was able to perform his obligation both in a legal and a factual sense. The doctrine of mistake only relates to facts that were in existence at the time when the contract was concluded, and is not applicable either.

III. Article 6.721 CC allows a party to terminate the contract without any reasons, but also establishes the duty of the client to pay part of the price and compensate the counter-party for any losses. If the reservation was made for the sole purpose of watching the coronation procession, the performance of the contract is meaningless for X. Thus, it could be stated that X is entitled to demand dissolution of the contract and exemption from his obligation as all requirements stipulated in Art. 6.204 CC are fulfilled: (i) The cancellation of the coronation procession took place after the conclusion of the contract; (ii) At the time when the contract was concluded, X could not have reasonably expected the occurrence of this event. Events of this kind usually are only cancelled due to extraordinary reasons, while an ordinary person may not be expected to predict all possible extraordinary cases; (iii) This circumstance was beyond X's control; (iv) X could not reasonably be required to assume the risk of such an extraordinary circumstance as mentioned in (ii). Regretfully, there is no relevant court practice or doctrine to support this conclusion.

Czech Republic

In every case X has the right to terminate the contract (cancel the reservation). But X is obliged to pay compensation for the loss caused by the cancellation if Y proves that he was not able to prevent the loss.

I. 1. For all four cases, Section 759(1) Civil Code is decisive; under this provision the accommodated guest may withdraw from the contract before the lapse of the agreed time. The guest must compensate the loss caused to the accommodation provider by the cancellation if the accommodation provider was not able to prevent the loss.

2. The provision applies to all of the cases in question, regardless of the reason for the cancellation of the reservation (contract) by the accommodated guest including the frustration of the contract's purpose.[574]

II. The solution chosen by the Czech legislator is very specific. It retains the freedom of the accommodated guest to unbind himself from the obligation at any time, whereupon the risk is shifted to the accommodation provider who is obliged to replace the guest who cancelled the accommodation contract. The accommodation provider also bears the burden of proof in respect of his obligation to avert loss resulting from the cancelled accommodation. However, the important thing is that the accommodated guest may in the end, pay the full price of the accommodation, even if it is increased ten times (as in the case of (d)) and only then may the issue of good morals be considered (as in the case of (d) and possibly also in the case of (b)).

Scandinavian jurisdictions

Sweden

X will be entitled to cancel the reservation in all the Cases (a)–(d), as a reservation is not regarded as binding in a Swedish hotel. If reservations were binding in this hotel, X would be entitled to cancel the contract, or have it adjusted in Cases (b) and (d), but not in Cases (a) or (c).

[574] See the wording of Section 759(1) Civil Code.

General

I. 1. X would normally be entitled to cancel the hotel reservation in all the Cases (a)–(d), because a reservation is generally not binding in a Swedish hotel. In some exceptional cases different procedures are used, e.g., a credit card number may be given as a guarantee. The hotel must then be informed on the planned day of arrival, or maybe even the day before, or payment has to be made, although only for the first night. At some hotels it is possible to contract for a binding reservation. These are exceptional cases, however: if X and Y have contracted for a binding reservation as an extraordinary arrangement, the aim of this would normally be that X assumes the risk of changed circumstances. If this is the case, X is not entitled to cancel the reservation.

2. Furthermore, it might be the case that Y for some reason always requires a binding reservation and X is aware of that. In all the four case alternatives, an ordinary performance assumption – which has to do with X's use of the performance received – has failed. Assumptions of this type are comparatively often of legal relevance in case law. Still, according to the general rule, they are not relevant.[575] None of the case alternatives (a)–(d) has been addressed in Swedish case law.

II. If X has contracted for a binding reservation, the first question is whether X has assumed the risk of changed circumstances. If so, the doctrine of assumptions cannot be applied as the basic prerequisite of good faith is not met. We will assume that this is not the case.

(a) Cancellation of the exhibition

I. The first alternative is a normal daily life situation and provided that Y has not issued a warranty or a clarification or acted in bad faith, it is difficult to argue that X would be entitled to cancel the binding reservation under the doctrine of assumptions. There are no good arguments why the reservation should not be binding.

(b) Terrorist movement

I. The second case, where a terrorist movement declares that it is to launch a campaign against tourists in a Swedish town, is on the other hand very extreme. Provided that this threat is to be taken seriously, X is not able to use the hotel room without risking his life and health. This is

[575] The issue whether Chapter 12 of the Code of Land Laws regarding rental of real estate ('hyra av fast egendom') is applicable to the rental of a hotel room is disputed. Regardless of which, the Code does not address the current issues.

likely to heavily influence the market price of the hotel room. If so, Y has made a profit at the expense of X, as the parties agreed on the regular price instead of the lower price that would have been agreed if the parties had known of these circumstances. X is therefore entitled to cancel the contract or have it adjusted under the doctrine of assumptions.

II. Section 36 Contracts Acts also allows for the introduction of a new rule that cancellation can take place on the basis that X is not able to use the hotel room without risking life and health.

(c) Strike at the airport

I. The third case is a normal daily life situation similar to Case (a), and it is difficult to find an argument to the effect that X would be entitled to cancel the reservation. There are no good arguments why the hotel reservation should not be binding.

(d) Coronation procession

I. The fourth case is a normal daily life situation too, but here the high price must also be considered as an argument. The parties assumed that the coronation procession would take place as planned. When it did not, Y made a profit at the expense of X, as the agreed price is ten times higher than the regular price which would normally have been agreed if X had booked the room knowing there would be no procession. X is therefore entitled to cancel the contract, or have it adjusted, under the doctrine of assumptions.

II. Under Section 36 Contracts Act, a hotel reservation can be modified or set aside if it is unreasonable with reference to the contents of the contract, the circumstances at the formation of the contract, circumstances arising later, and other circumstances. The contract is unreasonable with reference to the price and the changed conditions; the extremely high price is a good argument for adjusting the contract, but not necessarily for cancellation.

Denmark

Under Danish Law, X is not entitled to cancel the contract in Case 7(a). He may deduct the price by the amount of the expenses saved by Y. The result is uncertain in Cases 7(b) and 7(c). In Case 7(d), the coronation procession is treated as a condition of the contract. X will be required to pay the regular price but not the price raised due to the procession.

General

I. Traditionally, in Denmark it is possible to cancel a hotel reservation if the cancellation is made in due time before the person in question is supposed to use the room. Normally, a cancellation has to be announced at least twenty four hours before the reservation takes effect.

II. It seems that Danish case law does not have any cases which are similar to the ones in question. There is, however, a single case where the claimant claimed that a cancellation fee was a violation of Section 36 Contracts Act.[576] The hotel attached the cancellation conditions to the confirmation statement sent to the customer. The Højesteret stated that there had been no violation of Section 36 Contracts Act since such conditions are customary in the hotel sector in Denmark.

(a) Cancellation of the exhibition

I. It is not possible to invoke the rule of mistake in Section 32(1) Contracts Act unless the promisee in question – Y – has acted in bad faith. Pursuant to the case, there is no evidence that Y had acted in bad faith, in other words knowing at the time of the reservation that the exhibition would be cancelled.

II. Danish law does not contain any general or specific provisions on the risk of such unexpected circumstances as the one in question.

III. 1. X is not entitled to cancel the reservation, as it would be a violation of the main principle that agreements are binding. X could have made an agreement concening the issue, but in general that is very rare. X might invoke the use of the doctrine of assumptions, but it is very unlikely that any Danish court would recognise that all three conditions are fulfilled. It is very likely that X would never have wanted to book the hotel room had he known that the exhibition was going to be cancelled. However, the condition of perceptibility can hardly be regarded as having been met, since it must be considered very unlikely that the hotel would have any information about X's intention to visit the exhibition. Finally, the condition of relevance cannot be considered to have been fulfilled, since there is no argument as to why Y should bear the economic risk that the exhibition would be cancelled. In a case such as this, contracts that are concluded must be maintained.

[576] U 1985.23/2H.

2. Unless Y has the opportunity to rent the room to another customer in order to minimise the costs of X, X has to pay for the room in question but can deduct the amount which Y has saved due to the non-use of the room.

(b) Terrorist movement

I. In order to apply Section 36 Contracts Act, the agreed reservation must be considered unfair. It (also) applies to subsequent circumstances which make the fulfilment of the contract unreasonable. The application of Section 36 Contracts Act would probably lead to the result that X has the obligation to cover the costs, but not the lost profit which Y suffered as a result of the cancellation. Such an application, however, is arguable because it would solely transfer the risk to the hotel, which is not in a better position to evaluate the risk of terrorist threats.

II. The campaign launched by the terrorist movement is a subsequent circumstance, which the parties did not take into account when they concluded the contract. Thus, it is worth discussing whether the doctrine of assumptions could be applied. It is more than likely that X would not have booked the room if he had known about the campaign launched by the terror movement. The assumption is also to be considered perceptible for Y. Once again, the condition of relevance is the crucial requirement. With regard to this one may argue that the hotel will incur substantial losses if all the tourists who have booked a room are entitled to invoke the doctrine of assumptions, while the individual loss of each tourist is comparably low. Therefore, based on the facts of the case, the condition of relevance is not fulfilled in this case.

III. Traditionally, the principle of force majeure applies to acts of terrorism. As mentioned in the overview (Chapter 4), three conditions must be fulfilled in order to comply with the doctrine of force majeure in Danish law. Pursuant to the given case, X and Y were not aware that a terrorist campaign against tourists was about to be launched when the contract was concluded. Furthermore, such a threat must be considered to be an extraordinary event pursuant to the doctrine of force majeure. The crucial question is whether this extraordinary event prevents X from fulfilling the contract. This question depends upon an evaluation of the imminent risk. If the threat poses a relevant risk to X, he is not liable and the contract lapses.

(c) Strike at the airport

I. A strike preventing the fulfilment of the contract would normally be considered to be a case of force majeure in accordance with Danish law.

If, due to the strike, X has no possibility of reaching the hotel, he is not liable to pay damages. If the doctrine of force majeure is applied, X would still have to pay the costs incurred by Y in conjunction with the agreement. X must give notice to Y concerning the situation. If X is able to arrive at the hotel at a later stage, X has an obligation to fulfil that part of the contract and would otherwise be considered liable. Such an obligation is derived from the common principle of loyalty in Danish contract law.

(d) Coronation procession

I. X and Y have concluded an agreement, according to which X agrees to pay a very high price for the room in order to watch the coronation procession from the room. This must be considered as a contractual condition. Otherwise, X would never have agreed to pay ten times the regular price. Thus, the doctrine of assumptions is not applicable to the case. One cannot argue that Y has breached the contract, since the cancellation of the coronation procession is a subsequent circumstance beyond the control of Y. However, based on the mentioned contractual condition, X is under no obligation to pay the agreed price. Yet one could argue that X should pay the normal price for the room.

II. The cancellation of the coronation procession would not be considered to be force majeure pursuant to Danish law. In other words, force majeure is not relevant to the case.

Romanic-Mediterranean jurisdictions

Italy

If X cancels the reservation, Y is entitled to recover damages for the loss of profit due to the breach of contract in Cases (a) and (b). X is entitled to cancel the reservation without paying damages to Y in Cases (c) and (d).

(a) Cancellation of the exhibition

I. 1. X is not entitled to terminate the contract. It cannot be said that frustration of purpose has occurred since a visit to the cancelled exhibition was not even an implied condition of the agreement; the Italian doctrine of *presupposizione* would therefore not apply.

2. Scholars and courts affirm that under Italian law the individual purposes or motives of each party may not affect the contract, unless they are illegal and common to both parties (in such case the relevant

purposes render the contract null and void, Art. 1345 and 1418 CC). This is not the case with the visit of the exhibition, which is obviously neither illegal nor common to both parties. It is in the exclusive interest of X and rests within his/her individual grounds for the reservation of the room.

3. As a consequence of the cancellation X must pay damages to Y. However, on the basis of a general rule, Art. 1227 CC, Y has the duty of mitigation of the said losses and must try to use the room for other guests. In this case, the savings/profits of Y due must be deducted from the amount of the damages.

II. The solution would be different if Y had promoted a tourist special offer (e.g., travel plus hotel reservation) in connection with a visit to the exhibition. In this latter case a visit to the exhibition would not be an individual purpose of X alone.

(b) Terrorist movement

I. 1. The announcement of the terrorist movement against tourists is of course a good reason not to travel and therefore to cancel the reservation of the room, but this supervening event does not represent a case of impossibility.

2. In fact, in the case at hand, X's contractual obligation can actually be performed, and may not be considered impossible in principle. As has already been said,[577] termination for supervening impossibility is only operable if the performance becomes actually impossible in a strict sense, as the 'extraordinary difficulty' in rendering the performance is not a legitimate reason for terminating the contract under the rules of Arts. 1463 *et seq.* CC.

II. This is not a case of an excessive burden of the performance because the balance between the performances has not been altered. Neither does the doctrine of *presupposizione* apply since this legal concept ('*presupposizione*') concerns an implied assumption of the existence of some circumstances by both parties. In the case at issue the existence of the circumstances is unknown to the other party, and, on the other hand, it has been said that, in principle, under Italian law the individual purposes or motives of each party may not affect the contract (unless they are illegal and common to both parties). Accordingly, X is not entitled to terminate the contract, since his/her mere expectation may not be considered an assumption of the contract.

577 See Overview (Chapter 4).

(c) Strike at the airport

I. The unforeseeable strike of airport personnel entitles X to cancel the reservation without paying damages to Y, since the strike prevents X from travelling at the specified time to the city where the hotel is located. This is therefore a typical case of force majeure, although X's performance is not impossible in a technical sense (i.e., payment for the reserved room could still go ahead). Under Italian law there is no statutory provision explicitly dedicated to force majeure, but Art. 1218 CC provides rules about contractual responsibility and the discharge of the debtor. The supervening event obviously frustrates the contract.

II. Even if the rules about '*presupposizione*' consider the change of the circumstances as a reason for the legitimate dissolution or termination of the contract, this doctrine does not apply in the case at hand, because the absence of a strike cannot be considered as an implied assumption of the parties.

III. Needless to say that the remedy of the termination of the contract would also be available in favour of X because the performance has become excessively onerous (Art. 1467 CC), as travelling to the city where the hotel is located would be too expensive for X. As to the quantum of damages (deduction of savings/profits of Y for an alternative use of the room), see above, under Case 7(a).

(d) Coronation procession

I. X is not entitled to avoid the contract pursuant to the rules of mistake (Arts. 1427 *et seq.* CC), since the parties have never discussed the chance that the coronation procession would not take place. This is a supervening event.

II. Further, the circumstances prevent X from taking legal action in order to be discharged according to the rules of impossibility (Arts. 1463 *et seq.* CC). The performance is in fact not impossible with regard to both X and Y.

III. The most famous case of frustration examined by the English courts would be dealt with by Italian scholars and courts under the doctrine of implied assumptions ('*presupposizione*'), which requires that the parties have either shared these assumptions or at least one party was aware that the other considers them as a foundation of the contract. Nobody would have considered the coronation procession an irrelevant circumstance when X booked the room and accepted to pay a price ten times higher than the regular price. Accordingly, Art. 1467 CC would apply.

Spain

In Case 7(a)–(c) X has to bear the risk and is bound by the contract. In Case 7(d) he is entitled to cancel the reservation under Spanish law.

General

I. 1. All the variations of Case 7 would probably be solved by the Spanish courts not on the grounds of the '*cláusula rebus sic stantibus*' doctrine, but as cases where the '*causa*' of the contract has disappeared.

2. In Spanish law, the '*causa*' is an essential element of the contract; without a *causa* the contract is deemed not to exist (Art. 1261 CC). According to Art. 1274 CC, the *causa* for a party in onerous contracts is the performance of or the promise of performance by the other party. The *causa* is generally understood in an objective sense as the aim which is typically pursued by the parties to each contract (for instance, in sales contracts, the delivery of goods in exchange for payment).[578] However, the Spanish judiciary and doctrine admit that the subjective aims of the parties can have juridical relevance if they were known to both parties and the parties have formulated the contract on the basis of these grounds.[579]

3. The *causa*, as described above, is a condition for the validity of a contract. However, there are cases in which the *causa* is present at the moment the contract is concluded but disappears later on. In these cases, the doctrine of the disappearance of the basis of the contract will apply.

(a) Cancellation of the exhibition

I. This is not a case of (objective) impossibility to perform. Both parties can perform; the crucial question is only if performance is too onerous due to the circumstances.

II. Under Spanish law, there is no statutory provision providing for a specific risk allocation for these types of contracts. The risk that the exhibition is cancelled must be borne by X. His reasons are purely

[578] Código Civil Comentado, 1997, p. 551; L. Díez Picazo and B, Gullón, *Sistema de Derecho Civil* (Madrid: Tecnos, 2002), p. 47; Lacruz Berdejo *et al.*, *Elemeutos de derecho civil, Derecho de obligadciones*: Coutratus cuasicoutratos (Madrid: Dykensai, 2009), p. 143.

[579] Cf. STS of 30 June 1948 (RJ 1948, 1115), STS of 11 July 1984 (RJ 1984, 3939), STS of 30 December 1985 (RJ 1985, 6620), STS of 19 January 1990 (RJ 1990, 19), STS of 20 April 1994 (RJ 1994, 3216), STS of 30 June 2006 (RJ 2000, 6747), STS 10 April 2002 (Act. C. 2002, 492).

personal, that is to say reasons of a subjective nature that are not known to the other party and that were not relevant at the time the agreement was concluded. Therefore X has to pay the price.

(b) Terrorist movement

In Case 7(b), one can argue that, again, it is X who should bear the risk and pay for the room. The room does objectively fit the use stipulated in the contract. It is X who decides that he no longer has an interest in performance by the other party due to (subjective) security reasons. He is therefore not entitled to cancel the reservation.

(c) Strike at the airport

I. This solution also applies to Case 7(c), as the transport risk is generally attributed to the customer while there is no problem with regard to the hotel room.

(d) Coronation procession

I. This is not a case of impossibility. The party can perform; performance has only become much less valuable for X in the circumstances.

II. The case might, however, be qualified as a situation of a lacking *causa*, which is an essential element for the valid conclusion of a contract according to Art. 1261 CC. The existence of the *causa* element is to be assessed at the time the contract is concluded. If there is no *causa* (in its objective sense, that is, the aim which is typically pursued by the parties in each contract), the contract is null and void. However, in the case at hand, the *causa* disappears after the moment of concluding the contract. It is not a question of validity because the contract existed until the *causa* disappeared due to circumstances that took place after the contract was concluded.

III. Yet, X might be allowed to terminate the contract due to a subsequent disappearance of the *causa*. Different from the previous cases, X's special purpose in reserving the hotel room became part of the contract, as the agreed price was ten times higher than the regular price and both parties therefore knew the underlying reason for renting the room, namely providing a place to watch the procession. Due to the cancellation of the procession, the room was not fit for the stipulated use. On this basis, X is not compelled to pay. Therefore, the disappearance of the subjective '*causa*' of the contract will therefore not be understood by the Spanish judiciary as a ground for the annulment of the contract but as a ground for termination.

Portugal

In Case 7(a) the price must be paid fully, while in Case 7(b) it is debatable whether a terrorist threat against tourists would amount to a relevant change in the basis of the contract. Similarly, in Case 7(c) the outcome is not predictable. If the procession in 7(d) is cancelled or postponed there is a fundamental change of the foundation of the contract that justifies termination.[580]

(a) Cancellation of the exhibition

I. The fact that X wants to visit an exhibition and, as a result, booked a room at Y's hotel is, generally, a subjective motive which is irrelevant to the validity of the contract. It might have been ignored entirely by Y; but even Y's knowledge would not be sufficient as long as he did not agree that visiting the exhibition was a condition of the contract and as long as this visit does not represent an element of the basis of the contract, which is common to both parties. The answer could be different, however, if the visit to the exhibition and the booking of the hotel had been part of a package or if the hotel had offered a special price or special conditions and benefits to those who visited the exhibition.[581] Assuming not, the facts do not generally justify the refusal to pay the price or the cancellation of the booking at the very last moment. The very first requirement of Art. 437 CC is not fulfilled: there was no change in an element that was part of the basis of the contract for both parties.

(b) Terrorist movement

I. It is debatable whether a terrorist threat against tourists in a town would amount to a change in the basis of the contract. This depends largely on the facts of the case, mainly on how serious and

[580] The case is frequently quoted by the Portuguese literature as an example of the disappearance of the foundation of the contract: See, for instance, C. Mota Pinto, A. Pinto Monteiro and P. Mota Pinto, *Teoria Geral do Directo Civil* (Coimbra: Combra Editora, 4th edn, 2005), p. 515 and pp. 610–611; José de Oliveira Ascensão, 'Onerosidade Excessiva', p. 640, and António Pinto Monteiro, 'Erro e teoria da imprevisão', in: Alfredo Calderale (ed.), *Il nuovo codice civile brasiliano* (Milan: Giuffrè, 2003), pp. 65 *et seq.*

[581] Another example would be a hotel within a theme park (such as Eurodisney) where the visit to the park might be considered the basis of the contract. So if the park was subsequently closed to the public the booking of a hotel within the park for that period may also be cancelled.

unforeseeable the threat was. On the one hand, terrorist threats are largely unpredictable and amount to the political sphere of society.[582] On the other hand, terrorist threats are an almost daily event in our society and the fears must be justified in order to be a ground for termination of a contract. According to Art. 437 CC, only an anomalous change in a circumstance is relevant. In certain areas of the globe, political turmoil and terrorist attacks are rather frequent and would be predictable at the moment when the contract was concluded. If a court terminates the contract according to Art. 437 CC, the issue of damages does not emerge (namely reliance damages) since contractual liability normally requires that a party required to pay damages is responsible for an event and in a case of supervening events neither party is at fault.

(c) Strike at the airport

I. 1. It is very difficult to assess to what extent a strike of the airport personnel might be considered a cause or a justification for the termination of the contract or for its adaptation under Art. 437 CC. It is stated that the strike was unforeseeable and therefore we believe that it might provide such a ground. Again it might be said that in some countries strikes are a rather common event and one that belongs to the general risk of life.

2. It could also be argued that in such a contract the person who books the room bears the risk of transport to the location of the hotel.

(d) Coronation procession

I. The object of the lease was precisely to attend to the procession and the price was much higher than normal due to the coronation procession. Therefore, it is not only a subjective motive irrelevant to the fate of the contract. Quite in contrast, the procession was the common ground for the contract (and the price). The price itself shows that the procession was the main circumstance that represents the basis of the contract. It is still possible for the debtor to perform the obligation (the lease) but the purpose envisaged by both parties can no longer be attained.

II. Although there are cases of strict contractual liability in Portuguese law, the rule is that liability requires faulty behaviour

[582] A sharp increase in the level of terrorist activity or a dramatic and unforeseen event such as 9/11 would probably be accepted as a relevant change of circumstances.

(*'culpa'*). In these cases of supervening events that undermine the basis of the contract there is no fault of either of the contractual partners. As a result, it seems that each one will have to bear his/her own losses. So Y cannot claim any indemnification due to the cancelled reservation.

Greece

- **(a) Similarly to Case 6, X has no right to cancel the reservation.**
- **(b) X will not be entitled to cancel the reservation.**
- **(c) X has no right to cancel the reservation or terminate the contract.**
- **(d) X will be discharged from the contract.**

(a) Cancellation of the exhibition

I. Similarly to Case 6, X has no right to cancel the reservation. The 'secondary cause'[583] for X's visit has not become an explicit content of the contract. As there were no specific indications during the negotiation or formation of the contract, an implicit condition cannot be assumed. In particular, this specific purpose did not influence the contractual terms, especially on the rent (see below under (d)). Thus, the frustration of this purpose does not affect the validity of the contract (cf. Art. 143 AK).[584] There is no chance, whatsoever, for the application of Art. 388 AK, given that an onerous disproportion of the counter-performances is out of the question. There is no other remedy that could lead to termination or even to a deduction of Y's profits.

(b) Terrorist movement

I. The maintenance of the peace and social stability at the place of performance is one of the crucial facts, the absence of which could destroy excessively the balance of the contractual framework. Nevertheless, the declaration of a terrorist action can only under exceptional circumstances be considered as capable of overthrowing social stability. This assessment is always based on an objective point of view regardless of the personal feelings of the creditor. Thus, under this reservation of exceptional circumstances, X will not be entitled to cancel the reservation.

[583] See Case 5. [584] For the content of Art. 143 AK, see above, under Case 5.

(c) Strike at the airport

I. X has no right to cancel the reservation or terminate the contract. Due to the strike, X is unable to accept Y's offer to perform. As a consequence, X is in default of acceptance ('*mora creditoris*') regardless of his lack of fault (see Art. 349 AK).[585] Article 388 AK cannot be applied in favour of X. The frustration of X's plans to travel by plane is a risk that only this party should carry (unless there are explicit contractual clauses which indicate the opposite should apply). Any other opinion would be contrary to the objective prerequisites of creditor's default and, furthermore, the objective character of the circumstances, which are considered to be crucial in the framework of Art. 388.

(d) Coronation procession

I. Due to the agreed price, the 'secondary cause' of X became an implicit clause of the contract according to the rules of complementary interpretation.[586] Thus, the frustration of this cause does not affect the underlying basis of the contract, since it has already become its content.[587] Instead, it constitutes non-performance of the contract, here in the form of a non-fault impossibility,[588] since Y is irreversibly not in the position to provide the use of the leased room for the agreed purpose. In cases of impossibility both parties are released *ipso iure* (rule of common release; Art. 380 §1 AK) if neither party is at fault. If the counter-performance, here the rent, has already been fulfilled, it must be restituted by means of the provisions of unjust enrichment (Arts. 904 *et seq.* AK). Y is not entitled to compensation. Due to the serious increase in the price, he has undertaken the risk of the cancellation of the coronation procession.

[585] In that case, X – as any other creditor who is in default of acceptance – is obliged to pay the debtor's expenses for the ineffectual offer of the performance, as well as his expenses for safeguarding and maintaining the subject matter of performance for as long as the creditor's default of acceptance lasts (see Art. 358 AK).

[586] See Overview (Chapter 4) above.

[587] Therefore, it is best to avoid recognising a 'common', 'normative' or 'intersubjective' cause (either psychological or ontological), parallel to the 'exchange's cause' of the contract. An exceptional case remains the contract of partnership (Arts. 741, 772 AK). For the above approach see W. Flume, *Das Rechtsgeschäft* (Berlin: Springer, 4th edn. 1992), vol. II, p. 513.

[588] Franz Wieacker, 'Performance-act and performance-result in civil contract law', in: Rolf Dietz and Heinz Hübner (eds.), *Festschrift in honour of H. C. Nipperdey* (Munich: Beck, 1965), vol. I, p. 763, 811.

France and related jurisdictions

France

- **(a) X is not entitled to terminate the reservation. However, Y is only entitled to claim damages that were actually incurred.**
- **(b) X is entitled to terminate the contract.**
- **(c) The result is uncertain.**
- **(d) X is discharged from his obligation under the contract.**

(a) Cancellation of the exhibition

I. In principle, frustration of purpose does not allow for a revision or termination of the contract. After all, in this case, the room can be used for all kinds of purposes.

II. If the contract can be characterised as a lease, however, Art. 1722 Cciv could be invoked. This provision refers to cases where it is impossible to use the premises. In this case, the premises can still be used. The question is whether the agreed contractual use includes a right to visit the exhibition. The motive for the visit was not discussed during the negotiations. Even if Y was aware of the motive, it has not become part of the contractual agreement so that X has to bear the risk of the exhibition being cancelled. In order to be protected, the exhibition must have become a condition of the contract. If the contract at hand was to be treated as a service contract, Art. 1722 Cciv would not be applicable at all.

III. From an extensive interpretation of the contract (for instance, an exchange of correspondence indicating a guarantee from the hotel that the exhibition will take place) one could infer that the exhibition was an implied condition in the contract. Following this assumption, the cancellation of the exhibition leads to the annulment of the contract. The judge could also deduce by interpretation that the exhibition is a substantial element within the contract. As it cannot be performed, the contract could be cancelled due to force majeure. However, the facts of the case do not suggest such an interpretation.

IV. Assuming that X is bound by the contract, the question further arises whether X has to pay the entire price. Y would only be entitled to damages which were actually incurred. Thus, if Y can otherwise rent the room, he is not entitled to the total price but has to deduct the rent he would have obtained. On the other hand, he can add any administrative expenses arising from the cancellation.

(b) Terrorist movement

I. One could be inclined to provide the same solution as in Case 7(a). But it is possible that the judge would more readily admit the application of force majeure in this case. The debtor cannot be required to occupy a room that is unsafe. However, the doctrine of force majeure is subject to the following conditions: the event must be exterior, unexpected and irresistible. Under French law the courts apply a strict interpretation. In particular, in a case where a company had assigned an organiser to transport and accommodate its personnel at Marrakesh in January 1991, a court ruled that the Gulf War did not constitute a case of force majeure if the circumstances were not impossible to surmount.[589]

II. Assuming that the contract at hand is a service contract, Art. 1722 Cciv does not apply. It could be contrary to good faith (Art. 1134 Cciv) to oblige the parties to be exposed to a terrorist attack by performing the contract.

(c) Strike at the airport

I. The strike makes it impossible to occupy the room. This could be a force majeure case if the strike was not only unforeseeable but its effects were also beyond the control of X. In order to invoke force majeure the judge must also come to the conclusion that the strike at the airport is not part of X's contractual risks.

(d) Coronation procession

I. Frustration of purpose is not recognised under French law. Therefore the risk must generally be borne by X. However, this case can be interpreted as a situation of force majeure. According to the contract it was the obligation of the lessor to make a room available with a view of the coronation procession. The coronation actually taking place was part of the obligation. Therefore, the cancellation of the coronation was a new and unforeseeable circumstance that rendered the performance of the contract impossible. Thus force majeure has to be applied.[590] The contract is brought to an end and the financial consequences must be resolved on the basis of the principles of unjust enrichment. In other words, if payment has been made in advance, it must be refunded, apart from the administrative expenses incurred by Y.

[589] Cass., 1ère Civ., 8 December 1998, Bull. 1998, I, n° 346, p. 238 [590] *Ibid.*, p. 561.

Belgium

- **(a) X is not entitled to terminate the reservation. However, Y is only entitled to claim damages that were actually incurred.**
- **(b) X is entitled to terminate the contract.**
- **(c) The result is uncertain.**
- **(d) X is discharged from his obligation under the contract.**

(a) Cancellation of the exhibition

I. If the contract can be characterised as a lease, Art. 1722 Cciv could be invoked. This provision refers to cases where it is impossible to use the premises. For example, in a recent case in a lower court, a student had leased a room to study in Tournai. Shortly thereafter, the college refused to register him as a student. The judge considered this to be a case of force majeure.[591] In the case at hand, the premises can still be used. The question is whether the agreed contractual use includes a right to visit the exhibition. According to the facts, the subjective motive of the visit was not discussed during the negotiations. Even if Y was aware of such a motive, it did not become part of the contractual agreement. In order to be protected, X would have had to stipulate that the exhibition was a condition for the contract. If, however, the contract was to be qualified as a service contract, Art. 1722 Cciv would not apply anyhow.

II. A right to cancel the contract might be based on an interpretation of the contract or on an implied condition precedent.[592] From an extensive interpretation of the contract it could be inferred that visiting the exhibition was an implied condition of the contract. Accordingly, the contractual obligations extinguish if the exhibition does not take place. The judge could also deduce from the interpretation of the contract that the exhibition is a substantial element in this contract. The contract could then be cancelled due to force majeure. However, the facts of the case do not suggest any circumstances which could lead to such an interpretation.

III. In principle, frustration of purpose does not lead to a revision or termination of the contract.

IV. Therefore X cannot cancel the reservation. However, Y is only entitled to claim damages that were actually incurred. Thus, if Y can otherwise rent the room, he will not be entitled to claim the total price

[591] J.P. Tournai, 8 March 2008, *JLMB*, 2008, p. 522.

[592] See H. De Page, t.II, p. 549.

as the rent which has been otherwise obtained will be subtracted from the quantum of damages. On the other hand, he can add administrative expenses due to the cancellation of the room by X.

(b) Terrorist movement

I. One could be inclined to provide the same solution as in Case 7(a). But it is possible that the judge would more readily admit the application of force majeure in this case. It cannot be required that the debtor occupies a room which is unsafe. Its application is, however, submitted to the following conditions: the event must be exterior, unexpected and inevitable, in order to legitimate the cancellation of the reservation. With regard to a sudden terrorist threat, these requirements are met.

II. The principle of good faith (Art. 1134 Cciv) could also apply in this case, as it is contrary to good faith to oblige the parties to a contract to be exposed to a terrorist attack.

(c) Strike at the airport

I. The strike makes it impossible to occupy the room. It would be a case of force majeure if the strike was not only unforeseeable but its effects were also beyond the control of X. The judge must also consider that this strike at the airport does not enter into the field of the contractual risks to be borne by X. The result is very difficult to predict because the appreciation of the facts by the judge could be very broad in this case.

(d) Coronation procession

I. Frustration of purpose is not recognised under Belgian law. So the risk must generally be borne by X. However, this case can be interpreted as a situation of force majeure. The interpretation of the contract leads to the conclusion that the obligation of the lessor was to make a room available with a view of the coronation procession; this can be based on the fact that the price was ten times higher than normal. Therefore, the cancellation of the coronation was a new and unforeseeable circumstance which rendered the performance of the contract impossible. Thus, the principle of force majeure could apply.[593] The contract is brought to an end and the financial consequences must be resolved on the basis of the principles of unjust enrichment. In others words, if

[593] De Page, p. 561.

payment is made in advance it must be refunded. Y can, however, deduct any administrative expenses incurred.

England and related jurisdictions

England and Ireland

The central difference between Cases 7(a), 7(b), 7(c), on the one hand, and 7(d) on the other hand, lies in the notion of risk and consent to risk. The event in the first three situations, cancellation, terrorist threat and strike, are third party events that the hotelier did not have in mind when taking the reservation. In Case 7(d), the coronation procession was at the core of the negotiations and it is easier to foresee that the premium charged in 7(d) makes the risk of cancellation of the coronation an event that Y, the hotelier, may be deemed to have agreed will have a different consequence from 7(a), 7(b) and 7(c). Case law suggests that only in 7(d) will the contract be discharged.

General

I. 1. The four situations in this problem involve the question of the binding nature of a short term obligation that can be performed but that, because of a change of circumstances, will not now result in one contracting party securing a benefit which they expected from the contract. The most famous 'frustration of purpose' cases are undoubtedly the English 'coronation cases'.[594] These cases arose when the coronation of King Edward VII was postponed because of the illness of the King. For example, in *Krell* v. *Henry*[595] one Mr Henry entered into a contract for the hire of rooms overlooking the route of the coronation procession, for the days of the coronation procession. The contract itself made no mention of the coronation, but an advertisement in the window of the rooms said that they were to be let for viewing the procession and the rooms were hired for 'the days but not the nights' of the coronation procession. It was held in the English Court of Appeal that the cancellation of the coronation procession frustrated the contract, not because it was impossible to perform but because the room was no longer of any use for the mutually contemplated purpose. The

594 For a detailed analysis of these cases, see Treitel, *Frustration and Force Majeure* (1994), p. 286–96.

595 [1903] 2 KB 740.

cancellation prevented 'one party from supplying, and the other from obtaining, what the former had contracted to provide and the latter to acquire under the contract'.[596] An alternative way of looking at the case is to say that the foundation or basis of the contract, i.e., the coronation procession, no longer existed and so the contract was frustrated. The court contrasted the facts at hand with a situation where 'a cabman was engaged to take someone to Epsom on Derby Day at a suitable enhanced price for such a journey'. In this situation the happening of the race would not be the foundation of the contract, so the contract would not be frustrated if the race was cancelled:

> Whereas in the present case, where the rooms were offered and taken, by reason of their peculiar suitability from the position of the rooms for a view of the coronation procession, surely the view of the coronation procession was the foundation of the contract, which is a very different thing from the purpose of the man who engaged the cab – namely, to see the race – being held to be the foundation of the contract. Each case must be judged by its own circumstances.[597]

2. *Krell* v. *Henry* can be contrasted with the decision in *Herne Bay Steam Co* v. *Hutton*[598] where a contract for the hire of a steamboat was entered into 'for the purpose of viewing the naval review and for a day's cruise round the fleet'. The naval review was subsequently cancelled, again because of the illness of King Edward VII. The defendant refused to pay the balance owed under the contract, claiming that it had been frustrated. The Court of Appeal disagreed, stating that as the naval review had not been the sole basis or foundation of the contract, there had been no total failure of consideration and the defendant was still obliged to pay the full contract price. In other words, the contract was not frustrated because it was still possible to use the boat to cruise around the fleet, even though the defendant would not be able to get the full enjoyment they expected from the contract.[599]

II. 1. One final issue which emerged from the coronation cases has already been discussed in relation to Case 5 – namely, the effects of

[596] Treitel, *Frustration and Force Majeure*, p. 296.

[597] *Krell* v. *Henry* [1903] 2 KB 740 per Vaughan Williams LJ at 741.

[598] [1903] 2 KB 683.

[599] The court here also took into account the fact that the hiring of the steamboat was a commercial venture, as the defendant hoped to carry tourists and spectators on the boat for a fee. Hence the court was of the view that the defendant took the risk that the venture might fail because of the cancellation of the review. In contrast, the contract in *Krell* v. *Henry* could be viewed as a consumer contract, although it was not expressly stated to be one.

frustration. When the contracts in these cases were frustrated, both parties were excused from performing from the time of the cancellation, so one did not have to provide the room or stand, and the other did not have to pay the agreed price. However, frustration was said to operate prospectively only, and thus any obligations which accrued before the point of frustration still remained. This meant that in cases where the obligation to pay fell before the date of the cancellation of the coronation, the declaration of frustration offered little relief to the party who had hired out the room. For example, in *Chandler* v. *Webster*[600] a contract for the hire of a room to watch the coronation procession was frustrated when the procession was cancelled. The contract had provided that £141 15s. was to be paid in advance of the procession. This sum was due, and £100 of it had in fact been paid, before the cancellation. It was held in the Court of Appeal that although the contract was frustrated, the hirer was not only prevented from recovering his £100 but the liability to pay the remaining £41 15s. remained as it had accrued before the time of discharge.[601] Thus, the fact that the contract was frustrated made little difference to the hirer, who still had to pay even though he would receive nothing in return. This aspect of the decision in *Chandler* v. *Webster* was rightly overturned in *Fibrosa*,[602] where it was stated that the reasoning in *Chandler* v. *Webster* was contrary to 'endless examples which show that money can be recovered, as for a complete failure of consideration, in cases where the promise was given but could not be fulfilled'.[603] In England, the Law Reform (Frustrated Contracts) Act 1943 was enacted shortly after the *Fibrosa* decision, and thus the actual results of the coronation cases would now be determined according to that Act. In Ireland, as has already been mentioned, there has been no court decision or legislative provision providing for this situation, but the law of unjust enrichment would most likely provide for the return of money paid where there has

[600] [1904] 1 KB 493. See also *Blakely* v. *Muller & Co* [1903] 2 KB 760n, (1903) 88 LT 90; *Krell* v. *Henry* [1903] 2 KB 740.

[601] This liability to pay the accrued hire was based on the idea that a failure to perform (in this case, the failure to pay the £41 15s.) should not place a person in a better position than he would have been in had he performed. See the comments of Collins MR in *Chandler* v. *Webster* [1904] 1 KB 493, 497. See, however, the criticisms of this stance in Buckland, 'Casus and Frustration in Roman Law', (1932–1933) 46 *Harvard Law Review* 1281, 1290, 1294–5.

[602] *Fibrosa Spolka Akcyjna* v. *Fairbairn Lawson Combe Barbour Ltd* [1942] 2 All ER 122.

[603] *Ibid.*, per Viscount Simon LC at 129. See also [1942] 2 All ER 122, per Lord Atkin at 131.

been a total failure of consideration, subject to the possibility of a defence of change of position in suitable circumstances.

2. Turning now to the four situations at hand, it is difficult to see the justice behind permitting X to cancel the reservation in all but the last situation presented.

(a) Cancellation of the exhibition

I. 1. In this situation, X has booked a room at Y's hotel but the exhibition he wants to visit is cancelled at the very last moment. Unless there is an express stipulation in the contract giving X a cancellation right in this situation, X does not appear to have any basis for cancelling the reservation. The situation here would be seen as analogous to the situation where a cab is hired to drive to Epsom on Derby day when the race is cancelled, or the situation in *Herne Bay Steam Co* v. *Hutton*. In other words, the exhibition is not the foundation or basis of the contract – there is nothing 'special' about the room or the booking which would cause a court to believe that the booking was dependent or contingent on the holding of the exhibition. Nor has there been a failure of consideration, as it is still possible for X to use the room for other purposes. Nor could attendance at the exhibition be said to be a 'mutually contemplated purpose' of the contract, but rather X has a personal, and seemingly undisclosed, desire to use the room as a base from which to view the exhibition. Thus, this contract would not be frustrated by the cancellation of the exhibition. Nor would the doctrine of mistake have any impact here, as it only applies where a mistake relates to a fact in existence before the entering into of the contract. Mistake would thus be relevant if the exhibition was cancelled before X made the booking, and X was unaware of this fact, but even then it is doubtful that the courts would provide a remedy as it would most likely be held that X took the risk that it may have been cancelled.

2. Thus, X would be liable to pay for the cost of the room. However, if Y let the room to another person the third party income would be used to offset X's obligation to pay the monies due.

(b) Terrorist movement

I. 1. In this situation, X has booked a room at Y's hotel but a terrorist movement declares that it is to launch a campaign against tourists in that town. If the hotel was actually destroyed or seriously damaged in an attack, then the contract would clearly be frustrated, as per *Taylor* v. *Caldwell*. However, in a situation where the hotel has not actually been damaged, this question becomes more difficult to address. On the one hand, the situation could be viewed as one where X's desire to go to the town has simply been affected by his own fears of the possibility of a terrorist attack. There is nothing impossible about performance, but X simply does not wish to receive the bargained for performance in light of the change in circumstances. On this analysis, the contract would not be frustrated.

2. On the other hand, X could attempt to argue that the potential for personal injury or even death in this situation is so great that contractual performance should be deemed to be impossible and thus frustrated.[604] Such an argument would be given greater force if, for instance, there was a general evacuation of tourists from the town because of the risk to their safety. The hotel (Y) could still potentially rely on a series of English cases in which tenants were still liable to pay rent on leased premises even though they were prevented by legislation or government order from living there.[605] Arguably, these cases could be distinguished on the basis that there the landlord was still capable of performing, i.e., by offering the premises, whereas in the present case arguably the hotel is not capable of offering the rooms where there is a serious risk of personal injury or death. An unusual feature of the doctrine of frustration at common law is that it does not currently operate merely as a defence, but rather is said to arise automatically by operation of law. This means that either party is capable of relying on a frustrating event, even if it does not affect their own performance, and even if the party whose performance is affected is willing to continue with the contract.[606] In the absence of a government order requiring the closure of the hotel, however, the courts are likely to get around this technical aspect of the doctrine of frustration by finding that the threat

[604] See for example *Liston* v. *SS Carpathian (Owner)* [1915] 2 KB 42. Such an argument failed in the rather unusual circumstances of *Hall* v. *Wright* (1858) E B and E 765; 120 ER 695. This was an action for breach of a promise of marriage. The defendant claimed that due to illness he was incapable of marriage without great danger to his life, but he was still held liable for breach of contract. Actions for breach of a promise to marry are no longer allowed in either Ireland or England.

[605] See for example *London & Northern Estates Ltd* v. *Schlesinger* [1916] 1 KB 20. Although these cases can be partly explained on the basis that at the time English law did not recognise that the doctrine of frustration could apply to leases at all, Treitel contends that the majority would not be decided differently today, unless perhaps the lease was for a very short duration: *Frustration and Force Majeure* (1994), p. 304.

[606] See for example *Heilgers & Co* v. *Cambrian SN Co Ltd* (1917) 34 TLR 72.

of terrorist attacks is not so serious to constitute a frustrating event that can be relied upon by X.

3. On balance, it is unlikely in this instance that the contract would be frustrated, unless the threat of terrorist attacks and personal injury is so great that the hotel (Y) is deemed incapable of providing the rooms as agreed, in which case X would be able to rely upon Y's (excused) non-performance as a basis for his own failure to pay the agreed contract price. However, in such a situation it is likely that the hotel would not bring an action for the agreed price.

(c) Strike at the airport

I. 1. In this situation, an unforeseeable strike of airport personnel prevents X from travelling at the specified time to the city where the hotel is located. In the absence of an express provision in the contract dealing with this situation it is unlikely that X will be able to cancel the contract. A court would hold that in entering the contract, X took the risk that he might not be able to use the room booking. The situation would be the same if someone bought a ticket for a concert but was unable to attend because they fell ill on the day of the concert, or if a bride-to-be ordered a wedding dress and the wedding was called off by her fiancé. If X wishes to seek a remedy in this situation he must attempt to do so against the airline with whom he contracted to travel.[607]

2. An interesting case caused by airport delays is the Canadian decision of *Allen* v. *Taku Safari Inc.*[608] This case involved a claim for return of a deposit of CAN $3,383 which was paid towards a guided mountain goat hunt in September 2001. The plaintiff was to take one flight from Michigan to Alaska on 14 September, and another flight on to the hunt site on the 15 September. The first flight was cancelled after the New York terrorist attacks of 11 September 2001, and rescheduled for 16 September. As the delay meant that the plaintiff would not make the flight to the hunt site, he cancelled the trip and sought the return of his deposit. This claim was unsuccessful. It was held that the contract was not frustrated, as the unanticipated circumstances did not make performance impossible but simply delayed performance for two days. There was nothing critical about the timing of the contract, and the

[607] The airline may itself attempt to rely on the strike as an excuse for its failure to perform. However, the courts may find that such a strike was either the fault of or foreseeable by the airline: *McGuill* v. *Aer Lingus & United Airlines*, Unreported, 3 October 1983, Irish High Court.

[608] 2003 BCSC 516 CanLII (British Columbia Supreme Court).

fact that the plaintiff would be delayed two days arriving 'did not impose on the parties radically different obligations from those they assumed under the terms of their contract'.[609] Although this case differs from the problem posed (in the sense that in the hypothetical X is completely prevented from arriving at his destination) it illustrates the reluctance of the courts to offer a remedy to someone in this sort of situation.

(d) Coronation procession

I. 1. This situation bears a close resemblance to the facts of coronation cases such as *Krell* v. *Henry* and there is thus a strong likelihood that the contract would be frustrated by the cancellation of the coronation procession. The tenfold increase in the price of the room indicates that the room was hired for the purpose of viewing the procession and was thus the foundation or basis of the agreement.

2. The question then arises as to the effects of frustration. Frustration discharges both parties of the contractual obligations. Thus, if X was only to pay the hotel tariff upon registration or departure then X is absolved of any contractual obligations of any kind. Neither English nor Irish law would require X to pay for the room at the 'standard' rate as neither jurisdiction allows the courts to 're-write' the contract for the parties. As discussed above, a difficulty might arise if X paid in advance, or was required to pay a deposit, or X reserved the room from an agency that has debited X's credit card and the cancellation occurred after the charge was imposed. While in England, Section 1(2) of the Law Reform (Frustrated Contracts) Act 1943 determines that sums paid in advance can be recovered in the case of a frustrating event,[610] there is no Irish case law or legislative provisions on this issue. However, it is this author's view that also in Ireland, X would most likely be entitled to recover the full amount paid in advance, on the grounds that there was a total failure of consideration: *Fibrosa*.[611]

609 *Ibid.*, at para. 23.

610 Although under the Act the hotel could apply to the court to retain part of the sum paid in advance to cover its expenses it is unlikely that any such claim would be successful, particularly if X has also incurred expenses or loss: see *Gamerco* v. *ICM/Fair Warning* [1995] 1 WLR 1226. The probability of retaining a sum may be increased if, for example, the hotel underwent particular expenses at the request of X: see *Fong* v. *Kerwin* [1929] 3 DLR 612 (Ontario Court of Appeal).

611 *Fibrosa Spolka Akcyjna* v. *Fairbairn Lawson Combe Barbour Ltd* [1942] 2 All ER 122. Here, again, it is unlikely that the hotel could rely on the defence of change of position unless particular reliance on the advance payment could be shown.

Scotland

(a) X would be liable to Y in damages for breach of contract. Y should mitigate his loss by going into the market to seek replacement performance. The damages payable by X would be the difference between the contract price (payable by X) and the price Y has obtained, assuming that he has been able to find replacement performance in the market, (i.e., the price payable by the new guest).

(b) The same comments given at Case 7(a) above in relation to error apply equally here thus ruling out reduction of the contract on that particular ground. Nor is there any statutory risk allocation which would be available to X to reduce the contract. Again, the amount of damages payable by X to Y would be reduced by the amount recouped by Y through re-letting the room.

(c) The same comments given at Case 7(a) above in relation to error apply equally here in order to rule out reduction of the contract on that particular ground. Nor is there any statutory risk allocation which would be available to X to reduce the contract. As a result, the contract is not frustrated and X has no right to cancel his reservation. Again, the amount of damages payable by X to Y would be reduced by the amount recouped by Y through re-letting the room.

(d) In summary, although it is difficult to predict the outcome of Case 7(d), it is suggested that the elevation in price on its own is a weak ground on which to base the argument that the viewing of the procession is the foundation of the contract. The Scottish courts would find that the contract is not frustrated and X would not be entitled to cancel his reservation.

General

I. 1. *Tay Salmon Fisheries Co Ltd* v. *Speedie*[612] and *Mackeson* v. *Boyd*,[613] both discussed above, are illustrations of the concept of frustration of purpose in Scots law. Although it appears to be accepted that this concept is part of Scots law, it is undoubtedly difficult to apply. The purpose may be difficult to identify. Professor McBryde comments, 'Parties to a contract may not have the same purpose nor may each have a single purpose'.[614] Second, for frustration to operate, the purpose must be shared by both parties, although evidence to this effect may not be required if the purpose is so obvious that both parties must be aware

[612] 1929 SC 593. [613] 1942 SC 56. [614] McBryde, *Contract*, para. 21-32.

of it.[615] Examples of an obvious purpose are likely to be rare. Third, the shared purpose must be, in the eyes of both parties, the foundation of the contract.[616]

2. Smith's discussion of the English 'coronation cases,' which are discussed below, explains the rationale behind this approach:

> If seats are let to view a procession, and it does not take place owing (say) to illness of a personage in whose honour it is held, the shopkeeper is deprived of the use of the window for normal purposes. Moreover, had the parties contemplated the event at the time of contracting, it is probable that the purchaser of the seats would have been willing to accept the risk of the procession being cancelled.[617]

(a) Cancellation of the exhibition

I. 1. In this example, X has rented the room in order to visit the exhibition. It is highly unlikely that X has communicated this specific purpose to Y, and the purpose is so specific that it is unlikely that Y would be aware of it as a matter of general knowledge. There is therefore no shared purpose. Even if the purpose were shared between X and Y, it would additionally need to be the foundation of the contract. This being the case, X could not use frustration of purpose as grounds on which to reduce the contract or cancel his reservation.

2. None of the other grounds of frustration, such as impossibility or impracticability apply to this Case.

II. As a general rule, error is only relevant in Scots law where it prevents the parties from reaching *consensus* at the moment of formation of the contract.[618] It is difficult to rationalise X as labouring under an operative error simply because the exhibition has been cancelled (an event occurring post-formation). In any event, unilateral error is highly unlikely to provide a ground for reduction of a contract in Scots law.[619]

III. There is no statutory rule in Scots law concerning risk allocation which would apply to this type of contract. X would be liable to Y in damages for breach of contract. Y should mitigate his loss by going into the market to seek replacement performance. The damages payable by X would be the difference between the contract price (payable by X) and the price Y has obtained, assuming that he has been able to find

[615] *Ibid.*, para. 21–33. [616] *Herne Bay Steam Boat* v. *Hutton* [1903] 2 KB 638.
[617] Smith, *Short Commentary*, p. 849. [618] McBryde, *Contract*, paras. 15–01 – 15–02.
[619] *Ibid.*, para. 15.41.

replacement performance in the market, (i.e., the price payable by the new guest).

(b) Terrorist movement

I. As with Case 7(a) above, the terrorist threat does not affect the shared purpose of the contracting parties and so the doctrine of frustration of purpose does not apply. Nor is the contract frustrated on any other grounds such as impossibility or impracticability, indeed the possibility of X being affected by a terrorist threat is probably very minor. As a result, the contract is not frustrated and X has no right to cancel his reservation.

II. The same comments given at Case 7(a) above in relation to error apply equally here thus ruling out reduction of the contract on that particular ground. Nor is there any statutory risk allocation which would be available to X to reduce the contract. Again, the amount of damages payable by X to Y would be reduced by the amount recouped by Y through re-letting the room.

(c) Strike at the airport

I. Again, this example fails the test of whether X's ability to travel to the hotel affects both the common purpose and the foundation of the contract. Indeed, in this case it is not impracticable for X to travel to his destination given that he could use other means. The same comments given at Case 7(a) above in relation to error apply equally here in order to rule out reduction of the contract on that particular ground. Nor is there any statutory risk allocation which would be available to X to reduce the contract. As a result, the contract is not frustrated and X has no right to cancel his reservation. Again, the amount of damages payable by X to Y would be reduced by the amount recouped by Y through re-letting the room.

(d) Coronation procession

I. 1. Case 7(d) is a variation of the facts of two of the English 'coronation cases,' *Krell* v. *Henry*[620] and *Herne Bay Steam Boat* v. *Hutton*.[621]

2. The status of *Krell* in Scots law is controversial. Two of the most eminent Scottish authors on contract law have suggested that the

620 [1903] 2 KB 740. With regard to this case see the analysis in the English and Irish section.

621 [1903] 2 KB 638. See the English and Irish section.

Scottish courts would not reach the same result on the facts.[622] Nevertheless, one of those authors does not completely rule out the possibility that the courts would decide that a contract was frustrated in this type of situation. Gloag explains:

> If it can be shown either from the nature of the contract, or from external facts judicially known or proved, that foreknowledge of the events which have actually occurred would have precluded the contract, or materially altered its terms, it may be held that the basis of the contract is gone, and that neither party can enforce the contract.[623]

3. Even in English law, the authority of *Krell* is doubtful. It has been doubted by both the House of Lords[624] and the Privy Council.[625] The lack of cases of discharge of a contract through pure frustration of purpose since the coronation cases has been noted.[626] Taking all these issues into account, it seems unlikely that a Scottish court would follow *Krell*.

4. Even if one were to assume that *Krell* is binding in Scotland, it is distinguishable from Case 7(d) on the facts. In *Krell*, the contracts were concerned specifically with the viewing of the coronation procession: that was contemplated by both parties as the foundation of the contract. In Case 7(d) there is little to suggest that the rooms were hired specifically for this purpose. In *Krell* the rooms had been advertised specifically for this purpose, there had been pre-contractual enquiries as to the view of the procession from the window, and the hire was for the day only and not overnight. None of these factors is present in Case 7(d). The price is the only factor in Case 7(d) which might suggest that the rooms are being hired for a special purpose. A marginal rise in price might simply be caused by the staging of a major event, and may have nothing to do with the view from the window in question. However, a tenfold rise in price is so extreme that it might only be explicable on the basis of the special view from the window. Ultimately the issue for the court would be whether the view of the procession was the foundation of the contract, and this is, in essence, a factual question. The court may wish

622 Gloag, *Contract*, 352–3; Smith, *Short Commentary*, 849, who both rely on the Scottish case of *Trevalion* v. *Blanche* 1919 SC 617.

623 Gloag, *Contract*, p. 352.

624 *Joseph Constantine SS Line Ltd* v. *Imperial Smelting Corporation Ltd* [1942] AC 154; *Larrinaga & Co Ltd* v. *Société Franco-Americaine des Phosphates de Médulla* (1923) 39 TLR 316, per Viscount Finlay at 318.

625 *Maritime National Fish Ltd* v. *Ocean Trawlers Ltd* [1935] AC 524.

626 Peel, *Treitel's Law of Contract*, para. 19–043.

to compare prices charged at the time for rooms with views of the procession and prices charged for those without.

5. In summary, although it is difficult to predict the outcome of Case 7(d), it is suggested that the elevation in price on its own is a weak ground on which to base the argument that the viewing of the procession is the foundation of the contract. The Scottish courts would find that the contract is not frustrated and X would not be entitled to cancel his reservation.

Editors' comparative notes

The open jurisdictions

In situation (a) (exhibition cancelled), all open jurisdictions generally deny relief. X's intention to visit the exhibition has not been referred to in the contract. Therefore the rule applies that, as long as the contractual promise is unconditional, each party has to bear the risk that its envisaged purposes can be achieved under the contract.

Some reports like the Italian one, however, mention the fact that Y has a duty to mitigate the consequences by trying to use the room for other guests. If he can do so, Y's savings/profits must be deducted from the contract price. The same result is achieved in Lithuania, where X may cancel the reservation but has to compensate Y for lost profits if he cannot let the room to anyone else.

In situation (b) (terrorist threat), there is no clear tendency among the open jurisdictions, as the results largely depend on an assessment of the facts. In Austria, the Netherlands, Lithuania and Sweden, the terrorist threat is considered to constitute a relevant change of circumstances and therefore X may cancel the contract. In the other open systems, the threat is not deemed to be sufficient to frustrate the contract (cf. the German, Greek, Italian and Spanish report). Yet, some of these reports point out that relief could be granted, if the risk was sufficiently severe and if it was unforeseeable at the time the contract was concluded.

With regard to the details of the remedy, most reports only discuss termination. However, under German and Dutch law, the losses may be split between X and Y by equitable adjustment of the contract.

In situation (c) (strike by airport personnel), X is not entitled to cancel the contract in most of the open jurisdictions as X bears the risk of transport to the hotel. The Greek report points out that the rules on the creditor's failure of acceptance ('*mora creditoris*') apply regardless of the creditor's fault. Some reports (Austria, Italy) state that X can deduct from the contract price any benefits gained by Y. A different allocation of risk is only presented by the Italian and Lithuanian reports according to which X may cancel the contract if there is no other way for him to get to the hotel.

A clear tendency towards relief can be found in the reports on situation (d) (coronation procession cancelled). The cancellation of the procession is relevant because this event is reflected in the price agreement. X is accordingly entitled to cancel the contract in most jurisdictions. In Germany and Sweden, the contract may be adjusted to the normal price.

The closed jurisdictions

Like the open jurisdictions, all closed jurisdictions deny relief in situation (a) (exhibition cancelled). The reports also indicate that the claim of the hotel is reduced by any benefits gained from the cancellation (cf. Belgium, England and Ireland, France, Scotland and Slovenia).

In situation (b) (terrorist threat) there is no clear tendency amongst the 'closed' jurisdictions. The terrorist threat may justify cancellation in Belgium, the Czech Republic and France. Similarly, in Slovenia, the client only has to pay the reservation costs. On the other hand, the client is not entitled to cancel the contract in England, Ireland or Scotland because performance is still possible. The English and Irish report, however, indicates that the threat may justify frustration under more severe circumstances.

In situation (c) (strike by airport personnel), the client has to pay the contract price in England, Ireland, Scotland and Slovenia, because he bears the risk of transport.

Finally, in situation (d) (coronation procession cancelled), there is a strong tendency for relief. X is entitled to terminate the contract in Belgium and France on the basis of force majeure, and in England, Ireland and Slovenia because the contract has been frustrated. In Slovenia, the right to terminate is based on the fact that, due to the increased price, the purpose of the visit has become an element of the contract. A certain reluctance concerning relief is expressed by the Danish and the Scottish reports. According to Scottish law, the increased price is too weak a ground to assume that the purpose of the visit was part of the foundation of the contract. In Denmark, the contract price is reduced to the normal rate based on constructive interpretation of the contractual agreement.

Conclusion

There is clear tendency against relief across all jurisdictions in cases in which the individual purpose of the reservation has been frustrated (situation (a), exhibition cancelled). Likewise there is a broad consensus that the hotel guest has to bear the risk of transport and therefore no relief is available if he does not arrive in time due to a strike of the airport personnel (situation (c)).

In contrast, no clear tendency can be derived from the reports on the situation involving a terrorist threat (situation (b)). Some jurisdictions from both groups regard the threat (at least potentially) as force majeure and grant relief on the basis of their respective 'exceptional' doctrines. However, the relevance of the threats largely seems to depend on the facts (e.g., the probability and the foreseeability of the attacks).

A clear tendency for relief can be stated in the coronation case (situation (d)); most jurisdictions refer to the fact that the price reflects the procession and conclude that the hotel owner has to bear the risk. The predominant remedy is termination, while adjustment is discussed by the German and the Swedish report, as well as in the closed jurisdiction reports of Denmark (on the basis of constructive interpretation) and the Czech Republic (on the basis of public morality).

It is remarkable that the tendencies of the reports do not vary much with regard to the distinction of the open and the closed jurisdictions. The solutions mainly depend on how the contractual risk allocation is assessed by the courts in the different legal systems and on how serious the individual events are in light of the parties' expectations at the time of the agreement.

Case 8 Shop rental

Renting a retail outlet; unexpected business environment at a shopping centre

X is the owner of a bookshop. He contracts with Y to rent business accommodation in Y's shopping centre. The fixed period of the lease is five years. The shopping centre has just been built and a large part of the accommodation is still unoccupied. Both parties expect at the time of contracting that a variety of shops (the hotel and catering trade, retail sales) will be located there. One year later almost all the accommodation is rented, but three quarters of the shopping centre consists of restaurants and cafes. For that reason most potential customers visit the shopping centre after X closes the doors of his bookshop.

Is X entitled to an adjustment or to a termination of the contract?

Germany and related jurisdictions

Germany

X is not entitled to cancel or renegotiate the contract under German law.

I. X cannot avoid the contract according to §119 BGB.[627] §119 I BGB does not apply because the content of the contract reflects X's actual will at the time of closing. §119 II BGB does not apply either. Even though X made specific assumptions about the future occupation of the centre, they do not refer to a 'quality' of the contractual object.[628] First, it is doubtful whether the 'occupation of the centre' qualifies as 'quality' of the rented business accommodation as it is neither related to the nature of the premises nor a condition founded in its nature. Second, the mistake must not concern a *future* attribute of the subject-matter.[629] Hence, X's misconception about the occupation of the centre merely amounts to a non-operative mistake in the inducement.[630]

II. 1. The parties contracted for a fixed period of time.[631] According to §542 II BGB the lease can only be terminated early if there are grounds provided for by statute that justify a termination without notice. The right of termination without notice for an important reason is laid down in §543 BGB. According to §543 I 2 BGB an 'important reason' requires that it is unreasonable for one of the parties to be bound by the contract any longer considering all circumstances and balancing the interests of both parties.[632] Moreover, the important reason has to emanate from the sphere of the other party.[633]

627 According to some legal writers the rules of mistake do not apply after the lessee has possession of the good, cf. for an overview and further references V. Emmerich, 'Nichtigkeit und Anfechtung von Mietverträgen', (1998) *NZM*, 692 (694 *et seq.*).

628 For further details see Case 5.

629 Cf. Ellenberger, '§119', in: Palandt *et al.* (eds.), *Bürgerliches Gesetzbuch*, n. 24.

630 If the mistake concerns a 'quality' of the leased property according to some legal writers the rules of mistake are superseded by the warranty of quality, cf. for further references Emmerich, 'Nichtigkeit und Anfechtung von Mietverträgen', W. Weidenkaff, '§536', in: Palandt *et al.* (eds.), *Bürgerliches Gesetzbuch*, n. 12.

631 For an overview regarding the legal problems related to the lease of business premises in a shopping centre cf. W. E. Joachim, 'Wirklichkeit und Recht des Shopping – Centers bzw. Einkaufzentrums', (2000) *NZM*, 785 *et seq.*

632 Cf. Weidenkaff, '§543', in: Palandt *et al.* (eds.), *Bürgerliches Gesetzbuch*, nn. 31 *et seq.*

633 Cf. Weidenkaff, '§543', in: Palandt *et al.* (eds.), *Bürgerliches Gesetzbuch*, n. 5.

2. First, if there is a *substantial defect as to the quality* of the leased accommodation, it amounts to an 'important reason' and the lessee can terminate the lease without notice whether or not the lessor is at fault (§543 II no. 1 BGB). A defect as to the quality of the leased premises requires an imbalance between the condition of the leased good contractually agreed upon and its actual condition.[634] The unexpected occupation of the centre does not qualify as such a defect since it is neither *directly* related to the physical condition or nature of the premises nor does it *directly* relate to its actual conditions.[635] Additionally, the use of the premises is not affected by the different occupation. X can use the accommodation to sell books as agreed. Under this test, it is obvious that the fact that the sales volume is below the expectations does not render the premises defective.[636]

3. Second, the *general rule* on termination without notice due to an 'important reason' (§543 I 2 BGB) does not apply either since the different occupation in general does not qualify as an 'important reason'. In the given case, the risk of an adequate occupation is *not* allocated to the lessor. The parties did not contractually agree upon a certain occupational structure and Y did not promise to provide for it. Both parties merely expected a variety of shops. In principle, an 'important reason' requires a breach of the (contractual) obligation with regard to the other party's rights, legally protected interests and other interests (§241 II BGB), which affects the use of the leased property. If the use of the premises by X is construed narrowly, it is not affected by the occupation of the shopping centre.

III. Furthermore, X cannot rescind the contract on the ground that Y breached a pre-contractual duty to inform. In order to qualify as a breach of such a duty the lessor must convey intentionally or negligently false information with regard to the contractual subject or fail to disclose circumstances that are evidently material to the other party.[637] In that case, the lessee's claim for damages results in a rescission of the

[634] Cf. BGH NJW 2000, 1714 (1715); W. Schilling, §537, in: W. Krüger, H. P. Westermann *et al.*, *Münchener Kommentar zum Bürgerlichen Gesetzbuch* (Munich: Beck, 5th edn, 2008), vol. III, n. 5.

[635] Cf. BGH NJW 1981, 2405 *et seq.*; BGH NJW 2000, 1714 (1715); Joachim, 'Wirklichkeit und Recht des Shopping - Centers bzw. Einkaufzentrums', 785 (794 *et seq.*).

[636] Cf. Weidenkaff, '§536', in: Palandt *et al.* (eds.), *Bürgerliches Gesetzbuch*, n. 23; OLG Naumburg *NZM* 1998, 373.

[637] Cf. BGH NJW 2000, 1714 (1716); BGH NJW-RR 2000, 1535 (1536).

contract.[638] However, Y did not make false statements about the occupation of the other shops and he did not fail to disclose any material facts about the variety of shops in the centre.

IV. 1. Finally, X cannot cancel or renegotiate the contract on the concept of *Geschäftsgrundlage* (§313 BGB). This concept is applicable in so far as the statutory rules about warranty of quality (§§536 *et seq.* BGB) do not apply.[639]

2. X's expectation of gaining more profit from a shop in a prosperous shopping centre or the shared expectation of both parties that the centre will attract a variety of shops may qualify as the *Geschäftsgrundlage* of the contract. The issue at hand is, however, whether X is unreasonably burdened if the contract is upheld as originally concluded. This is not the case if X bears the risk that the shop is less profitable than expected and that the centre does not attract a variety of shops.[640]

3. According to the majority opinion, as a general rule, the lessee bears the risk that he can realise his purpose of use with the subject matter of a lease.[641] This general allocation of the risk on the lessee includes, in the case of a commercial lease, both teething troubles related to the shop opening as well as the risk that the business is not profitable at all in the rented business premises.[642] Nevertheless, there are some decisions that exceptionally and rarely suggest a different risk allocation if the impact of the change on the *Geschäftsgrundlage* leads to an 'existential crisis' of the business.[643] However, the general rule is *not* affected by the mere fact that the shop is located in a shopping centre even though both parties expect a promotional benefit and higher profits.[644] In general, the lessee has to weigh the chance of gaining higher profits because of additional customers against the risk that the business model of the shopping centre fails. Thus, in general, the

[638] Cf. BGH NJW 2000, 1714 (1718).

[639] Cf. BGH NJW 2000, 1714 (1716); BGH NJW-RR 2000, 1535 (1536).

[640] Cf. BGHZ 74, 370 (373); BGH NJW 2000, 1714 (1716).

[641] BGH NJW 1981, 2405 (2406); BGH NJW 1970, 1313; Roth, '§313', in: Krüger (ed.), *Münchener Kommentar zum Bürgerlichen Gesetzbuch*, n. 203; Grüneberg, '§313', in: Palandt *et al.* (eds.), *Bürgerliches Gesetzbuch*, n. 36.

[642] BGH NJW 2000, 1714 (1716); BGH NJW-RR 2000, 1535 (1536); BGH NJW 1981, 2405 (2406).

[643] Cf. BGH NJW 2000, 1714 (1716) for further references.

[644] Cf. BGH NJW 2000, 1714 (1716 *et seq.*); BGH NJW-RR 2000, 1535 (1536); BGH NJW 1981, 2405 (2406); for an overview cf. Joachim, 'Wirklichkeit und Recht des Shopping – Centers bzw. Einkaufzentrums'.

lessee bears the risk that the group of buyers alters in a way that is unfavourable to the lessee.[645]

V. A different allocation of the risk may result from the contractual provisions themselves (cf. §313 I BGB). The courts held that in some cases the contract may impliedly shift the risk from the lessee to the lessor.[646] Thus, if the contract contains narrow constraints for the lessee with regard to the assortment of goods, its presentation and the operation of the business that result in a conceptual integration of the shop into the shopping centre so that the shop merely resembles a part of a larger business, the risk may shift. In the given case, there are no such provisions in the contract.

Austria

X is neither entitled to cancel the contract nor to enforce renegotiations.

I. X is not entitled to terminate the contract because of mistake. Under Austrian law the frustrated expectation as to the kind of businesses settling in the shopping centre is a mistake of intention/motive, which does not affect the binding character of the agreement.[647] Only if Y had promised or told X that a particular kind of shops would settle down in the centre, would X have been entitled to terminate the contract.[648]

II. Where a lease contract is made for a definite period of time, no party is entitled to terminate the contract earlier unless there is a serious cause making the contract unreasonably burdensome for this party (extraordinary right of termination).[649] Under Austrian law, as a general rule, the change of commercial circumstances and marketing

[645] BGH NJW 1981, 2405 (2406); Roth, '§313', in: Krüger (ed.), *Münchener Kommentar zum Bürgerlichen Gesetzbuch*, vol. II, n. 203.

[646] Cf. BGH NJW 2000, 1714 (1717); BGH NJW-RR 2000, 1535 (1536); for an example cf. OLG Koblenz, NJW-RR 1989, 400: due to special provisions in the contract constraining substantially the lessees' sales activity the court considered the fact that all of the business premises in the shopping centre are occupied by shops as a *Geschäftsgrundlage* of the contract; cf. Roth, '§313', in: Krüger (ed.), *Münchener Kommentar zum Bürgerlichen Gesetzbuch*, vol. II, n. 203 and Grüneberg, '§313', in: Palandt *et al.* (eds.), *Bürgerliches Gesetzbuch*, n. 36 for further references.

[647] §901 ABGB; for the present case OGH 22.1.1986, SZ 59/17, for further details, see Sabine Kiesel, 'Kann der Bestandvertrag mit dem Betreiber eines Einkaufszentrums wegen Leerstehung vorzeitig aufgelöst werden?', (2003) *immolex*, 266 at 269.

[648] R. Pittl, 'Unternehmenspacht im Einkaufszentrum: Ansprüche des Bestandnehmers bei mangelnder Kundenfrequenz', (2001) *immolex*, 268.

[649] See §§1116, 1117 ABGB and Koziol and Welser, *Bürgerliches Recht*, vol. II, p. 9.

opportunities is not such a serious cause as to entitle a lease of business premises to be terminated ahead of time, since the parties were able to foresee such developments and accepted to bear this risk.[650]

III. Furthermore, the Austrian OGH held that mistaken expectations with regard to the future settling of shops in a shopping centre do not affect the '*Geschäftsgrundlage*' (basis) of the business lease contract.[651] The parties had to assume that the identity of future lessees is unknown when they entered into the contract. A lessee, who nevertheless contracts for a definite period of time, willingly accepts this risk. According to Austrian court decisions, the conclusion of a lease contract for a definite period of time when it is still unknown which kind of shops will settle down in the shopping centre, is a risky undertaking for the lessee including a speculative element.[652] Where a lessee refrains from reserving a special right of termination in the contract, he is presumed to have willingly assumed the risks (and chances) of the development of the market.[653]

The Netherlands

Under Dutch law, X is likely to be entitled to terminate or renegotiate the lease contract.

I. Cancellation, commonly translated as '*vernietiging*', is not possible, since it would have *ex tunc* effect (i.e., as from the date of entering into the lease agreement) leading to complications in determining the benefits which X did derive from the lease. More importantly, a termination cannot be based on the actual circumstances that were known or foreseeable at the time the contract was concluded, but rather on circumstances following that date. A renegotiation might be allowed but the likely outcome would probably not solve the fundamental problem: a bookstore located on an economically unattractive spot. Except for termination by mutual agreement, the Dutch Civil Code provides for early termination only in connection with persistent or material default by a party, or for specific termination rights concerning lease contracts that have lasted for longer than two years.

II. 1. The doctrine of unforeseen circumstances (Art. 6:258 Dutch Civil Code) can be applied according to the following criteria: (i) the

650 OGH, JBl 1982, 142.
651 OGH, SZ 59/17; similar OGH, *ecolex* 2003, 168 = RdW 2003/302.
652 OGH, *ecolex* 2003, 168 = RdW 2003/302.
653 §901 ABGB; for the present case OGH, SZ 59/17.

occupation of the shopping centre by restaurants and bars was not reasonably foreseeable (or, if foreseeable, the way the shopping centre has been occupied should not otherwise have been a subject that the parties had deemed to be too ineffectual to determine in sufficient detail); (ii) the change of circumstances or the development of circumstances contrary to the expectations of the parties are such that Y cannot reasonably expect the lease agreement to remain unchanged, which also implies that the adversely changed circumstances should not fall within X's sphere of responsibility. In particular the criterion under (i) must be applied by a court with reticence.[654]

2. The case embodies several facts and circumstances that all suggest that the contract may be terminated on the basis of Art. 6:258. First, the change of the (envisaged) nature of the shopping centre was entirely influenced by Y and is therefore a circumstance that falls within his sphere of responsibility. Second, if the current use of the shopping centre is considered to have been 'foreseeable' (and therefore a matter which X had to address in the lease agreement), one could argue that Y had to warn X of such a situation. The failure to warn would likely be for the risk and account of Y (and such a duty to warn would approximate to the doctrine of mistake but for the futuristic nature of the relevant circumstances). Third, a proper solution to X's problem is not likely to lie in the hands of X, except if X changes his core business: it is quite likely that only Y is capable of finding another lessee for the same location, and probably Y (if it is a large project development company) is able to propose suitable alternative locations to X, whether leased by Y itself, by affiliated companies, or by competitor project development companies. Finally, a solution to the vacated bookstore can more easily be found by Y: Y knows how to find potential lessees, whereas X does not. The case at hand has been the subject of litigation in the lower courts on several occasions. The courts have tended to award some compensation (also with retrospective effect) in the form of rent to the lessee or have even allowed him to terminate the contract if it appeared to be practicable to find a replacement lessee.

III. Appropriate legal remedies can offer X an incentive to make acceptable proposals: e.g., termination plus an obligation to compensate X for any investments in fittings or equipment. Compensation may not be awarded if Y has offered at least three reasonably feasible alternative bookstore locations. A court would be empowered to impose

[654] See, for instance: HR 20 February 1998, NJ 1998, 493 (*Briljant Schreuders* v. *ABP*).

such a solution on the basis of Art. 2:260: this statutory provision allows a court to impose conditional remedies as part of its decision to modify or terminate an agreement (based on Art. 6:258 Dutch Civil Code).

Eastern European jurisdictions

Slovenia

X is neither entitled to terminate the contract, nor to renegotiate it.

I. X is not allowed to demand annulment of the contract on grounds of mistake (Art. 46 CO), because his mistake relates to circumstances that were not present at the time of the conclusion of the contract, but occurred after the contract had been concluded. Slovenian law does not allow for an action on grounds of mistake if the mistake relates to future characteristics of the object of the contract.[655]

II. When a lease contract is concluded for a definite period of time, there are no general rules allowing for an extraordinary cancellation of the contract.[656] Under Slovenian law, it is not possible to terminate a contract that has been concluded for a defined period of time, except in cases of changed circumstances.

III. In the present case the contract, however, cannot be terminated on grounds of the '*clausula* rule' (Art. 112 CO). The termination of a contract on these grounds is only possible if the circumstances substantially change after a contract is concluded. In this case there is no change of circumstances, because at the time of conclusion most of the accommodation had not yet been rented. Instead, the case concerns a future development that should have been taken into account at the conclusion of the contract. If business expectations do not come true, this represents usual commercial risks parties should be aware of when concluding a contract.[657] By not inserting an appropriate clause in the contract, the lessee obviously assumed the risk that future developments would not be as favourable for him as he might have anticipated at the conclusion of the contract. It would not be just (in terms of

[655] N. Plavšak, M. Juhart and R. Vrenčur, *Obligacijsko pravo, splošni del* (Ljubljana: GV Založba, 2009), p. 205.

[656] Except in specific cases, stipulated by the CO.

[657] Dolenc in: Juhart and Plavšak (eds.), *Obligacijski zakonik*, vol. I, p. 603; Plavšak, Juhart and Vrenčur, *Obligacijsko pravo, splošni del*, p. 423.

Art. 112 CO) to let the lessor carry the burden of the fact that the lesee's future expectations have not been realised.

Lithuania

If the contract does not provide for the possibility of adjustment or the termination of the contract because of the change of marketing opportunities, X is not entitled to cancel or to renegotiate the contract.

I. There is no mistake in this case: according to Art. 1.90 CC, it is possible to be mistaken only in respect of facts that were in existence at the time when the contract was concluded. Neither can the reason for the conclusion of the contract be considered as a relevant mistake, unless both parties have discussed their intentions. Article 1.90(5) CC establishes that a contract cannot be avoided if a party made a mistake due to its gross negligence, or if the mistake was induced by events the risk of which was taken by that party. It is evident that X is a businessman, and, as businessmen perform at their own risk, X is bound to take upon himself the consequences of unsuccessful business as well.

II. According to Art. 6.498 CC, the lessee has the right to bring an action for dissolution of the lease contract before the term of lease ended under certain circumstances.[658] However, none of the grounds for the dissolution of a contract may be applied in this case as nothing prevents X from using the leased object. The contract does not provide for a possibility for its dissolution on the grounds of an inadequate number of clients, and X may respond to the lack of clients by changing the working hours of the bookshop, i.e., adapt them to the working hours of the restaurants and cafes.

[658] According to Article 6.498, the lessee has the right to bring an action for dissolution of a lease contract before the end of the period of time if:

(1) the lessor fails to carry out the repair work he is obliged to do;
(2) the leased object becomes unfit for use by virtue of circumstances for which the lessee is not liable;
(3) the lessor fails to transfer the leased object to the lessee or hinders the use of the leased object in accordance with its designation and the conditions of the contract;
(4) the leased object has defects which were not stipulated by the lessor and were unknown to the lessee and which render the object impossible to be used in accordance with its designation and the conditions of the contract;
(5) other grounds provided for by the lease contract occur.

III. In addition, as it was indicated in Case 4, Art. 6.487(5) CC provides that, unless otherwise provided for by the contract, the rent may be changed by agreement of the parties within the periods they agreed upon, but not more often than twice a year if the laws do not foresee otherwise. Thus, a modification of the rent could be possible only if it is provided for by the contract.

IV. In this situation, Art. 6.204 CC can hardly apply because: (i) X, as a businessman, could have reasonably predicted that the number of customers could turn out to be lower than he had expected; (ii) X was in the position to influence the unfavourable circumstances for his business by changing the working hours of the bookshop; (iii) X, as a businessman, was acting upon his own risk and had to accept the negative consequences of his business. This conclusion can indirectly be supported by a case heard before the Supreme Court where the Court rejected the claim of a purchaser of shares for the dissolution of the contract or a reduction of its price. The action was based upon the fact that, after the conclusion of the contract, the company whose shares he had purchased went bankrupt. The Court indicated that the purchaser was a businessman, thus he was acting on his own risk and had, therefore, to accept the negative consequences of his risk-laden activity.[659] Both Art. 6.204 and Art. 6.498 CC establish the right of a lessee to demand dissolution of the contract due to circumstances he is not liable for. Therefore he is not obliged to compensate the lessor for the losses incurred as a result of the dissolution of the contract. If the lessee dissolves a fixed period contract for reasons that are not serious, he is obliged to compensate the lessor for losses incurred (Art. 6.221(2) CC).

Czech Republic

X has no right to terminate or renegotiate the contract.

I. Under Czech law, this case does not constitute invalidity due to a mistake. Juridical acts may be invalidated due to a mistake only in the situations defined in Section 49a Civil Code, i.e., if undertaken mistakenly on facts crucial for the conclusion of the contract and if the person whom the juridical act addressed caused the mistake or must have been aware of the mistake.[660]

II. If X and Y have not agreed on a right to terminate the lease prior to the lapse of five years, e.g., by providing for an opportunity to withdraw,

[659] LAT, Judgment of 19 May 2003, Case No 3K-3-612/2003.
[660] See further Case 4.

the contract may not be terminated prior to the lapse of this definite period of time. This follows from Act No.116/1990 Coll., on the lease of non-residential premises (Section 9),[661] which applies here and only confirms the general rule of Czech law, namely that no party is entitled to terminate a contract concluded for a definite period of time (even if it is a long-term contract) before expiry of its term.

III. In the given case, the contract was not frustrated pursuant to Section 356(1) Commercial Code, since a change of economic or market conditions is not deemed to be a change in the relevant circumstances (Section 356(2) Commercial Code).[662]

Scandinavian jurisdictions

Sweden

X is not entitled to terminate the contract or to ask for a renegotiation.

I. There is no right, under Swedish law, to demand renegotiation if it is not contracted for. Nor is there any specific statutory provision for the extraordinary cancellation of lease contracts that are concluded for a fixed period of time. For contracts on rental of real estate there is extensive regulation in Chapter 12 of the Code of Land Laws. According to these rules the tenant is entitled to cancel the contract in some cases of the landlord's breach. None of these rules are applicable to the present case, however.

II. In this case an assumption regarding the fulfilment has failed. The assumption is a so-called ordinary 'performance assumption', which has nothing to do with the performance as such, but with X's use of the performance he receives from Y. Assumptions of this type are comparatively often deemed legally relevant in case law. However, according to the main rule, they are not relevant.

III. 1. In this case, there is no promise or warranty, nor any clarification. There is no strong indication that X is entitled to rely upon Y's better knowledge, nor any facts supporting the conclusion that Y has made any profit at the expense of X. However, a party's erroneous assumption is subject to relief under the doctrine of assumptions, which also applies the other party *negligently caused* the non-realisation of the assumption after the formation of the contract.[663]

[661] See Case 4. [662] See Case 4.

[663] See especially NJA 1936 p. 368 and hereto Lehrberg, *Förutsättningsläran*, pp. 527 *et seq.*

2. In Swedish case law, there is a kind of parallel case in NJA 1997 p. 5. A private person, X, contracted in summer 1991 with a co-operative building society for a co-operative flat in a new building that was constructed by the building society. A year later most of the apartments were still unoccupied. The building society then contracted with two housing companies, which acquired the unoccupied flats and rented them to the public by ordinary tenancy agreements. Thereafter only ten of a total of 225 flats were owned and used by private members of the co-operative building society. X then cancelled her contract. She argued that the apartment was defective and that a basic assumption had failed, as she would not get the kind of housing she had contracted for.

3. The Supreme Court upheld the contract. The apartment was not defective under Chapter 7 Section 1 of the Co-operative Housing Act,[664] as its fitness for use was not affected. The court accepted X's statement that it was a basic and visible assumption that she would acquire a flat in a co-operative living environment. This assumption could be of legal relevance if the building society had been blameworthy – and thus negligently had caused the non-realisation of the assumption. But this was not the case. The building society's measure to contract with the two housing companies was justified, as the demand for co-operative flats had fallen dramatically. The building society's goals, that the society survives and that the members (the owners of the co-operative apartments) receive their apartments without any extra payment, were achieved. It had not been proved that the building society would have been able to attain any other acceptable solution that would better provide for the interests of the society and the owners of the co-operative apartments.

4. It might have been of importance for the outcome of the case, that X did not only contract to acquire an apartment, but also to become a member of the co-operative building society. Thus, X was not only a buyer (or tenant) but was involved in a kind of joint venture with the building society. As a member, she could only demand that the building society looked after her interests as a member of the society, but not after her interests as a buyer. As a buyer, she could only demand a flat that was fit for use. One could, therefore, argue that the rules of the co-operative building society's responsibilities as a seller turned out to be too narrow, while the society's duties were not appropriate to protect X as a buyer. Only the limits of the seller's responsibilities under the

[664] Bostadsrättslagen (1991:614).

Co-operative Housing Act can justify that X's relying upon the society's better knowledge, or the profit the society made at the expense of X, did not render X's assumption legally relevant. As a consumer X would have deserved better protection.

5. In the case at hand, the conditions are somewhat different. This is a contract for normal tenancy, and none of the parties is a consumer. There is no obligation for Y to secure (or avoid) a certain type of tenant. In this case, it seems Y has not even had any real possibility of choosing the tenants. It is submitted that the contract would stand if this case was tried before a Swedish court.

Denmark

It is possible (but uncertain) that X would be entitled to termination or adjustment under Danish law.

Danish case law does not appear to have any cases which are similar to the one in question.

I. Danish law does not contain any general default rule concerning renegotiation. However, as already discussed in Case 4, Section 13 Commercial Tenancy Act[665] contains a provision on the obligation to pay the market rent. Unless the parties have agreed that Section 13 Commercial Tenancy Act is not applicable to the lease contract, X has an obligation to pay the rent for the fixed period of five years pursuant to the contract. If, on the contrary, the parties have agreed that Section 13 Commercial Tenancy Act is applicable to the contract, the tenant has the obligation to pay the market rent for the business premises, provided that the rent in question is substantially lower or higher than the market rent. In practice this will involve renegotiations between the parties. In the case at hand, the tenant unexpectedly experiences a substantial decrease in turnover, which entitles X to demand a rent comparable to the market rent. However, pursuant to Section 13(2), such a decrease in the market rent will first take effect four years after the conclusion of the contract and four years after X has invoked the decreased market rent.[666] Since the contract is concluded for a fixed period of five years and X reacts one year after the conclusion of the agreement, the Commercial Tenancy Act is not applicable in favour of X.

[665] Cf. Lov no. 934 20 December 1999 om leje af erhvervslokaler mv.

[666] For a more comprehensive discussion, see Laursen, *Erhvervslejeret*, and Frost, *Systematisk oversigt i lejeret*.

II. The rule of mistake pursuant to Section 32 Contracts Act is not applicable to the case, unless Y had acted in bad faith when the contract was concluded.

III. 1. Pursuant to Section 69 Commercial Tenancy Act the lessor is entitled to terminate the contract if the tenant commits a fundamental breach of contract. Various incidents are listed in Section 69 Commercial Tenancy Act, including situations where the rent is not paid in due time, the tenant transfers the right to the premises without permission, the tenant acts abnormally creating a lot of noise, annoying neighbours etc. However, the Commercial Tenancy Act has no provisions with respect to extraordinary cancellation in favour of the tenant.

2. It is clear that the business environment in the shopping centre has evolved in a completely different direction than the parties to the contract thought it would. X could argue that by renting out premises to various restaurants and cafes Y had notably changed X's opportunities for doing business in the shopping centre and by doing so had committed a breach of contract. Yet the claim of a fundamental breach of contract would most likely be rejected by the Danish courts, assuming that the lease contract did not contain any provisions on this issue. So unless Y violates the contract with X, he basically has the right to contract with the tenants of his choice despite the influence on X's business opportunities.

IV. X might be able to invoke the application of Section 36 Contracts Act. This is, however, an ordinary tenancy contract and there is no information to suggest that X might be considered to be the weaker party or that Y made any promise to X about future tenants in the shopping centre. There is no information supporting the contention that Y had any information about future tenants beforehand and thereby took advantage of X.

V. Again in this case, it is worth discussing the possible application of the doctrine of assumptions. More than likely, X would not have rented the business premises in the shopping centre if he had known about the kind of retail outlets located there one year after the conclusion of the agreement; at least, he would have required a lower rent compared to the one in question, since one must assume that X is paying rent which is equal to the market rent at the time of contracting. This assumption must also be considered perceptible to Y. In particular, there must have been a mutual expectation between the parties when the contract was concluded. Once again, the condition of relevance turns out to be the crucial condition. Things have evolved differently than expected, but to a lesser or greater degree have been influenced by the subsequent choices made by Y, in the sense that Y was the party who chose the future tenants of the shopping centre after concluding the agreement with X. From that perspective one could argue that Y is the more appropriate party to bear the risk that things have evolved differently than expected. From this point of view, it should be possible either to adjust and renegotiate the contract or to cancel it in favour of X.

VI. Alternatively, if a Danish court was presented with this case, it could just as well consider the lease contract to be a binding agreement, which X is obliged to perform in accordance with its terms. If the court delivered a judgment in favour of X, it would probably give X the right to terminate the lease contract with six months' notice taking into consideration the time-span of the lease contract, which is fairly long by Danish standards.

Romanic-Mediterranean jurisdictions

Italy

X is entitled to terminate the contract or to ask for a renegotiation.

The legal reasoning is rather similar to that made with regard to Case 7(a).

I. In principle, under Italian law the individual purposes or motives of each party may not affect the contract (unless they are illegal and common to both parties). Accordingly, X is neither entitled to terminate the contract nor to enforce a process of renegotiation, since the mere expectation of the parties may be not considered a condition of the contract.

II. The general provision related to long-term contracts is Art. 1373 CC, which provides that each party has a unilateral right to withdraw from the contract. In matters of lease contracts, Art. 4 l. 392/1978 also has to be taken into account. This provision allows each party to withdraw from the contract, the only requirement being a six-month notice period. This does not result in an indemnification for Y, unless otherwise provided for by the parties.

III. 1. However, if both the lessor and the lessee expected that a variety of shops (hotel and catering trade, retail sale) would lease premises at the time of contracting, this expectation would not only be an individual purpose of X, but it could be an implied condition of the agreement: the Italian doctrine of *presupposizione* could therefore be applied. The doctrine of implied assumptions requires that the parties have either shared these assumptions or at least one party is aware that the other considers them as a foundation of the contract. In particular, to invoke the *presupposizione*, the 'pre-supposed' event has to be a legal or factual situation external to the contract, not expressly mentioned in the contract and yet common to both parties (or, if only assumed by one party, and thus only reflecting the interest of the latter, at least known to the other party).[667] X would be entitled to cancel the contract on the basis of the *presupposizione* doctrine.

2. As far as the adaptation or renegotiation of the contract is concerned such relief is not explicitly provided by Italian law. However, some Italian scholars have maintained[668] that a duty to renegotiate with the aim of equitably adapting or modifying the affected contractual terms may be derived from the general duty to perform in good faith (Arts. 1175 and 1375 CC). This duty may require a party to enter into negotiations about an equitable modification of the contractual conditions (e.g., price or period of the lease). In this case, if the other party refuses to negotiate or breaks off the negotiations contrary to good faith and the rules of fair dealing, the court could award damages to the other party for the loss suffered, in addition to the equitable modification of the contractual terms.

Spain

X is not likely to be entitled to cancel the contract or to ask for a renegotiation.

I. There is no general statutory provision that allows an extraordinary cancellation of lease contracts concluded for a fixed period of time. The LAU[669] grants a right to cancel only to tenants who lease domestic property. Regarding commercial leases, a contract for a definite period cannot be cancelled before that period has expired. If the commercial parties want a specific regime they have to agree thereon.

II. According to the Spanish judiciary, an impossibility to use a good as it was contractually agreed is a relevant factor that may frustrate the contractual expectations of a party. This is illustrated by a judgment of the TS where the parties had concluded a contract for the sale of an outlet.[670] Both parties assumed that the buyer could open a cafe in the

[667] V. Roppo, 'Il contratto', in: G. Iudica and P. Zatti; *Trattato di diritto privato* (Milan: Giuffrè, 2001), p. 1039; Macario, 'Le sopravvenienze', p. 537.

[668] See above, Case 1 and Case 2, and Overview (Chapter 4).

[669] See Case 4. [670] 26 May 1990 (RJ 1990, 4852).

place to be sold. Subsequently the authorities did not grant the buyer the necessary permit. The buyer claimed damages. The Spanish Supreme Court stated that the seller should indemnify the buyer for the damage caused, as the latter could not use the shop for the purpose stipulated in the contract. On the basis of Art. 1258 CC, the seller should have informed the buyer that the outlet could not be used as the buyer intended. Article 1258 CC states that the contract requires the parties to perform their obligations that were expressly stipulated in the contract, but also those inferred from good faith. A court might come to the conclusion that Y has violated such an obligation when he let the unoccupied business premises only to cafes and restaurants. As a result, X might be entitled to claim the renegotiation of the contract in the case at hand.

III. X could also argue that the *causa* of the contract has ceased. Indeed, according to the facts in Case 8, the tenant's (X's) contractual aim is frustrated. The *causa* for X to contract was to open a bookshop and to sell books to customers. This is also known and admitted by the other party. If there are no customers who can buy books, one may assume that there is no *causa* for X to contract. The doctrine of the basis of the contract no longer being present probably applies if the following requirements are met: (i) the objective aim of the contract has disappeared; (ii) it is evident to the other party that the hustle and bustle of the shopping centre was a determinant for X to contract; and (iii) X, as the party who invokes the application of this doctrine, has had no control over the circumstances which have led to this situation. However, there are two strong counter-arguments against an application of the *causa* doctrine. First, the court may find that only the operation of the bookshop is the *causa* and not the volume of business and, second, it is uncertain whether the volume of business qualifies as an unforeseen circumstance. It may as well be attributed to the regular commercial risk as the tenant could have foreseen that this situation could occur and could have insisted on specific rules in the contract.

Portugal

X is not entitled to terminate the lease.

I. The lease was agreed upon under the common assumption that the shopping centre would be predominantly occupied by a large number of different shops. Even though this assumption proved to be wrong, it is doubtful whether such a turn of events qualifies as an error that affects the basis of the contract. The tenant merely had a certain expectation concerning the composition of the stores in the shopping centre and the type of customers who are attracted by such stores. But that expectation, even if shared by the lessor, was not subject to any contractual guarantee and was not provoked by *dolus* on the side of the lessor.

II. 1. Furthermore, it is doubtful whether this case qualifies as fundamental change of the basis or foundation of the contract.[671] There seems to be no unforeseeable or anomalous event: the parties might not have foreseen the development of the shopping centre. But it was certainly not an unforeseeable event or even outside the normal turn of events. The parties are required to take precautionary measures and to insert into the contract the necessary clauses to protect themselves against foreseeable changes that might aggrieve them.

2. The answer could be different if Y himself was responsible for the fact that most of the shops were restaurants and cafes (for instance providing beneficial conditions for this kind of shop) or if Y created in some way an appearance of diversity of shops that contributed to mislead X or if Y had promised such a result. As there are no indications for such conduct of Y, X is not entitled to terminate the lease.

Greece

X is not entitled to terminate the contract or to ask for a renegotiation.

I. X has no right to cancel or, even more, to renegotiate the contract (see Case 2), unless Y has agreed to lease only to specific kinds of enterprises.

II. There is no specific or general provision that could legitimate the extraordinary cancellation of the lease contract in the above case.

III. As mentioned before (in Case 5), the creditor of the performance always bears the economic loss, which is caused by the frustration of his purpose, unless exceptionally, by virtue of Art. 388 AK, this frustration demolishes the contractual allocation of risks. In the given case, this exception is not applicable: even if both parties were assuming certain facts, the crucial criterion is still the contract itself and the allocation of risks therein.[672]

[671] See António Pinto Monteiro, *Erro e vinculação negocial* (Coimbra: Coimbra Editora, 2002), pp. 16 *et seq.* and pp. 25 *et seq.*

[672] See Stathopoulos, 'Art. 388', in: Georgiadis and Stathopoulos (eds.), *AK*, n. 11; E. Kaufmann, *The Essence*, p. 107; Fikentscher, *Die Geschäftsgrundlage*, p. 16.

France and related jurisdictions

France

X can request the termination of the contract on a three-year basis. The notice must be given to the landlord at least six months in advance.

I. 1. In such a case, as a general rule, X has to bear the risk of the development of the shopping centre. But at the end of the day it is a question of interpreting the respective obligations of both parties; the judge could come to the conclusion that Y is responsible for the development of the shopping centre and therefore hold him liable.

2. The Cour de Cassation stressed that the landlord assumes no obligation concerning the maintenance of the commercial environment after the conclusion of the contract.[673] On the other hand, the Court of Appeal of Reims held that 'the lessor who is the owner of all the shops in a shopping gallery has more obligations than an ordinary lessor and must ensure that a favourable commercial environment is maintained'.[674] This decision (like others) has been overruled by the Cour de Cassation on two grounds, namely Arts. 1719 and 1134 Cciv. The Court held that the lessor of shops in a shopping gallery is only bound by an obligation to provide shop space in good working conditions and to ensure good usage. He is only obliged 'to ensure the maintenance of a favourable commercial environment' if specific stipulations had been included in the lease contract.[675]

II. 1. The decree of 1953 on commercial leases, which provides that rent can be revised every three years if there is a variation of more than 10 per cent between the rent and the actual rental value,[676] could be considered in this case. However, this article only applies if the circumstances are beyond the control of the parties. If Y runs the shopping centre and he is at fault (for instance, he only lets the other premises to

[673] Cass., 17 July 2000, Juris-data, 2000-002875; 20 June 1995, Revue Loyers, 1995, p. 513. JCP, 2002, Fasc.260, Code civil, 1708 to 1762. B. Boccara, 'Les centres commerciaux et les loyers du marché', (1983) AJPI 379; J. Lafond, (1997) JCP Ed E, n°40; Cass., 3è civ., 19 March 1980: JCP, 1980, IV, 212 C.A. Paris, 16e Ch. B, 1er October. 1992, Juris-Data n° 023017.

[674] C.A. Reims, 1st April 1993, *Sté Immofonds* v. *Sté Marge* (unreported).

[675] Cass., 3e civ., 12 October 1994, *Centre Achat Hutte Intersports France* v. *Centre commercial Afer*.

[676] The latter is based on the profitability of the hired premises.

cafes and restaurants),[677] the development of the business will not be an unforeseeable event, but one for which Y is contractually liable.

2. Thus the best legal ground for a revision would be the law on commercial leases.

Belgium

Under Belgian law, X will be entitled to renegotiate the contract after three years under Art. 6 of the Law on commercial leases.

I. As the contract in question has to be characterised as a lease contract, the application of Art. 6 of the Law on commercial leases can be envisioned. It provides for a revision of the rental charge every three years if there is a variation of more than 15 per cent between the rent and the actual rental value (the latter being based on the profitability of the hired premises). However, this article only applies if circumstances are beyond the control of the parties. If Y runs the shopping centre and he is at fault (for instance, because he hired the other premises only to cafes and restaurants), the decrease in business will not be an unforeseeable circumstance, but a circumstance for which Y is contractually liable.[678]

II. In this case, the normal solution would be that X has to bear the risk of the shopping centre being developed. But, at the end of the day, it is a question of the interpretation of the respective obligations of both parties. On the basis of Arts. 1156 *et seq.* CCiv,[679] the judge could come to the conclusion that Y is responsible for the development of the shopping centre and therefore hold him liable. But X's chances that this provision will be applied are limited.

III. A mistake could also be invoked if it appears that the format of the shops in the commercial centre (three quarters of them being cafes and restaurants) was already present when the contract was concluded. But according to the facts, large parts of the accommodation at the shopping centre were still unoccupied at the time of contracting.

[677] The landlord does not have an obligation to produce a certain result ('*obligation de résultat*') but only an obligation of means ('*obligation de moyen*').

[678] See on the obligation of the landlord the French case law under Case 8. C.E. de Fresart.

[679] See Overview (Chapter 4).

England and related jurisdictions

England and Ireland

In the absence of a misrepresentation by Y, or some breach of an express or implied term under which Y undertook to ensure a 'mixed' profile of business tenants, X cannot cancel or terminate the lease. There is no cancellation right for leases of this kind. Nor in the absence of contractual provision (such as a rent review clause) can X seek a renegotiation of the contract.

I. This is an interesting hypothetical situation. However, in practice it is likely that, in the absence of any express or implied undertakings or representations by Y as to the variety of shops in the centre, English or Irish courts would find in favour of Y and not allow X to cancel or renegotiate the contract.

II. It should be pointed out initially that the doctrine of frustration would not apply in this situation for two reasons. First, it is unlikely that a change in the profile of tenants, something that takes place over a period of time, would be regarded as a supervening event that frustrates the contract. Second, the law of frustration is not likely to apply because the event must be an event over which the parties have no control. In this situation, Y had control and responsibility because it is Y who is granting the leases. This suggests that the answer depends on whether Y is in breach of an express or implied term of the contract or has made an operative misrepresentation, i.e., a misrepresentation on which X can rely.

III. Turning then to the terms of the contract, if it was an express term of the contract that there would be a variety of shops in the centre then X may have a remedy against Y for breach of contract. However, the facts of the hypothetical question do not suggest that there is any such express term.

IV. 1. Alternatively, while there may not be an express contractual term about the 'mixed' nature of the tenants that are expected to take up accommodation in the shopping centre, any preliminary statements which are not contract terms but which would induce a reasonable person to believe that the shopping centre would have a specific tenancy profile could be actionable as a misrepresentation. Such an action was successful in the Irish case of *Donnellan* v. *Dungoyne Ltd.*[680] There, the

[680] Unreported, Irish High Court, 15 August 1994.

plaintiffs entered into a thirty-five year lease of a business unit in a shopping centre, beginning in October 1991. They alleged that the defendants had represented to them that all the units in the centre had been leased to tenants and that all would be occupied before Christmas 1991, when such representation was incorrect to the knowledge of the defendants. There was an evidential difficulty in ascertaining exactly what was represented to the plaintiffs, but O'Hanlon J in the High Court was satisfied that the plaintiffs were led to believe that lettings of all or almost all of the remaining units would be completed before Christmas or by the New Year, and that this amounted to a misrepresentation of the factual situation. Similarly, in the English case of *Esso Petroleum* v. *Mardon*[681] Esso was held liable for misrepresentation when its agent told a prospective tenant of a filling station that, in his opinion, a filling station would sell 200,000 gallons per annum by the third year of operation, when it knew that this was untrue.[682] It in fact only sold 78,000 gallons in its first fifteen months of business and subsequently closed.

2. However, it is not always possible to base an action on misrepresentation on such statements. There may be problems in proving such a statement was made, and the court may deem certain statements to be within the realm of acceptable 'sales talk' or 'sales puff'. If the contract is essentially speculative, it may be held that one party took the risk that the venture would not be a success. The court may alternatively hold that the contracting party to whom the representation was made should have known the truth and was not entitled to rely on the statement made.[683] On the facts of the hypothetical, it would have to be shown that a clear representation was made, which X was entitled to rely upon, and that X did not take a risk as to the profile of the tenants in the shopping centre.

3. If a misrepresentation has been made then the remedies available to X depend on whether it was made fraudulently, negligently or innocently. These remedies can be based in contract, tort[684] or

[681] [1976] QB 801.

[682] Esso had previously applied for planning permission, stating that 200,000 gallons would be sold, permission was subsequently refused and the station's pumps were in a different position, which presumably would reduce sales, but Esso did not revise their figure in negotiations with the tenant.

[683] See *Grafton Court* v. *Wadson Sales*, Unreported, Irish High Court, 17 February 1975 (Ire).

[684] For fraudulent misrepresentations the tort of deceit would apply. For negligent misrepresentations the tort of negligent misrepresentation would apply. A misrepresentation may give rise to an action in both tort and contract: *Henderson* v. *Merrett Syndicates* [1994] 3 All ER 506.

statute,[685] and include damages, rescission and the possibility of an abatement in price. Turning first to damages,[686] if a misrepresentation is fraudulent or negligent, then the measure of damages is generally tortious, i.e., the plaintiff should be restored to the position he would have been in had the representation not been made.[687] However, the court's assessment of the damages available tends to be more generous than in normal tortious actions and the House of Lords has held that the defendant is to 'make reparation for all the damage directly flowing from the transaction'[688] and not merely those losses which are reasonably foreseeable. In the case of an innocent misrepresentation, Section 2(2) of the English Misrepresentation Act 1967 provides that the court may award damages 'in lieu of rescission', although no guidance is given as to the exact measure of damages.[689]

4. It may be possible to rescind the contract, but this remedy will not always be available. For example, if a contract has been partly performed rescission may not be available unless it can be shown that Y fraudulently induced X to enter into the contract. In *Donnellan* v. *Dungoyne Ltd*[690] the remedy of rescission was not available because the court was not convinced that the tenants would not have entered into the contract if they had known the true situation, but was of the view that they would have negotiated a longer free-rent period with the landlord, and damages were awarded on this basis.[691] Finally, the plaintiff may be entitled to a price reduction under the remedy of an abatement of price which is available for misrepresentation.[692] In this

[685] In Ireland, Sections 43–6 Sale of Goods and Supply of Services Act 1980 deal with the remedies which are available following misrepresentation. These sections do not apply to leases and so are not relevant for the purpose of this question. In England, the Misrepresentation Act 1967 creates a statutory liability for misrepresentation, in particular non-fraudulent misrepresentation.

[686] See generally M. Furmston, *Cheshire, Fifoot & Furmston's Law of Contract* (Oxford University Press, 15th edn, 2007), pp. 362–9; Peel, *Treitel's Law of Contract*, pp. 374–401.

[687] This would also seem to apply where damages are awarded under Section 2(1) Misrepresentation Act 1967 and Section 45(1) Sale of Goods and Supply of Services Act 1980, although the point is not entirely settled.

[688] *Smith New Court Securities* v. *Scrimgeour Vickers (Asset Management) Ltd* [1996] 4 All ER 769 at 778 (House of Lords). See also *Doyle* v. *Olby (Ironmongers)* [1969] 2 QB 158.

[689] See *William Sindall plc* v. *Cambridgeshire County Council* [1994] 3 All ER 932. See also Section 45(2) Sale of Goods and Supply of Services Act 1980 (Ire), although as noted above this section does not apply to leases.

[690] Unreported, Irish High Court, 15 August 1994.

[691] See also *Grafton Court* v. *Wadson Sales*, Unreported, Irish High Court, 17 February 1975.

[692] See: *Conor* v. *Potts* [1897] 1 IR 534; *Doolan* v. *Murray*, Unreported, Irish High Court, December 21 1993; *Moran* v. *Orchanda*, Unreported, Irish High Court, 25 May 2000.

hypothetical situation, if a misrepresentation can be shown then it is likely that the remedy available would be damages or a reduction in the rent price, as in *Donnellan* v. *Dungoyne Ltd*.

V. Should misrepresentation not be established then X would be forced to argue that the lease between X and Y was the subject of an implied term. The argument would proceed along the following lines: Y has granted a leasehold contractual interest to X. Y is aware of the nature of X's business and X's needs for a retail clientele during business hours. These circumstances constrain the way in which Y is to grant leases to other users and by failing to take account of X's requirements Y is in derogation of this grant. Another way of putting forward this argument would be to argue that the contract is subject to an implied term on the basis of a 'business efficacy' test. The courts presume that both parties intended the contract to be workable, and will thus imply an unexpressed term into the contract where it is necessary to make the contract work.[693] X could argue that in order to make the lease contract work, Y is impliedly bound to exercise his rights to let shop units to other prospective tenants with due regard for the commercial expectations of X. However, it is unlikely that such an argument would succeed. It is not enough that such an implied term is 'reasonable' – it must in fact be necessary, and it is clear that this contract is still capable of operating without such an implied term, even though X is not making the profits he expected.

Scotland

No relief will be available under Scottish law.

I. As a general rule in Scots law, in order to be operative, an error must prevent the parties from reaching *consensus*. That issue is judged at the moment of formation of the contract.[694] In this case there is no error which prevents *consensus*, rather, the expectations of one of the parties to the contract are not fulfilled. Those expectations would only be legally relevant where they were the subject of an express term or warranty in the contract itself. Because that is not the case here, error does not provide a ground for reduction of the contract.

II. 1. The concept of frustration of purpose is potentially relevant here. As already noted, it is often difficult to identify the parties' shared purpose, and even then, the shared purpose must be the foundation of the contract. In this Case 8, from the landlord's perspective, the purpose

[693] *Sweeney* v. *Duggan* [1997] ILRM 211. [694] McBryde, *Contract*, para. 15–01.

of the lease is probably to provide the tenant with a building for occupation. The tenant would argue that the purpose is occupation of the building as a book shop. If he sought to argue that the purpose of the lease was frustrated, X would, in effect, be arguing that the purpose of the lease was the running of a successful bookshop business. The landlord does not, of course, warrant the success of his tenant's business. As a result, Case 8 is not a relevant case of frustration of purpose. X would not be entitled to cancel what has turned out to be a bad bargain on his part.

2. This example can be contrasted with Cases 5 and 6 above which are more clearly cases of frustration of purpose. What distinguishes those cases is that the frustrating event rendered performance of the contract utterly meaningless. In Case 8, the contract of lease can be performed. X can continue to run his business. It is true that most of his potential customers will visit the centre when his shop is closed. However, one quarter of the shopping centre is let to businesses other than shops and restaurants. As a result, a small number of people will visit the centre during the day, and those people are potential customers. As such, the contract is not meaningless, but simply less profitable than X had anticipated.

3. Frustration of purpose usually involves a shared assumption by the parties to the contract which turns out to be incorrect. It is true that X and Y shared an assumption relating to the type of businesses who would become tenants in the centre. However, that assumption is not sufficiently central to the purpose of the contract of lease to result in frustration of purpose.

III. There are practical ways in which X could have protected himself in this situation He could have sought an enforceable undertaking from Y in terms of which Y would undertake only to let the remaining units in the centre to a certain type of business. It is common for leases of units in shopping centres in the UK to contain 'keep-open' or continuous trading obligations. Such a clause binds the tenant to open for trade during certain core trading hours.[695] X could have asked the landlord to provide copies of the leases already granted to other tenants in the centre to check their obligations in relation to their core trading

[695] See A. McAllister, *An Introduction to the Scottish Law of Leases* (London: LexisNexis, 2002); L. Macgregor, 'Specific implement in Scots law', in: J. Smits *et al.* (eds.), *Specific Performance in Contract Law: National and Other Perspectives* (Antwerp: Intersentia, 2008), pp. 67–93.

hours. Alternatively, and if Y refused to grant the undertaking referred to above, X could have decided to wait until the centre had been more fully let before taking a lease from Y. There is also presumably nothing to stop X from opening in the evening when the centre is at its busiest.

Editors' comparative notes

The open jurisdictions

According to the majority of the open jurisdictions, X is not entitled to termination or adjustment of the contract because he assumed a commercial risk that was foreseeable for both parties when the contract was concluded. The mere expectation of both parties that a greater variety of shops would develop does not justify relief as the parties could have transformed their expectation into a contract term.

By contrast, relief is granted according to the Dutch and the Italian reports. In Italy, the doctrine of *presupposizione* may lead to termination of the contract. The Dutch report, based on a close analysis of the case law and the economic situation at hand, comes to the conclusion that X might be given a reduction on the rent or that he might be allowed to terminate the contract. This is justified by the consideration that it is easier for the lessor to provide for a profitable use of the shop by replacing the tenant.

The closed jurisdictions

X is not entitled to cancel or adjust the contract in any of the closed jurisdictions. The same rationales are applied as in the open jurisdictions, namely that X assumed a commercial risk (see Czech Republic, France, Scotland, Slovenia). Yet, the English and Irish report states that a misrepresentation as to the tenancy profile would be a potential basis for relief. However, the case at hand is inconclusive concerning this matter. In Belgium and France, specific legislation on commercial leases may again allow adjustment or cancellation.

Conclusion

Both groups of jurisdictions generally deny X the right to cancel or adjust the contract. The rationale generally referred to is that the commercial risk in question was foreseeable. Hence, in the absence of an express term, the risk of an unexpected business environment was allocated to X in the contract. A minority position is offered in the jurisdictions of Italy and the Netherlands and perhaps Denmark where X may be entitled to termination or adjustment of the contract.

Case 9 Beer supply agreement

Long-term supply of beer; beer sales are far below expectations

X, the owner of a bar, enters into an exclusive supply agreement with the brewery Y for a fixed period of fifteen years. Pursuant to the contract, X is obliged to accept and pay for a specific quantity of beer on a monthly basis, while he is allowed to use technical equipment and furnishings owned by Y. The consumption of beer, however, remains far below expectations. The bar is well attended but the 'Y beer' is unpopular amongst customers at X's bar. X requests an adjustment or the termination of the agreement.

Is X's claim justified?

Germany and related jurisdictions

Germany

The facts of the case at hand do not justify a shift of the risk on Y. Y is not entitled to claim termination or adjustment of the contract.

I. The parties entered into a binding agreement under German law. With regard to long-term contracts for the supply of beer, the courts consider a contract with a fixed period of fifteen years as valid.[696] Nevertheless, the contractual agreement does not provide for the unexpected low level of sales. A certain level of sales has not been stipulated as a condition of the contract. Furthermore, there is no legally relevant mistake.[697]

II. 1.The insufficient popularity of 'Y-beer' and the accordingly low level of sales do not affect the 'quality' of the beer, i.e., a 'quality' of the subject matter of the long-term sales contract at hand. Thus, Y is not liable under any warranty.

2. However, X may terminate the long-term contract under §314 BGB due to a serious cause without notice if X cannot be expected to

[696] Cf. BGH NJW 1992, 2145; BGHZ 74, 293; contracts exceeding this duration may be limited by the courts under §138 I BGB, cf. J. Ellenberger, '§138', in: Palandt *et al.* (eds.), *Bürgerliches Gesetzbuch*, n. 81.

[697] For details on §158 BGB and §119 BGB, see Case 5.

continue the contract.[698] Even though a substantial change of the relevant circumstances usually qualifies as a relevant reason for termination, §314 BGB does not apply if one party bears the risk of this substantial change.[699] A contract for long-term supply of beer may be terminated under §314 BGB if the building of the bar is destroyed without fault of the innkeeper.[700] But in general, the buyer bears the risk of the purpose of use. In this case there are no reasons to assign this risk to Y.[701]

III. 1. Finally, X cannot request an adjustment or termination under the rules of *Störung der Geschäftsgrundlage* (§313 BGB). It is doubtful whether the expected amount of sales constitutes a *Geschäftsgrundlage* of the contract since it is not a *basic assumption* of both parties at the time of contracting that is the basis of the contractual agreement. Not all elements of the parties' calculation amount to a fundamental assumption on which the contract is based. Thus, despite the expectation of X and Y with regard to a certain number of sales at the time of contracting, this sales number must be considered only as an element in the motivation of the parties that is irrelevant under the concept of *Störung der Geschäftsgrundlage*.

2. Even if the amount of sales were considered as a *Geschäftsgrundlage* (§313 BGB) of the contract, this would not lead to an adaptation or termination of the contract. There is no unreasonable burden for X because, according to the general rule, the buyer bears the risk of his purpose of use, e.g., if he fails to accomplish an intended resale or cannot sell the goods due to a slump in sales.[702] This is even true if there is a contractual clause on lump sum damages in case the buyer fails to buy the monthly minimum amount.[703] According to this risk allocation, even the termination of the lease of the bar by the lessor does *not* substantially affect the *Geschäftsgrundlage* with regard to the beer contract.[704]

[698] For further details on §314 BGB, see Case 9.

[699] Cf. BGH NJW 1991, 1828 (1829); Grüneberg, '§314', in: Palandt *et al.* (eds.), *Bürgerliches Gesetzbuch*, n. 9.

[700] Cf. BGH LM §242 BGB (Bb) n. 14.

[701] Cf. for a more specific analysis see III below because the risk allocation under §313 BGB equals §314 BGB.

[702] Cf. BGHZ 17, 327; BGH NJW 1990, 567, 569; Roth, '§313', in: Krüger (ed.), *Münchener Kommentar zum Bürgerlichen Gesetzbuch*, vol. II, n. 203; for further details see Case 5.

[703] Cf. for further references Bühler, 'Rechtsprechungsübersicht Getränkebezugsvertrag 1991/92', (1994) BB, 663 (664).

[704] BGH NJW 1985, 2693 (2694).

3. Under exceptional circumstances only this risk may be allocated to both parties. The shift of risk is extremely rarely triggered by the mere failing of an intended resale based on false expectations of one party or even of both parties with regard to economic development. The courts held that a shift of risk may be reasonable if – applying the diligence of a prudent businessman – it was not possible for the lessee to sell the monthly minimum amount of beer, the brewery is also the lessor of the bar *and*, due to the shortfall of the minimum sales level of beer, the rent of the bar is substantially increased.[705] In such cases the courts considered the minimum amount of monthly sales as a *Geschäftsgrundlage* of the contract and adapted the contract to the change of circumstances by a reduction of the monthly minimum sales. Nevertheless, in some cases, courts also applied the concept of *Geschäftsgrundlage* if the business in total is compromised by the unchanged contract of beer supply.[706]

Austria

Under Austrian law, X is entitled to terminate the supply agreement.

I. 1. First of all, the question is whether or not this long-term commitment to accept a certain quantity of beer for a certain price contradicts 'good faith' ('*gute Sitten*' in §879 ABGB – public morality). Similar to the German point of view, the Austrian OGH held that long-term beer supply contracts exceeding the ordinary duration of such contracts are against public policy (good faith) and therefore 'void', because they constitute a severe restriction of the economic freedom of the buyer.[707] Of course there are no fixed limits for the maximum duration of such contracts. The decision in the particular case depends on whether the brewery abused its dominant position and on the value of consideration. With regard to the supply of technical equipment and furnishing, a commitment of fifteen years was considered to be the maximum permissible duration of a beer supply contract by Austrian courts.[708]

[705] Cf. BGH NJW 1990, 567 (569).

[706] Cf. Roth, '§313', in: Krüger (ed.), *Münchener Kommentar zum Bürgerlichen Gesetzbuch*, vol. II, n. 216.

[707] OGH, SZ 32/133 = EvBl 1960/126 = JBl 1960, 384; OGH, EvBl 1983/13 = JBl 1983, 32; OGH, SZ 56/144; OGH, JBl 1992, 517 = RdW 1992, 236.

[708] OGH, SZ 56/144; OGH, JBl 1992, 517 = RdW 1992, 236.

2. In the present case X is additionally obliged to accept and pay for a fixed quantity of beer, which makes the agreement far more stringent and disadvantageous for X. According to the decisions of Austrian courts the long-term commitment in the present case is contrary to the standard of '*gute Sitten*' (public morality, 'good faith' according to §879 ABGB) and therefore 'voidable' by X. Due to the long-term nature of the contract X's right of avoidance can be exercised as an *ex nunc* termination of the agreement. X has no right to adjust the contract (unilaterally). He can ask Y to conclude a new agreement after the termination of the first contract or to modify the first contract by agreement. However, these new arrangements (modification or new contract) depend on Y's consent.

II. Prohibiting long-lasting and restrictive commitments in beer-supply contracts intends to protect the innkeeper's freedom of commercial action.[709] Austrian commentators refer to such agreements as gagging contracts ('*Knebelungsverträge*'), which are considered to be against '*gute Sitten*' (public morality, good faith).[710] This legal regime protects the usually economically weak innkeeper against the much stronger brewery, which is in the position to dictate contractual stipulations that are severely unfavourable to the weaker party.

The Netherlands

Under Dutch law, the courts are likely to intervene in this case. The most likely remedy is termination.

I. This case contains several interesting elements: first of all, it may be very difficult for X to establish the bar without investments from third parties, in this case the brewery. Second, the case contains several elements that are questionable from a competition law perspective.[711]

[709] OGH, EvBl 1983/13 = JBl 1983, 32; OGH, SZ 56/144.

[710] Koziol and Welser, *Bürgerliches Recht*, vol. I, p. 144; F. Bydlinski, *Zulässigkeit und Schranken*, p. 25.

[711] If brewery Y has a market share exceeding 30 per cent, the agreement does not benefit from the application of the antitrust 'block exemption regulation' (Regulation (EC) No. 2790/1999, 'the Block Exemption Regulation' (*Official Journal of the European Communities*, L 336, 29.12.1999)), which prohibits anti-competitive covenants extending beyond a five-year term (and extension of such a term must be freely and expressly made). There is an exception: when the brewery owns the bar or rents the bar from a third party not connected with the buyer, the five-year time limitation does not apply. Exclusive purchase obligations and volume commitments, or minimum purchase obligations, are anti-competitive covenants that fall outside the block exception. If the market share exceeds 30 per cent, the entire agreement is most likely null and void. If Y's market share is below 15 per cent, the agreement would normally

Since the brewery market is highly competitive with dominant parties with considerable market shares and relatively high barriers to entry, in most cases the cartel prohibition applies with the effect that the exclusive obligation between X and Y is null and void. In 2002, the Dutch Competition Authority (NMa) approved new 'exclusive purchase contracts' (vertical agreements) of the brewery Heineken. In 2002 this brewery had a market share of 50–60 per cent in the Netherlands. Under these new contracts Heineken invested in local bars and restaurants in exchange for single branding. These exclusive obligations would normally be null and void. In this case, however, the NMa did not object because the contracts allowed the bars to unilaterally cancel the contracts at any point in time. After cancelling the contract a bar would be able to sell other brands. The Eublock exemption allows breweries with a market share of less than 30 per cent to sign exclusive purchase agreements under the condition that the duration of the agreements does not exceed five years.

II. If neither the agreement nor the exclusivity obligation is invalid or unenforceable on the basis of competition law, it may nevertheless be an abuse of economic power. In such cases the agreement is voidable ('*vernietigbare*') or partially voidable based on Art. 3:44 Dutch Civil Code. However, the threshold for an abuse of power is high.[712]

III. 1. There are no provisions in the Dutch Civil Code specifically dealing with contracts of long duration or contracts for an indefinite term. X's right to amend or terminate the supply contract should therefore be based on general provisions, including provisions on unforeseen circumstances (i.e., of Art. 6:258 Dutch Civil Code). A case in which the facts are similar to those at hand is *Donkelaar* v. *Unigro*:[713] A supermarket franchisor had made significant investments in the supermarket of Donkelaar, the franchisee. Both parties had agreed that during a period of twenty-five years Donkelaar would buy at least 85 per cent of its required products from Unigro. The level of exclusivity was not considered high enough for Unigro to consider the interests of Donkelaar before agreeing or even proposing this. The Hoge Raad affirmed the consideration by the Court of Appeal that parties should seek legal

be outside the scope of European competition laws, see, Commission Notice on agreements of minor importance (*Official Journal of the European Communities*, C 368, 22.12.2001, p. 13). The standard threshold of 15 per cent is lowered to 5 per cent if, in the market, such exclusive purchase obligation is practised by more than one brewery.

[712] HR 2 November 1979, NJ 1980, 429 (*Brandwijk* v. *Bouwbureau Brandwijk*).

[713] HR 1 June 1990, NJ 1996, 53 (*Donkelaar* v. *Unigro*).

advice when they are negotiating a contract that has a considerable impact. They must understand that their experience is inadequate to properly consider their own interests. This may of course be different if one party is largely dependent on the other.

2. In such a case, the early termination of a contract for an agreed period of time may exceptionally be possible if (i) unforeseen circumstances have occurred, which were not considered at the time of the agreement and (ii) that are of such a nature that they do not occur in the sphere of one party only and must, furthermore, not remain for the risk and account of one party.[714] Such criteria, which implicitly refer to those of Art. 6:258 Dutch Civil Code (on unforeseen circumstances), should only be applied very reluctantly. In the current case of a brewery, where there is also some indication of a dominant market position, the fact that the beer is not very popular may well be attributed to brewery Y, which either fails to implement a successful marketing strategy or fails to brew a favourable beer. There is no doubt that this is a prevailing circumstance (which the parties had not foreseen and could not have been expected to foresee) which affects both parties. X may need to establish that the poor beer sales is not due to its own failure to promote the beer sufficiently. If it succeeds, a court may be inclined to amend the contract in terms of exclusivity or to provide for an early termination, in both cases subject to an obligation to repay brewery Y's investment to the extent not yet recovered.

3. It is important to emphasise that the poor sales must not have been due to X's behaviour, as the decision in the *Blom* v. *Skol* case shows.[715] The Hoge Raad confirmed a decision on appeal where a suretyship arrangement ('*borgtocht*') appeared not to be subject to early termination even though the underlying obligation (a loan) had been repaid. The suretyship was given by the brewery vis-à-vis a bank against a bar's obligation to purchase its beer exclusively from the brewery. At first sight, the early repayment of the loan principal may seem to be a justification for terminating the suretyship arrangement. This cannot be so because in practice each bar would then have a discretionary freedom to refinance such a loan with the surety of another brewery and thereby be able to influence its contractual obligations. (At the same time, one might very well doubt whether the same case of *Blom* v. *Skol*

[714] HR 21 October 1988, NJ 1990, 439 (*Mondia* v. *Calanda*); reconfirmed in HR 10 August 1994, NJ 1994, 688 (*Aerts* v. *Kneepkens*).

[715] HR 31 October 1986, NJ 1987, 270 (*Blom* v. *Skol*).

would still hold under current competition law: if the justification for the exclusivity falls by the wayside, competition should not continue to be unnecessarily restricted.)

Eastern European jurisdictions

Slovenia

Under Slovenian law, the supply agreement might be considered to be invalid. If it is valid, X is not entitled to termination.

I. The agreement might be null and void because it is contrary to good faith and/or good morals ('*gute Sitten*'). Article 5(1) CO requires that parties observe good faith when concluding and performing contracts and Art. 5(2) expressly mentions good faith. Article 86 CO provides, that a contract that contravenes the constitution, compulsory regulations or good morals is null and void. Here, the long duration of the contract in combination with the obligation to purchase a certain minimum quantity is problematic. As of yet there is no case law in Slovenia regarding beer supply contracts, but given the similarity of Austrian provisions of the ABGB (§879), it might be possible to refer to Austrian case law on this point.[716]

II. If the contract is nevertheless considered valid, the only possibility for a premature termination of a contract concluded for a defined period of time is an action on grounds of a change of circumstances (Art. 112 CO). X's obligation has become very difficult for him to perform, but the reason for this situation is not a change of circumstances, but the fact, that there is not enough demand for 'Y-beer'. This is a circumstance that already existed at the time of the conclusion of the contract. Assuming that Y-beer has already been on the market at the time of conclusion, X could (and should) have requested for information about the popularity of Y-beer. The reason for X's problems is his bad choice of beer-supplier, for which he has to bear the risk. It is also possible that he miscalculated the possibility of reaching a bigger market share for 'Y-beer'. Thus, there is no valid claim on the ground of the '*clausula* rule'.

Lithuania

X may terminate the contract but he may have to compensate Y for his damages.

I. Contracts of distribution are regulated by Arts. 6.796–6.806 CC. According to Art. 6.804(2) CC, a distributor is entitled to terminate a

[716] See the Austrian report.

fixed-term contract of distribution before it expires. The consequences of termination depend on its reason. If the distributor terminates a contract because of a fault of the producer, the distributor is entitled to claim compensation of damages, e.g., if X is able to prove that the beer produced by Y is not of the required quality. If Y may not be held liable for the termination of the contract, X may nevertheless terminate the contract. However, he will be obliged to compensate B for the losses incurred. Thus, X has the right to terminate the contract, but the consequences of this termination will depend on its reasons.

II. In theory, X may try to modify the terms of the contract by referring to the institute of hardship according to Art. 6.228 CC and the principles of justice, reasonableness and good faith according to Art. 1.5 CC. X will have to prove that Y was unjustifiably provided with excessive advantage by the contract and has also taken advantage of X's economic weakness, his difficult economic situation, inexperience, etc. X may also argue that the above mentioned clause in the long term contract substantially limits his private initiative and business freedom thus constituting a reason for declaring the clause null and void as contradictory to good faith and public policy (Art. 1.81 CC). It is difficult to predict whether the court would accept such arguments of X, as there are no court judgments taken in similar cases. According to Art. 6.801 CC, exclusive supply agreements must correspond to the mandatory requirements of competition law. Thus, the answer to the given question will also depend on the application and interpretation of competition law.

III. With regard to Art. 6.204 CC the situation under discussion resembles Case 8, though the difference lies in the fact that in Case 8 the contract was concluded for the term of five years, while in this case, the term is for fifteen years. A contract concluded for a term of fifteen years may be considered a long-term contract. Article 6.204 CC can hardly be applied in this situation as: (i) X, as businessman, could have reasonably predicted that he would not be able to sell such large quantities of beer; (ii) X could influence the unfavourable circumstances for his business by resorting to various marketing tools, e.g., advertising, etc.; (iii) X, as a businessman, was acting upon his own risks, thus he has to accept the negative consequences of business.

Czech Republic

X is not entitled to terminate the supply contract.

I. The problem is whether the supply contract in question contradicts the principle of good morals (public morality (Section 39 Civil Code).

This would be the case. Y should have known what success serving the beer produced by X would be possible. It was his duty – as a reasonable businessman – to check this basic fact. The doctrine of a reasonable businessman is found in Section 194(5) Commercial Code in respect of members of companies' boards, but can be applied in this case by analogy. A reasonable businessman is a person who possesses necessary knowledge and proficiency and who acts responsibly and conscientiously.[717]

II. As mentioned above (Case 8), the law only allow contracts concluded for an indefinite period of time to be terminated by notice (this follows *a contrario* from Section 582(1) Civil Code.[718]

III. This is not a situation which would involve any issue of force majeure, unexpected circumstances, or *rebus sic stantibus*. Neither is the frustration of the purpose of the contract at issue. The *pacta sunt servanda*, as a basic principle of contract law, applies and X will be obliged to accept and pay for the beer from Y for another fifteen years. Y has to bear the risk.

IV. Another matter is to what degree the conclusion of this supply contract is valid from the perspective of competition law. If abuse of a dominant position is involved, the agreement would be invalid for that reason. However, we do not have a sufficient factual basis to assess this problem.

Scandinavian jurisdictions

Sweden

X is not entitled to request termination or adjustment of the contract.

I. 1. This is a sales contract. There is no time limit for such a contract under Swedish law. Nor is the obligation to buy a certain quantity problematic as such. Under Swedish law there is no general right to terminate a long-term contract that is entered into for a specific period of time.

2. Under the Sales Act (Sections 17 *et seq.*) the seller is responsible for the quality of the assets delivered. These rules might be applied if there is something wrong with the beer, e.g., the taste is such that virtually nobody likes it. However, there is no indication of such a defect. The

[717] See Tomsa in: Štenglová, Plíva and Tomsa (eds.), *Obchodní zákoník Kaueutár*, p. 745.
[718] See the wording of Section 582(1) in Case 1.

main principle is that the buyer carries the loss when his ability to use the goods as planned is affected by circumstances which are not related to the quality of the goods.

II. By entering into a contract of this type, the buyer has assumed the risk of low sales. Therefore, the prerequisite of good faith is not fulfilled and the doctrine of assumptions cannot be applied. Of course, it is still possible that he has somehow been duped (e.g., to believe that he bought a popular beer when he did not) at the formation of the contract, and that he can rely on that. But, if that is not the case, it is not easy to find a relevant ground under Swedish law for the buyer's claim.

III. Section 36 Contracts Act allows for a contract term to be adjusted or disregarded in a particular case if it is unreasonable ('*oskäligt*') with reference to the contents of the contract, the circumstances at the formation of the contract, circumstances arising later, and other circumstances. However, this section is applied restrictively in relations between tradesmen, and is not principally aimed at correcting disturbances of the equilibrium under a trade contract. This is especially true when a tradesman, as in this case, has knowingly carried a risk. The buyer can argue that his losses are significant, that a lot of beer goes to waste and that Section 36 can be applied more often with regards to long-term contracts, but it is doubtful whether this would be sufficient.

IV. The principle regarding termination in the event of unexpected circumstances of an extraordinary magnitude, so-called '*viktig grund*' is most likely not applicable to a case like this, where the circumstances have not changed.

Denmark

Under Danish law the contract is likely to be adjusted by the court.

I. It might be possible to successfully argue that Y, the brewery, has acted fraudulently and thus violated Section 30 Contracts Act. This is the case if Y knew, upon the formation of the contract, that it is impossible to achieve a turnover comprising the specific quantity of beer set out in the contract between the parties. However, it would be quite difficult or impossible for X, the landlord, to prove that Y had acted in bad faith.

II. Danish law does not contain any provisions providing for restrictions on the duration of such contracts. Freedom of contract allows one to enter into contracts with a fixed period even though such a period might be of very long duration.[719] An obligation to buy a certain amount of beer is furthermore compatible with the freedom of contract, unless such a provision in the contract is considered to be a violation of Section 36 Contracts Act as it is unreasonable to X, the landlord.

III. If the beer can be considered defective in the sense of the Sale of Goods Act, X is entitled to terminate the contract if the defect is considered to be a fundamental breach of the contract and he can claim damages in accordance with the Sale of Goods Act.

IV. With regard to a long-term contract without any fixed period of time, either party is entitled to terminate the contract with six months' notice as discussed above in Case 1. If the parties have entered into an agreement for a fixed period of time, no matter how long, such a contract is considered binding upon the parties for the entire period. The termination of such a contract requires either a fundamental breach or a case of force majeure, where the extraordinary circumstances must last for more than six months. In such cases the long-term contract would be terminated. In the case at hand, a low consumption which is far below one's expectations is not considered to be force majeure in accordance with Danish law.

V. As the contract between X, the landlord, and Y, the brewery, contains a provision on the specific amount of beer, that X is obliged to receive and pay for on a monthly basis, such a provision must be regarded as a condition pursuant to the contract in accordance with Danish law. Thus, the doctrine of assumptions is not applicable in the case at hand.[720]

VI. However, if such a case is brought before a Danish court, there is no doubt that Section 36 Contracts Act will be invoked with good prospects. Especially considering the general turnover of the bar belonging to X, which is apparently quite good, and the time span of the contract, X has a strong case against Y. Furthermore, X, the landlord, must be considered to be the weaker party to the contract compared to Y, the brewery, which actually drafted the contract.[721] The Danish courts would most likely find in favour of X, in which case the obligation to buy a specific amount of beer would be adjusted (diminished) or, perhaps more unlikely, the whole contract would set aside. At the end of

[719] Cf. U 2004.2518V which is discussed in conjunction with Case 1.

[720] It might be difficult to make a clear distinction between an assumption and a condition. See for instance U 1988.500H.

[721] Cf. U 1979.931Ø and U 1981.870V.

the day, it is basically a decision as to whether such an obligation would be considered unfair in accordance with Section 36 Contracts Act.

Romanic-Mediterranean jurisdictions

Italy

X's claim would only be justified under special circumstances which are not present in this case.

I. 1. A long-term obligation to buy a certain quantity is valid under Italian law. If such an obligation is, as at hand, compensated by obligations of the other party, specific rules of the CC apply (Arts. 1559–70 CC; '*Somministrazione*').

2. Under Italian law there is no statutory provision providing for an extraordinary termination of long-term contracts. But in a case of a continuous or periodic performance of a long-term contract, Art. 1373 CC provides that each party has a unilateral right to withdraw from the contract. In the case at hand, Art. 1569 CC could also be applicable, which establishes a specific unilateral right to withdraw from a long-term sales contract.

II. 1. However, X's request of termination is, in principle, not justified under Italian law, unless Y is responsible for the low consumption of Y-beer (e.g., it depends on facts related to the production or the marketing of the beer). The supervening unpopularity of Y-beer is not, as such, a reason to ask for discharge. Italian courts would maintain that X assumed the contractual risk (in the case at issue, for sales below the expectations of the parties at the time of the agreement) and therefore the remedies against the excessive burden and/or the frustration of the contractual purposes would not be granted.

2. As far as the requests for an adjustment of the agreement is concerned, it is rather exceptional that, as a matter of fact, a long-term supply contract for a fixed period of fifteen years is not subject to adjustment or renegotiation clauses. However, if this is the case, Italian courts could decide both (i) that X assumed the contractual risk and therefore the remedies against the excessive onerousness and/or the frustration of the contractual purposes would not be granted (Art. 1467 CC not applicable), or (ii) that, according to some Italian scholars,[722] a duty to renegotiate with the aim of equitably adapting

[722] See Case 8.

or modifying the affected contractual provision may arise from the general duty to perform in good faith (Arts. 1175 and 1375 CC). Such a duty obliges Y to enter into negotiations with X in order to agree on an equitable modification of the contractual provision to accept and pay for a specific quantity of beer on a monthly basis.

3. It should be noted that the fact this is a long-term contract, would play a fundamental role in establishing a duty to renegotiate on the basis of the good faith principle, especially if X has negotiated as the weaker party and the duty of X to pay a specific quantity of beer on a monthly basis for fifteen years, as a matter of fact, has been imposed by the stronger party Y.

Spain

X's claim is not likely to be justified under Spanish law.

I. There are no restrictions under Spanish law regarding the duration of contracts for supply/distribution agreements. Exclusive purchasing clauses are typical in agreements in which the seller is concerned with the maintenance of the quality of the products. This is particularly true in this case, in which Y also provides the technical equipment to serve beer.

II. The buyer cannot unilaterally terminate the contract because it has been concluded for a definitive period. Indeed, in those cases, unlike in cases of contracts concluded for an indefinite period, the Spanish courts would only allow the buyer to unilaterally terminate the contract on the grounds established by the law, namely impossibility, non-performance or the existence of a contractual stipulation stating that the contract would terminate if the product turns out to be unpopular.[723] This approach is supported by the fact that the buyer is an independent entrepreneur who acts in his own name and for his own account and who assumes the risk of not being commercially successful.

III. X should have provided for this situation in the contract and reserved the right to terminate or adapt the contract. The *rebus* doctrine does not apply because the problems at hand are not considered to be unforeseen circumstances but commercial risks of which commercial parties are aware.

[723] Echebarría Saenz, p. 481.

Portugal

X's claim is not justified.

I. As was already previously stated, Portuguese law is generally reluctant to accept perpetual contractual obligations.[724] In most contracts there is no legal limit to its duration, the rule on leases being an exception. If a contract is not a fixed-term one, a party may terminate the contract at any time, provided notice is given within a reasonable period of time. However, that does not apply if the contract is limited in time.

II. In a situation like the one described in Case 9, Art. 437 CC probably could not be invoked successfully. The risk that the customers dislike the beer has been freely accepted by X. Therefore, the fact that the consumption of beer remained far below expectations will not allow X to terminate the contract or to ask for its adjustment. More precisely, even if there was a change in the taste of the customers, that change can hardly be considered anomalous and in any case it will probably fall within the risks inherent to the contract. A contract with a fixed-term duration of this kind is valid and the obligation to buy a certain quantity is equally valid.

Greece

X's claim to terminate or renegotiate the contract is not justified.

I. The agreement of exclusive supply is valid under Greek law. Article 5 §1 Greek Constitution (freedom of economic actions) and Art. 361 AK, which establishes the freedom of contracts, legitimates the validity of such an agreement.[725]

II. X's claim for adjustment or termination of the agreement is not justified under Art. 388 AK (see also Case 8). The long-term nature of the contract implies that the frustration of the creditor only concerns his motives, which are not essential for the validity of the contract.

[724] The Code allows, however, for so-called perpetual rent (*renda perpétua*), a contract in which one of the parties transfers to the other an amount of money or the ownership of an object or another right and the latter undertakes the obligation to pay a certain amount of money or other fungible object (Art. 1231 CC) periodically without any temporal limitation. Nevertheless, even in this case the debtor has the possibility of terminating the contract with a single payment (Art. 1236 CC) although that possibility can be excluded during the life of the first beneficiary or for no more than twenty years (Art. 1236, nr. 2 CC).

[725] See AP 53/2007 (unpubl.); 212/2006 (unpubl.); 139/2006, DEE 2006, 649.

III. Nevertheless, after the contract has been maintained for several years X will, inevitably, suffer serious economic losses and enormous damages. This result by itself might be considered as a substantial reason, that gives X the right to an extraordinary termination of the contract without notice pursuant to Art. 288 AK.[726] Of course, this is only a probable solution, which would require the financial ruin of X, a prerequisite which does not seem to be met in the above case.

France and related jurisdictions

France

The lease will expire after a period of ten years. The court may also require the brewery to renegotiate the contract.

I. In this case, a claim for a revision based on the law of commercial leases cannot be successfully invoked if one assumes that the rental value remains the same because the bar remains well attended. The decrease in sales is due to a factor (i.e., no sale of beer) which is irrelevant to the objective rental value.

II. In principle, the parties are free to agree upon the duration of the contract. However, there is a legal maximum limit: an old statute dating from 14 October 1943 (directed against certain providers of American materials) limits the duration of an exclusive supply contract to ten years. The duration of contracts providing for longer periods of exclusive supply is reduced to ten years. According to the European Regulation 2790/99, in the case of certain beer contracts the duration may be reduced if the exclusivity clause extends to other drinks as well. In our case, the contract for exclusive distribution is fixed at fifteen years. This period is excessive and may be reduced to the maximum limit of ten years according to Art. L330-1 of the Code of Commerce. If the exclusivity also covers other drinks, the duration can be reduced to ten years by virtue of the European regulation.[727]

[726] See Karakatsanis, 'Artt. 416–454', in: Georgiadis and Stathopoulos (eds.), *AK*, Introd. notes n. 23. The possibility of terminating a continuing contract based on a substantial reason according to the rules of good faith is supported by the majority of legal writers, see Stathopoulos, *Law of Obligations*, §21 n. 135; Ap. Georgiadis, *ContrLGenP*, §14 n. 32; Kapodistrias, 'Artt. 416–454', in: Introd. notes nn. 37 *et seq.*; Karakatsanis, 'Arts. 416–54', in: Georgiadis and Stathopoulos (eds.), *AK*, Introd. notes nn. 22 *et seq.* Contra Georgagopoulos, *The Law of Continuous Obligations* (Athens: Sakkoulas, 1979), p. 171.

[727] The application of the regulation is based on an economic analysis. See the Dutch report.

III. The parties have the obligation to perform their initial contractual obligations, even if the economic circumstances have radically changed. However, as already pointed out, in the specific domain of distribution contracts the Cour de Cassation required a petroleum company to renegotiate a contract in a similar situation (the *Huard* case).[728] This renegotiation is subject to there being unexpected circumstances. So the question is whether the change in the popularity of a beer was foreseeable or not.

Belgium

Under Belgian law, there is a distinct possibility that X would be allowed to terminate the contract.

I. If the contract is to be characterised as a lease, Art. 6 of the Law on Commercial Leases might again be relevant (see Case 8). X could invoke the decrease in the rental value due to a lack of consumption as far as the beer is concerned. One may argue that the objective rental value is not influenced by the poor sales of beer as the bar is still busy. According to this proposition, X cannot claim any adjustment or a termination on the basis of unexpected circumstances.

II. If X can prove, however, that the poor beer sales are due to faults in the management of Y's brewery, the contract can be terminated on the basis of breach of contract (Art. 1184 Cciv). Abuse of rights could also be invoked in this case because the loss suffered by X is disproportionate in relation to the benefit obtained by X.[729]

England and related jurisdictions

England and Ireland

X is bound to the contract and cannot claim adjustment or termination.

I. Exclusive supply agreements of this kind in the brewery business were at one time very common in Ireland and case law established that these agreements are enforceable at common law and are not the subject of the doctrine of restraint of trade: see *Murphy & Co* v.

[728] Cass., com 3 November 1992 *Sté Francaise des Pétrdes BP v. Huard*, JCP 1993, II, no. 22, 614.

[729] This answer does not take EU competition law into consideration, which also aims to guarantee the equilibrium between the respective obligations of the parties (see the French report on this point).

O'Donovan.[730] The hypothetical here is today not very commercially realistic, but in theory X is bound to continue to take the specified quantity of Y-beer. It is unlikely that X would be able to rely on the doctrine of mistake or frustration, as a court would most likely hold that X entered into a risky or speculative contract, and took the risk that Y-beer would not be popular with X's customers. However, a term allowing termination upon giving reasonable notice may be implied. For example, in *Irish Welding* v. *Philips Electrical (Ireland) Ltd*[731] a sole distributorship contract was terminable upon giving reasonable notice of nine months. However, this would probably only apply if the contract itself does not expressly deal with the right to terminate on giving reasonable notice.[732] In England and Ireland, the courts would most likely hold that a risky or speculative contract had been entered into, and would not imply a term to terminate the contract where the contract itself deals with the issue of termination.

Scotland

X has no right to terminate or adjust the contract.

I. Scots law contains no principle of commercial impossibility.[733] The fact that continued performance of the contract will be economically disadvantageous to one party does not mean that the contract is frustrated.[734] Lord Dundas commented:

> The difficulty which meets the defenders is well illustrated by the language in which they state their case, namely, that they are not bound to what is commercially impossible. That is a very far-reaching doctrine, and its application would lead to startling results.[735]

II. 1. In effect, one of the parties has made a 'bad bargain' and the courts will not intervene to prevent that party suffering the effects of the same. In this case, X's decision to enter into an agreement to accept the supply of beer is a commercial decision. As such, it would be made entirely at his own risk. Undoubtedly, he could have attempted to cut down this risk, for example by carrying out research into the level

730 [1939] IR 455. 731 Unreported, Irish High Court, October 8, 1976.

732 See Case 1 for more information on this. 733 McBryde, *Contract*, para. 21.20.

734 *Hong-Kong and Whampoa Dock Co Ltd* v. *Netherton Shipping Co Ltd* 1909 SC 34; *Tsakiraglou & Co* v. *Noblee & Thurl GmbH* [1962] AC 93; Gloag, *Contract* at 338–9; see also A. Forte, 'Economic Frustration of Commercial Contracts: A Comparative Analysis with Particular Reference to the United Kingdom', (1986) *Juridical Review* 1.

735 *Hong-Kong and Whampoa Dock Co Ltd* v. *Netherton Shipping Co Ltd* 1909 SC 34 at 40.

of popularity of the beer. If his commercial decision turns out to be an unprofitable one, the courts will not release him from his contract.

2. Scots law contains only an undeveloped idea of good faith in contract law.[736] It is not sufficiently wide as to impose obligations on X to act reasonably in the performance of this contract. Y therefore cannot reduce the contract on the basis that X has failed to act in good faith.

III. 1. As a general rule, there is no right to cancel long-term contracts in Scots law. The courts will not imply a term to this effect which would contradict an express term detailing the exact duration of the contract.[737] Y is therefore bound to perform this contract for its duration.

2. The obligation to supply and to accept the supply of the specific quantity of beer is valid. The quantity to be supplied is an express term of the contract and, this being the case, the court could not imply a term which contradicted the express term. Even if the courts were able to imply a term, the term required would be of an unusual nature, requiring, in effect, for the parties to renegotiate the quantity to be delivered. This type of 'agreement to agree' would fail the test of certainty applicable to implied terms.[738]

Editors' comparative notes

The open jurisdictions

In the open jurisdictions, there are two basic issues discussed with regard to the case at hand. The first one is the validity of the contract under the general standard of good morals and the second one is the application of the general doctrines addressing a change of circumstances (such as '*Geschäftsgrundlage*'). Yet, on both grounds, there is much reservation towards granting relief.

In some jurisdictions (Austria, Germany, Lithuania, the Netherlands), the issue is raised whether the contract violates the standard of good morals as X's economic freedom is strongly restricted by the fixed quantity of beer he has to buy from Y for such a long period of time. In Austria, for example, the contract would be held invalid under this consideration. However, some reporters indicate that immorality requires an abuse of power on the side of Y (see, e.g., Lithuania, the Netherlands). Similarly, the Italian report states that additional

[736] See *Smith* v. *Bank of Scotland* 1997 SC (HL) 111 and H. MacQueen, 'Good faith', in: H. MacQueen and R. Zimmermann (eds.), *European Contract Law: Scots and South African Perspectives* (Edinburgh University Press, 2006), pp. 43–73.

[737] McBryde, *Contract*, para. 9–10.

[738] MacQueen and Thomson, *Contract*, para 3.37.

circumstances are required in order to hold the long-term agreement invalid on the basis of good morals. In some other open jurisdictions that apply the standard of good morals to such contracts, the contract will be upheld as a fair business agreement (Germany and the Netherlands). The Lithuanian and the Dutch reports point out that rules of competition law might apply restricting long-term contracts which lead to the dependence of one party on a dominant supplier.

Germany, Greece, Portugal, Spain and Sweden mainly rely on their respective 'exceptional' doctrines addressing a change of circumstances in this case. However, under the facts of the case generally no relief is granted: the failure to sell the beer is regarded as a typical risk that X accepted under the agreement and that he should have been aware of. Relief based on these doctrines can only be granted under exceptional circumstances (Germany) or if X would otherwise be financially ruined (Germany and Greece).

The closed jurisdictions

In England and Ireland the courts tend to derive a term from the contract by implication allowing X to terminate the contract upon reasonable notice. In Slovenia, a long-term contract like the one in the given case appears to be regarded as in breach of good morals (the reasoning is also based on Austrian case law). In Denmark, the contract may be adjusted by the courts under Art. 36 Contracts Act (general unreasonableness clause).

In France, a specific provision on beer supply contracts will allow X to reduce the duration of the contract to ten years. Furthermore, a duty to renegotiate the contract might be imposed by the court. In Belgium, X can invoke an abuse of rights and there is a good chance that he would be allowed to terminate the contract.

Only the Czech Republic and Scotland deny a remedy based on the reasoning that X assumed the business risk in question under the contract. Unlike in England and Ireland, Scottish courts are very reluctant to imply a contractual right to terminate.

Conclusion

Surprisingly enough, in Case 9, the closed jurisdictions are more likely to grant relief (cf. Denmark, England and Ireland, Slovenia) than the open jurisdictions. Again, it seems that the outcome of the case rather relies on an overall assessment of the allocation of business risks than on the availability and choice of doctrines.

Another interesting observation is that the results of Cases 8 and 9 differ quite significantly even though they involve a fairly similar unexpected change of business development. While most of the reports on Case 8 leave the shop owner with no relief, a slight majority of the jurisdictions grants the landlord in Case 9 the right to terminate the contract. This distinction may be explained by the fact that the contract in Case 9 binds the parties for a longer time (fifteen as opposed to five years). Another aspect might be that the risk at issue in Case 9, the popularity of the beer, is regarded to fall within the sphere of the brewery.

Case 10 Export ban

Purchaser of technical equipment is affected by export ban

Firm X purchases technical equipment which is to be produced by firm Y. The parties know that firm X plans to resell the equipment to Iraq. At the time of contracting, exports to Iraq are illegal but the parties expect that the status quo will change before the time of delivery. The parties are aware that the equipment can only be sold to Iraq at a reasonable price. When firm Y has completed production and offers delivery, exports to Iraq are still illegal and no change is in sight. Firm X refuses acceptance and payment.

Is X's refusal to accept and pay justified?

Germany and related jurisdictions

Germany

X's refusal is likely to be justified under German law. However, he might have to partly indemnify Y for his expenses and his loss of profits.

I. In this case, the contract does not provide for a clause dealing explicitly with a lingering illegality of the export at the time of delivery nor does the contract contain an implicit provision for this situation. Thus, the possibility of exporting the technical equipment to Iraq is not a condition to the contract (§158 BGB).

II. The rules of impossibility (§§275, 311a I, 326 BGB) are not applicable either. Specific performance is still possible as there is no impediment to performance. The contractual obligation of Y only covers the production and delivery of the technical equipment in Germany, both of which are still possible.

III. The contract does not violate a statutory prohibition of sale and thus it is not void according to §134 BGB. The illegality of an export of technical equipment may render a contract void under §134 BGB and the Law on Foreign Trade and Payments (Außenwirtschaftsgesetz) if the contract contains the obligation of one party to export the goods. Here, the illegal export of the goods to Iraq is not covered by the contractual obligations.[739] The mere intention of one party to export the goods is beyond the scope of the contract and irrelevant under §134 BGB.[740]

IV. 1. X and Y entered into a contract for works, but, since Y is obliged to supply moveable things that are to be produced or manufactured (§651 BGB), the contract is covered in general by the provisions about the sale of goods. Thus, X can refuse acceptance and payment only if the goods do not meet the contractual requirements (§§434, 437 BGB). Under these rules X may refuse the delivery of defective goods. But a rescission of the contract is only allowed if a supplementary performance rendered by Y is also defective (§§437, 439 BGB).

2. However, the technical equipment is not defective according to §434 BGB. First, it is doubtful whether the possibility of exporting the goods is an element of the 'quality' of the contractual subject-matter. According to one opinion the 'quality' of the subject-matter must be directly related to the (physical) condition of the goods.[741] In this case, the possibility of exporting the goods lacks this close relation to the (physical) condition of the equipment. Second, the possibility of exporting the goods to Iraq is not a 'use specified in the contract' according to an interpretation of the contract in line with the interest of the parties (§434 I 1 nr. 1 BGB). Otherwise Y would have assumed the risk of the possibility of exporting the goods and X could terminate the contract or reduce the purchase price without any fault of Y. There are not sufficient grounds to conclude that Y assumed this risk. Additionally, the possibility of exporting the equipment is not an element of its 'normal use' nor an element of the quality 'that is usual with regard to objects of the same kind and that can be expected by the buyer by virtue of its nature' (§434 I 1 nr. 2 BGB).

[739] For further details and references on the Law on Foreign Trade and Payments cf. BGH NJW 1983, 2873; T. Mayer-Maly and C. Armbrüster, '§134', in: Säcker, *et al.*, *Münchener Kommentar zum Bürgerlichen Gesetzbuch*, vol. I/1, n. 63.

[740] Cf. BGH *LM* n. 1 to §15 WiStG 1949/52.

[741] Cf. H.-C. Grigoleit and C. Herresthal, 'Grundlagen der Sachmängelhaftung im Kaufrecht', (2003) JZ, 118 (122 *et seq.*).

III. 1. Thus, the core issue of the case is whether the concept of *Störung der Geschäftsgrundlage* (§313 BGB) is applicable. Since the contractual obligation of Y can be performed, while it has become practically useless with regard to the purposes of X, the *Vereitelung des Verwendungszwecks* (frustration of purpose) is the issue at hand.[742]

2. First, the lift of the export ban at the time of delivery must be a basic assumption shared by both parties at the time of contracting or at least an assumption of X recognisable to Y and uncontested by him. In the given case, both parties knew at the time of contracting that X intended to export the equipment to Iraq and that, as a prerequisite, the present export ban had to be lifted. Additionally, the equipment could only be sold to Iraq at a reasonable price. Thus, the lifting of the ban was a basic assumption shared by both parties.[743] Moreover, according to the prevailing view in legal literature and in the case law, the concept of *Geschäftsgrundlage* can also be applied to assumptions related to future circumstances if the contractual will of the parties is based on them.[744]

3. Additionally, the *Geschäftsgrundlage* of the contract must be *substantially* affected. This condition is met if the parties would have agreed on a different contract if they had known about the change in the circumstances at the time of formation. It is also sufficient that one party to the contract would have agreed only to a different contract and the other party would have agreed upon it as well. In the given case, the technical equipment can only be sold to Iraq at a reasonable price. Therefore, if the parties had anticipated the continuation of the export ban, X would not have entered into the contract without any provision dealing with an ongoing export ban.

4. As a further requirement for the application of §313 I BGB, X has to be *unreasonably burdened* if the contract is upheld as originally agreed upon. X is burdened by the fact that he cannot sell the goods at a reasonable price. Nevertheless, as a general rule, it is legally irrelevant whether or not either party can make use of the contractual subject matter in the way he expected, i.e., each party bears the risk that he can realise his purposes of use, unless the purpose in question is stipulated

[742] Cf. for further details on issue of frustration of purpose Case 5.

[743] Cf. for a similar case BGH *LM* §242 BGB (Bb) n. 12 (*Bohrhämmer*); BGH NJW 1998, 1701 (*Militärboote*).

[744] Cf. Roth, '§313', in: Krüger *et al.* (eds.), *Münchener Kommentar zum Bürgerlichen Gesetzbuch*, vol. II, n. 223 *et seq.*; e.g., BGH NJW 1984, 1746 (1747).

in the contract.[745] The courts have considered the frustration of purpose as *Störung der Geschäftsgrundlage* according to §313 BGB only in exceptional cases.[746] They have required a specific justification for the shift of the risk concerning the frustration of purpose.[747] It is not sufficient that the specific purpose of use is mentioned in the contract or communicated to the other party.[748] The purpose of use of one party must instead be so closely related to the other party's interest, that the latter party's claim of his contractual rights has to be qualified as *venire contra factum proprium* (§242 BGB).[749] Grave changes of political, economic and social conditions (e.g., government intervention) may justify a shift of the risk because the resulting burden on one of the parties is purely accidental (so-called '*Große Geschäftsgrundlage*').[750] Under this test, the courts applied the concept of *Geschäftsgrundlage* in cases where the buyer intended to resell the goods to a third party, specific performance of the resale became impossible without any contribution on the side of the buyer and the goods could not be sold otherwise.[751] In a similar decision, the courts held that there is also a relevant frustration of purpose if the buyer has no use for the furnishing of a restaurant because the lessor of the business accommodation does not perform without any contribution on the side of the buyer.[752] Legal scholars often shape the concept of *Geschäftsgrundlage* more narrowly.[753]

5. In the given case, Y knew about X's specific purpose of use. Y produced the goods knowing that the ban was still in effect. The technical equipment could only be sold to Iraq at a reasonable price.

[745] Cf. Roth, '§313', in: Krüger *et al.* (eds.), *Münchener Kommentar zum Bürgerlichen Gesetzbuch*, vol. II, n. 213; BGHZ 17, 327 (buyer has no use for the goods due to slump in sales); BGHZ 71, 293; BGHZ 74, 370 (374); BGH NJW 1985, 2693 (concept of *Geschäftsgrundlage* is not applicable if buyer has no use for long term beer supply due to termination of the restaurant lease).

[746] Cf. BGH *LM* §242 BGB (Bb) n. 12 (*Bohrhämmer*); BGH *JZ* 1966, 409 (*Fertighaus*); BGH *LM* §242 BGB (Bb) n. 54 (*Gaststätteninventar*); BGH NJW 1984, 1746 (*Iran*); BGH NJW 1998, 1701 (*Militärboote*).

[747] Cf. for further details Case 5. [748] BGH NJW-RR 1992, 182.

[749] Cf. Larenz, *Schuldrecht I*, §21 II; see also BGH *LM* §242 BGB (*Bb*) n. 54 (*Gaststätteninventar*); BGH *JZ* 1966, 409 (*Fertighaus*).

[750] Cf. for further details Case 5.

[751] Cf. BGH *LM* §242 BGB (Bb) n. 12 (*Bohrhämmer*); see also BGH NJW 1981, 1701.

[752] Cf. BGH *LM* §242 BGB (Bb) n. 54 (*Gaststätteninventar*).

[753] Cf. W. Flume, DJT 1960 I, S. 220 *et seq.*; F. Wieacker, in: *Festschrift zum 70. Geburtstag von Walter Schmidt-Rimpler* (Karlsruhe: C.F. Müller, 1957), pp. 229 (252 *et seq.*) with regard to the case of BGH *LM* §242 BGB (Bb) n. 12 (*Bohrhämmer*); for further references cf. Roth, '§313', in: Krüger (ed.), *Münchener Kommentar zum Bürgerlichen Gesetzbuch*, vol. II, n. 216.

Therefore the purpose of use is closely related to Y's interests. Without an alternative market Y would have to sell the goods to Iraq himself and be immediately affected by the export ban. Thus, Y's claim of his contractual rights may be qualified as *venire contra factum proprium*.[754]

6. Finally, the specific purpose is frustrated by the ongoing *export ban*. This suggests an analogy with cases in which a government intervention after the formation of the contract results in a frustration of purpose: in both cases the allocation of the loss is purely accidental. The solution may be different if the fact that the goods can only be sold to Iraq at a 'reasonable price' does not render the goods unsellable but merely amounts to some losses for X if he resells the goods to a third person.[755]

7. If there is a frustration of purpose, the contract is generally upheld and adapted to the unexpected circumstances (§313 I BGB). Only in exceptional cases, may the disadvantaged party be allowed to avoid the contract without paying any indemnity (§313 III BGB).[756] In cases similar to the given one, courts split the loss between the parties[757] or avoided the contract in return for indemnity.[758] Hence, if there is a possibility of selling the technical equipment to a third party, the contract may be upheld and adapted in a way that X's losses are split between both parties. If there are no specific circumstances, an equal allocation of the risk is equitable.[759] Otherwise the contract may be avoided and X may have to partly indemnify Y for his expenses and his loss of profits. Since there are no exceptional circumstances that justify a complete allocation of risk to Y, the other party cannot terminate the contract without paying any indemnity.

Austria

X is not entitled to terminate the contract and has to pay for the equipment.

I. 1. It is hard to draw the line between mistake of intention (§901 ABGB) and '*Wegfall der Geschäftsgrundlage*' in this case. The assumption

[754] In a similar case the court held that both parties took a risk by contracting; cf. BGH *LM* §242 BGB (Bb) n. 12 (*Bohrhämmer*).

[755] Cf. BGH ZIP 1997, 762 (764).

[756] Cf. for further details on the legal consequences in cases of frustration of purpose Case 5; see also Roth, '§313', in: Krüger *et al.* (eds.), *Münchener Kommentar zum Bürgerlichen Gesetzbuch*, vol. II, n. 217 for a precise allocation of those cases to the provisions of §313 I, III BGB.

[757] Cf. BGH *LM* §242 BGB (Bb) n. 12 (*Bohrhämmer*).

[758] Cf. BGH NJW 1998, 1701 (1705) (*Militärboote*).

[759] Cf. BGH NJW 1984, 1746 (1747).

that the status quo will change is not a usual mistake in intention/motive pertaining to the subjective motives of one party to conclude the contract. But anyhow, §901 ABGB (mistake of intention/motive) would not grant X any relief. The common expectation of the parties can be considered a general (objective) basis of their contract and thus falls within the scope of the doctrine of '*Wegfall der Geschäftsgrundlage*'. However, also according to this doctrine, X will not be entitled to terminate the agreement if the 'change of circumstances' is predictable or falls within his area of assumed risk.[760]

2. Under Austrian law, the solution of the case turns on whether or not the suspension of the export ban falls within X's own area of risk according to the contractual risk allocation (as interpreted or supplemented by the courts). The Austrian OGH held that where both parties knew that the leased property should be used to start up a drugstore, the administration's refusal to issue a business license entitled the lessee to cancel the contract.[761] This was justified by the argument that both parties had impliedly accepted the issuance of a licence as the basis of their agreement. On the other hand, the Austrian OGH held that denied housing subsidies expected by both parties do not entitle a party to terminate the purchase of an apartment.[762] As can be seen, Austrian court decisions are rather inconsistent and depend on the circumstances of the particular case.

3. In the present case, both parties must have known that the suspension of the export ban is not a certainty, i.e., the persistence of the boycott was, in fact, foreseeable. Furthermore Y did not accept the suspension of the export ban as a condition to the contract.[763] Therefore X entered willingly into a risky agreement. Even though Y knew that X wanted to export the technical equipment to Iraq, whether or not the export ban would be suspended is quite clearly a risk undertaken by X under the contract. As a result X is obliged to perform his contractual obligations.

II. Where the parties are aware of the fact that some of their assumptions are speculative, it is presumed that they willingly accept the binding character of the agreement irrespective of whether or not these assumptions turn out to be correct. If the seller does not agree to assume

[760] Apathy, '§901', in: Schwimann (ed.), *Kommentar zum ABGB*, vol. IV, n. 8; Bollenberger, '§901', in: Koziol, P. Bydlinski, and Bollenberger (eds.), *Kurzkommentar zum ABGB*, n. 7.

[761] OGH, Miet 40.064. [762] OGH, JBl 1982, 431; see also OGH, JBl 1995, 173.

[763] See OGH, Miet 40.064.

the risk by treating the expected speculative circumstances as a condition to the contract, the risk is borne by the purchaser. Private law will not interfere to alter the contractual distribution of risk retrospectively (unless there is a violation of '*gute Sitten*' §879 ABGB).

The Netherlands

Under Dutch law, it is unlikely that X's refusal to accept and pay will be justified.

I. The question might first of all be considered to be a case of a creditor's breach as addressed in Title 6.8 Dutch Civil Code: under this statutory title, the various consequences of non-performance by the creditor (in this case X) are addressed. The first article of the Title, Art. 6:58, stipulates that X defaults under its obligations if it does not cooperate with regard to Y's performance (i.e., the acceptance of delivery) or where a reason on the side of X prevents him from accepting the technical equipment, unless the reason for the hindrance cannot be attributed to X. It is questionable whether this would safeguard X: neither the unwillingness to accept at an agreed point of delivery nor an unwillingness to pay the purchase price are causes that would be attributable in any respect to Y.

II. 1. The question is whether Art. 6:258 Dutch Civil Code on unforeseen circumstances provides any leeway for firm X. Article 6:258 would entitle firm X to request an amendment of the purchase agreement. An essential criterion under this article is that it was not foreseen and not reasonably foreseeable at the time of entering into the agreement that the impossibility of exporting to Iraq would still exist at the agreed time of delivery. In other words, the foreseen change of circumstances (i.e., the repeal of the export ban) has not actually taken place. Generally, Dutch law deals with an unforeseen change of circumstances in exactly the same way as it deals with the unforeseen non-occurrence of an anticipated circumstance. For instance, in the case of *Briljant Schreuders* v. *ABP*,[764] the jeweller Briljant Schreuders (and ABP) anticipated that following the reconstruction of the road on which it rented its premises from ABP, the pavement would be adjacent to those premises. After the road reconstruction this expectation turned out to have been false, but the court refused to allow an amendment to or the termination of the lease. In the current case, the fact that the export ban remained in place would be such an unforeseen non-occurrence of

[764] HR 20 February 1998, NJ 1998, 493 (*Briljant Schreuders* v. *ABP*).

an anticipated circumstance. The difference with the *Briljant Schreuders* v. *ABP* case is, of course, that Briljant Schreuders still had the shop, whereas X has no sales at all: the contract is entirely useless.

2. Apparently, the parties have considered the circumstance of the illegality of transportation into Iraq. If the parties had foreseen this and had wanted to provide for the non-occurrence of such legalisation, this should have taken the form of a condition in the purchase agreement. As such a condition was not included, the question is whether the non-occurrence of legalisation may be invoked as a change of circumstances under Art. 6:258 Dutch Civil Code. If a court acknowledges that the current contract is completely useless for X and has not reached this decision by way of speculation, an amendment or termination might be allowed. Given the reluctance which must be applied by the courts under Art. 6:258, the facts and circumstances clearly point to such a solution. One may question whether this is currently the case.

Eastern European jurisdictions

Slovenia

No relief will be available under Slovenian law.

I. X is not allowed to an action on grounds of mistake, because his mistake refers to future circumstances that have not occurred as he anticipated.

II. 1. Article 112 CO might be applied to the case. In this case there is not a change of circumstances that makes the performance of X's obligation burdensome, but the fact that the circumstances, in spite of the common expectation, did *not* change. Still, the absence of an expected change of circumstances might be interpreted as a change of circumstances. It is the purpose of the contract (exportation to Iraq) that has been frustrated. It can also be said that due to the non-suspension of the export ban (contrary to expectations), the contract no longer complies with the expectations of the parties. At the time of conclusion of the contract, however, X should have taken into consideration that the export ban might not be suspended. He did not make the purchase of the equipment subject to the condition that the export ban would be lifted. Therefore he assumed the risk that the export restrictions would remain in force and he is not allowed to revert this risk on the seller.

2. Both parties were aware of the fact, that exportation to Iraq would only be possible when (and if) the export ban was be lifted. They also

should have been aware of the fact that it was not certain whether the boycott would be lifted.

Lithuania

X's refusal to accept the equipment and to pay the contract price is not justified.

I. This situation may not be qualified as a change of circumstances because the export ban existed at the moment of the conclusion of the contract and this fact was known to X. He has assumed the risk of the circumstance indicated above. Thus, X is under the duty to perform the contract and will be held liable for non-performance. Article 6.204 CC is not applicable in this event for three reasons. First, as the export ban was already in existence at the time when the contract was concluded, the continued effect of this ban may not be considered as a new circumstance that occurred after the conclusion of the contract. In accordance with Art. 6.204 CC, the circumstance that obstructs the performance of a contract has to occur or become known after the conclusion of the contract. Second, X could have reasonably predicted that the ban on export would not have been lifted by the time of performance. Finally, by concluding a contract under such circumstances, X was taking risks and has to assume the negative consequences of this risk. Regretfully, though, no relevant court practice or doctrine exists to support this conclusion.

II. This situation does not correspond to the criteria of force majeure either. In this case, the conditions for the application of Art. 6.212 CC are not met: (i) X could reasonably predict a protracted continuance of the ban; (ii) the export ban was already in effect at the time the contract was concluded and X was aware of this fact, while force majeure applies exclusively in the instances when a certain event, which could not have reasonably been predicted, occurs after the conclusion of a contract; (iii) X's actions ought to be qualified as an assumption of risks.

Czech Republic

X is not entitled to refuse to accept the equipment and must pay the purchase price.

I. 1. This is not a mistake under Section 49a Civil Code[765] or frustration of contract under Section 356 Commercial Code.[766] As indicated above, the Czech Civil Code construes mistake as a ground for the

[765] See the wording in Case 4(d). [766] See the wording in Case 4(c).

invalidity of a juridical act only if caused by the other party. In other words, wrong information, assumptions etc., however relevant they may be, do not constitute an error that would render the juridical act invalid under Czech civil law.

2. The contract is not to be regarded as frustrated unless the expectation of the parties regarding the cancellation of the ban on the export of equipment into Iraq has been expressed explicitly in the contract.

II. The contract does not contradict the law because it does not breach the ban on exports and, anyway, the parties and the exporter apparently do not intend to export despite the ban.

III. Both parties concluded a risky contract and thus are obliged to render their performances thereunder. It would not be sensible to consider any reallocation of risks. X simply has to bear the risk of the failure of the contract.

Scandinavian jurisdictions

Sweden

The buyer's refusal is most likely not justified under Swedish law.

I. 1. The parties have not contracted for this situation; i.e., the seller has not issued a guarantee (*'garanti'*), nor have the parties agreed on any other condition relevant to this case.

2. The supplementary rules of the Sales Act (Sections 17–21 and 41) regarding defective assets form the main limitations for the seller's responsibilities as to the delivered assets. These rules deal primarily with two principal kinds of defects; defects as to the physical character and quality (*'art och kvalitet'*) of the assets (*'faktiska fel'*), and defects as to the buyer's acquired title to the assets (*'rättsliga fel'*). A third category of defects relates to the buyer's rights over the assets, i.e., his rights under the law or government authorities' decisions to use the assets or to sell or otherwise legally dispose of them (*'rådighetsfel'*). Defects of this last category might alternatively constitute defects under the Sales Act, or be treated under the doctrine of assumptions. In this respect the Sales Act's scope of application is far from clear.[767] In our case, however, the

[767] See e.g., J. Hellner and J. Ramberg, *Speciell avtalsrätt I. Köprätt* (Stockholm: Juristförlaget, 2nd edn, 1991), pp. 167–71; T. Håstad, *Köprätt och annan kontraktsrätt* (Uppsala: Iustus förlag, 6th edn, 2009), pp. 133–42; B. Lehrberg, *Köprätt enligt 1990 års köplag* (Uppsala: IBA Institutet för Bank- och Affärsjuridik, 2008), pp. 341 *et seq.*

export ban was general and not directed at the object of the sale specifically, which is an argument against the application of the Sales Act.

II. One can identify the export expectations as an ordinary performance assumption, which has to do with X's use of the performance. Assumptions of this type are comparatively often deemed relevant in case law. However, the main rule is that they are not relevant. It might be considered that the buyer in this case has knowingly assumed the risk that the export ban would subsist. If so, the prerequisite of good faith is not fulfilled. More importantly, there is no specific ground on which to apply the doctrine of assumptions. No warranty or clarification was issued on the seller's side, nor has he acted in bad faith or negligently caused the ban to subsist, nor has the seller made a profit at the expense of the buyer.

III. Under Section 36 Contracts Act a contract term can be adjusted or disregarded in a particular case if it is unreasonable ('*oskälig*') with reference to the contents of the contract, the circumstances at the formation of the contract, circumstances arising later and other circumstances. However, this rule is normally not even discussed in relation to cases of the present category. The price is generally not adjusted because of this type of mistake.

Denmark

The contract will be upheld under Danish law.

I. 1. Despite the fact that the term 'export ban' is not directly mentioned in Section 24 Sale of Goods Act as a force majeure event, it is clear from the preparatory work that Section 24 constitutes an export ban.[768] The interpretation of Section 24 Sale of Goods Act implies, as mentioned in the general remarks, that any force majeure must be unforeseeable at the point in time when the contract was entered into. This is not the case between X and Y. At the time of contracting, X was fully aware that there was an export ban.

2. Even though the parties expect a suspension of the export ban, X is taking the economic risk in contracting with Y. X has an obligation to take delivery and pay the contract price in question. In general, contracting includes risks and the possibility of making gains in an economic sense. Specific stipulations in the contract might reduce the risks and enhance the possibility of economic gain. X should have kept that in mind when the company entered into the contract with Y. He

[768] Cf. U 1915.632SH, U 1917.470H, and U 1951.995H.

furthermore had an option not to conclude any contract at all. X cannot invoke Section 24 Sale of Goods Act.[769] There is, however, no case law which deals directly with the issue at hand.

II. 1. When the parties concluded the contract, they both expected the export ban to be abolished by the time the delivery of the technical equipment should have taken place. Thus, it is worth discussing the possible application of the doctrine of assumptions. It is very likely that X would not have chosen to conclude the contract with Y had he known that the export ban would not be abolished. This assumption is clearly perceptible to Y. However, is there any argument supporting the argument that Y is the most appropriate party to bear the risk and therefore that the assumption is relevant? In my opinion, the answer is no, since X concluded the agreement on a voluntary basis and, as a professional, he should have known that things do not necessarily evolve as expected. There is no argument that Y should bear the risk considering the facts of the case. The application of the doctrine of assumptions must be rejected.

2. If X should be entitled to invoke any of these legal provisions, it would be very difficult to maintain a legal system in which a contract could be binding. X is under the obligation to take delivery and to pay pursuant to the sales contract.

Romanic-Mediterranean jurisdictions

Italy

X's refusal to accept the equipment and to pay the contract price is justified.

I. 1. As already seen in Cases 7(a) and 8, the common expectation of the parties (the parties expect that the status quo will change by the time of delivery) or the awareness of both parties that an expectation that is the foundation of the contract for one of them (the parties are aware that the equipment can only be sold to Iraq at a reasonable price) could be qualified as an implied assumption to the agreement and the Italian doctrine of *presupposizione* could therefore be applied. It has also been said that the doctrine of implied assumptions requires in fact that the parties have either shared these assumptions or at least that one party was aware that the other considers them as foundation of the

[769] Cf. Jacob Nørager-Nielsen and Søren Theilgaard, *Købeloven med kommentarer*, pp. 319 *et seq*.

contract, as in the case at hand. X's refusal of acceptance and payment would be justified on the basis of the *presupposizione* doctrine.

2. In particular, according to the requirements of *presupposizione*, the 'pre-supposed' event is a factual situation external to the contract, not expressly mentioned in the contract and yet common to both parties (or, if only assumed by one party, and thus only reflecting the interest of the latter, at least known to the other party).[770]

3. If the risk deliberately assumed by X was unknown to Y, the termination of the contract would not be granted. But, as already seen, both parties expected the change of the situation with regard to exports to Iraq and this implied assumption can be considered a *presupposizione*.

Spain

X's claim will be refused under Spanish law.

I. 1. X's refusal to accept is not justified because the political situation in Iraq was not only foreseeable, but known. If X refuses to accept the equipment he will come into '*mora creditoris*'. If X does not pay he will be liable for non-performance because even though performance has become more onerous, the circumstances which have led to this situation were known beforehand. There was a clear risk that the export ban concerning Iraq would not change. If X had wanted to avoid the risk, he should have included a clause in the contract.

2. A similar case was decided by the TS:[771] X (a German company – the buyer) concluded a contract for the sale of steel beams with Y (a Spanish company – the seller). Y had to deliver the steel beams to X, who would then export them to Iran. Due to financial difficulties, Y did not deliver all the required goods and wanted to deliver the beams at a later stage and at a higher price and, relying on the *rebus* clause, wanted to modify the contract. The Spanish Supreme Court rejected Y's claim, because the parties, who were both experienced businessmen, could have foreseen these circumstances. Indeed, the first instance court stated that the non-performance had been due to problems in the production factory and that there was a lack of agreement as to how to adapt the contract to the situation in Iran. However, the TS indicated that this had not led to an extraordinary change of the status quo. There was no distortion of the

[770] Roppo, 'Il contratto', p. 1039; Macario, 'Le sopravvenienze', p. 537; Cass., 09 May 1981, n. 3074.

[771] Judgment of 27 June 1984, STS of 27 June 1984 (RJ 1984, 3438).

balance between the mutual obligations that could justify an adaptation of the contract.

Portugal

X's refusal of acceptance and payment is not justified under Portuguese law.

I. 1. The contract between X and Y is not void due to legal impossibility nor because it contravenes a legal prohibition. The technical equipment was built under the expectation that its subsequent resale to Iraq would be legal at the time of delivery.

2. The expectation of the suspension of the export ban may be common but there is no common undertaking. The risk is entirely assumed by X, and if the expectation proved to be correct X would be the only one to profit. It seems, therefore, that there is no justification for X to refuse acceptance and payment: he has 'gambled' and lost and X must not be allowed to shift the risk that he has freely undertaken to Y.

II. Again, it seems that the only remedy theoretically available to X could be Art. 437 CC. However, in this case a court would probably not allow for the termination or modification of the contract. It is not sufficient that a party suffered a significant hardship or economic loss as a result of the enforcement of the contract.[772] It is necessary that an anomalous supervening change has occurred and that the change goes beyond the risks inherent in the contract. The fact that the law did not change as expected (or did not change at the expected time) cannot be considered an anomalous event because there is a speculative element in this expectation.[773]

Greece

X's refusal is not justified.

I. By refusing to accept the purchased equipment and to pay for it, X commits a breach of the contract. The impossibility of exporting the equipment to Iraq constitutes a frustration of X's secondary cause to use the subject matter of performance in a specific manner, and, as has repeatedly been pointed out, this frustration does not influence the

[772] See Acórdão do Supremo Tribunal de Justiça de 30 June 1983 processo 070665, www.dgsi.pt.

[773] However, Almeida Costa, *Direito das Obrigações*, p. 337, applies Art. 437 CC in a similar case where an export ban was enacted after the formation of the contract. But in such a case it is easier to accept this event as an anomalous change than in a case where an already existing trade embargo is not lifted.

validity (Art. 143 AK) or the function of the contract (see also Case 5 above).

II. In the given case, X did not provide for a condition nor stipulate any clause related to the export of the merchandise. The fact that the goods can be exported has therefore not become an agreed quality of the merchandise, the absence or frustration of which would have characterised the merchandise as defective. X cannot terminate the contract according to Art. 540 §1 n. 3 AK.

III. There has not been a distortion of the contractual risk allocation scheme, which is a prerequisite for Art. 388 AK to apply: the impediments that prevent X from the exporting of the equipment were foreseeable. As mentioned in Case 2, the ability to foresee a risk always influences the risk allocation. The party that did foresee or could have foreseen the realisation of a risk is usually the one that bears the burden.

France and related jurisdictions

France

In general, the solution will depend on the factual details and the appreciation of the judge. It appears likely that the majority of judges will come to the conclusion that X should have inserted an express clause in the contract itself to reserve his rights. This position is all the more justified since the lifting of the ban was far from certain and its continuation was foreseeable since it was the actual situation at the time of concluding the contract. By not inserting such a clause, X did not act with care; he cannot invoke the concepts of mistake or good faith in such a case.

The lifting of the ban was a common assumption when the contract was concluded. This assumption can be examined from various angles.[774]

I. First, a judge might interpret the contract so that the lifting of the ban was an implied condition.[775] However, no definitive prediction is possible.

[774] See S. Pimont, *L'économie du contrat* (Presses Universitaires d'Aix Marseille, 2004), p. 83; Cass.civ., 11 February 1981, *Bull.civ.* III, 31.

[775] See Cass.civ., 3 August 1942: the motives concerning the future development of circumstances can only be taken into consideration when they are a condition precedent in the contract, DA 1943, 18.

II. Second, the lifting of the ban might be regarded as a mistake as to the motives of the contract. Such mistakes can be taken into consideration when they are shared by both parties and relate to a substantial element of the contract. Here, the substance of the goods sold is not affected by an error and therefore a mistake will probably not be recognised in this case.

III. Furthermore, the motives can also be considered under the doctrine of the *cause* of the contract (as defined in the overview (Chapter 4)) if they become part of the overall contractual agreement,[776] i.e., if they form part of the contractual equilibrium. In this regard, the same considerations apply as in connection with mistake. Thus, the concept of *cause* will probably not be applied in this case.

IV. A renegotiation of the contract could be ordered on the basis of Art. 1134-3 Cciv. As mentioned earlier, since the decision of the Cour de Cassation of 3 November 1992, in cases of unexpected circumstances the creditor will be required to renegotiate. The conditions of unexpected circumstances are always a matter of appreciation by the judge.

Belgium

X's refusal to accept the equipment and to pay the contract price is not justified under Belgian law.

The lifting of the ban on trade with Iraq was a common assumption at the time of entering into the contract. This assumption can be examined from various angles.[777]

I. First, the expectation that the ban will be suspended might be regarded as a mistake concerning the motives of the contract. Such mistakes can be taken into consideration when they are shared by both parties and relate to a substantial element of the contract. Here it is not certain that the mistake will be considered to relate to the substance of the contract as the substance of the goods sold is not affected by the mistake. It is therefore rather unlikely that a mistake will be recognised in this case.

II. Second, the motive may have become part of the contractual agreement,[778] i.e., it may form part of the contractual equilibrium and thereby give rise to the notion of *cause*. However, with regard to the

[776] See J. Ghestin, *Les obligations*, p. 63; D.M. Philippe, *Changement de circonstances*, p. 128.

[777] See Ghent, 5 April 1979, Rec Gen Enr Not 1980, pp. 436–41 and obs., n° 22551.

[778] See P. Van Ommeslaghe, 'Observations sur la théorie de la cause dans la jurisprudence et la doctrine moderne', note sub Cass., 13 November 1969, (1970) RCJB, pp. 326 *et seq.*

doctrine of *cause* the same objections must be considered as in connection with the concept of mistake. Thus, the doctrine of cause will probably not be applied in this case.

III. Finally, a judge might interpret the contract so that that the lifting of the ban was an implied condition. This conclusion leaves room for the judge's evaluation.

IV. The solution will thus depend on the appreciation of the judge. It appears to be more likely that the majority of judges will come to the conclusion that the buyer should have included an express clause in the contract itself to reserve his rights. This position is all the more justified as the lifting of the ban was far from certain and its continuation was all the more foreseeable since it was the actual and current situation at the time of concluding the contract. By not inserting such a clause, the buyer did not act with the necessary care; he cannot invoke the concepts of mistake, *cause*, interpretation or good faith in such a case.

England and related jurisdictions

England and Ireland

It is unlikely that X would be entitled to terminate the contract.

I. It is important here that, although both parties realise that exports to Iraq are illegal, the contract between X and Y does not in itself require the exportation of goods to Iraq or involve any element of illegality. Thus, the issue here is one of frustration of purpose rather than illegality.

II. Certain cases deal with the situation where the buyer of goods intends to export them to a country but that exportation is illegal or seriously restricted. In *D McMaster & Co* v. *Cox McEuen & Co*[779] the buyer of jute[780] intended to export the jute but was prevented from doing so by a supervening war-time restriction on exports. The House of Lords held that the contract was not discharged as the buyer could have disposed of the jute on the home market, albeit at a loss. Similarly, in *Congimex SARL (Lisbon)* v. *Continental Grain Export Corp (New York)*[781] a buyer who bought soya-bean meal with the intention of importing it into Portugal was not discharged from his contract when the importation was subsequently prohibited. Firm X faces a similar objection here – it could easily be argued that the equipment could be sold on the home market, or in

[779] 1921 SC (HL) 24. Cited in Treitel, *Frustration and Force Majeure*, p. 307.
[780] A strong coarse fibre from India. [781] [1979] 2 Lloyd's Reports 346 (Eng).

countries other than Iraq, albeit at a price which is lower than a 'reasonable price'. X would be deemed to take the risk of a loss of profit in this situation.

III. 1. A further difficulty faced by X is the fact that there is in fact no supervening illegality. The parties just expected the law to change and it didn't. It could not be said that the situation X now finds himself in was not foreseeable. It is likely that the courts will hold that X should have inserted a clause to protect himself in case the export ban to Iraq was not lifted and cannot now claim that the contract is frustrated. In the Canadian case of *Smale* v. *Van der Weer*[782] for example, the parties entered into an agreement for the sale of land in the knowledge that certain planning approval had not yet been given, but expecting such approval to be forthcoming. The contract was not frustrated when the approval was not given. This was not a case of a wholly unexpected event but of a misjudgment by the purchaser. Similarly in *Canadian Government Merchant Marine* v. *Canadian Trading Co*[783] it was stated in the Canadian Supreme Court: 'if the event which causes the impossibility could have been anticipated and guarded against in the contract, the party in default cannot claim relief because it has happened.' It is likely that a similar result would be reached in England and Ireland. In *McGuill* v. *Aer Lingus and United Airlines*[784] McWilliam J in the Irish High Court stated:

> If one party anticipated or should have anticipated the possibility of the event which is alleged to cause the frustration and did not incorporate a clause in the contract to deal with it, he should not be permitted to rely on the happening of the event as causing frustration.

On the facts of *McGuill*, only the defendant had anticipated the supervening event, a strike by its employees, but failed to inform the plaintiff of the possibility of a strike in case the other party would refuse to complete the contract.[785] It was held in the High Court that the defendant, in order to obtain the plaintiff's business, had taken the risk of entering into the contract 'without including a provision to safeguard its provision in the event of a strike taking place.'

[782] (1977) 80 DLR (3d) 704. [783] (1922) 68 DLR 544.

[784] Unreported, Irish High Court, 3 October 1983.

[785] *Walton Harvey Ltd* v. *Walker & Homfreys Ltd* [1931] 1 Ch 274 is another example of a case where one party, but not the other, could have foreseen the 'frustrating' event and thus the contract was not frustrated.

2. Here, *both* X and Y knew that exports to Iraq were illegal, and not just one of the parties. However, the failure to insert any provision dealing with a situation where exports continue to be illegal is likely to be fatal to X's chances of terminating the contract.

Scotland

The answer to this question depends on X's ability to prove the existence of an implied term. Bearing in mind the difficulty of this task, it is suggested that a court is likely to find that the contract has not been frustrated. Nevertheless, the contract may yet be unenforceable on different grounds. Y will be prevented from using both his normal contractual remedies and any remedies in unjustified enrichment because of his own illegal conduct in entering into the contract in contravention of the statute. Y therefore has no remedy in Scots law which will enable him to force X to accept the goods and make payment under the contract.

I. The particular facts of Case 10 raise an issue entirely separate from frustration of contract, i.e., whether the contract itself or the parties' conduct is illegal.[786] Whether the illegality affects the contract or the parties themselves, in both cases the parties may find themselves unable to use normal contractual remedies. In effect, in Case 10 the parties have knowingly entered into a contract in contravention of a statutory ban. The facts of the case imply that the parties expect the ban to be lifted before delivery. Nevertheless, it is likely to be difficult to convince a court that the parties have not acted illegally. Considering first the situation where the contract itself is treated as illegal because it is in contravention of the statute, the statute itself may expressly indicate the effect on the contract. The statute might render the contract void, or simply unenforceable, the latter term meaning that neither party has the ability to enforce the contract in the courts.[787] The contract may also be illegal as a matter of implication from the statute.[788] Finally, the statute may be entirely silent on the effect on the contract, but the parties may be denied access to their normal contractual remedies because their conduct involved illegality.

[786] For illegality in contract in Scots law generally see L. Macgregor, 'Pacta Illicita', in: K. G. C. Reid and R. Zimmermann (eds.), *A History of Private Law in Scotland* (Oxford University Press, 2000), vol. II, pp. 129–55.

[787] McBryde, *Contract*, paras. 19-28 to 19-32.

[788] *Ibid.*, para. 19-28, and see *St John Shipping Corp* v. *Joseph Rank Ltd* [1957] 1 QB 267.

II. 1. Where the parties are denied their contractual remedies on grounds of illegality, they may have access to remedies in unjustified enrichment.[789] In order to decide the availability of those remedies, the courts compare the degree to which each party's conduct could be said to involve 'moral turpitude' in accordance with the maxim *in pari causa potior est condition possidentis*.[790] If the court considers that each party is equally blameworthy (as may indeed be the case in Case 10), neither party has access to remedies in unjustified enrichment.

2. Applying these principles to the facts, and leaving to one side the issue of frustration for the moment, the contract may yet be unenforceable because of the illegal nature of the parties' conduct. This would prevent Y from using either specific performance to force X to accept the goods, or suing X for damages for X's breach of contract. Y's ability to make use of unjustified enrichment remedies will depend upon the court's view of the culpable nature of his conduct relative to X's conduct. If Y and X are considered to be equally blameworthy, Y will have no remedy in unjustified enrichment. Y is therefore left with no remedy as a result of the rules on illegal contracts.

III. Turning now to consider frustration, Case 10 may be an example of frustration of purpose. As such, the important issue is whether both parties viewed the purpose of exportation of the goods to Iraq as the foundation of the contract. This is a difficult test to satisfy. Case 10 may nevertheless be analogous with a case discussed by Gloag, who suggests that frustration may occur where 'the parties contracted on the assumption that a particular event would occur, and on the implied condition that the non-occurrence of the event would avoid the contract.'[791] There appears to be no express term which could operate as a resolutive condition, releasing the parties from their obligations when the condition is not fulfilled.[792] X would therefore require to prove that a resolutive condition existed as a matter of implication. Proving the existence of such an implied term is likely to be difficult. If the imminent lifting of the export ban is a shared assumption rather than a term

[789] See L. Macgregor, 'Illegal contracts and unjustified enrichment', (2000) *Edinburgh Law Review*, pp. 19–45.

[790] See *Cuthbertson* v. *Lowes* (1870) 8M. 1073; *Jamieson* v. *Watt's Trs* 1950 S.C. 265. These cases are difficult to reconcile, and the law in this area is far from clear, see L. Macgregor, 'Illegal contracts and unjustified enrichment', 19–45.

[791] Gloag, *Contract*, p. 352.

[792] On resolutive conditions and frustration see MacQueen and Thomson, *Contract Law*, paras. 3–59 to 3–62.

which constitutes a resolutive condition, it would not be legally relevant and frustration of purpose would not occur.

Editors' comparative notes

The open jurisdictions

In the majority of open jurisdictions, X's refusal is not justified. The main rationale is that, according to the facts of the case, at the time of contracting both parties were aware of the existing export ban and could have foreseen that it could be maintained. As X failed to insert a term into the contract addressing this risk he is deemed to have assumed it.

There are a few jurisdictions that come to a different conclusion. In Germany, X is entitled to adjust the contract, so that the loss is split if it is possible to sell the equipment to a third party. If X cannot sell the equipment at all, he only has to partially compensate Y for his expenses and losses. The assumption that the export ban would be lifted is considered to be an element of the underlying basis of the contract, the *Geschäftsgrundlage*. The rationale is that even though the parties were aware of the risk they shared the assumption that it would not materialise and therefore did not exclusively allocate the risk to X. Another important argument for setting aside the contract is the fact that the export ban is regarded as a government intervention that is beyond the control of either party. Similarly, in Italy, X may refuse acceptance and payment based on the doctrine of *presupposizione* without having to compensate Y. The reason for this is very similar to that in Germany, namely that the intention to resell the equipment is part of the basis of the contract and is shared by both parties.

The closed jurisdictions

In all of the closed jurisdictions, X is not granted relief and therefore his refusal to pay is not justified. The most common reason given for this is, again, X's awareness of the risk. Both parties knew about the risk and because they entered into the contract without any specific clause as to the possible lift of the export ban, X is regarded as having assumed the risk. Therefore, the contract is not frustrated.

Some reports (Belgium, Scotland) discuss the possibility of invoking an implied term. Even though such a solution is not ruled out in principle, it will be very hard to substantiate such a claim. The French report again mentions that the court might impose a duty to renegotiate on Y.

Conclusion

The majority of the open jurisdictions and all of the closed jurisdictions deny any form of relief. The reason for this is that the export ban was already present at the time of contracting. Hence, X was aware or should have been aware of the possibility that the export ban would not be lifted. Both parties agreed to the contract without including a term which addressed the risk of an enduring ban. Without such a term, the purchaser arguably assumes the risk of the ban because the use of the subject matter of the contract falls within his sphere of control. Under the majority opinion, misjudgment of an identified risk is not regarded to justify relief.

In the group of open jurisdictions two remarkable exceptions exist: Germany and Italy. In Italy, X is granted relief based on the doctrine of *presupposizione*. In Germany, the intention to resell the equipment to Iraq, including the lift of the export ban, is regarded as part of the foundation ('*Geschäftsgrundlage*') of the contract and the losses are divided between the parties by means of adjustment. The German example may be seen as an indication that jurisdictions offering a mechanism for adjustment of the contract as a primary remedy are more inclined to grant relief in hard cases because they are not faced with an all-or-nothing consequence. Nevertheless, other jurisdictions which recognise a mechanism for adjustment as an alternative are very reluctant to grant relief in the export ban case.

C. FRUSTRATION OF SPECIFIED PURPOSES (OTHER THAN A OR B)

Case 11 Sale of real estate involving expectation of cultural use

Use of real estate by transferee does not comply with expectations of the transferor

X sells his family home to Y at a price far below its market value. Both parties assume that Y would dedicate the house to cultural purposes only. However, this assumption was not inserted in the contract as an explicit condition. Y changes his mind and gives it to one of his daughters instead.

Is X entitled to ask for the difference between the agreed price and the market value or, alternatively, to reclaim the house?

Germany and related jurisdictions

Germany

Under German law X is entitled to ask to ask for the difference between the market value and the agreed price. If such an adjustment is unreasonable for either party, X may reclaim the property.

I. If the parties had consented to the dedication of the house for cultural purposes under the contract, they could have made use of various legal tools, which differ, in particular, to their legal consequences.[793] The contract, however, does not contain any explicit term as to the use of the house. It is impossible to derive a contractual clause by implication from the parties' action. This assessment would not be in compliance with the requirement that a real estate sales contract is officially recorded by a notary (§311b I BGB). This rule relates to all terms of the contract, regardless of whether they are essential or collateral.[794] Therefore, a *specific stipulation* concerning the use of the house must be by notarial deed.[795] A contractual term can be inferred *by implication* if the purpose in question is of some relevance to the parties but also if they had some specific legal consequences in mind, if the house was not used for cultural purposes.[796] Although in general complementary interpretation can be applied even in the case of notary deeds,[797] there is no information available about *how* the parties would have proceeded in case of the cultural purpose being frustrated. Thus, complementary interpretation does not provide for an unambiguous result.

[793] Cf. Overview (Chapter 4).

[794] Cf. RGZ 97, 220; BGHZ 63, 361; Grüneberg, '§311b', in: Palandt *et al.* (eds.), *Bürgerliches Gesetzbuch*, nn. 25 *et seq*.

[795] Cf. BGH ZIP 1999, 32 (Right of rescission); Grüneberg, '§311b', in: Palandt *et al.* (eds.), *Bürgerliches Gesetzbuch*, n. 31.

[796] Cf. H. Heinrichs and J. Ellenberger, 'Einf. v. §116', in: Palandt *et al.* (eds.), *Bürgerliches Gesetzbuch*, n. 6; K. Larenz and M. Wolf, *Allgemeiner Teil des Bürgerlichen Rechts* (Munich: Beck, 9th edn, 2004), §24 n. 16.

[797] According to the majority opinion complementary interpretation does not require compliance with rules related to formalities; cf. BGHZ 81, 135, 143; BGHZ 74, 370, 376; Ellenberger, '§157', in: Palandt *et al.* (eds.), *Bürgerliches Gesetzbuch*, n. 2a.

II. 1. Provided that the parties did not agree on the exclusive use of the house for cultural purposes under the contract, restitution according to the concept of *condictio ob rem* (§812 I 2 Alt. 2 BGB) appears to be a possible solution.

2. This doctrine requires that the use for cultural purposes be 'a result intended to be produced pursuant to the transaction'. According to the majority opinion, this refers to a specific behaviour of the transferee that the transferor cannot claim on the ground of a contractual obligation and that is part of the exchange. The reason for these narrow suppositions follows from the fact that otherwise the consequence of §812 I 2 Alt. 2 BGB - restitution - cannot be justified.[798] The result has to be intended to be produced 'pursuant to the transaction', i.e., the parties must have agreed that transfer depends on the respective result to be brought about by the transferee. This agreement is called '*Zweckvereinbarung*' (i.e., agreement on a certain purpose).[799] §812 I 2 Alt. 2 BGB covers agreements that cannot be reached by way of a binding contract and agreements that are not enforceable. For example, an exchange of the contractual subject matter related to a legal transaction that will take place or become effective in future falls within the scope of §812 I 2 Alt. 2 BGB.[800]

3. Accordingly, there may be reasons to apply §812 I 2 Alt. 2 BGB to the present case. The use of the house for cultural purposes is part of an exchange as the contract price was kept below the market price because of the envisaged purpose. One might be inclined to assume a *Zweckvereinbarung* between the parties since Y knew of the purpose of use intended by X and approved of it implicitly by acceptance of the performance.[801]

4. Yet, it is highly controversial whether the *condictio ob rem* according to §812 I 2 Alt. 2 BGB provides for a solution to cases like the given one as the cultural purpose is only an additional element within the framework of the contractual transaction. This problem is usually referred to by the expression '*angestaffelter Leistungszweck*' (additional purpose of

[798] Cf. K. Larenz and C.-W. Canaris, *Lehrbuch des Schuldrecht*, (Munich: Beck, 1994), vol. II/2, §68 I 3 a = S. 151.

[799] The legal structure of the *Zweckvereinbarung* and of *Rechtsgrundabrede* - as it is called in a more general sense - is controversial. Cf. Larenz and Canaris, *Schuldrecht II/1*, §68 I 3 a = S. 151 *et seq.*; BGH NJW 1984, 233.

[800] Cf. BGH BB 1990, 735 (*Absehen von einer Strafanzeige*); BGH MDR 1976, 38 (*schwebend unwirksamer Vertrag*); for further examples cf. H. Sprau, '§812', in: Palandt *et al.* (eds.), *Bürgerliches Gesetzbuch*, nn. 89 *et seq.*

[801] Cf. BGHZ 44, 321; BGH NJW 1984, 233.

performance). Some authors propose that §812 I 2 Alt. 2 BGB is applied nonetheless; as a consequence the whole contract will be rescinded if the agreed result is not produced.[802] As opposed to this, the majority opinion suggests applying the concept of *Geschäftsgrundlage* instead of *condictio ob rem*. Consequently, the contract will not be rescinded, but adjusted.[803] The decisive argument in favour of this position is that adjustment of contract is the more flexible solution, which serves the parties' interests better, as opposed to rescission of the contract as a whole. If one applied the doctrine of *condictio ob rem*, there would be an apparent contradiction between the idea of an implicit *Zweckvereinbarung* in the sense of §812 I 2 Alt. 2 BGB and the assumption (made above) that the parties have not provided for the respective purpose in the contract. The idea underlying §812 I 2 Alt. 2 BGB is that restitution of the exchange as a whole can be derived from the parties' consent. Finally, the preference for the concept of *Geschäftsgrundlage* can be based on reasons of legal method: at the time §812 I 2 Alt. 2 BGB was enacted, the doctrine of *Geschäftsgrundlage* was not yet established; now the rules of *Geschäftsgrundlage* refer specifically to contractual exchanges and provide for an adjustment of the contract as the primary legal consequence. Therefore, the doctrine of *Geschäftsgrundlage* may be considered *lex posterior* and *lex specialis*.

III. According to the majority opinion, the contract will be adjusted under §313 I BGB. The cultural purpose is the basis of the contract as defined by the concept of *Geschäftsgrundlage* (§313 I BGB) because the cultural purpose strongly influenced the contract price.[804] The use of the house for private purposes amounts to a fundamental change of the expected circumstances (§313 II BGB). Thus, X cannot reasonably be expected to continue the contract as originally concluded. The primary consequence under §313 BGB is the adaptation of the contract. According to §313 III BGB, restitution is only possible as far as adjustment is unreasonable for X (e.g., because he intended to sell the house exclusively for the purpose of promoting culture) or for Y (for instance because the market value is not affordable for him).

[802] Cf. M. Lieb, 'Bereicherungsanspruch wegen Mißerfolgs und Wegfall der Geschäftsgrundlage', (1978) JZ, 701; W. Fikentscher and A. Heinemann, *Schuldrecht* (Berlin: de Gruyter, 10th edn, 2006), n. 1457.

[803] Cf. BGH NJW 1975, 776; BGH NJW 1992, 2690; for different arguments cf. Larenz and Canaris, *Schuldrecht II/1*, §68 I 3 d = S. 153 *et seq.*; D. Reuter and M. Martinek, *Ungerechtfertige Bereicherung* (Tübingen: J.C.B. Mohr, 1983), pp. 155 *et seq.*

[804] For a detailed definition see the comments on Case 1.

Austria

Under Austrian law, X is entitled to reclaim the house or - depending on a further specification of the facts - to reclaim the benefit of the price reduction from Y (adjustment of the contract price to market value).

I. First of all, the question arises whether X and Y have inserted an implied (tacit) condition into their contract which makes the transfer dependent on the realisation of the cultural purposes by Y. This question can only be answered by interpretation of the contract. Under Austrian law, no formal requirements with respect to the validity of a sale of land exist. The contract does not even have to be in writing. Ownership in the land can, however, only be acquired by the transferee when he is registered as the new owner in the public land register; and this registration requires the contract to be in the form of a private or public document. Thus, X and Y might also have concluded an oral contract for the sale of the house. They chose not to insert such a condition into their (presumably) written contract, and they also did not agree on such a condition orally. Implied agreements must be judged under the standards of §863 ABGB: the behaviour of the parties must not leave any doubt that they wanted to make a legally binding declaration of will with the respective content. This is, however, not the case here. The parties' behaviour leaves reasonable doubt with respect to their intention to create such a condition. On the one hand, they agreed on a lower price - presumably because of the cultural purpose. On the other hand, they agreed not to mention this as a condition in the official contract. Because of these doubts, §863 ABGB excludes the existence of an implied condition.

II. 1. The next question that arises is whether or not X is entitled to avoid the contract because of mistake. The assumption that Y would dedicate the house to cultural purposes is a mistake of intention or motive. Such mistakes do not affect the validity of exchange contracts. By way of contrast, donation contracts can always be terminated because of mistake of motive (§901 ABGB).

2. Since both parties knew that the price of the house is far below its market value, the contract can be qualified as a '*gemischte Schenkung*' (mixed donation).[805] Whether or not the special provisions for donations apply to mixed donations depends on the prevailing character of

[805] Binder, '§938', in: Schwimann (ed.), *Kommentar zum ABGB*, vol. IV, n. 42; Bollenberger, '§938', in: Koziol, P. Bydlinski and Bollenberger (eds.), *Kurzkommentar zum ABGB*, n. 8.

the particular agreement.[806] Therefore, the mistake remedies discussed below only apply if the price is less than half of the market value of the house (which is not obvious in the case).

(i) *Avoidance of the whole contract*: If the contract was on the whole more a donation than a sale (price below half of market value) Austrian courts would allow X to avoid the contract because of mistake of intention/motive,[807] *if* X sold the house only because he wanted to see it dedicated to cultural purposes and would not have sold the house to Y otherwise.

(ii) *Adjustment of the contract price*: If X and Y would have agreed on a sale of the house even if it was not dedicated to cultural purposes, but would have stipulated the full market price in such a case, X can claim an *adjustment* of the contract on the basis of the doctrine of mistake (§872 ABGB). This adaptation of the contract will entitle him to claim the difference between the agreed price and the market value.

III. 1. If mistake remedies are not available because the prevailing character of the contract is rather that of a sale than a gift or donation, the *unjust enrichment* provision of §1435 ABGB can be applied. §1435 ABGB deals with the right to recover performances rendered under a contract that has been terminated (*condictio causa finita*):[808] 'Performances rendered on the basis of an obligation can be claimed back from the recipient if the legal ground to keep them has ended.' It provides a claim of unjust enrichment in cases where some value was given, transferred or rendered on the basis of a valid legal obligation which was terminated *ex nunc* later (not retroactively).[809] But the courts also extended §1435 ABGB to unjust enrichment claims where performances were rendered in pursuance of a particular purpose without any legal obligation to perform (*condictio causa data causa non secuta*) where this purpose is evident also for the enriched party and the purpose is frustrated.[810] This rule applies where both parties are aware of the

806 Schubert, '§938', in: Rummel (ed.), *Kommentar zum ABGB*, vol. I, n. 9a.

807 For a qualification as a gratuitous agreement in cases of doubt, see Binder, '§938', in: Schwimann (ed.), *Kommentar zum ABGB*, vol. IV, n. 42.

808 Koziol and Welser, *Bürgerliches Recht*, vol. II, p. 278; Rummel, '§1435', in: Rummel (ed.), *Kommentar zum ABGB* (2002), vol. II, nn. 1 *et seq.*; Peter Mader, '§1435', in: Schwimann (ed.), *Kommentar zum ABGB*, vol. VI, n. 1.

809 Koziol and Welser, *Bürgerliches Recht*, vol. II, p. 274; Rummel, '§1435', in: Rummel (ed.), *Kommentar zum ABGB*, vol. II, n. 2; Wilburg, in: Klang (ed.), *Kommentar zum ABGB* (1951), vol. VI, 466; Mader, '§1435', in: Schwimann (ed.), *Kommentar zum ABGB*, vol. VI, n. 22.

810 Rummel, '§1435', in: Rummel (ed.), *Kommentar zum ABGB*, vol. II, n. 4; Mader, '§1435', in: Schwimann (ed.), *Kommentar zum ABGB*, vol. VI, n. 11; Peter Rummel, 'Wegfall des Rechtsgrundes und Zweckverfehlung als Gründe der Kondiktion nach ABGB', (1978) *Juristische Blätter*, 449 at 454.

purpose irrespective of whether this purpose was inserted into the contract or not.[811]

2. The contract of sale, however, was not terminated in the (original) sense of §1435 ABGB (*condictio causa finita*). In so far as it still forms a basis for the transfer despite the frustration of the purpose of dedication, no unjust enrichment claim will be available. Rummel[812] suggests that in cases of frustration of purpose in which there is a contractual basis for the performance *condictio causa data causa non secuta* should not apply, but *condictio causa finita*. Before it can apply, the contract has to be avoided on the basis of '*Wegfall der Geschäftsgrundlage*'.

3. The *condictio causa data causa non secuta* would then only apply to cases where the *performance* (*not* the purpose or counter-performance) cannot be validly promised under a contract or other legal act or where it is not validly promised (no underlying obligation of performance). In the literature and the decisions, the borderline between *condictio causa finita* and *condictio causa data causa non secuta* is not clearly drawn.[813] If we follow Rummel's distinction in our case (for which we see good reasons), the *condictio* under §1435 ABGB will be only available if the doctrine of '*Wegfall der Geschäftsgrundlage*' allows us to avoid or modify the contract. If we apply *condictio causa data causa non secuta* of §1435 ABGB the question of whether the frustrated purpose will affect the whole performance (so that it can be claimed back) or not, will have to be decided on the basis of §1435 ABGB in the sense of *condictio causa data causa non secuta*.

4. In both alternatives (even though Rummel's solution is to be preferred as it is more consistent and plausible) we are confronted with the same problem as above with regard to the mistake remedies: either the whole contract is affected by the frustration of purpose (avoidance) or only parts of the contract - namely the price agreement. In this case partial remedy (modification, partial unjust enrichment claim) might be available.

5. By analogy with the mistake provisions of §§871, 872 ABGB the hypothetical intentions of the parties will determine whether the contract can be avoided or modified by X.[814] A solution based on the *condictio causa data causa non secuta* according to §1435 ABGB should

[811] Rummel, '§1435', in: Rummel (ed.), *Kommentar zum ABGB*, vol. II, n. 4.

[812] *Ibid.*, nn. 3, 4. [813] See examples in *ibid.*, n. 3.

[814] See Case 3 above, point II of this case above and Rummel, '§872', in: Rummel (ed.), *Kommentar zum ABGB*, vol. I, nn. 1, 7.

turn on the same grounds: if the dedication can be considered a purpose without which the whole transaction would not take place, the *condictio* should be granted for the recovery of the house and the contract price.

6. If the parties would have concluded a different contract in the awareness of the non-realisation of the dedication purpose – namely a sale of the house for its market value – (§§871, 872 ABGB by analogy) the doctrine of '*Wegfall der Geschäftsgrundlage*' and §1435 ABGB will allow for an adjustment of the contract price in that sense. In this case the frustrated purpose must be seen as being only connected to the benefit of a reduced contract price. X will be entitled to demand the difference between the agreed price and the market value of the house.

III. 1. If we apply *condictio causa finita* and '*Wegfall der Geschäftsgrundlage*' (Rummel) – the non-realisation of the dedication to cultural purposes can be considered to be for both parties an unforeseen change of circumstances which form the basis of their contract. This can be explained by the fact that X was pursuing a particular purpose when he sold the house to Y which was evident for both parties and formed a basis for the whole transaction or parts of it (price): X expected Y to dedicate the house to cultural purposes and Y frustrated this purpose willingly, which both parties or at least X could not foresee when they concluded the contract. Therefore, Y seems to be unjustly enriched when he keeps the house, uses it for his own purposes and at the same time profits from the price reduction.

2. Depending on the particular formulation of X's purpose (sale only for cultural purposes or sale anyway only at a different price) he may reclaim the house or only the benefit of the price reduction from Y according to §1435 ABGB.

The Netherlands

Under Dutch law, X will be entitled to terminate the contract or to have the price adjusted.

I. Dutch law protects X from several angles: (i) X could argue that, regardless of the written contract, the actual agreement between X and Y implied the condition relating to the use of the house as it was so evidently reflected in the price (or even that X rather naively expected that Y would use the house for cultural purposes and therefore had not insisted on making the joint expectation explicit); (ii) X can successfully claim that the agreed use of the house was not put in writing due to a mistake; (iii) Y's change of mind is an unforeseen circumstance that would entitle X to either demand an adjustment of the sale price or the restitution of the house. Either of these arguments should entitle X to cancel or dissolve the sales contract. Y will fail, however, to enforce a claim against Y or Y's daughter that the house must be used by Y's daughter for cultural purposes: the enforceability of such use would require that this had been registered as a qualitative obligation in the real estate register - Art. 6:252 Dutch Civil Code.

II. When arguing that the sales contract implied a condition relating to the use of the house (argument (i) above) X must provide evidence that such an implied condition had been agreed upon. This may be difficult and it does not entirely fit the facts of the case.

III. The argument under (ii) is stronger. The wording 'assumption' refers to facts or circumstances which the parties had in mind but did not as such 'incorporate' in their agreement. Such assumptions as to facts or circumstances trigger the application of the doctrine of mistake entitling X to declare the agreement null and void. Article 2:228 Dutch Civil Code, which codifies 'mistake,' requires that two criteria are met in order for X to nullify the agreement. First, X must establish that the sales agreement would not have been entered into under the current terms, including the price, if Y had informed X about the assumed fact or circumstance (i.e., that there was some likelihood that Y would not use the house for cultural purposes), and, second, Y ought to have known that the use of the house was of significance to X (Art. 6:228(1)(b)). X's mistake entitling him or her to nullify must have its roots at the moment of sale.[815]

IV.1. In the case of future changes in (assumed) facts or circumstances, the doctrine of unforeseen circumstances applies. Article 6:258, reflecting this doctrine, provides that in the case of a change or an occurrence of a fact or circumstance that is of such a nature that the other party cannot reasonably expect the contract to remain unmodified, each party may require the court to amend such a contract or terminate it in whole or in part. In the case at hand, Y's change of mind could potentially be such a change of circumstances, which X might wish to invoke. The additional requirement in Art. 6:258 that the change or occurrence should not fall within X's sphere of responsibility is also met: in the current case the circumstance is entirely attributable to Y. Since the change of mind was entirely that of Y, a claim based on Art. 6:258 should succeed.

[815] The mindset of Y, as assumed by X, regarding the use of the house should be entirely in the future, otherwise the doctrine of mistake does not apply (Art. 6:228 (2)).

2. If X bases his claim on unforeseen (or changed) circumstances, and not on mistake, the court should expressly stipulate that its modification of the sales contract has retrospective effect: the default effect of a successful claim for changed circumstances would be that Y had become the owner (also in hindsight this does not change) and was therefore free to sell or give the house to Y's daughter. Article 6:258 expressly gives the court the authority to declare that its modification or (partial) termination takes effect before the completion of the gift to Y's daughter. Since the gift is a valid title for the transfer of ownership, Y's daughter would have acquired the house from the owner Y. X's claim against Y would then result in an obligation for Y to either reacquire the house from his daughter and 'return' it to X, or to compensate X for damage (consisting of the difference between the sales price and the market value of the house). Anyhow, the court could possibly allow Y to have the option of terminating the sales contract pursuant to Art. 6:260. If the doctrine of mistake is applied, X could also nullify the sales contract with retroactive effect (Arts. 3:53 and 3:84 Dutch Civil Code). Consequently, in hindsight, Y has never become the owner of the house and Y could therefore neither sell nor give the house to anyone (including Y's daughter).

V. Alternatively, X can claim that the transfer of the house was to a large extent a gift, a legal concept elaborated in Title 7.3 on donation contracts. Ironically, a donation is a species of gifts. A gift is any act by a person with the effect (and the condition) that the receiving party is enriched by the gift (Art. 7:186(2) Dutch Civil Code). In the case at hand, the difference between the fair market value and the agreed sales price will likely qualify as a gift ('*negotia mixta cum donatione*'). If such a qualification is accepted, X may nullify the gift on the ground that Y is in default in performing the obligation related to the gift, provided that neither X nor a third party is entitled to enforce such performance (Art. 7:184 (1)(a), applicable by operation of Art. 7:187). In this case it is clear that Y is in default since he transferred the house to his daughter. Also, the case contains no particular aspects that entitle any person to require that Y will initiate cultural activities or even use the house for that purpose. Because the gift is part of a broader sales agreement, the nullification would result either in a partial nullity, the consequences of which are not unequivocally clear, or in mutual obligations to reverse all the consequences of the sale. In the latter case, however, it is not beyond doubt that Y's daughter's house will revert to X: in order to achieve this, X must prove that Y's daughter had not acted in good faith when she acquired the house from her father (i.e., in this case the crucial criterion of Art. 3:88 Dutch Civil Code). This establishment of a lack of good faith (based on Art. 3:11) is not without complications for X: Y's daughter must not have known or ought to have known that her father had acquired the house either subject to the condition of its specific use for cultural purposes or otherwise as a gift in connection with which he was obliged to perform in a certain agreed manner.

Eastern European jurisdictions

Slovenia

If the contract price amounts to less than 50 per cent of the market value, X is entitled to claim annulment of the contract. Y can (probably) prevent the annulment by paying the market value. If the contract price is more than 50 per cent of the market value, annulment is not possible, but X can claim the difference between the contract price and the market value.

I. According to Slovenian law, a contract for sale of real estate has to be concluded in written form (Art. 52 CO).[816] Since the written contract does not mention the future use of the house, this cannot be part of the contract.

II. 1. X's assumption, that Y would dedicate the house to cultural purposes, is a mistake *regarding the motive*. A mistake of motive does not entitle the mistaken party to demand nullification of a synallagmatic contract (Art. 40(1)). But in cases of *donation and other gratuitous* contracts, a mistake of motive is also relevant (Art. 47 CO).

2. Given the fact that the agreed price for the house was known by both parties to be 'far below its market value', the contract should be qualified as a mixed contract ('*donatio mixta*'). With regard to such contracts, the main question is which element (donation or sale) prevails. If the agreed price amounts to less than half the market value, the rules regarding donation prevail. In such a case, X can demand annulment of the contract on grounds of mistake (Arts. 46 and 47 CO), provided that his sole or prevailing motive for sale was the dedication to cultural purposes.

[816] Some even in the form of a notarial deed.

3. Due to the principle of *causality*,[817] established under Slovenian law (Art. 40 Property Code),[818] the annulment of the contract automatically has the effect that the transfer of property between X and Y becomes void with retroactive effect. According to this principle, X remained the owner of the house and Y was, consequently, not able to transfer the ownership to his daughter. However, if Y's daughter acted in good faith (i.e., did not know or ought to know the reason for the annulment)[819] she nevertheless acquired the ownership of the house. In this case the principle of reliance upon the data in the Land Register (codified in Art. 10 Property Code and Art. 8 Land Register Act[820]) prevails, which means, that the annulment of the contract between X and Y cannot affect her position.[821] The fact that Y donated the house to his daughter is not relevant to the question whether or not she remains the owner. In this case X is not in the position to reclaim the house. Therefore Y has to compensate him by payment of the market price.

4. X can only demand annulment of the contract, and not an adjustment of the price. But Art. 46(4) allows Y to counter X's claim by accepting the obligation to perform the contract as if there was no mistake. If X's intention was to sell the house anyway, but at the market price, Y would be allowed to avert X's claim by offering to pay the market value.[822]

III. If the donation element does not prevail, X does not have remedies based on the concept of mistake. In such a case, an action on grounds of unjust enrichment is possible. The Slovenian CO provides for general rules on unjust enrichment in Art. 190. According to para. 1 a party that has become enriched to the detriment of another without a legal ground has the obligation to make restitution of what was received. If restitution is not possible, the benefit has to be compensated for. In the present case, para. 3 is applicable, which relates to the specific case that the *benefit has been received in connection with a certain*

[817] This means that transfer of property is only valid when it is based upon a valid 'title contract'.

[818] Stvarnopravni zakonik, Official Gazette 87/2002.

[819] This is presumed, until proven otherwise by the party contesting the good faith (Art. 9 Property Code).

[820] Zakon o zemljiški knjigi, Official Gazette 58/2003.

[821] When she acquired the house, Y was registered in the Land Register as the owner of the house and she is allowed to rely on that information. This means that for her Y was the owner and the transfer between Y and her is considered to be valid.

[822] I.e., to create a situation, as it would be, if X did not want the house to be dedicated to cultural purposes only. Dolenc in: Juhart and Plavšak (eds.), *Obligacijski zakonik*, vol. I, p. 352.

purpose that did not come true (in this case the dedication to cultural purposes only). An action on grounds of Art. 190 CO against Y leaves the contract in force, but Y is under obligation to pay the market value in order to compensate X for the enrichment.

IV. 1. It might be possible to qualify the contract as a usurious contract if there is an obvious disparity between the contract price and the market value[823] and if X is able to prove that Y misused his inexperience or naivety and had no intentions to dedicate the house to cultural purposes when concluding the contract. Such contract is null and void (Art. 119(1) CO). The contract is, however, upheld if the disadvantaged party requests adjustment by a judicial decision. Consent of the other party is not required.[824]

2. An action on grounds of mistake leaves the contract valid, but subject to an annulment and gives Y the option to save the contract by offering to pay the market value. X is not allowed to decline such offer and is obliged to accept the adjustment of the price. Consequently, he is not able to endorse his wish to dedicate the house to cultural purposes only. If X takes action on grounds of Art. 119, the contract is null and void and X is free to chose between adjustment of the contract to the market value and leaving the contract void so he can reclaim the house. X can only reclaim the house from Y's daughter subject to the limitations described above (good or bad faith of Y's daughter). An action based on Article 119 CO, however, requires that X is able to prove the abuse, allegedly committed by Y, which is very unlikely.

V. It is not possible for X to invoke a change of circumstances because the change has occurred after the parties to the sales contract both performed their obligations. Thus, the contract has already been performed. As stated above, the buyer was not obliged to dedicate the house for cultural purposes according to the sales contract.

Lithuania

Relief is not very likely to be available in Lithuania.

I. 1. First, a decision in favour of X might be based on the assumption that there was an implied condition in the contract regarding the

823 The disparity must exist at the time of the conclusion of the contract. A disparity that occurs later is not relevant. Slovenian Supreme Court, II Ips 578/99.

824 The adjustment must be claimed in Court. The convalidated contract has the effect ex tunc. Juhart in: Juhart and Plavšak (eds.), *Obligacijski zakonik*, vol. I, p. 627; B. G. Blagojević and V. Krulj, *Komentar zakona o obligacionim odnosima* (Belgrade: Savremena Administracija, 1983), p. 418.

purpose of the use of the house: the transfer of the house by Y to his daughter would then constitute a breach of the contract. In addition, X may try to prove that, in reality, it was not a purchase sale contract that was concluded but a contract of gift under condition, as the price was considerably lower than the market price. If the contract can be qualified as a contract of gift, it would be possible to apply Art. 6.467 CC on gifts under condition. In accordance with this article, in case of a failure to perform the condition, the donor may demand annulment of the contract and return of the gift. Thus, in this case Art. 6.204 would not be applied but a special norm, i.e., Art. 6.467 CC. However, it would certainly be complicated to prove that such an implied condition of the contract really exists as contracts of gift for immovable property are concluded in notary form.

2. Therefore, the court may reject the arguments of X concerning the implied condition due to formal reasons, i.e., by stating that what is not included in a notary contract may not be considered a term of a contract. It should be noted that Art. 1.93 CC provides the court with a discretionary right to refuse the testimony of witnesses to prove such circumstances that had to be ratified by a written or notarial contract. Thus, it is not very likely that X would be able to rely on an implied condition by resorting to the testimony of witnesses. Consequently, if X fails to prove the existence of an implied condition of the contract related to the designation of the building, he would have no right to demand either the dissolution of the contract or the difference in price.

II. There is no mistake in this case as X was aware that he was selling the building at a price considerably lower than the market price. Had X erroneously believed that the agreed price conformed to the market price, he would have been under a misapprehension regarding the price, which is considered to be an essential condition of a contract (Art. 1.90 CC). However, the situation under discussion may be viewed as fraud if Y had really promised to use the building for a specific purpose while, actually, he never had any intention of doing so. In that case, the contract would have been concluded under particularly unfair conditions (Art. 1.91 CC).

III. The notion of unjust enrichment is not applicable in this case as: (i) a claim of unjust enrichment is subject to subsidiary application and is applied only if a problem cannot be resolved by the application of the provisions of contract or tort law;[825] (ii) unjust enrichment occurs

[825] Mikelenas, *Commentary on Book VI of the Civil Code*, p. 268.

in the cases where property or benefit is obtained without any legal grounds. In the case concerned, Y acquired the property on legal grounds, i.e., in accordance with a contract. Consequently, as long as the contract is valid, Y may not be considered as being unjustly enriched (Art. 6.237 CC).

IV. X might request modification of the contract or termination of the contract on the basis of gross disparity between the parties (Art. 6.228 CC). In such a case, however, X will have to prove that the contract, which he concluded under such unfavourable conditions, resulted either from his own inexperience or from fraudulent actions of Y. In any case, the interests of X must be protected according to the principles of justice, reasonableness and good faith (Art. 1.5 CC). In this case, Art. 6.228 CC could be invoked by X as the grounds for demanding the dissolution of the contract or compensation of the difference in prices.

V. Art. 6.204 CC is not applicable in this case for the following reasons: (i) X could have insisted on a clause with regard to the usage of the building and Y would then have been bound; (ii) By failing to do so, X assumed the possible risk of another usage; (iii) X could have reasonably predicted a change of the attitude on the part of Y.

VI. As Art. 6.204 CC may not be applied in this case due to the reasons indicated above, the most realistic option for X is to base his demand for the dissolution of the contract or compensation of the difference in prices on fraud (Art. 1.91 CC) or on a gross disparity between the parties (Art. 6.228 CC) and, in addition, in every instance to refer to the principles of justice, reasonableness and good faith (Art. 1.5 CC).

Czech Republic

It is possible but uncertain that X will be entitled to reclaim the house.

I. Contracts on transfer of real estate are valid only if made in writing (Sections 40(1) and 46(1) Civil Code)[826]. Terms agreed by the parties but not incorporated into the contract do not form a part of the contract.[827] Y does not expressly breach the contract by changing his decision after the real estate is transferred.

[826] See Section 40(1): 'Where an juridical act was not executed in the form required by law or by agreement of the parties, it shall be null and void', and Section 46(1): 'A contract on transfer of real estate, as well as other contracts, for which the law or agreement between the parties requires a written form, must be made in writing'.

[827] See J. Švestka in: Jehlička *et al.* (eds.), *Občanský zákoík kaueutář (Civil Code Commentary)* (Prague: ASPI, 9th edn, 2004), p. 270.

II. As mentioned above, contracts are not invalid per se due to mistakes. Mistakes are relevant only at the moment of execution of the contract, so application of Section 49a Civil Code on mistakes is out of the question in this case.

III. However, the above-mentioned agreement can be classified as a mixed agreement – partly donation and partly purchase – as it should be interpreted in compliance with the parties' will (Section 35(2) Civil Code).

IV. Under Section 630 Civil Code the donor may claim that the donation be returned (reclaimed) if the recipient of the donation treats the donor in a way that contradicts good morals.

V. In principle, the prenuptial agreement of X and Y can be interpreted based on the subsequent behaviour of the parties. One can even see in the behaviour of the parties a contractual agreement on resolution of their reciprocal claims.

Scandinavian jurisdictions

Sweden

Under Swedish law, X is not entitled to ask for the difference between the agreed price and the market value, nor is he entitled to reclaim the house.

I. The parties did only assume – and not agree – that the house would be dedicated to cultural purposes only. If this had been an (unwritten) condition, the situation would have been different. However, according to Chapter 4 Section 3 Code of Land Laws[828] the contract cannot be made dependent on a condition that is not mentioned in the written contract, which has to be signed. This rule applies also if the contract would qualify as a contract for a gift (Chapter 4 Section 29), but not if the house is not real estate.

II. 1. With regard to the doctrine of assumptions, this case gives a typical example of the category of 'assumptions regarding objectives other than economic values'. Assumptions of this kind are traditionally not normally relevant. The main grounds for the application of the doctrine of assumptions would be that Y has *made a profit* at the expense of X. However, this ground is not likely to be applicable, as the assumption was that the house was to be dedicated to cultural purposes, which

[828] Jordabalken.

would probably not be to the benefit of X. And even if it was, it is doubtful whether this would be enough to render the assumption legally relevant.

2. This requirement was met in case NJA 1943 p. 109, which concerned economic values, and still the assumption was not deemed to be relevant. A town district sold real estate to an association, which promised to build a first class hotel on the land. Since the association's application for permission to build the hotel had been rejected by the permission authority, the town district claimed for cancellation of the contract. The claim was rejected on the grounds that (i) the purchase was not subject to the condition that the association would be able to build the hotel; (ii) the association's inability to do so did not grant the town district the right to cancel the contract; and (iii) there was no ground to cancel the contract on the basis of failed assumptions. In this case it was really the claimant's (seller's) assumption regarding an objective of the contract other than the performance (the building of the hotel) that failed.

3. A party's erroneous assumption is subject to relief under the doctrine of assumptions when the other party after the formation of the contract *negligently caused* the non-realisation of the assumption.[829] However, the general rule is that a party to a contract is free to protect their own interests as they wish. This general rule would most likely be applied if the case was tried before a Swedish court, as there is no specific norm, such as trade customs, which Y has violated.

III. The case has not been tried, but it is most unlikely that the absence of a condition in the contract could be considered an unreasonable contract term under Section 36 Contracts Act.

Denmark

X is entitled to reclaim the house and demand reliance damages from Y.

I. The parties did not insert a provision in the sales contract making it a condition that the house must be used for cultural purposes. However, the condition may be regarded as an implied term, since Y bought the house at a price which was far below the market price. Danish law does not have any specific formality rules with respect to real estate sales contracts. The parties can conclude an oral agreement, but in Denmark

[829] See especially NJA 1936 p. 368 and Lehrberg, *Förutsättningsläran*, pp. 527–8.

such a contract is normally concluded in writing, especially if the sale takes place through an estate agent.

II. Depending on the circumstances at the time when the contract was entered into, it might be worth taking into consideration whether the promisee to the contract (Y) already knew that he was going to give the house to his daughter. If that is the case, the promisee has acted fraudulently, which is a violation of Section 30 Contracts Act. In such a case, the general rule is that the contract is void unless the daughter had acted in good faith. However, if the third person involved, i.e., in this case the daughter, receives the subject matter of the contract as a gift, the contract is void, even if she has acted in good faith. With regard to gifts the security of trade does not require protection.

III. 1. If it is not possible to establish fraud, X would most probably invoke the doctrine of assumptions or perhaps Section 36 Contracts Act. In that case, he is not entitled to claim damages for a breach of contract (expectation damages), as the application of the doctrine of assumptions (or Section 36 and for that matter also Section 30 Contracts Act) implies that damages can only be claimed as negative contractual interest. Thus X is not entitled to claim the difference between the agreed price and the market value.

2. However, if it is possible to apply the doctrine of assumptions and thereby to avoid the contract, X could reclaim the house. As mentioned in the overview (Chapter 4), three cumulative conditions must be fulfilled in order to apply the doctrine of assumptions. It can be considered more than likely that X never would have made the promise if he had known that Y would subsequently donate the house to his daughter. Furthermore, Y could have realised that this assumption is crucial for X. Finally, the assumption is also relevant, as Y, under the circumstances, must bear the risk that the assumption fails.

Romanic-Mediterranean jurisdictions

Italy

X is entitled to either reclaim the house or to require Y to dedicate the house to cultural purposes.

I. 1. If we assume that the contract is a sale (rather than a mixed donation, see above), one can say that Y is contractually obliged to use the house for the agreed purpose. According to the interpretation of the parties' intention, provided that such obligation is essential and it has actually induced X to sell the house at a low price, he has several rights if Y does not comply with this obligation: X has the right (i) to enforce X's obligation or (ii) to terminate due to breach of contract, i.e., the non-performance of B's obligation (Art. 1453 CC).

2. However, the doctrine of the legal irrelevance of the parties' individual motives can question this result. The rules on the interpretation of the intention of the parties, which play a decisive role in the case at issue, allow the construction of contractual terms even beyond the explicit wording used by the parties (Art. 1362 CC). In other words, in the absence of an explicit conditional clause, which as far as the transfer of property is concerned, subordinates the effectiveness of the sale, to the event specifically considered, the court has to ascertain whether or not the agreement was actually reached on the assumption of the alleged implicit condition. Further, it should be noted that a specific provision amongst the rules of the interpretation of contracts (Art. 1366 CC) rests on the general principle of good faith and it is quite clear that on the basis of such a rule Y would be obliged to perform according to the expectations of X, as far as they shall be deemed implicitly inserted in the contract. In this case, X would otherwise not have sold the house at that price. In summary, the mere fact that the assumption of the parties about the use of the house was not formally inserted into the contract as an explicit condition should not allow Y to change his mind.

3. The basic concept, on which the doctrine of *presupposizione* has been developed, is that of the implied condition and the purpose of this doctrine is actually to give legal significance to the implied assumptions between the parties independently of the nature of the contract.

4. In the case at issue, a difficulty in the application of the doctrine of *presupposizione* could *prima facie* derive from the requirement that the contract at issue, i.e., sale of an immovable, has to be in written form, under the sanction of its invalidity (Art. 1350 CC). Should the said requirement relate to all terms, the parties would actually be prevented from enforcing a stipulation deducted from the parties' intention by implication. However, Italian case law confirms the applicability of the doctrine of *presupposizione* also to contracts that are subject to the requirement of the written form, since the fundamental question of the interpretation of the parties' intention prevails over other issues. This question relates to the contract intended as a relationship between the parties and not as a formal (i.e., notarial) deed. The above theory is based on the consideration that formal

rules affect the structure of the deed and not the contractual relationship, i.e., they do not affect the prevailing intent of the parties whose determination is paramount with respect to the construction of the hypothetical will.

II. Furthermore, it must be said that X would not be entitled to ask for the difference between the agreed price and the market value, in terms of judicial adaptation of the contract and/or as a result of the general rules on unjustified enrichment (Art. 2041 CC), which under Italian law have a very strict application. X may instead sue Y asking for specific performance, provided that X can give proof that both parties had assumed that Y would dedicate the sold house to cultural purposes only and this (bilateral and therefore objective) assumption determined the low price of the sale. Alternatively or even subordinately to the first instance for specific performance, Y may terminate the contract due to a breach by X. The restitution of the house to X would be subject, under Italian law, to the judicial declaration of termination of the contract for non-performance (according to the law of restitution, see Arts. 1458 and 2033 *et seq*. CC).

III. Under Italian law, a fundamental question in the case at issue concerns the nature of the contract, since the sale at a price far below the market value could determine the qualification of the agreement as donation instead of as sales contract. In such case, the donation could include a burden (onus, charge) and X would be entitled to take legal action against Y asking for the performance of the contractual burden to dedicate the house for cultural purposes. In the case of non-performance, X could not claim the difference between the agreed price and the market value (because of the qualification of the contract as donation), but he could terminate the contract and, as a consequence of the dissolution of the contract, ask for the restitution of the house (Art. 793 CC).

IV. Even if the assumption of the use of the house is not an explicit condition, Y is not allowed to change his mind, and the doctrine of *presupposizione* would apply. If X can proove that both parties had assumed that Y would have dedicated the house to cultural purposes only and this assumption determined the low price of the sale, X can ask for specific performance or, alternatively, for the termination of the contract for non-performance resulting in the restitution of the house (according to the law of restitution, see Arts. 1458 and 2033 *et seq*. CC). However, X would not be entitled to ask for the difference between the agreed price and the market value.

Spain

X can either claim adjustment or termination of the contract under Spanish law.

I. This is a case that could be decided by interpreting the will of the parties to the contract, or by applying the good faith principle. In Spanish law, obligations do not only arise from the express content of the contract, but also from the law, general usage and the principle of good faith (Art. 1258 CC). Regardless of whether it is explicit or implicit, if X sues Y for non-performance, he will have to prove that such a clause had been agreed upon. Otherwise, Y can use the house as he likes. If an interpretation of the contract leads the court to the conclusion that there had been an implicit clause stating a condition as to the purposes of the sale (as it seems from the facts of the case), X could claim specific performance (Y has to use the house for cultural purposes) or termination of the contract on the basis of Art. 1124 CC. He would also be entitled to claim damages in both cases.

II. Another approach could be taken if the contract is considered to be a mixed contract of sale and donation. According to Art. 647 CC, a donation can be revoked if the person receiving the gift breaches the obligations established by the donor in the donation contract.

Portugal

The most appropriate legal answer to these cases is an adjustment of the contract (namely an increase of the price) on the basis of Art. 437 CC.

I. 1. In one opinion,[830] situations of this kind can be subject to various interpretations. It is essential from the outset to determine the exact meaning of the agreement between the parties by means of the interpretation of the contract (Art. 236 CC). First of all, the contract should be qualified as a sale and not a mixed sale and donation. In our opinion, the low price of the house as such does not allow for a (partial) application of the rules of donation. The mere fact that the price is below, and even far below, the market value of the asset, is not sufficient to qualify the transaction as a donation. Under Portuguese law, the intention to benefit the other party ('*animus donandi*') must be proven as a general rule. Furthermore, the treatment of mixed gifts remains debatable,

[830] This opinion is explained in a recently published work: see António Pinto Monteiro, *Erro e vinculação negocial*.

i.e., whether they are treated as single contracts[831] or as a combination of contracts. Furthermore, the possibility of revoking a gift in Portugal is somewhat restricted.

2. A sale and purchase contract, in itself, is neutral with regard to the purposes and motives of the contracting parties. Therefore, in most cases, the buyer pays the price and takes possession of the property and uses it for whatever purpose he sees fit. But the situation can be different if the use of the property is stated or if there is an agreement by the parties in this respect. Then there is a need to determine the exact meaning of such an agreement through interpretation. One may find that the seller has protected himself by means of a condition or a resolutive clause, which allows him to reclaim the property if the buyer does not use it for the agreed purpose (Arts. 270 and 432 CC, respectively).

II. 1. If the use of the property has not been stipulated in this way, two very different positions can be taken: either the use of the property has no specific legal, transactional significance as it is a matter of mere motivation. Or, one could argue that the use is the object of a legally binding agreement. Under this approach, the agreement must relate to the use of the property, even if it is not the object of an explicit condition. Thus, there can be an agreement by the terms of which the buyer must not only pay the price but must also use the object of purchase for a certain purpose, so that he assumes an additional or secondary obligation. This additional purpose, however, must not necessarily be conceived as a condition by the parties.

2. Regardless of this option, there are other obligations to be respected, which are determined by the principle of good faith, having regard to the context of the transaction and the contractual purpose (Arts. 762, n°2, and 239 CC). Furthermore, the contract also comprises duties, which are established by the principle of good faith and are necessary for the contract to be fulfilled.[832] In this situation, the so-called '*deveres laterais*' or '*deveres acessórios de conduta*' (duties of care) emerge.[833] So if a certain use of the object of purchase is an obligation

[831] Defending the proposition that the mixed gift must be treated as a single contract and not split up in a gift and a sale, see Antunes Varela, *Das obrigações em geral*, vol. I, p. 295.

[832] António Pinto Monteiro, *Erro e vinculação negocial* (Coimbra: Almedina, 2002), pp. 40 *et seq.*, especially p. 43; Paulo Mota Pinto, *Declaração tácita e comportamento concludente no negócio jurídico* (Coimbra: Almedina, 1995), pp. 132 *et seq.*

[833] These correspond to the so-called '*Nebenpflichten*' of German legal science, equally acceptable in Portuguese law: see especially Carlos Mota Pinto, *Cessão da posição*

for the buyer, even if established via good faith, the non-compliance with this obligation will permit the seller to terminate the contract (Arts. 801, n°2, and 802, n°1 CC) with the consequent right to obtain restitution of the property (Arts. 433 and 434 CC). However, X must prove that he would never have sold the house otherwise. If he can only prove that he would still have sold the house at a higher price, he can claim the difference between the market price and the actual price. This solution is imposed by the principle of good faith, bearing in mind the context of the transaction and the contractual purpose, based on the integration of the contract (Art. 239 CC) or on 'complementary interpretation'.[834]

III. 1. It should be considered, however, that in certain cases the purpose is not included in the contract. Then the purpose will be irrelevant in principle, only being each party's individual motive for the contract, unless the purpose forms part of the basis of the transaction. In such a case recourse to the rules concerning the alteration of circumstances is possible (Art. 437 CC).[835]

2. Similar cases have been tried before Portuguese tribunals, mainly concerning the sale of land. Three classic cases analysed have in common the fact that they were decided by the application of the rules on *mistake*. In each of these three cases the buyer stated that he was buying the property for a specific purpose (street development, public garden, camping site) and then used it for a different purpose. The courts annulled the contracts arguing that if the seller had known in any of the cases that the object of purchase was going to be used for a different purpose than he had expected, he would not have agreed on the

contractual (Coimbra: Almedina, 1970), pp. 337 *et seq.* and 402 *et seq.*, Antunes Varela, *Das Obrigações em geral*, vol. I, pp. 121 *et seq.*, Almeida Costa, *Direito das Obrigações*, pp. 73 *et seq.*, and Antonio Menezes Cordeiro, *Da Boa Fé ne direitocivil* (Coimbra: Almedina, 1984), pp. 586 *et seq.* With regard to the inclusion of the purpose of the creditor in a contractual relationship by means of '*deveres laterais*', see Köhler, *Unmöglichkeit und Geschäftsgrundlage bei Zweckstörungen in Schuldverhältnis*, pp. 139–40.

834 K. Larenz, 'Ergänzende Vertragsauslegung und dispositives Recht', (1963) NJW, 737 *et seq.* On recourse to Art. 239 CC for legal interpretation in Portuguese law via integration of the transaction, secondary or lateral duties ('*deveres acessórios ou laterais*') based on good faith and in the light of the contractual purpose and of the context of the transaction, see for all, C. Mota Pinto, A. Pinto Monteiro and P. Mota Pinto, *Teoria Geral*, pp. 459 *et seq.*

835 And it appears that this is the only case: see Pinto Monteiro, *Erro e vinculação negocial*, pp. 25 *et seq.* and 38, and Ulrich Huber, 'Verpflichtungszweck, Vertragsinhalt und Geschäftsgrundlage', (1972) *Juristische Schulung*, 57–8 and 64–5.

transaction.[836] This perspective, however, is not the most appropriate for the cases being considered.[837]

3. Such situations can also be settled applying the rules on unjust enrichment (Art. 473 CC), which still are of a subsidiary nature in Portuguese law (Art. 474 CC).[838] Thus, these rules should only be considered if it is not possible to have recourse to one of the other demonstrated routes. Unjust enrichment is subsidiary in the sense that it can only be invoked if the law does not allow for any other way of ensuring the reparation of a loss or restitution. It seems that it is subsidiary even with regard to Art. 437 CC and a change of circumstances. If it is not possible to obtain a modification or a rescission of the contract on the basis of Art. 437 CC (since its conditions were not met), it is not possible to invoke unjust enrichment, as a rule. After all, a valid contract provides a legal ground or cause for the benefit of one of the parties.

4. In this case, the seller is not ignorant of the facts nor have they been falsely or defectively represented. Therefore the rules on mistake do not apply. In Portuguese law, a defective prediction of the evolution of circumstances – an '*error in futurum*' – is a problem of presupposition (as in the schedule of Art. 437 CC), not of error.

5. This would have been the correct interpretation of the previously mentioned cases. So if it can be proven that the use of the objects of purchase was part of the basis of the transaction ('*base do negócio*'), the solution is the termination of the contract or its modification as set out in Art. 437 CC. The change occurred after the contract was concluded. As already stated, there is no consensus among legal writers whether the

[836] See respectively Acórdão do Supremo Tribunal de Justiça of 2 February 1971, *Boletim do Ministério da Justiça* 204, 131 *et seq.*, Acórdão do STJ of 2 November 1977, *Boletim do Ministério da Justiça* 271, 190 *et seq.* and the Acórdão do Tribunal da Relação do Porto of 8 May 1986, *Colectânea de Juisprudência*, XI, 3, 190. More recently Acórdão do STJ of 26 May 1994, *Boletim do Ministério da Justiça*, 437, 486 *et seq.*

[837] But we admit that in certain cases the correct interpretation is error. This would be the case for example if the seller was mistaken as to the meaning of the declaration of the buyer, who never intended to use it for the purpose that the seller had expected. In such a case there would be a fault in the formation of the will ('*formação de vontade*') and not a change in the use of the property. There may even have been deceit ('*dolo*') on the part of the buyer if he acted with the intention of deceiving the other party when he made the declaration about the use of the property.

[838] See, e.g., Diogo Leite de Campos, *A subsidiariedade da obrigação de restituir o enriquecimento* (Coimbra: Coimbra Editora, 1974), F. Pereira Coelho, 'Um problema de enriquecimento sem causa', (1970) 17 *Revista de Direito e de Estudos Sociais*, 351, Júlio Gomes, *O conceito de enriquecimento, o enriquecimento forçado e os vários paradigmas do enriquecimento sem causa* (Porto: UCP, 1998), pp. 415 *et seq.* and 496 and Menezes Leitão, *O enriquecimento sem causa no direito civil*, (Lisbon: CEF, 1996), pp. 545 *et seq.*

termination of the contract or its modification has priority: a minority view holds that as long as one of the parties objects to a modification, termination would be the only possible outcome. In contrast, the dominant point of view is that the court may choose modification of the contract in spite of the opposition of one of the parties, at least if that opposition is contrary to good faith.[839]

Greece

X is entitled to demand either an increase of the price or to terminate the contract and, in consequence, reclaim the house.

I. The contract is neither a mixed donation nor a donation under a condition (in German, '*Schenkung unter Auflage*'). No valid condition has been stipulated, because this substantial term of the contract must become a clear and undeniable part of the notarial deed, which is required in case of a donation (Art. 498 §1 AK).[840] An implied condition should also be excluded. According to the prevailing opinion,[841] terms can only be implied in the case of a formal contract if a third person can identify them based on objective criteria. In any case, the contract at hand cannot be qualified as a mixed donation given that X has no *causa donandi* whatsoever. The *cause* of the above contract is the common assumption that the house would be dedicated to cultural purposes. Therefore, the contract is a mere sale and X has no right, whatsoever, to revoke it.

II. The above case is not a mere frustration of the unilateral expectations of a party, regarding the use of the contractual object, which would be legally irrelevant (Art. 143 AK). In fact, this is a subsequent collapse of the underlying basis of the transaction according to Art. 388 AK. Y's intention to use X's family house for cultural purposes has become a crucial part of the contractual basis. This approach applies not because the parties have based their contractual relationship on it (subjective criterion), but, mostly, because the specific manner of using

839 If the plaintiff asks for the rescission of the contract, under Art. 437 CC, the defendant may, according to Art. 437-2 CC, apply for the modification of the contract. On the other hand the plaintiff may from the beginning of the legal action ask for modification. The only case where a court may not impose modification of the contract occurs when the plaintiff sues asking only for rescission and the defendant accepts that request (see Almeida Costa, *Direito das Obrigações*, p. 348).

840 See AP 1029/1988, HellDni 1990, 65; Kornilakis, *Law of Obligations*, I, p. 65.

841 See AP 329/2006, HellDni 2006, 783; 1867/2006 (unpubl.); Stathopoulos, 'Art. 200', in: Ap. Georgiadis and Stathopoulos (eds.), *AK*, n. 21; Ap. Georgiadis, *General Principles*, §40 n. 34.

this house has affected a substantial part of the contract, that is the price (cf. Case 2). As a result, X can either seek judicial adjustment (here increase) of the price or terminate the contract and reclaim the house according to the provisions of unjust enrichment (Arts. 904 *et seq.*). The fact that Y is responsible for this collapse of the contractual basis does not prevent X from invoking Art. 388 AK.[842]

III. Another suitable solution could be the application of the *condictio ob rem*, which is – in general terms – a claim of restitution in case a *cause* has not been accomplished. The result of this solution would be the direct application of the rules of unjust enrichment (Arts. 904 *et seq.* AK). This would set aside Art. 388 AK and the institution of the unforeseen change of circumstances. Indeed, the dedication of the house to cultural purposes could be considered as a non-compulsory obligation of Y, which motivated X to sell his house at a low price.[843] According to this solution, X has no right to seek an adjustment. The total dissolution of the contract and the return of the performances that already have been exchanged would be the only remedy. This is, of course, a disadvantage for the interests of the parties in comparison to Art. 388 AK, which not only provides for a dissolution but also an adjustment of the contract.[844] Therefore, it would be preferable to bring the case under Art. 388 AK, as already mentioned.

France and related jurisdictions

France

Under French law, it is possible but uncertain that X will be held entitled to claim a higher price or to terminate the contract.

The solution will depend on the qualification of the contract.[845]

I. X might claim that the contract contains an implied condition (see Case 10). Similarly, the judge can consider that the dedication linked to the low price is part of the contractual framework. So, dedicating the house for cultural purposes could be part of the contract even though it is not expressly stipulated. In this case, Y would be contractually liable and X could enforce the change of use or terminate the contract.

842 See also Overview (Chapter 4).

843 See Filios, *Law of Obligations, Special Part* (Athens-Komotini: Sakkoulas, 5th edn, 2005), vol. II, §144 p. 241.

844 See in general Stathopoulos, *Law of Obligations*, §19 n. 57 with further references.

845 See Cass., 16 November 1989, Rôle 8402 Justel N-19891116–15.

However, it is far from certain that the judge would go this far in his interpretation.

II. If the court comes to the conclusion that the contract is a donation, it can be revoked on the basis of Arts. 953 and 954 Cciv if conditions that are linked to the donation are not met. The assessment of the contract will depend on the qualification of the parties' implied assumptions. Most judges will come to the conclusion that the contract at hand is a sales contract so that a revocation on the basis of Arts. 953 and 954 Cciv is excluded.

III. Unjust enrichment cannot be invoked as this doctrine only applies if no other rules can be used, as explained in the overview (Chapter 4). Here, the case must be settled on the basis of contractual rules.

IV. Finally, the principle of good faith might be relevant to the solution of the case. The seller could argue that in changing the use of the premises the buyer did not act in conformity with the principle of good faith as required by Art. 1134/3 Cciv. He could then request a readjustment of the price. However, it is not likely that this solution will prevail as the parties have abstained from inserting such a condition in the contract.

Belgium

Under Belgian law, it is possible but uncertain that X will be held to be entitled to request the difference between the market value and the contract price or to request termination of the contract.

I. The solution will depend on how the contract is qualified:[846] if the court comes to the conclusion that the contract is a donation, it can be revoked on the basis of Arts. 953 and 954 Cciv if the conditions that are linked to the donation are not met. But more likely, the contract will be characterised as a sales contract and the answer will depend on the qualification of X's implied assumption. The judge can consider that the dedication linked to the lower price is part of the contractual agreement.

II. The dedication of the house for cultural purposes could also be interpreted as an implied condition precedent (see Case 10), which must be respected by Y. In this case, Y would be contractually liable and X could force him to use the house as agreed or terminate the contract.

[846] See Cass., 16 November 1989, Rôle 8402 Justel N-19891116-15

III. A solution might also be found in the law of unjust enrichment. But these rules only apply if no other concepts are relevant, as pointed out in the overview (Chapter 4). Here the case should rather be settled on the basis of contractual rules.

IV. Finally, the principle of good faith might be relevant for the solution of the case. The seller could argue that in changing the designation for cultural purposes, which was part of the contractual framework, the buyer did not act in conformity with Art. 1134/3 Cciv, according to which the contract must be performed in good faith. He could then ask for a readjustment of the price. However, as the parties had abstained from an explicit condition, it is not likely that this solution would prevail.

England and related jurisdictions

England and Ireland

X will only have a remedy if a term is implied into the contract that Y was to use the house for cultural purposes only.

I. In the absence of an express term requiring Y to use the property in the way intended, there are only a limited number of concepts that could be utilised by X. In this situation it is critical to note that at the time of formation of the contact both X and Y were of one mind: each believed the property would be dedicated for cultural purposes only, hence the below market value consideration. However, Y, at the date of the formation of the contract, did not misrepresent his intention, nor was he in any way acting with *mala fides*. Y's change of heart occurs after the formation of the contract.

II. 1. First, it is very unlikely that the law of contractual mistake would apply to this situation. The bargain may have been struck in circumstances where the parties believed that the result of the contract would be the creation of a cultural centre, but this is an error as to assumptions or consequences and not one as to terms. The fact that Y's change of mind occurs after the conclusion of the contract further strengthens the view that, at the time of the agreement, there was no operative mistake.[847] Nor would the doctrine of frustration be of any use to X here, as it presupposes that there is a supervening event outside the control of *both* parties. The doctrine will not generally apply if one of the

[847] *Fitzsimons* v. *O'Hanlon* [1999] 2 ILRM 551; see generally Clark, *Contract Law in Ireland* (Dublin: Roundhall, 6th edn, 2008), pp. 218–23.

contracting parties has control over the event, even if it is not the party attempting to rely on frustration.[848]

2. X could attempt to argue that the contract is subject to an implied term that the property was to be used for the intended cultural purposes that motivated the parties to enter into the contract. The juridical basis for implying a term into a contract for the sale of real property is whether the term is needed to give the contract 'business efficacy'.[849] In other words, if the contract would not function as intended but for the implied term then such a term may be implied. The English and Irish courts apply the test of the hypothetical officious bystander who is used in order to gauge the presumed intention of the parties. So, applying this test, if the officious bystander were to say to the parties 'if the property is not used for the intended cultural purpose the buyer cannot retain the property', and the reaction of the parties to such a hypothesis, judged at the time of the contract, would be to say 'Yes, of course!', then the courts will imply that term. On these facts we think it quite possible that a court could hold the contract to be subject to an implied term.

3. There are arguments the other way. First, an implied term that has the result of making a contract work is favoured over terms which have the effect of destroying or terminating the contract.[850] The courts may not wish to imply a term if the effect of this would be to allow X to rescind the contract and reclaim the house. X's claim may thus be stronger if he simply argues for damages for breach of the term, and does not seek to 'undo' the contract entirely, by claiming rescission. Second, contracts for the sale of real property and buildings do not normally contain implied terms as to fitness for purpose, which indicates the potential reluctance of the courts to find 'obvious' implied terms in contracts of this kind. However, given the facts, and in particular the reduction in the price of the house, it is possible that the courts would imply an obligation on the part of Y to use the house for cultural purposes only. It is unlikely that there would be any problems regarding

[848] An exception to this rule arises in the context of employment contracts, where it has been held that the party claiming frustration (the employer) will be successful in such a claim even if the frustrating event was caused by the employee: see *FC Shepherd & Co Ltd* v. *Jerrom* [1987] QB 301. The rule and its exception have both been criticised: C. Kelly, 'Frustration and Employment Contracts', (2004) 11(11) *Commercial Law Practitioner* 286.

[849] *Butler* v. *McAlpine* [1904] 2 IR 445; *Ward* v. *Spivack Ltd*. [1957] IR 40; *Tradax (Ireland) Ltd* v. *Irish Grain Board Ltd* [1984] IR 1; *Sweeney* v. *Duggan* [1997] 2 ILRM 211.

[850] See *Karim Aga Khan* v. *Firestone* [1992] ILRM 31.

formalities in this situation. The Statute of Frauds[851] provides that for a contract for an interest in the sale of land to be enforceable there must be a 'memorandum or note' in writing of the contract, and this memorandum should contain the terms which the parties consider essential. However, implied terms do not necessarily have to be expressed in the memorandum.[852]

4. The question of implied terms leads on to a further possibility. Good faith obligations have been held to arise under English and Irish law at least in relation to the formation of a contract.[853] However, good faith obligations in the performance of a contract are much more problematical. The most likely avenue to explore is that of improvident or unconscionable bargain. Under this doctrine, if it can be shown that the transaction – whether a contract or a voluntary deed – was so ill-advised that no person, properly advised, would enter into it, then it can be set aside. In such cases, if the parties are not meeting on equal terms, the courts of equity may infer that the party contracting at undervalue did not understand the transaction. Although appearing initially to be quite wide ranging, this jurisdiction is found in only a limited range of cases.[854] There is little to suggest that X and Y here do not contract on equal terms and the absence of a clause allowing X to rescind the contract is not evidence of improvidence. It must be remembered that when parties contract on equal terms and there is no evidence of duress or undue influence, the courts will not interfere with the agreement reached: 'If there be a fair and *bona fide* consideration, the court will not enter minutely into it, and see that it is full and ample'.[855]

Scotland

It is likely that the courts would find that X had simply made a bad bargain. X having failed to incorporate a term into the

[851] The Statute of Frauds 1677 (Eng); The Statute of Frauds (Ireland) 1695 (Ire).

[852] See *Supermacs Ireland Ltd* v. *Katesan (Naas) Ltd* [2001] ILRM 401.

[853] *Rooney* v. *Byrne* [1933] IR 609; *Blackpool & Flyde Aero Club Ltd* v. *Blackpool Borough Council* [1990] 3 All ER 25. There is no general duty to negotiate in good faith, however: *Walford* v. *Miles* [1992] 1 All ER 453.

[854] See R. Clark, *Contract Law in Ireland*, pp. 298–302; the Irish Supreme Court decision in *Carroll* v. *Carroll* [2000] 1 ILRM 210 and the Northern Ireland case of *Buckley* v. *Irwin* [1960] NI 98. See also *Portman Building Society* v. *Dunsangh* [2000] 2 All ER (Comm) 221 (Eng) in which on the facts the transaction was held not to be unconscionable.

[855] *Grogan* v. *Cooke* (1812) 2 Ball & B 230 at 234 per Manners LC.

contract limiting the use of the premises to cultural purposes, the courts will not come to his aid. Scots law does not provide X with a remedy on these facts.

I. The proposed use of the house for cultural purposes was an unexpressed assumption shared by the contracting parties. The assumption was not inserted as an express term in the written contract for sale of the house. Even despite the shared nature of the assumption, it would be extremely difficult to argue that the assumption was in fact an oral term of the contract because of the parole evidence rule. In terms of this rule, a written contract is presumed to be the expression of the entire agreement between the parties, ruling out the existence of further orally agreed terms.[856]

II. 1. Nor can the doctrine of implied terms provide a solution to X here. The implication of terms is subject to stringent rules, in effect, limiting the exercise of the power to cases in which the implied term is necessary to make the contract work or for reasons of business efficacy.[857] This is not the case here, and a court would refuse to imply a term limiting the use of the premises to cultural purposes only.

2. It makes little difference that the contract is one for the sale of heritable property. It is possible for terms to be implied in such contracts. The circumstances in Case 11 are simply not ones in which a Scottish court would imply such a term.

III. The rules on error are not relevant to Case 11. As a general rule in Scots law, in order to be operative, an error must prevent the parties from reaching consensus judged at the moment of formation of the contract.[858] In Case 11 there is no error which prevents consensus. The contracting parties' shared assumption is likely to be treated by the courts as lacking legal relevance.

IV. As already stated, Scots law possesses an undeveloped idea of good faith in contract.[859] It is not sufficiently wide to enable X to argue that Y has acted in a manner which is contrary to good faith, and therefore that the contract should be reduced.

[856] Gloag, *Contract*, pp. 365–6; see also D. M. Walker, *The Law of Contract and Related Obligations in Scotland* (London: T & T Clark, 3rd edn, 1995), para. 24.13.

[857] MacQueen and Thomson, *Contract Law*, para. 3–36. See *Crawford* v. *Bruce* 1992 SLT 524 per Lord President Hope at 531or *McWhirter* v. *Longmuir* 1948 SC 577.

[858] McBryde, *Contract*, para. 15–01.

[859] See *Smith* v. *Bank of Scotland* 1997 SC (HL) 111 and MacQueen, 'Good faith', pp. 43–73.

Editors' comparative notes

The open jurisdictions

With the exception of Sweden (and potentially Lithuania), most of the open jurisdictions offer some relief allowing X either to adjust (increase the price) or to terminate the contract. In Italy, X may only terminate the contract but cannot claim adjustment of the price agreement. In all jurisdictions where adjustment is admissible, termination of the contract is available as an alternative. However, in Germany, the contract may only be terminated if Y refuses the adjustment.

The solutions are based on four different approaches: (i) constructive interpretation of the contractual agreement; (ii) unjust enrichment; (iii) specific provisions on donations; and (iv) 'exceptional' doctrines specifically addressing a change of circumstances (in particular in Austria, Germany, Greece, the Netherlands and Portugal).

(i) In Sweden, a legal rule applies stating that an implied condition cannot affect a contract involving real estate. Some other reports point out that, even in the jurisdictions that allow constructive interpretation of real-estate agreements, it might be difficult to prove such an implied term (see. Austria, Germany, Lithuania).

(ii) Another solution that is discussed is a claim for unjust enrichment ('*condictio causa data causa non secuta*'). This rule basically refers to a separate agreement ('*causa data*') on the cultural use of the real estate. However, the doctrine of *condictio causa data causa non secuta* is generally in conflict with the contract concluded by the parties and with the exclusive character of the contract (see Austria, Germany, Greece, Portugal).

(iii) In some jurisdictions the contract at hand can also be qualified as a mixed donation and special provisions from the law of donations apply if the donation is the predominant element of the contract. These rules may provide for the enforceability of the condition (Italy), adjustment (Austria) or termination (Austria, Italy, Lithuania, the Netherlands and Spain) of the contract.

(iv) Austria, Germany, the Netherlands and Italy apply their respective 'exceptional' doctrines.

Sweden is an exception in the group of the open jurisdictions. Here, X is neither entitled to termination nor to adjustment of the contract. The rationale for this position is the above-mentioned provision of Swedish law under which an implied condition cannot affect a contract involving real estate. Furthermore, X's assumptions are considered to be irrelevant under the doctrine of assumptions in Sweden. Relief is also unlikely to be granted in Lithuania although, as the reporter explains, it is not ruled out in principle.

The closed jurisdictions

The majority of the closed jurisdictions offer some form of relief to X. However, relief is generally restricted to termination. In most jurisdictions (Belgium, Czech Republic, Denmark, Slovenia), X may terminate the contract. Whether X may reclaim the house may in some jurisdictions also depend on good faith on the side of Y's daughter (Czech Republic, Slovenia).

The rationales for this result vary. In Belgium, Denmark and France, constructive interpretation is regarded as a likely solution. In other closed jurisdictions, specific rules on donations apply to this contract which may be qualified as a mixed donation (Belgium, Czech Republic, France, Slovenia). The *clausula* doctrine does not justify relief in Slovenia because the contractual obligations have already been performed. The doctrine of assumptions could, however, be applied in Denmark leading to a right to terminate the contract. In Belgium and France, the concept of good faith may also lead to a readjustment of the price.

England and Ireland are unlikely to offer a remedy to X. In these jurisdictions, the only basis of relief for X would be to argue that the use of the house for cultural purposes was an implied term of the contract. Even though the reporter believes that such a term could be implied by the courts, this result is considered to be far from certain. The English and Irish reporter explains that a claim for damages for breach of a contractual term would be more promising for X than a claim for termination. Under Scottish law, no term can be implied because the doctrine of implied terms is subject to stringent conditions that are not met according the facts of the case at hand.

Conclusion

In the group of the open legal systems, most of the jurisdictions provide relief either in the form of adjustment or in the form of termination of the contract. Most of the closed jurisdictions also offer some form of relief, generally only in the form of termination.

The most common basis for these remedies in both the open and closed jurisdictions is constructive interpretation, based on the fact that

X only sold his house at a price below market value because both parties assumed that Y would use the real estate exclusively for cultural purposes. It appears to be decisive for the legal relevance of this mutual assumption that the cultural purpose is reflected by the price agreement. Some jurisdictions also have specific rules on donation contracts which are applied if a contract can be qualified as a mixed donation. In some (of the open) jurisdictions, unjust enrichment is discussed as a possible solution but generally rejected in the light of the contractual agreement that is still in force.

In the case at hand, the correlation between (constructive) interpretation and the 'exceptional' doctrines becomes evident: 'exceptional' doctrines addressing a change of circumstances seem to be less important in the open jurisdictions as the case is primarily solved on the basis of constructive interpretation. In the open jurisdictions, the courts seem more willing to adjust the contract based on constructive interpretation than in the closed jurisdictions. In Austria, Germany, Greece, Italy, Lithuania and the Netherlands, however, constructive interpretation is less likely to be applied and relief can only be granted based on the 'exceptional' doctrines.

Only very few jurisdictions are reluctant to take the parties' assumptions into account. In England and Ireland, it is uncertain whether the courts would accept an implied term. Scotland and the open jurisdiction of Sweden do not offer any remedy at all.

Case 12 Investment in spouse's house is frustrated by divorce

Equitable compensation if divorce laws lack a basis for compensation

Before X and Y marry, they enter into a prenuptial agreement, in which they agree on the separation of property. During the marriage X buys a house and X and Y use the house as their family home. The price of the house is €500,000. X is the sole proprietor of the house, but Y has contributed €100,000 to the purchase price. In addition, Y carries out extensive renovation work before they move in. The renovation would have cost €50,000 if professional services had been employed. After X and Y have lived together in the house for one year, they separate and then divorce. Divorce law does not provide a basis for compensation.

Is Y entitled to compensation for his contributions to the family home?

Germany and related jurisdictions

Germany

Y will receive compensation for his contributions to the family home.

I. 1. Y is not entitled to compensation for his renovation work based on the provisions on service contracts (§611 BGB) or contracts for works (§631 BGB).[860] Though spouses may enter into a legally binding contract of service[861] or for works, by working for the (small) business of the other spouse or building or renovating the family home owned by the other spouse, they do not generally intend to create a binding agreement. Usually, both parties consider the exchange of services and goods during the marriage as contribution to the matrimonial consortium and a moral obligation during the marriage.[862] For this reason, the rules of §§612 I, 632 BGB, which provide that remuneration is deemed to have been tacitly agreed upon if the performance of the service (§612 I BGB) or the production of the work (§632 BGB) is to be expected only for remuneration, do not apply in this case in the absence of a contractual agreement. Applying this objective test, remuneration cannot be expected during the marriage. As a result, there have to be clear indications of the will of the spouses to enter a legally binding contract of the kind mentioned above. Such indications are not present in the given case.

2. Y cannot claim reimbursement for contributions to an undisclosed partnership of the spouses after its liquidation (§733 III BGB). As a general rule, spouses may enter into a contract of partnership if they agree to promote the attainment of a common goal as specified by the contract. The parties can even implicitly agree on this contractual obligation.[863] But in order to establish a partnership agreement

[860] Cf. BGHZ 84, 361 (366 *et seq.*); BGHZ 127, 48; J. Gernhuber and D. Coester-Waltjen, *Familienrecht* (Munich: Beck, 5th edn, 2006), §20 III 4 = pp. 183 *et seq.*; for an overview A. Wacke, '§1356', in: Säcker, *et al.*, *Münchener Kommentar zum Bürgerlichen Gesetzbuch*, vol. VII, nn. 23 *et seq.*

[861] Cf. BVerfGE 13, 290; J. Gernhuber and D. Coester-Waltjen, *Familienrecht*, §20 III 4 = pp. 183 *et seq.*

[862] Cf. BGHZ 84, 361, (366 *et seq.*); J. Gernhuber and D. Coester-Waltjen, *Familienrecht*, §20 III 4 = pp. 183 *et seq.*

[863] Cf. BGH NJW 1995, 3383 (3384); BGHZ 84, 361 (366 *et seq.*); A. Wacke, '§1356', in: F. J. Säcker, R. Rixecker *et al.*, *Münchener Kommentar zum Bürgerlichen Gesetzbuch*, vol. VII, n. 25; for an overview cf. U. Haas, 'Ehegatteninnengesellschaft und familienrechtlicher Vertrag sui generis', (2002) *FamRZ* 2002, 217 *et seq.*

(§705 BGB), spouses first have to promote a 'common object' that differs from the common promotion of the matrimonial consortium and of family life and, second, they have to agree that both parties will profit from the resulting income or gains.[864] Common goals of a contractual agreement under this test are, e.g., the set-up and operation of a business or the common exercise of a profession. However, the building or renovation of the family home is only covered by a mere promotion of the matrimonial consortium.[865]

3. B has no claim for compensation according to the provisions on the revocation of gifts (§§530 *et seq.* BGB) because the service or work rendered by him does not qualify as a gift according to §516 BGB. A gift requires that Y confers a benefit on X out of his own property and that both parties agree that the disposition is gratuitous. First, according to the courts and the prevailing view in legal literature,[866] §516 BGB requires that a property asset is transferred ('*Vermögenswert*') and manpower is not regarded as such.[867] Second, according to the courts and the prevailing view in legal literature, the transfer is not gratuitous in the case of services or work rendered during marriage, because, in general, both parties agree implicitly that the service or work is rendered in support of the matrimonial consortium. Thus, even though the disposition is gratuitous from an objective point of view, there is no corresponding (implicit) agreement of the spouses on the gratuitous nature of the transfer. The majority opinion qualifies the (implicit) agreement of the spouses as a mutual consent about a *non*-gratuitous transfer.[868]

II. Additionally, the rules on unjust enrichment (§§812, 818 II BGB) do not apply in this case. Y cannot claim restitution for the value of his services or work according to the principles of *condictio ob causam finitam*

864 BGH NJW 1999, 2962 (2966); BGH NJW 1995, 3383; BGHZ 84, 361 (366); H. Sprau, '§705', in: Palandt *et al.* (eds.), *Bürgerliches Gesetzbuch* n. 39; for critics see Gernhuber and Coester-Waltjen, *Familienrecht*, §20 III 6 = pp. 184 *et seq.*; P. Ulmer, 'Vor §705', in: Säcker, Rixecker *et al.*, *Münchener Kommentar zum Bürgerlichen Gesetzbuch*, nn. 76 *et seq.*

865 BGH NJW 1999, 2962 (2964); BGHZ 84, 361 (366).

866 Cf. BGHZ 84, 361 (366); J. Koch, '§516 BGB', in: W. Krüger, H. P. Westermann *et al.* (eds.), *Münchener Kommentar zum Bürgerlichen Gesetzbuch*, nn. 5 *et seq.*

867 BGHZ 127, 48.

868 Cf. BGHZ 127, 48; BGHZ 84, 361 (364 *et seq.*); BGH NJW 1999, 2962 (2965); Weidenkaff, '§516', in: Palandt *et al.* (eds.), *Bürgerliches Gesetzbuch*, n. 10; for a different opinion cf. U. Seif, 'Ehebezogene Zuwendungen als Schenkungen unter Ehegatten', (2000) *FamRZ*, 1193; H. Kollhosser, 'Ehebezogene Zuwendungen und Schenkungen unter Ehegatten', (1994) NJW, 2313 *et seq.*

(§812 I 2 Alt. 2 BGB) or the concept of *condictio ob rem* (§812 I 2 Alt. 2 BGB).[869] It is true that Y was under no contractual obligation to perform his services or work and he did not render it to meet a contractual obligation. However, the principles of *condictio ob causam finitam* are triggered only by the cessation of a (contractual) obligation as a legal ground according to §812 I BGB and a *condictio ob rem* (§812 I 2 Alt. 2 BGB) requires that a 'result intended to be produced pursuant to the transaction' is not achieved. Additionally, the result to be brought about has to become part of an agreement pursuant to the contractual agreement ('*Zweckvereinbarung*' or agreement on a certain purpose). If one qualifies building a family home as such a result, this result was actually accomplished.[870] The continuation of the marriage, on the other hand, cannot qualify as a *Zweckvereinbarung* as the parties did not *explicitly* or *implicitly* agree on such a purpose. In order to qualify as a *Zweckvereinbarung*, the specific result must have been known to the other party who must have agreed that the transfer would only be valid if the result is attained. Since the service or work is rendered primarily on the basis of the marriage and of the matrimonial consortium, X's acceptance does not qualify as an agreement that the rendering of the services and works shall be subject to the continuation of the marriage.

III. 1. Nevertheless, according to the courts, the concept of *Störung der Geschäftsgrundlage* (§313 BGB) applies in the given case.[871] If one spouse confers a benefit on the other that clearly exceeds mere favours and reasonable matrimonial support (§§1360 *et seq.* BGB) and the mutual obligations to assist and support the other spouse, the courts infer that the spouses implicitly enter into an agreement.

2. This agreement is referred to as 'agreement *sui generis* governed by family law' ('*familienrechtlicher Vertrag sui generis*'). This concept is applied if the work or services of one spouse result in certain assets for the family, e.g., a family home, or if one spouse works, at least for a certain period of time, in the company of the other spouse.[872] Even though the

[869] Cf. BGHZ 84, 361; H. Sprau, '§812', in: Palandt *et al.* (eds.), *Bürgerliches Gesetzbuch*, n. 90.

[870] Cf. BGHZ 84, 361.

[871] Cf. BGHZ 84, 361 (368); BGHZ 127, 48; BGH NJW 1999, 2962 (2965); Grüneberg, '§313', in: Palandt *et al.* (eds.), *Bürgerliches Gesetzbuch*, n. 51, G. Brudermüller, '§1372', in: Palandt *et al.* (eds.), *Bürgerliches Gesetzbuch*, n. 4; Gernhuber and Coester-Waltjen, *Familienrecht*, §19 V 5 = pp. 174 *et seq.*, §20 III 7 = pp. 185 *et seq.*; for critcs see R. Hepting, *Ehevereinbarungen – Die autonome Ausgestaltung der ehelichen Lebensgemeinschaft und ihr Verhältnis zu Eherecht, Rechtsgeschäftslehre und Schuldrecht* (Munich: Beck, 1984), pp. 162 *et seq.*

[872] Cf. BGHZ 84, 361 (368); BGHZ 127, 48.

spouses may, in theory, explicitly or implicitly shape this special contractual agreement in accordance with their situation, the main function of the concept of an implicit contract between spouses is to provide for a contractual basis for the application of the concept of *Störung der Geschäftsgrundlage* (§313 BGB) in case of a divorce.

3. In the given case, the extensive renovation work went beyond the usual matrimonial obligations to support the family and transfers a benefit on the owner of the building, X. Thus, the persistence of the marriage qualifies as *Geschäftsgrundlage* of the above-mentioned implicit agreement *sui generis* governed by family law.[873] It is a basic assumption shared by both parties at the time of contracting or at least an assumption of Y recognisable to X and uncontested by her, since it was obvious for her that Y's service or work were rendered on the basis of the matrimonial consortium. This *Geschäftsgrundlage* is substantially affected by the divorce.[874]

4. Whether there is an *undue burden* for the spouse that rendered the service or work depends on the matrimonial property regime. If the marriage is subject to the statutory matrimonial property regime,[875] those rules govern the winding-up of the marriage exhaustively, in principle. The concept of *Störung der Geschäftsgrundlage* may only apply in very rare cases.[876] If separation of property was agreed upon between the spouses, this doctrine may apply if the assets of one spouse are still substantially increased at the time of divorce due to the services or work of the other spouse and this allocation is not equitable to the other spouse. All the circumstances of the case have to be taken into consideration, especially the duration of the marriage, the age of the spouses, the kind and amount of the services or work rendered, the remaining increase of the assets of the other spouse, the expenses saved and the living standard of the parties.[877]

5. In case of a transfer of property assets, i.e., other than services or work, the courts refer to a concept of so-called '*ehebezogene Zuwendung*'

[873] Cf. BGHZ 84, 361 (368); BGHZ 127, 48; Grüneberg, '§313', in: Palandt *et al.* (eds.), *Bürgerliches Gesetzbuch*, nn. 50 *et seq.*

[874] Whether there is fault on the side of one spouse with regard to the end of the marriage influence neither the answer to the question whether there is a claim for compensation nor its amount, cf. BGH NJW 1992, 427.

[875] Cf. for details Gernhuber and Coester-Waltjen, *Familienrecht*, §34 = pp. 358 *et seq.*

[876] Cf. BGHZ 115, 132, (135 *et seq.*); BGH NJW 1997, 2747; Roth, '§313', in: Krüger (ed.), *Münchener Kommentar zum Bürgerlichen Gesetzbuch*, vol. II, n. 234.

[877] Cf. BGHZ 84, 361 (368); BGHZ 127, 48; BGH NJW 1999, 2692 (2695); Grüneberg, '§313', in: Palandt *et al.* (eds.), *Bürgerliches Gesetzbuch*, n. 52.

(attribution with regard to the marriage).[878] This doctrine requires a transfer of property assets from one spouse to the other for the sake of the marriage and as a contribution to the matrimonial consortium. Additionally, the spouse must expect that the matrimonial consortium will continue and thus he himself will continue to participate in the transferred property assets.[879] This concept may be qualified as a contractual basis for the disposition that provides for the cause in law for the transfer. Nevertheless, according to the majority opinion, the agreement does not include the above-mentioned expectation of the spouse because this expectation is considered as *Geschäftsgrundlage* of the *ehebezogene Zuwendung*. As a result, the divorce only triggers the principle of §313 BGB and the agreement may be adapted under §313 BGB. Thus, the main function of this concept is to provide an agreement that the doctrine *Störung der Geschäftsgrundlage* (§313 BGB) can be applied to.

With regard to the questions whether and how the agreement is adapted, i.e., whether there is a claim for remuneration and with regard to its amount, the relevant circumstances mentioned above apply too.[880] Moreover, the claim is limited to the transferred amount and the amount the property of X is increased at the time of divorce.[881] In this case, X's property is still increased by the transfer at the time of divorce since X still holds title to the house.

IV. In the given case, the marriage was only of short duration but Y's work was of substantial value. Moreover, it is likely that the assets of X are still increased at the time of divorce. Thus, Y can ask for an amendment of the implicit agreement *sui generis* governed by family law, i.e., claim for compensation. This claim is limited both by the amount of expenses saved by X and by the remaining increase of X's assets at the time of divorce.[882] Y can also claim at least half of his contribution to the purchase price.

Austria

If the parties make additional arrangements concerning their co-operation in investing into the house, the courts will find an implied partnership agreement (§§863, 1175 *et seq*. ABGB). Then the rules for distribution of the partnership's assets after

[878] For a summary of the lines of cases cf. BGHZ 116, 167 (169); for critics cf. Gernhuber and Coester-Waltjen, *Familienrecht*, §19 V 5 = pp. 175 *et seq*.

[879] Cf. BGH NJW 1999, 2962 (2965).

[880] Cf. BGH NJW 1999, 2962 (2965); BGHZ 127, 48 (50).

[881] BGH NJW 1999, 2962 (2965).

[882] Cf. BGHZ 84, 361 (369); BGHZ 127, 48; BGH NJW 1999, 2962 (2965).

termination of the partnership will grant Y a claim for compensation of his financial and labour contributions. In the absence of such an implied agreement, Y is entitled to compensation for his contributions to the family home on the basis of §1435 ABGB (unjust enrichment) under the condition that Y has not frustrated the continuity of the marriage by acting against good faith. The exact amount of compensation awarded to Y depends on the relative contributions (fault) of the spouses to the breakdown of the marriage.

I. 1. If the parties make additional arrangements concerning their co-operation in investing into the house, the courts will find an implied partnership agreement (§§863, 1175 *et seq.* ABGB). Under appropriate circumstances, Austrian courts see an implied partnership agreement in joint contributions of both spouses to the building and furnishing of a marital house[883] ('*Gesellschaft bürgerlichen Rechts*' under §§1175 *et seq.* ABGB).[884] To find an implied partnership agreement the parties must have shown that they are willing to combine their labour and property for their joint benefit[885] and that they set up a minimum common organisation for their co-operation.[886] In case of termination of the partnership the distribution of the assets follows §§1215, 841 *et seq.* ABGB.[887] In the absence of a particular agreement, the assets have to be distributed among the partners according to their contributions to the partnership. The value of contributions of labour and services has to be taken into account as well.[888]

2. In the absence of a tacit (implied) agreement in the above mentioned sense (§863 ABGB), Y is entitled to compensation for his contributions to the family home on the basis of §1435 ABGB (unjust enrichment) under the condition that Y has not frustrated the continuity of the marriage by acting against good faith.

3. Y contributes money and services for a certain purpose which is evident to both parties: the joint usage of the home by both married spouses. If this purpose is frustrated by divorce, X as the sole owner of the house appears to be unjustly enriched in the light of §1435

[883] §863 ABGB: implied agreements arise where the behaviour of the parties does not leave any reasonable doubt that the parties wanted to be bound by a certain agreement.

[884] Mader, '§1435', in: Schwimann (ed.), *Kommentar zum ABGB*, vol. VI, n. 17; Martin Stefula, 'Der gemeinsame Hausbau bei der Auflösung von Ehe und Lebensgemeinschaft (Teil I)', (2001/2002) *Juristische Ausbildung und Praxisvorbereitung*, 138.

[885] *Ibid.* [886] *Ibid.*, 138 at 140. [887] *Ibid.*, 138 at 140. [888] *Ibid.*, 138 at 141.

ABGB.[889] In the absence of an agreement on the legal grounds for the transfer of the benefits in question, payments rendered and services performed with regard to a certain purpose may justify a claim of unjust enrichment on the basis of §1435 ABGB (*condictio causa data causa non secuta*) if this purpose is frustrated.[890] Any payment or service which goes beyond the general obligation of support may be subject to this claim.[891]

4. The right to demand return on the grounds of frustration of purpose is barred, if the party who claims unjust enrichment under §1435 ABGB has prevented the realisation of the purpose by acting in bad faith ('*wider Treu und Glauben*').[892] The question of what constitutes an action in bad faith in that sense cannot be answered by simply referring to the statement of fault in the decree of divorce.[893] Even if the marriage was dissolved on the basis of the sole fault of the claiming party, this will not necessarily exclude his claim under §1435 ABGB due to a violation of good faith.[894] The claimant violates good faith, however, if he acts fraudulently or if he leaves the common dwelling to live with his extra-marital boy/girl-friend.[895]

5. The exact amount of compensation awarded to Y depends on the relative contributions (fault) of the spouses to the breakdown of the marriage. In the absence of any fault on the part of the claiming party, he will be awarded a reasonable remuneration for his contributions

[889] Koziol and Welser, *Bürgerliches Recht*, vol. II, p. 279; Rummel, '§1435', in: Rummel (ed.), *Kommentar zum ABGB*, vol. II, nn. 1, 4; Mader, '§1435', in: Schwimann (ed.), *Kommentar zum ABGB*, vol. VI, n. 1; OGH, 8 Ob 617/87; F. Bydlinski, 'Lohn- und Kondiktionsansprüche aus zweckverfehlenden Arbeitsleistungen', in *Festschrift zum 60. Geburtstag von Walter Wilburg* (Graz: Leykam, 1965), 45 at 46; Wilburg, in: Klang (ed.), *Kommentar zum ABGB*, vol. VI, p. 466; OGH, 2 Ob 111/02s; OGH 24 March 1987, 2 Ob 583/86; OGH, EvBl 1988/149; P. Rummel, 'Wegfall des Rechtsgrundes und Zweckverfehlung als Gründe der Kondiktion nach §1435 ABGB', (1978) *Juristische Blätter*, 449 at 454.

[890] For an introduction into §1435 ABGB see Case 11 above; Mader, '§1435', in: Schwimann (ed.), *Kommentar zum ABGB*, vol. VI, n. 22; OGH, 8 Ob 38/75; OGH, 9 Ob A207/98a; OGH, JBl 1991, 588.

[891] Mader, '§1435', in: Schwimann (ed.), *Kommentar zum ABGB*, vol. VI, n. 22; OGH 25 September 2003, 2 Ob 111/02s.

[892] Rummel, '§1435', in: Rummel (ed.), *Kommentar zum ABGB*, vol. II, n. 9; Mader, '§1435', in: Schwimann (ed.), *Kommentar zum ABGB*, vol. VI, nn. 1, 23; OGH, 8 Ob 617/87; OGH, JBl 1991, 588.

[893] Mader, '§1435', in: Schwimann (ed.), *Kommentar zum ABGB*, vol. VI, n. 23.

[894] *Ibid.*, n. 22; OGH, 2 Ob 111/02s.

[895] Stefula, 'Der gemeinsame Hausbau bei der Auflösung von Ehe und Lebensgemeinschaft (Teil I)', 138 at 142 *et seq.*

independent of the recipient's enrichment.[896] If the claiming party is to be blamed for the frustration of purpose (no violation of good faith in the above sense is required here) his demand is limited to the benefit received by the unjustly enriched party.[897] If both parties are responsible for the frustration to an equal degree, the claiming party will be awarded an amount between reasonable remuneration and received benefit.[898]

II. The relationship between the *condictio causa data causa non secuta* and the doctrine of '*Wegfall der Geschäftsgrundlage*' is not easy to determine. In court decisions, the two legal instruments are used alternatively and no clear dividing line can be found.[899] As already explained in Case 11, Rummel proposed the following distinction: where there is a legal relationship (a valid contract) between the two parties, the doctrine of '*Wegfall der Geschäftsgrundlage*' should be applied to determine whether the contract can be set aside or not. If it can, §1435 ABGB as *condictio causa finita* will give the parties the right to reclaim their performances. Thus, §1435 ABGB as *condictio causa data causa non secuta* should, according to Rummel, only apply where there is no valid legal relationship (contract) between the parties, and the parties' common orientation towards a particular purpose has to be respected nevertheless.[900] Case 12 falls within this latter category provided that courts cannot find a tacit (implied) partnership agreement.

III. In summary, Austrian law provides two possible grounds for Y's claim of compensation for his money as well as for his labour contributions to the house. The rules for the distribution of assets after the termination of a partnership contract (after divorce) only apply if the behaviour of the parties – especially the arrangements they make with respect to their rights and duties in their common undertaking – allows the court to find an implied partnership agreement (§§863, 1175 *et seq.*

[896] Koziol, '§1435', in: Koziol, P. Bydlinski, and Bollenberger (eds.), *Kurzkommentar zum ABGB*, n. 7; Mader, '§1435', in: Schwimann (ed.), *Kommentar zum ABGB*, vol. VI, n. 22; OGH, 8 Ob 38/75; OGH 10 April 1991 JBl 1991, 588.

[897] Mader, '§1435', in: Schwimann (ed.), *Kommentar zum ABGB*, vol. VI, n. 22; OGH, 8 Ob 38/75; OGH 2 September 1998, 9 Ob A207/98a; OGH, JBl 1991, 588; F. Bydlinski, 'Lohn- und Kondiktionsansprüche aus zweckverfehlenden Arbeitsleistungen', in *Festschrift zum 60. Geburtstag von Walter Wilburg*, 45 at 76.

[898] Mader, '§1435', in: Schwimann (ed.), *Kommentar zum ABGB*, vol. VI, n. 22; OGH, 8 Ob 38/75; OGH, 8 Ob 617/87.

[899] Rummel, '§901', in: Rummel (ed.), *Kommentar zum ABGB*, vol. I, n. 7 with further references.

[900] *Ibid.*, vol. I, §901 n. 7.

ABGB). In the absence of such indications for an implied partnership agreement, Y's claim for compensation will be based on the law of unjust enrichment (§1435 ABGB). Y's investments in the common use of the house during the marriage, which were not made on the basis of a legal obligation, become frustrated by the divorce and they are (unjustified) unilateral benefits for X as the sole owner of the house. If Y did not cause the marital breakdown in bad faith, he will be entitled to compensation for his contributions.

The Netherlands

Y is entitled to compensation for his contributions.

I. Dutch case law has formulated a rule which is applicable to the current case: a provision in a valid and otherwise enforceable prenuptial agreement is not applicable if such a provision would have led to consequences that were unacceptable pursuant to the principle of reasonableness and fairness under the then current circumstances.[901] Whether consequences are 'unacceptable pursuant to the principle of reasonableness and fairness' may depend particularly on the fact that such a provision implies a substantial exclusion from patrimonial rights that have been created (at least substantially) due to the efforts of the so-excluded person (i.e., in this case Y). This exception would not affect X's ownership rights as such.[902] Nevertheless, if by virtue of a mandate, Y acquired the house in his own name but for the risk and account of X, then X may claim (and enforce) ownership from Y.[903]

II. If, as in the current case, Y has provided financial means (or has otherwise contributed to the value of X's house), X and Y may be deemed to have entered into an (implied) set-off arrangement. Such a set-off arrangement implies a contractual right to set off any entitlements as if the parties had acquired the relative goods (i.e., the house) in co-ownership. Accordingly, the parties share in value increases (or decreases).[904] If a court does not qualify the financing arrangement (partly) as a set-off arrangement, the same solution could be achieved

[901] HR 25 November 1988, NJ 1989, 529 (*Cafébedrijf*); and HR 5 October 1990, NJ 1991, 576.
[902] HR 2 April 1976, NJ 1976, 450 (*Modehuis Nolly I*), determining that publicly registered ownership rights are determinative.
[903] *Ibid*., see also: HR 16 March 1984, NJ 1984, 556 (*Modehuis Nolly II*).
[904] As developed in the case law: HR 15 February 1985, NJ 1985, 885 (*Verrekeningsbedingarrest*); HR 22 July 1988, NJ 1988, 912 (*Concubinant v. successors*); HR 26 May 1989, NJ 1990, 23 (*Kermisklanten*).

by analogy on the basis of relevant statutory provisions,[905] except that Y would be entitled merely to the nominal amount of his actual contribution (although compensation for Y may exceptionally be based on the principle of reasonableness and fairness and therefore diminish the effect of no set-off arrangement being in place).[906] The compensation for Y should be pro rata according to his contribution, meaning that at least 20 per cent (i.e., €100,000 of €500,000) of the fair market value at the date of divorce should be paid, possibly, but not very likely, increased by the remaining 7.2 per cent.[907]

III. The aforementioned solution is based on Dutch case law, which is still not a completely solid basis for assessing the great variety of cases and is therefore the subject of currently pending legislation (with a likelihood of enactment).[908]

Eastern European jurisdictions

Slovenia

B is entitled to compensation of the money and labour invested in the house.[909]

I. Y's claim should be based on unjust enrichment. As the sole proprietor of the house, X is enriched by Y's contribution in money, as well as in performing services. The Code of Property Law (CPL) of 2003 has specific unjust enrichment rules regarding improvements of immovable property that belongs to another person (Art. 48 CPL). These rules primarily apply in the case of an investment of labour and/or construction materials and equipment, but they are also applicable in cases of contributions to the purchase price. The nature of the relationship between the investor and the owner and the investor's motives are not relevant. The investment must be performed with the owner's consent, which can in practice be proven by the fact that he allowed the contribution. The investor has a right to compensation equal to the

[905] E.g., Art. 1:95 section 2, 1:96 section 2, 1:127 Dutch Civil Code.

[906] For example: HR 12 June 1987, NJ 1988, 150 (*Kriek Smit*).

[907] There is case law rejecting a 50/50 share (HR 25 November 1988, NJ 1989, 529 (*Cafébedrijf*)), but for a substantiated cost of construction work (i.e., the €50,000 fair market price) a court may decide otherwise.

[908] Parliamentary documents EK 2008/2009, 28 867 D ('Wet aanpassing gemeenschap van goederen').

[909] As prenuptial agreements are not allowed, no case law regarding such contracts exist in Slovenia.

owner's enrichment. The amount of compensation does not depend on the kind of relationship between the parties nor on the reasons for which the common purposes of the parties were not (entirely) realised. Y therefore has a right to claim compensation. The reasons for which their marriage has become frustrated, or his/her possible 'bad faith' in this respect, are irrelevant for the calculation of the amount. Y has the right to recover €100,000 plus the value of the labour he performed.

II. In the present case an action on the basis of the '*clausula* rule' (Art. 112 CO) will not prevail because the dissolution of a marriage is a circumstance that should be taken into consideration by the spouses when making property arrangement regarding their marriage, as proven by the relatively high divorce rate in Slovenia.[910]

Lithuania

Y is entitled to compensation in accordance with the rules of family law (Arts. 3.90 and 3.98 CC).

I. Mutual relationships between spouses are regulated by Book III CC. Thus the provisions of contract law are applied only in those cases where the norms of family law do not provide for special regulation. Prenuptial agreements are allowed in Lithuania by Art. 3.102 CC. In such marriage contracts, spouses are also entitled to determine the division of property on divorce (Art. 3.104 CC). The issue will be resolved in accordance with the norms of Book III CC. Pursuant to Arts. 3.90 and 3.98 CC, in cases where a spouse has used his or her individual funds or work for the improvement of the individual property of the other spouse, the spouse who has made the investment is entitled to compensation. Thus, in accordance with the provisions of family law, Y is entitled to compensation.[910]

II. If Y's right to demand compensation was not provided for by the provisions of family law, Y would be entitled to payments on the basis of unjust enrichment. The institute of unjust enrichment is applicable in this case: (i) The absence of the resolution of this issue in family or contract law entails the subsidiary application of Art. 6.237 CC; (ii) the ground for the investment is not effective any longer; as the basis for the investment was marriage, its dissolution resulted in the lapse of the legal basis for X's enrichment. Nevertheless, in Lithuania, there would be no need to apply the institute of unjust enrichment as this issue is regulated by family law.

[910] LAT, Judgment of 15 February 2006, Case No 3K-3-126/2006.

III. Art. 6.204 CC is a general norm applicable in the instances where the facts are not governed by special rules. As the mutual property relationships of spouses are regulated by the provisions of Book III, Art. 6.204 CC is not applicable in this case. Article 6.204 CC is also not applicable in these cases for the reason that the prenuptial agreement determined only the legal regime of the property of spouses and was not associated with its performance.

Czech Republic

Provided that he acted in good faith, Y is entitled to claim the amount by which his contributions have increased the value of his spouse's house.

I. Whether a restitution claim of one of the parties can be asserted depends on the contract itself.

II. If no solution based on the agreement is feasible, then the general provision of Section 451 Civil Code regarding unjustified enrichment applies, namely as regards the benefit acquired by performance in respect of a legal ground which has disappeared. The reason for Y's contribution was the matrimonial cohabitation of X and Y in X's house. Therefore in good faith and by his own acts, Y made improvements to the house and provided X with a sum for the purchase thereof, without, however, becoming a co-owner of the house on the basis of that interest. Y's *bona fide* reliance was grounded, but the grounds lapsed when the spouses divorced. Y's claim exists regardless of his/her part in the divorce, provided that Y's contributions were made in good faith.

III. No rules on unexpected circumstances are applicable in this case.

Scandinavian jurisdictions

Sweden

Y has acquired a so-called concealed joint title to the property and Y has to be compensated as joint owner of the property.

I. In Swedish law, problems of this type are solved by the application of certain case law-based rules of so-called 'concealed title' ('*dold äganderätt*'); basically rules of commission.[911] For these rules to apply

[911] See in case law NJA 1980 p. 705; NJA 1981 p. 693; and NJA 1982 p. 589. See also Agell, A., *Äganderätten till fastighet för makar och samboende. En studie av kommissionsköp* (Stockholm: Norstedts, 1985).

there are four prerequisites, here outlined briefly. First, either of the spouses has acquired assets, or property, in his or her name but for common use. Second, the other spouse has made the purchase possible, or at least easier, through a financial contribution – which is then, when nothing else is said, presumed to be based on a wish to acquire joint title to the assets. Third, the first spouse is presumed to have perceived this wish. Fourth, on the basis of this, a joint will of the spouses to establish a joint title for the contributing spouse is presumed. If these prerequisites are fulfilled, X and Y will be considered joint owners. These requirements appear to be met in this case.

II. If the above rules are not applied, the Swedish Law of Marriage may provide further rules. According to Chapter 12 Section 3 Law of Marriage,[912] a term or condition of a marriage settlement may be modified or set aside if such term or condition is unreasonable with reference to the contents of the agreement, the circumstances at the time the agreement was concluded, circumstances arising later and other circumstances.

III. The doctrine of assumptions, or Section 36 Contracts Act, may be applied (analogously) as a complement to the rules in the Code of Marriage. The divorce might, for example, be invoked as a failure of a basic assumption, as the house was acquired for common use.

Denmark

Y is entitled to receive compensation pursuant to the principle of unjust enrichment equal to a sum of €150,000 with a fair deduction considering his one-year stay in the house.

I. Apart from the prenuptial agreement between the spouses, there is no contract between the parties with respect to the contributions provided by Y, comprising the contribution of €100,000 to the purchase price and the renovation work estimated at €50,000. From a Danish legal point of view, it is not possible to support the idea of any contractual agreement between the former spouses.

II. Danish law does not contain any general rules on unjust enrichment, even though the Marketing Act contains a provision on unjust enrichment. Since the amount in question is substantial and the spouses have only lived in the house for a year, it seems quite reasonable to apply the principle of unjust enrichment in the case at hand, which implies that the spouse is entitled to compensation.

[912] Äktenskapsbalken.

III. Neither the Legal Effects of the Marriage Act nor the Act of Marriage contains provisions about compensation for contributions to the family home.

IV. 1. So far, no case law has supported the use of the doctrine of assumptions, and if the doctrine of assumptions is invoked by one of the spouses it must be in conjunction with the establishment of the prenuptial agreement, but before the registration at the court-house takes place.[913] However, in a couple of cases the Højesteret has used Section 36 Contracts Act to set aside a prenuptial agreement.[914] In both cases, one of the spouses was experiencing a severe personal crisis at the time when the prenuptial agreement was concluded, and they did not receive any sort of consideration for signing the prenuptial agreement. These specific circumstances are not present in the given case.

2. As mentioned under I, the issue is not likely to be considered as a contractual issue, which makes it impossible to apply Section 36 Contracts Act directly. No case law so far supports an analogy with Section 36 Contracts Act dealing with cases of tort, and this case is more likely to be considered as a tort case.

Romanic-Mediterranean jurisdictions

Italy

Y might be entitled to compensation.

I. Y is, at least in principle, not entitled to compensation, since the divorce law as such does not provide for a basis of compensation in similar cases. Neither is Y entitled to ask for compensation for his contributions on the assumption of a contract of service or a contract of work ('*appalto di servizi*' or '*contratto d'opera*'), since the exchange of services during the marriage results from the duty to contribute (in money or in nature) to the matrimonial family life (Art. 143 CC). Such exchange of services may not be considered as a gift subject to the rules of revocation.

II. Although the case at issue should not be deemed to be a case of unjustified enrichment (Art. 2041 CC) outside the scope of contract law, however, the contribution given by Y in terms of both money (as part of

913 Cf. Ingrid Lund-Andersen, Noe Munck and Irene Nørgaard, *Familieret* (Stockholm: Norstedts Juridik, 5th edn, 2003), p. 418.

914 Cf. U 1999.1365H and U 2002.1933Ø.

the purchase price) and of renovation work for the benefit of the family home can be partially recovered. Provided that X and Y have both the above-mentioned duty to contribute (in money or in nature) to the *ménage* of the family (Art. 143 CC), the court could grant compensation (obviously lower than the expenses or the loss of profit suffered by Y) in case of divorce, according to the rules set forth to protect the possessor (in the case at issue of the family home) who met expenses for the benefit of the owner in good faith (Art. 1150 CC).[915]

III. Under Italian law this question is unlikely to be answered applying the general rules of contract law, as marriage is not considered a contract and the supervening events (such as separation and divorce) are subject to ad hoc rules. For this reason Italian courts would not apply the doctrine of implied assumptions between the parties (i.e., *presupposizione*).

Spain

Y is entitled to compensation for the work and the amount contributed. He is likely to recover one third of the value of his contribution.

I. Under Spanish law this is a case of unjust enrichment. Unjust enrichment is not expressly regulated in the Spanish Civil Code, but is acknowledged as a general principle, which has been developed by the Spanish judiciary and legal doctrine.[916] According to these rules Y would be entitled to compensation for his contributions to the family home on the basis of the unjust enrichment of X. The same conclusion was reached by the TS in a decision of 17 January 2003.[917] In this case an unmarried couple decided to separate after several years. The TS decided that the wife had the right to receive one third of the goods owned by the husband, because she had worked for the family during this time instead of working in her own profession.

[915] Cass., 26 May 1995, n. 5866.

[916] Diez Picazo and Gullar, *Sistema de Derecho Civil*, V. II, p. 577; J. A. Álvarez Caperochipi, *El enriquecimiento sin causa* (Granada: AND, 1989); L. Díez Picazo and Cámara, *Dos estudios sobre el enriquecimiento sin causa* (Madrid: Tirant, 1988); Núñez Lagos, *El enriquecimiento sin causa en el Derecho español* (Madrid: 1934). It has, however, been codified in Art. 65 of the Spanish statute regarding bills of exchange and cheques – Ley Cambiaria y del Cheque.

[917] STS of 17 January 2003 (RJ 4, 2003). In the same direction STS of 11 December 1992 (RJ 9733).

Portugal

A claim for compensation may be based on the rules of unjust enrichment. However, it might be easier to obtain compensation for the financial contribution than for the work.

I. A loan for the amount in question would have to meet formal requirements. In any case, no contract seems to have been explicitly concluded concerning the invested money since there was no intention to be legally bound. As there is no valid contract, there is no room to invoke Art. 437 CC.

II. A distinction must be drawn between the portion of the purchase price contributed by Y, on the one hand, and the renovation work, on the other. The financial assistance from Y was contributed under the assumption that the marriage would last and that all the family would benefit from the purchase; it was not an unconditional gift. It seems that unjust enrichment may be invoked (probably *condictio ob rem*) as the assumed state of affairs subsequently ceased and the house became the exclusive property of X. This results in an enrichment of one of the partners (X) at the expense of the other (Y) who contributed to the price but has no property rights with regard to the house.

III. As far as the renovation work is concerned, the rules on improvements only apply to cases of possession or certain cases of detention to which the law has extended the rules on possession. Article 1273 to 1275 CC contemplate a number of rights of the possessor who made improvements to an object. However, possession normally requires an exclusive domain over the object, which does not seem to be present in such a case.

IV. It is doubtful whether the rules of agency ('*negotiorum gestio*') might be successfully invoked. It could be argued that Y acted on his own initiative and according to his duties under the marriage contract. In a marriage, each of the parties is expected to contribute to the maintenance of the family. If Y had acted according to his duties under the marriage contract it is out of the question to invoke agency. In any case, agency does not provide a ground for the payment of work done by Y himself. Only a professional *gestor* is entitled to claim the value of his/her labour.[918] It seems that, again, unjust enrichment might be invoked by Y as a last resort. With regard to the renovation work, a claim can be

[918] On the rules of *negotiorum gestio* in Portuguese law, see, for instance, recently, Júlio Gomes, 'A gestão de negócios: a Oeste nada de novo?', in: *Comemorações dos 35 Anos do Código Civil e dos 25 Anos da Reforma de 1977, Direito das Obrigações* (Coimbra: Coimbra Editora, 2007), vol. III, pp. 39 *et seq*.

justified at least to the extent that the renovation work has increased the value of the building or to the extent necessary expenses were saved.[919]

Greece

Y is not entitled to compensation according to Greek case law. Relief could, however, be granted based on Art. 288 AK.

I. The benefits that Y grants to X go beyond the limit of his legitimate obligation to contribute to the family affairs according to Art. 1386 AK.[920] Therefore, if a common intention of the parties can be inferred, the grants should be considered as a donation pursuant to Art. 496 AK. Such a common intention emerges from an objective interpretation of the parties' behaviour (Art. 200 AK). Pursuant to the requirements of good faith and common usages, the marriage of the parties should be considered as the underlying basis of this donation. Therefore, by the dissolution of the marriage, the underlying basis of the donation has lapsed in the sense of Art. 288. As a result, the cause of the transaction is *ipso iure* terminated and Y acquires the right to reclaim €150,000 according to the provisions on unjust enrichment (Arts. 904 *et seq.* AK). The prevailing case law, however, suggests a different solution but is, at the same time, rather ambiguous. According to the Areios Pagos[921] and the courts of first degrees,[922] the former husband has no right whatsoever to reclaim the benefits from the spouse, first, because the agreement is based on his free (and rather still valid) will (which implies enrichment with cause) and, second, because this benefit did not satisfy any true needs of the spouse (which implies the absence of any enrichment whatsoever).

France and related jurisdictions

France

Under French law Y is entitled to compensation.

I. In this case, there is no contract between the parties and from their behaviour no contractual agreement can be inferred. The question of compensation in the case of divorce is covered by Art. 1469 Cciv. However, this provision is not applicable if the parties agreed to a

[919] Menezes Leitão, *O enriquecimento sem causa no direito civil*, pp. 514 and 517 and Júlio Gomes, *O conceito de enriquecimento*, pp. 322 *et seq.*

[920] See AP 1356/1992 HellDni 1995, 349; EfPir 744/2002 PirNom 2002, 457.

[921] See AP 180/2000 HellDni 2000, 1005.

[922] See EfAth 2393/2001 DEE 2002, 193.

separation of property. In this case, the general principles of the law of unjust enrichment will apply.

II. The conditions for unjust enrichment as described above must be fulfilled. First, X has to be enriched. This requirement is met as X is the sole owner; the enrichment consists of at least €50,000 (the value of the work) with a €100,000 contribution by the spouse. Second, this enrichment must have been at Y's expense. Y invested time and services (€50,000) and made a financial contribution of €100,000. There is also a causal link between X's enrichment and Y's expenses. Finally, the requirement of subsidiarity is also met. Of course, the problem could have been foreseen in the prenuptial agreement, but if there is no other rule regulating this case and no other legal basis, the rules on unjust enrichment can apply.

Belgium

Under Belgian law Y is entitled to compensation.

I. In this case, there is no contract between the parties and no contractual agreement can be inferred from the parties' behaviour. The question of compensation in the case of divorce is covered by Art. 1428 *et seq.* Cciv. However, this provision is not applicable if the parties have agreed on a separation of property.

II. In this case, the general principles of the law of unjust enrichment will apply. X as the sole owner of the house is enriched; the enrichment consists of at least €50,000 (the value of the work) and the €100,000 contribution by the spouse. X received this enrichment at the expense of Y. Y invested time and services (€50,000) and made a financial contribution of €100,000. There is also a causal link between X's enrichment and Y's investment. Finally, the requirement of subsidiarity is also met. As a matter of course the problem could have been foreseen in the prenuptial agreement, but if there is no other rule regulating this case and no other legal basis, the rules on unjust enrichment may apply.

England and related jurisdictions

England and Ireland

In England and in Ireland relief may be available on the basis of a trust.

In this case X and Y have entered into a prenuptial agreement in which they agree on separation of property. The constitutional protection of marriage in Ireland means that it is appropriate to deal with the law in England and Ireland separately.

(a) Ireland

I. 1. It is unclear whether prenuptial agreements are enforceable in Ireland. This uncertainty is caused in part by Article 41.3.1° of the Constitution, Bunreacht na hÉireann, which provides that the state is to 'guard with special care the institution of marriage' and to 'protect it against attack', and in part by Article 41.3.2° which provides that, on the dissolution of marriage, the courts must make 'proper' provision for the spouses and any children.[923] In Ireland, marriage is regarded as a constitutionally protected institution and not a mere contractual arrangement, and thus, the argument goes, a contract which undermines marriage,[924] or which attempts to provide for the consequences of its dissolution and reduce the discretion of the courts to make 'proper provision' for the spouses and children is against public policy and therefore void. However, there is no court decision to expressly back up the view that prenuptial agreements are unenforceable. Nor do the legislative provisions governing divorce provide a solution. For example, the Family Law (Divorce) Act 1996 provides that, when granting a decree of divorce, the court should make 'proper' provision for the spouses and any dependent children, having regard 'in particular' to certain factors.[925] While this list of factors which can be taken into account by the court includes any separation agreement entered into by the spouses, there is no specific mention of whether the courts should take into account any prenuptial agreement which was entered into. However, the list of factors to be taken into account by the court is

[923] The dissolution of marriage (divorce) is specifically provided for in Article 41.3.2°, which was inserted by virtue of the Fifteenth Amendment of the Constitution Act 1995 after a Constitutional Referendum on the issue of divorce.

[924] See *Ennis* v. *Butterly* [1996] 1 IR 426.

[925] Factors to be taken into account include the income, earning capacity, property and other financial resources which each of the spouses concerned has; the financial needs, obligations and responsibilities which each of the spouses has or is likely to have in the foreseeable future; the standard of living enjoyed by the family concerned; the age of each of the spouses, the duration of their marriage and the length of time during which the spouses lived with one another; and the contributions which each of the spouses has made or is likely in the foreseeable future to make to the welfare of the family, including any contribution made by each of them to the income, earning capacity, property and financial resources of the other spouse and any contribution made by either of them by looking after the home or caring for the family.

non-exhaustive, so the failure to mention prenuptial agreements does not necessarily mean that they are excluded or unenforceable.

2. In 2006 a Study Group on Prenuptial Agreements was set up to report to the Government on the law relating to prenuptial agreements. Although the Study Group was of the opinion that prenuptial agreements were enforceable under the current law, at least in the sense that they could be taken into account by a court, in the absence of any court decision to this effect the Group recommended an amendment to the Family Law (Divorce) Act 1996[926] to expressly provide for the recognition of prenuptial agreements.[927] To date such amendment has not occurred and – as the findings of the Group are not binding, and, indeed, have been questioned – the law is still fraught with uncertainty.[928]

3. It has already been mentioned that the Family Law (Divorce) Act 1996 provides for ancillary relief on a declaration of divorce, and that proper provision must be made for both spouses and any children of either spouse.[929] In the given hypothetical scenario, however, divorce law does not provide a basis of compensation, and so it is necessary to turn to equity to provide a solution to the problem at hand. These equitable principles could apply in Ireland to unmarried cohabitants, or where spouses decide to separate without obtaining a divorce or judicial separation, or where spouses obtain a civil annulment.[930] Even though in the question it is provided that X is the sole proprietor (which we take to mean that legal ownership is vested in X alone) Irish law will recognise Y's contribution towards the property as follows. Firstly, Y has contributed part of the purchase price and under Irish law this direct contribution will require X, as the legal owner, to hold the home as a trustee in favour of both X and Y. The proportion of the contribution made will be important in determining the scope of each party's equitable interest. This principle was outlined in the case of *W* v. *W*, where Finlay P stated:

> Where a wife contributes by money to the purchase of property by her husband in his sole name in the absence of evidence of some inconsistent agreement or arrangement the court will decide that the wife is entitled to an equitable

[926] An amendment to the Family Law Act 1995 would also be necessary.

[927] *Report of the Study Group on Pre-nuptial Agreements* (April 2007), p. 71.

[928] See Coulter, 'Caution advised over prenuptial deals', *The Irish Times*, 26 November 2007.

[929] See *T* v. *T*, Unreported, Supreme Court, October 14, 2002; *LB* v. *Ireland*, Unreported, High Court, McMenamin J, 7 July 2006.

[930] H. Delaney, *Equity and the Law of Trusts in Ireland* (Dublin: Roundhall/Sweet & Maxwell, 3rd edn, 2007), p. 177.

interest in the property approximately proportionate to the extent of her contribution as against the total value of the property at the time the contribution was made.[931]

4. Applying this principle to the hypothetical given, Y would, by virtue of his contribution to the purchase of the property, have a proportionate equitable interest in the house. However, this is subject to a contrary agreement, and the prenuptial agreement entered into by X and Y might be evidence of this agreement. This would depend first, on whether the agreement is enforceable by the courts, and, second, on the proper interpretation of the agreement, and in particular on what was meant by the phrase 'separation of property', which is quite ambiguous and could, depending on the meaning attributed to it, either support or weaken Y's argument. As presumably prenuptial agreements are entered into in contemplation of the possibility of the failure of the marriage, there would be no room for any argument that it should not apply because of a change in circumstances, i.e., because of the failure of the marriage.

5. Turning to Y's second contribution to the home, namely the renovation work, in *W* v. *W* it was stated that a wife is entitled to a beneficial interest proportionate to the extent of her indirect contributions to a 'general family fund', again provided that there is no inconsistent agreement or arrangement.[932] For example, if one spouse (X) pays the mortgage on a house, and the other spouse (Y) uses their salary to pay for things such as items for the house or to pay household expenses, and by doing so releases X from the obligation to pay for these goods, this is regarded as an indirect contribution by Y to the mortgage and so, in the absence of an alternative arrangement, Y is entitled to an equitable interest in the property approximately proportionate to the contribution. However, in *W* v. *W*, it was held by the Irish High Court that improvements to property were not indirect contributions, and would not create such an equitable interest in a spouse (wife) unless it was specifically agreed that she would gain such an interest, or she was led to believe by virtue of the surrounding circumstances that she would be recompensed.[933] Any such claim would be limited to monetary

[931] [1981] ILRM 202, at 204.

[932] Contrast the view in England where no interest will arise in the *absence* of an express agreement or arrangement: *Lloyd's Bank plc* v. *Rossett* [1991] 1 AC 107.

[933] See Delaney, *Equity and the Law of Trusts in Ireland*, p. 187–9.

compensation and could not give rise to an interest in the property itself. In the majority of cases a spouse claiming compensation as a result of their contribution to improvements to property will not be able to provide evidence of such an agreement, and in the hypothetical scenario there would appear to be no such agreement. Thus, Y could not claim for the renovation work done to the family home unless this was provided for in the prenuptial agreement.

(b) England

I. As is the case in Ireland, in England the courts have a statutory jurisdiction to order a distribution of the property on the dissolution of the marriage.[934] This aside, there is an equitable jurisdiction to deal with the problem at hand, and in this regard English law will recognise Y's contribution to the family home in a similar fashion to Irish law.[935] In relation to the financial contribution Y made to the purchase of the home, a resulting trust will arise in favour of Y, who will have a beneficial interest in the home.[936] If, as in this case, there is a direct financial contribution, an intention to share the interest in the property may be presumed. However, the presumption may be rebutted and on the facts of this case the prenuptial agreement may constitute evidence of a contrary agreement which may defeat Y's claim to the property. On the other hand, if there was a common intention that Y should have a beneficial interest, this may result in Y obtaining a proportion of the interest greater than that which he contributed (i.e., greater than one fifth). The court will impute a common intention as to what their shares should be, on the basis of what is fair in the circumstances, taking into account later conduct, such as housekeeping.[937] This aside, indirect contributions such as the renovations carried out by Y are not recognised in equity,[938] at least not unless there is an express agreement to

[934] Matrimonial Causes Act 1973, as amended by the Family Law Act 1996. See also Section 72 and Schedules 5–7 of the Civil Partnership Act in relation to same sex couples.

[935] See generally J. Martin, *Hanbury and Martin's Modern Equity* (Cardaró: Thomson Sweet & Maxwell, 17th edn, 2005), pp. 271 – 299.

[936] In some cases this has been viewed as a constructive, rather than a resulting, trust: see *Lloyd's Bank plc v Rossett* [1991] 1 AC 107.

[937] Martin, *Hanbury and Martin's Modern Equity*, p. 279. See for example *Drake* v. *Whipp* [1996] 1 FLR 826; *Springette* v. *Defoe* (1992) 65 P & CR 1.

[938] See *Gissing* v. *Gissing* [1971] AC 886; *Burns* v. *Burns* [1984] Ch 317. The decisions are not entirely consistent: see for example *Cooke* v. *Head* [1972] 1 WLR 518.

that effect.[939] There is statutory provision, however, to recognise the beneficial interest in the home by a husband or wife who 'contributes in money or money's worth to the improvement' of property in which one of them has an interest.[940] This is, however, also subject to contrary agreement, be it express or implied.

II. The question which thus arises in relation to Y's position under English law is whether the prenuptial agreement entered into by X and Y can rebut the presumption that, by directly contributing to the purchase of the family home, Y is entitled to a beneficial interest in that home. In England, prenuptial agreements were once regarded as contrary to public policy, but today the court will give effect to a nuptial agreement that is freely entered into by each party with a full appreciation of its implications unless, in the circumstances prevailing, it would not be fair to hold the parties to their agreement.[941] Elements which are taken into account in deciding whether it is 'fair' to hold the parties to their agreement include the welfare and interests of any children, the need to respect the autonomy of the parties and the length of the marriage, including any changes in circumstances since the agreement was entered into. In circumstances such as these, if the agreement is interpreted as meaning that X and Y had no intention of giving Y a beneficial interest in the home, it is likely that that would be sufficient to rebut the presumption that there was such an intention. As mentioned above in relation to Irish law, the agreement would continue to apply despite the change in circumstances, i.e., because of the failure of the marriage.

Scotland

Under Scottish law, Y is not entitled to compensation.

I. 1. The facts of this case resemble a well-known Scottish case, *Shilliday* v. *Smith*.[942] In that case a cohabiting couple who were engaged to be married lived in a cottage, title to which was in the name of Mr Smith only. Mrs Shilliday contributed sums towards the upkeep of the property. Eventually, Mr Smith indicated that he did not intend to marry Mrs Shilliday. She raised an enrichment action against him

[939] See for example *Drake* v. *Whipp* [1996] 1 FLR 826; *Thomas* v. *Fuller* [1988] 1 FLR 237 (although in this case the claim failed as the necessary common intention could not be found).

[940] See Section 37 Matrimonial Proceedings and Property Act 1970.

[941] *Radmacher (formerly Granatino)* v. *Granatino* [2010] UKSC 42 at para. 74 per Lord Phillips.

[942] 1998 SC 725.

using the *condictio causa data causa non secuta* as a basis. This action is available to a party in order to recover something given for a purpose or cause which later fails.[943] Mrs Shilliday argued that she would not have expended the sums on the property had Mr Smith not promised to marry her. The purpose was therefore the marriage, which then failed, entitling her to repayment of the sums expended.

2. The facts of *Shilliday* are not entirely analogous to Case 12. Importantly, Case 12 lacks the essential aspect of *Shilliday*, namely the purpose (the promise to marry) which has failed. The parties are already married when the expenditure is made, and so Y cannot argue that the expenditure was made for the purpose of the marriage. A court is likely to conclude that the sums were expended by Y for the benefit of Y and X. They are therefore expended, at least in part, '*in suo*' (for Y's own benefit). Y's situation does not fall within the parameters of *Shilliday* and he would not be able to recover his expenditure using this case as a basis.

3. The Scottish courts would be unlikely to find that Case 12 is an example of an implied contract. The Scottish courts are less willing to use this concept as a solution compared to their English counterparts. *Shilliday* is likely to be identified as the governing authority in cases of this type. Because the parties do not fall within the parameters of that case, Y has no remedy in contract law.

4. Case 12 indicates that divorce law does not provide for a basis of compensation. The case therefore implies that family law and divorce law are not relevant to this question. Nevertheless, it may be worth noting that the financial sum which Y has contributed towards the cost of the house might be considered a relevant factor under Section 9 Family Law (Scotland) Act 1985 in determining what financial provision Y is entitled to on divorce.

Editors' comparative notes

The open jurisdictions

Y is entitled to compensation in all of the open jurisdictions except for Greece. However, the underlying rationale for this solution varies. In Austria, Lithuania, Portugal and Spain relief can be based on the rules on unjustified enrichment and in particular the doctrine of *condictio*

[943] On this action see G. D. MacCormack, 'The Condictio Causa Data Causa Non Secuta', in: R. Evans-Jones (ed.), *The Civil Law Tradition in Scotland* (Edinburgh: The Stair Society, 1995), 253.

causa data causa non secuta because the reason for the investment – the marriage – has ceased to exist. As a result of the application of the rules of unjust enrichment the amount granted may be lower than the amount invested (e.g., Italy). Some of the open jurisdictions, however, are reluctant to apply the rules of unjust enrichment because Y's contributions may be justified by his duty to contribute to the matrimonial consortium (cf. in particular Germany, Italy).

As an alternative to the rules of unfair enrichment, some reporters discuss a claim resulting from an implied contract. In Austria, for example, the courts have referred to an implied partnership agreement under similar circumstances. Under German law, the courts have derived an implied agreement from transactions between spouses and they have applied the doctrine of *Geschäftsgrundlage* to this contract in the case of divorce. In the Netherlands, the courts may derive by implication from the investment a (separate) contract between the parties overriding the initial prenuptial agreement as far as the transferred benefits are concerned. Alternatively, they might grant relief by analogy with relevant statutory provisions.

In Sweden, X and Y will be considered joint owners based on the doctrine of 'concealed title'; furthermore, specific provisions of the Law of Marriage and (unlike in Denmark) the doctrine of assumptions could apply. In Greece, relief could only be granted based on the provisions relating to donations. However, according to the Greek report, it is very unlikely under the facts of the given case that Y will succeed with his claim under these rules.

A remarkable peculiarity is mentioned in the Austrian report as Y's role in the marital breakdown may be relevant for the claim resulting from the investment. If Y is held responsible for the marital breakdown, even though it is valid in principle, his claim may be excluded on the basis of acting in bad faith.

The closed jurisdictions

In the majority of the closed jurisdictions, this case is dealt with in a similar way as in the open jurisdictions. The Belgian, Czech, Danish, French and Slovenian reports explicitly state that the reason entitling Y to compensation is the unjustified enrichment of X. In Denmark, the prenuptial agreement can also be set aside under Art. 36 Contracts Act.

The English and Irish reporter presents a very particular approach. Because of Y's contributions to the house, X holds the house as a trustee for both X and Y. Therefore, Y is entitled to compensation under equity. Under English and Irish law, the prenuptial agreement could, however, prevent equitable remedies. According to the English and Irish report, it would be impossible to disregard such an agreement due to a change of circumstances since it was entered into in contemplation of the fact that the marriage could fail. The courts might, however, conclude that there was a (subsequent) common intention that Y should have a beneficial interest. The solution in the common law jurisdictions is also largely dependent on an interpretation of the parties' behaviour and on their assumed intention.

The only closed jurisdiction in which Y is not granted any compensation is Scotland. The conditions for implying an agreement are very restrictive according to Scottish case law and they are not met in the case at hand.

Conclusion

The main issue in this case is whether one spouse's investment to the benefit of the other can be reclaimed after a divorce even if the spouses have agreed on a prenuptial agreement that is essentially aimed at excluding monetary compensation. In both groups of jurisdictions, there is a clear tendency for compensation. The claim for compensation is denied only in Greece and Scotland. In Scotland, the courts are reluctant to assume an implied contract. The Greek report states that a remedy could only be based on the rules on donation, which are unlikely to be applied by the courts in this case.

As far as the doctrinal basis of compensation is concerned, many jurisdictions (both open and closed) refer to the rules of unjustified enrichment. The marriage is considered to be the legal ground for the investment and, therefore, after the marriage failed, the benefits from the investment are no longer justified.

In some of the jurisdictions, the rules on unjust enrichment seem to be applied even in the light of the prenuptial agreement. In many jurisdictions, however, the courts are more reluctant to provide compensation as a prenuptial agreement can preclude this regime as well. As a consequence, the courts may assume an (additional) implied agreement between the spouses that is derived from the investment. Some jurisdictions apply their respective 'exceptional' doctrines on a change of circumstances to the implied agreement, arguing that the separation eliminates the justification for the transfer of the benefits which can accordingly be reclaimed.

In England and Ireland, Y's right to compensation is considered to be the result of a trust structure in which X has become a trustee of the house for both X and Y. However, the courts in these jurisdictions will also take into account the prenuptial agreement. The reporter on the English and Irish law finds it hard to predict whether the courts would give preference to the prenuptial agreement or whether equitable relief would be granted.

As a result, regardless of the different doctrines applied, the solutions depend on each jurisdiction's willingness to accept an implied agreement, (similarly) a (legally relevant) mutual assumption or a relevant change of circumstances that overrides the original regime of the prenuptial agreement. The general tendency towards relief may be attributed to the consideration that the investment is based on the reliance in the durability of the marriage and that this reliance is worthy of legal protection.

D. MUTUAL MISTAKE CONCERNING THE CALCULATION UNDERLYING THE CONTRACT

Case 13 Share deal – mutual mistake

False determination of the market value in a share deal

X holds shares of Z corporation. He agrees to sell the shares to Y at the current price as listed by the stock exchange on the day of contracting. In the written contract, the parties set a price of €10 per share. However, the actual price per share on the day of contracting is €12. The internet service, from which the parties derived the price, had displayed an incorrect number. When X discovers the correct price, he demands that the purchase price is to be increased to €12.

Can X ask for a price of €12 per share? Can he, alternatively, terminate the contract?

Germany and related jurisdictions

Germany

X is entitled to ask for a price of €12 per share or – alternatively – to terminate the contract if Y refuses to pay this price.

I. 1. If the contract itself does not only contain the price of €10 per share but also provides for the mode of calculation – i.e., the current market value – then both the mode of calculation and the price (wrongfully) fixed by the parties are part of the agreement. It is a matter of interpretation (§§133, 157 BGB) whether the resulting ambiguity in the parties' declarations can be solved. The test to be applied refers to what a reasonable promisee would have regarded as decisive taking into consideration all the circumstances of the given case: the mode of calculation or the actually stated price. In the former case, the agreement relates to the official current price, in the latter to the price (wrongfully) stated in the contract. If the two elements are to be regarded as of equal weight, the declarations remain ambiguous and are therefore void per se.[944]

2. In the given case, the contract contains an express provision how the price is to be calculated. This implies that the parties wanted the mode of calculation to be the decisive criterion.[945] As a result, the price evidenced in the contract is an irrelevant *falsa demonstratio* and the payment is determined only on the basis of the current market value. However, this would not apply if the contract at hand only states the price of €10 per share without an express provision about the mode of calculation. In this case, the interpretation of the contract is conclusive: the agreement relates to the price of €10 per share and not to the current market value.[946] It is true that the parties were aware of the fact that the price was to be calculated on the basis of the current market value. However, the mode of calculation only influenced the parties' will prior to contracting and did not become part of the contractual agreement. A different result cannot be derived from the rules of complementary interpretation of the contract on the basis of §§133, 157 BGB either. These rules are only applicable if the agreement is incomplete and if the parties failed to notice the incompleteness.

II. 1. In the given case, however, the agreement is complete and the parties are merely mistaken. However, it is now common ground – as opposed to earlier decisions[947] – that X cannot avoid the contract on the

[944] Cf. Larenz and Wolf, *Allgemeiner Teil*, §36 nn. 60 *et seq.*; D. Medicus, *Allgemeiner Teil des BGB* (Munich: Müller, 9th edn, 2006), n. 759; for another opinion cf. E. A. Kramer, '§119', in: Säcker, Rixecker *et al.* (eds.), *Münchener Kommentar zum Bürgerlichen Gesetzbuch*, vol. I/1, n. 89, who refers to a disagreement.

[945] Cf. Larenz and Wolf, *Allgemeiner Teil*, §36; n. 64; Kramer, '§119', in: Säcker, Rixecker *et al.* (eds.), *Münchenes Kommentar zuni Bürgerlichen Gesetzbuch*, n. 92; Medicus, *Allgemeiner Teil*, n. 758.

[946] Cf. Kramer, '§119', in: Säcker, Rixecker *et al.* (eds.), *Münchener Kommentar zum Bürgerlichen Gesetzbuch*, vol. I/1, n. 90.

[947] Cf. RGZ 105, 406 (*Rubelfall*); RGZ 94, 65 (67); 97, 138 (140); 101, 51 (53); 116, 15 (18) (*Börsenkursfälle*) holding that the party can avoid the contract because of an *Inhaltsirrtum*.

basis of §119 BGB.[948] §119 I BGB entitles a party to avoid the contract if it is mistaken as to the objective meaning of its declaration (*'Inhaltsirrtum'*). In the given case, however, the parties were not in error as to the meaning of their declarations (since they knew the content of their agreement was a price of €10 per share) but they were mistaken as to external facts (the market value of the shares).

2. According to some scholars, mutual mistakes as to the price fall within the scope of §119 II BGB.[949] The party who sustains disadvantages may then avoid the contract without being liable under §122 BGB for the losses the other party sustained by relying on the agreement (cf. in particular §122 II BGB). The contract may be upheld only under the terms erroneously assumed by the disadvantaged party if the other party accepts these terms immediately.[950] However, it is a well-recognised rule that *unilateral* errors as to the price do not fall within the scope of §119 II BGB because the price is not a 'quality' of the contractual subject matter, which is a prerequisite for a relevant error under §119 II BGB (*'Eigenschaftsirrtum'*). Moreover, it is a basic rule of a free market system that each party must bear the risk of making a bad bargain by fixing an unfavourable price. It cannot be inferred from §119 II BGB that this proposition ought not to apply to *mutual* mistakes.[951]

III. 1. The courts[952] and the majority of scholars[953] apply the doctrine of *Störung der Geschäftsgrundlage* so that the contract is to be adjusted under the conditions of §313 I, II BGB. The *Geschäftsgrundlage* encompasses all basic assumptions shared by both parties at the time of contracting; if the assumption is held by only one party, it must be recognisable to and not contested by the other party. The assumption may refer to present or future circumstances as far as they are relevant

[948] Cf. BGH JZ 1999, 365; Larenz and Wolf, *Allgemeiner Teil*, § 36 n. 65; Medicus, *Allgemeiner Teil*, n. 758; see also R. Singer, 'Kalkulationsirrtum – ein Fall für Treu und Glauben', (1999) JZ, 342 *et seq.*

[949] Cf. Kramer, '§119', in: Säcker, Rixecker *et al.* (eds.), *Münchener Kommentar zum Bürgerlichen Gesetzbuch*, vol. I/1, nn. 93 *et seq.*, who applies §119 II BGB by analogy to a mutual mistake of the parties that relates to assumed facts; likewise H.-M. Pawlowski, 'Kalkulationsirrtum – Fehler zwischen Motiv und Erklärung', (1997) JZ, 741 (746).

[950] For this general possibility cf. Kramer, '§119', in: Säcker, Rixecker *et al.* (eds.), *Münchener Kommentar zum Bürgerlichen Gesetzbuch*, vol. I/1, n. 142; Larenz and Wolf, *Allgemeiner Teil*, §36 n. 126; for a similar result based on different reasons cf. Flume, *Allgemeiner Teil*, vol. II, §26/4b.

[951] Cf. BGHZ 16, 54 (57); for further details with regard to §119 II BGB, cf. Case 1.

[952] BGH NJW-RR 1995, 1360; BGH NJW 1952, 137.

[953] Cf. Ellenberger, '§119', in: Palandt *et al.* (eds.), *Bürgerliches Gesetzbuch*, n. 21a; Larenz and Wolf, *Allgemeiner Teil*, §29 nn. 82 *et seq.*

to the contractual will, even though it may not be expressly provided for in the contract.[954] Thus, a common mistake as to circumstances which are decisive for the parties' will is covered by the doctrine of *Geschäftsgrundlage*.[955] X and Y intended to calculate the price on the basis of the current market value and it was decisive to determine the value of the shares. Since the actual current market value was higher at the time of the formation of the contract, the *Geschäftsgrundlage* is affected. The frustration of the *Geschäftsgrundlage* is also substantial since the discrepancy amounts to 16 per cent of the market value. Neither the contract itself nor general legal rules allocate the risk of miscalculation to only one of the parties. Thus, as a general rule, the price for the shares provided for in the contract is to be adjusted on the basis of §313 I, II BGB to the actual current market value at the time of contracting.

2. Some legal writers contest such adjustment on the ground that it violates Y's contractual autonomy to force him to pay a higher price than he had expressly consented to and that he might have been able to pay.[956] This argument is compelling but it can be accounted for as the party burdened by the adjustment – in this case Y, due to the price increase – should be allowed to refuse adjustment. Such a right is not expressly provided for in §313 III BGB. However, the adjustment must present a reasonable solution to *both* parties. If the party favoured by the original contract refuses adjustment, the party affected by the frustration of the *Geschäftsgrundlage* may only rescind the contract as a whole.

Austria

X was mistaken and may demand an appropriate adjustment of the contract which will entitle him to demand the price of €12 per share. X is not entitled to terminate the contract because, in the absence of the mistake, the parties would not have rejected the contract, but would have contracted at a different price (€12).

I. The parties made two seemingly contradictory agreements on the contract price: (orally) the current listed price of the day (€12) and (written) €10 were agreed upon. Albeit not in writing, the prevailing

[954] Cf. BGH NJW 2001, 1204 (1205). [955] Cf. BGHZ 25, 392; BGH NJW 1976, 566.

[956] Cf. K. Larenz, *Geschäftsgrundlage und Vertragserfüllung* (Munich: Beck, 3rd edn,1963), S. 173; similarly J. Esser and E. Schmidt, *Schuldrecht – Allgemeiner Teil* (Heidelberg: Müller 8th edn, 2000), I 2, §24 III 1.

agreement is the current price agreement, the second (written) agreement was only made to execute the current price agreement. Therefore, the erroneous agreement on €10 per share is completely absorbed by the agreement on the current listed price which was the only price both parties really wanted to agree on. The price owed under the contract is therefore €12 per share (oral agreement). By inserting €10 per share into the written contract, X and Y determined the price not in accordance with the real and correct contractual price stipulation (current price). Consequently X can demand the price difference of €2 per share. An adaptation of the contract is not necessary.

II. 1. Alternatively, when X and Y fixed a price of €10 thinking that this is the current price as listed by the stock exchange on the day of contracting, they were (both) mistaken with respect to the subject matter of their contract ('*Geschäftsirrtum*' of §871 ABGB).[957] According to §871 ABGB, the mistaken party can invoke such a mistake if one of three alternative requirements is fulfilled: (i) the mistake was caused by the other party, (ii) the mistake was evident for the other party due the circumstances, or (iii) the mistake was discovered in due time ('*rechtzeitig aufgeklärt*').[958] In our case the mistake was neither caused by Y nor must it have been evident to him. Probably the mistake was discovered in due time, but the facts do not clearly show that this was the case.

2. If we qualify Y's mistake as a mistake caused by a third person, §875 ABGB provides that no avoidance of the contract will be possible unless the other party took part in the third person's causation of the mistake or must have evidently been aware of it.[959] Therefore, the argument of a third person's causation of the mistake provides no basis for the avoidance or adaptation of the contract.

3. In addition, the Austrian OGH and older scholars grant a right to invoke the mistake also in cases of a mutual mistake if none of the three above-mentioned requirements is met.[960] This is justified by the

[957] Rummel, '§871', in: Rummel (ed.), *Kommentar zum ABGB*, vol. I, n. 11; Apathy, '§871', in: Schwimann (ed.), *Kommentar zum ABGB*, vol. IV, n. 11.

[958] Koziol and Welser, *Bürgerliches Recht*, vol. I, pp. 156 *et seq.*; Apathy, '§871', in: Schwimann (ed.), *Kommentar zum ABGB*, vol. IV, nn. 19 *et seq.*

[959] Gschnitzer, '§875', in: Klang (ed.), *Kommentar zum ABGB*, vol. IV/1, p. 152; Reichel, 'Checkliste bürgerliches Recht (Teil II) sonstige zentrale Privatrechte', (1997/98) *Juristische Ausbildung und Praxisvorbereitung*, 223 at 223.

[960] Koziol and Welser, *Bürgerliches Recht*, vol. I, p. 158; Rummel, '§871', in: Rummel (ed.), *Kommentar zum ABGB*, vol. I, n. 18; Apathy, '§871', in: Schwimann (ed.), *Kommentar zum ABGB*, vol. IV, n. 28; Gschnitzer, in: Klang (ed.), *Kommentar zum ABGB*, vol. IV, p. 133; OGH, JBl 1976, 646; OGH, JBl 1974, 144; OGH, 8 Ob 122/66; OGH, KRES 7/31.

argument that in cases of mutual mistake one party's reliance on the validity of a declaration of intention of the other side is not worthy of protection (because party one shared the mistake).[961] According to this view, which is heavily criticised by a number of contemporary authors,[962] a mutual mistake entitles both parties to demand avoidance or adjustment of the contract.[963]

4. The arguments advanced against this view are the following: the fact that party one was mistaken as well does not make his interest in upholding the contract less legitimate.[964] Mutual mistakes are not consistent with the underlying rationale of the other three requirements (where the other party is closer to the mistake or is not burdened by its invocation).[965] According to this opinion opposing the jurisdiction of the Oberster Gerichtshof, mutual mistakes do not provide any basis for avoidance or adjustment of the contract.

5. The key question is whether the other (also mistaken) party Y has a legitimate interest in relying on the contract as concluded. Y will want to preserve the contract concluded under a mutual mistake if he is the one who accidentally profits from the mistake. His windfall gain does not seem legitimate as such. However, assuming that Y may have made dispositions in reliance on the content of the contract as concluded in the first place and might consequently have suffered additional damages in case of avoidance or adaptation of the contract, his interest in sticking to the contract appears in a different light and may well seem justified. It is therefore rather difficult to strike a balance between the interests of the parties X and Y in cases of mutual mistakes. In our case, Y declared that he would accept the current market price of the day. He would have received a windfall gain from the mutual mistake, and he probably would not have made any special dispositions in reliance on the erroneous price determination to make his claim more legitimate.

961 Gschnitzer, in: Klang (ed.), *Kommentar zum ABGB*, vol. IV, p. 134; P. Rummel, 'Anmerkungen zum gemeinsamen Irrtum und zur Geschäftsgrundlage', (1981) *Juristische Blätter*, 1 at 2.

962 *Ibid.*, 1 at 2; Raphael Thunhart, 'Die Beachtlichkeit des Irrtums als Interessenabwägung – § 871 ABGB', (2000) *Österreichische Juristen-Zeitung*, 447 at 449; Ferdinand Kerschner, 'Anm zu OGH 19.1.1982, 4 Ob 1/82', (1983) *Das Recht der Arbeit*, 365 at 370; Apathy, '§871', in: Schwimann (ed.), *Kommentar zum ABGB*, vol. IV, n. 28.

963 OGH, KRES 7/31; Gschnitzer, in: Klang (ed.), *Kommentar zum ABGB*, vol. IV, p. 141.

964 Koziol and Welser, *Bürgerliches Recht*, vol. I, p. 158; Rummel, '§871', in: Rummel (ed.), *Kommentar zum ABGB*, vol. I, n. 18.

965 OGH, KRES 7/31; Rummel '§871', in: Rummel (ed.), *Kommentar zum ABGB*, vol. I, n. 18; Kerschner, 'Anm zu OGH 19.1.1982, 4 Ob 1/82', 365 at 370.

Recognising mutual mistakes in accordance with the Austrian OGH therefore seems a fair solution in this case.

6. Mistakes can be categorised into fundamental and non-fundamental mistakes, depending on whether the parties would not have concluded the contract without the mistake or whether they would have concluded it with a different content.[966] X's and Y's mistake is non-fundamental: in the absence of the mistake the parties would have concluded the contract at a price of €12 per share. Therefore, X can demand adjustment of the price, but has no possibility of avoiding the entire contract[967] (provided that we do not follow the opposing opinion of the literature which would deny X any remedy). Therefore, the contract will be adapted.

III. Under Austrian law, this is not a case of '*Wegfall/Fehlen der Geschäftsgrundlage*'. The parties made a mistake in determining the current price at the stock exchange. This current price is not a mere 'circumstance' (on which the intention of the parties to conclude the contract is based), but an essential part of the contractual exchange itself. The price agreement is a part of the contract, and a mistake with respect to it is considered a '*Geschäftsirrtum*' (§871 ABGB) and not a mistake about unforeseeable future events, ('*Motivirrtum*', §901 ABGB). The rule of §871 ABGB (subject matter mistake) excludes the doctrine of '*Wegfall der Geschäftsgrundlage*', which is only a subsidiary instrument.

IV. Under Austrian law, the same solution, namely X's claim for an additional €2 per share, is reached according to two different lines of reasoning.

(i) An *interpretation* of the stipulation of the current listed price of the day of contracting (namely €12) leads to the conclusion that this is the predominant or only price agreement of the contract. The subsequent erroneous determination of the price of €10 per share does not change the actual price owed under the agreement, which is the price of €12 per share.

(ii) According to the doctrine of *mistake*, the court has to strike a balance between the interests of the two parties by using the concept of 'mutual mistake'. In our case Y clearly declared that he would accept the current market price of the day. As he would receive a windfall gain

[966] Koziol and Welser, *Bürgerliches Recht*, vol. I, pp. 137 *et seq.*; Apathy, '§871', in: Schwimann (ed.), *Kommentar zum ABGB*, vol. IV, n. 16.

[967] Koziol and Welser, *Bürgerliches Recht*, vol. I, p. 159; Rummel, '§872', in: Rummel (ed.), *Kommentar zum ABGB*, vol. I, nn. 1, 7; Apathy, '§871', in: Schwimann (ed.), *Kommentar zum ABGB*, vol. IV, n. 16; Gschnitzer, in: Klang (ed.), *Kommentar zum ABGB*, vol. IV, p. 141.

from the mutual mistake and probably has not made any special dispositions in reliance on the erroneous price, he has no legitimate interest in upholding the written agreement. The Austrian OGH's acceptance of mutual mistakes, therefore, seems a fair solution for the case. The contract has to be adapted on the basis of the doctrine of mistake (§§871, 872 ABGB).

The Netherlands

Under Dutch law, X will be entitled to ask for a price of €12 per share; alternatively the agreement might be terminated.

I. 1. Under Dutch law, what is agreed between the parties is determinative for what applies amongst them. It is irrelevant whether or not their agreement is stipulated in writing (albeit a written form may obviously constitute more convincing evidence). Agreements and their contents are established by means of offer and acceptance (Art. 6:217 Dutch Civil Code). The precise scope of the offer and the acceptance must be interpreted on the basis of their declaration taking into account the context and all the circumstances on the recipient's side (Arts. 3:33 and 35 Dutch Civil Code). In the current case, it is clear that the parties agreed on the listing price.

2. The case suggests that the written form was created after the parties had reached an agreement. Therefore, the fact that the parties erroneously stipulated their agreement in writing (i.e., based on a false representation of the actual share price on the website) is as such no longer relevant. Although the written contract is strong evidence, if X can prove that the stock exchange listing was the reference agreed upon, the latter will prevail over the written form. The case itself suggests that such evidence is not difficult to adduce (i.e., the case concedes that the website displayed an incorrect number). Even if the written contract contains an 'entire agreement clause' (i.e., a miscellaneous provision which declares all preceding understandings invalid and unenforceable), under Dutch case law it is questionable whether the written number will prevail.[968] The agreement is therefore enforceable on the basis of a purchase price of €12.

II. Under Dutch law, it is doubtful whether the contract can be cancelled. Pursuant to the above line of reasoning, the legal concept of

[968] There is recent case law on entire agreement clauses, which does not confirm such clause's apparent scope: HR 19 January 2007, NJ 2007, 575.

'mistake' (Art. 6:228) does not apply since, strictly speaking, there was no mistake at the moment of entering into the agreement. The agreement was not entered into at the moment of the acceptance or execution of the written form, but before this when Y's acceptance was received by X (compare Arts. 6:217, 6:224 and 3:37 Section 3). This is only different if that latter moment coincided with the price establishment by the parties on the basis of the website. In such a case, the written reference to the incorrect amount (i.e., €10) could establish a (mutual or unilateral) mistake. Such a mistake would be the legal ground on which X or Y could cancel the contract. As regards mistake (either unilateral or mutual), according to Art. 6:228(1)(a) an agreement that would not have been entered into but for a true representation of the facts may be declared void in several cases. In the current case, this would be possible if Y had acted upon the same error as X, unless Y must not have understood that even in case of an accurate representation of facts, X would not have entered into the agreement. In other words, if Y ought to have understood that X would not enter into the agreement if the listing price were €10, X may declare the agreement null and void.[969]

III. Y might argue that the establishment of the amount of €10 qualifies as a settlement agreement. A settlement agreement is a 'special contract' (governed by Title 7.15 Dutch Civil Code) entered into for the purpose of ending an uncertainty, or settling an as yet uncertain fact. The settlement remains effective even if the previously existing legal context ultimately appears to differ from what was settled (Art. 7:900 Dutch Civil Code). In other words, even if the parties had agreed that the actual listing price would apply rather than the amount of €10, a settlement agreement would prevail because it would settle an uncertainty. (The uncertainty would be the listing price, which was as such unknown.) On the other hand, X may well argue that even if the written establishment of the sales agreement applied, both parties anyhow assumed that the website accurately reflected the price of the shares in Z-company. This cannot be rectified by reference to their agreement being a settlement agreement and is then nevertheless a mistake.

[969] Art. 6:228 furthermore requires that declaring a contract or provision 'null and void' cannot be based on a mistake that relates entirely to a future circumstance (i.e., for which Art. 6:258 on changed circumstances applies), or that should remain at the risk and for the account of the mistaken party by virtue of the nature of the agreement, the generally prevailing opinion ('*verkeersopvattingen*') or the particular circumstances of the case. None of these would apply here.

Eastern European jurisdictions

Slovenia

X is entitled to ask for €12 per share or to demand termination of the contract. By offering €12 Y can save the contract.

I. The parties orally agreed that the shares would be sold at the current price as listed by the stock-exchange, which is €12. The principle of informality is established under Slovenian law (Art. 18 CO),[970] and, therefore, the oral agreement, stipulating the essential elements of a sales contract (the object of the sale and the criterion for establishing the contract price) makes a perfect contract (Art. 15 CO).[971] The function of the written agreement is only to confirm the previous oral agreement. In this case it is obvious that the setting of the price to €10 is based on false information about the current price and is not meant to be a change to the former oral contract. Accordingly, the real contract price is €12 and not €10 as erroneously stated in the written contract. Consequently, X is entitled to ask €12 under the contract.

II. 1. If the court does not take the view that the contract can be interpreted in the way that the actual agreed share price is €12, X might rely on the rules on mistake instead. The Slovenian CO does not have any specific provisions regarding mutual mistake. Still, the general rules are, in principle, applicable. In the present case the mistake relates to the value of the shares, which can be considered as a decisive element of a contract of sale. If the parties were correctly informed of the price, they would have concluded the contract with a different content (€12 per share).

2. A mistake in the value of the object of sale is generally considered as a mistake regarding the motive and in accordance with Art. 40(1) CO such mistakes do not affect the validity of a contract. This would preclude an action on grounds of mistake. But in some cases, it is difficult to distinguish between a genuine mistake in motive and a mistake as to the basis of the contract (*causa*, *Geschäftsgrundlage*). A mistake as to the *causa* is relevant and allows an action on grounds of mistake. Generally it can be assumed that a motive concerns only one of the parties and that the other party usually does not know it. In contrast, the *causa* is a 'motive' that is necessarily known to the other party. The other party is also

[970] Kranjc in: Juhart and Plavšak (eds.), *Obligacijski zakonik*, vol. I, pp. 218–19.
[971] *Ibid*. Kranjc in: Juhart and Plavšak (eds.), *Obligacijski zakonik*, vol. I, p. 207.

aware of the fact that the *causa* is an essential element of the contract.[972] In the present case the parties have agreed for the current price listed on the stock exchange, and this price has been incorrectly published on the internet. Therefore the correct current price was an essential element, the *causa* of the contract. This means, that an action on grounds of mistake can be justified. X can demand annulment of the contract on the basis of Art. 46(1), (2) CO. Y, who was mistaken as well, can reverse the annulment of the contract by offering to pay the price the parties would have agreed upon if there had been no mistake (Art. 46(4) CO), i.e., €12 per share.

III. The rules regarding change of circumstances are not applicable, since there are no circumstances that have changed and make the performance of one of the parties more difficult.

Lithuania

X is entitled to demand €12 per share because it was a mutual intention of both parties to set this price.

I. The parties have agreed on the price that would be quoted on the stock exchange. According to Art. 6.193 CC, in interpreting a contract, it is necessary to seek the real intentions of the parties without being limited by the literal meaning of the words. Both parties intended that the shares should be sold at the market price, which is usually displayed correctly on the stock exchange list. The agreement on the basis of an incorrectly displayed price constitutes a mutual mistake. As the intentions of both parties coincide in this case, the contract is to be interpreted on the assumption that the contract price conforms to the market price. Thus, the real intention of the parties was to fix the price at €12 per share. Article 1.90(7) CC provides that the mistaken party cannot claim annulment of a contract if his rights and interests may be adequately protected by invoking other remedies; hence the claim for the difference in price will be the primary remedy.

Czech Republic

X has the right to claim the price of €12 per share.

I. Under Section 35(2) Civil Code, juridical acts expressed in words must be interpreted not only according to their verbal expression, but

[972] Cigoj, *Komentar obligacijskih razmerij*, p. 252; Dolenc in: Juhart and Plavšak (eds.), *Obligacijski zakonik*, vol. I, pp. 343–4.

in particular according to the will of the person who made the act, unless this contradicts the verbal expression. In the given case, it may be concluded that the will of both parties was directed at selling the shares at their market price at the time of the execution of the purchase agreement. The joint will was directed at the actual, correct price in the amount of €12 per share, and not €10, which was an incorrect figure due to an error made by an electronic device. In the light of Section 37(3) Civil Code, juridical acts are not invalid due to typing or calculation errors, provided that their meaning is beyond doubt. So, the agreement may be interpreted so that the purchase price per share amounts to €12, but it cannot be cancelled unilaterally.

II. No case like this has been analysed in the literature nor provided for in Czech statutory and case law.

III. It will be problematical to enforce the rights of X using the doctrine of mistake, because the Czech conception of it does not recognise 'mutual mistake'.[973]

Scandinavian jurisdictions

Sweden

Y cannot terminate or modify the contract as the parties have most likely agreed on a price of €12, and this price prevails under Swedish law.

I. This is not a case concerning changed circumstances, but an example of mistake at the formation of a contract. It first calls for an interpretation of the contract. It is explicitly stated that the shares are sold 'at the current price as listed by the stock exchange on the day of contracting'. This agreement is probably oral, but an oral agreement is binding. Such an agreement is often difficult to prove in a Swedish court, as the standards of proof are high, but that does not seem to be a problem here. Under such circumstances, it normally does not matter that something different has been included in the written contract. The document is not the contract, merely a mutual confirmation, and X can ask for a price of €12 per share pursuant to the contract.

It is also possible, however, that when the contract was signed at the price of €10, the parties concluded a new contract, modifying the

[973] See Case 4(d).

content of their agreement.[974] Nevertheless, there is no reason to assume this was the case here. The parties did not intend to amend the agreement, but only to confirm and give effect to its original content. Therefore, the written contract is not a new agreement, and the agreed price is still €12.[975]

II. 1. The next question is whether the purchaser Y has a claim for relief on the basis of the common mistake. Y might claim that he made a mistake as to the content of the contract. In the event of such a mistake, the contract is invalid under Section 32(1) Contracts Act if the other party knew or ought to have known about the mistake. In this case, nothing indicates that X had such actual or constructive knowledge. Therefore, the contract will stand under this rule.

2. If this is true, Y still has entered into the contract under an erroneous assumption. He actually thought the market price was €10, not €12, per share and apparently had good reason to believe so. However, at the time the written contract was concluded, the market price was already contracted for; consequently the erroneous information in the written contract probably did not affect Y's motives for entering into the contract; nor did the subsequent erroneous information as such constitute a relevant change of the circumstances after the contract was concluded.[976] However, it is uncertain when exactly the parties received the erroneous information; thus there is a possibility that Y actually concluded the first oral contract under the erroneous assumption that the current market price was €10.

III. 1. The contracted price of €12 would probably not be considered unreasonable under Section 36 Contracts Act, as it equals the market price, but the doctrine of assumptions may apply as Y made a mistake as to what was the set price. Nonetheless, here the requirement of good faith on the side of the party claiming relief on the basis of an erroneous

[974] If this was the case, the first agreement on the current market price might be perceived as an aim the parties wanted to realise with their contract. Such an aim is considered at the interpretation of the contract, and can even be decisive for it, although in this case this appears unlikely as the written contract clearly deviates from the first agreement.

[975] A third possibility, disregarded here, is that both the term 'current price' and '€10' actually constitute part of the contract; this would call for a more advanced interpretation to settle the difference between the conflicting price clauses.

[976] Still, there is a slight possibility that it would, provided that Y took action on the basis of the information and that his actions resulted in more intervening consequences, severe enough to render the contract price unreasonable under Section 36. However, this possibility is disregarded here as nothing in the case outline indicates that such was the case in this instance.

assumption must be considered. A party is not entitled to invoke the assumption if he knew, or ought to have known, that it was erroneous – or that there was a considerable risk that it was. This involves 'conscious risk-taking' ('*medvetet risktagande*'), where the claimant knowingly carries the risk of the assumption proving to be erroneous. In this case, Y might have believed that the current market price actually was €10, but still did not contract for €10, only for 'the current price as listed by the stock exchange on the day of contracting'. When entering into such an agreement, a party typically knowingly assumes the risk that the market price might change to his disadvantage. There is no reason to believe this was not the aim of this clause in this contract. Therefore, it must be concluded that the doctrine of assumptions cannot be applied.

2. Still, the possibility that there was no conscious risk-taking cannot be entirely ruled out. The parties might have agreed on the current market price while they thought they knew the market price was €10. If that was the case, it is very likely that interpretation would hold that the agreed price was actually €10. However, the opposite conclusion cannot be entirely excluded. Notwithstanding the conclusion just reached, it should therefore also be mentioned that there is a tendency in Swedish law to render an erroneous assumption relevant when it has been of immediate relevance to the contents of the contract. For this situation, case law is illustrative.

3. In NJA 1947 p. 150 a seller, who had sold all the shares of a corporation owning real estate, had overlooked some payments that had been made on the corporation's debts. As the parties had based the calculation of the price on the figures provided by the seller, the price consequently became too low. The price was adjusted by the Supreme Court, which argued that the price was in fact settled in the contract to be the equivalent of the difference between the assets and the debts of the corporation. However, it is doubtful if this was really the truth. It would seem more realistic to apply the doctrine of assumptions on the basis that the defendant, as a result of the fact that the assumption was erroneous, made a profit at the expense of the claimant. On the other hand, the price cannot be increased under the doctrine of assumptions, as it only leads to avoidance and not to increasing a party's liability under a contract. However, in academic commentaries it has been argued that the doctrine of assumptions applies in some situations closely related to contract interpretation, where a party would, had it considered or investigated what could come to pass, have assumed a condition for the contract, and the other party should not reasonably

have had any objections to this.[977] It is possible that in such exceptional cases, the liability can be increased under the doctrine of assumptions.

IV. Should the interpretation of the contract instead result in the conclusion that the written contract is to be adapted, i.e., that the agreed price is €10 and not the current price as listed by the stock exchange on the day of contracting, a similar problem can occur for X. However, X's mistake would then not concern his motives for entering into the contract, but the content of the contract. In the event of such a mistake, the contract is invalid under Section 32(1) Contracts Act if the other party knew or ought to have known about the mistake. In this case, nothing indicates that the purchaser Y had such actual or constructive knowledge. Therefore, the contract will stand.

Had X instead agreed to sell the shares at a price of €10, based on the erroneous assumption that this was the market price, the situation would have resembled that in case NJA 1947 p. 150. X's assumption would then most likely have been legally relevant on the basis of the profit Y gained at X's expense. However, as stated above, the doctrine of assumptions does not normally provide for an increase in price, so termination may have been X's only option. On the other hand, this may have qualified as such an exceptional case where a liability may be increased under the doctrine of assumptions (see above).

Denmark

X is entitled to ask for a price of €12 per share because the parties have concluded a binding contract, under which the reference to the stock exchange prices will prevail.

I. 1. There is no Danish case law similar to the case at hand. The rules of interpretation as developed in Danish case law do not provide much assistance, even though a substantial number of principles can be derived in Danish law dealing with conflicting provisions in a contract.[978]

2. X has agreed to sell his shares to Y pursuant to the price on the stock exchange on the day of contracting. In my opinion, this is a clear and unambiguous provision in the contract. X and Y received incorrect information about the actual price, which was incorporated in the

[977] See H. Guldberg, 'Om bristande förutsättningar vid avtal', (1953) *Svensk Juristtidning*, 1 *et seq*. 9. See also, Hj. Karlgren, *Avtalsrättsliga spörsmål* (Stockholm: Norstedts, 2nd edn, 1954), p. 81 and Hj. Karlgren, *Kutym och rättsregel* (Stockholm: Norstedts, 1960), pp. 62 *et seq*. (n. 4).

[978] Cf. Lennart Lynge Andersen and Palle Bo Madsen, *Aftaler og mellemmænd*, (Copenhagen, Thomson, 5th edn, 2006), pp. 411 *et seq*.

contract. Which provision in the contract should prevail? In my view, the original basis for price-setting should prevail by which X is entitled to receive a price of €12 per share.

II. 1. Assuming that the court declines this interpretation of the contract, X might refer to Section 32(1) Contracts Act, which deals with the issue of mistake. In Danish law a mistake is considered a weak ground for nullity, which implies that the contract is binding upon the parties if the promisee to the contract acts in good faith. If a party claims damages in conjunction with a mistake, it is only possible to claim damages equal to the negative contractual interest.

2. Considering the case in question, there is some doubt as to whether it falls within the scope of Section 32(1) Contracts Act, since it deals with the question of mutual mistake and not a mistake made by the promisor. Even though the case is not within the scope of Section 32(1) Contracts Act, it would be possible to use the provision by analogy. Apparently, there is no doubt that Y as the promisee has acted in good faith. If X announces the mistake to Y as soon as it is discovered, Section 32(1) Contracts Act is likely to be invoked, depending on whether it was possible for X to provide the necessary information.

Romanic–Mediterranean jurisdictions

Italy

X can ask for a price of €12 per share.

I. 1. First, the rules on the interpretation of contracts (Arts. 1362 *et seq.* CC) state, as a basic general rule, that one must seek to ascertain the parties' mutual intention, without limiting the construction to the strict meaning of the wording used by the parties. The apparent ambiguity in the parties' declarations could therefore be solved by means of interpretation, so that the agreed mode of calculation should prevail over the formally fixed price.

2. The fact that the contract does not make an express provision as to how the price is to be calculated implies that the parties did not want the mode of calculation to be the decisive criterion. Otherwise, if the price were evidenced in the contract the payment would be determined only on the basis of the current market value. The contract between X and Y has only stated the price of €10 per share without making express provision for the mode of calculation. In this case the interpretation of the contract cannot lead to the modification of the indicated price: the agreement relates to the price of €10 per share and not to the current market value;

this discrepancy is, in fact, perfectly legitimate since it rests on the principle of contractual freedom. Even if the parties negotiated that the price was to be calculated on the basis of the current market value, a court would say that the mode of calculation only influenced the parties' intention prior to contracting and did not become part of the agreement.

II. 1. Under Italian law the case at issue would at first glance be treated under the doctrine of mutual or bilateral mistake (although the Civil Code does not contain ad hoc rules). In general terms, the mistaken party may claim invalidity only if the mistake is (i) fundamental (i.e., it must fall on the object and/or the parties of the contract) (Art. 1429 CC) and (ii) recognisable to the other party (Art. 1431 CC). The doctrine of mutual mistake allows the plaintiff to supersede the second requirement, since it is implied in the concept of bilateral mistake. In the selected case, since the contract does not provide for the mode of calculation (the current market value) of the price of the sold shares, the mistake in wrongfully fixing the contractual amount for the shares to €10 is not clear enough, because there is no proof that it is mutual and recognisable.

2. However, Art. 1430 CC provides that a 'calculation mistake' ('*errore di calcolo*') does not lead to an annulment of the contract, since it can be rectified, provided that it does not relate to the quantity as the determining reason of the agreement (but this does not seem to be the case). In other words, under Italian law the mistake in calculation prevents a party from claiming invalidity in so far as the rectified contract objectively expresses the common intention of the parties. If X shows that the agreed price was the current price as listed by the stock exchange on the day of contracting, the incorrect number displayed by the internet service could be treated as a mistake in the calculation pursuant to Art. 1430 CC. X could ask, in this case, for the price of €12 per share.

III. Instead, the doctrine of *presupposizione* could be applicable because both parties agreed that the price of the shares should be the one listed by the stock exchange on the day of contracting. Even if the mode of calculation is not part of the agreement, it may be considered an implied assumption in their intention.

Spain

The contract price is €12 per share but X can avoid the contract if the mistake was essential for the formation of consent (Art. 1266 CC).

I. An interpretation of the contract probably leads to the result that the parties have concluded the contract at a price of €12 instead of €10 per share. After all, they agreed that the current price as listed by the stock exchange should be decisive. That the written agreement of €10 was influenced by the wrong display is irrelevant and the true price of €12 applies.

II. 1. Under Spanish law, if X claims the higher price, Y can refuse payment and claim an annulment of the contract based on the doctrine of mistaken consent (Art. 1301 CC). The provisions supporting Y's claim are Art. 1261 CC, according to which the requirements for a valid contract are *causa*, object and consent, and Art. 1265 CC providing that consent is null and void when it is given by mistake, violence, deterrence or dolus. Furthermore, he can rely on Art. 1266(1), which states that a mistake invalidates consent when it refers to the substance of the contract ('*error in substancia*'). According to Diez Picazo,[979] the substance relates to all those qualities of the goods (shares) which lead the party to enter into the contract (subjective criterion).[980]

2. In order to succeed, Y must provide evidence that the price was an essential element of the contract. He has to prove that if he had known the true price, he would not have entered into the contract or would have concluded the contract on different terms ('*error propio*').[981] Furthermore, he must show that the mistake regarding the price does not derive from his negligent behaviour.[982]

3. The contract cannot be modified on the ground of mistake, as the legal consequence is the avoidance of the contract (Arts. 1300 *et seq*. CC).[983]

Portugal

X can terminate the agreement unless Y is willing to pay €12 per share.

I. 1. With regard to mistakes, the Portuguese Civil Code distinguishes between '*erro na declaração*' and '*erro-vício*'. An '*erro na declaração*', a mistake in declaration, is present in cases of an unintentional divergence between the will and the declaration.[984] In the words of Mota Pinto, 'the

[979] Diez Picazo, *Fundamentos del Derecho*, p. 57.
[980] STS of 25 November 1932 and 8 June 1968.
[981] See for instance STS of 19 February 1996 (RJ 1605) or STS of 27 May 1983 (RJ 2914).
[982] See for instance STS of 17 July 2000 (RJ 6803).
[983] This remedy could, however, be applied according to the Principles of European Contract Law, see Art. 4:105: Adaptation of Contract.
[984] James Gordley, *Foundations of Private Law* (Oxford University Press, 2006), pp. 310–12.

offeror makes the declaration which diverges from the real intent *without being aware* of this lack of coincidence'.[985] With regard to mistake in declaration, Art. 247 CC determines that a declaration is voidable if, due to an error, the declared intention does not correspond to the author's real intention and the addressee knew or should not have ignored the importance of the erroneous point for the offeror. Rendering a contract void is thus admitted or allowed on fairly broad terms. The mistake is not required to be excusable, known to the other party or able to be perceived by him/her.[986]

2. In the case at hand, we are convinced that a Portuguese Court would apply Art. 247 CC, since we are dealing with a mistake in declaration. Such a mistake renders the agreement voidable, as long as the other party knew or should have known the importance of the erroneous point. Here, the error related to the price, which should always be considered an essential element of a sale. The other party cannot be ignorant as far as this is concerned. Annulment can, however, be avoided if the addressee accepts the agreement as the author intended (Art. 248 CC). It would suffice for the other party to declare that he is prepared to accept the contract at the real stock market price for the agreement to stand.

Greece

X is entitled to either ask for the payment of a price of €12 per share; alternatively, he may terminate the contract.

I. If the parties have agreed primarily on the pricing procedure, and, only indirectly, on the finally declared price, this is a case of a mutual error as to the declaration ('*falsa demonstratio non nocet*'). Then the declared price - i.e., €10 - should be substituted *ipso iure* by the price, which would have been stipulated if the procedure had been applied correctly. In this case that is the price of €12.[987]

[985] C. Mota Pinto, A. Pinto Monteiro and P. Mota Pinto, *Teoria Geral*, p. 459. See also M.E Hörster, *A Parte Geral* (Coimbra: Almedina, 1992), p. 561; Manuel de Andrade, *Teoria Geral da Relação Jurídica*, vol. II, *Facto Jurídico, em especial Negócio Jurídico* (Coimbra: Almedina, 7th reprint 1992), pp. 220–1, n. 3; José de Oliveira Ascensão, *Direito Civil, Teoria Geral*, Vol. II, *Acções e factos Jurídicos* (Coimbra Editora, 1999), p. 183. See, in English, João António Pinto Monteiro, 'Portuguese Case Note – House of Lords, 19 November 2003, *Shogun Finance Limited* v. *Hudson*', (2005) 13 *European Review of Private Law*, 545 *et seq*.

[986] See Hörster, *A Parte Geral*, p. 563, and principally P. Mota Pinto's critique on the solution admitted by this rule: *Teoria Geral*, pp. 493–4.

[987] See Paul Oertmann, 'Bilateral error during the conclusion of a contract', AcP 117, 289–91; Heinrich Titze, 'About the so-called error in motivation', in: Justus Wilhelm

II. If the parties, however, contracted relying – as must usually be assumed – on the final price, and not on the procedure, according to which the price has been determined, this is a case of a mutual error in the motivation. The Civil Code does not address this problem. According to the judiciary[988] and a part of legal literature,[989] this lacuna has to be dealt with by applying the provisions on mistake by analogy (Arts. 140 *et seq.* AK). The party who suffers loss due to the mistake has the right to annul the contract. This right is normally accompanied by an obligation to compensate the other party, whose reliance on the validity of the first party's declaration will have been frustrated by annulment (see Art. 145 AK). In the case of a common error, however, none of the parties has the obligation to compensate the other, regardless of who takes the initiative to annul (pursuant to the prevailing opinion in legal literature).[990]

III. According to another and more expedient approach, the problem should be dealt with by the application of the principles of the underlying basis of the contract or even by analogy with Art. 388 AK. This provision can only be applied by analogy as there has been no subsequent 'change of circumstances'.[991] Perhaps it is even more correct to apply Art. 288 AK[992] as it can be applied directly and, therefore, there is no need for an analogy with Art. 388 AK. The benefits of the latter approach are the following: (i) it does not distinguish between an initial and a subsequent disproportion of the obligations;[993] (ii) in contrast to annulment, it allows for adjustment to the contract and can thereby

Hedemann (ed.), *Festschrift für E. Heymann* (Weimar: Böhlau, 1940), vol. II, p. 87; Flume, *Allgemeines Teil*, pp. 501–2.

988 See AP (plenary session) 35/1998, HellD 39, p. 1268 = NoV 1999, p. 251, 251; AP 526/1997, HellD 27, p. 1357; 5/1990, HellD 1990, p. 551, 551 I = NoV 1990, p. 1318, 1319.

989 See Balis, *Law of Obligations General Part*, p. 140; Litzeropoulos, *Elements*, vol. II, p. 301 f.; Stathopoulos, *Law of Obligations*, §22 n. 21–23.

990 S. AP (plenary session) 35/1998, NoB 47, p. 251, 251/2 = HellD 39, p. 1268, 1268 I/II; AP (plenary session) 5/1990, HellD 31, p. 551, 551 I = NoB 38, p. 1318, 1319; AP 526/1997, HellD 37, 1357. Contra Flume, *Algemeines Teil*, pp. 488 *et seq.*

991 See George Simonetos, *The disturbance of the obligation* (Athens: Petrou Dimitrakou, 1939), p. 52; A. Gazis, *Enueneia tou Astikar Kodikos* (Commentary to the Greek civil code), Arts. 335–348 Introd. Notes n. 32; Karakatsanis 'Art. 143', in: Georgiadis and Stathopoulos, *AK*, n. 8.

992 See Ap. Georgiadis, *General Principles*, §43 nn. 10, 13, 20; Papanikolaou, 'The Measure of Onerousity of the Performance', 942–3.

993 See Zepos, 'Frustration of contract', (1948) 11 *The Modern Law Review* 43 *et seq.*; Simonetos, *The Disturbance*, p. 52; Karakatsanis, in: Georgiadis and Stathopoulos, *AK*, Art. 143 n. 8.

address the parties' interests more adequately;[994] and, finally, (iii) it excludes, without any doctrinal problems, the possibility of compensation.[995] In this context, X is entitled to demand either the payment of an adjusted price of €12 per share, or the common release of the parties from the contract.[996]

France and related jurisdictions

France

The contract price is €12 per share but Y may be entitled to terminate the contract due to mistake under French law.

I. The contractual agreement cannot be interpreted so that X is entitled to demand the market price, i.e., €12 per share.

II. A common mistake can lead to the cancellation of the contract if the mistake relates to a substantial characteristic of the contract. This is a mistake as to a material fact at the time of concluding the contract. A mistake as to the price is not recognised,[997] but in this case one can argue that the mistake relates to a material fact on which the contract was based – displaying the current price by the internet service. Such a mistake is relevant unless the mistaken person was at fault ('*erreur inexcusable*'). But such a fault is not present according to the facts of the case. The incorrect information was due to an error by the provider of the internet service.[998]

Belgium

The contract price is €12 per share. X may be entitled to terminate the contract due to mistake under Belgian law.

[994] See Papanikolaou, 'The Measure of Onerousity of the Performance', 942–3.

[995] See *ibid.*, 943, n. 20.

[996] If Y refuses to perform his obligation, X can resort to the court and ask for the judicial recognition of the modified contract or, exceptionally, for termination. In the above case, where Art. 288 AK is applicable, judicial intervention will only have an affirmative character, but not a constitutive one as under Art. 388 AK. See Stathopoulos, in: Georgiadis and Stathopoulos (eds.), *AK*, Art. 288 n. 21. See also above in the Overview (Chapter 4).

[997] J. Ghestin, *La notion d'erreur*, p. 23.

[998] We can refer to the recent decision of the Cour de Cassation of 4 July 2007. The price during a sale was incorrectly displayed due to an erroneous conversion of Francs into Euros. The Court of Appeal declared the contract null and void on the basis of the mistake. The Cour de Cassation overruled this decision arguing that a professional seller had to pay attention to the conversion mechanism for the price. However, the case is different because in our case the parties could not easily detect the error.

I. The contractual agreement cannot be interpreted so that X is entitled to demand the market price, i.e., €12 per share.

II. A common mistake can be the basis for terminating the contract if this mistake relates to a substantial element of the contract. This is a mistake relating to a material fact which is present at the time of concluding the contract. A mistake as to the price is generally not recognised,[999] but in this case we are dealing with a mistake as to a material fact on which the contract was based – displaying the current price by the internet service. This mistake is relevant and leads to the nullity of the contract but not, in principle, to a price adaptation. We can deduce from the facts that the contract would not have been concluded if there had been no mistake as to the price. This mistake could not be taken into consideration if fault could be attributed to the mistaken person ('*erreur inexcusable*'). But here this is not the case: the incorrect information was due to an error by the provider of the internet service.

England and related jurisdictions

England and Ireland

It is unlikely that the contract would be set aside on the basis of a common or shared mistake by an Irish court. This result seems to be even more obvious under English law which rejects the broader approach of the equitable jurisdiction. X may, however, be able to seek rectification of the written document, if he can prove that it does not reflect the oral contract which was agreed between the parties.

I. 1. In this hypothetical situation, the oral agreement between X and Y is that X will sell the shares at the price listed by the stock exchange on the day of contracting, i.e., €12. However, an internet site gives them the wrong information about the price on the day of contracting, and the written contract states that the price is €10. There are a number of different ways of approaching this problem.

2. First, the court could hold that the bargain was to fix the consideration at the stock exchange price on a particular day. The price obtained from the internet site could thus be said not to reflect the agreed formula. In such a situation, where the written agreement does

[999] See comm., Mons, 26 April 2004.

not reflect the oral agreement reached, it may be possible to get rectification of the written document.[1000] It is important to note that only a mistake in the record of the agreement can be corrected and that the contract itself cannot be changed or varied. In *Collen Bros* v. *Dublin County Council*[1001] for example Dublin County Council entered into a contract where the price was to be calculated according to a particular formula, but owing to a clerical mistake the final written price did not reflect this formula. The price was adjusted to reflect the agreement originally made. However, English and Irish courts will not reform a written contract unless there is convincing proof that the contract, as a result of a mistake, has failed to give effect to the common intention of the parties, and the burden of proof lies on those seeking rectification.[1002]

II. 1. Alternatively, the position of X and Y in relation to this share purchase agreement presents a problem that could be resolved by reference to the law of mistake. The solution to the problem will depend on how the court chooses to characterise the mistake. This mistake is a mistake of fact which is shared by both parties. If the mistake is operative at common law, i.e., if it can be relied upon by X, then the contract will be declared *void ab initio*. In *Western Potato Co-operative* v. *Durnan* the test to be applied was stated as follows:

> Where the parties contract under a false and fundamental assumption, going to the root of the contract, and which both of them must be taken to have in mind at the time they entered into it, as the basis of their agreement, the contract may be avoided.[1003]

However, the factual situations that lead a court to declare a contract a nullity because of common mistake are extremely limited[1004] and a court would be unlikely to find that an error as to the consideration to be paid for the contractual subject matter satisfies this test.

2. On the other hand, there is a separate equitable jurisdiction that has been adopted in Ireland in both nineteenth-century[1005] and twentieth-century case law[1006] that allows equity to set aside a contract

[1000] See for example *Nolan* v. *Graves & Hamilton* [1946] IR 376. [1001] [1908] IR 503.
[1002] *The Olympic Pride* [1980] 2 Lloyd's Rep 67, 73 (Eng). See *Irish Life* v. *Dublin Land Securities* [1989] IR 253, where the burden of proof was not met.
[1003] [1985] ILRM5; *Clark* (1984) 19 Ir. Jur. 101.
[1004] See *Bell* v. *Lever Brothers* [1932] AC 161. [1005] *Cooper* v. *Phibbs* (1865) 17 IR. Ch. R.73.
[1006] *O'Neill* v. *Ryan* [1991] 1 ILRM 673, affirmed by the Supreme Court at [1992] 1 IR 166.

on the ground of common mistake. In *O'Neill* v. *Ryan*[1007] Costello J approved of the following passage from the English case of *Solle* v. *Butcher*:[1008]

> A contract is also liable in equity to be set aside if the parties were under a common misapprehension either as to facts or as to their relative and respective rights, provided that the misapprehension was fundamental and that the party seeking to set it aside was not himself at fault.

The equitable jurisdiction to set a contract aside for mistake is wider than the common law doctrine of mistake which will render it void *ab initio*. In England, the recent Court of Appeal decision in the *Great Peace*[1009] case has rejected this equitable jurisdiction associated with *Solle* v. *Butcher*, in favour of the narrow common law doctrine of mistake set out in *Bell* v. *Lever Brothers*.[1010] However, Irish courts continue to operate a broader equitable jurisdiction. The *Great Peace* decision was based in part upon the need to reconcile the House of Lords decision in *Bell* v. *Lever Bros*[1011] with the more liberal equitable line of cases in the lower courts. An Irish court would not be hampered by such precedent, and, it is submitted, is likely not to follow the reasoning in *Great Peace*, thus opting for a more flexible approach to this issue. However, even this more flexible set approach will not necessarily mean that the courts will offer a remedy. In *Fitzsimons* v. *O'Hanlon* litigation over the estate of a deceased person was compromised on the basis that the plaintiff would get £60,000 and the rest (approximately £150,000) would go to the defendants. It subsequently emerged that the deceased had £58,000 in a separate bank account and the plaintiff sought to set aside the agreement on the grounds of mistake. The court refused to set aside the contract, stating that it is 'in the interest of commercial convenience that, in general, apparent contracts should be enforced'.[1012] It was foreseeable that additional amounts would be found even though the parties believed all the deceased's assets had been found.

3. Thus, while this equitable jurisdiction to rescind the contract is broader than that found at common law, it is again our view that the error here is unlikely to provide a basis for rescinding the contract. There are strong policy considerations that support this. First, neither A nor B appear to have acted improperly; there was candour and honesty at the formation of the contract. Second, public policy requires that

[1007] [1992] 1 IR at 185. [1008] [1950] 1 KB 671.
[1009] *Great Peace Shipping Ltd* v. *Tsavliris Salvage (International) Ltd* [2002] 4 All ER 689.
[1010] [1932] AC 161. [1011] [1932] AC 161.
[1012] [1999] 2 ILRM 551 at 558 per Budd J.

an apparent bargain should be upheld. Third, it is not necessarily just or fair that X should be able to compel Y to pay a higher price than that which had been agreed between them, or that X should be able to cancel the contract and thus deprive Y of a bargain that had been freely struck as between X and Y.

Scotland

Applying the principles of the Scottish law of error to this case, X and Y have made a common error as to price. The error is essential and, at least in the traditional view, the contract is void. On the more modern view, the contract is voidable only, meaning that X would need to raise an action of reduction. As part of such an action, *restitution in integrum* must be possible, i.e., Y must return the shares to X, and X must return the price to Y.

I. The parties may have reached *consensus in idem* orally. A term of that orally agreed contract provided a formula for calculating the price. The parties' agreement was then incorrectly reflected in the written version of their contract. Because the error is contained in a written contract, X's ability to challenge the term is severely limited. This is as a result of the parole evidence rule which dictates that '... where the parties have reduced the terms of their agreement to writing, the obligations they have undertaken must be ascertained from the terms of that writing without the aid of extrinsic evidence'.[1013] To bring evidence of the formula which was orally agreed and incorrectly applied would be to attempt to contradict the terms of the written contract. The parole evidence rule is subject to many exceptions, one of which is that it will not apply where the contract is admittedly inaccurate.[1014] However, X and Y are unlikely to agree that the written contract is inaccurate and so this rule is unlikely to be helpful to X in practice. The Contract (Scotland) Act 1997 amended the parole evidence rule by creating a rebuttable presumption that a contract forms the sole expression of the terms of the contract where that appears to be the case.[1015] Evidence can now be led to show that there are terms in addition to the written terms, but not to contradict the actual written terms.[1016]

II. There are statutory provisions providing a mechanism in Scots law for the rectification of an error in a contract.[1017] A contract can be

[1013] Gloag, *Contract*, p. 365. [1014] Gloag, *Contract*, p. 377. [1015] Section 1(1).
[1016] Section 1(1) and Section 2 Contract (Scotland) Act 1997.
[1017] Law Reform (Miscellaneous Provisions) (Scotland) Act 1985, Sections 8 and 9.

rectified so that it properly expresses the contracting parties' common intention assessed objectively,[1018] although the court has discretion whether or not to rectify.[1019] In theory, X could lead evidence to persuade the court that the written contract does not accurately reflect the agreement of the parties and the court could rectify the contract so that the price was correctly stated as €12 per share. In practice, applications to rectify using this legislation are rare, and success is even more rare. X's chance of success depends upon the strength of the evidence he can lead concerning the true nature of his agreement with Y.

II. 1. Alternatively, X could argue that the written contract is affected by a common error, i.e., that both parties were, at the time of formation, labouring under the same error as to the price. The Scots law of error is in an unsatisfactory state, and has been described as 'bordering on chaos'.[1020] There is confusion as to the meaning of 'common' and 'mutual error',[1021] although it seems that the latter should be reserved for cases in which each party labours under a different error.[1022] To be operative, the error must be 'essential' or '*in substantialibus*',[1023] i.e., go to the root of the contract. Bell classified essential error into five categories, namely error in relation to the subject matter of the contract or obligation; the person undertaking the obligation; the price; the quality of the thing to be delivered should this be essential to the bargain; and the nature of the contract.[1024] The traditional view dictates that if an error is essential, then the contract is void.[1025] Modern commentators have criticised Bell's explanation given that it fails to distinguish between contracts which are void and those which are merely voidable.[1026]

2. An error may also be treated as so fundamental that it has prevented the parties from reaching consensus. In a case of this type, known as '*dissensus*' then, in theory, the contract will be void. By contrast, if the

[1018] *Shaw* v. *William Grant (Minerals) Ltd* 1989 SLT 121 (note); *Rehman* v. *Ahmad* 1993 SLT 741.

[1019] Section 8(1) Law Reform (Miscellaneaus Provisions) (Scotland) Act 1985.

[1020] J.J. Gow, 'Mistake and Error', (1952) 1 *International and Comparative Law Quarterly* 472, 475.

[1021] See McBryde, *Contract*, para. 15.34.

[1022] A.D.M. Forte, 'Frustration', in: Sir Thomas Smith *et al.* (eds.), *The Laws of Scotland: Stair Memorial Encyclopaedia* (Edinburgh: Butterworths/Law Society of Scotland, 1987–96), paras. 690 and 691.

[1023] Stair, 1st Viscount (James Dalrymple), *Institutions of the Law of Scotland* (The University Presses of Glasgow and Edinburgh, 6th edn, 1981), 1,10,13; and Bell, *Principles*, p. 11.

[1024] *Ibid.*, p. 11. [1025] Forte, 'Frustration', para. 690.

[1026] MacQueen and Thomson, *Contract Law*, para. 4.45.

parties have indeed reached *consensus in idem*, then the modern view is that the error is more likely to render the contract voidable. In practice, the Scottish courts are very reluctant to find that there has been *dissensus* given the extreme result, and are more likely to find that the parties have reached *consensus*, but that the error renders the contract voidable rather than void.

3. Some argue that a further requirement ought to be added, namely that the error must be an error in transaction and not an error in motive.[1027] Others have criticised this as an unhelpful distinction.[1028] An error in transaction must relate to the provisions of the contract, whereas an error in motive focuses on the reasons for entering into the contract. An uninduced error in transaction can result in reduction of the contract, whereas an error in motive must be induced before it can result in reduction. The error in this case is an error in transaction, and so this requirement is fulfilled.

Editors' comparative notes

The open jurisdictions

In most open jurisdictions, X can generally claim adjustment of the (written) contract and demand payment of the price difference between the price inserted in the document and the 'true value' of the shares (Austria, Germany, Greece, Italy, Lithuania, the Netherlands, Spain, Sweden). As the basis for the claim, the reports primarily refer to the rules of interpretation or to an 'exceptional' doctrine (e.g., *Geschäftsgrundlage*). A claim for adjustment is denied in Portugal; here, Y is primarily granted a right to terminate the contract and adjustment only comes into force if X demands to uphold the contract under the increased price reflecting the 'true value' of the shares. In Greece, the Netherlands and in Spain, X appears to be allowed to choose between adjustment and termination. Such an elective right is explicitly denied in the Austrian, Italian and Lithuanian reports.

In most of the jurisdictions that grant adjustment, there is some caveat aimed at protecting the other party's (Y's) interests (e.g., Austria, Germany, Spain, Sweden). This protection is based on the consideration that Y should not be forced to pay a price for the shares which he did not agree with. On the basis of this rationale, Y may be entitled to

[1027] *Ibid.*, para. 4.45; Forte, 'Frustration', para. 686; see also *Angus* v. *Bryden* 1992 SLT 884.
[1028] McBryde, *Contract*, para. 15.21.

refuse adjustment in this case and X has a right to terminate the contract (cf. Germany). In other jurisdictions, Y may cancel the (adjusted) contract at €12 per share if he proves that he would not have contracted at this price and/or if he has made dispositions in reliance on the lower price (cf. Austria, Sweden).

From the doctrinal perspective, three approaches can be identified in this case in the open jurisdictions: (i) interpretation, (ii) mistake and (iii) 'exceptional' doctrines (e.g., *Geschäftsgrundlage*):

(i) Cases of mutual mistake are often solved by reference to the rules of interpretation arguing that the wording of the contract is false and therefore irrelevant (*falsa demonstratio non nocet*) because – subject to proof – the parties intended to contract at a price reflecting the 'true value'. Some jurisdictions give preference to the oral agreement reached before the drafting of the written document.

    Many jurisdictions, however, refuse to give priority to the mode of calculation (current price/true value) as in the written agreement only the result of the calculation was included. Accordingly, the mode of calculation is regarded as a mere motive (Germany, Greece, Italy). Similarly, the Swedish report argues that it may be difficult to prove an unequivocal common intention in the light of a written agreement (cf. the Swedish report). If the mode of calculation does not prevail under the rules of interpretation, the focus shifts to the provisions of mistake.

(ii) As far as mistake is concerned, we can distinguish between jurisdictions in which mutual mistakes are governed by the general rules on mistakes (the Netherlands, Portugal, Spain, Sweden) and jurisdictions that solve this problem by reference to *Geschäftsgrundlage* or similar 'exceptional' doctrines (Austria, Germany, Greece). In Italy, there is a specific provision in the Civil Code addressed at mistakes of calculation ('*errore di calcolo*', Art. 1430 CC).

(iii) The main rationale for referring to 'exceptional' doctrines is that these concepts may allow for a more flexible solution than the general rules of mistake. In many jurisdictions, the general rules on mistake are based on the notion of one-sided responsibility for the mistake. Furthermore, the rules of mistake often do not provide for adjustment of the contract as a remedy, but only for termination. Consequently, there is no need to apply 'exceptional' doctrines to mutual mistakes if the general rules on mistake account for the issue of mutual responsibility and allow the courts to adjust the contract.

The reason why most reports do not simply refer to the rules of interpretation is the fact that they can only offer an all-or-nothing approach: the contract is concluded either at a price agreement of €10 or €12 per share. A price agreement of €10 neglects the parties' reference to the current market price; an agreement at €12 may unjustly affect Y's interests as he may have made dispositions in reliance on the written contract price of €10. The rules on mistake and *Geschäftsgrundlage* may offer a more flexible remedy of adjustment as well as a right to avoid the contract.

The closed jurisdictions

Adjustment is most likely to be available in the Czech Republic, Denmark and Slovenia on the basis of constructive interpretation and termination is available in Belgium and France. Under Scottish law, even though adjustment may be available in principle, termination is probably the only remedy in this case. In England and Ireland, (most likely) no remedy will be available to X.

Like in the closed jurisdictions, the doctrines mainly applied in the closed jurisdictions are (i) interpretation and (ii) mistake. 'Exceptional' doctrines, on the other hand, are of little relevance in the closed jurisdictions.

(i) The rules of interpretation are the main basis for resolving the case at hand in the Czech Republic, in Denmark and in Slovenia. In Scotland and in the common law jurisdictions, it is reported to be very unlikely that a written contract will be rectified based on common intentions according to the so-called parol evidence rule (cf. Scotland).

(ii) In Belgium, Denmark and France, the general rules on mistake are applied to mutual mistakes; Denmark and Slovenia allow for some modifications in the case of mutual mistakes. In Slovenia (like in Portugal), X may terminate the contract based on mistake as to the *causa* and Y may avoid termination by offering to uphold the contract at the assumed price of €12. In the Czech Republic, there are no rules on mutual mistakes and thus the report resorts primarily to the rules of interpretation.

The reasons presented to establish the relevance of the mistake vary: some reports qualify the mistake as relating to a material fact (Belgium and France); others accentuate the reference of the mistake to the *causa* (Slovenia) or qualify it as an essential error in transaction (Scotland). In Ireland the doctrine of mistake in equity is broader than the rules of mistake under common law. However, the Irish courts require a relevant mistake to be related to a fundamental fact and they are reluctant to rebut the presumption of an apparent bargain. This approach is shared by the English courts (which have abandoned the doctrine of mistake in equity).

Conclusions

In the case of a mutual mistake, there is a clear tendency to grant relief, i.e., not to uphold the written price agreement, amongst both the 'open' as well as the 'closed' jurisdictions. Only under English and Irish law, the contract will (most likely) be upheld on the basis of the written price agreement.

While all the open jurisdictions offer a remedy generally leading to an adjustment of the (written) agreement, amongst the closed jurisdictions, adjustment is available only in the Czech Republic, Denmark and Slovenia. Belgium and France merely offer termination. In both the open and the closed jurisdictions, three doctrinal solutions are applied to cases of mutual mistake: (i) interpretation, (ii) mistake and (iii) 'exceptional' doctrines (e.g., *Geschäftsgrundlage*).

(i) The rules of interpretation may lead to an adjustment of the written price agreement if the mode of calculation (i.e. reference to the 'true value') is deemed to have priority over the (false) result specified in the contract document. Yet, the rules of interpretation are somewhat limited as they neglect either the parties' reference to the current market price (if the price given in the document prevails) or Y's reliance in the price specified in the document.

(ii) Therefore, most jurisdictions do not rely solely on interpretation but refer to the general doctrines of mistake and to 'exceptional' doctrines. The relationship of these concepts appears to depend on the nature of the general rules on mistake. In many jurisdictions, they are designed only to apply to situations of one-sided responsibility and offer only termination as a remedy.

(iii) Thus, a recourse to 'exceptional' doctrines such as *Geschäftsgrundlage* may be considered as a means to overcome the shortcomings of the rules on mistake. Such doctrines provide a balanced and flexible approach including a mechanism of adjustment that may take into account the respective expectations and losses of the parties in the individual case.

However, it should be mentioned that the tendency to challenge the binding force of the written price agreement is not unanimous. From the group of the closed systems, the common law jurisdictions of England and Ireland and the mixed jurisdiction of Scotland are reluctant to take into account considerations based on the alleged intentions of the parties and are more likely to rely on the terms specified in the written agreement.

E. MISCELLANEOUS ISSUES

Case 14 Impediments of production beyond seller's control

Production of contractual goods is inhibited by a strike/ restriction of electricity supplies

X agrees to deliver some goods to Y at a certain date, but:

(a) *the workers of a subcontractor go on strike.*
(b) *due to problems with the state energy production and distribution system the government decides to cut the electricity supply at night thereby making it impossible to work at night.*

As a result, X cannot deliver the goods for an uncertain period of time. Is Y entitled to terminate the contract and to ask for damages?

Germany and related jurisdictions

Germany

X is entitled to terminate the contract and – depending on the assessment of the facts – may be entitled to damages.

I. 1. First, it is necessary to establish whether or not specific performance is impossible or grossly disproportionate due to the strike. As far as specific performance is impossible or grossly disproportionate, X is not obliged to deliver the goods (§275 I, II BGB) and Y, as a consequence, is not obliged to pay the agreed price (§326 I 1 BGB). Restitution of the contract beyond the scope of §275 BGB requires, in principle, a time limit to be set. The starting point in determining whether or not impossibility or disproportionality can be established, is the contractual definition of the debtor's obligation.

2. If the parties did not stipulate a duty of X to deliver goods from his production or supplies exclusively, then the contractual agreement between X and Y contains a so-called '*marktbezogene Gattungsschuld*' (general obligation in kind).[1029] It implies that X's duty to procure the goods extends to the entire market. As long as the goods can possibly be procured by a market transaction, there is no impossibility according

[1029] Cf. Grüneberg, '§276', in: Palandt *et al.* (eds.), *Bürgerliches Gesetzbuch*, n. 31; Larenz, *Schuldrecht I*, §21 I d; V. Emmerich, '§243', in: Krüger (ed.), *Münchener Kommentar zum Bürgerlichen Gesetzbuch*, vol. II, nn. 5 *et seq.*

to §275 I BGB.[1030] In this case, performance by X usually cannot be grossly disproportionate according to §275 II BGB as the value of goods will normally increase if the expenses of procuring the respective goods are increased. Thus, the increased burden on X corresponds with an equivalent advantage for Y and such a correspondence takes the case beyond the scope of disproportionality in the sense of §275 II BGB.

3. If impossibility does not apply, Y can rescind the contract under §323 I BGB. In principle, §323 BGB requires him to set an adequate time limit for X to perform, and after its expiration, Y is entitled to rescind the contract. The contractual duties then cease to exist and the contractual rules on restitution apply (§346 I BGB).[1031] The right of Y to rescind the contract does not require any fault on the part of X.

4. The situation is fundamentally different if the parties have agreed on a so-called '*Vorratsschuld*' or '*Produktionsschuld*' (obligation in kind restricted to own supplies). In the case of such an agreement, X only has to deliver goods as taken from his own production or supplies. Accordingly, he is not burdened with the risk of procuring goods in the market.[1032] However, an actual intention of the parties to restrict X's obligation to his production or supplies must be derived from the contract by means of interpretation. Usually, there is a *Vorratsschuld* if the manufacturer agrees to deliver goods of a kind that he produces.[1033]

5. In the case of a *Vorratsschuld*, performance is impossible for X during the strike (§275 I BGB). Strikes, however, are purely temporary impediments to performance. Nonetheless, temporary impediments are treated like permanent impediments if it is uncertain how long they will extend for and if the other party (in our case, Y) cannot reasonably be expected to stand by any longer.[1034] This must be judged on the individual facts. Therefore, if the end to the strike is uncertain and Y cannot be expected to stand by any longer, performance by X must be

[1030] Cf. C. Grüneberg, '§276', in: Palandt *et al.* (eds.), *Bürgerliches Gesetzbuch*, n. 31; Regierungsbegründung BT-Ds. 14/6040, p. 129.

[1031] Cf. BGH NJW 1976, 1931; C. Grüneberg, '§346', in: Palandt *et al.* (eds.), *Bürgerliches Gesetzbuch*, n. 4.

[1032] Cf. Grüneberg, '§276', in: Palandt *et al.* (eds.), *Bürgerliches Gesetzbuch*, n. 31; Emmerich, §243, in: Krüger (ed.), *Münchener Kommentar zum Bürgerlichen Gesetzbuch*, vol. II, n. 13 *et seq.*; RGZ 108, 420.

[1033] Cf. Emmerich, '§243', in: Krüger (ed.), *Münchener Kommentar zum Brgerlichen Gesetzbuch*, vol. II, n. 14.

[1034] Cf. BGHZ 47, 50; BGHZ 83, 200; V. Emmerich, '§275', in: Krüger (ed.), *Münchener Kommentar zum Bürgerlichen Gesetzbuch*, vol. II, n. 39 *et seq.*; Grüneberg, '§275', in: Palandt *et al.* (eds.), *Bürgerliches Gesetzbuch*, n. 11.

considered impossible according to §275 I BGB. Consequently, Y is relieved from his obligation to pay the agreed sum (§326 I 1 BGB). Besides, in cases of permanent impossibility Y is also entitled to rescind the contract under §326 V BGB without having to fix an additional period for performance. In both cases – relief according to §326 I 1 BGB and rescission of the contract according to §326 V BGB – the legal consequences are determined according to the rules governing the rescission of contracts (§326 IV BGB). This relief does not require that X is responsible for the impediment.

II. The second question is whether there is any opportunity for Y to claim damages, regardless of whether or not he rescinds the contract under §281 I 1 or §283 BGB. Both provisions require that X is responsible for the impossibility or delay of performance due to strike. There is a rebuttable presumption that the debtor is responsible (§280 I 2 BGB), i.e., X bears the burden of proof. According to §276 BGB the debtor's responsibility is to be assessed on the basis of the contractual agreement, in particular on the basis of whether or not the debtor assumed the risk of procuring the goods. At this point, the so-called '*marktbezogene Gattungsschuld*' (general obligation in kind) has to be distinguished once again from a '*Vorratsschuld*' (obligation in kind restricted to own supplies).

(a) Strike

I. 1. In case of a '*marktbezogene Gattungsschuld*' (general obligation in kind), the debtor implicitly assumed all risks arising from his duty to procure the goods, i.e., all risks usually related to the procurement of goods.[1035] This also encompasses loss of production or complications in purchasing goods in the market, both being caused by strike of the subcontractor's workers.[1036] In order to avoid such risks the debtor may insert a clause into the contract which purports to limit his liability for interference with the contract.[1037]

1035 Cf. RGZ 99, 1; Emmerich, '§279', in: Krüger (ed.), *Münchener Kommentar zum Bürgerlichen Gesetzbuch*, vol. II, nn. 10 *et seq.*; Grüneberg, '§276', in: Palandt *et al.* (eds.), *Bürgerliches Gesetzbuch*, n. 32.

1036 R. Richardi, 'Auswirkungen eines Arbeitskampfes auf Schuldverhältnisse mit Dritten', (1984) *JuS* 1984, 825 (827); for dissenting opinion cf. Grüneberg, '§276', in: Palandt *et al.* (eds.), *Bürgerliches Gesetzbuch*, n. 32; S. Kreissl, 'Die Gattungsschuld – zur Anwendung des §279 BGB bei Arbeitskampf, bedingten Lieferstörungen', (1994) MDR 958.

1037 Cf. for further details M. Löwisch, '§276', in: J. v. Staudinger *et al.* (eds.), *Kommentar zum Bürgerlichen Gesetzbuch und dem Einführungsgesetze* (Munich: Sellier and Berlin: de Gruyter 2004), n. 152.

2. Assuming that there is a *Vorratsschuld* (obligation in kind restricted to own supplies), the debtor's responsibility is governed by general principles. Therefore the decisive question is whether X – in exercise of due care – could reasonably be expected to have foreseen and avoided the danger of delay or impossibility of performance due to the strike (§276 BGB).[1038] This must be decided on the facts of the case, i.e., whether a labour dispute was foreseeable or whether X had an opportunity to stock up on goods. For instance, the latter is not possible for a newspaper publisher, and in some instances it might not be reasonably expected of a car supplier due to high storage costs.

(b) Cut of power supply by the state

I. In the case of a cut of power supply, assuming a '*marktbezogene Gattungsschuld*', X is considered to have assumed all the usual risks of procuring the goods. This also covers the risk of loss of production due to limited power supply. This is because the obligation of X to procure the goods in the market is exactly the characteristic of a '*marktbezogene Gattungsschuld*'. Thus, it is an impediment to performance that is typical of any obligation to procure goods. In case of a '*Vorratsschuld*', the crucial question is whether or not X – in exercise of due care – could reasonably be expected to have foreseen and avoided the cut of the power supply. In the given case, this cannot be asserted on the basis of the facts.

2. Y also has the right to claim compensation for the damage incurred due to the delay of performance according to §§280 I, III, 286 BGB. This, again, is subject to X being responsible for the delay, following the rules outlined above.

II. Accordingly, significant hardship for the debtor might occur if the parties have stipulated a '*marktbezogene Gattungsschuld*'. In order to alleviate such hardship, courts and the majority of legal writers apply the doctrine of *Geschäftsgrundlage* (§313 BGB) in such cases if the labour dispute has rendered performance extraordinarily burdensome.[1039]

[1038] Cf. M. Löwisch, 'Arbeitskampf und Vertragserfüllung', (1974) 74 *AcP*, 202 (257).

[1039] Cf. BGH NJW 1972, 1702; BGH NJW 1994, 515; Grüneberg, '§276', in: Palandt *et al.* (eds.), *Bürgerliches Gesetzbuch*, n. 32; for different solutions cf. H.P. Westermann, '§276', in: O. Palandt *et al* (eds.), *Erman – BGB* (Cologne: Schmidt, 12th edn, 2008), n. 21.

(a) Strike

I. The parties have at least implicitly assumed that there will be no labour dispute and thus, it is true that the strike interferes with the '*Geschäftsgrundlage*'. The concept of '*Geschäftsgrundlage*', however, in addition, requires that this risk is not allocated by statute or by contract to one of the parties (§313 I BGB). This must be judged on the facts of the case. Regularly, this is the case if there is a labour dispute in the business of the subcontractor because a '*marktbezogene Gattungsschuld*' basically allocates the risk of impediments to the debtor. Conversely, the debtor is free to stipulate a '*Vorratsschuld*' or '*Produktionsschuld*' (obligation in kind restricted to own supplies) in order to alleviate the risk of procuring goods.[1040] Therefore the concept of '*Geschäftsgrundlage*' may only be applied under exceptional circumstances in cases like the one at hand. For example, performance and counter-performance might be grossly disproportionate due to strike, or – to put it differently – the increased costs of procuring goods on the part of X most significantly exceed the payment owed by Y.[1041]

(b) Cut of power supply by the state

The cut of power supply, if it stands alone, does not, in general, justify the application of the concept of *Geschäftsgrundlage*. Rather, the duty of X to perform is required to be found unreasonable due to the cut of power supply. For example, this requirement might be met if the entire industry is subject to the cut of power supply and if, consequently, the increased costs of procuring the goods on the side of X are grossly disproportionate to the payment of Y. Anything less than a grossly disproportionate relation constitutes a risk that is contractually allocated to the debtor X.

Austria

In Case 14(a) Y is entitled to terminate the contract (after some additional time). Y is entitled to claim damages from X if X is held responsible for the impediment of production. In Case 14(b) Y may terminate the contract but he is not entitled to claim damages. If X was under the contractual duty to procure the

[1040] Without differentiations Grüneberg, '§313', in: Palandt *et al.* (eds.), *Bürgerliches Gesetzbuch*, n. 32.

[1041] Cf. *ibid.*, n. 32.

goods promised to Y on the general market, he will be held liable for Y's damages in both variants (a) and (b).

I. 1. Since Y is not able to deliver in due time, he is in *delay* according to §918 ABGB. This is not a case of factual or economic impossibility (§920 ABGB) of performance (in which case Y would be entitled to avoid the contract right away). The case law and the doctrine distinguish between 'objective delay' and 'subjective delay'. 'Subjective delay' is a delay caused by negligent or intentional conduct either by the debtor or a person the debtor is held responsible for (vicarious liability), whereas an 'objective delay' was not caused by such conduct.[1042] In both cases the creditor (Y) is entitled to *terminate* the contract under the following requirements: (i) the debtor either declares that he will not perform or it is otherwise clear that there will be no performance or, alternatively, (ii) the creditor fixes an additional period of time for performance in vain.[1043] Such a time period has to be of reasonable length, i.e., under normal circumstances the debtor has to be given a realistic chance to fulfil his obligation within the time allowed.[1044]

2. The creditor can claim damages only in cases of 'subjective' delay.[1045] However, with regard to the question of fault, X bears the burden of proof according to §1298 ABGB:[1046] X has to prove that the delay was not caused by his negligent or intentional conduct (act or forbearance).

(a) Strike

I. 1. X is not able to deliver in time due to the strike of workers of a subcontractor: Y can terminate the contract after a reasonable period of time (fixed by him) has elapsed without performance having been rendered.

2. X is liable for damages due to his own culpable conduct only if he could have foreseen the strike of the workers at the time of

1042 Koziol and Welser, *Bürgerliches Recht*, vol. II, p. 55.

1043 *Ibid.*, pp. 53 *et seq.*; OGH 28 August 1985, 1 Ob 589/85; Wimmer, 'Die Einrede der Unsicherheit in Zielschuldverhältnissen', (1980) *Österreichische Juristen-Zeitung*, 449 at 454.

1044 Koziol and Welser, *Bürgerliches Recht*, vol. II, pp. 53 *et seq.*; OGH 28 August 1985, 1 Ob 589/85.

1045 Koziol and Welser, *Bürgerliches Recht*, vol. II, p. 55; OGH 28 August 1985, 1 Ob 589/85; OGH 31 August 1988, 1 Ob 629/88; Wimmer, 'Die Einrede der Unsicherheit in Zielschuldverhältnissen', 449 at 454.

1046 OGH, JBl 1982, 431; OGH, SZ 55/185 = EvBl 1983/101; OGH, 5 Ob 40/85; OGH, 7 Ob 539/86.

contracting,[1047] if he could have avoided the strike by his own conduct, or if he could have avoided the consequences of a foreseeable strike by stocking up on goods. If the goods owed to Y are '*specific*', X cannot be held liable if he did not procure the goods on the market. A court will assume a duty to supply specific goods if they (i) are produced only by X and are not available elsewhere on the market or (ii) if they are available elsewhere, if the contract does not oblige X to procure them on the market but only to produce them himself. If, however, X's obligation to deliver the goods is formulated more openly in the way of an obligation for delivery of '*generic*' goods which are available elsewhere on the market, he will be held liable to pay damages to Y, if he does not procure the goods by buying them from other suppliers on the market.

3. According to the rules on vicarious liability, X can also be held liable for the culpable conduct of persons that assist X with the performance of the contract according to §§1313a ABGB ('*Gehilfenhaftung*').[1048] Vicarious liability under a contract does not require an employment relationship (labour contract) between the debtor and the person assisting, it extends also to the culpable conduct of a person acting in *economic independence* who is 'employed' by X to perform one of X's contractual duties owed to Y.[1049] In our case it does not seem unlikely that the 'subcontractor' himself is responsible for the strike of his workers. According to the Austrian OGH an enterprise that cannot deliver the sold goods in time due to a strike of his workers will be held liable to pay damages to the buyer if the strike was caused by the enterprise's unlawful refusal to pay the full amount of wages the workers were entitled to.[1050]

4. A 'subcontractor' employed by the main contractor on a construction site is a typical example of the main contractor's vicarious liability for another independent enterprise.[1051] The main contractor promised the construction of the whole building to his contract partner. If he 'employs' different subcontractors to execute parts of the construction work, he will be liable for the culpable conduct of these subcontractors in relation to his contract partner. On the other hand, a mere supplier of components or materials needed by X to produce the goods sold to Y, or

[1047] OGH, SZ 55/185 = EvBl 1983/101.

[1048] Koziol and Welser, *Bürgerliches Recht*, vol. II, pp. 355 *et seq.*

[1049] Reischauer, '§1313a', in: Rummel (ed.), *Kommentar zum ABGB* (2004), vol. II/2b, n. 8; Karner, '§1313a', in: Koziol, P. Bydlinski, and Bollenberger (eds.), *Kurzkommentar zum ABGB*, n. 4.

[1050] OGH, SZ 61/190. [1051] OGH, *ecolex* 1990, 406.

a wholesaler who delivers already produced goods to a retailer, are not considered to act as assistants in the sense of §1313a ABGB, because they do not perform duties that X or the retailer himself owe to Y or the second buyer.[1052] If we, therefore, assume that the 'subcontractor' of our case is a 'mere supplier' of components or materials needed by X to produce the goods, X cannot be held liable for the culpable conduct of the subcontractor.

5. If X can be held liable under the above-stated conditions (for his own culpable conduct), Y can claim the damages caused to him by non-performance of the contract: as for instance the extra costs of concluding a substitute transaction.[1053] Y has to be put financially in the same position he would have been in case of proper performance ('*Erfüllungsinteresse*', *expectation damages*).[1054] Only if X should have or had foreseen the strike at the time of the conclusion of the contract (but could not prevent the strike), would the requirement of causation of damage lead to a different result: in that case X only caused the damages incurred by Y in reliance on a contract which would not have been concluded if X had told him about the risk of a strike ('*Vertrauensinteresse*', *reliance damages*).[1055] X violated a pre-contractual duty of information. The compliance with this duty would have caused Y not to conclude the contract with X. 'Reliance damages' in that sense may be the costs incurred by Y because he did not conclude a contract with another supplier right away.

(b) Cut of power supply by the state

I. If the electricity supply is reduced, the rules of delay, as explained above, will apply again: Y can fix an additional period of time and after its expiry without performance terminate the contract (§918 ABGB). The award of damages again requires the existence of culpable conduct by X or a person he is held responsible for. X cannot be blamed for the cut of electricity supply and the electricity supplier is not a person X is held responsible for in the sense of §1313a ABGB. It seems unlikely that X could have foreseen the electricity problems and could have avoided its negative consequences on his production. If X was not obliged to or

[1052] OGH, SZ 55/31.
[1053] Koziol and Welser, *Bürgerliches Recht*, vol. II, p. 55; OGH, 1 Ob 629/88; 11 June 1985, 5 Ob 40/85.
[1054] OGH, SZ 55/185 = EvBl 1983/101; Koziol and Welser, *Bürgerliches Recht*, vol. II, p. 55.
[1055] *Ibid.*, vol. II, p. 19; Reischauer, 'Vor §918', in: Rummel (ed.), *Kommentar zum ABGB*, vol. I, n. 16 with further references.

could not procure the goods elsewhere on the market ('specific' goods obligation), Y will not be entitled to claim any damages from X. X is obliged to pay damages only if he had the contractual duty to procure the goods elsewhere on the market ('generic' goods obligation), but did not do so.

II. In so far as contract law (ABGB or specific statutes) distributes the risk of future developments, there is no space for the application of the doctrine of '*Wegfall der Geschäftsgrundlage*'.[1056] The legal issues of the case are covered by the rules on delay of performance (§§918 *et seq.* ABGB). If the debtor is unable to deliver the goods within a reasonable time period after delivery was due, the creditor cannot be reasonably expected to wait any longer and may terminate the contract. The debtor will thus lose his profits under the contract. However, he will only have to compensate the creditor for the damages he incurred (expectation or reliance damages) *if* the damages were caused intentionally or negligently (including vicarious liability under §1313a ABGB as described above). If the 'subcontractor' in case (a) is a mere supplier of materials or components needed by X to produce the goods owed to Y, X will not be held liable for the 'subcontractor's' conduct. In case (b) no culpable conduct can be found on the side of X and he will therefore not be held liable for Y's damages. If X was under the contractual duty to procure the goods promised to Y on the general market if he cannot produce them himself, he will be held liable for Y's damages in both variants (a) and (b), because he negligently or intentionally violated this contractual duty to procure the goods for Y in time.

The Netherlands

Under Dutch law, Y may terminate the contract and will be awarded damages in Case 14(a); the amount of damages payable may, however, be reduced. Unless the non-performance (or a delay in the delivery) by X is insignificant, Y is entitled to terminate the agreement in Case 14(b).

[1056] OGH, SZ 54/71; 14 June 2000, 7 Ob 40/99d; Rummel, '§901', in: Rummel (ed.), *Kommentar zum ABGB*, vol. I, n. 4, 6 with further references; Gschnitzer, in: Klang (ed.), *Kommentar zum ABGB*, vol. IV, p. 335; Peter Rummel, 'Anmerkungen zum gemeinsamen Irrtum und zur Geschäftsgrundlage', 1 at 7, 10; Koziol and Welser, *Bürgerliches Recht*, vol. I, pp. 163 *et seq.*; Apathy, '§901', in: Schwimann (ed.), *Kommentar zum ABGB*, vol. IV, n. 11.

(a) Strike

I. Under Dutch law, every breach of a contractual obligation entitles the creditor to claim damages suffered as a result of such breach, unless the breach cannot be attributed to the debtor (Art. 6:74 Dutch Civil Code). Therefore the basis for claiming damages is the legal provisions on breach of contract, which embrace the concept of (temporary) impossibility and force majeure. The engagement of a subcontractor is a matter that falls within the debtor's sphere of responsibility (X), as is expressed in Art. 6:76. Accordingly, a strike by the contractor's employees cannot be attributed to Y. This might be different if Y imposed an obligation on X to contract with the relevant contractor (but even then it would depend on the contract between X and Y whether the consequences of the strike should be attributed to Y at all). In certain industries, this can be considered as normal, but the current case contains no facts or references allowing for such an interpretation.

II. Although the impossibility of X's subcontractor delivering to X could arguably be substituted for X's own impossibility of delivering in good time to Y, such impossibility would still be a circumstance falling within X's sphere of responsibility. The excusable scope of force majeure is limited to external events or circumstances but would not include strikes on the side of the (sub-)contractor (Art. 6:74, as elaborated in Art. 75[1057]). The impossibility of X's subcontractor remains attributable to X (and X or X's subcontractor only). Many similar cases have been decided in connection with construction contracts, where the engagement of subcontractors is very common. In a case of even greater hardship, the competent arbitral tribunal decided that a temporary impossibility or a delay in the delivery of raw materials on the side of the contractor is something that the contractor should take into account, despite any reassuring reports from the subcontractor, even if the ultimate cause of such impossibility or delay is the outbreak of a civil war in the area from which the raw materials are sourced.[1058]

III. 1. Y has a right to dissolve the supply contract with X, partly or wholly, on the basis of X's breach of contract, unless the dissolution and its consequences do not justify such a dissolution in view of the particular or relatively insignificant nature of the breach (Art. 6:265 Dutch Civil Code). To the extent that performance by X is not permanently or temporarily impossible, Y's entitlement to invoke dissolution comes

[1057] See expressly for strikes: Parliamentary notes to Art. 6:75.

[1058] RvA 20 June 1988, no. 13.311, BR 1988, p. 706.

into existence only when X is actually in default (Art. 6:265(2)). To determine whether this is the case, it is important to establish whether or not the delivery date was crucial for Y (i.e., if 'time is of the essence') – see Subtitle 6.1.9 Dutch Civil Code (Art. 6:81–7). In the current case, Y may first need to give notice of the default before the (mere written) termination notice (Art. 6:267).

2. Obviously, the nature of the strike, its impact on the production processes of X and the subsequent timing of the delivery by X's subcontractor to X and thereafter by X to Y (e.g., including X's possible preference for resuming deliveries to third party customers first and only then to Y) are relevant to determine whether Y may dissolve the supply contract. The consequence will be that both parties will reverse those acts already implemented, in connection with which X shall be liable to compensate Y's damage suffered as a consequence of X's breach and the dissolution (Arts. 6:271, 277 and Arts. 6:95 *et seq.* to determine which damages are eligible for such indemnification).

3. One should note that the supply contract may complicate the case considerably. Typically, such contracts expand the scope of definition of force majeure to include strikes by employees or interruptions in the supply by their suppliers of raw materials. On the other hand, the exposure to extensive damages will probably be limited because most contracts exclude indirect and consequential damages (e.g., where a delay in delivery will often result in rather remote damages on the side of the customers).

(b) Cut of power supply by the state

I. 1. If a government decided to cut the supply, this would be so onerous and triggered by such supervening circumstances that this must be considered a force majeure event that cannot be attributed to X. Under Dutch law, this is important because, in that case, X would not be liable for a breach of contract and hence not liable for the damages suffered by Y (Arts. 6:74 and 75 Dutch Civil Code). The solution may be illustrated by the case of *Badaway* v. *Atlanta*,[1059] in which the Egyptian government had imposed import restrictions on the agreed delivery of certain goods. The Hoge Raad considered that the import restriction was of a temporary nature, albeit of a long duration, and that upon its repeal the parties were in principle obliged to continue performance under the contract, probably with appropriate amendments.

[1059] HR 16 January 2004, *NJ* 2004, 164 (*Badaway* v. *Atlanta*).

X's only 'liability' would exist to the extent that X obtains a benefit from the breach of contract that he would not have otherwise enjoyed (Art. 6:78).

2. The question whether Y is entitled to terminate (i.e., dissolve) the contract is subject to a different criterion. Article 6:265(1) determines that each breach in the performance of a party's obligations under a contract entitles the (affected) party to dissolve that contract in whole or in part, unless the breach, in view of its special nature or insignificance, does not justify the dissolution. To the extent that the performance is not of a permanent nature or only temporarily impossible, the entitlement to dissolve exists only as of the moment from which the breaching party is in default (Art. 6:265 Section 2). But since the performance is temporarily impossible due to the unavailability of electricity, this exception does not apply.

Eastern European jurisdictions

Slovenia

Y is entitled to terminate the contract. He is most likely entitled to ask for damages in the case of strike (a) but not in the case of power-shortage (b).

I. 1. For the assessment of Y's rights, it is important to know whether or not the delivery of the goods on the specified date is an essential element of the contract.[1060] If the date is essential, the contract is terminated automatically (*ex lege, ipso iure*) without any action on Y's side (Art. 104(1) CO). Y can, however, prevent this consequence if he demands performance of the contract immediately after the delivery period has expired. If he sets a period of time for delivery and X does not deliver within this period, the contract is dissolved automatically. If Y only demands performance without setting a deadline and X does not perform within a reasonable period of time, Y has the right to terminate the contract by notice, Art. 104 CO).[1061]

2. If the time is not of the essence under the contract (which is more likely in the present case), the expiry of the delivery period does not affect the validity of the contract automatically. X remains entitled to

[1060] This should be determined on the basis of the contract, the will of the parties and can also depend on the nature of the contract. Juhart in: Juhart and Plavšak (eds.), *Obligacijski zakonik*, vol. I, pp. 568–9.

[1061] *Ibid.*, pp. 570–1.

performance. Y is not allowed to terminate the contract immediately, but only after fixing a reasonable additional period of time for the performance. Fixing an additional period of time has the same effect as an agreement that time is of the essence under the contract. If X does not deliver the goods within the additional period of time, the contract is terminated automatically (Art. 105).[1062]

II. Under Slovenian law, a party is liable for damages arising from non-performance or an incorrect performance of a contract (Art. 239(2) CO). The term incorrect performance covers cases of untimely performance and defective performance (e.g., delivery of a defective machine). The general requirements for contractual liability are (i) the violation of a contractual obligation (ii) arising from *the sphere* of the debtor (fault or risk). Furthermore, (iii) damages must have occurred to the creditor that are (iv) causally linked to the violation of the contract.[1063] It is important to note that it is presumed that the impediment arises from the sphere of the non-performing party. Fault (not even negligence) is not a requirement for liability.[1064] A party is only excused if it proves its inability to perform its obligation due to an impediment that occurred after the conclusion of the contract and which the party could not have prevented, eliminated or avoided (Art. 240 CO).[1065]

(a) Strike

In the present case the reason for non-performance within the stipulated period of time is a strike at X's subcontractor. It is generally accepted that impediments concerning subcontractors are considered to arise from the sphere of the main contractor, since the latter bears the risk of choice of his subcontractors ('*culpa in eligendo*').[1066] This means that X is liable for damages, arising out of the untimely performance (or non-performance), unless he can prove that the impediment was inevitable for him. This depends on many circumstances, the relevant questions being whether the subcontractor in question was the seller or the producer of the goods, whether he is the only possible supplier or whether he had a choice between several possible producers

[1062] Again, Y has the possibilty of declaring that he still wants the contract to be performed.

[1063] Plavšak in: Juhart and Plavšak (eds.), *Obligacijski zakonik*, vol. I, pp. 207–8.

[1064] *Ibid.*, pp. 207–8.

[1065] It is, however, not required that the performance should be impeded due to an extraneous event.

[1066] Plavšak in: Juhart and Plavšak (eds.), *Obligacijski zakonik*, vol. I, p. 216.

and/or sellers. Furthermore it may depend on whether a strike could have been taken into account by X when contracting with the subcontractor.[1067] Assuming that X is not able to prove the impediment was inevitable, he will be held liable for non-performance (or untimely performance, if the contract is still to be performed later).

(b) Cut of power supply by the state

The power-shortage is a consequence of government intervention. Government intervention is one of the most typical cases of impossibility of performance (force majeure) regulated in Art. 116 CO. If the performance of one of the parties to a synallagmatic contract has become impossible due to an event for which none of the parties is liable, the contract terminates by operation of law. It terminates when performance of one of the parties becomes impossible and both parties are released from their contractual obligations.[1068] In accordance with Art. 240 CO, X will have to prove that the reason for the impediment does not arise from his sphere. If Y has already performed parts of his obligation (e.g., a downpayment), he is entitled to claim restitution, in accordance with the rules of unjust enrichment (Art. 190 CO). He is not entitled to claim damages.

Lithuania

Y is entitled to terminate the contract and demand damages only if Y fails to prove that the strike and the government acts amount to force majeure. The difference between the situations (a) and (b) lies in the fact that in Case (a) X is liable for the subcontractor's performance. In this case, X will therefore have to prove the absence of fault on the side of the subcontractor, so that in respect of both the subcontractor and X the strike amounts to force majeure. With regard to Case (b), however, the courts tend to regard government acts as force majeure without any further conditions. In addition, in alternative (b), Y is entitled to question the government acts and claim compensation from the state if the government acts were unlawful (Art. 6.127(3) CC).

[1067] E.g., Is the subcontractor known for labour disturbances; is his trade or profession known for labour disturbances?

[1068] Juhart in: Juhart and Plavšak (eds.), *Obligacijski zakonik*, vol. I, p. 613.

I. The fixing of a specified date for the delivery of the goods means that the time of performance is an essential contract term. Consequently, the failure to deliver the goods at this specified date will be considered an essential violation of the contract enabling Y to unilaterally dissolve the contract (Art. 6.217 CC). If X is a businessman, he is liable for the failure to perform his obligation in all cases with the exception of force majeure (Art. 6.256(4) CC). Thus, the risk of failure to perform the contract is borne by X, except in cases of impossibility of performance or force majeure.

II. If X uses the assistance of other persons to perform his obligations, he is liable for the actions of these persons as for his own according to Art. 6.38(4) CC. Hence, X is also liable for the subcontractor's non-performance. Y's right to terminate the contract and compensation of damages will depend on how one distributes the risk of strike. If the strike is considered to be an event that makes it objectively impossible for X to perform, then, pursuant to Arts. 6.62 and 6.127 CC, X's obligation is void. In this case, accordingly, Art. 6.212 CC is also applicable, pursuant to which the strike will be regarded as force majeure. Consequently, Y will have no right to claim compensation of damages. If the strike does not render X's performance objectively impossible, it does not lead to an impossibility of performance and hence cannot be regarded as force majeure. In such a case, Y is entitled to unilaterally dissolve the contract due to an essential breach and claim compensation of damages in accordance with Art. 6.217 CC.

III. However, X can invoke the defence of impossibility of performance and force majeure. It should be noted that the Lithuanian doctrine of law views impossibility of performance in the objective sense. Therefore, X will have to prove that the strike or the government acts would have rendered it impossible to perform not only for him but equally for any other person. Hence, if the strike or the government acts did not result in making the performance objectively impossible, these circumstances would not be qualified as impossibility of performance or force majeure. In such case Y is entitled to cancel the contract and claim damages.

(a) Strike

I. If the strike of the subcontractor's workers amounts to force majeure, X may be released from civil liability towards Y. The strike amounts to an event of force majeure only if the employer cannot be held responsible for the strike and, consequently, if the strike was totally unjustified. If the strike was justified by some violations made by the employer, the strike does not constitute force majeure.[1069] Thus, in this case, Y is not entitled to claim compensation of damages.

(b) Cut of power supply by the state

I. Government acts are qualified as force majeure and, therefore, X is not liable (Art. 6.212 CC) in alternative (b).

Czech Republic

In Case 14(a) and (b) Y is entitled to terminate the contract but he is not entitled to claim damages if the condition of force majeure in Section 374 and those in Section 375 Commercial Code are met.

I. If X's delay constitutes a material breach of his obligation Y is entitled to withdraw from the contract, provided Y notified X of the withdrawal without undue delay, once Y learned of X's breach (Section 345(1) Commercial Code).[1070]

II. Y is in both situations (a) and (b) entitled to damages. The extent of indemnity is governed by Section 373 Commercial Code, according to which 'whoever breaches a duty arising from a contractual relationship is obliged to provide compensation for the damage caused to the other party, unless it proves that the breach was caused by circumstances excluding the liability'. The liability of X shall be excluded by

> obstacles which arise independently of the obligated (liable) party's will and which prevent the party from performing its obligation, provided that it cannot be reasonably expected that the obligated party could avert or overcome the obstacle or its consequences, and further that the occurrence of such an obstacle was unpredictable at the time when the obligated party undertook to perform the obligation. (Section 374(1) Commercial Code)

III. In situation (a), another decisive provision is Section 375 Commercial Code stipulating that if a breach of obligations is caused by a third party (subcontractor) to whom X entrusted the fulfilment of its obligation, the

[1069] Mikelenas, *Commentary on Book VI of the Civil Code*, p. 362.

[1070] Essential breach of contract is defined in Section 345(2) Commercial Code: 'The party breaching the contract knew, or could have reasonably predicted, at the time of its conclusion, taking into account the purpose of the contract as evident from its contents, or the circumstances under which it was concluded, that the other party would not be interested in performance of the obligation in the event of such a breach.'

liability of X is excluded only if his own liability under Section 374 is also excluded, and the third party would not be held liable under that provision if it had been bound directly instead of X.[1071] This has to be applied *mutatis mutandis* to situation (b).

IV. 1. The question whether X is liable for damages must be considered with regard to the specific circumstances, in particular whether X was aware that the subcontractor faced the possibility of strikes, taking into account the overall situation of the enterprise, and whether he would be able to reasonably fulfil his obligation otherwise.

2. This applies to X in situation (b) similarly. If X could have foreseen that the supply of electricity would be cut off, he could undoubtedly foresee the damage and he would also be liable for the damage even if he could have distributed the production without major obstacles so as to avoid the need for night-time electricity supplies.

Scandinavian jurisdictions

Sweden

Y is entitled to terminate the contract, provided there is a delay that amounts to a fundamental breach, or that it is obvious such breach will be committed. However, Y is not entitled to claim damages.

I. 1. This is a sales contract, and under Swedish law the current problems are dealt with in the Sales Act.[1072] The seller's delay in delivery of the goods is one of the major categories of breach of contract. The main principle, as set forth in Section 22, is that if the goods are not delivered, or not delivered on time, and this does not depend on the seller or some circumstances on his side, the buyer is, under Sections 23–9, entitled to require performance by the seller or to terminate the contract. He is also entitled to damages under Sections 27–8. Furthermore, he is, under Section 42, entitled to withhold payment to an amount equivalent to the claim.

[1071] Section 451(2): 'Unjustified enrichment means a benefit acquired by performance of an act for which there was no legal reason, by performance based on a void legal act or by performance based on a legal ground which disapeared, as well as benefit acquired from dishonest resources.' This is the wording of Section 375 Commercial Code.

[1072] Köplagen (1990:931).

2. The buyer's right to require performance by the seller under Section 23 will not apply if there is an obstacle which the seller is unable to overcome, or if delivery demands sacrifices that are not reasonable with regards to the buyer's interest in receiving the goods. But again, the buyer is entitled to demand delivery should the impediment cease to exist within a reasonable time. The right to request delivery is lost however, if the buyer does not exercise that right within reasonable time.[1073]

II. 1. The main rule as to termination of the contract on the basis of the seller's delay is stated in Section 25. The buyer is entitled to terminate the contract if the breach is of fundamental importance to him, and the seller knew or ought to have known this. The buyer may also choose to fix an additional period of time for delivery. If the time limit is not unreasonably short, the buyer may terminate the contract if the goods have not been delivered within the additional time period. During the additional time period, the buyer is, on the other hand, only entitled to terminate the contract if the seller informs him that delivery will not be on time.[1074]

2. If the time of delivery has not yet passed, the delay that can, in this case, be foreseen is what is commonly referred to as an anticipatory breach of contract. If prior to the date for performance of the contract it is clear that the seller will commit a fundamental breach of contract, the buyer may terminate the contract under Section 62. However, termination is ineffective as a remedy if the seller immediately provides adequate assurance of his performance.

3. In this case it is impossible to tell from the submitted information which rules are applicable, or if the prerequisites are met. However, it can be concluded that Y is entitled to terminate the contract, provided

[1073] Under Section 24, the seller is entitled to ask the buyer whether he, despite the delay, will accept delivery within a certain time limit. If the buyer does not respond within a reasonable time after receiving the seller's message, the buyer may not terminate the contract as long as the seller delivers within that time. The same rule applies if the seller has merely informed the buyer that he is going to deliver within a certain time limit.

[1074] If the goods are to be manufactured or procured for the buyer exclusively according to his instructions or wishes, and it is impossible for the seller to utilise the goods in any other way without a major loss, the buyer's right to terminate the contract is limited under Section 26. This section states that the buyer is entitled to terminate the contract only if the purpose the buyer had in entering into the contract is fundamentally not feasible.

there is already a delay that amounts to a fundamental breach, or that it is obvious that such breach is imminent.

III. 1. The main rule concerning damages under Section 27 is that the buyer is entitled to compensation for his direct losses caused by the seller's breach of contract, where the seller is unable to prove that the delay is caused by an obstacle outside of his control which he could not reasonably have foreseen, and the consequences of which he could not reasonably have avoided or overcome. If the delay is caused by a subcontractor, the seller does not have to pay damages if the subcontractor would also have been excused under the same rule. The buyer's right to damages for indirect losses applies only when the delay, or the loss, is caused by the seller's negligence.

2. When the seller is prevented from delivering the goods, under Section 28, he is obliged to inform the buyer of the obstacle and its effects on his ability to fulfil the contract. If the buyer does not receive such a message within a reasonable time after the seller has, or should have, acquired knowledge of the obstacle, the buyer is entitled to damages for the loss that could have been prevented, had the message been received in time.

3. If the goods have been delivered late, the buyer is, under Section 29, obliged to give the seller notice of his intention to terminate the contract or claim for damages. If such notice has not been given within a reasonable time after the buyer acquired knowledge of the delivery, the buyer may not terminate the contract or claim damages on the basis of the delay. However, the buyer does not have to give special notice of his intention to claim damages, provided he has informed the seller that he will terminate the contract. In addition, the buyer is always entitled to damages, when the delay or the loss is caused by the seller's negligence.

4. When, after the conclusion of the contract, it becomes apparent that the seller will not perform a substantial part of his obligations, Section 61 entitles the buyer to withhold payment. He then has to inform the seller immediately, or the seller is entitled to damages for his loss which could have been prevented had he received the message in time. The buyer must continue with performance if the seller provides adequate assurance of his performance.

5. In light of the above, it follows that the main prerequisites in respect of the buyer's right to damages is if the seller is able to prove that the delay has been caused by an obstacle beyond his control, which he could not reasonably have foreseen and the consequences of which

he could not reasonably have avoided or overcome. When, as is the case here, the delay is caused by a subcontractor, the seller does not have to pay damages if the subcontractor would also have been excused under the same rule.

(a) Strike

I. A strike of a subcontractor's own workers will generally not be considered to be under the subcontractor's control. An exceptional case is probably at hand if the subcontractor caused the strike by clearly violating rules of law or collective bargaining agreements. There has also been some discussion of whether a local strike, which is strictly local and does not form part of general negotiations of collective agreements, is really impossible for the employer to overcome.

(b) Cut of power supply by the state

I. The situation concerning problems with the state energy production and distribution system which makes it impossible to work during night time has to be tested against the circumstances in the specific case. In this case X appears to be totally dependent on state energy supply, while it is not possible to buy energy from other suppliers, or to arrange for other sources of energy. If this is true, this is a situation outside X's control.

Denmark

Y is entitled to terminate the contract, since the non-delivery of the goods is considered to be a fundamental breach of contract. Additionally, Y is entitled to claim damages, because the circumstances leading to the non-delivery of the goods can hardly be considered as force majeure pursuant to Section 24 Sale of Goods Act.

I. The non-delivery of goods is dealt with by the Sale of Goods Act and is considered to be a delay by the vendor and thus a breach of contract. As a general rule, any delay between merchants is considered a fundamental breach of contract, which entitles the purchaser to terminate the sales contract; cf. Section 21 Sale of Goods Act.[1075] This principle is also applicable despite the delay being caused by unexpected circumstances such as a strike.

[1075] Alternatively, the purchaser can require performance, unless it is impossible to deliver the goods in question.

II. If the goods in question are generic goods, the seller is strictly liable (cf. Section 24 Sale of Goods Act as discussed more comprehensively in the overview (Chapter 4)). Nevertheless, the seller has no obligation to pay damages if he can prove that the obstacle causing the delay amounts to force majeure or the sales contract contains an exemption clause.

III. The seller is not liable if it can be proven that the delay by the subcontractor is caused by force majeure.[1076]

(a) Strike

I. Whether the purchaser is entitled to receive damages depends on the question of to what extent a strike can qualify as force majeure. A strike would normally be regarded as force majeure if it is a widespread strike. However, if the strike takes place solely at the place of the subcontractor, it would not be considered as force majeure. If the seller is liable, the purchaser is entitled to claim damages for breach of contract (expectation damages).

(b) Cut of power supply by the state

I. 1. If it is only possible for X to produce the goods in question during the night, such a restriction would be considered a force majeure event in accordance with Section 24 Sale of Goods Act. X is not liable towards Y. As mentioned above, the non-delivery of the goods is considered a delay in accordance with Danish law and thus a breach of contract. Y would be entitled to cancel the contract, since any delay in accordance with the Sale of Goods Act is considered fundamental between merchants.

2. On the other hand, if it is possible for X to produce the goods during the daytime, but if it is not possible to perform all the contracts which X has entered into, the situation is slightly more difficult. Such circumstances would be regarded as a partial frustration. Then X has an obligation to deliver as many goods as possible in accordance with the principle of a pro rata share among his customers. In doing so X must not give any preference to certain customers e.g., with regard to the time of delivery or the time of contracting.[1077] If X violates this principle, he is contractually liable for the goods in question that were not

[1076] See U 1977.489 H.

[1077] Cf. Jacob Nørager-Nielsen and Søren Theilgaard, *Købeloven med kommentarer*, p. 370.

delivered, and Y can claim damages for breach of contract. The case law on partial frustration is quite substantial.[1078]

Romanic–Mediterranean jurisdictions

Italy

If X's contractual duty is held to be a general obligation in kind, Y will be entitled to terminate the contract for non-performance of X. Consequently, Y will be entitled to claim damages.

If the obligation is considered to be restricted to X's own supplies, X will not be burdened with the risk (and the cost) of procuring goods on the market. Y is entitled to terminate the contract, provided that the delay in the performance renders it useless for him.

I. 1. If performance is impossible, X will be discharged from the contractual duty to deliver the goods (Art. 1256 CC, the obligation extinguishes because of the objective impossibility) and Y, as a consequence, will not be obliged to pay the agreed price to X (Art. 1463 CC, the contract is automatically terminated because of the objective impossibility). In short, both parties will be released and none of them could ask for damages.[1079]

2. It should also be noted that in order to decide whether or not a case of impossibility occurs, it is important to define the precise content of the debtor's obligation. If X is obliged to deliver goods of a certain kind without any other specification (general obligation in kind), he is under the duty to procure the goods in the market even if this will increase the cost of the performance. As long as the goods can be purchased through a market transaction, there will be no impossibility and therefore no reason to discharge X. If the contract does not include a hardship clause or the assumption of impossibility due to strike, Y will be entitled to terminate the contract

[1078] See for instance U 1941.134H and U 1953.973SH.

[1079] If there is a temporary impossibility of the performance, the obligation does not extinguish until the performance may no longer be reasonably requested or the creditor has no longer an interest thereto (Art. 1256(2) CC). The impossibility of performance could also only be partial. In the latter case, the debtor remains bound to the possible part of the performance (Art. 1258 CC), but the counter-party has the right to a corresponding reduction of the counter-performance and may also withdraw if there is no longer a relevant interest in the partial performance (Art. 1464 CC).

for non-performance of X. Consequently, Y shall be entitled to claim damages, which could also be requested for the simple delay in the performance (even if the contract is not terminated).

3. The situation could be different if the parties have agreed upon an obligation in kind restricted to X's own supplies. If X is obliged to deliver goods from his own production or supplies, he will not be burdened with the risk (and the cost) of procuring goods on the market. Of course, the actual parties' intention to restrict the duty of X to his production or supplies must be derived from the contract by means of interpretation.

(a) Strike

I. With regard to the case at issue, assuming that X cannot deliver the goods for a certain period of time, Y is entitled to cancel the contract, provided that the delay in the performance renders it useless for Y (i.e., pursuant to the provision of Art. 1464 CC, there is no longer an interest for the creditor). The crucial question is if X - in exercise of due care - could reasonably be expected to have foreseen and avoided the danger of delay or impossibility of performance due to the strike. In that case, the extraordinary and unforeseeable nature of the events is decisive. The test of the 'extraordinary and unforeseeable' character of the event may be applied only on a case-by-case basis. Pursuant to Italian case law, it cannot be excluded that the said rule applies to the case at issue (and therefore the dissolution of the contract would take place) if the supervening events were so exceptional and unforeseeable that they frustrate even the agreed clause.[1080] The application of the remedy would be excluded in case of an aleatory contract.

II. 1. If X's performance is not impossible but only more expensive, Art. 1467 CC could apply. However, Art. 1467 CC provides that, in the case of contracts that involve a continuing or a periodical performance or a delayed performance, the debtor may ask for the termination of the contract only if the performance has become extremely burdensome following extraordinary and unforeseeable events, and only if the supervening hardship exceeds the usual contractual risk (Art. 1467(2) CC). The limits fixed by the legislator determine a rather strict application of said rule by Italian courts.

2. Since the circumstances must be evaluated on a case-by-case basis, the strike of the workers could be considered neither extraordinary nor

[1080] Cass., 29 June 1981, n. 4249; Cass., 28 November 1958, n. 1373.

unforeseeable, taking into account that the supplier bears the risk of the organisation of the enterprise (i.e., the strike could not exceed the usual contractual risk). As a matter of fact, many supply contracts, particularly if they are long-term contracts, have hardship clauses, which usually provide for the risk of the strike of the workers (among other various contractual risks). Once again, the crucial question is whether X – in exercise of due care – could reasonably be expected to have foreseen and avoided the risk of the increase of the cost of the performance due to the strike.

(b) Cut of power supply by the state

I. As to the cut of power supply, it is necessary once again to determine whether or not the performance is impossible (this question, again, depends on whether the obligation in kind is restricted to the debtor's own supplies or the parties agreed upon a general obligation in kind). The questions of the temporary impossibility and the supervening increase of the cost of performance (which has become excessively onerous) are to be treated the same way as the previous case of the workers' strike.

Spain

There is a possibility that Y will be entitled to terminate the contract and claim damages under Spanish law in both Case 14(a) and 14(b).

I. 1. Since X has not fulfilled the obligation to deliver, Y may rely on X's non-performance of contractual obligations.

2. In alternative (a), Y could claim the termination of the contract and damages on the basis of Art. 1124 CC. If X is found to be liable, he will have to indemnify Y for any damage (Arts. 1101 *et seq.* CC). However, X might argue that he has not been able to perform due to external circumstances beyond his control and that he is therefore excused (Art. 1105 CC).

3. In the case at hand, X agrees to deliver some goods to Y on a certain date, but the workers of a subcontractor go on strike; X is excused if the strike is beyond his control and he has not expressly assumed the risk in the contract. In a similar case, a court rejected the application of the doctrine of *cláusula rebus sic stantibus*.[1081] The debtor demanded the modification of the contract because a strike by his workers did not

[1081] STS of 16 June 1983 (RJ 1983, 3632).

allow him to perform in time and led to higher costs than expected. However, in this case, the strike was expressly established in the contract as a risk assumed by the debtor. In further decisions, the courts have denied the application of Art. 1105 CC (force majeure) in cases of strike. In one case, the TS argued that this was not an unforeseeable circumstance.[1082] In another case, a court held that the risk of a strike was borne by the debtor when he concluded the contract.[1083]

II. Alternative (b) relates to a temporary impossibility to perform. The TS has dealt with a situation of a temporary impossibility to perform for one of the parties due to an administrative provision. The defendant claimed that forcing him to perform the obligation constituted an imbalance between obligations and that the new circumstances made his performance excessively onerous. The TS indicated that although the costs of construction might have increased during that period, the prices of the houses had increased as well, and, accordingly, the profits and losses were compensated.

III. Whether on the basis of this judgment Y would be granted a right to terminate is unclear. Respect for the principle of the sanctity of contracts usually leads the courts to maintain the contract as agreed by the parties, even if the performance is carried out after the agreed period for performance has expired. Only when performance becomes useless for Y may the court apply the doctrine of cessation of the contractual basis and terminate the contract.

Portugal

Under Portuguese law it can be argued that a strike, particularly if unlawful and without warning, represents an unforeseeable event which constitutes an excuse for the seller in Case 14(a). In 14(b) it is likely that an interruption in the power supply will be qualified as a change in the basis of the contract according to Art. 437 CC.

(a) Strike

I. 1. In the case of non-performance, there is a general presumption that the debtor is responsible. This presumption can be rebutted if the debtor shows that the failure to perform was due to a fact that he is not responsible for – an expression which is broader than merely

[1082] TS of 14 March 2001 (RJ 2001, 5977). [1083] 17 November 1997 (RJ 1997, 8129).

referring to an unexpected circumstance and force majeure. However, Art. 800, n°1 CC states that the provider is responsible for the actions of auxiliary persons he deploys to perform the contract as if he was acting himself.[1084] This is independent from any liability for the selection, control or instruction of auxiliaries. 'The creditor trusts that in performing the obligation, due care and competence should be exercised by the debtor, and he therefore expects the same level of expertise and diligence on the part of the auxiliaries'.[1085]

2. The described situation certainly relates to a subcontract, but it seems that the same rule that applies to the actual auxiliaries should apply in the case of non-performance of a subcontractor. Pedro Romano Martinez agrees, stating that 'the contractor is then objectively responsible under the terms of Art. 800 because the subcontractor is a person used for the purposes of performing his obligation'.[1086] This applies even though it is recognised that the situation of the subcontractor, like all those who are not part of the provider's own production system, is not exactly the same as that of a worker employed by the provider.[1087] So it appears that the contracting firm will be responsible to the same extent as the subcontracting firm.

II. 1. Furthermore, the question arises whether a strike at a subcontractor can be invoked as a cause for excusing non-performance as a case of force majeure or as an event that causes an objective impossibility to perform for reasons unrelated to any fault of the debtor (Art. 790 CC). Opinions on this matter differ considerably. António Nunes de Carvalho correctly maintains that the resolution of this problem usually lies in one of two opposing premises, which are 'like poles of natural attraction . . ., either one of which is able to offer a logical and reasonable basis for examination'.[1088] One can either seek to integrate a strike in the scope of the obligation by means of fundamental principles and rules of performance because of the civil justice fact of non-performance, or conversely view the strike as an essential matter and

[1084] Cf. António Pinto Monteiro, *Cláusulas Limitativas e de Exclusão de Responsabilidade Civil*, (Almedina: Coimbra, 1985), pp. 258 *et seq.*

[1085] *Ibid.*, p. 262.

[1086] Pedro Romano Martinez, *O Subcontrato* (Almedina: Coimbra, 1989), p. 142. Romano Martinez expressly excludes this rule equating subcontractors with auxiliaries in the fulfilment of certain kinds of subcontracts, such as, for example, in subletting or in '*subcomodato*' (contrary to the opinion of Larenz quoted at pp. 138–9).

[1087] See António Pinto Monteiro, *Cláusulas Limitativas*, p. 287.

[1088] António Nunes de Carvalho, 'Responsabilidade civil do empresário e greve', (1986) *Revista de Direito e de Estudos Sociais*, n°3, 367 *et seq* and n°4, 571 *et seq*, 382.

as a constitutionally sanctioned right and a legitimate method of self-protecting collective interests.

2. One may be tempted to say that a strike should not be an excuse for non-performance, for the simple reason that a lawful strike is a legally accepted method to produce loss. The employer should not be able to escape this loss by invoking the strike as an excuse for not fulfilling his contractual obligations which he owes to a third party. Otherwise the strike would not be effective. In reality, a strike action is a normal phenomenon, which occurs frequently in modern society. Therefore it cannot be considered unforeseeable – in fact a lawful strike is normally preceded by a warning.[1089] Thus, at least with regard to lawful strikes, it seems that they fall within the general risks of life or within the company's risk, and should not be invoked to excuse non-performance.

3. The situation is or can be very different in the case of a strike within a company: here, the strike may have been caused by unlawful conduct of the employer who, for example, may have violated the collective union agreement or may not have complied with his legal duty to renegotiate it. In these cases, at least, the strike, which he is ultimately responsible for, should not excuse his non-performance. And even if it is not an employer's unlawful action that led to the strike, consideration must be given to whether the employer (or his association) could have avoided the strike by accepting the demands. However, this is the most controversial scenario, as the employer cannot be considered as having been at fault if the demands were unrealistic, for example.

(b) Cut of power supply by the state

I. 1. In a situation of a power cut, the first task of the judge is always to determine the contractual distribution of risks, based on the

[1089] It is necessary to distinguish between lawful and unlawful strikes: unlawful strikes are usually uncontrollable and even unforeseeable for an employer. Without a doubt strike action is a relatively frequent phenomenon today, but this does not mean that a particular strike (or its intensity or duration) can be considered foreseeable. With regard to lawful strikes, it is once again important to distinguish between those which occur on an external level beyond the company (for example a general strike) or which are not related to a particular company (for example a sympathy or protest strike against working conditions affecting the whole industry – for those who consider this to be lawful). Such strikes cannot be avoided by an employer and we even consider them to be almost a '*fait du prince*'. They are part of the so-called overall basis of the agreement, to use Kegel's expression.

interpretation of the contract, in order to assess whether one of the parties had assumed that risk in any way. In fact, there is nothing in the exercise of private autonomy that prevents a party to an agreement from assuming an obligation to guarantee a determined result.[1090] In the words of Almeida Costa, 'it is possible for the contracting parties to remove or limit the application of Art. 437 CC, and assume greater risks'.[1091]

2. If such a risk was not included in the normal risks of the contract as concluded by the parties, it could then be argued that a power cut of this kind could qualify as a supervening alteration of circumstances. It could be said that power cuts are normal occurrences and that they should be considered. The same applies to inflation,[1092] for example. Today, this is not usually considered as an admissible supervening alteration but much more an ordinary fact of life. However, the possibility of a situation in which there was a sudden and enormous increase in the rate of inflation cannot be completely dismissed; in the same way, this power cut, because of its scale, is a completely anomalous occurrence – and the concept of anomaly is broader than the concept of the unforeseeable – and a '*fait du prince*', which no individual can control or avoid. It is part of the '*grande base negocial*', and should be relevant in our legal order, allowing for the termination or modification of the contract under the terms of Art. 437 CC.

Greece

The answer to Case 14 cannot be stated definitely as the legal assessment depends on various factors that remain ambiguous in our case.

I. If according to the contract X is obliged to purchase the goods only from the specific subcontractor (obligation in restricted kind), there are different scenarios to consider. If the performance has to be effected only at a specific time and a later performance would be useless to the creditor (absolutely fixed-date contract) the performance should be considered impossible.[1093] There is a rebuttable presumption that the

[1090] See Pinto Monteiro, *Cláusula penal e indemnização* (Coimbra Editora, 1990, reprinted in 1999), pp. 265 *et seq.*
[1091] Almeida Costa, *Direito das Obrigações*, p. 341.
[1092] See António Pinto Monteiro, *Inflação e Direito Civil* (Almedina: Coimbra Editora, 1984).
[1093] See Balis, *Law of Obligations*, pp. 160/1, 330/1; Gazis, *ErmAK*, Art. 401 n. 7; Stathopoulos, *Law of Obligations*, §17 n. 15; Ap. Georgiadis, *Law of Obligations*, §24 n. 36, §52 n. 36.

debtor is at fault, as in any kind of breach of a contract the following distinctions should be made:

(a) Strike

I. 1. Thus, if X can prove that the impossibility to perform is not due to his fault (because he has neither foreseen nor could have foreseen the strike of his subcontractor's workers), he is released from his obligations and discharged from any liability. Y is also released from his obligations (rule of common release - see Art. 380 AK), but he has no right, whatsoever, to compensation.

2. If, however, X cannot prove, that he was not at fault, Y either has the right to demand a common release (see Art. 380 AK) according to Art. 382 AK, or full compensation of his positive interest (non-performance damages), or he has a right to terminate the contract and to receive equitable compensation (see Art. 387 AK). Pursuant to the prevailing opinion,[1094] this kind of compensation covers his negative interest or, pursuant to another version,[1095] either negative or positive interest, based on judicial discretion.

(b) Cut of power supply by the state

I. If the contract is an absolutely fixed-time one, performance is impossible without X being at fault (the cut of the power supply due to the statutory intervention is undoubtedly an incident of force majeure). Thus, the prerequisites for the application of Art. 380 AK are met and both parties are released from their contractual obligations.

II. 1. If the performance has to be effected at a specific time, but a later performance is not useless for the creditor (relative fixed-date contract), after the expiration of the contractual deadline, X is considered to be in delay (his fault is assumed). Thus, Y, primarily, has the right to insist on performance and to receive compensation (positive interest) for the damages he suffered from the delay (see Art. 343 §1 AK). If, however, Y proves no longer to have an interest in the delayed performance, he can seek full compensation for his non-performance damages (positive interest- see Art. 343 §2 AK). Under such circumstances, Y is not released from his duty to perform, unless he seeks compensation according to the 'difference theory'. Furthermore, according to Art. 383 AK, Y has the

[1094] See George Mantzoufas, *Law of Obligations* (Athens: Sakkoulas, 1969), p. 85–6.

[1095] See AP 1417/1999, HellD 41, pp. 767, 767 II; Michailidis and Nouaros, *ErmAK*, Art. 387 n. 6; Stathopoulos 'Art. 387', in: Georgiadis and Stathopoulos (eds.), *AK*, n. 3.

right to ask for full compensation (positive interest) or to rescind the contract and ask for reasonable compensation (see Art. 387 AK). Nevertheless, Y does not acquire these rights immediately, as in the case of impossibility. First, he must fix a reasonable additional period for the debtor to perform, unless the whole attitude of the debtor demonstrates that this would be pointless (Art. 385 n. 1 AK), or he proves to have no further interest in the performance of the contract (Art. 385 n. 2 AK).

2. However, if X was not responsible for the delay, Y has no right to compensation. He is, nevertheless, entitled to rescind the contract. According to Art. 401 §1 AK, the creditor is entitled to rescind a fixed-date contract if the performance was not effected in time, independent of the debtor's fault.

III. If X has to deliver the purchased goods to Y without any special clause concerning the origin of the products (genuine obligation in kind), X is obliged to obtain the goods from another contractor within the agreed period of time. If X does not comply with this obligation, he is in breach of the contract. The specific form of breach, again, depends on whether the contract is stipulated as absolutely or relatively fixed-dated. If the contract is an absolute fixed-date contract, the non-compliance of X renders the performance impossible due to X's fault. Thus, Y has the rights under Art. 382 AK (common release, compensation or rescission cumulatively with reasonable compensation, see above). If there is a relative fixed-date contract, the non-compliance of X results in a situation of debtors' delay. As a result, Y has the rights of Art. 383 AK (compensation or rescission cumulatively with reasonable compensation only if a reasonable time-limit expired without effect, see above).

IV. In the case of a genuine obligation in kind, X is at fault, since he should have obtained the purchased goods, even from another country. Nevertheless, there is always the possibility that the cost for this action requires expenses that are extremely onerous for the debtor. Such an assessment can be influenced by the object of the performance, the importance of the creditor's interest and, in general, by the purpose of the obligation. If performance has become extremely onerous, then, according to a view of modern literature,[1096] the underlying basis of the contract is considered to have collapsed. According to another opinion,

[1096] See Stathopoulos, *Law of Obligations*, §19 nn. 58–9.

which is not indisputable,[1097] the debtor is released *ipso iure* due to a non-faulty (economic) impossibility to perform (see Art. 380 AK).[1098]

France and related jurisdictions

France

In Case 14(a) Y is likely to be entitled to damages as the doctrine of force majeure will only be applied to exceptional strikes, whereas in Case 14(b) the contract will be terminated or suspended under the doctrine of force majeure and Y will not be entitled to damages.

(a) Strike

I. A strike is not a case of force majeure because it is not an external event. This is even true for strikes at a subcontractor. Such events are part of X's sphere of responsibility. In exceptional situations, one can come to a different conclusion, for instance if the strike is part of a national strike.[1099] If the application of the doctrine of force majeure is rejected, the buyer will be entitled to damages. Should a case of force majeure be recognised, the buyer will not be entitled to damages and, if time is of the essence, the contract will be terminated. If time is not of the essence, the contract will be suspended.

(b) Cut of power supply by the state

I. In this case, force majeure (Art. 1148 Cciv) applies as the circumstances were unforeseeable and beyond the control of the parties. A different view has to be taken if the contract can normally be performed without working at night, which does not seem to be the case here. The contract will in principle not be terminated in this situation[1100] but be suspended until delivery except when time is of the essence. If time is of the essence, the contract can be brought to an end.

[1097] See above in the Overview (Chapter 4).

[1098] See Balis, *Law of Obligations*, §47; Litzeropoulos, *Elements*, vol. II, §156; Zepos, *Law of Obligations – General Part* (Athens: Sakkoula, 3rd edn, 1969), pp. 128 *et seq.*; Ap. Georgiadis, *Law of Obligations*, §24 n. 5.

[1099] Paris, 4 June 1980, JCP, 1980, II, n°19411 and the conclusions of Av.Gen Besnard and G. Cornu, RTD Civ, 1980, p. 1711; H. Sinay, 'La grève', in: G. H. Camerlynck (ed.), *Traité de droit du travail* (Paris: Dalloz, 1966), 313; Philippe, *Changement de circonstances*, 149.

[1100] *Ibid.*

Belgium

In Case 14(a) Y is likely to be entitled to damages, as the doctrine of force majeure will only be applied to exceptional strikes, whereas in Case 14(b) the contract will be terminated or suspended under the doctrine of force majeure and Y will not be entitled to damages.

(a) Strike

I. A strike, as a general rule, is not a case of force majeure under Belgian law because it is not an external event. This is even true for strikes experienced by a subcontractor; these events also fall within X's sphere of influence. Therefore the buyer is entitled to damages.

II. In exceptional situations, however, a strike can be qualified as force majeure, for instance if the strike is part of a nationwide strike.[1101] If force majeure applies, the buyer will not be entitled to damages and, if time is of the essence, the contract will be terminated. If time is not of the essence, the contract will be suspended.

(b) Cut of power supply by the state

I. In this variation, force majeure (Art. 1148 Cciv) applies as the circumstances are unforeseeable and beyond the control of the parties. A different view can only be taken if the contract can normally be performed without working at night which does not seem to be the case here.

England and related jurisdictions

England and Ireland

In both situations Y will most likely be entitled to terminate the contract for breach of contract and to recover damages. The chances of a frustration argument are low. They are stronger in the second scenario.

I. In general terms, the failure of X to deliver the goods constitutes a breach of contract.

[1101] D. Philippe and S. Michaux, 'La force majeure', in: *Traité de droit des obligations*, (Deventer: Kluwer, 2002); D. Philippe, *Changement de circonstances*, 207. Liège, 6 July 1949, *Jurisprudence de Liège*, 1949–1950, p. 83; Comm. Anvers, 17 April 1956, RW, 1955–56, 2029; comm. Liège, 3 March 1962, *Jurisprudence de Liège*, 1962, p. 172 and obs. M.H.; 24 January 1978, *Jurisprudence de Liège*, 1977–8, 190.

II. 1. If the contract is one for the sale of goods, it would be governed in Ireland by Section 27 Sale of Goods Act 1893, and, in England by Section 27 Sale of Goods Act 1979. The wording of these provisions is identical and as follows:

It is the duty of the seller to deliver the goods, and of the buyer to accept and pay for them, in accordance with the terms of the contract of sale.

2. If, as in this example, a time is fixed for the delivery of the goods and the goods are delivered late, the seller (X) would be in breach of contract. Whether or not the buyer (Y) can terminate the contract would depend on whether the time of delivery is said to be 'of the essence'. In *Hartley* v. *Hymans*[1102] it was stated that in ordinary commercial contracts for the sale of goods the rule is that time is *prima facie* of the essence with respect to delivery. Thus, if delivery is late the buyer may reject the goods, terminate the contract and sue for damages, even if the delay is slight.[1103] However, this is only a *prima facie* presumption, and depends on the construction and terms of the contract.[1104] Similar principles would apply if the contract was not one for the sale of goods, but simply a contract for the delivery of goods. The court would ask whether time was 'of the essence' i.e., whether the time of delivery was of such importance that a delay would justify terminating the contract.

3. If Y chooses to accept the goods, he is entitled to claim damages for late delivery. There is no indication in the legislation of how damages for late delivery should be assessed, so general contract law principles must apply. According to the rule in *Hadley* v. *Baxendale*, the measure of damages 'should be such as may fairly and reasonably be considered either arising naturally, i.e., according to the usual course of things, from such breach of contract or such as may reasonably be supposed to have been in the contemplation of both parties, at the time they made the contract, as the probable result of the breach of it.'[1105] This rule is illustrated in *Victoria Laundry (Windsor) Ltd* v. *Newman Industries Ltd*[1106] where the owner of a laundry business was entitled to claim loss of general profits suffered when a boiler which was supposed to be delivered in June was in fact delivered in November. However, the plaintiff

1102 [1920] KB 475.

1103 Alternatively, the buyer may waive the date of delivery and accept the goods late: *Charles Rickards* v. *Oppenhaim* [1950] 1 KB 616.

1104 See Section 10 Sale of Goods Act 1893.

1105 (1854) 9 Ex 341 at 354 per Alderson B.

1106 [1949] 2 KB 528.

could not claim for extra profits which would have resulted from a lucrative government contract because these contracts were exceptional and the defendant did not know about them.

4. If Y terminates the contract, he is still entitled to claim damages for non-delivery of the goods (a rejection of the goods is equated with non-delivery). If the contract is one for the sale of goods, it would be governed by Section 51 Sale of Goods Act 1893 which states:

> (2) The measure of damages is the estimated loss directly and naturally resulting, in the ordinary course of events, from the seller's breach of contract.
>
> (3) Where there is an available market for the goods in question the measure of damages is prima facie to be ascertained by the difference between the contract price and the market or current price of the goods at the time or times when they ought to have been delivered, or, if no time was fixed, then at the time of the refusal to deliver.

5. Section 51(2) essentially reflects the common law rule in *Hadley* v. *Baxendale* and the law would essentially be the same even if it wasn't a contract for the sale of goods. In applying Section 53(3), the court is interested in the market value of the goods at the time of delivery, and it makes no difference if the plaintiff did not in fact buy replacement goods, or if the plaintiff bought (or sold) goods at a more expensive rate than the market rate.[1107]

III. However, the situation could be different if X was entitled to plead frustration of contract. If X pleaded frustration of contract, X and Y would be discharged of their contractual obligations, so X would not have to deliver the goods and Y would (most likely) not have to pay the contract price. Unlike the situation with breach, Y would not be able to 'opt' to continue with the contract, and would not be able to insist on delivery at a later stage. Nor would Y be able to claim damages. It must then be asked whether X could claim the contract is frustrated in either situation presented.

(a) Strike

I. 1. A contract for the sale of goods involves strict liability on the part of the seller. The fact that the defendant has not acted carelessly, and that the defendant can put forward a plausible explanation for defective performance, is no defence in a contract action, and the courts would

[1107] *Williams* v. *Agius* [1914] AC 510.

most likely hold that the contract is not frustrated. This is graphically illustrated by the 1874 case of *Leeson* v. *North British Oil and Candle Company*.[1108] The defendants were sued for the non-delivery of a consignment of paraffin that they had agreed to sell to the plaintiffs. The defendants pleaded that their failure to deliver the paraffin was due to a strike at the premises of their own suppliers. This was held not to provide a defence to the plaintiff's claim in damages.

2. The specific issue of whether a strike can frustrate a service contract was examined by McWilliam J in *McGuill* v. *Aer Lingus and United Airlines*.[1109] McGuill booked a holiday package for a group of persons, the holiday envisaging a flight from Ireland with Aer Lingus and onward internal flights with United. At the time the flights were booked United employees had served strike notice and the strike went ahead, disrupting the internal travel arrangements made with the plaintiffs. It was held that United could not plead frustration of the contract because there was knowledge on the part of United that a strike was foreseeable but United had failed to advise the plaintiff of this risk. However, McWilliam J did say: 'I do not accept the argument made on behalf of the plaintiff that a strike by the employees of a party cannot cause frustration of a contract. In my opinion it depends entirely on the circumstances whether it does nor not.' The decision in *McGuill* really turns upon the fact that the event was known by one party and, absent a specific provision in the contract, such an event should not frustrate a contract.

3. It will be very difficult to make out a frustration defence. In *Zuphen and Others* v. *Kelly Technical Services (Ireland) Ltd*[1110] Murphy J said:

> It is not hardship or inconvenience or a material loss itself which calls the principles of frustration into play. There must have been such a change in the significance of the obligation that the thing undertaken would, if performed, be a different thing from that contracted for.

4. In this case it is likely that the courts would hold that the strike is just a hardship or inconvenience, and not a frustrating event.

[1108] [1874] 8 IRCL 309.

[1109] Unreported, Irish High Court, October 3, 1983, extracts can be found in R. Clark and B. Clarke, *Contract – Cases and Materials* (Dublin: Gill and MacMillan, 4th edn, 2000), pp. 984–7.

[1110] [2000] ELR 277, 291.

(b) Cut of power supply by the state

I. 1. While the interruption of the supply of electricity would appear to present a similar scenario to that of the strike, it is possible to see this as a supervening event for frustration purposes, especially if the scale of the disruption is unprecedented.[1111] The difference between the two situations is essentially that in (a) a strike would be seen as a normal, foreseeable risk in contracting, which should be provided for in the contract, whereas in this situation a decision by the government to cut the electricity during the night would be an unforeseen event for which the parties would not necessarily expect to provide. The situation is somewhat similar to the Australian case of *Codelfa Construction Pty Ltd* v. *State Rail Authority of New South Wales*.[1112] There a construction company had contracted with the railway authority to perform excavations for the construction of an underground railway, the work to be performed within a fixed period. A third party obtained an injunction against the plaintiff, preventing it from carrying out certain work between 10 pm and 6 am and on Sundays. The construction company claimed that the contract was frustrated by the grant of the injunction. The High Court held that the injunction which prevented night time work meant that performance of the contract was radically different from that which has been originally contemplated.

2. However, if in the situation in question the supplier of the goods is producing a volume of goods and providing these to some of his customers, but is not supplying Y because the volume of production is below the anticipated level, then the decision to supply A, B and C, for example, but not Y, is not a frustrating event: see *Maritime National Fish Ltd* v. *Ocean Trawlers Ltd*.[1113]

Scotland

Assuming that the contract in Case 14 does not contain a force majeure clause, in both Cases (a) and (b) the contract is not frustrated. Y is entitled to terminate the contract (assuming that the breach is a material one) and claim damages from X.

I. There is very little authority in Scots law on whether strikes frustrate contracts. This may be because in many commercial contracts the parties will have inserted a force majeure clause to regulate the outcome in such situations. For example, in shipping law, the contract of

[1111] *Metropolitan Water Board* v. *Dick Kerr & Co* [1918] AC 119 (Eng).
[1112] (1982) 149 CLR 337. [1113] [1935] AC 524 (Eng).

charter-party usually excludes the charterer's obligation to discharge the cargo at a dock in a strike situation. In most of the reported cases therefore the important issue for consideration is usually whether the facts of the situation fall within the ambit of the force majeure clause excluding the charterer from liability. One such example is *Horsley Line Ltd* v. *Roechling Bros.*[1114] A ship was prevented from discharging her cargo because it was moored end-on a quay and to discharge the cargo in this position would have been contrary to a declaration of the presidents of two cooperative societies of labour. Under the charter-party, the charterers were excluded from their obligation to discharge in cases of strikes. It was held that the actual occurrence could not be construed as a strike within the meaning of that contractual clause.[1115] It is clear that the Scottish courts interpret such clauses strictly, and will only absolve the contracting party of its obligations under a force majeure clause if the circumstances fall clearly within the terms of the clause.[1116]

II. 1. The issue of strikes and frustration were considered in the case of *Milligan* v. *Ayr Harbour Trs.*[1117] In this case an argument was, raised that circumstances had made the contract practically impossible to perform. That attempt failed, and their Lordships definitively rejected the suggestion that contracts can ever be frustrated as a result of practical impossibility.[1118] Because of the operation of private Acts of Parliament, the defender was bound either to supply labour for the unloading of ships or to provide unloading facilities for use by workers supplied by the shipowner. The defenders refused to do either on the grounds that their labourers had refused to work on the particular ship and if facilities were provided for outside labourers, there would be a strike. The contract was found not to be frustrated and the defenders were held liable in damages.

2. Walker confirms this strict approach: '... unless the contract provides it, it is no excuse that performance has been delayed or prevented by weather, shortage of materials, delay by suppliers, industrial action by employees, or the like.'[1119] It is likely that the Scottish courts would exhibit a similarly strict attitude to lack of performance due to

[1114] 1908 SC 866.

[1115] See also *Budgett & Co* v. *Binnington* [1891] 1 QB 35; *Forrester's Trustee* v. *McKelvie* (1895) 22 R. 437 and *Arden Steamship Co Ltd* v. *William Mathwin & Son* 1912 SC 211.

[1116] Walker, *Contract*, para. 31.44 and cases cited above.

[1117] 1915 SC 937.

[1118] 1915 SC 937 per the Lord Justice - Clerk at 948; Lord Dundas at 949–50; Lord Salvesan at 952.

[1119] Walker, *Contract*, at para. 31.44; see also Gloag, *Contract*, p. 352.

non-availability of the electricity supply. This would also fall within the category of contracts which cannot be performed through practical impossibility.

Editors' comparative notes

The open jurisdictions

Y is generally allowed to terminate the contract in all of the open jurisdictions under their respective rules on breach of contract. There are some variations with regard to the question whether or not Y's right to terminate the contract is subject to fixing an additional (reasonable) period for performance.

The more interesting question is whether X is liable to pay damages to Y or whether he is excused due to the character of the impediments to performance. The issue of excuse depends on many factors, in particular on the interpretation of the agreement and on the assessment of events (a) and (b). The complex interplay of these factors and their assessment based on the fact pattern of the case at hand makes it difficult to identify clear tendencies with regard to the results of the cases. However, it may be stated that the open jurisdictions appear to grant relief more readily in case (b) than in case (a) (cf., e.g., Austria, Greece, Portugal, Spain).

Three factors appear to be of relevance in assessing X's liability: (i) the character of X's duty under the contract, (ii) his responsibility for the events under the contract and (iii) mechanisms that allow for a re-allocation of this risk due to the extraordinary character of the impediments.

(i) As a starting point, the character of X's obligation under the contract is discussed by most reporters. Many jurisdictions distinguish between general obligations and obligations restricted to the sellers own supplies (cf. Austria, Germany, Greece, Italy). In the case of a general obligation X is obliged to procure goods in the entire market whereas under an obligation restricted to own supplies the obligation is limited to his own production facilities. The character of the seller's duty usually depends on the contractual agreement as interpreted by the courts. In the case of a general obligation in kind, X has to bear the risk of both events, in principle, whereas in case of an obligation restricted to his own supplies, X's liability depends on whether or not he is responsible for the impediment.

(ii) The dominant position among the open jurisdictions is that liability for damages requires fault (typically negligence) on the side of the debtor.

However, in most jurisdictions, the debtor bears the burden of proof with regard to his excuse. As far as Case (a) (the strike) is concerned, many reports state that X's responsibility depends on whether or not he could have foreseen the strike and taken action to prevent it. Alternatively some reporters discuss vicarious liability and hold X responsible for the strike if his subcontractor is responsible for the strike (Austria, Germany, Lithuania, the Netherlands, Portugal, Sweden). In Case (b) (the power supply), the main question similarly seems to be whether X could have foreseen and overcome this event (cf. in particular the German report).

(iii) The extraordinary character of the impediments to production is considered under different doctrinal aspects. One may distinguish three points of reference: (a) Most jurisdictions refer to the extraordinary character of the impediment when assessing the issue of fault as an element of a contractual claim for damages. (b) In some jurisdictions the impediments may relieve X from his contractual liability on the basis of the concept of (economic) impossibility. In Germany, however, this can only apply if Y's interest in the goods is grossly disproportionate to the costs of X, which is not the case here. In Lithuania, impossibility will only apply if performance is impossible for anyone. (c) In some jurisdictions, the character of the impediment does not just exclude X's contractual liability for damages but it may justify the application of 'exceptional' doctrines (e.g., *Geschäftsgrundlage*, cf. Germany, Greece), potentially resulting in a flexible distribution of the losses by adjustment.

The closed jurisdictions

According to all of the closed jurisdictions, the purchaser, Y, may terminate the contract. Y is also entitled to damages in most of the closed jurisdictions based on their strict liability rules on breach of contract. There are very few conceptual approaches in the closed jurisdictions that will unburden X from his contractual liability.

The common law jurisdictions and Scotland, in particular, assume strict liability and therefore X is liable in damages even if he is not at fault with regard to the impediments (i.e., could not have foreseen and avoided them). X can only be excused under common law and Scottish law if the contract is frustrated, which is not likely to be the case in any of the three jurisdictions. However, the English and Irish report does not rule out the possibility that a contract could be frustrated due to a strike or a cut of power supply under circumstances more exceptional than those presented in the fact pattern.

In the Czech Republic and in Denmark, the result is similar to the one in the common law jurisdictions: the doctrine of force majeure is not deemed applicable and therefore X is liable for damages. The French and Belgian report stresses that X can only be excused under exceptional circumstances, i.e., if the strike is launched at a national level.

Conclusion

In all the jurisdictions, Y is entitled to terminate the contract. Thus, X's interest in carrying out the contract after the impediment has ceased to exist is unanimously disregarded irrespective of the extraordinary nature of the impediments.

Therefore, the dominant issue is whether or not Y is entitled to damages for breach of contract. It is quite remarkable, yet not surprising, that the distinction between open and closed jurisdictions is in line with the division between systems that apply a fault liability regime with regard to contractual damages and systems that assume strict liability. With regard to both distinctions, a different approach materialises with regard to balancing the principle of *pacta sunt servanda* with equity considerations. The higher degree of flexibility that is characteristic for the open jurisdictions in dealing with unexpected circumstances corresponds with more flexible conditions with regard to liability for breach of contract.

On the basis of their strict liability regime, there is a clear tendency among the closed jurisdiction to hold X liable for damages. The findings of the open jurisdictions remain somewhat vague due to the limited fact basis of the given case. However, subject to the factual details, X has a strong case in challenging his liability in many of the open jurisdictions. In particular, he may argue that, due to the external and exceptional impediments, he is not at fault and therefore the conditions of the damages claim are not met. Furthermore, he may be relieved from his contractual liability on the basis of the 'exceptional' doctrines (e.g., *Geschäftsgrundlage*).

Case 15 Disclaimer

Disclaimer concerning the rights arising from unexpected circumstances; other clauses related to unexpected circumstances

The construction company X agrees to build a double-floor building on Y's land for the price of €2,000,000. In the contract the parties stipulate a disclaimer which excludes 'all the rights of both parties arising from unexpected circumstances'. Two weeks after the construction work has begun a granite rock, which could not have been detected by the parties before the conclusion of the contract, is revealed on Y's land. As a result the costs of the construction increase by 300 per cent.

Can X ask for an adjustment of the contract or can he terminate the contract in spite of the disclaimer?

Germany and related jurisdictions

Germany

X is not entitled to ask for adjustment or termination of the contract.

I. 1. X cannot refuse performance based on §275 II BGB. According to this rule, the debtor may refuse to perform if specific performance requires expenditures that are manifestly disproportionate to the other party's interest in performance. Whether this is the case has to be determined with regard to the subject matter of the obligation and the principle of good faith. In the case at hand the aggravation of performance by the granite rock probably does not increase the value of the completed building and thus might result in disproportionality between X's expenditure and Y's interest in performance.

2. However, first, according to the majority of legal writers[1120] §275 II BGB is *not* applicable if the aggravation of performance is caused by a distortion in the equivalence of exchange, since in those cases §275 II BGB is superseded by §313 BGB. The reason is that the latter provision takes the interests of both parties into consideration. Secondly, it is doubtful whether the increase of 300 per cent qualifies as a *manifest* disproportionality since §275 II BGB applies only in exceptional cases.[1121] With regard to the disclaimer, there is no manifest disproportionality at all because whether there is a relevant disproportionality has to be determined on the basis of the contractual allocation of risks.[1122] This allocation of risks must be specified by an interpretation

[1120] Cf. C.-W. Canaris, 'Sondertagung Schuldrechtsmodernisierung', 501; Grüneberg, '§313', in: Palandt *et al.* (eds.), *Bürgerliches Gesetzbuch*, n. 41.

[1121] Cf. Grüneberg, '§275', in: Palandt *et al.* (eds.), *Bürgerliches Gesetzbuch*, n. 27; for a manifest disproportionality cf. BGH NJW 1988, 699.

[1122] U. Huber, 'Die Schadensersatzhaftung des Verkäufers wegen Nichterfüllung der Nacherfüllungspflicht und die Haftungsbegrenzung des § 275 Abs. 2 BGB neuer Fassung', in: G. Hager and I. Schwenzer (eds.), *Festschrift für Peter Schlechtriem zum 70.*

of the contractual disclaimer. The issue is whether the disclaimer mutually allocates all unforeseen risks to the affected party or whether there are limits to this contractual risk allocation. In any case, the aggravation caused by the granite rock is covered by the disclaimer since neither the cause of the aggravation nor its extent are clearly beyond the coverage of the clause.

II. Additionally, X has no right to terminate the contract or ask for its adaptation applying the concept of *Störung der Geschäftsgrundlage* (§313 BGB). This is true even if a normal constitution of the soil may qualify as *Geschäftsgrundlage* of the contract which is substantially affected by the granite rock. In the given case, there is no undue burden for X. The extent to which X has to bear the risk of this substantial distortion of the equivalence of exchange by the unexpected circumstance is governed by all the circumstances of the specific case, in particular the statutory or contractual allocation of risks.[1123] An example for the latter one are ventures. Moreover, without a doubt, the parties can explicitly or even implicitly stipulate the allocation of the risk of unexpected circumstances[1124] and exclude the adaptation of the contract in the case of an unexpected circumstance on the basis of the concept of *Störung der Geschäftsgrundlage* (§313 BGB).[1125] Under this agreement every party bears the risk of unexpected circumstances that interfere with its contractual rights or obligations. The judge may not interfere with a valid contractual allocation of the risk invoking equity.[1126] However, contractual clauses that allocate such risks are subject to interpretation according to §§133, 157 BGB. Thus it has to be determined whether the clause covers the risk at hand.[1127] A clause may be construed narrowly if it relates to risks that were foreseen by the parties

Geburtstag (Tübingen: Mohr, 2003), pp. 521 *et seq.*; Grüneberg, '§275', in: Palandt *et al.* (eds.), *Bürgerliches Gesetzbuch*, n. 28.

1123 Cf. for the contractual allocation of the risk as general foundation of the concept of *Störung der Geschäftsgrundlage*, H. Köhler, '*Störung des Geschäftsgrundlage*', in: Canaris *et al.* (eds.), *50 Jahre Bundesgerichtshof – Festgabe aus der Wissenschaft*, vol. I, pp. 295 (300).

1124 Cf. Roth, '§313', in: Krüger (ed.), *Münchener Kommentar zum Bürgerlichen Gesetzbuch*, vol. II, nn. 28 *et seq.*; Grüneberg, '§313', in: Palandt *et al.* (eds.), *Bürgerliches Gesetzbuch*, n. 20; an implicit allocation of the risk may result from a fixed price contract cf. BGHZ 129, 236 (253); Köhler, '*Störung de Geschaftsgrundlage*', in: Canaris *et al.* (eds.), *50 Jahre Bundesgerichtshof – Festgabe aus der Wissenschaft*, vol. I, pp. 295 (302 *et seq.*).

1125 Cf. BGH LM §242 BGB (Bb) n. 162; BGHZ 2, 379 (383); Roth, '§313', in: Krüger (ed.), *Münchener Kommentar zum Bürgerlichen Gesetzbuch*, vol. II, n. 34, 40.

1126 Cf. BGHZ 121, 378 (392); BGHZ 74, 370; Roth, '§313', in: Krüger (ed.), *Münchener Kommentar zum Bürgerlichen Gesetzbuch*, n. 37.

1127 Cf. *ibid.*, vol. II, nn. 34, 36 *et seq.*

at the time of formation. Additionally, if the contract includes a risk premium this may indicate the extent of the clause.

III. 1. Recently, in the scholarly discussion, the issue whether the contractual allocation of the risk itself is subject to an adaptation by the concept of *Störung der Geschäftsgrundlage* was addressed. According to some legal writers, the results of the economic analysis of law as well as of the scientific risk analysis reveal structural limits of the parties' ability to evaluate the risk at hand. According to this minority opinion these limits may justify a judicial allocation of the risk at hand on the basis of §313 BGB even though it seems to be covered by a contractual risk allocation.[1128]

2. In the given case the contractual provision covers the risk at hand. The risk is within the explicit wording of the clause and the price may be computed including the resulting risk allocation. Additionally, the unexpected condition of the soil qualifies clearly as a 'usual' risk in contracts for building. Thus it is covered by the will of the parties at the time of formation and there is no reason to disregard this will on the ground of the economic analysis of law.

Austria

X has no right to claim adjustment of the contract. However, despite the disclaimer X will be entitled to avoid the contract if Y does not pay for the additional costs of construction.

I. 1. The unexpected granite rock in the soil leads to a gross inequivalence of performance and counter-performance in the proportion of 1:3. Under Austrian law this inequivalence could be treated as an issue of impossibility of performance (§920 ABGB), as '*laesio enormis*' (§934 ABGB) or as '*Wegfall/Fehlen der Geschäftsgrundlage*' (alternatively 'mutual mistake').

2. As the granite rock was there from the beginning this must be considered a case of 'initial impossibility' ('*anfängliche Unmöglichkeit*'). 'Impossibility' does not only cover factual or legal impossibility, but also 'economic impossibility' in the sense of '*Unerschwinglichkeit*' (i.e., 'unaffordability') the latter concept covers cases in which the debtor is able to perform, but performance would be so extremely costly

[1128] Cf. for further details, *ibid.*, nn. 38 *et seq.*; H. Köhler, '*Zur ökonomischen Analyse des Regeln über die Geschäftsgrundlage*', in: H.-B. Schäfer and C. Ott (eds.), *Allokationseffizienz in der Rechtsordnung* (Berlin: Springer, 1989), S. 148 (1959); H.-B. Schäfer and C. Ott, *Lehrbuch der ökonomischen Analyse des Zivilrechts* (Berlin: Springer, 4th edn, 2005), SS. 250 *et seq.*

or otherwise burdensome for him that he cannot reasonably be expected to perform under the circumstances.[1129] 'Economic impossibility' entitles X to avoid the contract. The typical case of 'economic impossibility' ('unaffordability') can be described as follows: the increased costs of a party's performance are due to a change of the general economic circumstances in a market (e.g., the seller can procure the goods in the market only for a much higher price due to excessive inflation or other grave changes in the market) and the party risks insolvency or financial ruin if he were forced to perform under these circumstances.[1130]

3. It is disputed whether 'economic impossibility' also covers other cases than the above-mentioned typical case of 'unaffordability'.[1131] F. Bydlinski suggests using the rule of '*laesio enormis*' (§934 AGBG) also when applying other private law rules in gross imbalance of performance cases:[1132] §934 ABGB entitles a party to avoid a contract if there is an initial imbalance between the values of the performances of more than 1:2. F. Bydlinski aims to apply this rule in combination with the financial ruin rule of 'unaffordability' in cases of '*Wegfall der Geschäftsgrundlage*'. In this case, the difference of €4,000,000 between the two prices could cause X's financial ruin in the sense mentioned above. If this was the case, Austrian courts would clearly qualify the situation as 'economic impossibility'. If X was *not* threatened by financial ruin as a consequence of the performance of the contract, it is uncertain whether Austrian courts would still find a situation of 'economic impossibility'. It is uncertain whether they would take up F. Bydlinski's argument. In the light of '*laesio enormis*' an imbalance of performances promised by the parties of 1:3 (which is far more than 1:2) must seriously put the validity of the transaction in question (and would amount to an 'impossibility').

3. The *laesio enormis* provisions apply to exchange contracts (synallagmatic contracts) where one party receives from the other party not even half the value of what he himself has given. This objective disproportion

1129 Reischauer, '§920', in: Rummel (ed.), *Kommentar zum ABGB*, vol. I, n. 4 with further references.

1130 With further references F. Bydlinski, 'Zum Wegfall der Geschäftsgrundlage im österreichischen Recht' (1996) *Österreichisches Bankarchiv*, 499 at 507; Reischauer, '§920', in: Rummel (ed.), *Kommentar zum ABGB*, vol. I, n. 4.

1131 *Ibid.*, vol. I, n. 4.

1132 F. Bydlinski, 'Zum Wegfall der Geschäftsgrundlage im österreichischen Recht', 499 at 507.

of performance and counter-performance must exist at the time of the conclusion of the contract.[1133] In our case the contract obliges X to perform construction work and services worth 300 per cent of the contract price, whereas Y has to pay only 100 per cent. In the case of '*laesio enormis*' the disadvantaged party can terminate/avoid the contract. The other party can save the contract by paying to the disadvantaged party the difference between the agreed performance (price) and the market value of the counter-performance (three times the price). In our case Y would have to pay three times the contract price to X (€6,000,000) in order to keep up the contract. If Y refuses to do so, X would be entitled to terminate the contract.

4. As the doctrine of '*Wegfall der Geschäftsgrundlage*'[1134] is – in a strict sense – applicable only subsidiarily, §934 ABGB would exclude this doctrine. There is, however, no clear indication in the decisions that §934 ABGB must necessarily exclude the doctrine of '*Wegfall der Geschäftsgrundlage*'. And the rules on impossibility do not necessarily apply in this case either (mere 'economic impossibility' if not 'unaffordability'). The doctrine of '*Wegfall der Geschäftsgrundlage*' could, therefore, play a decisive role in this case.

5. The fact that the soil is of a normal quality could be considered as a '*Geschäftsgrundlage*' in this case. The doctrine of '*Wegfall/Fehlen der Geschäftsgrundlage*' would entitle X to avoid the contract. If the parties would have contracted at a different price if they had known from the beginning that there was a granite rock, X could claim the adjustment of the price.[1135] In this case it seems very unlikely that Y would have accepted a price that was three times the initial contract price and X would not have accepted a lower price than 300 per cent because it would not even allow him to cover his costs of construction. Therefore X would only be entitled to avoid the contract.

[1133] Reischauer, '§934', in: Rummel (ed.), *Kommentar zum ABGB*, vol. I, n. 5; P. Bydlinski, '§934', in: Koziol, P. Bydlinski and Bollenberger (ed.), *Kurzkommentar zum ABGB*, n. 1.

[1134] Reischauer, '§901', in: Rummel (ed.), *Kommentar zum ABGB*, vol. I, n. 6 with further references; Gschnitzer, in: Klang (ed.), *Kommentar zum ABGB*, vol. IV, p. 335; Rummel, 'Anmerkungen zum gemeinsamen Irrtum und zur Geschäftsgrundlage', 1 at 7, 10; Koziol and Welser, *Bürgerliches Recht*, vol. I, pp. 163 *et seq.*; Apathy, '§901', in: Schwimann (ed.), *Kommentar zum ABGB*, vol. IV, n. 11; Franz Bydlinski, 'Vertragsrechtliche Grundfragen des Industrieanlagenbaus', in: Aicher and Korinek (eds.), *Rechtsfragen des nationalen und internationalen Industrieanlagenbaus* (Vienna: LexisNexis, 1991), p. 67 at 115.

[1135] By analogy with the law of mistake: Koziol and Welser, *Bürgerliches Recht*, vol. I, p. 165; Rummel, '§872', in: Rummel (ed.), *Kommentar zum ABGB*, vol. I, nn. 1, 7.

6. However, the doctrine of '*Wegfall/Fehlen der Geschäftsgrundlage*' is only applicable if we are not dealing with a 'mutual mistake' under the Austrian law of mistake (see Case 13 above).[1136] If one assumes that the erroneous expectations of the parties concern the subject matter of the contract or an important characteristic of it, the law of mistake applies (§§871 *et seq.* ABGB '*Geschäftsirrtum*'). If one assumes that they do not concern the subject matter of the contract but its general basis and wider circumstances, the law of mistake does not apply, but the doctrine of '*Wegfall/Fehlen der Geschäftsgrundlage*' does.[1137] Krejci[1138] assumes that in most building contracts the quality of the soil is an important factor for the planning, calculation and construction of the building and is therefore an integrated part of the building contract itself. If both parties are mistaken with respect to the quality of the soil, the rules of mutual mistake (see Case 13 above) entitle the parties to avoid or adjust the contract. If one follows Krejci's approach, §871 ABGB entitles X to avoid the contract and the doctrine of '*Wegfall der Geschäftsgrundlage*' is not applicable.

7. However, in other cases it may well be possible that the quality of the soil was not included into the contract by the parties. In our case the parties did not discuss the quality of the soil because they may have had good reasons to expect it to be normal. Therefore, the quality of the soil cannot be considered to be part of the main object of the contract or an important characteristic of it in the sense of §871 ABGB. The doctrine of '*Wegfall/Fehlen der Geschäftsgrundlage*' will apply. Both approaches (mutual mistake and '*Wegfall/Fehlen der Geschäftsgrundlage*') lead to the same result: X is entitled to avoid the contract with *ex tunc* effect (retrospective effect).

II. 1. The next question is whether these provisions can be derogated from by a contractual exclusion of 'all rights of both parties arising from unexpected circumstances'.

2. The rules of impossibility and '*Wegfall/Fehlen der Geschäftsgrundlage*' can be altered or excluded by party agreement. The rules on '*laesio enormis*' (§§934, 935 ABGB) can be waived by (disadvantaged) parties who are merchants in the sense of the Austrian Commercial Code (§351 UGB). Here we can assume that X is a merchant and a waiver

[1136] OGH, SZ 54/71.

[1137] Rummel, '§901', in: Rummel (ed.), *Kommentar zum ABGB*, vol. I, n. 6.

[1138] Heinz Krejci, 'Die bauvertragliche Pflicht der Baugrundrisikotragung', (1988) *wirtschaftsrechtliche blätter*, 425.

would, therefore, be valid. However, all disclaimers are subject to the general clause of '*gute Sitten*' (good faith, public morality) in §879(1) ABGB. A provision violating the standard of '*gute Sitten*' will be invalid (voidable by the disadvantaged party). §879(3) ABGB contains a special rule for contractual provisions that are part of standard forms: a standard form provision which does not determine the main performances of the parties will be invalid if it unilaterally places one party at a gross disadvantage.

3. In our case, the disclaimer is probably not part of the standard terms of one of the parties but an individually negotiated provision. It is, at first sight, not a provision constituting a *unilateral* disadvantage of one party, because it excludes the 'rights of *both* parties arising from unexpected circumstances'. The relevant provisions for building contracts in the ABGB (especially §§1168, 1168a) state as a general rule that the ordering party (Y) is liable for circumstances belonging to its sphere of responsibility that prevent the execution of the work or make it more difficult. The soil, as well as the examination of the soil, fall within the ordering party's sphere of responsibility.[1139] If the ordering party loses its interest in the building contract for reasons connected with the qualities of the site (see Case 5 above), he can prevent the execution of X's work and pay the contract price minus the costs saved by X (§1168 ABGB). The risk that the building is destroyed (before acceptance) due to defects of the soil has to be borne by the ordering party (§1168a ABGB). Equally, additional construction costs caused by the problematic quality of the soil have to be borne by the ordering party. Even the agreement on a lump sum price does not shift the risk of the unexpected problematic quality of the soil to the constructor of the building.[1140] Additionally, all above-mentioned provisions (impossibility, '*laesio enormis*', mutual mistake, '*Geschäftsgrundlage*') would give X the right to avoid the contract.

4. This leads us to the conclusion that the disclaimer of rights arising from unexpected circumstances is – at least with respect to the quality of the soil – unilaterally burdensome for X, because – if valid – it would deprive him of all his rights under the ABGB regime which would remove the gross inequivalence of performances.

[1139] *Ibid.*; Krejci, '§1168a', in: Rummel (ed.), *Kommentar zum ABGB*, vol. I, n. 19, 34d; OGH, wbl 1987, 219; OGH, *ecolex* 1998, 204 = RdW 1998, 66; OGH, JBl 2001, 786.

[1140] Krejci, '§1168a', in: Rummel (ed.), *Kommentar zum ABGB*, vol. I, n. 19.

5. X can certainly be required to unilaterally bear the increased costs due to the unexpected problematic quality of the soil, if these additional costs are not exorbitant (but here they exceed three times the contract price) and do not lead to a gross imbalance between the performances thus putting X in a very desperate situation.

6. Another problem arises from the fact that the disclaimer is phrased in very general terms. According to court decisions the risk of the quality of soil can, in principle, be attributed to the construction company by the contractual provisions.[1141] Such a contractual reallocation of the risk in question from the ordering party to the construction company must, however, be formulated with reasonable clearness. The risk that the quality of the soil turns out to be problematic and that construction costs can increase considerably must be expressly mentioned in the contract. Furthermore, even such a clearly formulated disclaimer would be subject to the clause of '*gute Sitten*' (public morality) if it led to extreme results.[1142]

7. Considering the gross unilateral imbalance between the performances caused by the disclaimer clause and its general formulation, which does not ensure that the construction company could really be aware of the risk of inappropriate soil it thereby undertook to bear unilaterally, the disclaimer must be seen as a violation of the clause of '*gute Sitten*' in §879(1) ABGB and is voidable by X. Therefore, the above mentioned rights of X rest intact.

8. An obligation to renegotiate exists only if it is provided by the contract.[1143] In our case, X can ask Y to renegotiate the contract; Y can do so voluntarily (in order to 'save' the contract). But if Y refuses to renegotiate the contract, X cannot legally compel him to do so.

III. The case reveals an initial gross imbalance between the main performances of the contract of the relation 1 (contract price):3 (costs of performance). The major instrument to guard against such gross imbalances under Austrian law is the instrument of '*laesio enormis*'. It may be assisted by other provisions and doctrines like 'economic

[1141] OGH, *ecolex* 1998, 204 = RdW 1998; OGH, JBl 2001, 786.

[1142] Krejci, 'Zulässigkeitsgrenzen bauvertraglicher Risikoverschiebungen zu Lasten des Auftragnehmers', (1999) *wirtschaftsrechtliche blätter*, 385 at 393; Peter Rummel, 'Das "Baugrundrisiko", ein neuer Rechtsbegriff?', in: *Festschrift für Rudolf Strasser zum 70. Geburtstag* (Vienna: Manz, 1993), 309 at 310; Bollenberger, '§879', in: Koziol, P. Bydlinski, and Bollenberger (eds.), *Kurzkommentar zum ABGB*, n. 24.

[1143] F. Bydlinski, in: Aicher and Korinek (eds.), *Rechtsfragen des nationalen und internationalen Industrieanlagenbaus*, 67 at 108.

impossibility', '*Fehlen der Geschäftsgrundlage*' or 'mutual mistake'. They all give the disadvantaged party the right to avoid the contract or to adjust the contract if the other party is willing to pay the increased costs. The general provisions of distribution of risk in a construction contract will lead to similar conclusions: the ordering party (Y) bears the risk of the quality of the soil, has to pay additional costs or withdraw from the contract. The key question of the case is whether the parties can waive these rules by party agreement, i.e., whether they can validly assign the risk of an unexpected problematic quality of the soil to the construction company (X). The answer is yes, but only if the risks allocated to the construction company are clearly indicated in the contract and if the contractual risk allocation scheme is not an exorbitant unilateral burden for the construction company. This would be contrary to the standard of public morality ('*gute Sitten*'). In our case these requirements do not seem to be met and consequently the disclaimer clause in the contract has to be considered invalid.

The Netherlands

Under Dutch law, it is not entirely clear whether a court would allocate the risk in question to the construction company X or the principal Y. It is unlikely that a general exclusion of remedies resulting from unexpected circumstances will be considered to effectively allocate the whole risk to the construction company. The courts will probably take the disclaimer into account in assessing the risks that the parties assumed under the contract.

I. X and Y cannot entirely contract away the right of a party to amend or terminate a contract on the basis of unforeseen circumstances. Such an exclusionary clause may reduce the scope of the default rule of Art. 7:753 but it cannot exclude the applicability of the doctrine of changed circumstances, as codified in Arts. 6:258 *et seq*. Dutch Civil Code. Article 7:753 is a provision in Title 7.12 Dutch Civil Code on 'contracting for (construction) work', and is often considered as an elaboration of the broader Art. 6:258. An important difference between the two is that Art. 7:753 provides for a default rule, the scope of which can be mitigated, as in the case at hand, whereas Art. 6:258 is mandatory law,[1144] thereby implying that the courts are more reluctant to amend contracts. Despite the mandatory nature of Art. 6:258, the parties can

[1144] By operation of Art. 6:250 Dutch Civil Code.

elaborate the scope or allocation of any particular circumstances that should or should not affect the contents or effects of their agreement. Obviously, such an elaboration does not limit the scope of Arts. 6:258 *et seq.*, but rather has the effect of identifying or determining any circumstances and the way they may or may not affect the agreement: in other words, when parties elaborate certain circumstances, they must be deemed to have taken them into consideration and therefore they must be deemed to have embodied them in their agreement.

II. Although one may question the applicability of Art. 6:753 in view of the contractual exclusion in the construction contract between X and Y, the article provides an inevitable guidance in applying the doctrine of unforeseen circumstances. In particular, Art. 7:753 provides that:

> if, after entering into an agreement, circumstances change or come to light, which increase the costs for completing the (construction) work whereas such occurrence or coming to light should not be attributed to the contractor, the court will adjust the contracted fee in part or in whole, provided that the contractor must not have taken into account the chance that such circumstances would occur or come to light.

The words 'must not have taken into account the chance' refer to what construction companies should generally investigate or provide for, so that the benefit of any doubt is not in favour of the contractor, X. The formulation as a precondition to the rule indicates that the benefit of the doubt is in favour of the contracting party (Y). Although the case lacks sufficient details, the presence of the granite rock must be exceptional in the area in order for X to be at all successful in his claim. Extrapolating this elaboration of Art. 7:753 to Art. 6:258, it would be contrary to the general principle of reasonableness and fairness to allow for any modification of the contract if it was reasonably likely that the granite rock would be in the ground.

III. In the current case, a mere sentence excluding a contractual amendment on the basis of unexpected circumstances is insufficient to have the general and unlimited effect it apparently attempts to achieve. However, such a broad and abstract sentence does provide important indications as to how the parties generally wanted to allocate any risks amongst each other. This is important in case X or Y actually invoke Art. 6:258: a court shall amend (or cancel) a contract, and therefore allow a renegotiation, if the circumstances (or context) surrounding (the performance of a party under) a contract change and (i) the circumstances have not been foreseen, and were not reasonably foreseeable, and (ii) the unforeseen circumstances are of such a nature that the other party (here, Y) may not expect the agreement to remain unmodified. In the current case, X and Y have specifically agreed that any unforeseen circumstance should be at the risk and for the account of X. This suggests that a greater level of investigation by X, or a greater level of care in excluding any 'chances of unforeseen circumstances', may be expected than would otherwise be the case. Accordingly, it would make it less likely that the contract should be renegotiated, modified or terminated if the presence of the granite rock is not highly exceptional or highly unlikely and if, furthermore, the (un)foreseeability of the presence of the granite rock is of such nature that the other party (here, Y) may not expect the agreement to remain unmodified.

IV. In itself, the impossibility for parties to exclude any amendment because of unforeseen circumstances would also follow from the overriding principle of reasonableness and fairness codified in Arts. 3:12 and 6:248 Dutch Civil Code. Also the doctrine of mistake (Art. 6:228) could lead to the (partial) invalidity of a contractual provision of such extensive scope or nature if the other party may not reasonably expect the agreement to remain in full force and effect. Because the doctrine of mistake (applicable when either or both parties have erred in facts or circumstances as of the date of the agreement) does not lead to a different result under the doctrine of unforeseen circumstances, the following will deal with the latter doctrine.

V. Finally, the case could also be addressed by referring to Arts 6:75 and 6:76 (on impossibility due to force majeure). As discussed in connection with Case 14, the courts are very reluctant in assuming that events of hardship or an impossibility to perform are not at the risk and for the account of, in this case, the contractor. However, in *Wasscher* v. *LBU*[1145] the Amsterdam Court of Appeals dealt with a case which is very similar to the one at hand: a drilling company agreed to drill a pipeline underneath a canal. During the drilling work, the ground (i.e., shell sand) appeared to be very difficult to penetrate, resulting in a number of drill chucks being damaged and a delay in the drilling work of over ten days. Ultimately, the parties sought another location for the pipeline construction. Furthermore, the presence of the shell sand was not known from soil investigations in the neighbourhood and there were no other factors indicating that there

[1145] Hof Amsterdam 7 March 1996, case no. 1047/94, BR 1997/1032 (*Wasscher* v. *LBU*).

was shell sand underneath the canal. This led the court to establish that the presence of shell sand was not a circumstance which was attributable to the drilling company. In the current case, the parties have somehow attempted to contract away risks such as the presence of granite rock under the ground.

Eastern European jurisdictions

Slovenia

X has no right to ask for an adjustment of the contract. He may be entitled to termination of the contract unless Y is prepared to pay a price that would reflect the increased costs of the construction.

I. In Slovenian law the principle of equal value of performances ('*iustum pretium*', '*laesio enormis*', 'gross disparity') has been declared to be one of the general principles of contract law that applies to synallagmatic contracts (Art. 8 CO, cf. above in the overview (Chapter 4)).[1146] In this case, X can invoke the rule of *laesio enormis* (Art. 118 CO), which is considered a mistake in the value of the performances. He can claim annulment of the contract unless Y is prepared to pay a price based on the factual costs of the construction. X is not entitled to claim the adjustment of the price, but he cannot achieve annulment if Y is prepared to adjust the price.[1147]

II. A party is allowed to demand the annulment of a contract that has been concluded under the influence of mistake, if the mistake relates to (among others) essential characteristics of the object of the contract (Art. 46(1), (2) CO). We can assume that in this case, beside the mistake regarding the value of performances (discussed above), there is also a mistake relating to the characteristics of the object of the contract, i.e., the characteristics (the quality) of the soil, where the construction should take place. According to the facts of the case, the rock could not have been detected beforehand, which means that this is a case of mutual mistake. Consequently, X has the choice between invoking the *laesio enormis* (Art. 118 CO) as a mistake in the value of the performances and an action on grounds of the mistake, which relates to the characteristics of the soil (Art. 46 CO). The consequences are the same. In both cases he can claim annulment of the contract unless Y is prepared to pay

1146 Juhart in: Juhart and Plavšak (eds.), *Obligacijski zakonik*, vol. I, p. 618.
1147 *Ibid.*, vol. I, p. 622.

a price based on the factual costs of the construction. X is not entitled to claim adjustment of the price, but he cannot achieve an annulment, if Y is prepared to adjust the price.[1148]

III. X is not entitled to claim the dissolution of the contract on grounds of the '*clausula* rule' (Art. 112 CO). There has been no change of circumstances that has occurred after the conclusion of the contract. The rock was there at the moment of the conclusion of the contract, only the parties did not know that.

IV. 1. According to the provision of Art. 115 CO, the parties to a contract can waive the possibility of an action, based on a change of certain circumstances in advance (e.g., at the conclusion of the contract). Such waiver may, however, be contrary to good faith ('*Treu und Glauben*'). This rule, which was already codified in the Yugoslav Obligations Act of 1978, solved the dilemma in the case law, which had not taken a firm position as regards the validity of such waiver.[1149]

2. It should be pointed out, that such a disclaimer is only effective if it relates to changes of circumstances that are *specified* by the disclaimer. This means that the party declaring the waiver should also specify the circumstances that are subject to the disclaimer.[1150] In accordance with general principles of Slovenian contract law, a party cannot waive all the possibilities of dissolution or annulment of a contract in advance, whatever the reasons. Such a disclaimer would interfere with the waiving party's freedom to act.[1151] Therefore, X's waiver is null and void. In accordance with the rules of partial nullity (Art. 88 CO), the contract remains valid unless the void provision was an essential part of the contract (which does not seem to be the case).

Lithuania

X is entitled to ask for an adjustment of the price of work or to terminate the contract. The disclaimer is invalid under Lithuanian law.

[1148] *Ibid.*, vol. I, p. 622.

[1149] E.g., the decisions Yugoslav Supreme Commercial Court Sl 588/56 and Sl 2244/63; cited by Juhart, in: Juhart and Plavšak (eds.), *Obligacijski zakonik*, vol. I, p. 610.

[1150] E.g.: 'I waive the right to an action on grounds of a change of circumstances, if it turns out, that the actual costs of construction would turn out to be . . . % higher than the costs of the construction.'

[1151] R. Kovačević-Koštrunović, 'Klavzula rebius sic stantibus po zakonu o obligacionim odnosima', (1979) *Zbornik radova PF u Nišu*, p. 302; Cigoj, *Komentar obligacijskih razmerij*, p. 451; Juhart in: Juhat and Plavšak (eds.), *Obligacijski zakonik*, pp. 610–11.

I. The principle of freedom of contract enables the parties to agree on the distribution of possible risks. The parties, for instance, may make an agreement that each of them assumes the possible risks and will not claim compensation for any damages. This principle also enables the parties to agree on the attainment of certain results. Article 6.204 CC does not preclude an agreement according to which a contract has to be performed despite any newly emerged circumstances that obstruct its performance. Nevertheless, any agreement of the parties is subject to the requirement of good faith prescribed by Arts. 1.5, 6.4, 6.158 and 6.200 CC. Article 6.158 CC imperatively forbids abolishing the duty of good faith. Therefore, any agreements of the parties in respect of the assumption of risk and its distribution may be interpreted and evaluated on the basis of the principle of good faith. Even if the parties agreed not to have Art. 6.204 CC applied, the court may hold such an agreement invalid if it finds that it is contrary to the principle of good faith and, consequently, constitutes a violation of the imperative norm established in Art. 6.158 CC.

II. The doctrines of impossibility and force majeure cannot be invoked in this case because the performance is possible. Therefore, X may invoke Art. 6.204 CC as the performance of the contract has become considerably obstructed (the price of the work has increased by 300 per cent). However, X's position is aggravated by the fact that the parties have agreed on the non-application of Art. 6.204 CC. Article 6.204 CC can only be applied if the disclaimer has to be regarded as invalid. Such a disclaimer violates the principle of good faith, because it imposes a limitation on the use of remedies provided by law. It is important to mention Art. 2.6(2) CC according to which transactions limiting the active or passive capacity of persons to make legal agreements are null and void.

III. Having the disclaimer annulled by the court, X may refer to Art. 6.204 CC and ask it either to modify the contract or to dissolve it, because the prerequisites of Art. 6.204 are met in the case at hand. However, a special rule (Art. 6.653(5) CC), which is applicable to contracts of independent work, could be of importance in this case. Pursuant to this article, if a fixed price for the work to be fulfilled is indicated in the contract, the independent work contractor has no right to increase the price, nor has the customer any right to reduce it. This provision has been applied in court practice: the Supreme Court of Lithuania indicated that if the parties have agreed on a fixed price, they have to assume any negative consequences of such an agreement. The court held that a fixed price might be changed only in exclusive circumstances, e.g., upon an essential increase in the price of materials, if it is necessary to perform unforeseen work or if the increase in the price of the work exceeds 15 per cent.[1152] As in the case under discussion the price has increased by 300 per cent, Art. 6.653(5) CC ought not to be applied. Consequently, X is entitled to demand, in accordance with Art. 6.204 CC, the revision of the price of work or rescission of the contract.

Czech Republic

X is not entitled to request an adjustment of the contract. However, he may be entitled to termination.

I. The allocation of the risks is based on the institution of initial impossibility to perform (Section 37(2) Civil Code)[1153] and the invalidity of contract or contractual arrangement that contradicts good morals (Section 39 Civil Code).[1154]

II. Under Section 37(2), any juridical act whose subject matter is an impossible performance is invalid. Although no literature or case law exists on the matter, one can consider a burden consisting in the 300 per cent increase of costs to constitute impossibility to perform. Some definitions of impossible performance are contained in Sections 575(2) and 576 Civil Code. Performance is not deemed to be impossible if it can be rendered under difficult conditions, with higher costs or after the agreed period of time. Generic performances are never considered to be impossible. Substantially higher costs are paramount in the given case – they may be considered such an economic burden that the impossibility to perform may be involved.

III. 1. A 300 per cent increase of costs means a clear imbalance of performance. Czech law does not contain a provision on *laesio enormis*; however, it tends to express this in the principle of good morals. Section 39 Civil Code on avoidance of contracts that contradict good morals may thus be applied in this case.

2. Clauses that rule out claims for protection against the consequences of unforeseen circumstances may be used unless they affect

[1152] LAT, Judgment of 30 October 2006, Case No 3K-3-543/2006.

[1153] 'A juridical act is void if the subject of its performance is impossible.' Section 451(1): 'Any person, who to the detriment of somebody else, is unjustly enriched must return what he has obtained'.

[1154] 'Juridical act is void if its content or purpose contradicts or circurvents the law, or if such act contravenes good morals'.

mandatory provisions that must be insisted on. Such mandatory provisions include rules on the invalidity of juridical acts due to the impossibility of performance, and good morals.

Scandinavian jurisdictions

Sweden

X is entitled to terminate the contract, but cannot request adjustment.

I. 1. Swedish law lacks supplementary legislation regarding commercial construction contracts.[1155] In case law, the Sales Act[1156] has often been applied analogously. In contract practice, detailed standard forms, which deal with most upcoming issues, are commonly used. The so-called AB-contracts[1157] are pre-dominant, and the principles laid down therein are often so strongly established that they form an alternative to supplementary law. It has even been suggested that these principles should be applied as supplementary law in this area.[1158]

2. The AB contracts differ significantly from supplementary law when it comes to unexpected circumstances requiring extra work or a time extension. Such unexpected circumstances are normally treated like alterations and additions ordered by the employer. For example, when information related to the construction site or the area affected by the work in total is lacking, the circumstances shall be assumed to be such as could have been expected to prevail after expert assessment (Chapter 1 §8 AB 04, the English version). Work caused by deviations from this assumption is considered equivalent to alterations and additions (Chapter 2 §3). Thus, the employer is basically responsible for unexpected conditions regarding the relevant conditions for the work. The contractor is entitled to extension (Chapter 4 §2), as well as payment for the extra work (Chapter 6 §1); and in the event of a substantial disruption of the conditions for the execution of the total work, a cost adjustment shall be

[1155] In consumer contracts, the Consumer Services Act (Konsumenttjänstlagen (1985:716)) applies.

[1156] Köplagen (1990:931).

[1157] 'AB' stands for 'General conditions'. The main contract is traditionally '*AB 04. Allmänna bestämmelser för byggnads- anläggnings- och installationsentreprenader*'. These are also available in an English version; 'AB 04. General Conditions of Contract for Building and Civil Engineering Works and Building Services'.

[1158] See e.g., Källenius, *Entreprenadjuridik* (Stockholm: Norstedts, 1960), p. 14.

made (Chapter 6 §5). The contractor also has a right and duty to carry out the work, unless otherwise prescribed by statute (Chapter 2 §3).

3. Under supplementary law, the basic problem instead concerns X's assumption that his own fulfilment will not be unexpectedly burdensome. Under the old Sales Act 1905, relief was granted when performance could be considered impossible due to a circumstance which could not have been taken into account when the contract was concluded, such as the destruction of all goods of the kind the seller was to deliver, war, embargo on import, or some other comparable circumstance. This rule still prevails as a general principle of contract law.

4. The rules of the Sales Act 1990 differ from this. Section 23 states, as the main rule, that the buyer's right to require performance does not apply if there is an obstacle which the seller is unable to overcome, or if delivery would demand unreasonable sacrifices with respect to the buyer's interest in receiving the goods. The Sales Act's solution regarding damages is that, under Section 27, the buyer is entitled to compensation for direct losses caused by the seller's breach, when the seller is unable to prove that the delay is caused by an obstacle ('hinder') outside the sellers control, which could not reasonably have been foreseen and the consequences of which could not reasonably have been avoided or overcome. The granite rock could not have been detected by the parties before the conclusion of the contract. One also has to assume that the consequences of its presence could not reasonably have been avoided or overcome by the contractor. The cost of the construction would be four times as high as initially expected. Therefore, it should be possible to cancel the contract without damages under these rules.

5. However, the Sales Act rules do not automatically constitute general principles of contract law. The issue to what extent they do was left for the courts to decide in the preparatory works,[1159] and is not yet settled when it comes to these rules. An important part of the problem is that the rules regarding which losses are compensated for differ from general principles. Traditionally, there is no limitation when it comes to the types of losses that are compensated for in the event of a breach; all the deprived party's losses are compensated for. However, under the Sales Act 1990, only direct losses are generally compensated for, while compensation for indirect losses requires warranty or negligence (Sections 40, 27 and 57). The Sales Act is not directly applicable in this case, and the limitations regarding indirect losses cannot be applied

[1159] See Prop. 1988/89:76 pp. 23–4, compare p. 22.

analogously as they are not supported by other legislation, e.g., the Consumer Services Act.[1160] Therefore, it cannot be taken for granted that the rules regarding obstacles can be applied analogously.

II. This case might also be tried under the doctrine of assumptions. The contractor will then argue he made a mistake at the conclusion of the contract. The contractor was not knowingly assuming the risk of the ground conditions, and the rock was impossible to detect. However, it is difficult to find a convincing argument for considering the assumption legally relevant. This would probably require that the construction company had some reason to rely on the better knowledge of the employer as to the ground conditions, or that the employer knew, or ought to have known, of the rock (which is not the case here).

III. 1. Exemption clauses ('*friskrivningsklausuler*'), where a party's responsibility is limited in relation to what follows from supplementary law, or from other provisions of the contract, are generally accepted in Swedish law, but are treated restrictively in several respects. First, a higher level of clarity is required when it comes to the incorporation into a contract of clauses which appear oppressive ('*tyngande*') or unexpected ('*överraskande*').[1161] Second, a higher level of clarity is required with respect to the interpretation of such clauses, such as disclaimers. Thus, if a contract clause is intended to be interpreted in a way that differs from what follows from supplementary legislation, the clause needs to be clearly and unambiguously stated.[1162] Similarly, clauses which appear oppressive or unexpected are generally interpreted restrictively.[1163]

3. As far as the disclaimer is concerned, it is necessary to first address the issue of interpretation. It deals only with rights arising from 'unexpected circumstances', while the problem is due to an error in motives, and not a change in the circumstances. If the wording 'unexpected circumstances' is to be understood as 'changed circumstances' (including expected changes that have not come to pass), the disclaimer cannot

[1160] See J. Hellner, R. Hager and A. H. Persson, *Speciell avtalsrätt II. Kontraktsrätt 2. Allmänna ämnen* (Stockholm: Novstedts Juridik, 4th edn, 2006), p. 221.

[1161] See B. Lehrberg, *Avtalstolkning* (Uppsala: IBA Institutet för Bank- och Affärsjuridik, 5th edn, 2009), pp. 69–74, and in case law NJA 1919 p. 359, NJA 1970 p. 478, NJA 1971 p. 36, NJA 1975 p. 545, NJA 1978 p. 432 and NJA 1979 p. 401.

[1162] See Lehrberg, *Avtalstolkning*, pp. 152–8, and in case law NJA 1942 p. 548, NJA 1963 p. 683.

[1163] See Lehrberg, *Avtalstolkning*, pp. 183–6; Hellner, Hager, Persson, *Speciell avtalsrätt II. Kontraktsrätt 2. Allmänna ämnen*, p. 119, and in case law NJA 1946 p. 666, and NJA 1985 p. 397 II.

be applied. If the expression is to be understood as 'unknown or changed circumstances', the disclaimer is on the other hand applicable. This latter view will be applied in the following text, although disclaimers are interpreted restrictively.

3. In the practical situation, where an AB contract is used, the consequences of the disclaimer may appear somewhat surprising. Here, the rules concerning what is generally known as unexpected circumstances form an integrated part of the contract, and the risk is basically allocated to the employer, who would therefore be the party most interested in introducing special stipulations regarding unexpected circumstances. Contractor X would then – on the basis of the rules governing AB contracts – most likely have no reason to ask for termination or re-negotiation. Therefore, this option will be disregarded from now on.

IV. 1. The main method of dealing with these types of clauses is through the application of Section 36 Contracts Act. Disclaimers are one of the most typical examples of clauses at risk of being considered unreasonable ('*oskäliga*') and thus adjusted under this rule.[1164] Under Section 36, a contract term can be adjusted or disregarded in a particular case if it is unreasonable with reference to the contents of the contract, the circumstances at the conclusion of the contract, later arising circumstances, and 'other circumstances'. If the unfair term is of such importance to the contract that the rest of it could not fairly be upheld unchanged, the contract can be adjusted in other parts or disregarded in its entirety. By the application of the prerequisite 'unreasonable' the need to protect a consumer or another inferior party is to be especially taken into consideration. From this it follows that Section 36 is applied restrictively in commercial contracts.

2. The preparatory works distinguish between two major *categories* of exemption clauses.[1165] Clauses in the first category impose a limitation on a party's responsibility in relation to the character or quality of his performance ('*egenskapsfriskrivning*'). If a disclaimer of this type is general in wording, such as 'the good is to be delivered as it is', it runs an increased risk of being considered unclear, and thus interpreted in favour of the party entitled to the performance. The second type of disclaimer refers to the remedies due to a breach. A clause like the

[1164] See SOU 1974:83 pp. 174–84.

[1165] For the following, see SOU 1974:83 pp. 176 *et seq*. See also cases NJA 1975 p. 545, and NJA 1976 p. 217.

one at hand, which eliminates all remedies, is of course clear enough, but its effects can be most radical and it therefore runs the risk of being considered unreasonable. A main rule is that it is unreasonable to apply a disclaimer in favour of a party who has caused the breach intentionally or by gross negligence.[1166]

3. Under Section 36, a contract clause may be considered unreasonable as such, notwithstanding the situation in which it is to be applied. This is obviously not the case with the disclaimer in question. It may also be important whether the contract contains other clauses that have an impact on the importance of the disclaimer. Here, one can assume there are no such clauses. The most important argument in favour of the application of Section 36 is, of course, that the presence of the rock imposes an extreme burden on the contractor, thus fundamentally altering the equilibrium of the contract. This is because the cost of the construction company's performance has increased manifold, compared to what could have been expected at the formation of the contract. Another relevant argument is that the disclaimer leaves the employer without a remedy for breach caused by unexpected circumstances on the contractor's side.

4. A significant argument against the application of Section 36 is that this is a commercial contract, and that the parties knew what they where contracting for. The construction company has also entered into the contract with eyes open as to its meaning, consequently knowingly assuming the risk of obstacles in the construction work. Still, there is a good chance the heavy burden that would otherwise be implied on the contractor will be considered to render the clause unreasonable. As the problem cannot be solved through adjustment of the contract, termination appears the only remedy available.

V. There is no right, under Swedish law, to demand renegotiation unless contracted for.

Denmark

It is possible that X would be granted relief on the basis of Section 36 Contracts Act. The assessment of the disclaimer is uncertain as there is no representative case law.

[1166] See SOU 1972:28 pp. 19 f; Prop. 1973:138 pp. 137 ff; SOU 1974:83 p. 177; and Prop. 1975/76:81 p. 144. See also e.g., U. Bernitz, *Standardavtalsrätt* (Stockholm: Juristförlaget, 7th edn, 2008), p. 96, and T. Lundmark, *Friskrivningsklausuler. Giltighet och räckvidd* (Uppsala: Iustus Förlag, 1996), pp. 133 *et seq.*

I. This case is outside the scope of the Sale of Goods Act, as the contract would be considered to be a contract for work and materials. As discussed, the parties would normally apply AB 92 (General Conditions for building and construction activities). In accordance with Section 27(3) of AB 92, cf. the principle in Section 24 Sale of Goods Act, it is ambiguous whether X can invoke economic force majeure or not. There is no case law on this issue. In accordance with the contract, X would most likely be obliged to perform or otherwise pay damages for breach of contract.

II. Alternatively, X could invoke the application of Section 36 Contracts Act. This is probably the most likely source of law supporting a judgment in favour of X. So far, case law concerning the application of Section 36 Contracts Act has apparently not dealt with a case like the one in question. Once again the crucial issue to be determined is whether upholding the contract in question can be considered unfair. Generally, a construction company must be aware of the possibility that the ground might contain major obstacles that the company must overcome in order to fulfil its obligations. Despite the fact that the granite rock would not have been discovered through an investigation, it is hardly uncommon that unexpected circumstances arise during the performance of the contract. The construction company could have reserved the right in the contract to charge the other party in case of additional costs. It is normal for a construction company to have insurance cover dealing with an issue like the one at hand. On the other hand, the balance of power between the parties must be taken into account. If X can be considered to be the weaker party compared to Y with respect to bargaining power, turnover, the number of employees etc., it could be argued that X is the weaker party in the contract. Did Y use his bargaining power in conjunction with the original contract negotiations? Does the contract as a whole favour Y? Did Y draft the contract? Did Y use his standard terms? Will X eventually become bankrupt if performance has to take place? If these and other questions clearly reveal that X is the weaker party and that the fulfilment of the contract might threaten X's existence, it is very likely that Section 36 Contracts Act would apply.

II. 1. If the parties do not renegotiate the contract on their own initiative, the case requires further legal discussion. After all, the application of Section 36 Contracts Act could be excluded by a disclaimer agreed between the parties. Such a condition is binding upon the parties. They have considered the issue of unexpected circumstances by inserting a provision to that effect in the contract. It could therefore be argued that this construction makes it impossible to apply the doctrine of assumptions, since the parties have agreed on a disclaimer (a condition) with regard to a certain situation, which would traditionally comprise of the doctrine of assumptions. A traditional interpretation of the contract would lead to the result that X is not entitled to claim any money for the increased costs of removing the granite rock.

2. The question remains whether the granite rock in the ground can be considered an unexpected circumstance, as it had been there all the time. In that sense, the circumstances have not changed, thus making it impossible to apply the disclaimer in the contract. If an 'unexpected circumstance' must be interpreted as something completely unfamiliar to the parties, the disclaimer can be applied. The interpretation of the disclaimer is thus crucial if the case is presented to a Danish court. In a number of cases, Danish courts have used the 'right' interpretation of disclaimers to reach what would be considered a fair judgment. If that is the case, X would be entitled to cancel the contract, as maintaining the contract would not create a 'just' result.

III. In general, case law does not provide evidence or any clear indications that the parties to a contract address the question of unexpected circumstances. Danish case law, for instance, does not contain any cases concerning hardship or the use of hardship provisions.[1167]

Romanic-Mediterranean jurisdictions

Italy

X may not terminate the contract, but a claim for just compensation is justified (according to Art. 1664(2) CC). The disclaimer is likely to be held ineffective as it is too vague.

I. 1. It has already been said that a duty to renegotiate as such, with the aim of equitably adapting or modifying the affected contractual terms (in the case at issue, the increased construction costs), is not provided by Italian law. Nonetheless it can be argued that, under the circumstances provided for by Art. 1467 CC, if a court allows a party charged by the unjustified and excessive burden of performance (which is certainly the case for the increase of the construction cost by

[1167] For a further discussion about Danish law, see Kim Østergaard, *Anvendelsen af hardshipklausuler i et erhvervsjuridisk perspektiv* (Julebog: 1st edn, 2005), pp. 213–28.

300 per cent) to terminate the contract, the other party is entitled to enter into negotiations in order to obtain an equitable modification of the contractual conditions (Art. 1467(3) CC). In this case, the refusal to negotiate or the break off of negotiations contrary to good faith and the rules of fair dealing, entitles the burdened party to claim damages for the suffered loss, in addition to the equitable modification of the contractual terms. This conclusion can be justified by reference to the general duty to perform in good faith (Arts. 1175 and 1375 CC).

2. It has been said that a principle of keeping the contract in force by means of modification of its terms and conditions can be recognised under Italian law within the rules of the contracts in general and it could be said that such a principle prevails on those rules which lead to the complete dissolution of the agreement (including of course those in case of hardship, Art. 1467 C.C., specifically Art. 1467(3) for the equitable modification of the conditions). Furthermore, rules governing impossibility (e.g., partial impossibility, Art. 1464 CC) and mistake (e.g., maintenance of the rectified contract, Art. 1432 CC) seem to confirm this underlying principle in the CC. One must also consider the rules set forth for specific contracts, where this attitude of the Italian law appears even clearer and hardly disputable.

3. A meaningful example of the above-mentioned attitude of the Italian legislator is given by the already-mentioned Art. 1664 CC,[1168] which is applicable to cases of hardship in the performance of building contracts such as in the case at issue. Article 1664 CC considers the supervening hardship or difficulty in performance and provides a remedy very different from that provided by the general rules on the excessive onerousness (Arts. 1467–9 CC). If, as a result of unforeseeable circumstances, such an increase or a reduction in the cost of the materials or of labour occurs so as to cause an increase or reduction by more than 10 per cent of the total price, the independent contractor or the customer can request that the price is revised. The revision can only be granted for that part of the difference which exceeds 10 per cent.

4. Furthermore, if difficulties are revealed in the course of the work deriving from geological conditions, water or other similar causes not foreseen by the parties, which made the performance of the contractor considerably more onerous, he is entitled to just compensation (Art. 1664(2) CC). The latter would in principle apply to the case at issue (geological surprise which renders the performance of the contractor

[1168] See Case 1 and Overview (Chapter 4).

considerably more onerous), considering that the Italian case law has extensively interpreted the said rule. Only events due to the *factum principis* or to third parties[1169] have been excluded from the 'similar causes'.

5. Pursuant to Art. 1664 CC Italian law provides for a fixed percentage of increase or reduction of the total price agreed upon (one-tenth) which the parties have to bear as a risk of supervening events, but once this limit has been exceeded, the entitled party can request that the price is revised. Of course, this remedy excludes any demand of dissolution (pursuant to Art. 1467 CC[1170]) in consideration of the prevailing interests (in principle of both parties) for the maintenance of the contract.

II. 1. The above rule stated by Art. 1664 CC is, however, considered a default one, so that the parties are free to agree upon a different range or percentage of risk and they may also exclude any influence of the change of circumstances affecting the performance (i.e., exclude the right to claim a just compensation pursuant to Art. 1664(2) CC).[1171] In principle, this was decided by the parties of the contract at issue through the stipulation of a disclaimer which excludes 'all the rights of both parties arising from unexpected circumstances'. Italian scholars and courts affirm that an agreed derogation from Art. 1664 CC is valid and that it does per se alter the structure and the function of the building contract (in the sense that it would become fully aleatory by the intention of the parties). It is furthermore not deemed abusive and therefore ineffective without specific approval in writing.[1172]

2. Some difficulties arise, however, with regard to such clauses, pursuant to Italian case law: provided that the discovery of the granite rock on Y's ground two weeks after the construction work has begun (which could not have been detected by the parties before conclusion of the contract), falls within the 'unexpected circumstances' and is not a good reason for challenging the contract under the rules of mutual mistake (the granite rock was already there when the agreement was concluded and therefore may be not considered a supervening event),[1173] Italian

1169 Cass., 26 January 1985, n. 387; Cass., 19 March 1980, n. 1818.

1170 It is commonly recognised that Art. 1664 CC overcomes, as a specific rule according to the principle of *lex specialis*, the general provision of Art. 1467 CC. See Cass., 19 March 1980, n. 1818; Cass., 5 March 1979, n. 1364.

1171 Cass., 26 November 1984, n. 6106 and many others, hereinafter indicated.

1172 Pursuant to Art. 1341 CC, relating to general contractual clauses unilaterally drafted: Cass., 23 April 1981, n. 2403.

1173 See Case 13.

courts in fact request that these circumstances are exactly indicated: in other words, the intention of the parties to derogate from Art. 1664 CC must be clear.[1174]

III. 1. In summary, the questions posed by the case at issue under Italian law are (i) whether or not the detection of the granite rock may be considered an 'unexpected circumstance' according to the intention of the contracting parties (alternatively, the rules on mutual mistake could play a role); (ii) provided that the disclaimer covers also the geological surprise (i.e., this falls within the unexpected circumstances), whether or not the derogation from the default rule stated by Art. 1664(2) CC is valid and effective in consideration of the vagueness of the clause.

2. The answer to question (i), which involves the interpretation of the contract, should be in the affirmative, since Art. 1664 CC considers the difficulties due to geological causes among the supervening events determining the right of the builder to claim a just compensation. As far as question (ii) is concerned, the clause at hand is too vague to derogate from the default rule stated by Art. 1664(2) CC, in accordance with the prevailing opinion among the Italian scholars and courts, and therefore this latter default rule of the CC would apply.

Spain

Under Spanish law X can, in principle, request an adjustment of the contract. However, a contractual allocation of risks has to be respected by the courts.

I. A very similar case was decided by the Audiencia Provincial of Lleida:[1175] a construction company was faced with an extraordinary difficulty in performance because of the consistency of the soil. The parties did not know about this at the time the contract was concluded. The court stated that performance was excessively burdensome for the construction company and considered that it had made sufficient efforts to perform its obligations; after all, the construction company had spent PTA 5,000,000 on performing the contract. The court held that the problems in performing could be equated with the impossibility to perform (Art. 1184 CC), and that the legal consequence should be the modification of the contract.

[1174] Cass., 22 February 1974, n. 259; Cass., 25 November 1977, n. 5137; Cass., 6 June 1977, n. 2326; Cass., 5 March 1979, n. 1364; Cass., 14 July 1980, n. 4514.

[1175] Judgment of 19 March 1998; SAP Lleida 19 March 1998 (AC 576).

II. However, if the parties have excluded 'all the rights of both parties arising from unexpected circumstances', one could conclude that the court could neither terminate nor modify the contract because a condition for the application of the '*cláusula rebus sic stantibus*' is that none of the parties has assumed the risk of changed circumstances. This approach has explicitly been codified by the legislator as regards the application of Art. 1105 CC on force majeure. This provision indicates that the debtor is excused unless indicated otherwise by the law or by the contract, that is, if the parties have agreed that the risk shall be assigned to the debtor.[1176]

Portugal

Due to the excessive increase in cost, X may be granted relief. Yet, the disclaimer will be upheld and thus X is bound to perform under the conditions of the contract.

I. 1. The existence of a granite rock, undetectable by the parties before the conclusion of the contract, will generally result in the need for more work than initially assessed. This sort of extra work is unavoidable in order to successfully complete the building. According to Art. 1215 CC, if technical rules demand changes to the initial project and if the parties do not come to an agreement, it is up to the court to determine which changes are imperative and to adjust both the price and the time of completion. If the price is increased by more than 20 per cent as a result of the court order, X can choose to terminate the contract. The underlying assumption of this legal rule is that if the price is increased by more than 20 per cent, the nature of the work to be done is significantly altered. Therefore, X must have an opportunity to decide if it still wishes to complete the contract (X may feel that it is no longer technically or financially prepared to complete the task). If X decides to 'bail out' of the contract, the court will decide what amount of indemnification the contractor X will be entitled to according to equity. This rule might apply in this case, as it seems that neither party was responsible for the event. Both the contractor and the builder probably had no reasons to suspect the abnormal composition of the terrain and therefore acted with due care.

2. It seems that, in the absence of a subsequent agreement on the new conditions, X might choose to terminate the contract if the price set by

[1176] X. O'Callaghan, *Compendio de Derecho civil*, vol. II, Derecho de obligaciones, V. I, Teoría general de la obligación, del contrato y del acto ilícito (Madrid: Revista de Derecho Privado, 2nd edn, 1994).

the court is 20 per cent higher. However, Y will have to pay an indemnification to contractor X, the equitable amount of which will be assessed by the court.

3. Y may also decide to terminate the contract. As a matter of fact Y can terminate the contract at any given moment without having to present any reason. But if Y terminates the contract, the contractor X may, under Art. 1229 CC, ask for damages that will take into account his expenses for materials and labour and his loss of profit.

II. However, in our case, the parties have excluded 'all the rights of both parties arising from unexpected circumstances'. This stipulation is permitted (except perhaps in adhesion contracts) as one party may contractually assume the risk.[1177] Article 437 CC, by the way, is subsidiary to the contractual rules of risk distribution and such a disclaimer might be construed as a clause in which each party assumes the risk of supervening events.

Greece

X has the right to an appropriate adjustment (by raising the price) or to terminate the contract pursuant to Art. 288 AK.

I. If the agreed price of €2,000,000 is stipulated on the ground of a budget or schedule listing the cost of the work containing a detailed record of the services that need to be accomplished, and of the material, which needs to be employed,[1178] the budget must be considered guaranteed in terms of Art. 696 AK. Thus, we are dealing with a budget, the precision of which is guaranteed by the contractor. Naturally, there is no explicit declaration of such contractual will. Nevertheless, according to an opinion of Greek writers, this guarantee can also be declared implicitly, pursuant to the rules of the complementary interpretation of contracts.[1179] According to Art. 696 AK, the contractor who operates on the basis of a guaranteed budget has no right, whatsoever, to an increase of the price, if the evaluation of his services turns out to be false. Nevertheless, this rule only applies under the basic reservation of

[1177] See Menezes Cordeiro, *Da alteração das circunstâncias*, pp. 47 *et seq.*, Carvalho Fernandes, *A teoria da imprevisão no direito civil português* (Lisbon: Quid Juris reprint with updates, 2001), p. 99 and António Pinto Monteiro, *Cláusula penal e indemnização*, p. 269.

[1178] See Filios, *Law of Obligations Special Part*, vol. I, p. 336; Kardaras 'Artt. 696–697', in: Georgiadis and Stathopoulos, *AK*, n. 2.

[1179] This implicit guarantee will result indirectly from a disclaimer of the contractor from any right in case of an unexpected change of circumstances. The above case may be considered as a case of a conversion, which is regulated by Art. 182 AK.

Art. 388 AK, and, generally, under the reservation of the initial lack or the subsequent collapse of the underlying basis of the contract.[1180]

II. At hand, the detection of the granite rock, which could not have been predicted, includes an initial lack of the underlying basis of the contract, which has to be dealt with according to Art. 288 AK (see also Case 13 and overview (Chapter 4)). Due to the increase of the construction costs by 300 per cent, the contractor's obligation to perform without any previous adjustment of the price constitutes an extremely onerous burden, which exceeds the limits of good faith (Art. 288 AK). This is an approach already adopted by the majority of the Greek judiciary on public construction work.[1181] Furthermore, the above solution applies even if the price is not stipulated on the ground of a budget but on the ground of a total evaluation of the work.

III. The disclaimer depriving both the parties of their rights 'arising from unexpected circumstances' does not influence this approach. Pursuant to the majority of the Greek judiciary and literature,[1182] the original total waiver from the legal protection provided by Arts. 288 and 388 AK, is null and void. In contrast, a disclaimer according to which a party accepts to bear a specified risk is valid, and the application of Arts. 288 and 388 AK is out of the question, since in that case we are not dealing with an unexpected circumstance.

France and related jurisdictions

France

The disclaimer will normally be valid in civil law. Therefore X cannot request that the contract be adjusted or terminated.

[1180] See I. Deligiannis, in: I. Deligiannis and P. Kornilakis, *Law of Obligations – Special Part*, (Thessalonica: 1992), vol. II, p. 116–18.

[1181] See *ibid*., p. 118.

[1182] See ad hoc for the contract for work AP (plenary session) 350/1985, NoB 33, p. 1187; AP 16/1983, NoB 31, p. 1368; Deligiannis, in: Deligiannis and Kornilakis, *Law of Obligations – Special Part*, vol. II, p. 116–7, and generally Balis, *Law of Obligations*, §88 p. 316; Michailidis-Nouaros, *Law of Obligations*, p. 218; Oikonomopoulos, 'Unforeseen change of circumstances', (1972) 28, 321, 324; Papantoniou, *The Good Faith*, p. 180; Stathopoulos, *Law of Obligations*, §22 n. 40; Ast. Georgiadis, *Law of Obligations– General Part* (Athens/Thess alarika:Sakkoula, 3rd edn, 2000), vol. II, pp. 135–7; Ap. Georgiadis, *Contract Law General Part*, §33 n. 25 ; Theodoropoulos Panagiotis, *The Unforeseen Change*, pp. 176–8. See also AP (plenary session) 350/1985, HellD 26, 468 = NoV 33, 1197. The non-mandatory character of Art. 388 AK was supported by Sakketas, 'Art. 388', in: *ErmAK*, n. 53; Fourkiotis, *Greek Law of Obligations*, 1972, p. 693/4; Zepos, *Law of Obligations*, p. 567.

I. Leaving aside the effect of the disclaimer, the contractor will only be entitled to equitable compensation on the basis of *imprévision* under administrative law. On the grounds of this doctrine, compensation would cover the increased costs minus 5 per cent as this threshold represents the contractual risk borne by the contractor. In civil law, however, the doctrine of *imprévision* is not accepted and only the – familiar, but not identical – concept of *sujétions imprévues* applies. In this case, the conditions for *sujétions imprévues* are indeed met: X is confronted with unforeseen natural circumstances, namely a granite rock that could not have been initially detected. Furthermore, the contractual balance is disrupted by the 300 per cent increase in construction costs.

II. 1. Assuming that X, in principle, is not bound by the contract due to the detection of the granite rock, the further question arises whether the introduction of the disclaimer in the contract leads to a different result. In administrative law, some authors hold the view that *imprévision* is part of public policy and cannot be derogated from. They invoke the continuity of public services.[1183] The highest administrative court considered that compensation based on unexpected circumstances can be granted even in the presence of a clause excluding a price revision.[1184]

2. In contrast, as French civil law is quite reluctant to consider unexpected circumstances, a clause excluding such concepts must *a fortiori* be effective. This is also true in the case of the special doctrine of *sujétions imprévues* although there are no cases dealing with this question. Any revision of the price would normally be rejected. However, the judge could possibly deduce from interpreting the will of the parties (Art. 1156 Cciv) that they did not intend to exclude all possibilities to revise the price by inserting this clause.

Belgium

I. The most likely outcome of the dispute is that X cannot request adjustment or termination of the contract. But it is not impossible that the courts will conclude that the price is to be adjusted by interpretation.

II. Leaving aside the effect of the disclaimer, the concept of *sujétions imprévues* applies: X is confronted with unforeseen natural circumstances, namely a granite rock which could not have been initially detected.

[1183] A. De Laubadère, *Traité de droit administratif* (Paris), pp. 115–16.
[1184] Cons. Et.,10 March 1948, Hospice de Vienne, *Recueil*, 1948, 124.

Furthermore, the contractual balance is disrupted by an increase of 300 per cent in construction costs.

III. 1. The disclaimer could lead to a different solution, however. As Belgian law is quite reluctant to consider unexpected circumstances, a clause excluding such concepts must *a fortiori* be effective. This is also true in the case of the exceptional applicability of *sujétions imprévues*, although there seem to be no published cases dealing with this question. So any revision of the price would normally be rejected.

2. However, by an interpretation of the contract (under Art. 1156 Cciv.) the judge could possibly deduce that the parties did not intend to exclude any revision of the price by inserting this clause. For example, even in the case of a contract providing for a lump-sum payment (Art. 1793 Cciv.), the doctrine of *sujétions imprévues* can be applied in Belgian law.[1185]

England and related jurisdictions

England and Ireland

Whether the clause will prevent the frustration of the contract depends (i) on whether it can be proved that it was the intention of the parties that the clause should have this effect, given the ambiguous nature of its wording and (ii) whether the clause can in fact apply in the circumstances which occurred. There is no issue of illegality here, but it is still at least arguable that the clause was not meant to have effect where there was such a high rise in costs.

I. 1. Leaving aside for the moment the issue of the disclaimer, in this situation it is possible that the detection of the granite rock and subsequent increase in construction costs is capable of frustrating the contract and discharging the parties from their contractual obligations. It would have to be shown, however, that the supervening event (i.e., the detection of the granite rock) caused more than mere 'hardship or inconvenience or material loss', but rather caused 'such a change in the significance of the obligation that the thing undertaken would, if performed, be a different thing from that contracted for'.[1186]

1185 See D. Philippe, 653 (advocating the possibility of revising the contract, even with the presence of such a clause).

1186 Per Lord Radcliffe in *Davis Contractors Ltd* v. *Fareham Urban District Council*, cited with approval by Murphy J in *Zuphen and Others* v *Kelly Technical Services Ltd* [2000] ELR 277, 291.

Alternatively, it is possible that the contract is capable of being void for common mistake, as both parties contracted in the belief that there would be no granite rock in the ground. However, in deciding whether either the doctrine of frustration or mistake would apply, the court will examine the allocation of risk in the contract, to determine if either X or Y took the risk that there could be problems such as the one incurred. If either X or Y took the risk that there would be granite rock, the doctrines of mistake or frustration would not apply.[1187]

2. In ascertaining the allocation of risk under the contract, the court would have regard to the terms of the contract. However, a clause which excludes 'all the rights of both parties arising from unexpected circumstances' is quite vague and ambiguous. It could arguably be interpreted as excluding the right to bring an action for breach of contract; as excluding the right to rescind the contract; as excluding the right to restitution after discharge of the contract; or as excluding the doctrine of frustration regardless of how difficult a contractual obligation is to perform. Any term expressly excluding the doctrine of frustration (or, indeed, mistake) is unlikely to be expressed in this way. In fact, it should be pointed out that the common law doctrine of frustration does not confer a 'right' to rescind on any one party, but rather is said to occur automatically, regardless of the wishes of the parties: 'Frustration is not a right; it is a legal doctrine, the effect of which is to determine the rights and obligations arising under the contract which is frustrated.'[1188]

3. However, if it was established that the clause was intended to exclude the operation of the doctrine of frustration, it would most likely be upheld. The general approach of the courts as regards contract terms which allocate the risk of supervening events is to uphold them. The contract was freely entered into by two commercial entities, who were capable of qualifying their obligation to perform (for example, by the inclusion of a force majeure clause) but who instead expressly contracted to perform regardless of future events. The House of Lords in *Joseph Constantine SS Line Ltd* v. *Imperial Smelting Co Ltd*[1189] confirmed that such an express term would exclude the operation of the doctrine of frustration:

[1187] See *Amalgamated Investments* v. *John Walker* [1976] 3 All ER 509; *William Sindall* v. *Cambridgeshire CC* [1994] 3 All ER 932.

[1188] *BP* v. *Hunt* [1979] 1 WLR 783 per Goff J at 809.

[1189] [1942] AC 154 per Lord Simon at 163.

There can be no discharge by supervening impossibility if the express terms of the contract bind the parties to performance, notwithstanding that the supervening event may occur.

However, it may be held that the express term excluding frustration does not cover the unexpected event which has occurred. In other words, it may be held that although the parties were prepared to take the risk of *certain* events occurring making performance more difficult, they could not possibly have anticipated or taken on the risk of the *specific event which did occur*. Therefore, the disclaimer will have no effect and the doctrine of frustration will operate as though it was not there. For example, in *Fibrosa*[1190] the House of Lords held that a clause which, on the face of it, seemed to deal with the situation which occurred, did not in fact prevent the contract from being frustrated. In July 1939 an English company contracted to deliver certain machinery to a company in Poland. A clause in a contract of sale provided that if delivery should be delayed by 'any cause beyond our reasonable control,' including war, 'a reasonable extension of time shall be granted.' In September Germany invaded Poland, which was later declared an enemy occupied territory. The Polish company brought an action against the English company, claiming damages for breach of contract and the return of £1,000 which had been paid in advance. It was held in the House of Lords that the state of war meant it was both impossible and illegal to deliver the machinery, and that thus the contract was frustrated. Viscount Simon LC rejected the idea that the clause providing for an extension of time precluded the frustration of the contract. First, the delay referred to in the clause could not be taken to include a prolonged and definite interruption such as that caused by the war. Second, it was in fact illegal for the British company to trade with an enemy. In such circumstances the parties cannot unilaterally agree that the contract is to continue, and thus the provision for an extension of time could not have application.

4. Similarly, in *Metropolitan Water Board* v. *Dick Kerr & Co*[1191] a contract was made in 1914 for the construction of a reservoir. The contract provided that in the event of delays 'howsoever occasioned' the contractors were to be given an extension of time. In 1916 the contractors were prevented from working and forced to sell their business by government order. It was held that the contract was frustrated in spite

[1190] *Fibrosa Spolka Akcyjna* v. *Fairbairn Lawson Combe Barbour Ltd* [1942] 2 All ER 122.
[1191] [1918] AC 119. See Treitel, *Frustration and Force Majeure*, p. 420.

of the clause providing for delays, which would have seemed to provide for the situation at hand. The clause did not apply as it did not 'cover the case in which the interruption is of such a character and duration that it vitally and fundamentally changes the conditions of the contract and could not possibly have been in the contemplation of the parties when it was made'.[1192]

Scotland

X cannot ask for an adjustment of the contract, nor may he terminate the contract. The disclaimer will have little effect. It presupposes that the parties have rights in this situation whereas, under Scottish law, no remedy will be available to X.

I. 1. The facts in Case 15 are unlikely to be considered an example of frustration. Rather it is a case of uninduced error. The impossibility or impracticability which has occurred here is not supervening, but antecedent. In other words, this is not a case where an event has occurred which was not anticipated by the parties. Rather, the parties have contracted in ignorance of specific conditions already present, though concealed, at the moment of formation. Gloag explains that the contractor takes the risk that the cost of the work will increase due to conditions which were present when the contract was concluded but which neither party was aware of.[1193] This factual situation is analysed in Scottish textbooks sometimes as an issue of error and sometimes as frustration.[1194]

2. The leading case is *Boyd & Forrest* v. *Glasgow and South Western Railway Company*.[1195] The facts of this case are similar in certain respects to Case 15. The Glasgow and South-Western Railway Company (GSW) contracted with Boyd & Forrest (BF) for the latter to construct a railway line. BF were entitled to have sight of records of various samples taken from the rock strata, with the express reservation that GSW did not guarantee their accuracy. The contract provided that BF were solely responsible for satisfying themselves as to the strata and nature of the work. The records provided failed accurately to reflect the content of certain samples due to amendments made to the raw data by GSW's engineer (who, it was held, had not acted fraudulently). Construction of the railway was consequently significantly more difficult and expensive than BF had first anticipated.

1192 [1918] AC 119, 126. 1193 Gloag, *Contract*, p. 359.
1194 See, for example, Gloag, *Contract*, p. 359. 1195 1915 SC (HL) 20.

3. In this case a strict approach was taken, the House of Lords refusing to release BF from its obligations. The same rationale was identified both at Inner House and House of Lords level. The view was expressed that if one were prepared to release parties from their obligations on the ground that performance had proved to be more expensive than anticipated, one must equally be prepared to release the parties where performance turned out to be less expensive than anticipated.[1196] Nevertheless, the Inner House recognised that in certain cases the parties might be released where the increase in cost is so severe that the contract is entirely different from what was contemplated. The facts of *Boyd & Forrest* were not sufficiently severe to merit such an outcome. It is, however, difficult to find support for this particular view in the speeches in the House of Lords.

4. There is academic support for this more lenient approach. It has also been suggested that contractors may claim extra payment where the work which they have been obliged to carry out is so different from that contracted for that it is not covered by the contract at all.[1197] Some academics concede, however, that this view is difficult to reconcile with *Boyd & Forrest*.[1198] Nevertheless, in at least one of the cases they cite, the extra work is not treated as forming part of the original contract, but rather as falling under a new agreement, express or implied, under which the contractor will be paid on a *quantum meruit* basis.[1199] It seems clear that, if the contractor seeks to argue that he is due extra payment on a *quantum meruit* basis, he must raise this issue with the employer at the time it becomes clear that the work will involve extra costs.[1200]

II. In spite of the arguments detailed above, the weight of authority points towards a strict approach, exemplified by the House of Lords

[1196] 1914 SC 472 at 491 per Lord Justice-Clerk Macdonald; 1915 SC (HL) 20 per Lord Parmoor at 39.

[1197] See J. Arnott and J. Wolffe, 'Building Contracts', in: Sir Thomas Smith, *et al.* (eds.), *The Laws of Scotland: Stair Memorial Encyclopaedia* (Edinburgh: Butterworths/Law Society of Scotland, 1987–96), vol. III, para. 27.

[1198] *Smellie* v. *Caledonian Railway Co* (1916) 53 SLR 336; *Quin* v. *Gardner* (1888) 15 R. 776; *Smail* v. *Potts* (1847) 9 D. 1043.

[1199] *Smellie* v. *Caledonian Railway Co* (1916) 53 SLR 336 per the Lord Ordinary Dewar at 341.

[1200] This is implied by the speech of Lord Chancellor Cairns in *Thorn* v. *London Corporation* (1876) 1 App. Cas. 120 given that he reserves his opinion on whether the contractor might make such a claim once he has actually completed the works; see also Lord MacKenzie in *Smellie* v. *Caledonian Railway Co* (1916) 53 SLR 336 at 343. Arnott and Wolffe's explanation is also consistent with this view, see 'Building Contracts', para. 27.

decision in *Boyd & Forrest*. The 'inclusive price' principle which forms part of English law also adopts a strict approach. Hudson's Building and Engineering Contracts states:

> . . . by virtue of the inclusive price principle, all contingently necessary expenditure incurred in order to overcome difficulties and bring the described work to satisfactory completion will, in the absence of express provision, be regarded as included in the contractor's price or prices for the described permanent work. This will mean, among other things, that overcoming whatever physical difficulties may be encountered on a particular site in order to construct the required permanent works will prima facie be included in the contractor's prices.[1201]

There is Scottish authority which supports this view.[1202]

Editors' comparative notes

The open jurisdictions

No clear tendency can be stated in the open jurisdictions with regard to this case. In spite of the disclaimer X is likely to be granted relief in Austria, Greece, Italy, Lithuania and Sweden. Greece and Lithuania will grant adjustment and termination, Italy only offers adjustment, while the other jurisdictions (Austria and Sweden) only offer termination. However, in jurisdictions that discuss relief in form of termination, Y can generally save the agreement if he agrees to pay the increased price (cf. Austria). A duty to renegotiate is potentially available in Italy and the Netherlands. No relief will be granted in Germany, Spain and, perhaps, in Portugal, mainly because the disclaimer is likely to be considered valid.

As far as the doctrinal approaches are concerned, we are dealing with three different but interconnected issues: (i) The contractual allocation of risks in contracts for works, (ii) the assessment of the unexpected circumstance in question and (iii) the validity of the disclaimer.

(i) Generally, the parties of a contract for works are free to determine a risk allocation scheme and the fact that they have agreed on a fixed price means that costs and risks of performance are attributed to the contractor (cf. Greece, Lithuania). In some jurisdictions (Italy, Portugal,

[1201] I. N. Duncan Wallace, *Hudson's Building and Engineering Contracts* (London: Sweet & Maxwell, 11th edn, 1995), para. 8-060, see also para. 4-036.

[1202] *Tharsis Sulphur & Copper Co* v. *McElroy & Sons* (1878) 5 R. 171 per Lord Blackburn at 177.

Sweden), however, specific rules exist that divide unforeseen costs between the parties of such contracts. These rules will apply in lack of a specific agreement. Whether or not such rules are derogated from in the contractual agreement and which risk allocation scheme applies is determined by interpretation. At this stage, most reports take the disclaimer into account in their assessment of the allocation of risks arising from performance to X.

(ii) Without having regard to the disclaimer, in most jurisdictions the case is solved either based on specific rules addressing unexpected circumstances in contracts for work (Italy, Portugal, Sweden) or with reference to general 'exceptional' doctrines on unexpected circumstances (*Geschäftsgrundlage* or *clausula rebus sic stantibus*). In Austria, the doctrine of '*laesio enormis*' is applied because there is an imbalance between the values of the performances of 1:3. In Germany, 'economic' or 'practical' impossibility is discussed but does not apply, as the creditor's interest in performance has not become grossly disproportionate compared to the creditor's costs. Leaving the disclaimer aside, most jurisdictions tend to grant some form of relief based on the 'exceptional' doctrines. Yet, the German report states that the conditions of *Wegfall der Geschäftsgrundlage* are not met in the case at hand.

(iii) In most of the open jurisdictions, the disclaimer is regarded as invalid. This is justified by reference to the principle of good faith (Lithuania, the Netherlands), a general fairness clause (Section 36 Swedish Contracts Act) and public morality (Austria). However, many jurisdictions do accept derogations from rules on unexpected circumstance, as a general rule, as long as the disclaimer is specific enough, i.e., if the parties show that they have taken into account the particular risk in question (cf. Austria, Greece, Italy). The disclaimer is regarded to be valid in Germany, Portugal and Spain. In Portugal and Spain, relief (modification or termination) is accordingly excluded, whereas, according to the German report, relief would not have been likely in the first place.

The closed jurisdictions

In the group of the closed jurisdictions, the Czech Republic, Denmark and Slovenia will potentially allow X to terminate the contract. In England and Ireland, there is a good chance that frustration will apply in spite of the disclaimer and that the contract will be discharged by operation of law. In Belgium and France, the disclaimer will be held valid and it derogates from the potential right to terminate the contract based on *sujétions imprévues*. A right of adjustment or a right to renegotiate is not offered in any of the closed jurisdictions. In Scotland, there is no right to terminate on the grounds of the cost increase and the disclaimer is therefore superfluous.

Let us first disregard the disclaimer and turn to the general issue of relief. While the result of granting relief is (except for Scotland) quite uniform, the doctrinal approaches differ. In Denmark, the Czech Republic and Slovenia, the legal arguments for relief are, once again, very similar to those applied in the open jurisdictions. In Denmark, like in Sweden, general terms and conditions for construction contracts may apply. In lack of such general contract terms, the case would be solved based on the general unreasonableness clause (Art. 36 Contracts Act) and, perhaps, based on the doctrine of assumptions. Article 36 Contracts Act will, however, only apply if X can be regarded as the 'weaker' party. Under Slovenian law, X is entitled to terminate the contract based on the doctrine of '*laesio enormis*' (like in Austria) or based on a relevant mistake as to the characteristics of the soil. Y can save the contract if he agrees to pay an increased price. In the Czech Republic, the doctrine of (economic) impossibility may be applied. In Belgium and France, the doctrine of *sujétions imprévues* applies, leading to a right to terminate the contract.

In England and Ireland, the contract is likely to be regarded as frustrated because the increase in price renders X's obligation radically different from what was envisaged in the contract. An alternative ground for relief is the parties' mutual mistake with regard to the structure of the land and to the efforts required to carry out the works. Similar rules are applied in Scotland where the case is considered to be a case of *uninduced error*. However, due to the so-called 'inclusive principle', all necessary expenditure for performance will be regarded as included in the contractor's price in absence of an express provision. A similar reasoning can also be found in the report of the open jurisdictions of Greece and Lithuania.

As a result, without having regard to the disclaimer, termination is likely to be granted in all of the closed jurisdictions except for Scotland.

The disclaimer will only exclude relief in Belgium and France, where the courts would enforce it in line with their general reluctance to grant relief in cases of unexpected circumstances. In the other closed jurisdictions, the disclaimer is very likely to be held invalid. In Denmark, England and Ireland, the clause might be disregarded by interpretation because it is not specific enough. There is some case law suggesting that such exclusionary clauses will be interpreted narrowly and will have no effect on the doctrine of frustration. In Slovenia, based on the standard of good faith, the courts will also only accept exclusionary clauses that specify the events included. In the Czech Republic, the disclaimer is likely to be disregarded based on the standard of public morality.

Conclusion

The issue in this case is whether a general disclaimer will influence the burdened party's rights arising from unexpected circumstances. In most jurisdictions, both open and closed, the disclaimer is held to be invalid. The exceptions are Belgium and France from the group of the closed jurisdictions and Portugal, Spain and Germany from the group of the open jurisdictions where the courts will respect the disclaimer. In Scotland, relief will not be granted in the first place and the disclaimer will therefore not influence the solution. In Germany, relief is also not very likely to be granted regardless of the disclaimer. Alternatively, the German report states that if the case supported relief, the disclaimer would be treated as valid and would therefore exclude relief.

Even though the doctrinal solutions and the outcomes differ, the reasoning is very similar in both the open and the closed jurisdictions: the contractual risk allocation and perhaps specific rules on contracts for work are the starting point. The fact that construction contracts are prone to undergo considerable changes is generally taken into account by the application of specific or general rules on unexpected circumstances to such contracts. The only exception seems to be Scotland where case law is very reluctant to take these circumstances into account based on the 'inclusive principle', i.e., by the assumption that in the case of a fixed price contracts the contractor assumes all risks of performance. However, this approach is disputed in Scottish legal literature.

Under a clear majority of the jurisdictions in both the open as well as the closed legal systems, the disclaimer is held invalid, at least in the general form presented in our case. Three different rationales can be distinguished that render the disclaimer ineffective: (i) the disclaimer will either be interpreted narrowly, (ii) it will be considered not to be precise enough to actually attribute specific contractual risks on X or (iii) it will be regarded as too great a disadvantage to one party and therefore contrary to public morality or good faith. The underlying rationale for the majority perspective is that unexpected events are beyond the parties' imagination and thus beyond their disposition. One may also draw the conclusion that the equity principles from which the doctrines governing unexpected circumstances are derived qualify as *ius cogens*.

However, the discussions in the reports show that most jurisdictions are more willing to accept a disclaimer addressing specific risks in particular if there is some evidence that the parties contemplated such risks when the contract was concluded (cf. the English and Irish report). This is most likely to be accepted if the contract price shows that such risks were taken into account.

The distinction between termination and adjustment does not seem to play a decisive role in this case. In general, jurisdictions that only grant termination will allow the other party to save the contract if he is willing to pay the increased price. Likewise, if adjustment is the primary remedy, most jurisdictions will allow termination if the other party is not willing to accept the increased price. A duty to renegotiate is only discussed in the Italian and the Dutch report. In Italy, the courts will, in fact, assume such a duty in this case.

PART IV

General comparative remarks

7 General comparative remarks: Converging tendencies, remaining differences and the unsolved mystery of adjustment

EWOUD HONDIUS AND
HANS CHRISTOPH GRIGOLEIT

1. 'Open' versus 'closed' legal systems, the variety of doctrines and the difficulty of identifying clear tendencies

In the Introduction, we drew an initial distinction between 'open' and 'closed' legal systems. This distinction was based on the criterion whether or not a jurisdiction recognises a general rule under which the contract can be adjusted to unexpected circumstances by the courts. The distinction led to the following groups: as 'open' legal systems we have qualified those of Austria, Germany, Greece, Italy, Lithuania, the Netherlands, Portugal and Sweden and we have characterised as 'closed' jurisdictions those of Belgium, Denmark, England, France, Ireland, Scotland and Slovenia. To a certain extent this distinction goes along with the classic division into legal families. Not very surprisingly, the common law tradition, the French influence ('closed' jurisdictions) and the German tradition ('open' jurisdictions) lead to similarities in the doctrinal approach to cases of unexpected circumstances. There is one exception. The Nordic legal systems use the same concepts but arrive at different ends of the spectrum.

However, the distinction between 'open' and 'closed' jurisdictions did not survive the test wholly unscathed as far as the outcome of our cases is concerned. Thus, the distinction between 'open' and 'closed' jurisdictions is a rough doctrinal approach rather than a clear indication of differences with regard to the result of a certain case. Yet, the strict requirements for relief and the variety of other legal concepts dilute the effects of any particular doctrine. The distinction was drawn based on doctrinal aspects and the differences between the two groups remain on a doctrinal level. In a jurisdiction such as the Netherlands, for example, where a provision in the Civil Code allows adjustment of the contract in the case of a change of circumstances, this provision is used so rarely that one may occasionally ask whether this is not a 'closed' system instead. Likewise, Slovenia, which we have qualified as a 'closed' jurisdiction, seems to be on the borderline with the 'open' systems.

This rather diffuse picture with regard to results in the 'open' and 'closed' legal systems can be explained by the complex interference of different legal concepts that are applied to cases involving unexpected circumstances. Even if a jurisdiction does not recognise an 'exceptional' doctrine allowing for an adjustment of the contract, 'conventional' doctrines may be applied with similar results. In addition, in many jurisdictions specific legislation exists that is directed at dealing with the consequences of certain exceptional events on the contractual exchange. This complex interference of concepts complicates conclusions on a general level and makes a clear distinction between the groups difficult as far as the results are concerned.

Yet, it seems fair to say that the recognition of a general and flexible rule providing for relief in cases of unexpected circumstances may make it easier for the courts to set aside a contract. Across all the cases, the 'open' jurisdictions actually seem to be more open towards equitable relief than the 'closed' ones while the latter systems express a higher esteem for the principle of *pacta sunt servanda*. It is also interesting to see that this division corresponds remarkably with the distinction between fault liability ('open' jurisdictions) and strict liability ('closed' jurisdictions – see Case 14).

2. Convergence as to the general issue of suspending (or upholding) the binding character of the contract terms

Before we turn to a more systematic analysis of the doctrinal concepts, it is remarkable to observe that, in most cases, there is a clear tendency as far as the results are concerned, i.e., whether or not a certain unexpected event justifies suspending the binding character of the terms of the contract and limiting the principle of *pacta sunt servanda*. It should be noted, however, that these tendencies only relate to the suspending effect as such while the legal consequences (adjustment or termination) may vary in detail. We shall examine these tendencies in the five different groups that we have established for our cases:

A. *Equivalence of exchange is substantially affected*

(i) With regard to the first group of cases in which the 'equivalence of the exchange has been affected' we can conclude that under the law of all jurisdictions long-term agreements can lose their binding effect if, in the course of time, the initially fixed price grows out of proportion compared with the value of the object (Case 1). In many jurisdictions, the right to terminate long-term contracts is an essential element of contract law. Such a right is, in effect, based on the rationale that in the course of long-term agreements unexpected effects can occur that cannot be provided for by the parties in advance. This correspondence becomes evident under the German rules on unexpected circumstances which contain a separate section dealing with the effects of unexpected events on long-term contracts (§314 BGB) besides the general provision on *Wegfall der Geschäftsgrundlage* (§313 BGB).

(ii) There is generally much reservation as to the question whether extraordinary inflation can affect credit agreements. Only some of the 'open' jurisdictions mitigate the consequences for the burdened party while applying very strict standards (Case 2). This reservation can be referred to as the nominal value principle under which the amount of a monetary debt is based on its nominal and not on its 'real' value. Inflation is a ubiquitous phenomenon of the economy and distinctions between regular and excessive conditions are hard to draw. Unsurprisingly, due to its speculative nature, the jurisdictions are even more reluctant to grant relief in the case of a foreign currency agreement (Case 2(b)).

(iii) We can observe a tendency towards relief in cases in which government intervention has strongly affected the contractual equilibrium (Case 3), even though the 'closed' jurisdictions are more reluctant to grant relief. This trend can be attributed to the consideration that government action is often elementary to the parties' interests and evidently beyond their control.

(iv) Under a majority of jurisdictions, unexpected benefits do not trigger any form of relief, even if the benefits are out of proportion with the consideration (Case 4). It appears that one-sided windfall profits arising from the contract do not elicit the same inclination for equitable compensation as excessive losses.

B. *Recipient's use of goods or services is substantially affected*

(i) In the cases from group B where the 'recipient's use of goods or services is substantially affected', government intervention seems to be, again, a clear case for judicial intervention: relief is predominantly granted if the lease of a petrol station becomes worthless to the lessee as petrol is no longer available due to confiscation in wartime (Case 6). However, in the majority of the jurisdictions an export ban that is already present at the time of contracting does not justify relief for the burdened party even if both parties expected that the ban would be suspended (Case 10). The reason for upholding the contract in this case is that the parties knew about the risk of the ban and the misjudgment of an identified risk is held not to justify a relief.

(ii) When a promised work of construction (in our case, a cellar) becomes useless to the client due to a natural disaster (destruction of the rest of the building), all legal systems give him the right to cancel the completion of the work because it has become useless. With regard to the question of compensation, the jurisdictions are basically divided into two groups: under one approach, the contractor remains entitled to the full contract price less the expenses he saves by not having to carry out the work, e.g., wages, material etc. (Belgium, Czech Republic, Denmark, France and Slovenia). Thereby the contractor is awarded his contractual profits and the risk that the contract has become useless is allocated to the client. The argument for this is that the house is in his sphere of risk and control. In other jurisdictions, the contractor's claim for his contractual profits is reduced by some form of equitable adjustment and therefore the risk is distributed between both parties (e.g., Germany, the Netherlands, Portugal, England and Ireland). This solution is based upon the notion that the risk in question is not rooted in the house itself but in the natural disaster which is beyond either party's control (Case 5).

(iii) In the hotel reservation case the four presented events (Case 7(a) to (d)) display different tendencies: there is broad correspondence with regard to the conclusion that the frustration of individual purposes (exhibition cancelled, Case 7(a)) and disturbances in transport (strike, Case 7(c)) do not relieve the customer from his contractual obligations as these risks fall in the sphere of the customer. There is a certain tendency towards relief in the case involving terrorist threats (Case 7 (b)); however, much seems to depend on the facts (e.g., the probability and the foreseeability of the attacks). A clear tendency for relief can be stated in the coronation case: the fact that the price reflects the procession leads most reports to conclude that the hotel owner has to bear the risk (Case 7(d)).

(iv) With regard to the shop rental case, a clear majority of the jurisdictions denies relief to the shop owner who claims that the business environment has developed unfavourably. This risk is considered not to be unusual and therefore the shop owner could and should have provided for it by implementing a protective term (Case 8). The jurisdictions under scrutiny are more likely to grant relief, however, if the owner of a bar is bound under a long-term supply agreement to sell only one kind of beer and this beer turns out to be unpopular among the guests (Case 9). Here, the long-term character of the contract may strengthen the case for relief as well as the fact that the risk in question (the popularity of the beer) might be qualified as falling within the sphere of the brewery.

C. *Failure of a specified purpose (other than A and B)*

Both of the cases that we have dealt with under the heading 'failure of a specified purpose' show a tendency in favour of relief:

(i) The assumption that the sold property will be used for cultural purposes will suffice for setting aside the agreement if it is used for other purposes because this assumption is – similarly to the coronation case – reflected in the price (Case 11). Here, the requirements of equity can quite easily be reconciled with the principle of *pacta sunt servanda* on the basis of 'conventional' doctrines (especially constructive interpretation).

(ii) In the case of divorce, the investment of one spouse in the property of the other one can give rise to a claim for compensation in most jurisdictions if divorce law does not provide for just results (Case 12). This solution can be based on the consideration that the reliance in the durability of the marriage should be legally protected.

D. *Mutual mistake*

(i) A clear tendency can be stated in the case in which the parties to a share deal made a mutual mistake concerning the market value of shares (Case 13). Here, the burdened party is generally entitled to set aside the agreement on the fixed price, as both parties share the responsibility for the mistake. Another tendency is that the party burdened by the false price setting is not entitled to enforce a price agreement that reflects the 'true value' because the other party's reliance on the written price agreement must equally be taken into account. Notable exceptions are the common law jurisdictions of England and Ireland where no remedy is granted and thereby the risk of the mutual mistake is allocated only to the party burdened by the 'false' price calculation in the written contract.

E. *Miscellaneous issues*

(i) In Case 14, the effect of unexpected circumstances on the respective rules on breach of contract was analysed. The question here was whether the seller would be excused from his liability in damages due to the unexpected nature of the impediment. Even though many jurisdictions tend to solve this case on the basis of their ('conventional') doctrines on breach of contract, a clear distinction between the 'open' and 'closed' jurisdictions can be observed. The main reason for this is that the distinction between the 'open' and the 'closed' jurisdictions is in line with the division between systems that apply a fault liability regime with regard to contractual damages and those jurisdictions that provide for strict liability. On the basis of their strict liability regime, there is a clear tendency towards holding X liable for damages among the 'closed' jurisdictions. The findings of the 'open' jurisdictions remain somewhat vague due to the limited fact basis of the given case. However, it becomes quite clear that, subject to the factual details of the case, X has strong arguments to challenge his liability in many of the 'open' jurisdictions. The lack of a clear tendency reflects the division as to the liability regime, but also the ambivalence of the risks in question. While neither strikes nor the energy supply is under the complete control of the seller, one may argue that he is closer to these sources of risk than the purchaser.

(ii) With regard to Case 15, it is remarkable to note that a general disclaimer will predominantly be regarded as invalid in both the 'open' and in the 'closed' jurisdictions. There are, however, some exceptions (Belgium and France from the group of the 'closed' and Germany, Portugal and Spain from the group of the 'open' jurisdictions). The rationale for the majority perspective is that unexpected events are beyond the parties' imagination and thus beyond their dispositions. One may also draw the conclusion that the equity principles from which the doctrines governing unexpected circumstances are derived are qualified as *ius cogens*.

3. The preference for openly addressing the conflict between the principle of *pacta sunt servanda* and the goal of a fair allocation of risks

Let us now turn to the doctrinal distinction between 'conventional' and 'exceptional' concepts. The doctrines that specifically address the issue of unexpected circumstances and identify the unexpected event as the source for relief (e.g., *Wegfall der Geschäftsgrundlage*, doctrine of assumptions, *clausula rebus sic stantibus*) have been referred to as 'exceptional' doctrines. 'Conventional' doctrines, on the other hand, are the traditional doctrines of contract law, which are based on the parties' (hypothetical) intentions or on flaws in the mechanism of contracting. Such doctrines can address unexpected events with reference to the contractual agreement (e.g., interpretation, mistake, impossibility of performance and *laesio enormis;* see Introduction, sections 4 and 5).

In favour of the 'conventional' concepts one may argue that they are in harmony with the principle of *pacta sunt servanda*: if the parties' (hypothetical) intentions can be referred to as the basis of relief or if flaws can be identified in the contracting process, there is no conflict between the contract and an equitable allocation of risks. The harmonising character of the 'conventional' concepts may make it easier for the courts to set the contract aside.

However, quite often the 'conventional' concepts provide no precise and persuasive rationale for relief in cases of unexpected circumstances - even if they are referred to by the courts. If the contract does not address the unexpected event explicitly or by clear implication, relief cannot be based on the parties' actual intentions. Hence, 'conventional' concepts are always dealing with hypothetical assumptions as to what the parties would have agreed upon if they had foreseen the event. This reconstruction of the parties' hypothetical intentions will often be fictional. If the parties have not foreseen the risk in question, it is equally fictional to qualify their non-perception as a mistake. Therefore, in many cases of unexpected circumstances applying a 'conventional' doctrine amounts to concealing the essential equitable conflict between the (flawless but silent) contract and the extrinsic effect caused by the unexpected event in question.

The 'exceptional' doctrines, on the other hand, openly address the conflict between the contract and the requirements of equity in the light of the unexpected event in question. These doctrines and their application reveal that in most cases the problem of unexpected circumstances cannot be solved with reference to the intention of the parties and that an external standard of law is to be applied in the assessment of the event and its consequences for the contract. This becomes evident in the 'open' jurisdictions, where on the basis of a general 'exceptional' doctrine the contractual agreement itself can be adjusted to match the requirements of equity.

The European model rules on contract law presented so far (see Introduction, section 8) all propose to recognise such a general 'exceptional' doctrine. The conflict between the principle of *pacta sunt servanda* and the requirements of equity is particularly evident in the rules of the DCFR, which are based on the PECL. In Art. III.-1:110 DCFR and Art. 6.111 PECL the principle of sanctity of the contract is confirmed as the general rule. However, at the same time, it is confronted with the relevant exceptions in the case of a change of circumstances.

4. Minimum requirements of setting aside the contract

As we have already mentioned and as our national reports illustrate there are various 'exceptional' doctrines, i.e., concepts specifically addressing the issue of unexpected circumstances both in the 'open' and in the 'closed' jurisdictions. In the 'open' jurisdictions, these doctrines will allow for termination as well as adjustment of the contract, while in the 'closed' jurisdictions termination is generally the only remedy available.

Even though the different concepts vary strongly in detail, we can identify three basic prerequisites for the application of such 'exceptional' doctrines, as far as their doctrinal justification is concerned:

(i) The transaction must have been affected *fundamentally* by a certain event. This requirement expresses the general idea that the principle of *pacta sunt servanda* and the stability of the contract may only be disregarded in exceptional cases.
(ii) The event affecting the transaction *must not have been provided for in the contract or foreseen by both parties* at the time of the conclusion of the contract. This requirement reflects the prevalence of the parties' specific dispositions within the scope of their foresight.
(iii) The burden resulting from the event may *not be attributed to one party by any particular legal rule*. This postulate accounts for the principle of *lex specialis derogat legi generali*: the law provides rules for certain unexpected events and these rules demand priority over a general doctrine on unexpected circumstances.

These requirements can be characterised as 'minimum conditions': even though further restrictions may (and often do) apply under the law of the individual jurisdictions, these requirements must be met in any case if the contract is to be challenged successfully.

Evidently, the 'minimum conditions' are phrased in general and ambiguous terms and they cannot guarantee convergence with regard to the findings in a certain case as the complementary rules vary throughout the jurisdictions. But this ambiguity and divergence often reflect the complex and manifold character of the problem of unexpected circumstances rather than diverging concepts in the different legal systems which admittedly exist as well. Even if the complementary rules were identical, the question of what amounts to a 'fundamental effect' or which contractual risks are provided for in the agreement or by a particular rule of law is largely based on the individual appreciation of the event in question. The fundamental conflict between legal security and the binding force of contract on the one hand and equity on the other hand will always leave room for diverging judgments.

5. Distinction between issues of initial mistake and of unexpected events arising after the conclusion of the contract

A mistake of one party or a mutual mistake of both parties with regard to factors that were already present before or at the time the contract was concluded differs significantly from the occurrence of unexpected events arising after the conclusion of the contract. A clear distinction between pre-existing and supervening factors is meaningful for the doctrinal treatment of unexpected circumstances because it is generally easier for the parties to recognise and control pre-existing factors than future developments. Furthermore, by submitting themselves to a contractual agreement, the parties are aware that they generally assume the risk of future changes and they may only be relieved from this risk under exceptional circumstances. A lack of information about pre-existing factors, on the other hand, will in most jurisdictions allow parties to terminate a contract even if they are not heavily burdened by its stipulations. The absence of a relevant mistake is a precondition for the binding effect of the contract and the assumption of risks provided therein. Hence, if a party is mistaken about certain factors that were present at the time of contracting, the case should only be treated according to the respective rules on mistake.

If some jurisdictions tend to apply their 'exceptional' doctrines on unexpected circumstances in cases of mistakes as to pre-existing factors, this can mainly be explained by certain deficiencies in their respective law of mistake. Germany, where the rules on *Geschäftsgrundlage* are applied in cases of mutual mistakes, may serve as an example because the rules on mistake in the BGB were only designed for cases of one-sided responsibility for the mistake and the principles on *Geschäftsgrundlage* offer a more flexible instrument that is necessary in cases of mutual mistake. From a doctrinal point of view, these problems can be solved more adequately by refining the rules on mistake.

However, the fact that the problem of initial mistake and the issue of supervening unexpected circumstances both tend to be approached on the same doctrinal basis shows that they are in fact similar with regard to the issue of remedies. In both types of cases, the binding force of the agreement is disregarded because one or both parties have failed to take into account certain factors that were of relevance for the contract. And both cases can essentially be solved with two remedies: the contract can either be discharged or it can be adjusted to take into account the relevant aspect. A legal system therefore has to answer this question with regard to both constellations discussed. It is suggested that, in a legal system with a systematic approach, both problems should be addressed on the basis of uniform principles.

6. Legal Consequences – the unsolved mystery of 'adjustment'

The convergences of the court findings (see section 2) and the similarities in the doctrinal approach (see section 4) only concern the primary issue whether or not the contract is suspended due to unexpected circumstances. With regard to the secondary issue, i.e., the precise definition of the legal consequences, it is very hard to identify convergence between the different jurisdictions. At a closer look, this obscurity is not due to the comparative perspective; rather, the cause for this can be traced back to the legal systems themselves as none of them presents a clear, systematic, complete and convincing concept with regard to the legal consequences that apply once an unexpected event suspends the binding effect of the contract terms. The same holds true for the various European model codes of contract law.

As we have pointed out in the Introduction, the remedy of termination is quite simple and does not involve much judicial discretion. It is not surprising that this remedy is widely available in cases of unexpected circumstances in all jurisdictions. However, in a large number of cases termination does not achieve fair results as it may distribute the losses arising from the unexpected event arbitrarily to one party. Therefore, it can be said that the recognition of a mechanism of adjustment is a postulate of equity if the contract is set aside due to unexpected circumstances.

This conclusion is explicitly drawn in the 'open' jurisdictions and in the model codes (e.g., Art. III. – 1:110 DCFR; Art. 6:111 PECL), as there are established sets of rules under which the burdened party may seek adjustment of the contract in cases of unexpected circumstances. Even in the 'closed' jurisdictions, where there are no such mechanisms established as a general rule, the reports show that the courts may find a way to reach results that amount to adjustment of the contractual terms, e.g., on the basis of constructive interpretation or by granting ad hoc compensation based on the standards of equity and good faith. Also, the development of the doctrine of frustration in England shows that the all-or-nothing approach of termination (or discharge) is inadequate for dealing with all the issues of unexpected circumstances. In England, the strict effects of the common law doctrine of frustration leading to a discharge of the contract had to be amended by the Law Reform (Frustrated Contracts) Act 1943 granting the judge a wide amount of discretion in order to achieve just results.

The details of adjustment, however, involve a number of difficult issues:

(i) The *relation between termination and adjustment* (i.e., the conditions under which termination or adjustment is the appropriate remedy): this aspect also includes the question whether the party that is not burdened by the unexpected event in question is entitled to object to the adjustment and can thereby compel termination.
(ii) The *form of adjustment*: it must be determined whether the adjustment may interfere with the contractual obligations in kind or whether there is only monetary compensation available.
(iii) The *standard for determining the extent of adjustment*: this issue raises the difficult question whether the burdened party has to bear the losses from the unexpected circumstances up to a reasonable extent or whether – alternatively – the losses are to be divided equally among the parties.
(iv) The *technical implementation of adjustment*: it must be determined whether adjustment comes into force by operation of law (determined by the court) or whether the burdened party has a right to claim adjustment by specifying the contents of the adjustment. In addition, it must be decided whether adjustment must be preceded by a renegotiation process and whether and how such a renegotiation process can be governed by rules of law.

The reports show that these issues have not yet been fully resolved in any one of the jurisdictions explored in this volume. Hence, it is unsurprising that convergent and convincing solutions cannot be identified from the comparative perspective. It appears that the conditions for adjusting the contract are the unsolved mystery of the legal rules on unexpected circumstances. This unresolved issue is of great influence for the entire problem as the willingness to grant relief depends very much on reliable consequences of the remedy available.

In order to provide fair solutions it is unavoidable to recognise a legal regime for the adjustment of a contract that is affected by relevant unexpected circumstances. One may resort to judicial discretion which is relied upon by all of the 'open' as well as the 'closed' jurisdictions to a certain extent. But if more precise guidelines are required, the material is inconclusive. Thus, the conditions of adjustment appear to be the most important topic for further research in the field of unexpected circumstances.

7. Uncertainty, the lack of precedents and harmonisation by advancing the legal discourse

As we have mentioned, the uncertainty of judgments on unexpected circumstances is an unavoidable characteristic of the conflict between legal security and the binding force of contract on the one hand and the requirements of equity on the other. There are possibilities of strengthening certainty on the comparative level by further harmonisation with regard to the doctrinal background in general and the mechanism of adjustment in particular. Yet, there is another structural source of uncertainty that is particularly important in cases of unexpected circumstances: the lack of reliable precedents in many jurisdictions.

The cases in which relief on the basis of unexpected circumstances is discussed are quite eccentric and rare. Some national reporters have had difficulties in identifying precedents similar to our cases at hand and some may have had to go back several decades. Especially in continental countries, the question may be raised whether 'old' precedents still have – persuasive – value as they reflect an antiquated legal and social background and could arguably be overruled if they were submitted to the respective Supreme Court today.[1]

Further harmonisation of the law in Europe may enlarge the basis of precedents. It would mean that instead of a meagre trickle of cases, every member state would fully profit from the case law of the other member states of the European Union. However, the harmonisation on the basis of precedents does not necessarily depend on a common Civil Code.[2] The American example shows that the various states of the Union refer to the case law of other states. The process of harmonisation by precedents may be enhanced by a restatement of European contract law without binding effect. In fact, in Europe several model codes are available such as the DCFR, the PECL, the Principles of the Association Henri Capitant des Amis de la Culture Juridique Française and the

[1] Ewoud Hondius (ed.), *Precedent and the Law/Les précédents et le droit* (Brussels: Bruylant, 2007), p. 19.

[2] See Ilka Klöckner, *Grenzüberschreitende Bindung an zivilgerichtliche Präjudizien*, PhD Thesis Freiburg 2005, (Tübingen: Mohr, 2006), 254 pp.

Société de Législation Comparée, the Acquis-Principles, the Gandolfi Code, as well as other international instruments, such as the UNIDROIT Principles for International Commercial Contracts.

We have already seen that there is a considerable amount of similarity between the different European legal systems both in terms of the results achieved as well as in terms of their doctrinal approach (cf sections 2 and 4). Hence, even without a uniform mandatory European rule on unexpected circumstances, courts and practitioners are very likely to profit from an analysis of cases from other European legal systems. Such an exchange is particularly important in cases of unexpected circumstances as, due to the variety of the potentially relevant factors, the legal doctrines applied and their requirements are necessarily vague and it may always be argued that the solution will greatly depend on the facts of the individual case. Furthermore, it should be stressed again that, as far as precise doctrinal guidelines are concerned, no legal system seems to have presented a convincing approach to the problem of unexpected circumstances as a whole so far. Therefore, this volume is intended to serve as a guide that may help to improve the understanding between the different European legal systems and to refine the rules on unexpected circumstances, either on the national level of or with regard to harmonisation projects.

Of course, the process of harmonisation on the basis of precedents involves the problem of languages. An Estonian case on change of circumstances will have little impact in Portugal if it is not available in a language which is accessible to Portuguese lawyers. A database in the present European *lingua franca* – and ideally in more than just one language – would therefore be necessary. This need not necessarily be a database in the formal sense, such as CLAB.[3] A more user-friendly option is ECTIL's Yearbook of Tort Law, which is discussed at annual meetings in Vienna. Likewise, Trento could be the platform, long after the Common Core project has finished, for annual updates as to national case law on the various topics, such as unexpected circumstances.

[3] DG SANCO's database on unfair contract terms (*clauses abusives*) – see Thomas Wilhelmsson, in: Torbjörn Andersson and Bengt Lindell (eds.), *Festskrift till Per Henrik Lindblom* (Stockholm: Iustus, 2004), pp. 781–800.

APPENDIX

Some Texts on Change of Circumstances

Although contractual hardship clauses are not yet considered to be part of the *lex mercatoria*, they are becoming more and more usual. The difference with statutory provisions is that while the latter – if they do exist – usually provide for intervention by the court, a hardship clause confers such powers upon the parties themselves. A Restatement of hardship clauses may be found in Article 6.111 of the PECL and the similar Articles 6.2.1–6.2.3 in UNIDROIT's Principles of International Commercial Contracts (PICC).

1 Principles of European Contract Law (PECL)

Article 6:111: Change of Circumstances

(1) *A party is bound to fulfil its obligation even if performance has become more onerous, whether because the cost of performance has increased or because the value of the performance it receives has diminished.*

(2) *If, however, performance of the contract becomes excessively onerous because of a change of circumstances, the parties are bound to enter into negotiations with a view to adapting the contract or ending it, provided that:*

   (a) *the change of cirumstances occurred after the time of conclusion of the contract,*

   (b) *the possibility of a change of circumstances was not one which could reasonably have been taken into account at the time of conclusion of the contract, and*

   (c) *the risk of the change of circumstances is not one which, according to the contract, the party affected should be required to bear.*

(3) *If the parties fail to reach agreement within a reasonable period, the court may:*

   (a) *end the contract at a date and on terms to be determined by the court; or*

(b) *adapt the contract in order to distribute between the parties in a just and equitable manner the losses and gains resulting from the change of circumstances.*

In either case, the court may award damages for the loss suffered through a party refusing to negotiate or breaking off negotiations contrary to good faith and fair dealing.[1]

2. UNIDROIT Principles of International Commercial Contrats (PICC)

Article 6.2.1 (Contract to be observed)

Where the performance of a contract becomes more onerous for one of the parties, that party is nevertheless bound to perform its obligations subject to the following provisions on hardship.[2]

Article 6.2.2 (Definition of hardship)

There is hardship where the occurrence of events fundamentally alters the equilibrium of the contract either because the cost of a party's performance has increased or because the value of the performance a party receives has diminished, and

(a) *the events occur or become known to the disadvantaged party after the conclusion of the contract;*
(b) *the events could not reasonably have been taken into account by the disadvantaged party at the time of the conclusion of the contract;*
(c) *the events are beyond the control of the disadvantaged party; and*
(d) *the risk of the events was not assumed by the disadvantaged party.*

Article 6.2.3 (Effects of hardship)

(1) *In case of hardship the disadvantaged party is entitled to request renegotiations. The request shall be made without undue delay and shall indicate the grounds on which it is based.*
(2) *The request for renegotiation does not in itself entitle the disadvantaged party to withhold performance.*
(3) *Upon failure to reach agreement within a reasonable time either party may resort to the court.*
(4) *If the court finds hardship it may, if reasonable*
    (a) *terminate the contract at a date and on terms to be fixed, or*
    (b) *adapt the contract with a view to restoring its equilibrium.*

[1] Ole Lando and Hugh Beale (eds.), *Principles of European Contract Law Parts I and II* (The Hague: Kluwer Law International, 2000) pp. 322–8.

[2] UNIDROIT, *Principles of International Commercial Contracts* (Rome: UNIDROIT, 1994), pp. 145–55 (unchanged in the 2004 edition).

3. Draft Common Frame of Reference (DCFR)

Art. III.-1:110: Variation or termination by court on a change of circumstances

(1) *An obligation must be performed even if performance has become more onerous, whether because the cost of performance has increased or because the value of what is to be received in return has diminished.*

(2) *If, however, performance of a contractual obligation or of an obligation arising from a unilateral juridical act becomes so onerous because of an exceptional change of circumstances that it would be manifestly unjust to hold the debtor to the obligation a court may:*
- (a) *vary the obligation in order to make it reasonable and equitable in the new circumstances; or*
- (b) *terminate the obligation at a date and on terms to be determined by the court.*

(3) *Paragraph (2) applies only if:*
- (a) *the change of circumstances occurred after the time when the obligation was incurred;*
- (b) *the debtor did not at that time take into account, and could not reasonably be expected to have taken into account, the possibility or scale of that change of circumstances;*
- (c) *the debtor did not assume, and cannot reasonably be regarded as having assumed, the risk of that change of circumstances; and*
- (d) *the debtor has attempted, reasonably and in good faith, to achieve by negotiation a reasonable and equitable adjustment of the terms regulating the obligation.*

4. Association Henri Capitant des Amis de la Culture Juridique Française and the Société de Législation Comparée

Article 7:101: Change of cirumstances

(1) *If a contract becomes deeply unbalanced during its execution due to a change of cirumstances that could not reasonably be foreseen, the parties must renegotiate it in order to revise or terminate the contract.*

(2) *If, in spite of the good faith of the contracting parties, the renegotiations do not succeed within a reasonable time, the parties can terminate the contract by common agreement; if this does not happen, a court can equitably revise the contract or deprive it of future effect.*

Article 7:102: Clauses relating to the allocation of risk

A clause which allocates the major part of the risk of a change of circumstances to one of the parties is only valid where it does not bring about unreasonable consequences for that party. The clause cannot be applied when the change of circumstances is due, either completely or in part, to the party to whose benefit such a clause operates.[3]

5. Avant-projet de Code européen des contrats (Gandolfi project)

Art. 157: Re-negotiation of contract

(1) *If extraordinary unforeseen events occur, such as those in Art. 97 para.1, the party who intends to avail himself of the right provided for therein must communicate to the other party a declaration with all necessary information specifying - under penalty of nullity - the different conditions that he proposes in order to keep the contract alive. The declaration is covered by the provisions of Articles 21 and 36 para. 2.*

(2) *No action can be brought until after six (three) months have elapsed from receipt of said declaration, in order to enable the parties to settle the question out of court. The right nevertheless is unaffected to apply to the court for the measures of Art. 172 below to be applied in emergency.*

(3) *If the event covered by para. 1 occurs, the other party can intimate to the party entitled to exercise the power there set out notice to declare within a period of not less than sixty days when he intends to claim renegotiation of the contract. After this time limit has elapsed in vain the party entitled is deemed to have abandoned renegotiation. The intimation is covered by the provisions of Articles 21 and 36 para 2.*

(4) *If the parties are unable to agree within the time limit at para. 2, the person entitled must - within the subsequent sixty days on pain of forfeiture - present said request to the court according to the procedure applicable in the place where the contract is to be performed.*

(5) *After evaluating the cirumstances and taking into consideration the interests and requests of the parties, the judge, with possible expert assistance, can alter or dissolve the contract as a whole or in its non-performed part and, if required, and it is the case, order return of goods or award damages for loss.*[4]

6. International Chamber of Commerce (ICC): model hardship clause 2003

1. *A party to a contract is bound to perform its contractual duties even if events have rendered performance more onerous than could reasonably have been anticipated at the time of the conclusion of the contract.*

[3] Bénédicte Fauvarque-Cosson and Denis Mazeaud (eds.), *European Contract Law/Materials for a Common Frame of Reference: Terminology, Guiding Principles, Model Rules* (Munich: Sellier, 2008), pp. 594–5. See also the French original in: Laura Sautonie-Laguionie and Frédéric Bujoli, *Principes contractuels communs* (Paris: Société de législation comparée, 2008), pp. 527–39.

[4] Giuseppe Gandolfi, *Code européen des contrats/Avant-projet I* (Milan: Giuffrè, 2004), p. 579.

2. *Notwithstanding paragraph 1 of this Clause, where a party to a contract proves that:*
   (a) *the continued performance of its contractual duties has become excessively onerous due to an event beyond its reasonable control which it could not reasonably have been expected to have taken into account at the time of the conclusion of the contract, and that*
   (b) *it could not reasonably have avoided or overcome the event or its consequences,*

   the parties are bound, within a reasonable time of the invocation of this Clause, to negotiate alternative contractual terms which reasonably allow for the consequences of the event.
3. *Where paragraph 2 of this Clause applies, but where alternative contractual terms which reasonably allow for the consequences of the event are not agreed by the other party to the contract as provided in that paragraph, the party invoking this Clause is entitled to termination of the contract.*

7. Vienna Convention of the Law of Treaties of 1969

Article 61: Supervening impossibility of performance

1. *A party may invoke the impossibility of performing a treaty as a ground for terminating or withdrawing from it if the impossibility results from the permanent disappearance or destruction of an object indispensable for the execution of the treaty. If the impossibility is temporary, it may be invoked only as a ground for suspending the operation of the treaty.*
2. *Impossibility of performance may not be invoked by a party as a ground for terminating, withdrawing from or suspending the operation of a treaty if the impossibility is the result of a breach by that party either of an obligation under the treaty or of any other international obligation owed to any other party to the treaty.*

Article 62: Fundamental change of cirumstances

1. *A fundamental change of cirumstances which has occurred with regard to those existing at the time of the conclusion of a treaty, and which was not foreseen by the parties, may not be invoked as a ground for terminating or withdrawing from the treaty unless:*
   (a) *the existence of those circumstances consitituted an essential basis of the consent of the parties to be bound by the treaty; and*
   (b) *the effect of the change is radically to transform the extent of obligations still to be performed under the treaty.*
2. *A fundamental change of circumstances may not be invoked as a ground for terminating or withdrawing from a treaty:*
   (a) *if the treaty establishes a boundary; or*

(b) *if the fundamental change is the result of a breach by the party invoking it either of an obligation under the treaty or of any other international obligation owed to any party to the treaty.*

3. *If, under the foregoing paragraphs, a party may invoke a fundamental change of cirumstances as a ground for terminating or withdrawing from a treaty it may also invoke the change as a ground for suspending the operation of the treaty.*

Selected bibliography

Abas, P. *Rebus sic stantibus* (Deventes: Kluwer, 1989).

Akerlof, G. A. 'The Markets for Lemons: Qualitative Uncertainty and the Market Mechanism', (1970) 84 *Quarterly Journal of Economics*, 488–500.

Ambrosoli, M. *La sopravvenienza contrattuale* (Milan: Giuffrè, 2002).

Berger, K. 'Renegotiations and Adaptation of International Investment Contracts: the Role of Contract Drafters and Arbitrators', (2003) 36 *Vanderbilt Journal of Transnational Law* 1347–80.

Bruce, C. L. 'An Economic Analysis of the Impossibility Doctrine', (1982) 11 *Journal of Legal Studies* 311 (1982).

Brunner, C. *Force Majeure and Hardship under General Contract Principles/Exemption for Non-performance in International Arbitration* (Alphen aan den Rijn: Kluwer, 2009).

Cooter, R. and T. Ulen, *Law and Economics* (Reading, MA: Pearson, Addison Wesley, 5th edn, 2008).

De Geest, G. 'Specific Performance, Damages and Unforeseen Contingencies in the Draft Common Frame of Reference', in: P. Larouche and F. Chirico (eds.), *Economic Analysis of the DCFR/The Work of the Economic Impact Group within CoPECL* (New York: Sellier/de Gruyter, 2010), pp. 123–32.

Draetta, U. 'Les clauses de force majeure et de hardship dans les contrats internationaux', 15 (2001) *Diritto del commercio internazionale* 297–308.

Dutoit, B. 'Le droit des contrats face à la globalisation des relations humaines', in: *Festschrift für Peter Gauch zum 65. Geburtstag* (Zurich: Schulthess Juristische Medien, 2004), pp. 379–393.

Fauvarque-Cosson, B. and D. Mazeaud (eds.), *European Contract Law/Materials for a Common Frame of Reference: Terminology, Guiding Principles, Model Rules* (Munich: Sellier, 2008), pp. 594–595.

Fontaine, M. 'Les dispositions relatives au hardship et à la force majeure', in: M. J. Bonell, and F. Bonelli (eds.), *Contratti commerciali internazionali e Principi UNIDROIT* (Milan: 1997), pp. 183–191.

Gallo, P. *Sopravvenienza contrattuale e problemi di gestione del contratto* (Milan: Giuffrè, 1992).

Gandolfi, G. *Code européen des contrats/Avant-projet I* (Milan: Giuffrè, 2004).

Gordley, J. *Foundations of Private Law/Property, Tort, Contract, Unjust Enrichment* (Oxford University Press, 2006).

Gordley, J. 'Impossibility and Changed and Unforeseen Circumstances', (2004) 52 *American Journal of Comparative Law* 513.

Joskow, P. 'Commercial Impossibility, the Uranium Market, and the "Westinghouse" Case', (1976) 6 *Journal of Legal Studies* 119.

Karampatzos, A. 'Supervening Hardship as Subdivision of the General Frustration Rule: A Comparative Analysis with Reference to Anglo-American, German, French and Greek Law', (2007) *European Review of Private Law* 105–47.

Kim, N. 'Mistakes Changed Circumstances and Intent', (January 22, 2007).

Lando, O. and Beale M. (eds.), *Principles of European Contract Law Parts I and II* (The Hague: Kluwer Law International, 2000), pp. 322–8.

McKendrick, E. '*Hardship*', in: S. Vogenauer and J. Kleinheisterkamp (eds.), *Commentary on the Unidroit Principles of International Commercial Contracts (PICC)* (Oxford University Press, 2009), pp. 709–25.

Maskow, D. 'Hardship and Force Majeure', (1992) 40 *American Journal of Comparative Law* 657–669.

Mekki, M. and M. Kloepfer-Pelēse,'Hardship and Modification (or "Revision") of the Contract', in: A. Hartkamp *et al.* (eds.), *Towards a European Civil Code* (Nijmegen: Ars Aequi Libri, 2010), pp. 651–80.

Momberg Uribe, R. *The Effect of a Change of Circumstances on the Binding Force of Contracts* (PhD Utrecht, 2011).

Nassar, N. *Sanctity of Contracts Revisited/A Study in the Theory and Practice of Long-Term International Commercial Transactions* (Dordrecht: Maarius Mijhoff, 1995).

Pardolesi, R. 'Regole di "default" e razionalità limitata: per un (diverso) approccio di analisi economica al diritto dei contratti', (1996) *Rivista critica del diritto privato* 451.

Parisi, F. 'The Harmonization of Legal Warranties in European Sales Law: An Economic Analysis', (2004) 52 *American Journal of Comparative Law*, 403–31.

Perillo, J. M. 'Hardship and its Impact on Contractual Obligations: A Comparative Analysis' (Rome, April 1996).

Posner, R. A. and A. M. Rosenfield, 'Impossibility and Related Doctrine in Contract Law: An Economic Analysis', (1977) 6 *Journal of Legal Studies* 83.

Priest, G. L. 'A Theory of the Consumer Product Warranty', (1981) 90 *Yale Law Journal*, 1297–352, reprinted in Victor P. Goldberg (ed.), *Readings in the Economics of Contract Law* (Cambridge University Press, 1989), pp. 174–84.

Rippen, E. E. 'Verandering van omstandigheden in het Engelse contractenrecht: een vergelijking met de UNIDROIT-Principles en de Principles of European Contract Law', in: K. Grosheide and W. Boele-Woelki (eds.) *Europees Privaat-recht* (Lelystad: Molengrafica, 1996), pp. 3–45.

Sautonie-Laguionie, L. and F. Bujoli, *Principes contractuels commune*, Projet de cadre Commun de référence (Paris: Société de législation comparée, 2008), pp. 527–39.

Schwartz, A. 'Law and Economics: l'approccio alla teoria del contratto', (1996) *Rivista critica del diritto privato*, 427, 446.
Schwartz, A. 'Relational Contracts in the Courts: An Analysis of Incomplete Agreements and Judicial Strategies', (1992) 21 *Journal of Legal Studies* 271.
Schwenzer, I. '*Die clausula* und das CISG', in: *Tradition mit Weltsicht: Festschrift fur Eugen Bucher zum 80 Geburtstag* (Bem: Stampfli, 2009), pp. 723–41.
Shavell, S. 'Damage Measures for Breach of Contract', (1980) 11 *Bell Journal of Economics* 466.
Spence, M. 'Consumer Misperceptions, Product Failure and Producer Liability', (1977) 44 *Review of Economic Studies* 561–72.
Sykes, A. O. 'The Doctrine of Commercial Impracticability in a Second-best World', (1990) 19 *Journal of Legal Studies* 443.
Tallon, D. 'Hardship', in: A. Hartkamp *et al* (eds), *Towards a European Civil Code* (Nijmegen: Ars Aequi Libri, 2004), pp. 499–504.
Trimarchi, P. 'Commercial Impracticability in Contract Law: An Economic Analysis', (1991) 11 *International Review of Law and Economics* 63.
Trimarchi, P. 'Transfers, Uncertainty and the Cost of Disruption', (2003) 23 *International Review of Law and Economics* 49–62.
UNIDROIT, *Principles of International Commercial Contracts* (Rame: UNIDROIT, 1994) (unchanged in the 2004 edition).
Vogenauer, S. and J. Kleinheisterkamp (eds.), *Commentary on the Unidroit Principles of International Commercial Contracts (PICC)* (Oxford University Press, 2009).
Wehrt, K. '*Warranties*', in: B. Bouckaert and G. De Geest (eds.), *Encyclopedia of Law and Economics* (Aldershot: Elgar, 2000), vol. III, pp. 179–95.
White, M. J. 'Contract Breach and Contract Discharge due to Impossibility: A Unified Theory', (1988) 17 *Journal of Legal Studies* 353.
Zimmermann, R. and S. Whittaker, *Good Faith in European Contract Law*, (Cambridge University Press, 2000), pp. 557–77.

Index